Life Histories of North American Cuckoos, Goatsuckers, Hummingbirds, and Their Allies

by

Arthur Cleveland Bent

Two Volumes Bound as One

DOVER PUBLICATIONS, INC.

NEW YORK

Published in Canada by General Publishing Company, Ltd., 30 Lesmill Road, Don Mills, Toronto, Ontario.

Published in the United Kingdom by Constable and Company, Ltd., 10 Orange Street, London, WC2H 7EG.

This Dover edition, first published in 1989, is an unabridged republication in one volume of the work first reprinted by Dover Publications, Inc. in 1964 in two volumes. The work was first published in 1940 by the United States Government Printing Office as Smithsonian Institution United States National Museum *Bulletin 176*.

Manufactured in the United States of America
Dover Publications, Inc., 31 East 2nd Street, Mineola, N.Y. 11501

International Standard Book Number: 0-486-26029-1
Library of Congress Catalog Card Number: 64-14301

PART ONE

ADVERTISEMENT

The scientific publications of the National Museum include two series, known, respectively, as *Proceedings* and *Bulletin*.

The *Proceedings* series, begun in 1878, is intended primarily as a medium for the publication of original papers, based on the collections of the National Museum, that set forth newly acquired facts in biology, anthropology, and geology, with descriptions of new forms and revisions of limited groups. Copies of each paper, in pamphlet form, are distributed as published to libraries and scientific organizations and to specialists and others interested in the different subjects. The dates at which these separate papers are published are recorded in the table of contents of each of the volumes.

The series of *Bulletins*, the first of which was issued in 1875, contains separate publications comprising monographs of large zoological groups and other general systematic treatises (occasionally in several volumes), faunal works, reports of expeditions, catalogs of type specimens, special collections, and other material of similar nature. The majority of the volumes are octavo in size, but a quarto size has been adopted in a few instances in which large plates were regarded as indispensable. In the *Bulletin* series appear volumes under the heading *Contributions from the United States National Herbarium*, in octavo form, published by the National Museum since 1902, which contain papers relating to the botanical collections of the Museum.

The present work forms No. 176 of the *Bulletin* series.

ALEXANDER WETMORE,
Assistant Secretary, Smithsonian Institution.

WASHINGTON, D. C., *May 3, 1940.*

CONTENTS

INTRODUCTION

This is the thirteenth in a series of bulletins of the United States National Museum on the life histories of North American birds. Previous numbers have been issued as follows:

107. Life Histories of North American Diving Birds, August 1, 1919.

113. Life Histories of North American Gulls and Terns, August 27, 1921.

121. Life Histories of North American Petrels and Pelicans and their Allies, October 19, 1922.

126. Life Histories of North American Wild Fowl (part), May 25, 1923.

130. Life Histories of North American Wild Fowl (part), June 27, 1925.

135. Life Histories of North American Marsh Birds, March 11, 1927.

142. Life Histories of North American Shore Birds (pt. 1), December 31, 1927.

146. Life Histories of North American Shore Birds (pt. 2), March 24, 1929.

162. Life Histories of North American Gallinaceous Birds, May 25, 1932.

167. Life Histories of North American Birds of Prey (pt. 1), May 3, 1937.

170. Life Histories of North American Birds of Prey (pt. 2), August 8, 1938.

174. Life Histories of North American Woodpeckers, May 23, 1939.

The same general plan has been followed, as explained in previous bulletins, and the same sources of information have been utilized. The nomenclature of the 1931 check-list of the American Ornithologists' Union has been followed.

An attempt has been made to give as full a life history as possible of the best-known subspecies of each species and to avoid duplication by writing briefly of the others, giving only the characters of the subspecies, its range, and any habits peculiar to it. In many cases certain habits, probably common to the species as a whole have been recorded for only one subspecies; such habits are mentioned under the subspecies on which the observations were made. The distribution gives the range of the species as a whole, with only rough outlines of the ranges of the subspecies, which in many cases cannot be accurately defined.

The egg dates are the condensed results from a mass of records taken from the data in a large number of the best collections in the country, as well as from contributed field notes and from a few published sources. They indicate the dates on which eggs have been found in various parts of the country, showing the earliest and latest dates and the limits between which half the dates fall, indicating the height of the season.

The plumages are described in only enough detail to enable the reader to trace the sequence of molts and plumages from birth to maturity and to recognize the birds in the different stages and at the different seasons.

No attempt has been made to describe fully the adult plumages; this has been well done already in the many manuals. The names of colors, when in quotation marks, are taken from Ridgway's Color Standards and Nomenclature (1912). In the measurements of eggs the four extremes are printed in boldface type.

Many who have contributed material for previous volumes have continued to cooperate. Receipt of material from over 450 contributors has been acknowledged previously. In addition to these, our thanks are due to the following new contributors: E. C. Aldrich, Mrs. H. P. Bracelin, Maurice Brooks, Mildred Campbell, R. T. Congdon, Murl Deusing, S. S. Dickey, H. E. Edgerton, W. G. F. Harris, L. B. Howsley, Charles Macnamara, R. F. Mason, Jr., R. T. Moore, A. R. Phillips, A. J. Pinckney, O. P. Silliman, A. F. Skutch, Emily Smith, W. P. Steinbeck, R. R. Talmadge, H. O. Todd, Jr., B. P. Tyler, L. O. Williams, G. R. Wilson, and H. B. Wood. As the demand for these bulletins is greater than the supply, the names of those who have not contributed to the work during the previous ten years may be dropped from the author's mailing list.

Dr. Winsor M. Tyler rendered valuable assistance in reading and indexing, for these groups, a large part of the literature on North American birds, and contributed three complete life histories. E. C. Stuart Baker and Alexander F. Skutch each contributed two complete life histories; and Dr. Alfred O. Gross, the Rev. F. C. R. Jourdain, Alexander Sprunt, Jr., Dr. George M. Sutton, and Robert S. Woods contributed one each. Our thanks are also due F. Seymour Hersey for figuring egg measurements. Egg measurements were furnished, especially for this volume, by Dean Amadon, A. M. Bailey, American Museum of Natural History, Griffing Bancroft, R. M. Barnes, I. McT. Cowan, H. G. Deignan, C. E. Doe, J. H. Gillin, W. C. Hanna, R. C. Harlow, R. T. Moore, R. T. Orr, P. B. Philipp, M. S. Ray, J. H. Riley, G. H. Stuart, 3d, and Miss M. W. Wythe.

Through the courtesy of the Bureau of Biological Survey, the services of Frederick C. Lincoln were again obtained to compile the distribution paragraphs. With the matchless files of the Survey at his disposal, his many hours of careful work have produced results far more satisfactory than could have been attained by the author, who claims no credit and assumes no responsibility for this part of the work.

The manuscript for this bulletin was completed in March 1939. Contributions received since then will be acknowledged later. Only information of great importance could be added. The reader is reminded again that this is a cooperative work; if he fails to find in these volumes anything that he knows about the birds, he can blame himself for not having sent the information to—

THE AUTHOR.

Life Histories of North American
Cuckoos, Goatsuckers, Hummingbirds,
and Their Allies

LIFE HISTORIES OF NORTH AMERICAN CUCKOOS, GOATSUCKERS, HUMMINGBIRDS, AND THEIR ALLIES.

ORDERS PSITTACIFORMES, CUCULIFORMES, TROGONIFORMES, CORACIIFORMES, CAPRIMULGIFORMES, AND MICROPODIIFORMES

By Arthur Cleveland Bent

Taunton, Mass.

Order PSITTACIFORMES

Family PSITTACIDAE: Parrots and Parakeets

CONUROPSIS CAROLINENSIS CAROLINENSIS (Linnaeus)

CAROLINA PARAKEET

HABITS

Many of the glories of North American bird life have gone, never to return. The spread of civilization, the selfish greed of human interests, and the lust to kill have wiped out some of the most spectacular and beautiful features in our formerly abundant bird life. The countless millions of passenger pigeons that formerly darkened the sky in their seasonal migrations are gone forever. And the great flocks of gorgeous parakeets that formerly roamed over nearly all the eastern part of our country will be seen no more. This was the only representative of the parrot family that lived and bred within the United States; it gave a touch of tropical character to our avifauna and a vivid tinge of color to the landscape; its loss is much to be regretted. Never again may be seen the glorious sights witnessed by Wilson, Audubon, and other early writers, as great flocks of these gorgeous birds wheeled through the air, in close formation, their long tails streaming out in straight flight or spreading as they turned, and their brilliant colors, red, yellow, bright green, and soft blue, gleaming in the sunlight. As Wilson (1832) says: "They came screaming through the woods in the morning, about an hour after sunrise, to drink the salt water, of which they, as well as the pigeons, are remarkably fond. When they alighted on the ground, it appeared at a distance as if covered with a carpet of richest green,

1

orange, and yellow: they afterwards settled, in one body, on a neighbouring tree, which stood detached from any other, covering almost every twig of it, and the sun, shining strongly on their gay and glossy plumage, produced a very beautiful and splendid appearance."

Conuropsis carolinensis, as a species, covered a wide range in eastern North America, from the vicinity of the Great Lakes southward to Florida and the Gulf States, and from Colorado (rarely) to the Atlantic coast. For a full account, given in detail, of the former range of the species and its gradual disappearance, the reader is referred to a comprehensive article on the subject by Edwin M. Hasbrouck (1891). As the species has been divided into two subspecies since this was written, we shall consider here only the former distribution of the eastern race, *Conuropsis c. carolinensis*. The oldest and northernmost records, of what was probably this race, appeared in Bartram's Fragments (1799) in the following words:

The two first of these birds were seen in the neighbourhood of Philadelphia, between thirty and forty years ago. The Psittacus, most probably the Psittacus pertinax, Illinois Parrot, or the Psittacus carolinensis, Carolina Parrot, has been occasionally observed in Shareman's Valley, on Shareman's Creek, a branch of the river Susquehanna, within twenty miles of the town of Carlisle. This last fact seems to contradict the observation of Mr. William Bartram, who says, "The parakeets (Psittacus carolinensis) never reach so far north as Pennsylvania, which to me is unaccountable, considering they are a bird of such singular rapid flight, they could easily perform the journey in ten or twelve hours from North-Carolina, where they are very numerous, and we abound with all the fruits which they delight in." * * * I may add, that a very large flight of parakeets, which came from the westward, was seen a few years ago, about twenty-five miles to the north-west of Albany, in the State of New-York.

The arrival of these birds in the depth of winter (January, 1780) was, indeed, a very remarkable circumstance. The more ignorant Dutch settlers were exceedingly alarmed. They imagined, in dreadful consternation, that it portended nothing less calamitous than the destruction of the world.

DeKay (1844) places this New York record as occurring in 1795. The only record we have for New Jersey is one recently published by Warren F. Eaton (1936); Albert E. Hedden (1841–1915) told his son and nephew "of the occurrence of this species in East Orange, Essex County, New Jersey, when he was a boy. They placed the time between 1850 and 1860, and both recall exactly the same story. The Paroquets occurred probably twice at least in hot weather (I suspect September) and were considered very destructive to the small household apple orchards, maintained by the family at that time. The birds occurred in flocks and tore the apple fruit apart, extracting the seeds." There seems to be no record for Delaware, but in Audubon's time they were found as far north as the boundary line between Virginia and Maryland, where a flock was seen and specimens were shot as recently as September 1865 (Smith and Palmer, 1888). They apparently were common in the Carolinas up to 1850, or perhaps 1860, but must have disappeared from there soon after that. For Georgia, there seem to be no records since 1849. In Florida, the species made its last stand; parakeets were evidently common throughout the State up to the 1860's, but during the next 20 years all observers reported them as becoming rarer and more restricted in range. In the early 1890's it was still common in certain remote localities in Florida. Arthur H. Howell (1932) has this to say about the last records of this vanishing bird:

E. J. Brown reported the birds plentiful in March, 1896, near Campbell, Osceola County. Dr. E. A. Mearns took 6 specimens on Padget Creek, Brevard County, April 18, 1901. Apparently the last stronghold was in the vicinity of Taylor Creek, on the northeastern side of Okeechobee Lake. Here on February 29, 1896, Robert Ridgway collected 13 specimens, and in April, 1904, Frank M. Chapman saw two flocks aggregating 13 birds (1912, p. 318). W. W. Worthington hunted along both sides of Taylor Creek on March 26, 1907, without seeing any Paroquets. * * * Capt. F. W. Sams, an old resident of Florida, told Dr. Amos W. Butler that he saw a flock of 8 or 10 Paroquets in 1909 at Cabbage Slough, on the west side of Turnbull Hammock, about 12 or 15 miles southwest of New Smyrna. E. Stewart Hyer, of Orlando, reports seeing one bird at Istokpoga Lake on February 16, 1910. A late and apparently authentic record is published by Chapman (Bird Lore, 1915, p. 453) on the authority of W. J. F. McCormick, who claims to have seen about a dozen birds in March and April, 1915. Henry Redding, who knows the birds well, reported a flock of about 30 seen on Fort Drum Creek in February, 1920.

The causes that led to the extermination of the parakeet are not hard to find. It was a bad actor, regarded by fruit growers and agriculturists as a destructive pest, doing extensive damage to their crops. Consequently it was slaughtered in enormous numbers on every opportunity. It was more or less hunted as a game bird, for it was abundant and its flesh was said to be very palatable. It was shot in enormous numbers for mere sport, or for practice. Hundreds were captured by professional bird catchers and sent north, as cage birds or pets, and many were killed for their plumage. Furthermore, it has always retreated before the spread of civilization and seemed incapable of surviving in settled regions, probably for the reasons mentioned above.

W. E. D. Scott (1889) says that "they were wantonly mischievous and cut hundreds of young *green oranges*, peaches, and the like, from the trees almost as soon as the fruit was formed." Many were shot by farmers in their cornfields, where the birds had formed the bad habit of feeding on the tender corn on the ears, thus destroying, or injuring, a large part of the crop.

According to Audubon (1842) they ate or destroyed almost every kind of fruit indiscriminately and on this account were always unwelcome visitors "to the planter, the farmer, or the gardener." He says:

The stacks of grain put up in the field are resorted to by flocks of these birds, which frequently cover them so entirely, that they present to the eye the same effect as if a brilliantly coloured carpet had been thrown over them. They cling around the whole stack, pull out the straws, and destroy twice as much of the grain as would suffice to satisfy their hunger. They assail the pear and apple-trees, when the fruit is yet very small and far from being ripe, and this merely for the sake of the seeds. As on the stalks of corn, they alight on the apple-trees of our orchards, or the pear-trees in the gardens, in great numbers; and, as if through mere mischief, pluck off the fruits, open them up to the core, and, disappointed at the sight of the seeds, which are yet soft and of a milky consistence, drop the apple or pear, and pluck another, passing from branch to branch, until the trees which were before so promising, are left completely stripped. * * * They visit the mulberries, pecan-nuts, grapes, and even the seeds of the dog-wood, before they are ripe, and on all commit similar depredations. * * *

Do not imagine, reader, that all these outrages are borne without severe retaliation on the part of the planters. So far from this, the Parakeets are destroyed in great numbers, for whilst busily engaged in plucking off the fruits or tearing the grain from the stacks, the husbandman approaches them with perfect ease, and commits great slaughter among them. All the survivors rise, shriek, fly around about for a few minutes, and again alight on the very place of most imminent danger. The gun is kept at work; eight or ten, or even twenty, are killed at every discharge. The living birds, as if conscious of the death of their companions, sweep over their bodies, screaming as loud as ever, but still return to the stack to be shot at, until so few remain alive, that the farmer does not consider it worth his while to spend more of his ammunition. I have seen several hundreds destroyed in this manner in the course of a few hours.

This fatal habit of hovering over their fallen companions has helped, more than any one thing, to bring about their extermination. Their social disposition has been their undoing. C. J. Maynard (1896) says of this trait: "This is not a mere liking for company, as they are actually fond of one another, for, if one out of a flock be wounded, the survivors attracted by its screams, will return to hover over it and, even if constantly shot at, will not leave as long as their distressed friend calls for assistance; in fact, I have seen every individual in a flock killed one after the other, and the last bird betrayed as much anxiety for the fate of its prostrate friends which were strewed upon the ground, as it did when the first fell."

Nesting.—Nothing very definite seems to be known about the nesting habits of the Carolina parakeet. No competent ornithologist has ever seen a nest. Even Wilson and Audubon, who lived in the days when these birds were so abundant, never saw a nest; and all they wrote about it was based on hearsay. Most observers seemed to agree that the parakeets nested in hollow trees, but some of the accounts were rather fantastic. For example, Wilson (1832) wrote: "One man assured me that he cut down a large beech tree, which was hollow, and in which he found the broken fragments of upwards of twenty parakeets' eggs, which were of a greenish yellow colour. The nests, though destroyed in their texture by the falling of the tree, appeared, he said, to be formed of small twigs glued to each other, and to the side of the tree, in the manner of the Chimney Swallow." Audubon (1842) says: "Their nest, or the place in which they deposit their eggs, is simply the bottom of such cavities in trees as those to which they usually retire at night. Many females deposit their eggs together."

Maynard (1896) was told by some cedar hunters that a large number of parakeets nested in a hollow in a huge cypress tree in the depths of a great cypress swamp. He offered them a good sum to procure the eggs, which they attempted to do; but, on opening the tree, about which they saw a large number of the parakeets, they were disappointed to find only young birds. H. B. Bailey (1883) had in his collection a set of two eggs, which he felt sure were eggs of the Carolina parakeet. "The eggs, which were taken April 26, 1855, were deposited in a hollow tree, on the chips at bottom. One of them was sent to Mr. Ridgway who has kindly compared it with identified eggs, and who confirms the identification." There was an apparently authentic set in the John Lewis Childs (1906b) collection, taken in the wild, of which he writes:

The set consists of three eggs which were taken on April 2, 1896, by Dr. H. E. Pendry. They were found in a cavity of a sycamore tree forty feet up on the outskirts of the Great Swamp near the head of the Caloosahatchee River and west of Lake Okechobee, De Soto County, Florida. Dr. Pendry was not sure of the identity of these eggs, as he saw no Paroquets at the nest, but they were in the swamp and he had frequently seen and taken young birds in the same locality. * * * The eggs were sent to us for identification, and there seems to be not the slightest doubt but that they are genuine. They measure as follows: 1.35 x 1.06–1.26 x 1.06, 1.25 x 1.05 [34.3 by 27.1, 32.1 by 27.1, and 31.8 by 26.8 millimeters].

William Brewster (1889) published the following account, which seemed to him "to rest on evidence sufficiently good to warrant its publication." He questioned everybody he met about the nesting of the parakeet and was told by two professional hunters of alligators and plume birds that they had "seen Parrakeets' nests, which they described as flimsy structures built of twigs and placed on the branches of cypress trees." He goes on to say:

This account was so widely at variance with what has been previously recorded regarding the manner of nesting of this species that I considered it, at the time, as a mere fabrication, but afterwards it was unexpectedly and most strongly corroborated by Judge R. L. Long of Tallahassee. The latter gentleman, who, by the way, has a very good general knowledge of the birds of our Northern

States, assured me that he had examined many nests of the Parrakeet built precisely as above described. Formerly, when the birds were abundant in the surrounding region, he used to find them breeding in large colonies in the cypress swamps. Several of these colonies contained at least a thousand birds each. They nested invariably in small cypress trees, the favorite position being on a fork near the end of a slender horizontal branch. Every fork would be occupied, and he has seen as many as forty or fifty nests in one small tree. Their nests closely resembled those of the Carolina Dove, being similarly composed of cypress twigs put together so loosely that the eggs were often visible from the ground beneath. The twigs of the cypress seemed to be preferred to those of any other kind of tree. The height at which the nests were placed varied from five or six feet to twenty or thirty feet. Mr. Long described the eggs as being of a greenish white color, unspotted. He did not remember the maximum number which he had found in one set, but thought it was at least four or five. He had often taken young birds from the nests to rear or to give to his friends.

Several times parakeets have been known to breed in captivity or attempt to do so. Robert Ridgway brought several birds from Florida that laid at least 13 eggs in captivity; most of the eggs now in American collections are the product of these birds. Dr. William C. Herman writes to me that parakeets bred successfully in the Cincinnati Zoological Garden, where some were kept for 20 or more years; the last one died in September 1914. "Some of these birds bred in captivity. Dozens of young birds were raised, especially when others recently captured were added." Dr. Nowotny (1898) purchased a pair of Carolina parakeets in Vienna and tried to breed them in captivity. The female laid in all ten eggs; the first five were put in a breeding box, but never hatched, as they were "picked and sucked," presumably by the birds. Two more eggs were placed under a hen but were destroyed through carelessness. The other three were placed in the breeding box and incubated by the parakeets; three young were hatched, but they did not live to maturity.

Eggs.—It is not definitely known how many eggs were laid by the Carolina parakeet in a normal set, but indications point to two and three as being the commonest numbers. Bendire (1895) says, of the eggs laid by Mr. Ridgway's birds in captivity:

None of these eggs can be called round; they vary from ovate to short ovate, and are rather pointed. They are white, with the faintest yellowish tint, ivory-like and quite glossy; the shell is rather thick, close grained, and deeply pitted, not unlike the eggs of the African Ostrich (*Struthio camelus*), but of course not as noticeable. Holding the eggs in a strong light, the inside appears to be pale yellow. * * *

The deep pitting is noticeable in every specimen, and there can be no possible doubt about the identity of these eggs. * * * There is no difficulty whatever in distinguishing these eggs from those of the Burrowing Owl or the Kingfisher, both of which are occasionally substituted for them.

Mr. Childs (1905) figures the three eggs sent to him by Mr. Ridgway and describes them as "color pure white with ivory gloss surpassing that of the Ivory-billed Woodpecker." One of Mr. Ridgway's eggs, in the John E. Thayer collection, I should describe as ovate in shape and dull white in color, with a very slight gloss. The measurements of 24 eggs average 34.23 by 27.80 millimeters; the eggs showing the four extremes measure 37 by 38, 33 by 30.2, 32.1 by 27.1, and 34.4 by 25.8 millimeters.

Young.—We do not know much about the development and care of the young in the wild state, but in captivity the birds seem to be very careless or indifferent in the care and feeding of the young. Dr. Nowotny's eggs were hatched, after continuous incubation, in about 19 or 20 days, but the young all eventually died from neglect.

Mr. Ridgway wrote to Mr. Childs (1905), under date of November 13, 1902: "My female Parakeet laid only six eggs the past summer and I shall never get any more, as the bird is now dead. The first she laid is the one I sent you. The remaining five hatched, but I have only two young ones left, a rat having carried off one, another was starved by the parents when half grown, and the third I gave to a friend who had time and disposition to take care of it in order to save it from starving."

Plumages.—I have never seen the downy young or nestling plumages and doubt if there are any such in collections. Audubon (1840) says that "the young are at first covered with soft down, such as is seen on young Owls. During the first season, the whole plumage is green; but towards autumn a frontlet of carmine appears. Two years, however, are passed before the male or female are in full plumage." His plate shows a bird with a wholly green head.

Dr. Nowotny's (1898) young birds, when between five and six weeks old, "had already attained green wings and tail; the older one also had red feathers above the bill and on the under parts. * * * The oldest young one had already attained many dense strong red feathers above the bill at the age of eight weeks". This does not agree with Audubon's account, or with C. J. Maynard's (1896) who says, of the young of the year: "Head and neck, wholly green, and the tail is short." He says, of the nestling: "One of my collectors, who found the young in the nest, informs me that they are covered with a grayish down." I have never seen a young bird with a wholly green head; those that I have seen, some nine in number, were in first winter plumage, and were collected between October 7 and April 3, indicating that this plumage is worn all through the first winter. These are much like adults, but with no yellow on the head, thighs, or anal region, and only greenish yellow on the edge of the wing; the forehead and front of the crown up to the front edges of the eyes are "flame scarlet" or "cadmium orange," shading off to dull brownish orange on the lores and to dull brown on the cheeks. Specimens taken in February show yellow feathers coming in on the head, and progressive changes toward maturity continue all through the spring months until, by summer, the yellow head is fully acquired. Audubon (1840) says that the young bird requires two years to attain its full plumage, and Maynard (1896) says that it is acquired during the third year, but the material examined does not indicate this.

Adults have a complete molt in fall, from September to November. Dr. Frank M. Chapman's (1890) captive bird began to molt in September, "and by November had acquired an entirely new plumage." Arthur T. Wayne (1910) says that they "commence to molt about October 5, and require at least six weeks to acquire their perfect plumage."

Food.—Much has been said about the food of the Carolina parakeet in the earlier part of this account, as its feeding habits were so destructive in fruit orchards and grain fields that the birds were unmercifully slaughtered by the planters, thus hastening the extermination of the species. But before the lands were so extensively cultivated, the parakeets lived on their natural, wild food. C. J. Maynard (1896) writes:

I observed a large flock of Parokeets moving along the ground. * * * At first, I could not make out what they were doing but soon found that they were busily engaged in eating cockspurs, the seeds of a species of grass which grows very abundantly in old fields. They walked quite well for birds having such short legs and, in pressing forward, moved side by side in a long rank, looking exactly like miniature soldiers. After a few moments, something startled them and they arose, wheeled about, darting rapidly up and down, precisely like pigeons, at the same time, uttering loud cries; then settled quietly down again and resumed their meal, as composedly as if nothing had occurred to interrupt.

This is the only time that I ever chanced to see the Parokeets feed on the ground but I have been informed by the inhabitants of Florida, that they are very fond of cockspurs and will frequently alight in the fields in order to eat them. Early in winter, they visit the swamps, where they feed upon the cypress balls. Then it is very difficult to find them as they often remain for weeks in the impenetrable fastnesses of the vast wooded tracts which, at this season, are submerged in water. Later, about the first of February, the Parokeets emerge from the swamps in small flocks and enter the open woods to search for the seeds of the pine cones which are then ripe. At this time, they may be met with quite frequently but the best opportunity to procure specimens occurs about the middle of February, when they may be found in large companies, feeding upon the green seeds of the maples and elms which grow along the rivers.

Dr. Chapman (1890) found these parakeets feeding on the prairies near the Sebastian River in Florida, of which he says:

About these "prairies" and at the borders of small streams or low ground grew in abundance a species of thistle (*Cirsium Lecontei*, T. & G.) the seeds of which, so far as I could learn, constituted at this season [February] the entire food of *Conurus*. Not a patch of thistles did we find which had not been visited by them, the headless stalks showing clearly where the thistles had been neatly severed by the sharp chisel-like bill, while the ground beneath favorite trees would be strewn with the scattered down. * * *

Two days passed before I again met *Conurus*, and this time to better advantage. It was a wet and drizzling morning when we found a flock of six birds feeding on thistles at the edge of a "prairie." Perched on the leafless branches of the tree before us, their brilliant green plumage showed to the best advantage, as we approached through the pines without difficulty. Several were skillfully dissecting the thistles they held in their feet, biting out the milky seed while the released fluffy down floated away beneath them. There was a sound of suppressed conversation; half articulate calls. * * *

There was an evident regularity in the habits of the birds we afterwards observed—in all about fifty, in flocks of from six to twenty. At an early hour they left their roost in the hummock bordering the river and passed out into the pines to feed, always, so far as I observed, selecting thistle patches, and eating the seeds only when in the milky stage. At about ten o'clock they returned to the hummock and apparently to some favorite tree, here to pass the rest of the morning and early afternoon, when they again started out to feed, returning to the roost just before sunset. A flock of these birds feeding among the thistles is a most beautiful and animated sight; one is almost persuaded not to disturb them. There is constant movement as they fly from plant to plant, or when securing thistles they fly with them in their bills to a neighboring tree, there to dissect them at their leisure. The loud rolling call was apparently uttered only when on the wing, but when at rest, or feeding, there was a loud conversational murmur of half articulate, querulous notes and calls.

Cottam and Knappen (1939) examined the stomach and crop of one bird, of which they say: "Except for two rabbit hairs, two bits of the bird's own feathers, and two fragments of an indeterminable ant, which formed only traces, the entire content consisted of the remains of no fewer than thirty-two seeds of loblolly pine (*Pinus taeda*)."

Behavior.—Audubon (1842) writes:

The flight of the Parakeet is rapid, straight, and continued through the forests, or over fields and rivers, and is accompanied by inclinations of the body which enable the observer to see alternately their upper and under parts. They deviate from a direct course only when impediments occur, such as the trunks of trees or houses, in which case they glance aside in a very graceful manner, merely as much as may be necessary. A general cry is kept up by the party, and it is seldom that one of these birds is on wing for ever so short a space without uttering its cry. On reaching a spot which affords a supply of food, instead of alighting at once, as many other birds do, the Parakeets take a good survey of the neighborhood, passing over it in circles of great extent, first above the trees, and then gradually lowering until they almost touch the ground, when suddenly re-ascending they all settle on the tree that bears the fruit of which they are in quest, or on one close to the field in which they expect to regale themselves.

They are quite at ease on trees or any kind of plant, moving sidewise, climbing or hanging in every imaginable posture, assisting themselves very dexterously in all their motions with their bills. They usually alight extremely close together. I have seen branches of trees as completely covered by them as they could possibly be. If approached before they begin their plundering, they appear shy and distrustful, and often at a single cry from one of them, the whole take wing, and probably may not return to the same place that day.

Maynard (1896) says:

I have remarked that the Parokeets scream very loudly when flying; so loudly, in fact, that their shrill cries can be heard for miles. They come dashing along, moving in a most eccentric manner; now near the ground, then high over the tree tops, seeming about to alight a dozen times but still without settling, each in the company endeavoring to excel the other in producing the most discordant yells, when they will all pitch, at once, into some tree and a sudden silence ensues. So great had been the din but a second before that the comparative stillness is quite bewildering, then too, the large flock of highly colored birds, lately so conspicuous, have disappeared completely. I well remember my first experience of this nature; I stood, gun in hand, watching the evolutions of a large company as it wheeled about, awaiting an opportunity to shoot, when, of a sudden, they all alighted in a large live-oak which stood a few rods away. I cautiously approached the tree, ready to slaughter half the flock at a single discharge, if possible, when, what was my surprise upon going within a suitable distance, not to perceive a bird. Neither could I see so much as a feather of the desired game although I walked around the tree several times and even went beneath its branches to peer up between them. After spending some time in these fruitless efforts, my patience became quite exhausted and I threw a large oyster shell up into the tree. This certainly produced an effect, not just what I intended, however, for, in an instant, out darted the entire body of screaming birds but on the opposite side of the thick tree; thus I could only stand and watch them as they disappeared in the neighboring swamp.

Audubon (1842) says:

Their roosting-place is in hollow trees, and the holes excavated by the larger species of Woodpeckers, as far as these can be filled by them. At dusk, a flock of Parakeets may be seen alighting against the trunk of a large sycamore or any other tree, when a considerable excavation exists within it. Immediately below the entrance the birds all cling to the bark, and crawl into the hole to pass the night. When such a hole does not prove sufficient to hold the whole flock, those around the entrance hook themselves on by their claws, and the tip of the upper mandible, and look as if hanging by the bill. I have frequently seen them in such positions by means of a glass, and am satisfied that the bill is not the only support used in such cases.

Dr. William C. Herman writes to me, of the parakeets in the Cincinnati Zoological Garden: "The parakeets were well adapted to being caged, some were in the zoo for 20 or more years. A hollow tree was provided for the birds for roosting. Here they hung for the night; that is, they used their beaks for holding to the interior of the tree trunk and so rested for the night."

DISTRIBUTION

Range.—Southeastern United States; probably extinct.

The range of the Carolina parakeet extended **north** to casually northeastern Colorado (Little Thompson River); eastern Nebraska (Omaha and Brownville); casually Iowa (Spirit Lake and Decatur County); casually southern Wisconsin (Lake Koskonong and Waukesha County); Ohio (Columbus and Summit County); and Pennsylvania (Juniata River and Shermans Valley). East to Pennsylvania (Shermans Valley); casually the District of Columbia (Washington); casually West Virginia (White Sulphur Springs); South Carolina (Pine Barrens and Edding Island); Georgia; and Florida (Oklawaha River, Wekiva River, and Micco); south to Florida (Micco, Lake Okeechobee, Tampa, Tarpon Springs, Old Town, and Tallahassee); southern Louisiana (Bayou Sara and St. Mary); and central Texas (Brownwood). West to central Texas (Brownwood); eastern Oklahoma (Caddo and Fort Gibson); and casually eastern Colorado (Fort Lyon, Denver, and the Little Thompson River).

Casual records.—Several of the records that figure in the range as above outlined can be considered as little more than casual occurrences, but this status must be accorded a flock reported 25 miles northwest of Albany, N. Y., in January 1780, and to flocks observed "many years ago" at Buffalo and West Seneca, N. Y. There also is an indefinite record of this species in East Orange, Essex County, N. J., sometime between 1850 and 1860.

Systematists now consider the species as separable into two geographic races, the true Carolina parakeet, *C. c. carolinensis*, being the eastern form that ranged west to Alabama, while the Louisiana parakeet, *C. c. ludovicianus*, ranged westward from Mississippi, Tennessee, Kentucky, and Ohio.

Egg dates.—Florida: 2 records, April 2 and 26.

CONUROPSIS CAROLINENSIS LUDOVICIANUS Gmelin

LOUISIANA PARAKEET

HABITS

In describing this pale race of *Conuropsis*, Outram Bangs (1913) says: "For many years it has been common knowledge among the older set of American ornithologists that the Carolina paroquet divided into two very distinct geographical races." He says of its characters: "A much paler bird than *Conuropsis c. carolinensis* (Linn.); yellow portions of head and neck pale lemon yellow or picric yellow, instead of lemon yellow or lemon chrome; green of upper parts much paler and more bluish, verdigris green to variscite green on wing coverts and sides of neck; under parts dull green-yellow glossed with variscite green; bend of wing and feathers of tibia paler, purer yellow, less orange." Mr. Ridgway (1916) adds: "Greater wing-coverts, proximal secondaries, and basal portion of outer webs of primaries more pronouncedly and more extensively yellowish, contrasting more strongly with the general green color; size averaging decidedly greater." The latter author says of its former range: "Formerly inhabiting the entire Mississippi Valley (except open prairies and plains), from West Virginia to eastern Colorado, north to the southern shores of Lake Erie and Lake Michigan, south to the Gulf coast."

This parakeet is now, doubtless, quite extinct throughout all this wide range. Though formerly abundant over most of this region, it had begun to disappear even in Audubon's time, for he (1842) says: "Our Parakeets are very rapidly diminishing in number; and in some districts, where twenty-five years ago they were plentiful, scarcely any are now to be seen. At that period, they could be procured as far up the tributary waters of the Ohio as the Great Kenhawa, the Scioto, the heads of the Miami, the mouth of the Manimee at its junction with Lake Erie, on the Illinois River, and sometimes as far north-east as Lake Ontario. * * * At the present day, very few are to be found higher than Cincinnati, nor is it until you reach the mouth of the Ohio that Parakeets are met with in considerable numbers. I should think that along the Mississippi there is not now half the number that existed fifteen years ago."

Myron H. Swenk (1934), in a comprehensive paper on this parakeet of the interior, sums up its disappearance in the following words: "By 1840 they were practically gone in West Virginia and Ohio. They disappeared from Indiana about 1858 and from Illinois about 1861. The Colorado birds were gone by about 1862. In Kansas they were gone by about 1867, and during the years 1875–1880 they disappeared from Kentucky, Tennessee, Louisiana, Mississippi and Alabama. Their last stand was made in Missouri and along the Arkansas River and its tributaries in Arkansas and central Oklahoma, but by 1890 they were practically gone in these localities also. * * * The very last records of living Interior Carolina Paroquets are of lone individuals shot at Atchison, Kansas, in 1904, and seen at Notch, Stone County, Missouri, in 1905 (*vide* Widmann, * * * 1907)."

Since that time there have been at least two sight records reported. Harry Harris (1919) says that "in some unaccountable manner a lone bird strayed into the Courtney bottoms in 1912 and was observed by Bush for several weeks before it finally disappeared." Dr. Daniel S. Gage has sent me a letter from Prof. Elliot R. Downing, of the University of Chicago, reporting that he saw a Carolina parakeet in the sand-dune region on the shore of Lake Michigan, not far from Chicago, on June 11, 1912, His letter states that he saw the parakeet "on a Juneberry tree, a small one, on the margin of an interdunal pond. I remember the observation very clearly. I was within 20 feet of the bird and had a chance to observe it with my bird glasses for 10 or 15 minutes. I am therefore quite confident that there was no error in the observation."

Both of these records might well be based on escaped cage birds, as there were a number in captivity at that time, and the wild birds had long since disappeared.

Wilson (1832) suggests certain reasons why the inland parakeet enjoyed a wider and more northern distribution than its relative on the Atlantic coast. He writes:

The preference, however, which this bird gives to the western countries, lying in the same parallel of latitude with those eastward of the Alleghany mountains, which it rarely or never visits, is worthy of remark; and has been adduced, by different writers, as a proof of the superior mildness of climate in the former to that of the latter. But there are other reasons for this partiality equally powerful, though hitherto overlooked; namely, certain peculiar features of country to which these birds are particularly and strongly attached; these are, low, rich, alluvial bottoms, along the borders of creeks, covered with a gigantic growth of sycamore trees, or button-wood; deep, and almost inpenetrable swamps, where the vast and tower-cypress lifts its still more majestic head; and those singular salines, or, as they are usually called, *licks*, so generally interspersed over that country, and which are regularly and eagerly visited by the Paroquets. A still greater inducement is the superior abundance of their favorite fruits. That food which the paroquet prefers to all others is the seeds of the cockle bur, a plant rarely found in the lower parts of Pennsylvania or New York; but which unfortunately grows in too great abundance along the shores of the Ohio and Mississippi.

Nesting.—We have no more positive information on the nesting habits of this parakeet than we have of the eastern race, beyond the following statement by Col. N. S. Goss (1891): "Their nests are usually placed in holes or hollow cavities of trees. In the spring of 1858, a small flock reared their young in a large hollow limb of a giant sycamore tree, on the banks of the Neosho River, near Neosho Falls, Kansas. I have never been able to procure their eggs."

Eggs.—What few eggs of this race are in existence are indistinguishable from those of the Carolina parakeet. The measurements of the only four eggs that I have been able to locate are 36 by 27, 35 by 27.5, 35 by 26.5, and 36 by 26.5 millimeters.

Food.—Prof. Myron H. Swenk (1934) says of the food of this parakeet:

The food of the Interior Carolina Paroquet, though all vegetable was highly varied, and they seemed to delight in the fruits of spiny or thorny plants. One of the most relished foods was the seeds of the cocklebur (*Xanthium canadense*), and they fed also on the seeds of the sand-bur grass (*Cenchrus tribuloides*) and of the various species of thistles (*Cirsium*). In the fall they ate the seeds of the honey locust (*Gleditsia triacanthos*) and the tender buds and fruit of the osage orange (*Maclura pomifera*). In the spring they ate the buds of the red maple (*Acer rubrum*) and birch (*Betula* spp.). During the summer they ate much fruit, especially mulberries, wild grapes, hackberries and pawpaws, and, after the planting of cultivated apple orchards, were likely to visit them and peck out the apple seeds in the fall, sometimes doing injury in this way. Corn in the milk was also sometimes injured, but not extensively. Other favorite items of food were the seed balls of the sycamore and beech and pecan nuts. In the South cypress seeds were much eaten.

Dr. Amos W. Butler (1892), quoting from W. B. Seward, thus describes the parakeet's method of eating the cocklebur seeds: "In eating, the bird picked up a burr with its beak, this was then delivered to one foot raised to receive it. Then one end of the burr was cut off with the sharp-ended under beak, the burr being held with the foot and the under side of the upper beak while two small kernels were extracted with the assistance of the tongue and the husk was thrown away."

Dr. Butler, elsewhere (1898), adds to the items of food mentioned above cherries, persimmons, black-gum berries, haws, and acorns.

Voice.—Mr. Swenk (1934) says: "The common call notes consisted of a loud, shrill series of rapidly uttered, discordant cries, given incessently when the birds were in flight, resembling *qui-qui, qui, qui, qui, qui-i-i-i,* with a rising inflection on each *i* and the last cry drawn out. Another call resembled the shrill cry of a goose and was frequently uttered for minutes at a time. When at rest they had a low, conversational chatter."

Winter.—The Carolina parakeet was evidently a very hardy bird, a remarkable quality, quite unique among parrots. Wilson (1832) saw them "in the month of February, along the banks of the Ohio, in a snow storm, flying about like pigeons, and in full cry." Dr. Butler (1898) was furnished the following note by Prof. John Collett:

In 1842, Return Richmond, of Lodi (Parke County), Ind., cut down, in the cold weather of winter, a sycamore tree some four feet in diameter. In its hollow trunk he found hundreds of Parakeets in a quiescent or semi-torpid condition. The weather was too cold for the birds to fly or even to make any exertion to escape. Mr. Richmond cut off with his saw a section of the hollow trunk some five feet long, cut out a doorway one foot by two in size, nailed it over a wire screen of his fanning mill, rolled this cumbersome cage into the house and placed in it a dozen of the birds. They soon began to enjoy the feed of fruit, huckleberries and nuts he gave them, and he had the pleasure of settling absolutely the disputed question of how they slept. At night they never rested on a perch, but suspended themselves by their beaks, and with their feet on the side of their cage. This was repeated night after night during their captivity.

RHYNCHOPSITTA PACHYRHYNCHA (Swainson)

THICK-BILLED PARROT

HABITS

This fine, large parrot is a Mexican species that claims a place on our list as an irregular visitor across our southwestern border in southern Arizona and New Mexico. Charles T. Vorhies (1934) has published an account of all the Arizona records that he was able to find, which probably tells the whole story. R. D. Lusk (1900) reported that a flock of nine or ten of these parrots came into the Chiricahua Mountains, just north of the Mexican border, about the middle of June 1900. He collected two specimens, and some pole-cutters killed several others. "They appeared to come up the large canon, at the head of which I was encamped, to about midway of the mountain's height, where the oaks begin to give way to pine, and there they tarried."

Austin Paul Smith (1907) reported "an immense flock of this species, * * * observed by miners at Bonita Park, near Cochise head in the Chiricahua Mountains, during the month of August, 1904. * * * This flock was estimated at from 700 to 1,000, by those who observed the birds. Among these were a number of young birds, easily distinguished by plumage and small size."

The next occurrence of these parrots, and probably the last definite record, was in the winter of 1917–18, of which Percy Hands wrote to Professor Vorhies as follows: "The Mexican Thick-billed Parrots were first noticed on my ranch in lower Pinery Canyon in mid-September. About 250—counted over 200—in one flock. They have been on my ranch at irregular intervals since then up to March 27. They roosted here seven times during late October and early November. The longest period they were away was about three weeks before they appeared March 27. There were about 70, rough count, at that appearance."

The thick-billed parrot may have occurred elsewhere in Arizona, but Professor Vorhies was unable to find any definite records for any locality outside of the Chiricahuas. The New Mexico records are both hearsay, sight records. Mrs. Bailey (1928) reports: "In 1919, Dr. Alexander Wetmore was told by R. Winkler that in recent years his son had at times seen parrots on Animas Mountain, above Deer Creek. * * * A confirmatory record was given Aldo Leopold by Forest Ranger Don S. Sullivan, who said that in 1917 some large Parrots were seen near the Elvey Ranch. * * * on the Animas Division of the Coronado Forest near the Mexican boundary."

The main range of the thick-billed parrot is in the mountains bordering the Mexican tableland. Dr. W. H. Bergtold (1906) writes:

This bird is increasingly common from Chuichupa southward, and was especially an everyday sight during the trip, in 1904, to the mountains west of Parral. * * * In the higher mountains west of Parral, a region varying in altitude from 4,000 to 10,000 feet, the Thick-billed Parrot is far more common than northward in the country west of Cases Grandes; in fact it is the characteristic bird of these high places, as much so as is the Magpie part of the local color of our Western Plains. * * * In whatever section we saw them, these parrots were most abundant in the pines. They frequented the tops of dead pines, and were, a good part of the time, going in and out of abandoned woodpecker nests, nests which we took to be those of the Imperial

Woodpecker (*Campophilus imperialis*), for this splendid woodpecker is relatively common in the same neighborhood, and is the only woodpecker which excavates such a large hole.

Nesting.—Practically all we know about the nesting habits of the thick-billed parrot is contained in the report of Col. John E. Thayer (1906) on some ten nests of this species examined by Wilmot W. Brown, Jr., in 1905, in the mountains near Colonia Pachaco and Colonia Garcia, Chihuahua, Mexico. The breeding grounds were at altitudes varying from 6,500 to 7,500 feet, and all the nests were in the tall pines, characteristic of the region. The parrots occupied the old nests of the imperial woodpecker, which had been excavated at heights ranging from 50 to 80 feet above ground; one nest was in a living longleaf pine, but all the others were in dead, dry, or rotten pines. The entrance to the hole was usually circular and 6 or 7 inches in diameter; the holes varied in depth from 18 to 24 inches, and the inner cavity measured from 8 to 10 inches in diameter. No nesting material had been brought in, the eggs having been laid on the bare wood dust left by woodpeckers. One nest, found on August 20, contained two big young ones and one fresh egg; another found on August 28, held two young ones. All the other nests, found between August 11 and 25, contained one or two eggs. Mr. Brown wrote to Colonel Thayer (1906) that the first tree he climbed was "located on a flat-topped mountain at an altitude of 7,500 feet above the sea. * * * The tree was about one hundred feet high and was thirty-six inches in diameter at the base and was so dry that the bark had all peeled off. It was very difficult to climb, not to mention the danger." The nest was 80 feet from the ground.

Eggs.—I have examined the eggs referred to above, which, with the entire Thayer collection, are now in the Museum of Comparative Zoology, in Cambridge. They vary in shape from ovate to rounded-ovate, are pure white in color, and are decidedly glossy; the shell is hard and thick. The measurments of 20 eggs average 39.49 by 30.63 millimeters; the eggs showing the four extremes measure 42 by 31, 39.2 by 32, 37.6 by 30.6, and 38.2 by 29 millimeters.

Plumages.—Aside from the alcoholic specimens in the Thayer collection, which are unsuitable for description, I have seen no nestlings of this species. The immature bird is similar to the adult, but the red of the forehead is more restricted, and the red is lacking on the bend of the wing and on the lower thighs. Nothing seems to be known about the length of time that the immature plumage is worn, or about subsequent molts and plumages.

Food.—The birds observed by R. D. Lusk (1900) "were very busily engaged with the pine cones, and investigation of their stomachs showed nothing but a plentiful quantity of very immature pinones wrested from their cavities in the hearts of the hard, green cones by their powerful beaks. The beaks, at their bases, as well as nearly the entire under parts of the birds, were more or less begummed with the resin of the cones." The birds reported by Austin Paul Smith (1907) were first noticed when "feeding on pinyon nuts. Some of the birds were on the ground, searching for the fallen nuts." During their sojourn in Arizona, these parrots have been reported as feeding on pinyon nuts and acorns, after they had exhausted the supply of pine cones.

The stomachs of two birds examined by Cottam and Knappen (1939) contained 136 and 284 or more seeds of the Chihuahua pine (*Pinus chihuahuana*). "The pine seeds were in all stages from entire seeds to a pulverized mast-like débris."

Behavior.—All observers seem to agree that the thick-billed parrot is very tame and unsuspicious, probably owing to its unfamiliarity with man.

William Beebe (1905) says: "It is either a very stupid bird or controlled by its curiosity, for the flocks followed us everywhere."

Dr. Bergtold (1906) writes:

It was a great surprise to see how different is a wild parrot from a tame one; one must need get an idea from the latter that a parrot is a slow, lumbering climber, able to use its wings perhaps, yet little given to prolonged and vigorous flight. On the contrary, this Thick-billed Parrot flew across deep barrancas, from mountain to mountain, as swift and strong on wing as a duck, going often in large flocks, which were noticeably divided in pairs, each couple flying one above another as closely as beating wings allowed. Its loud squawk resounded overhead, across the barrancas, and in the pines all day long, from dawn till dusk; and many and many a time a flock could be heard long before it was in sight. The birds were not at all shy, as one could walk up under a tree and watch a pair climbing in it without disturbing them in the least. Here they seemed natural, at least to one whose previous knowledge of parrots came via the cage bird, for they climbed about precisely as does the domesticated species, using bill and feet in the familiar way; on the wing the birds seemed anything but parrots.

Dr. Alexander Wetmore (1935) obtained considerable information from reliable observers about the occurrence of this parrot in Arizona and its habits; regarding its movements and behavior, he writes:

According to all accounts Thick-billed Parrots gathered at night to roost in flocks and then spread out in small bands to feed during the day. In Pinery Canyon they roosted somewhere on the upper mountain slopes during summer and fall. Morning and evening they were seen in two large flocks. As the weather became colder the roosting place was changed to one at a lower altitude. In Rucker Canyon the birds came at night to the mountain side above the site of old Camp Rucker.

As there were a thousand or more here, their morning and evening flights were quite impressive. In the Dragoon Range the parrots roosted somewhere near the head of Cochise Stronghold and made a morning flight that often carried them directly out over the plains to the east.

In feeding, the large bands usually broke up into smaller parties. In winter such flocks at times came down to perch on broken sandstone ledges where they clambered about or basked in the sun. In Rucker Canyon toward evening flocks often flew down to the river to drink before passing on to their roost. In the Chiricahua Mountains during late fall and winter the birds came down into the foothills to an altitude of between 5000 and 5500 feet though earlier they were confined to the higher basins.

The birds were noisy and their coming was heralded by their loud calls that were said to be readily audible at a distance of more than a mile. Like parrots elsewhere they were said to show much fear of hawks (though it seems strange that a bird with so powerful a bill and so muscular a body should show such fear); when a red-tail or a hawk of some other species appeared they rose in flocks and circled in the air, doubling the volume of their ordinary screeching calls.

He was told by F. Hands that "as cold weather came during the fall some of the birds disappeared. Others remained during the entire winter, although at one time the ground was covered by six inches of snow for over two weeks and the birds were forced to seek their food on the ground where this covering had blown partly away."

DISTRIBUTION

Range.—Southeastern Arizona and southwestern New Mexico (casually) and the mountainous area adjacent to the tableland of Mexico.

The range of the thick-billed parrot extends **north** to (casually) southeastern Arizona (probably near Mowry, Pinery Canyon, Cochise Head, and Paradise); (casually) southwestern New Mexico (Animas Mountain); eastern Chihuahua (Ciudad Chihuahua); and Veracruz (Perote). **East** to Veracruz (Perote and Jalapa). **South** to central Veracruz (Jalapa); Mexico (Popocatapetl); and southern Durango (Canyon Rio San Juan). **West** to Durango (Canyon Rio San Juan, Cuidad Durango, and Arroyo del Buey); western Chihuahua (Guadalupe y Calvo, Jesus Maria, and Colonia Garcia); and southeastern Arizona (Nogales and probably Mowry).

While the range as outlined includes the entire region over which the species is known to occur, it has actually been found breeding only in the Mexican States of Chihuahua and Durango. At irregular intervals flocks that sometimes are of large size travel northward and invade the mountain ranges of southeastern Arizona. Such invasions took place in 1900, 1904, and 1917.

Egg dates.—Mexico: 10 records, May 10 to August 25; 7 records, August 11 to 25.

Order CUCULIFORMES

Family CUCULIDAE: Cuckoos, Roadrunners, and Anis

CROTOPHAGA ANI Linnaeus

SMOOTH-BILLED ANI

HABITS

This curious member of the cuckoo family is a tropical species of rare, or perhaps only casual, occurrence within the limits of the United States; a few may occur more or less regularly in southern Florida or Louisiana, but to find it in abundance one must visit the West Indies or South America. It has a variety of local names, such as black ani, black witch, blackbird, savanna blackbird, and tickbird, the last from its habit of eating the ticks that infest cattle. Charles B. Taylor sent some interesting notes on this bird to W. E. D. Scott (1892); regarding its haunts in Jamaica, he says:

The Ani appears to be abundant in all parts of the island. It is one of the commonest birds near Kingston; and in most open and sparsely wooded lands, or in the vicinity of cultivated clearings, little groups or companies may nearly always be seen. Blackbirds are invariably present wherever cattle are pastured. I cannot recollect an instance in which I have noted a herd of cows at pasture without a flock of these birds appearing in company with them or in their immediate vicinity. This association is doubtless chiefly for the purpose of feeding on the ticks and other parasites on the animals, a good work largely shared by the Grackles (*Quiscalus crassirostris*). It is most interesting to watch a company of Blackbirds when thus engaged. Many are perched on the backs of the cattle (two or three sometimes on one cow), others are on the ground hopping about fearlessly among the grazing herd, searching for insects at the roots of the herbage or capturing those disturbed by the feet of the cattle.

Nesting.—He says on this subject:

Their nesting habits are exceedingly curious and interesting. Many individuals (possibly members of one flock) work together in the construction of a large nest in which all the females of the company lay their eggs. The number of eggs deposited in different nests varies greatly but is of course dependent on the number of birds in a company. Six and eight eggs are commonly found. I once took eleven, and in August last year I saw a clutch of twenty-one that had been taken from a single nest! It is probable that normally not more than two eggs are deposited by each bird, but nothing definite can be said on this point. The nest, which is usually placed high up in a tall tree, very frequently in a clump of mistletoe on a "bastard cedar", is a large, loosely constructed mass of twigs, entirely lined with dried leaves. But the most remarkable circumstance in connection with the nesting of these birds is the deposition of the eggs in *regular layers* with leaves between. This custom I had long heard of before an opportunity offered for personal observation. In the first nest I examined, the eggs were in two distinct layers, separated by a deep bed of dry leaves; the bottom layer consisted of four eggs and these, strange to say, were all infertile. I believe this singular habit is practised in all cases where a large number of birds resort to the same nest.

Dr. Alexander Wetmore (1927) writes:

Although this species often builds a communal nest, this is not always the case. Near Cayey [Porto Rico], January 22, two anis were seen constructing a nest in a tree about thirty feet above a small stream, the male sitting on a limb above while the female was in the nest, as yet only a loose mass of sticks and weeds. She moved and turned to shape it to her body, with her long tail sticking nearly straight up in the air. Near Bayamón, July 25, a single bird slipped quietly from a bulky nest in a clump of bamboos and only its mate appeared to join it. The nests were all large and bulky and were located from six to thirty feet above the ground. Bowdish reports a communal nest found near Aguadilla, August 13, built eight feet from the ground, in a thicket of bushes and trees. This nest contained twenty eggs, placed in layers of four or five, each layer being covered with dead leaves to separate it from the next lot of eggs above. Eight of the eggs were partly incubated and twelve were fresh.

John G. Wells (1902) says: "A flat nest is first built and about 6 or 7 eggs laid in it; then these are covered over and more eggs laid, and so on until four or five layers of nests have been constructed one over the other.

"I have seen four of these birds sitting on the nest together. When the top layer of eggs is hatched, and the young fledged, it is scraped off and incubation goes on with each succeeding layer, until all the eggs are hatched."

Eggs.—On account of its communal nesting habits, the number of eggs laid by each individual ani does not seem to be known; nor is anything known about the period of incubation. The number of eggs found in a nest varies greatly, from 4 or 5 up to 20 or more, depending on the number of females laying in the nest. I have in my collection a set of 18, there is a set of 19 in the Thayer collection, and sets of 20 and 21 are mentioned above.

The eggs vary in shape from oval to elliptical-oval. Bendire (1895) says that the eggs "are glaucous-blue in color, and this is overlaid and hidden by a thin, chalky, white deposit; as incubation advances the eggs become more or less scratched and the blue underneath is then plainly visible in places, giving them a very peculiar appearance." The underlying color of some of the eggs that I have seen is "pale Nile blue"; others have described them as green.

The eggs are often very much nest stained. Mr. Taylor (Scott, 1892) makes the following interesting observation regarding the scratches: "What seems very singular is that comparatively little of this chalky covering gets rubbed off the sides, where from the turning over of the eggs in the nest we should expect to see the greatest extent of denudation, whereas *one* or *both ends* are nearly always *wholly* denuded. * * * So cleanly and evenly is it done, and to such an extent, that I feel confident it is the work of the birds themselves, their beaks alone being able to accomplish it. At the same time it is easy to see that the marks and scratches at the sides are the result of friction with the twigs and leaves of the nest."

The measurements of 63 eggs average 35.03 by 26.27 millimeters; the eggs showing the four extremes measure 40.4 by 28, 36.5 by 30, and 29.21 by 23.37 millimeters.

Young.—Alexander F. Skutch has sent me the following notes on the development of young smooth-billed anis, as observed by him on Barro Colorado Island, Panama: "The newly hatched ani is covered with black skin quite devoid of any trace of feathers. Its eyes are tightly closed. The development of this naked, helpless, little creature is amazingly rapid. By the second day the sheaths of the flight plumes have already begun to sprout. By the third day the eyes are open, and the sheaths of the contour feathers have begun to push out from the skin. The pinfeathers grow rapidly and become very long before they begin to release the true feathers which they enclose. When the young ani is 5 days old, the body feathers peep from the ends of their sheaths. At this age, the nestling could hang by one foot from my finger, and pull itself up by the use of its feet and bill, which was hooked over the support. When placed on the ground, it attempted to crawl away through the grass, and might have succeeded in escaping if I had not watched it carefully. Returned to the nest, it would not remain in the bowl, but climbed out to perch on the rim, where it uttered a little whine.

"When I approached the nest on the following day, the 6-day-old youngster hopped out and began to climb through the thorny branches of the orange tree, but soon it lost its hold and fell to the ground. When I picked it up, it uttered a weak imitation of the parents' usual call. The flight feathers, as well as the body feathers, were now pushing forth from their sheaths, and the latter were longer than on the preceding day. Much bare skin was, however, still visible between them. On the following morning the nest was empty; and I could not discover what had befallen the occupant."

Plumages.—The youngest bird I have seen is about half grown and fully feathered. The contour plumage is soft and short, "bone brown" on the under parts and somewhat darker above; the wings and tail are glossy, purplish black, much like those of the adult; the bill is smaller and less specialized than that of the adult. On account of the extended breeding season, it is difficult to give any definite dates for the molts. I have seen a young male, taken March 7, that was just completing the molt of the wings and tail, but the body plumage was still juvenal; from this I infer that the juvenal plumage may be worn for the whole of the first year. Maynard (1896) took some birds that had just completed molting on March 8; also some that had just begun to molt on April 24. I have seen young birds molting into adult plumage in December.

Food.—P. H. Gosse (1847) says of the food of the ani in Jamaica:

The food of our Blackbird, though consisting mainly of insects, is not confined to them. We usually find the stomach distended with caterpillars, moths, grasshoppers, beetles, and other insects, to such a degree that we wonder how the mass could have been forced in. But I have found these contents mixed up with, and stained by the berries of the snake-withe; and in July I have found the stomach crammed with the berries of the fiddle-wood, (*Cytharaxylon*) which had stained the whole inner surface a bright crimson. Flocks of these birds were at that time feeding on the glowing clusters profusely ripe upon the trees. Stationary insects are the staple food; to obtain which, they hop about grassy places, and are often seen to jump, or to run eagerly at their prey; on which occasions the long tail, continuing the given motion after the body has stopped, is thrown forward in an odd manner, sometimes nearly turning the bird head over heels. * * *

One day I noticed a cow lying down, around which were four or five Black-birds, hopping on or off her neck, and eagerly picking the insects from her body; which service seemed in no wise unpleasing to her. I have also seen them leaping up on cows when grazing; and, on another occasion, jumping to and from a horse's back; and my lad Sam has repeatedly observed them clinging to a cow's tail, and picking insects from it, as far down as the terminal tuft. * * *

But stationary insects are not the only prey of the Crotophaga; in December, I have seen little groups of them engaged in the evenings, leaping up from the pasture about a yard into the air, doubtless after flying insects, which they seemed to catch. * * * I have seen one with a dragon-fly in its beak, which it had just caught, but it may have been while resting. At another time I saw that a Blackbird had actually made prey of one of our little nimble lizards (*Anolis*).

Maynard (1896) says that "anis live largely on locusts, especially a large species, which is quite common on the Bahamas, and which has a peculiar, rather disagreeable odor, which is imparted to the birds." W. E. Clyde Todd (1916) says that, on the Isle of Pines, "it is fond of following in the wake of brush-fires, picking up the roasted lizards, snails, and insects." Dr. Wetmore (1916) reports that the stomachs of 41 birds from Puerto Rico contained 91.3 percent animal matter, mostly harmful insects and arachnids, including mole crickets, other crickets, locusts, sugar-cane root-borers, leaf beetles, other beetles, squashbugs, other bugs, caterpillars, and spiders; the other 8.7 percent was vegetable matter, mostly seeds and fruits of 7 species of wild plants. He also says elsewhere (1927): "On May 20 near Yauco three anis were seen in a tree in which several mazambiques had nests. The anis were very near these nests, and the blackbirds, together with a pair of gray kingbirds, were much excited, but appeared to be unable to drive out the intruders.   It was certain that the anis were bent on robbing the nests, and one was shot in the act of gulping down something which was later found to be an egg.   No other instances of this evil habit were observed."

Behavior.—Gosse (1847) writes:

Though its usual mode of progression on the ground is by hopping, or rather bounding, the feet being lifted together, the Blackbird is seen occasionally to *run* in a headlong manner for a short distance, moving the feet alternately.   He is fond of sitting in the morning sun on a low tree with the wings expanded; remaining there perfectly still for a considerable time.   In the heat of the day, in July and August, many may be seen in the lowland plains, sitting on the fences and logwood hedges with the beaks wide open, as if gasping for air; they then forget their usual loquacity and wariness.   Often two or three will sit in the centre of a thick bush, overhung with a matted drapery of convolvolus, whence they utter their singular cry in a calling tone, as if they were playing at hide-and-seek, and requiring their fellows to come and find them.

Several observers have noted that anis roost at night huddled close together on a branch, like domestic fowls, and that they often bunch together in this way during a rain.   Dr. Wetmore (1927) writes:

These strange birds are found in flocks that contain from half a dozen to twenty or more individuals, ranging mainly in pasture-lands, but going also into the cane-fields and orange groves to feed.   In pastures they remain near the cattle, keeping ahead of them with long hops, in order to get the insects that the cattle scare up.   Any intruder is greeted with a querulous call, and the whole flock flies in a straggling line across the fields to perch in a bush or low tree, where they crowd together and peer out curiously, their long tails and arched beaks giving them an odd appearance.   In the early morning, when the grass is wet, they frequently sit in the sun with the wings extended in order to dry them or to absorb heat.   The wings are small for the size of the bird, and the flight, accomplished by a series of steady wing beats alternating with short sails, is not strong.   In a heavy wind the birds are almost helpless, and they seldom rise high from the ground at any time.   When on the wing, the back appears concave from the fact that the head and tail are held on a higher level.

C. J. Maynard (1896) says:

In flight they most nearly resemble a Canada or Florida Jay, alternately flopping and sailing, moving in a straight forward flight from tree to tree with great rapidity, uttering their mournful notes as they quickly disappear in the distance.   *   *   *

A careful study of the Anis convinced me of the fact that a number of females are led by two or three males, and these males take great care of their charges.   They utter cries of alarm when they perceive an intruder, and drive the females before them into a place of safety.   I have even seen males fly against females or young birds which did not attempt to escape soon enough, and knock them off the limb on which they sat and then accompany them to a distant thicket.

I am inclined to think that the Ani is polygamous and this habit of the males taking care of a number of females would appear to confirm this idea.

Mr. Taylor (Scott, 1892) gives a somewhat different impression, thus:

The Blackbirds at their best have a very lean and shabby appearance, and are slow and awkward in their movements. I have watched an individual make several ineffectual attempts to alight on the frond of a cocoanut palm; but even among the branches of other trees their actions appear awkward. Their flight is slow and gliding, somewhat labored, and of little duration, the birds often appearing to fall short of the point originally aimed at. Yet they will chase the large yellow butterflies, and I was shown a large green locust that one of these birds was seen to capture in flight and afterwards drop. In the progress of a flock from place to place they do not usually fly all together, but move away in straggling groups or couples. One or more individuals first start off with their wailing call, followed soon after by two or three; after a little delay then two more go; another pause, then one, then three, and so on. If a tree has very dense foliage they alight (with much awkward scrambling) on the tops or extremities of the highest branches, where they may gain a clear and uninterrupted view, and this is usually the case when they are traversing very open country.

Voice.—The note of the ani has been called a wailing or a whining whistle; it has been said to resemble the notes of the wood duck. Dr. Wetmore (1927) says: "The ordinary call-notes are a low *kur-r-rk* and a querulous *quee ick, quee ick,* varied by low chuckling notes. When the birds are at all wild, they serve to alarm the entire country, as they begin to call on the slightest provocation." It has also been expressed as *que-yuch, que-yuch, que-yuch* by Gosse (1847) and similarly by others.

Field marks.—The ani is such a peculiar and unique bird that it could hardly be mistaken for anything else. It is the only long, slender, black bird, with a long tail, short wings, and a huge bill, that is to be found within its range, so far as I know. Its shape and its manner of flight are quite different from those of the grackles; its concave back in flight, referred to above, is distinctive. Gosse (1847) says: "The appearance of the bird in its sliding flights is unusual; the body is slender, the head large, and the beak enormous; and as in flying it assumes a perfectly straight form, with the long tail in the same line, without flapping the wings, it takes the aspect, on a side view, rather of a fish than of a bird."

Where our two small species of anis come together in Panama, they are likely to be confused, but the voices of the two are quite distinct; the call of the groove-billed is softer and higher in pitch, while that of the smooth-billed is more raucous and whining. The grooves in the bill of the former are not easily seen, except under favorable circumstances, but the culmen of the bill in the smooth-billed is much higher and sharper than in the groove-billed.

DISTRIBUTION

Range.—South America and the West Indies; casual in winter in eastern Central America and casual or accidental in Florida, Louisiana, North Carolina, and Pennsylvania.

The normal range of the smooth-billed ani extends **north** to western Cuba (Los Indios and Nueva Gerona); the Bahama Islands (Little Abaco and Nassau); Haiti (Jacmel); the Dominican Republic (Sesua and Ciudad Trujillo); Puerto Rico (Aguidillo and Rio Piedras); and the Virgin Islands (Cuelebra, Vieques, and St. Croix). **East** to the Virgin Islands (St. Croix); the Lesser Antilles (Grenada and Trinidad); British Guiana (Georgetown); Surinam (Paramaribo); and eastern Brazil (Ilha Mexiana, Maranhao, Bahia, Sapetiba, Canatgallo, Rio de Janeiro, and Iguape). **South** to southeastern Brazil (Iguape); and northern Argentina (Posadas, the Chaco District, and San Jose). **West** to northwestern Argentina (San Jose, Concepcion, and Salta); Peru (Huanuco and Iquitos); northwestern Colombia (the Cauca River Valley); Panama (Gatun, Perme, and Obaldia); Jamaica (Port Henderson, Spanish Town, Grand Cayman, and Little Cayman); and western Cuba (Los Indios).

This species occurs in other parts of Central America only in winter, when it has been recorded from Costa Rica (Rio Coto); Nicaragua (Great and Little Corn Islands); Honduras (Ruatan Island); and Quintana Roo, Mexico (Cozumel Island).

Casual records.—The following are among the several records the species has for Florida: Flamingo, a specimen taken in June 1916; Pass-a-Grille, a specimen collected on February 25, 1929; Dry Tortugas, three seen June 18 and 19, 1935; and Miami Beach, a small flock seen on February 24, 1937. Undated specimens also are available for Brevard County, Tortugas, Pepper Hammock near the head of the Banana River, and Charlotte Harbor.

A specimen was collected on July 18, 1893, at Diamond, and several have been reported from the vicinity of Buras, St. Bernard Parish, La. A specimen was collected previous to 1866 at Edenton, N. C., while individuals were reported from Piney Creek in the western part of that State on July 17, 1932, June 1, 1933, and June 25, 1934. There also is an old record of the occurrence of this species on Pettys Island in the Delaware River, opposite Kensington, Pa.

Egg dates.—Bahamas: 2 records, June 14.

Brazil: 3 records, October 1 to November 18.

British Guiana: 3 records, January 14 to July 2.

Cuba: 4 records, February 22 to August 20.

Jamaica: 7 records, May 29 to July 30.

Puerto Rico: 2 records, July 25 and August 13.

CROTOPHAGA SULCIROSTRIS SULCIROSTRIS Swainson

GROOVE-BILLED ANI

PLATES 1, 2

HABITS

This Central and South American species was added to our fauna by George B. Sennett (1879), who secured a fine male on May 19, 1878, near Lomita, Tex., while it was "flying about the low bushes in open chaparral. It was very shy, flying in and about the bushes, and was shot on the wing." The only one I have ever seen did not seem at all shy. I was sitting down, quietly watching some Texas sparrows that were hopping around on the ground near me, in some thick brush bordering a resaca near Brownsville, Tex., when one of these curious birds appeared. It seemed more curious than shy, as it moved about slowly in the bushes, looking me over; it remained in my vicinity for some time and I could have shot it easily. It is said to show a preference for thick underbrush in the vicinity of water, or for lightly wooded swamps.

In his proposed work on the birds of the Caribbean lowlands, Alexander F. Skutch devotes two long and very interesting chapters to the home life of the groove-billed ani. He has kindly placed at my disposal his unpublished manuscript and allowed me to quote freely from it. As to its haunts, he writes: "The variety of the habitat of the anis is enormous and their only restriction seems to be that they do not tolerate the forest and are never seen there. They are birds of open country but seem nearly indifferent to its type. In the inhabited districts of the humid coastal regions they are one of the most conspicuous species. Their favorite haunts are bushy pastures, orchards, the lighter second growth, and even lawns and clearings about the native huts. Marshland is as acceptable to them as a well-drained hillside, and they are numerous in such extensive stands of sawgrass as that surrounding the Toloa Lagoon in Honduras, although it is probable that they do not venture far from some outstanding hummock or ridge which supports a few low bushes in which they can roost and nest. In the semidesert regions of the interior, where their associates of the coast lands, if present at all, are as a rule rare and restricted to the moist thickets along the rivers, they are among the most numerous of birds, and live among scattered cacti and acacias as successfully as amid the rankest vegetation of the districts watered by 12 feet of rainfall in the year. In altitude they range upward to 5,000 feet, but are not nearly so numerous in the elevated districts as in the lowlands."

Nesting.—Dr. Charles W. Richmond, drawing on his experience with it near Bluefields, Nicaragua, sent some elaborate notes on the groove-billed ani to Major Bendire (1895), from which I quote as follows:

It appears to breed at various times during the year, as I have found fresh eggs July 6, 1892, and young birds, recently from the nest, November 29, the breeding season spreading over seven months of the year at least, as it begins nesting earlier than the date of taking my first eggs. Nests are frequently built in the heart of a thick, thorny orange or lemon tree, and this appears to be a favorite situation. In this case the nest is from 4 to 7 feet from the ground, and, besides being difficult to get at, is somewhat protected from invasion the wasps which almost invariably take up their abode in the same tree. In going through a small lemon grove I found an old nest of this species. In the cavity there were no eggs, but on poking the nest to pieces six badly decayed eggs rolled out.

One nest containing three eggs in the proper place and two others at the bottom, under the lining of green leaves, was located in a bamboo about 12 feet from the ground. The eggs were fresh, and more would probably have been deposited; the leaves forming the lining were still green. The parent birds were away at the time. Another nest was situated in some vines which had over-run an old tree stub, and was about 15 feet from the ground.

It may be that where numerous eggs are deposited in one nest only those eggs that are deposited in the proper place and directly influenced by the incubating bird are hatched, while those placed among the sticks forming the bulky exterior are left unhatched. It would be interesting to watch the progress of a large nestful of eggs and note results. The nests found by me were all composed of dead black twigs, rather loosely put together, very bulky and conspicuous structures, lined with green leaves, or, if old nests, with leaves that had the appearance of having been picked green.

One of Dr. Richmond's nests is described by Major Bendire (1895) as "a rather loose structure, about 10 inches in diameter and 4 inches in height. The inner cup measures 4 inches in diameter by 2½ inches in depth."

According to George K. Cherrie (1892) Señor Don Anastasio Alfaro says of the nests he collected in Costa Rica:

The structure is voluminous, composed chiefly of coarse dead twigs, but presents one peculiarity not observed in any other bird, namely the nest being lined with fresh green leaves. My three specimens were all placed in low trees, and neither was found at a greater height than three meters. One had been built above an old nest of one of the larger Tyrannidae.

It will not be without interest, I think, to insert my observations relative to one of these nests. On the 20th of May I noticed a Zopilotillo with a dry stick in its bill, which was immediately carried to a point in the hedge-row where it was deposited with three others. After assuring myself that the bird was building its nest there, I retired, with the intention of returning at a more opportune moment. And when one week later I returned to the same spot, what was my surprise to see not only the nest completed and containing six eggs, but more than this: in the thorns and leaves about it were scattered seven more eggs! As a consequence, if that collection was not the work of the Zopilotillos collectively, the poor owner would have had to deposit three eggs daily! In the finding of some of the eggs scattered in the leaves was revealed one of the architect's peculiarities. A hole had been left in the centre of the nest and only recently filled with leaves whose fresh green color testified that they had been cut and placed there later than the others forming the carpeting to the bottom of this common incubator.

Alden H. Miller (1932) writes of his experience with the nesting habits of the groove-billed ani in El Salvador:

Several nests were watched from the time there was one egg until there were nine, or in one case eleven, eggs. The eggs were deposited regularly at one day intervals and there was no certain indication in any of the sets, of two females contributing to the same nest as has been claimed by other observers. My findings, however, do not prove conclusively that community nests may not exist, at least occasionally. Incubation is uniform within a set and, correspondingly, birds were found to be incubating regularly only after the sets were completed. In the set of thirteen the eggs were resting in three layers in the necessarily ample cup of the nest.

Nest sites were from two feet to twenty-five feet above ground in almost any kind of bush or tree. Usually they were located between six and twelve feet above ground in thorny tangles or close twiggery. One nest was found, however, in an open crotch of a fan of a royal palm. Adult birds are not much in evidence around nests which are being built or around sets of incomplete eggs. When flushed from sets of complete eggs, they may approach within five feet of the intruder and utter their feeble, squeaking notes of protest.

A. J. van Rossem (1938) found several nests, on July 29, 1925, "in the mimosa scrub in the marsh along the north shore of Lake Olomega," in El Salvador. "These nests were all in similar situations, that is, they were rather conspicuously placed in mimosa bushes and more than six feet above the mud or water."

Mr. Skutch devoted considerable time to studying the communal nesting habits of the groove-billed ani. He found them to be among the latest birds to breed, remaining together in small flocks from February to May while the other birds of the region were raising their broods. During June he watched the construction of a communal nest, on which three pairs worked in perfect harmony, operating in pairs and not as a unit. One of the pair remained on the nest while its mate brought in the material. There was not the least jealousy between the pairs, and "two or more pairs often perched quietly in the same bush. Each pair preferred to work alone at the nest, and if a second pair flew into the nesting tree, the first often quietly withdrew. This was not always their conduct, and sometimes one of the second pair (probably the female) took a place on the nest beside one of the first pair, while their two mates perched near by, or else brought them sticks.

"The normal set of eggs for each female is three, or more commonly four. Nests belonging to a single pair generally contain this number, and the nests belonging to two pairs, which I encountered, contained a maximum of eight. Once I found a nest with 12 eggs, which covered the bottom two layers deep, and six birds were interested in them. * * * Of ten nests which I found in Honduras and Guatemala and was able to watch for an adequate period, four were the property of single pairs, five of two pairs together, and one belonged to three pairs in common."

All the birds of both sexes took turns in incubating the eggs, but their shifts on the nest had no regular order and no fixed duration. "Just as the parents cooperate in incubating the eggs, they all join in the care of the nestlings. I have watched three nests, each belonging to two pairs, during the time they contained young. Two of them, I made quite sure, were attended by four adults, but at the other I could not convince myself that there were more than three attendants. Possibly some calamity had befallen the fourth bird, or possibly also I failed to recognize it, since the anis at this nest were unmarked and indistinguishable."

Eggs.—The groove-billed ani lays 4 to 13 eggs, the smaller numbers being apparently commoner. The eggs vary in shape from oval to elliptical-oval, or rarely to elliptical-ovate or rounded-ovate. The ground color, when visible, varies from "glaucous-blue" to "Nile blue" or "pale Nile blue"; when first laid, the ground color is completely covered with a thin layer of dull white, chalky deposit, which eventually becomes somewhat discolored; as incubation progresses this chalky covering becomes more or less scratched, by contact with the twigs in the nest or by the action of the bird's feet in turning the eggs, or in relining the nest, so that ultimately much or nearly all of the blue ground color is visible; even then the shell is not glossy. The measurements of 51 eggs average 30.93 by 24.06 millimeters; the eggs showing the four extremes measure 35 by 25, 32 by 26, and 27.68 by 21.84 millimeters.

Young.—Mr. Skutch determined, by close observation of marked birds and by noting which individual of a marked pair laid the eggs, that both sexes share in the duties of incubation. They were very impatient sitters, constantly changing about; 30 minutes was the longest time that he saw one incubate, during the early stages, and they sometimes left the nest unguarded for 10 or 20 minutes, while they enjoyed each other's company; during the last two days of incubation they lengthened their periods on the eggs to from 30 minutes to an hour. He describes the hatching process in detail:

"Fourteen days after the last egg had been laid, I held one in my hand while the birdling worked its way out of it. When I first took it up there was a gap in the larger end, which extended about a third of the way around the circumference. The little bird's short, thick bill was in this gap, and so pressed out of position that the lower mandible overshot the upper, only a temporary condition.

At intervals the struggling prisoner drew its bill farther into the egg, then suddenly pushed it outward, bringing the keeled upper edge, armed with a rather insignificant egg-tooth or 'pip,' against the edge of the shell at one end of the hole, and breaking off a small fragment at the outward thrust. In its squirmings the bird, impelling itself in some manner I could not determine, rotated imperceptibly slowly in the shell, in such a way that the head, turned under one wing, moved backward and the upper edge of the bill was constantly brought to bear upon a fresh portion of the shell, which was chipped off at the next outward thrust. Occasionally the struggling birdling emitted a weak cry. Thus bit by bit the ragged-margined aperture was lengthened until it extended about two-thirds of the way around the egg, when the struggles of the bird succeeded in cracking the remainder, and the large end of the shell fell off as a cap. Then the naked creature wormed its way out into my palm, where it lay exhausted by its continued effort."

In another nest the last egg to be laid hatched in 13 days. The young, when first hatched, "were blind, black-skinned, and without any trace of feathers." When the nestlings were 6 days old they were "both bristling with long pinfeathers. The plumes of the one that was the older by a few hours were already beginning to peep through the tips of these pinfeathers." Later in the day, the feathers had burst their sheaths with amazing rapidity, and the young bird "was already well covered. The back and belly, save for a naked line down the middle of the latter, bore a soft, downy black plumage. Broad ends of the flight feathers of both wings and tail now showed."

From this time on, the young birds became more lively and left the nest when approached, climbing about among the branches or down onto the ground to hide in the grass. They were brooded by one of the parents until they were a week old, returning to the nest at night. But "the following two nights they remained in the nesting tree but did not return to the nest to sleep. They could not yet fly and had entered a half scansorial, half terrestrial stage of existence. When they were 10 days old I tried to catch them for a photograph, but they hopped from limb to limb with such agility that, protected as they were by the sharp thorns, I was unable to secure them. When they were 10 days old they could make short flights from branch to branch of the same bush. Their bills were smooth, without any grooves, and their cheeks were bare of feathers."

All through his account Mr. Skutch emphasizes the affection that is shown by all the members of the ani family for one another. While he was watching the second nest of the pair on which the above observations were made, something very unusual, if not entirely unique, happened. One of the young from the previous brood, now nearly fully grown, "was the constant companion of his parents during the period in which they were busy with their second brood." He frequently perched on the rim of the nest while one of his parents was incubating, and twice he was seen to offer food to the parent on the nest. After the young had hatched, "the youngster fed the nestlings regularly, but not so often as his parents." During four hours and a quarter, he saw the male, always the more attentive parent, bring food to the nestlings 29 times, the female 14, and the young assistant 8 times. "The young bird not only fed the nestlings but was ardent in protecting them, flying up close to me and uttering an angry *grrr-rr-rr* whenever I came near them. In the absence of the parents he attempted to defend them alone."

Plumages.—The young nestling and the development of its first plumage are described above. In this juvenal plumage the contour feathers are short and soft, "bone brown" below and darker above; the wings and tail are much like those of the adult; the bill is less specialized and not grooved.

Van Rossem (1938) says:

The postjuvenal plumage, attained by a complete body and tail and a partial wing molt, is not different from that of the adults except that the rectrices are noticeably narrower. An irregular molt of the primaries takes place at this time, although some of the juvenal quills (though their number and location varies) are held over till the following spring. In March and April of the next year there is a partial body, tail, and wing molt in which an irregular number of rectrices are renewed and such juvenile remiges as have been held over from the previous fall are replaced by new ones. The adult plumage with wide rectrices follows in the second fall, that is, at the first annual molt. The time of the annual molt extends from the middle of July to the first of October, the younger (one-year-old) birds molting earlier than the older ones. The spring molt of the adults includes some of the rectrices and secondaries.

Food.—Mr. Skutch writes (MS.): "The food of the anis consists largely of insects, which they secure both from the ground and among the foliage of bushes, and to a smaller extent of fruit and berries. Often they hunt grasshoppers and other creatures among the long grass or tall weeds, where they are completely hidden from view except when occasionally they leap a foot or so above the herbage to snatch up an insect which has tried to escape by flight. Perhaps their favorite method of foraging is beside a grazing cow or mule. Several together remain close to the head of the beast, moving along by awkward hops as it moves and just managing to escape its jaws and forefeet, ever on the alert to snatch up the insects frightened from their retreat in the grass by the passage of the herbivore. It is frequently stated in books, and affirmed by the residents of the countries where the anis live, that they alight upon cattle and pluck ticks and other vermin from their skin—hence the name *garrapatero* (tick-eater) given them in Costa Rica.

"While this is doubtless true in certain parts of the ani's range, I have watched them in the neighborhood of cattle from Panama to Guatemala and only once in three years have I seen an ani alight on a cow. Since the ani associates so much with cattle without alighting upon them, and the giant cowbird, another black bird of approximately the same size, does frequently perch upon them and relieve them of their vermin, it seems likely that the ani may be often credited with the acts of the cowbird, especially since the latter is shier and less known. I have occasionally questioned one who informed me that the ani plucks ticks from the grazing animals, only to find that he was unaware of the existence of the giant cowbird. At a little distance such a person might easily suppose that the birds upon the animal's back were the same as those about its feet, and since his closer approach would leave only the latter, the illusion would probably persist."

He has also seen a group of anis excitedly following a battalion of army ants, probably not to feed on such fiery morsels as the ants, but to pick up "the cockroaches, spiders, and other small creatures driven from their retreat among the dead leaves by the relentless hordes." Again he says: "After the first heavy rain of the season has sent the winged brood of the termites forth from their nests in countless millions, one can watch the anis everywhere feeding like flycatchers, making ungraceful darts, not exceeding a few feet, from low twigs and fences; but the insects are so numerous on these occasions that they can catch many without quitting their perches."

Major Bendire (1895) quotes Dr. Richmond as saying: "The food of those examined by me on banana plantations consisted almost entirely of small grasshoppers, the stomachs being much distended with these insects. From the fresh earth found on the bill and feet of these birds, I should judge they also feed on the ground."

Prof. A. L. Herrara, of the City of Mexico, wrote to Bendire that "it is a social bird, being usually found in small companies of from six to fifteen individuals, absolutely monogamous, sedentary, and of semidomesticated habits, frequenting the haciendas and the fields and pastures in their vicinity, and as it is considered very useful because of its habit of destroying large numbers of parasites infesting the cattle, it is not molested by the inhabitants, and becomes very tame. It extracts the *Ixodes* and other *Acaridans* with remarkable skill, without causing ulcerations which might result from the proboscis or sucker remaining in the fibres of the skin, and it must be regarded as one of the most useful birds of Mexico, especially in warm regions, so abounding in parasites of all kinds."

Behavior.—Dr. Richmond (Bendire, 1895) says:

At Mr. Haymond's plantation, on the Escondido River, above Bluefields, this species was unusually plentiful, owing, no doubt, to a large number of cattle kept there. The birds follow these animals as they meander over the pastures, hopping along on each side of an animal, catching grasshoppers and other insects which the cow disturbs as it moves along. Frequently the cow moves too rapidly and the birds lag behind, when they make short flights to the front again, passing over one another after the manner of the Grackles when feeding in a field. Only half a dozen birds or so follow a cow usually, and not many congregate in a flock, except when roosting. On this plantation, where the species is more abundant than usual, the birds appear to roost in numbers. An orange tree near the house was a favorite place where thirty or forty birds came to pass the night, flying in from the surrounding pasture about dusk, and after a few short flights from one tree to another, passed into the roost one or two at a time, hopping about as if seeking a favorable perch, uttering their peculiar note meanwhile. Out of this roost I shot seventeen birds one evening, and the males greatly predominated; there were only five females in the lot. The note of this species reminds one somewhat of the Flicker, *Colaptes auratus*, but may be better represented by the combination "plee-co," rapidly repeated, with the accent usually on the first syllable, but sometimes on the last. I have frequently found one of the small flocks resting on a bush or bamboo along the water's edge, perfectly silent, until my near approach started them off, one or two at a time, scolding as they went. Their flight is even, slow, as short as possible, and consists of a few flaps of the wings, followed by a short sail, then a few more flaps, etc.

Mr. Skutch writes (MS.) : "Their flight is as perfectly characteristic of the birds as any other of their peculiar habits. A long journey, say anything much in excess of a hundred yards, is seldom made by a continuous flight, but the bird advances with frequent pauses in conveniently situated trees and bushes. As he alights on one of the lower branches, the momentum of the long tail carries it forward above the head with an abrupt jerk. Recovering his balance, he remains here for some moments, looking around with caution and calling in his high-pitched voice. Then, satisfied that the path ahead is clear, with a *tuc tuc tuc, pihuy pihuy pihuy*, he launches himself upon the next stage of his journey. A few rapid beats of his short wings serve to impart the requisite momentum, and he sets them for a long glide. In this manner he can cover surprisingly long distances, on a slightly descending course, without further muscular effort. If his ultimate destination is a certain perch in a tree or bush, he will often arrest his flight on another considerably below it. By a few queer, rapid, sideways hops along the branch, and some bounds, or better bounces, from limb to limb, he gains the desired position where, as likely as not, he spreads his wings to the morning sun."

Mr. van Rossem (1938) says: "They feed side by side with never a sign of friction or argument over the choicer insects, and at night roost in low trees or bushes, pressed shoulder to shoulder to the limit of available space. We not infrequently found them thus when hunting at night. During the time just preceding nesting it was noticeable that they were inclined to roost two and two instead of in a long line. In some cases the pair was sitting in close contact, even though there might be plenty of room to perch comfortably."

Voice.—Dr. Richmond's impression of the note of the groove-billed ani is mentioned above. Señor Alfaro says, in his notes given Mr. Cherrie (1892), that, in Costa Rica, it is "known as 'Tijo, tijo' (tée-ho) in imitation of its peculiar notes which seem to repeat the word *tijo* over and over again." Dr. Chapman (1896) says: "Its note is a prolonged *chee-wyyah*, easily distinguishable from the single whining whistle of *C. ani.*" Mr. van Rossem (1938) says: "The ordinary or 'conversational' notes are a series of very liquid and what can best be described as 'contented' bubblings and cluckings. The louder, often repeated 'chee-múy-o-chee-múy-o' is the alarm note."

DISTRIBUTION

Range.—Lower Rio Grande Valley of Texas and Baja California, south to northern South America.

The range of the groove-billed ani extends **north** to southern Baja California (San Pedro and Santiago) ; southern Sinaloa (Mazatlan) ; southern Texas (Lomita and Corpus Christi) ; and Yucatan (Progreso and Chichen-Itza). **East** to Yucatan (Chichen-Itza) ; British Honduras (Cayo) ; Honduras (La Ceiba) ; Colombia (Santa Marta) ; and Venezuela (Altagracia, Curaçao, and Caicara). **South** to Venezuela (Caicara) ; and Peru (Chachapoyas and Lima). **West** to Peru (Lima and Cutervo) ; Ecuador (Tumbez) ; Costa Rica (San Jose and La Palma) ; El Salvador (Sonsonate) ; western Guatemala (Lake Amatitlan) ; southwestern Chiapas (Tapachula) ; Nayarit (San Blas) ; and southern Baja California (San Jose del Cabo and San Pedro).

The birds found in the cape district of Baja California have been separated subspecifically and are known as the San Lucas ani, *C. s. pallidula.*

Casual records.—In Louisiana a specimen was collected near New Orleans about 1890; another was taken at Ostrica during the winter of 1919; a third was obtained without date of collection near Houma; a fourth was taken at Cottonport on December 11, 1932; while a fifth was collected on Grand Isle on April 23, 1935. A specimen was taken at Huachucas, Ariz., 10 miles from the Mexican border, in May 1888, and it was noted at a point 20 miles north of Tucson on August 21, 1932. About November 1, 1904, a specimen was taken near Emporia, Kans., and on October 12, 1913, one was killed on an island about 9 miles north of Red Wing, Minn. A specimen was obtained at Jupiter Inlet, Fla., during the first week in January

1891, and there is also a somewhat indefinite record of its occurrence in the early part of January in the vicinity of Kingston, Jamaica.

Egg dates.—Central America: 4 records, May 27 to July 29.

Baja California: 6 records, April 1 to September 3.

Mexico: 40 records, March 20 to August 14; 20 records, May 16 to June 30, indicating the height of the season.

Texas: 7 records, March 17 to July 15.

CROTOPHAGA SULCIROSTRIS PALLIDULA Bangs and Penard

SAN LUCAS ANI

HABITS

The groove-billed ani of the Cape region of Lower California, Mexico, was described and given the above name by Bangs and Penard (1921), based on a series of 18 specimens from San José del Cabo. It is said to be—

similar to *Crotophaga sulcirostris sulcirostris* Swainson of Mexico, and of about the same size, but much paler and with less purplish iridescence; the U-shaped iridescent markings of the back and breast paler and duller greenish, not so brilliant; the dull purplish bronze of the head and neck of true *sulcirostris* replaced by paler, more grayish bronze; the lustreless parts of the body-feathers grayish brownish black instead of dull black. * * *

Eighteen adults of this new form, laid out beside a series of nearly double that number from various points in Mexico and Central America, are strikingly different; the pale, dull colors of the Lower California bird cannot be matched by any specimen in our series of true *sulcirostris*. The difference is noticeable at a glance but rather difficult to describe. Brewster (1902), in his account of the birds of the Cape Region of Lower California, states that the Groove-billed Ani is not known to occur in central and northern Lower California, and that the colonies which have become established in the Cape region were probably originated by birds which came from western Mexico. However this may be, the isolated colony of Cape St. Lucas has developed into a very distinct form, worthy of recognition.

Griffing Bancroft writes to me, on August 6, 1937, that he is "as nearly satisfied as it is possible to be from negative evidence" that this form of the groove-billed ani is extinct.

Nesting.—Lyman Belding (1883) writes: "The 1st of April I discovered four of these birds in a marsh, in which was a rank growth of *tule*, flags, and reeds. Having shot one of them, and the others were not molested, they remained in the marsh until May 15, or later. A nest found April 29 contained eight eggs. It was fastened to upright reeds, and was composed of coarse weed stalks and mesquite twigs, lined with green leaves. The female, while incubating, was very wary, slipping quietly away from the nest and returning to it very stealthily, below the tops of the reeds."

William Brewster (1902) says that the nest "taken by Mr. Frazar was in a willow about twenty feet above the ground. It is a flat-loose, but withal rather neat structure, formed outwardly of dead twigs and very substantially lined with cottonwood and willow leaves, which look as if they must have been dry when gathered. * * * This nest measures about six inches across the top, and the cavity is nearly an inch in depth. * * * Mr. Frazar met with the Groove-billed Ani only at San José del Cabo, where a flock of about thirty frequented some thick brush about pools of water near the mouth of the river."

Eggs.—The eggs of this race are apparently just like those of the species elsewhere. The measurements of 9 eggs average 31.99 by 24.00 millimeters; the eggs showing the four extremes measure **33.5** by 23, 31.8 by **24.9,** and **30.5** by 23 millimeters.

GEOCOCCYX CALIFORNIANUS (Lesson)

ROADRUNNER

PLATES 3-6

HABITS

CONTRIBUTED BY GEORGE MIKSCH SUTTON

Most ornithologists are to some extent acquainted with the road-runner. They have read about him. They have heard strange stories about him. Perhaps, driving along some road in the South-western United States, they have even seen him. But he who really knows the roadrunner has risen morning after morning with the desert sun; thrilled at the brilliance of the desert stars; seen day turned to sudden night by the dust-storm; pulled cactus spines from his shins. He who knows the roadrunner, he who has measured the breadth and the depth of this unique bird personality, has lived with him—not for an hour or so, not for a day, but week after week after week.

First impressions almost invariably give us an inadequate concept of this strange bird. We hear him scuttle through dry leaves ahead of us, catch a glimpse of him as he slips back of a rock, know from the flight of a grasshopper that he has gone a certain way, and that is all. Or, coming upon him suddenly, we surprise him into flight; note his short, rounded wings, long tail, and coarsely streaked plumage; watch him sail down the arroyo; and marvel that with the shutting of his wings and reckless plunge into the thicket he is so instantly lost to view.

Sometimes, traveling in a motorcar, we come upon him perched on a fence post or telegraph pole close to the highway. Now we have opportunity to observe how slim he is, how long his legs, how notice-able his crest. But as we pass he leaps to the ground, swings off through the cactus clumps, and is gone. Once more only a glimpse! Once more only the retreat of a timid desert creature that appears to be half bird, half reptile.

But lie in wait for the roadrunner! Watch him race across the sand, full speed, after a lizard. Watch him put out a wing, change his course, throw up his tail, change his course again, plunge head-long into a clump of cactus, and emerge, whacking his limp victim on the ground. Watch him jerk a slender snake from the grass, fling it into the air, grasp it by the head or neck, pummel it with his hard mandibles, and gulp it head first. Watch him stalk a grasshopper, slipping quietly forward, making a sudden rush with wings and tail fully spread, frightening the doomed insect into flight, then leaping 3 or 4 feet in air to snatch it flycatcherwise in his long bill. Watch the roadrunner for an hour at his daily business of catching food and you will deem him among the most amazing of all the desert's amazing creatures. Snake-killer indeed! Chaparral cock! Not by sitting quietly on fence posts, not by slipping shyly from the path, has the roadrunner earned for himself these blood-stirring names!

So odd, so even *funny* a creature is the roadrunner that it is natural to caricature him a bit in describing him. This J. L. Sloanaker (1913) has done when he writes:

Of all the birds on our list the Roadrunner is doubtless the most unique; indeed, he is *queer*, and would certainly take first prize in the freak class at the Arizona state fair. He is about two feet in length, with a tail as long as his body, color above brown streaked with black, bare spaces around eyes blue and orange, feathers of head and neck bristle-tipped, eyelids lashed, * * * his whole plumage coarse and harsh. Could you imagine such a looking creature? Try and think of a long striped snake on two legs, a feather duster on his head and another trailing behind; or a tall, slim tramp in a swallow-tailed coat, a black and blue eye, and a head of hair standing straight on end! There you are!

Elliott Coues (1903) describes roadrunners as "singular birds—cuckoos compounded of a chicken and a Magpie." Mrs. Bailey (1902) considers them among the "most original and entertaining of western birds." Other writers call them "odd," "anomalous," and "unique." They are.

Throughout much of his range the roadrunner is known as the chaparral cock, or merely the chaparral. He also is called lizard bird, ground cuckoo, cock of the desert, and, as we have stated above, snake killer. The Mexicans call him the *paisano* or the *correo del camino*. The first of these names means *compatriot* or *fellow country-man;* according to some writers it expresses affectionate regard, and is to be freely translated "little friend." The latter is almost the equivalent of our name roadrunner.

That the roadrunner has at times been known as the *churca* we learn from an interesting note by Elliott Coues (1900) who quotes from an anonymous Franciscan priest the following description, published in 1790: "The *Churca* is a kind of pheasant which has a long bill, dark plumage, a handsome tail and *four feet*. It has these latter facing outward in such fashion that when it runs it leaves the track of two feet going forward and two going backward."

Coues himself calls attention to the fact that the word "toes" must replace the word "feet" in the above paragraph if the description is to fit the roadrunner. The error may well have been the translator's. At any rate, anyone who has observed a roadrunner's tracks in the sand knows how faithfully these record the zygodactylism of the bird's foot.

Many a fanciful tale is told of the roadrunner. According to the best known of these, the bird builds a fence of cactus spines about a sleeping rattler, letting the doomed reptile buffet itself to weariness until finally, in desperation, it is impaled on the spines or bites itself to death! According to other stories (some of which probably have a grain of truth in them), the bird will deliberately race the swiftest horse across the plains!

The speed of the roadrunner *is* remarkable. Not when he is flying —a flying roadrunner is as much out of his element as a swimming chicken—but when he is afoot. A. W. Anthony (1892) tells us of a pair of birds that apparently enjoyed being chased by a hound that could never catch them. He says:

At Hatchita [New Mexico] a pair came regularly to one of the mines for water, a small pool having been formed near the shaft, from the pumps. The visit was made at nearly the same hour each forenoon, and was eagerly looked forward to by a foxhound owned by one of the workmen. The dog never failed to give chase as soon as the birds were sighted, and the race was as much enjoyed by the birds as by the dog; they seemed to have no difficulty whatever in keeping well out of danger without taking wing, and usually found time during the chase to stop at the water hole and get their daily drink, after which they quickly disappeared.

H. C. Bryant (1916) quotes from Heermann that the roadrunner "may, however, be overtaken when followed on horseback over the vast open plains," and Heermann is known to have seen "one captured by a couple of dogs."

Richard Hunt (1920), who was able to check with a speedometer the actual speed of a roadrunner encountered "en route from Soledad to the Galiban Range" in California, writes: "At the top speed to which we provoked our victim, the famous runner was moving at the tremendous rate of 10 miles an hour on a practically level piece of road."

H. H. Sheldon (1922a), who also checked the roadrunner's running speed with a speedometer, writes of the incident: "The car gained on the bird until about five yards separated us, and I saw it was running at its utmost speed. I instructed my friend, who was driving, not to press him further, and for fully three hundred yards the bird ran from the big monster in pursuit, the while the speedometer registered exactly fifteen miles per hour. When finally we approached very closely, the bird gave up and flew into a palm, where I plainly saw it, beak agape and apparently very much fatigued from the unusual exertion."

There is no doubt in my own mind that a fully adult roadrunner, can, for short distances, run faster than 15 miles an hour. Athletic directors tell us that an average man (not an athlete) can run 9 yards a second, or about 18 miles an hour. I know I can run as fast as the average man, and I know I have failed many a time to gain on a roadrunner that happened to appear on the road a short distance ahead of me. I distinctly recall catching two *young* roadrunners (with tails 7 or 8 inches long) in a little gully near Fort Worth, Tex., in about the year 1913. I had quite a chase and might never have caught them had they not been forced to run up a steep embankment.

Spring.—We have seen the roadrunner sneak off through the weeds—a frightened bird. We have seen him capture lizards, snakes, scorpions, centipedes, tarantulas—a veritable monster. But not until we have heard him sing do we know the finer side (as Aldrovandus of old would say) of his nature. On fine spring mornings he sings as the sun rises, and he may continue his fervent if somewhat monotonous performance for an hour or more. His favorite song-perch is the eastern rim of a mesa where, full in the fresh sunlight, he can see far and wide. If there is no mesa, he chooses a dead tree or a high cactus. Here, directing his bill downward until it almost touches his toes, he begins to coo. *Coo, coo, coo, ooh, ooh, ooh, ooh, ooh,* he calls, pumping out the syllables in a hoarse, throaty voice, his head rising a little with each *coo,* until the bill points upward, the pitch of the song meanwhile dropping gradually lower. So he starts with head low and coo high, and ends vice versa. Cattlemen say that before he begins his song he "lays his beak on the rock."

The pumped-out series of coos we have just described doubtless is the roadrunner's love song. Before giving it he may parade in a prominent place, strutting with head held stiff and high, and wings and tail drooping. On May 2, 1914, I witnessed what I believe were certain courtship antics of the male before the female not far from Fort Worth, Tex. According to the published account (Sutton, 1922) of this performance, the bird's "wings were spread, and he may have been preening and taking a sun bath, but circumstances * * * led me to think otherwise. Now and then he bowed, and affected a close examination of his feet, only to raise his head again, drop his wings, lift them again and spread his tail. * * * Before I knew it [I] was discovered * * * and then, without wings spread, leaped from the dead branch to the next lower one, whence on outstretched wings he sailed to the ground. I rushed up to where he had been, and was surprised to see two birds scuttling * * * off through the vines."

Nesting.—The nest, which usually is situated in a low tree, thicket, or clump of cactus 3 or 4 to 15 feet from the ground, is a rather compact, though not deeply cupped affair, about a foot in diameter and 6 to 8 inches high, with foundation of sticks and lining of leaves, grass, feathers, mesquite pods, snakeskin, roots, and dry flakes of cattle and horse manure. It is sometimes well hidden, sometimes not. In the Black Mesa country of the far western Oklahoma Panhandle John Semple and I found several nests in small cedar trees that grew on the mesa sides. Here the nests were well hidden, and since cedar trees were numerous our usual method of locating nests was watching the parent birds.

Rarely the nest is built on the ground. Such a nest, containing six eggs, was found by W. W. Brown in Sonora, Mexico, on May 15, 1905. This nest is preserved in the John E. Thayer collection.

A. C. Bent writes me of a nest found by F. C. Willard in Cochise County, Ariz., on April 23, 1916, "7 feet from the ground on a packrat's nest in a dense thicket of hawthorn." This nest was "merely a few leaves, etc., in a slight hollow in the rubbish of the rat's nest." While Mr. Bent was hunting ravens' nests among the abandoned oil derricks in the Kettleman Hills, Calif., his companion, J. R. Pemberton, told him that roadrunners sometimes built their nests in the lower parts of the derricks, using the sticks dropped by the ravens. Griffing Bancroft (1930) describes a nest with complete set of two eggs found in Lower California in the heart of a date palm * * * so well concealed that it could not be seen until much of the foliage had been cut away."

Eggs.—Roadrunner nests contain, as a rule, three to five or six eggs. Occasionally two eggs comprise a complete set; and sets with as many as 12 eggs have been recorded. Where large numbers of eggs are found in one nest it is supposed that more than one female has deposited them. Coues (1903) describes the eggs as "ovate or elliptical, white in ground color with an overlying chalky film which may take a slight yellowish tint, ranging in length from 1.45 to 1.75, averaging 1.55 x 1.20. They are laid at considerable intervals; incubation begins as soon as a few are deposited, and is believed to last 18 days for each egg. The development of the chicks is rapid;

perfectly fresh eggs and newly-hatched young may be found together; and by the time the last young are breaking the shell the
others may be graded up to half the size of the adult."

[AUTHOR'S NOTE: The measurements of 55 eggs average 39.2 by
30.1 millimeters; the eggs showing the four extremes measure 44 by
30, 41 by 32, and 34 by 27.5 millimeters.]

William L. and Irene Finley (1915) describe a typical nest in
which there were "one fresh egg, one egg just ready to hatch, two
featherless, greasy, black young, and two young ones about grown
and ready to leave home." These authors were in a position to watch
this nest almost continuously for several days. They did not observe
more than one female parent. If, then, the several eggs were laid
by more than one female, it may be supposed that the species is to
some extent parasitic or promiscuous in this regard, as the yellow-
billed and black-billed cuckoos also are thought to be.

Frank L. Burns (1915) also gives the period of incubation as "18
days." It is supposed that only the female incubates. That incubation sometimes begins with the laying of the first egg rather than
"as soon as a few are deposited" (see above quotation from Coues)
has been observed by M. French Gilman (1915), who tells us of a
nest with four eggs in which "one hatched July 20, the others on the
three succeeding days." In cases of this sort it is natural to suppose
that all eggs are laid by the same female.

Eggs are usually laid in April and May. W. E. D. Scott (1886)
tells us, however, of several nests found on the San Pedro slope of
the Catalina Mountains in Arizona, the earliest of which, discovered
March 17, 1885, at an elevation of 3,000 feet, contained two fresh
eggs. That two broods of young are sometimes, if not frequently,
reared in one season has been reported by numerous authors, though
I believe it has not been proved beyond doubt that fresh eggs found
in July are laid by females that have already succeeded in bringing
out one brood.

Young.—Newly hatched young are odd, "featherless, greasy,
black" creatures with a reptilian appearance. I had a good deal
to do with young roadrunners in the vicinity of Fort Worth, Tex.,
as a boy, so I quote my own description here (1922):

The nestling bird, be it ever so young, has an unmistakable cuckoo-like expression in its face, though its eyes, upon which a good portion of the facial expression depends, are quite different from those of the adult, being of a deep dull
brown with a bluish pupil. * * * The eyelashes are small, in fact scarcely
apparent. Its whole external appearance is very sombre, and rather dirty-
looking, as though the creature had been bathed in some unrefined oil, which
had not been properly administered. The white hairs, each of which marks a
coming feather, all lie in rows and look as if they had been rudely combed into
place. The rather large, pale blue-gray feet are strong in the toes, but very

weak at the heel, so that the birds cling to the fingers or the twigs of their nest with some power, but are quite unable to rise. Whenever there were very many young birds in the nest they presented a peculiarly scrambled appearance, due, I believe, to the constant disturbance at feeding time more than to restlessness, for they usually lie quite still. By May 1 [the birds were taken from the nest on April 29] feathers were appearing rapidly on my young birds, first on the top of the head, back, and wings, and then on the belly, tail, and throat. Once the blood-quills had started to burst, development was very rapid. On May 4 the birds were quite well feathered, the tails being one and one-half inches long, and they were quite able to walk unsteadily. It is at this period, or a little before, that the young leave the nest, though there must be innumerable dangers for the rather weak-legged creatures. Several times I have come across young birds able to run well, but still in trees, which leads me to believe that the young may, like young Green Herons, spend a portion of their early active life climbing about from branch to branch.

During the spring and summer of 1914 I reared these two young roadrunners, feeding them uncounted hundreds of grasshoppers, cave crickets, tarantulas, centipedes, scorpions, lizards, snakes, mice, cotton rats, and small birds. They were the most entertaining pets I ever had. Eventually they learned to capture their own food. Concerning this period of their life I have published the following paragraphs (1936):

After three weeks they became sturdy enough to catch part of their own food. With patient coaxing they were taught to pick up grasshoppers tossed to them, and finally to run after and capture crippled insects. Content at first, perforce, with sluggish, wingless nymphs which were abundant, they stole about through the weeds, wings pressed neatly against their slender bodies, snapping up the insects as fast as they could find them. Grasshoppers, often still alive and kicking, they swallowed with a toss of the head and a hollow gulp. Large green or gray cave crickets, which live in piles of boards, or in damp, shadowy places, were especially prized. When a yellow- or coral-winged grasshopper rose noisily from the path, the birds crouched in momentary fear, but soon began to mark the return to earth of the clackety aeronaut and to steal up behind clumps of grass, intent upon a killing.

Finally they learned to capture the biggest, noisiest, and wariest grasshoppers on the prairies. They would watch a coral-wing in his courtship flight and, running stealthily, wait until the performer dropped to the ground. With a bound over low weeds, a dart across the open, and a final rush with outspread wings and tail, they would frighten their prey into the air, leap nimbly after him, nab him unerringly with their bills, and descend gracefully on outspread wings to beat him to insensibility with a whack or two on a stone.

Once they had learned to capture grasshoppers, their food problem was largely solved and, since they showed no inclination to run away, they were at liberty most of the time. They ran about the yard, playing with each other, or catching insects. In the heat of mid-day they sought the shelter of broad, cool leaves, and sprawled in the sand. Daily, often many times daily, I took them for a walk across the prairie. Following me closely or running at my side, they watched the big world with eyes far keener than my own. Grasshoppers which I frightened from the grass they captured in side expeditions. If I paused near a flat stone, they urged me on with grunts, bit gently at my hands, and raced back and forth in an ecstasy of anticipation.

I entertained misgivings concerning these flat stones. What savage creatures might not they conceal? Could young Road-Runners manage swift-tailed scorpions, sharp-toothed mice, or poisonous spiders? Under the first stone there were scorpions. The Road-Runners hesitated an instant, as if permitting an untried instinct to take possession of their brains, then rushed forward, thrust out their heads, and attacked the scorpions precisely at their tails. Perhaps these venomous tails received more than the usual number of benumbing blows, but the scorpions were swallowed with gusto.

I had not supposed that a Road-Runner would capture and devour a tarantula. One day, however, we paused at the tunnel of one of these big, furred spiders. Somewhat in the spirit of experimentation, and following the method known to all Texas boys, I teased the black Arachnid from her lair by twirling a wisp of grass in her face. She popped out viciously and jumped a good ten inches to one side. With a dash one bird was upon the monster before she had opportunity to leap a second time. A toss of the bird's head and one of the eight legs was gone. Free again, the spider leaped upon her captor. The other bird now entered the combat, snatched up the spider, and flicked off another leg. One by one the legs went down, and finally the two birds pulled apart and gulped the sable torso.

Plumages.—The newly hatched roadrunner's only plumage is coarse, long, white or whitish hairs. These do not by any means cover the dark-skinned body, but they apparently give the bird all the protection it needs. At this stage the light-colored egg tooth is noticeable, the feet are dark colored like the rest of the body, the mouth lining has a peculiarly blotched appearance, and the irides are dull brown.

As blood quills replace the long white hairs, the egg tooth disappears, the legs and feet turn blue-gray, the skin about and back of the eye lightens, and the blotching of the mouth lining becomes less conspicuous. The sprouting feathers now bear at their tips the white hairs of babyhood. Some of these hairs cling to the plumage long after the bird leaves the nest.

When young roadrunners begin to capture their own food they wear a plumage that is much like that of the adult. J. A. Allen (Scott, 1886) describes this plumage thus: "The chief difference in color consists in the broad shaft stripes of the feathers of the neck and breast being less sharply defined in the young than in the adult, and in the brown edgings bordering the shaft stripes being paler."

At this stage the bare skin about the eye becomes pale blue, and the naked patch back of the eye light orange. Too, the eye itself changes, a light-colored ring, which contrasts sharply with the brown or gray-brown of the rest of the iris, forming about the pupil. As the bird becomes older the bare skin of the face brightens. Fully adult males, at the height of the nesting season, are fairly resplendent with their high, steel-blue crest, brilliant eye, and bright orange patch back of the eye.

The plumage worn by the young bird after it loses its natal hairs is apparently the first winter plumage. Judging from such specimens as I have seen, the postnuptial molt is the only complete molt of the adult bird. Whether there is a partial prenuptial molt in young or adult birds I cannot say. The roadrunner's life is so strenuous that he doubtless loses feathers frequently. Spring birds with half-grown tail feathers may therefore not be performing a molt in the usual sense of the word.

Food.—Lizards (including the armored horned "toad"), small snakes, scorpions, tarantulas and other spiders, centipedes and millipedes, mice, cotton rats, ground-inhabiting small birds and their eggs and young, young quail, insects of all sorts, various fruits and seeds, including pricklypears: all these are eaten by the roadrunner; and this considerable list but hints at the rapacity and digestive powers of the gaunt bird. One of the most thorough-going reports on the roadrunner's food habits is that by Dr. Harold C. Bryant (1916). Informing us that animal food makes up slightly over 90 percent of the total food of the species in California, Dr. Bryant says:

Almost any animal, from the smaller rodents down to tiny insects, appears to be relished by this bird. Although the stomachs examined showed no large percentage of vertebrates, other published records show that reptiles sometimes form a large part, if not the entire diet. Even these larger elements of food are usually swallowed whole at one gulp. That the digestive apparatus is powerful is evidenced by the fact that bone, hair, and feathers pass through the digestive tract, and are not thrown back out through the mouth in the form of pellets, as is the case with some hawks and most owls.

A diagram in Dr. Bryant's paper makes it plain that grasshoppers and crickets form a considerable part (36.82 percent) of the roadrunner's food in California. Beetles form 18.2 percent; and seeds and fruits, cutworms and caterpillars, bugs, ants, bees, wasps, scorpions, lizards, mammals, fly larvae, birds, and "miscellaneous" items go to make up the rest.

Game officials are usually opposed to the roadrunner, for the bird is reputed to be an enemy of young quail. Regarding the bird's reputation as a quail destroyer, W. L. McAtee (1931) tells us that "the Road-runner is persecuted almost throughout its range * * * as an alleged destroyer of Quail eggs, and state bounties are even paid for its destruction. Yet the Road-runner never has been known to be a special enemy of Quail," and it doubtless "eats more scorpions, centipedes, and tarantulas, those poisonous nuisances of the Southwest, than it does Quail eggs."

Aldo Leopold (1922) writes of shooting a roadrunner "with a light-colored object in his bill." Examining the spot where the bird had fallen he "found a dead [quail] chick, still limber and warm but unmutilated * * * still in the downy stage, with ⅛-inch pin feathers on the wing—smaller than a domestic chick when hatched."

S. S. Visher (1910) writing of birds found by him in Pima County, Ariz., tells us that roadrunners "have been seen leaving the nest of Gambel's Quails carrying an egg in their beak."

That the roadrunner will occasionally capture birds as large as a mockingbird is apparent from several published accounts including that by Robert S. Woods (1927a) who tells us of "an immature but full-grown mockingbird" captured though not actually killed by a roadrunner near Azusa, Calif.; and that by Dr. W. K. Fisher (1904) who reports that a roadrunner was seen to "remove from a nest a young mockingbird and devour it" in Mission Valley, near San Diego, Calif.

In a letter to A. C. Bent, Mr. Woods (who is quoted above) speaks of a short article written by the late Rev. St. John O'Sullivan, of San Juan Capistrano Mission, "describing a roadrunner's method of killing a swift by lying in wait in a creek-bed near Palm Springs and suddenly springing into the air to knock down one of the birds which passed within its reach." This capturing swifts in air seems perfectly plausible to me, for I recall seeing my captive roadrunners capturing English sparrows in much the same manner. Walking about with a noncommittal air that was comically suggestive of the chickens that fed nearby, they gradually grew nearer to a sparrow, then with a dash to one side and a tremendous leap snatched the fleeing victim from the air.

A. W. Anthony (1896) tells us of suddenly coming upon a road-runner that had just finished despatching a wood rat (*Neotoma*). "The bird reluctantly withdrew as I came upon the scene," he writes, "leaving the rat, which I found to be quite dead."

My own captive birds caught and killed a cotton rat (*Sigmodon*) that lived in a stone wall near our house in Fort Worth, Tex. Two or three times a day this rat scurried across a gap in this wall, and the birds came to look upon him as a possible meal. At first his speed and considerable size kept the enemy at a safe distance, but their interest sharpened daily, and eventually they formed the habit of loitering near the runway. One day I heard a squeal of terror and ran up in time to see the bewildered animal running this way and that, trying to escape two lightning-quick demons who never really held him, but pinched him, tossed him, dealt him blows, buffeted him, made him weary with fighting for life. Over his limp form the roadrunners had an argument. He was heavy. No sooner would one bird start to swallow than the other would be tugging at the hind foot or tail, and down he would drop. I finally cut the rat in two.

Carroll Dewilton Scott has contributed a note concerning roadrunners that catch half-grown "gophers" in his garden at Pacific Beach, Calif. Describing one of the birds he says: "Finally, after ridiculous gulpings and twistings of his neck he got the gopher down, balanced his tail, and ambled away from another conquest."

Mrs. Bailey (1928) tells us of two roadrunners observed at Carlsbad, N. Mex., that "snapped their bills and chased each other up into a cottonwood on the bank where there were caterpillar nests. To determine what they had been eating, one was shot and its gizzard was found to contain not only caterpillar skins but a number of large grasshoppers, a large black cricket, beetles, a centipede six inches long, and part of a garter snake a foot long. The rest of the snake was down in the crop and the barely swallowed end up near the bill."

Regarding the economic status of the roadrunner in California, Dr. Bryant (1916) says: "A preponderance of evidence favors the bird. The destruction of such unquestioned pests as grasshoppers, cutworms, caterpillars, and wireworms and of such rodents as mice is to be desired even if the amount of destruction be relatively small. The taking of this sort of food on wild land is evidence that this bird when feeding in cultivated fields is likely to be distinctly beneficial."

Behavior.—Anyone who has observed the roadrunner closely knows what an entertaining creature it is. Its voracity keeps it on the alert for food. To capture a grasshopper one moment, a race-runner lizard the next, and a tarantula the next requires strength, speed, and prowess. If nymph grasshoppers are numerous, the bird has no trouble in obtaining a meal. But flying grasshoppers are difficult to overtake; lizards escape because of the brittleness of their tails; and tarantulas have burrows into which they can pop when danger threatens.

Not often does one see a wild roadrunner capturing its food. I recall watching one a year or two ago, not far from Packsaddle Lake, a small, artificial body of water in western Oklahoma. I had climbed a sandy mound. Peering through the sagebrush, I saw a roadrunner under a bush not far away, busy feeding. He ran out into the sunlight now and then, but his attention was directed principally to grasshoppers that must have been feeding on the leaves. These he snatched, with nimble leaps upward, in the tip of his bill. To reach the insects that were in the midst of the bush, he scrambled noisily through the twigs, caught a few, then sprang back to the ground to catch those that had fallen or jumped out.

W. E. Allen (1932) gives us a breezy description of the capture of a small bird by a roadrunner that had been running just ahead of him. He says:

Before we had gone as much as a hundred yards, however, his [the road-runner's] pacing routine was broken by a sudden dash from a slouchy pose and the development of a brown streak across the road which ended in his emergence on a bank beyond a parked automobile. Somewhere beneath the car he had struck a full-fledged young bird (probably a "California Linnet") at full speed * * *. The victim appeared to have been caught by the neck, which probably accounts for the fact that it made no outcry. It must have been badly stunned also by the stroke of the heavy beak because it struggled only feebly.

After becoming satisfied that I was not disposed to interfere, the captor moved on to a point about 10 feet farther away. Here he hammered the hard ground two or three times with the body of his victim, evidently destroying all signs of life. Then he dropped it, grasped a wing near its base, and with a skilful jerk stripped nearly every feather from it * * *. After stripping the wing he spent three or four minutes in picking at the birdling's body with some hammering and jerking mixed in. Apparently this was for the purpose of getting rid of feathers. At any rate, they were thrown around profusely, and the movements were different from those a little later which seemed to be devoted to mauling and crushing the body into a shapeless mass.

Finally this mass (which seemed to be about as large as the roadrunner's head) was picked up with a kind of tossing motion which landed it in the back of his mouth. The first effort at swallowing, consisting of tossings of the head and spasmodic movements of the jaws and throat, only resulted in getting the mass started into the throat. After a short rest another series of these movements shifted it along to a visible extent but it was not till the fourth series was finished that the food appeared to have been swallowed completely. After this was accomplished the bird turned toward me and slouched into a curious pose of indifference mixed with satisfaction.

A roadrunner's program is full enough with only himself to feed. But when he has a nestful of hungry young he must indeed wear himself ragged catching insects and lizards and snakes. These he brings from near and far, going and coming in such a way as to keep himself hidden. With what satisfaction must he start a foot-long garter snake on its way down the gullet of one of his offspring, knowing that one voice at least will be stilled so long as any of that snake remains to be swallowed!

Many an interesting account has been written of the roadrunner's foraging activities. A. Brazier Howell (1916) tells us of difficulties he had in retrieving small bird specimens before roadrunners stole them. He writes:

While I was out collecting, these abundant birds would often be seen skulking about with eyes open for any opportunity, and it was always necessary, in such cases, to make a dash for a specimen after it was shot. On two occasions a roadrunner darted in and grabbed a bird when I had almost reached it, once hopping two feet in air to nip a sparrow that had lodged in the branches of a bush. At another time I was watching a small flock of sparrows as they busily fed in the brush, when I noted a roadrunner stealing up like a cat, taking advantage of every bit of cover. When at the proper distance, it rushed out and sprang into the air at the retreating sparrows.

J. Eugene Law (1923) tells us of a roadrunner that tried to pull a dead golden-crowned sparrow through the ¾-inch-mesh wire of a sparrow trap. This writer states that he did not actually see the roadrunner kill the sparrow, though an autopsy showed "the entire brain area" to be "dark with blood infusion."

My pet roadrunners did not capture horned "frogs" unless other food was difficult to obtain. They killed and ate these well-armored reptiles, however. A horned lizard, confronted by its ancient foe, would flatten out, rise high on its legs, and sway back and forth as if about to leap or inflict a dangerous bite. But a roadrunner is not to be bluffed. Grasping his tough victim by the head or back he beat it against a convenient stone. Thirty or forty blows were needed to render it sufficiently quiescent for ingestion. If swallowed while yet alive it had to be coughed up for further battering.

When not engaged in pursuing food a roadrunner may rest, seeking either a cool spot on the ground or the shadowy heart of a tree. In the morning it sometimes takes a sunbath. Henry W. Henshaw (1875) tells us that "it loves to meet the first rays of the rising sun, ascending for this purpose to the top of the mesquite trees, and, standing erect on the topmost branch, loosens its feathers, and appears to catch all the grateful warmth possible, remaining in this attitude for many minutes." My captive roadrunners took sunbaths every day, spreading their wings and exposing the featherless tracts of their backs.

The roadrunner has a streak of domesticity in his nature. Mrs. Bailey (1922) has given us a delightful account of a remarkably tame though uncaged bird that lived about camp. Concerning this bird (which was known as "Koo"), Mrs. Bailey says:

It was not his potential usefulness as a camp watchman or killer of "varmints" but his ready friendliness and attractive ways which attached us to our rare camp visitor. If we were busy when he came he would call *koo, koo*, and then wait for us to discover him. Sometimes we would look hard before finding him and finally make him out standing on the mesquite slope above us, his feathers puffed out spreading the streaks on his chest till they and his light underparts toned in perfectly with a background of straw-colored ground and dry weed-stalks—completely camouflaging him. It was astonishing to see how such a large, marked bird could disappear in its background. And what a contrast that round, bird-like form made to the grotesque running figure we were familiar with—long neck, slender body, and long tail, one straight line.

J. K. Jensen (1923) tells us of a pair of roadrunners that fed "with the chickens on a ranch near Santa Fe," that "came regularly for a 'hand out' and often went to roost in the poultry house." This author does not specify what the "hand out" was. Needless to say, it hardly could have been corn or wheat.

Frightened from the nest a roadrunner may scuttle off to remain hidden for some time. Again, it may stay close by, attempting to lure the intruder away. M. French Gilman (1915) describes a mother bird that was "very anxious about the eggs," that "ran around close to me in a mammalian sort of way, flat on the ground, tail dragging, and head stretched out in front only about three inches from the soil. She did not look like a bird at all, and though making no fluttering demonstration, her antics were calculated to excite curiosity and distract attention from the nest."

J. R. Pemberton (1916) describing a "variation of the broken-wing stunt" by a roadrunner, writes:

As I was climbing near the nest the bird hopped to the ground. Immediately it began to squirm, scramble, and drag itself away across an open space and in full view. The bird was simulating a broken leg instead of the conventional broken wing! The bird held its wings closed throughout the demonstration though frequently falling over on its side in its enthusiasm. The whole performance was kept entirely in my view, the bird gradually working away from the tree until it was some 35 feet distant when it immediately ran back to the base of the tree and repeated the whole show. I had been so interested up to now that I had failed to examine the nest which when looked into contained five young probably a week old. When I got to the ground the bird continued its stunt rather more frantically than before and in order to encourage the bird I followed, and was pleased to see it remain highly consistent until I was decoyed to a point well outside the grove. Here the bird suddenly ran away at full speed and in a direction still away from the nest.

Voice.—We have already described the spring song of the roadrunner. Howard Lacey (1911) tells us that the bird "makes a loud chuckling crowing noise * * * and also a cooing noise that might easily be mistaken for the voice of some kind of dove; it also makes a sort of purring sound in its throat, *perrp, perrp, perrp.*"

As for this "purring sound," I am not at all sure that it is *vocal*. One of the roadrunner's most characteristic alarm sounds is not a cry at all; it is an incisive, clackety noise made by rolling the mandibles together rapidly and sharply. Even young birds just out of the nest can produce this sound, though the softness of the bill muffles the sharpness somewhat.

Young birds in the nest make a buzzing sound when begging for food. Well do I remember a nestful of these "infant dragons" that I found in April 1914. Concerning these I have written (1936): "Accidentally I touched an upturned beak and four great mouths, wobbling uncertainly on scrawny necks, rose in unison. I jerked back my hand—the pink-blotched lining of those mouths had an almost poisonous appearance. From the depths of the small frames came a hoarse, many-toned buzzing which gave the impression that a colony of winged insects had been stirred to anger."

Enemies.—There is little doubt in my mind that the roadrunner's worst enemy is man. Man wants quail to shoot. Man sees a roadrunner chasing young quail or finds a young quail in a roadrunner's stomach and lo, thumbs turn down, another name goes on the black list, and the roadrunner's doom is sealed. In many a southwestern State there have been chaparral-cock drives and contests, bounty on roadrunners, newspaper stories and editorials defaming the bird. Too, there are those who *eat* roadrunners, or who chase and shoot them for "sport." In populated sections the roadrunner has a hard time. Where man appears the roadrunner all too frequently disappears.

Certain predatory birds and mammals doubtless prey occasionally on the roadrunner, though adult birds usually are swift or wary enough to evade such enemies as coyotes and hawks. Crows and ravens doubtless eat some roadrunner eggs and young. Even the snakes themselves may take a hand in keeping the snake killer tribe from becoming too numerous. Remains of a roadrunner were found in the stomach of a red-tailed hawk collected by Dr. Josselyn Van Tyne in Brewster County, Tex., February 28, 1935 (Van Tyne and Sutton, 1937).

W. L. McAtee (1931) in his timely "Little Essay on Vermin" so justly states the case of roadrunner *versus* mankind that his comments are of special significance here:

The Road-runner is persecuted almost throughout its range * * * as an alleged destroyer of Quail eggs, and state bounties are even paid for its destruction. Yet the Road-runner never has been shown to be a special enemy of Quail, and it cannot eat their eggs except during a brief season. The Road-runner is as nearly omnivorous as any of our birds, eating anything in its habitat that is readily available and swallowable. No doubt it will eat Quail eggs, but it is equally certain that not one meal in a thousand of all the birds at all times consists of Quail eggs.

The Road-runner actually lives up to its repute of killing rattlesnakes; without doubt, it eats more scorpions, centipedes, and tarantulas * * * than it does Quail eggs, and it is a voracious consumer of grasshoppers. It is a unique bird, not only in our fauna but in that of the world, has extremely interesting habits, and in its choice of food in the long run undoubtedly does more good than harm. Its persecution is all but baseless and is thoroughly unjustified.

DISTRIBUTION

Range.—Southwestern United States south to central Mexico.

The range of the roadrunner extends **north** to north-central California (Navarro River, Owens River, and Death Valley); Colorado (Meeker, Canon City, and Las Animas); and southern Kansas (probably Caldwell and Arkansas City). **East** to Kansas (Arkansas City); central Oklahoma (Norman); Texas (Fort Worth, Kerrville, and San Antonio); Tamaulipas (Matamoras, Soto La Marina, and Tampico); and Pueblo (San Salvador). **South** to Puebla (San Salvador); Mexico (Tenango); and Jalisco (Zapotlan). **West** to Jalisco (Zapotlan); Baja California (Cape San Lucas, San Cristobal Bay, and Rosario) ; and California (San Diego, Mentone, Santa Barbara, Sebastopol, and Navarro River).

Casual records.—The roadrunner is not known outside of its normal range, but a remarkable occurrence was the finding of a specimen at Marshall Pass, Colo., at an elevation of about 10,000 feet, on October 12, 1907.

Egg dates.—Arizona: 20 records, April 5 to June 24; 10 records, April 20 to June 3, indicating the height of the season.

California: 73 records, March 4 to July 16; 37 records, March 25 to May 2.

Mexico: 5 records, April 16 to May 16.

Texas: 57 records, March 18 to July 5; 29 records, May 3 to June 1.

COCCYZUS MINOR MAYNARDI Ridgway

MAYNARD'S CUCKOO

HABITS

The mangrove cuckoo (*Coccyzus minor minor*) long remained on the A. O. U. Check-list, including the third edition, based on Audubon's record of a specimen taken on Key West and figured in his Birds of America. Ridgway (1916) examined this specimen and identified it as the Jamaican mangrove cuckoo (*C. minor nesiotes*). Now the 1931 Check-list makes the statement that all Florida records prove to be referable to *C. minor maynardi*, and excludes both of the above races from the list.

The mangrove cuckoo, of which Maynard's is a subspecies, is well named, for all races of the species seem to be confined almost exclusively to the mangroves. The only one I ever saw was encountered on our way to Alligator Lake through the mangrove forests near Cape Sable, Fla. Arthur H. Howell (1932) collected the only two he ever saw "in a black mangrove swamp near the mouth of Allens River, below Everglade."

Nesting.—Audubon (1842) says: "The nest is slightly constructed of dry twigs, and is almost flat, nearly resembling that of the Yellow-billed Cuckoo." Mr. Howell (1932) says that "a set of two fresh eggs (now in the Florida State Museum), which the female was beginning to incubate, was taken at Chokoloskee, June 4, 1903, from a nest 7 feet up in a red mangrove."

Oscar E. Baynard tells me that he took two sets of two eggs each, on May 25 and 26, 1912, in a dense stand of extra large mangroves in Pinellas County, Fla.

Eggs.—The eggs of Maynard's cuckoo are practically indistinguishable from those of the yellow-billed cuckoo. The measurements of 20 eggs average 30.77 by 23.18 millimeters; the eggs showing the four extremes measure **33.1** by 22.6, 31.4 by **24.3, 27.9** by 22, and 30 by **21.6** millimeters.

Young.—Audubon (1842) says that this cuckoo "raises two broods in the season, and feeds its young on insects until they are able to go abroad."

Plumages.—I have seen no nestlings of this species, but a fully grown juvenal, taken in the Bahamas on June 23, has the upper parts everywhere "buffy brown" to "wood brown," including the crown, which in the adult is grayer than the back; there are narrow white tips on the secondaries, tertials, and all the wing coverts; there are still narrower white tips on the primaries, which soon wear away; the black space below and behind the eye, so conspicuous in the adult, is lacking; the central tail feathers are paler grayish brown terminally than in the adult, and the lateral tail feathers are pale "wood brown," instead of black, with whitish, instead of pure white, tips, which are also less clearly defined than in the adult. I have seen young birds in this plumage in July, August, and September. The body plumage is probably molted during the fall, but the juvenal wings and tail are apparently retained until the following spring or summer; I have seen young birds molting wings and tail in February, June, and August, thus assuming a fully adult plumage.

Food.—The food of Maynard's cuckoo consists mainly of caterpillars, spiders, moths, flies, grasshoppers, and other insects; probably a few small fruits and wild berries are eaten at times. Mr. Howell (1932) says: "The stomachs of two birds taken at Everglade, Florida, in March, were examined in the Biological Survey; the food in one consisted mainly of hairy caterpillars (Arctiidae), the stomach being well lined with caterpillar spines; the remains of 3 mantids (*Stagmomantis*) composed the remainder. The other stomach contained 4 long-horned grasshoppers, lepidopterous larvae, locustid eggs, mantids, and spiders."

Behavior.—Maynard (1896) says of the habits of this cuckoo in the Bahamas:

They frequent thickets near fields, and often venture into the open grounds to feed, but usually when taken by surprise in such places, quickly retreat to the thickets, into which they glide easily. Once within the cover of the shrubbery, their movements are quite deliberate, but when approached, they will jump from branch to branch, and although not appearing to hasten, will manage to elude their pursuer, and become quickly lost in the foliage.

The flight of this Cuckoo is rapid, the wings being moved quickly, much more so than in the Black or Yellow Billed Cuckoos. They generally move straight forward, without doubling, and when they wish to alight, they do so suddenly without any preliminary lessening of their speed, and as soon as their feet touch the branch the tail is dropped perpendicularly. As a rule, this Cuckoo is rather shy, especially when in open fields, but I once came across one near Mathewstown, Inagua, that was feeding in an old field, that was very tame, allowing me to approach within ten feet of it, as it deliberately searched for food among the remains of partly decayed stubs of trees which stood in the clearing.

Voice.—On this subject Maynard says:

All through the winter Maynard's Cuckoo is rather silent, but as spring approaches they begin to utter their singular cries, and at times, more especially before rain, are quite noisy. The notes may be represented by the syllables "ou, ou, ou, ou, qua, qua, qua, coo, coo, coo."

The "ous" are given very rapidly, with a decided Cuckoo-like intonation.

The "quas" are harsher, more like the notes of the Bahama tree frog, and are not hurriedly given. The last three notes are more Cuckoo-like than any of the others. The first four notes are often omitted, then the harshly and gravely given "quas" begin the song and on occasions these quaint sounds are not followed by any other notes, then it is sometimes difficult to distinguish the notes uttered from some of those uttered by the large Andros Island Cuckoo, Saurothera andrea. This varied song is uttered in the early morning with rather more energy than at any other time in the day.

Field marks.—The Maynard's cuckoo might easily be mistaken for a yellow-billed cuckoo, as it doubtless often has been, the tail markings being practically the same. But the underparts are decidedly washed with "pinkish buff" and "cinnamon-buff," though these parts are not so deeply colored as in the mangrove cuckoo. If clearly seen at close range, the grayish crown and the black area behind and, narrowly, below the eye are good field marks.

DISTRIBUTION

Range.—Northeastern South America, Central America to central Mexico, the West Indies, and southern Florida.

The range of the mangrove cuckoo extends **north** to Nayarit (Tres Marias Islands and San Blas); Tamaulipas (Alta Mira); Yucatan (Izamal, Temax, Chichen-Itza, Cozumel Island, and Mujeres Island); western Cuba (Isle of Pines); Florida (Anclote Keys and Cape Florida); the Bahama Islands (Berry, Eleuthera, and Watling Islands); the Dominican Republic (Monte Cristi, Sosua, and Seibo); Puerto Rico (Desecheo, Culebra, and Vieques Islands); and the Virgin Islands (St. Thomas, Tortola, and Virgin Gorda). **East** to the Virgin Islands (Virgin Gorda); the Leeward and Windward Islands (Antigua, Guadeloupe, Dominica, Martinique, Santa Lucia, St. Vincent, and Grenada); and Trinidad. **South** to Trinidad; northern Venezuela (Aruba Island); Panama (Chiriqui); and Costa Rica (San Jose and Puntarenas). **West** to Costa Rica (Puntarenas, Pozo del Rio Grande, and Tigres), Nicaragua (Greytown and Chinandega); Honduras (Roatan Island and Puerto Caballo); El Salvador (La Libertad); western Guatemala (near Ocos); Oaxaca (Cacoprieto); and Nayarit (Tres Marias Islands).

The range as outlined is for the entire species, which has been separated into several subspecies, only one of which is found in North America. This race, known as Maynard's cuckoo, *C. m. maynardi*, is found in the Bahamas, Cuba, and the southern part of Florida, including the Florida Keys.

Migration.—Apparently only Maynard's cuckoo is migratory, and this only in the Florida part of its range. Early dates of arrival in Florida are: Gator Lake in Monroe County, March 22, and Punta Rossa, March 29. A late date of departure from Key West is September 19.

Egg dates.—Florida and the Keys: 13 records, May 17 to July 10.

COCCYZUS AMERICANUS AMERICANUS (Linnaeus)

YELLOW-BILLED CUCKOO

PLATES 6, 7

HABITS

The yellow-billed cuckoo, with its western subspecies, covers practically all the United States and some of southern Canada. It is mainly a bird of the Austral Zone, being much commoner in the Southern States than in the northern portions of its range. In New England it is not so common as the black-billed cuckoo, though in some seasons it seems to be a familiar bird. Originally it was probably a woodland bird, but, like many other species, it has learned to frequent the haunts of man, where it is not molested and where it finds an abundant food supply in our shade trees, orchards, and gardens. Its favorite haunts are still the woodland thickets, where the tree growth is not too heavy, brush-grown lanes, shady roadsides, dense thickets along small streams, and apple orchards in rural districts. In dense, heavy woods it is seldom seen.

Nesting.—Unlike the European cuckoo, both of our North American species usually build their own nests and rear their own young, though they are very poor nest builders and are often careless about laying in each other's nests or the nests of other species. Major Bendire (1895) gives the following very good account of the nesting habits of the yellow-billed cuckoo:

The Yellow-billed Cuckoo is one of the poorest nest builders known to me, and undoubtedly the slovenly manner in which it constructs its nest causes the contents of many to be accidentally destroyed, and this probably accounts to some extent for the many apparent irregularities in their nesting habits. The nests are shallow, frail platforms, composed of small rootlets, sticks, or twigs, few of these being over 4 or 5 inches in length, and among them a few dry leaves and bits of mosses; rags, etc., are occasionally mixed in, and the surface is lined with dry blossoms of the horse-chestnut and other flowering plants, the male aments or catkins of oaks, willows, etc., tufts of grasses, pine and spruce needles, and mosses of different kinds. These materials are loosely placed on the top of the little platform, which is frequently so small that the extremities of the bird project on both sides, and there is scarcely any depression to keep the eggs from rolling out even in only a moderate windstorm, unless one of the parents sits on the nest, and it is therefore not a rare occurrence to find broken eggs lying under the trees or bushes in which the nests are placed. Some of these are so slightly built that the eggs can be readily seen through the bottom. An average nest measures about 5 inches in outer diameter by 1½ inches in depth. They are rarely placed over 20 feet from the ground, generally from 4 to 8 feet upon horizontal limbs of oak, beech, gum, dogwood, hawthorn, mulberry, pine, cedar, fir, apple, orange, fig, and other trees. Thick bushes particularly such as are overrun with wild grape and other vines as well as hedgerows, especially those of osage orange are most frequently selected for nesting sites. The nests are ordinarily well concealed by the overhanging and surrounding foliage and while usually shy and timid at other times, the Yellow-billed Cuckoo is generally courageous and bold in the defense of its chosen home; the bird on the nest not unfrequently will raise its feathers at right angles from the body and occasionally even fly at the intruder.

Of five Massachusetts nests, on which I have notes, the lowest was only 2 feet above the ground in some bushes, and the highest was 12 feet up in a crotch near the top of an oak sapling in a swampy thicket near a brook. Owen Durfee mentions in his notes a nest 5 feet up in a juniper on the edge of a swamp. The others were at low elevations in thickets along brooks.

A. D. DuBois has sent me his notes on five Illinois nests; one of these was on the end of a branch of an apple tree, 8 feet from the ground, near a country schoolhouse; this nest contained 3 eggs of the cuckoo and a robin's egg. Another was near the end of a branch in an osage-orange hedge, 10 feet up; still another was in an isolated clump of willows, between a field and a pasture, 6 feet from the ground.

But cuckoos do not always nest in such low situations; there are several records of their nesting well up in elm trees. Grant Foreman (1924) tells of a pair that nested on his place in Muskogee, Okla., for one or two years, high up in an elm tree; he says: "The next year after nesting in this inaccessible place, they built their nest in a little elm tree in the parking, in a low limb overhanging the curb on an asphalt street where hundreds of automobiles were passing every day, and here in this exposed, noisy place they raised a brood of young. This year they built their nest in a little hackberry tree in the parking along the side of my lot; but here also the nest was on a low limb overhanging the curb on a paved street, and the ice wagon stopped every morning directly under this nest, which was so low down that the driver might have put his hand in it."

George Finlay Simmons (1915) mentions a nest that he found near Houston, Tex., on the horizontal limb of a young pine near the edge of some woods. He says of it: "The nest was a slight platform about eleven feet up, through which I could see with ease; it was composed of small pine twigs, about an eighth of an inch in diameter and averaging six or eight inches long, and was much more concave than I had expected. This shallow saucer was neatly, though quite thinly lined with a few pine needles, a small quantity of Spanish moss and several tiny buds."

George B. Sennett (1879) says that in the Lower Rio Grande region of Texas "ebony trees near the ranch, mesquites among cactuses, thorny bushes in open chaparral, and open woodland, were favored breeding places."

Wright and Harper (1913) found a well-made nest in Okefinokee Swamp, in a tupelo tree at the margin of the Suwannee. "It was placed in a cluster of mistletoe on a horizontal branch four feet above the water, and consisted of sticks interwoven with Spanish 'moss' (*Tillandsia usneoides*)."

Dr. Harry C. Oberholser (1896) gives the measurements of four nests; the average height of the nests was 4 inches, and the greatest outside diameters averaged 7.63 by 6.25 inches.

Both species of North American cuckoos often lay their eggs in each other's nests. The eggs of the yellow-billed cuckoo have been found several times in nests of the robin and catbird. H. P. Attwater (1892) writes: "In 1884 I found a Dickcissel's nest which contained five eggs and one Yellow-billed Cuckoo's egg. The next year some boys brought me three Black-throated Sparrow's eggs and one Yellow-billed Cuckoo's, from the same field, which they said they found all together in one nest." J. L. Davison (1887) says: "I also found a nest of *Merula migratoria*, taken possession of by *Coccyzus americanus* before it was finished, which was filled nearly full of rootlets; and in this condition the Robin laid one egg and the Cuckoo laid two and commenced incubation, when a Mourning Dove (*Zenaidura macroura*) also occupied it and laid two eggs and commenced incubation with the Cuckoo. I found both birds on the nest at the same time, when I secured nest and eggs. The eggs of the Robin and Cuckoo were slightly incubated; those of the Mourning Dove were fresh."

Bendire (1895) adds the wood thrush, cedar waxwing, and cardinal to the list of birds that have been imposed upon, and says: "Such instances appear to be much rarer, however, than those in which they interlay with each other, and the majority of these may well be due to accident, their own nest having possibly been capsized, and necessity compelled the bird to deposit its egg elsewhere. Such instances do occur at times with species that can not possibly be charged with parasitic tendencies."

Marcia B. Clay (1929) thus describes the cuckoo's method of gathering twigs for her nest:

Flying into an adjacent apple tree containing a considerable quantity of dead material, the Cuckoo landed on a limb, selected a dead twig, and grasping it in her bill bent it back and forth until it snapped from the limb, whereupon she flew with it to her nesting-site in the next tree, arranged this twig and quickly returned for another. As she tugged at a stubborn twig, her back was arched and her long tail curved under or waved about. If a twig resisted too well her attack, the bird desisted at once and tried another. Always she worked rapidly with great energy, attacking a twig as soon as she landed in the tree, never carrying more than one twig at a time, holding it squarely at right angles to her bill and flying rapidly with long tail streaming.

The Cuckoo's concentration in the work, coupled with her indifference to observers, was remarkable. Not once did she descend to the ground for material. Not once did she gather material in the tree in which her nest was located. With two exceptions the twigs were all gathered from the same tree. Working thus off and on for an hour or two at a time, the bird completed the nest. The third night the Cuckoo was sitting on the nest at dusk, but after two days she deserted.

Eggs.—The yellow-billed cuckoo lays ordinarily three or four eggs, sometimes only one and rarely five; as many as six, seven, or even eight eggs have been found in a nest, but these larger numbers may be the product of more than one female. The eggs vary in shape from elliptical-oval to oval, oftener nearer the former, and about equally rounded at both ends. The shell is smooth, but without gloss. Bendire (1895) says that the "color varies from a uniform Nile blue to pale greenish blue when fresh, fading out in time to a pale greenish yellow." Eggs that I have examined in collections vary in color from "pale glaucous green" to "pale fluorite green." The measurements of 53 eggs average 30.4 by 23 millimeters; the eggs showing the four extremes measure **34.64** by 23.11, 33.53 by **25.40, 27.43** by 22.86, and 29.21 by **20.83** millimeters.

Young.—The period of incubation is said to be about 14 days; it is shared to some extent by both sexes, but is probably performed mainly by the female. The eggs are sometimes laid on succeeding days, but oftener at more or less infrequent intervals; the young, therefore, frequently hatch at irregular intervals, and young of different ages are often found in the nest.

Snyder and Logier (1931) say of a brood of young that they examined: "The young were quite active when disturbed. They scrambled about the bush, using the wings and bill for climbing. One young which was brought to our camp demonstrated a remarkable reptile-like behaviour. When it was placed on the table and one reached to pick it up, it erected its somewhat horny plumage and emitted a buzzing hiss like the sound of bees escaping from a tunnel in dry grass. This performance was certainly unbirdlike in all respects."

Francis H. Allen writes to me: "I found a young one in an open field on the ground. I was attracted to the spot by its loud rasping

cry.   It fluttered along when I approached, but it could not fly from
that position, in rather long grass, though wings and tail were
pretty well fledged.   When I picked it up, it pecked at my finger
angrily.   It seemed as fierce as a young hawk, and its rasping cry was
probably calculated to inspire terror in its enemies.   I placed the
bird on a bough of a Norway spruce, where it took a characteristic
cuckoo attitude and seemed much more at home than on the ground."

Dr. Lawrence H. Walkinshaw has sent me some notes on the
weights and development of young yellow-billed cuckoos.   One
"well-grown" young was weighed for three days in succession before
it left the nest, at 6 a. m. each morning.   It weighed 28.8 grams the
first morning, 31 grams the second, and only 26 grams on the third,
August 6.   The interesting point is that the loss of weight came with
the sudden development of the plumage, of which he says: "When I
visited the nest on August 5, at 6 a. m., his feathers resembled the
quills of a porcupine, long and bluish, stretched out over his wings
and back.   At 7 p. m., these quills had all opened and the bird had
taken on the resemblance of an adult cuckoo.   Correspondingly, the
following morning, he had lost 5 grams in weight.   He left the
nest on August 6."

At another nest a young bird weighed 25 grams on August 25,
27.6 on the 26th, 32.9 on the 27th, and only 28.9 grams on the 28th;
this bird left the nest on August 29, with feathers unsheathed.   He
says that during the unsheathing process the young bird dressed its
feathers continually; "the wings, the tail, the scapulars, the rump,
and breast all shared alike, then with the feet he would work about
the head and throat.   When hungry he would pause and call a low
cuk-cuk-cuk-cur-r-r-r-rrr.   If the parent did not come soon, these
calls increased in number.   While feeding, his wings would vibrate
rapidly, and after the parent left his call was more of contentment,
a short *curr*, or a *cuk-currrrr*.   When excreting, he simply backed
up to the edge of the nest."

Plumages.—Bendire (1895) says: "The young when first hatched
are repulsive, black, and greasy-looking creatures, nearly naked, and
the sprouting quills only add to their general ugliness."   This is a
very good description, and the young birds do not improve much
in appearance during the period of early growth.   The body is well
covered with the long, pointed feather sheaths until the young bird
is more than half grown.   But the sheaths burst, the juvenal plumage appears, and the young bird is well feathered before the time
comes to leave the nest.

Dr. A. H. Cordier (1923) describes this process very well as
follows:

At the end of seven days the young Cuckoo resembled a porcupine more than a bird. I now cut the limb holding the nest and brought it to the ground. Within three feet of it I then put up the umbrella tent that I might at close range observe minutely the rapid transition of the porcupine-looking object into a fully feathered, beautiful Rain Crow. * * *

The first picture was made at nine o'clock. * * * This shows the young by the unhatched egg; the horny, sheathed feathers were fully two inches long, making the bird look like a porcupine. About ten-thirty the sheaths began to burst, and with each split a fully formed feather was liberated. This process took place with such rapidity that it reminded me of the commotion in a corn popper or a rapidly blooming flower. All the while I was within three feet of the bird, and could see every new feather, as it blossomed, so to speak.

At three p. m., six hours after the first picture was taken, I made another photograph, showing this same bird in the full plumage of a Cuckoo, except the long tail.

In this first plumage the young cuckoo looks very much like the adult, perhaps slightly paler above and with a slight wash of tawny or pale buff on the throat and breast; but the tail is quite different, lacking the conspicuous black and white markings so prominent on the sides of the adult tail; in the young bird the dark spaces in the tail are not black, but dark gray or lighter gray, variable in different individuals or in different feathers in the same individual; the light spaces are not so sharply defined as in the adult and are grayish white instead of pure white.

The juvenal body plumage appears to be molted in fall, from August to October; but the juvenal wings and tail are worn through the first winter at least; I have not been able to detect this plumage in spring birds, so I suppose that a more or less complete molt occurs while the birds are in their winter homes, producing a practically adult plumage before they return in the spring. Adults have a complete molt between July and October, and possibly a more or less complete molt in spring before they arrive here, but winter specimens to show it are lacking.

Food.—Cuckoos are among the most useful of our birds, mainly because of their fondness for caterpillars, which are some of our most injurious insect pests and which constitute the principal food of these birds during their seasons of abundance. Edward H. Forbush (1907) writes:

The Cuckoos are of the greatest service to the farmer, by reason of their well-known fondness for caterpillars, particularly the hairy species. No caterpillars are safe from the Cuckoo. It does not matter how hairy or spiny they are, or how well they may be protected by webs. Often the stomach of the Cuckoo will be found lined with a felted mass of caterpillar hairs, and sometimes its intestines are pierced by the spines of the noxious caterpillars that it has swallowed. Wherever caterpillar outbreaks occur we hear the calls of the Cuckoos. There they stay; there they bring their newly fledged young;

and the number of caterpillars they eat is incredible. Professor Beal states that two thousand, seven hundred and seventy-one caterpillars were found in the stomachs of one hundred and twenty-one Cuckoos—an average of more than twenty-one each. Dr. Otto Lugger found several hundred small hairy caterpillars in the stomach of a single bird. The poisonous, spined caterpillars of the Io moth, the almost equally disagreeable caterpillars of the brown-tail moth, and the spiny elm caterpillar, are eaten with avidity.

He says elsewhere (1927) :

When, in time, the inside of the bird's stomach becomes so felted with a mass of hairs and spines that it obstructs digestion, the bird can shed the entire stomach-lining, meanwhile growing a new one. * * * Mr. Mosher, a competent observer, watched a Yellow-billed Cuckoo eat 41 gypsy caterpillars in fifteen minutes, and later he saw another consume 47 forest tent caterpillars in six minutes. * * * Dr. Amos W. Butler [1897] says that he has known these Cuckoos to destroy every tent caterpillar in a badly infested orchard and tear up all the nests in half a day. This species frequently feeds on or near the ground, and there gets an enormous number of locusts and other pests. In summer and autumn it feeds to some extent on small wild fruits, such as the raspberry, blackberry and wild grape.

The fall webworm is a destructive pest on certain trees, but few birds will eat it. Dr. Sylvester D. Judd (1902) noted that, on a Maryland farm, "a pair of yellow-billed cuckoos continually extracted them from the webs. The destruction of this insect is an habitual practice with the cuckoo. In a single stomach of the species examined by Professor Beal there were 325 of the larvæ."

Henry C. Denslow writes to me that he fed many hairy caterpillars to a cuckoo that he had in captivity, and says: "Many of these this bird sheared the hairs from by slowly moving them from end to end through its beak by a side-shifting motion of the mandibles. The removed hairs collected in a little bunch and, at the end of the caterpillar, fell to the floor. Most of the hairs were thus shorn from these caterpillars. Other caterpillars were swallowed entire, as I gave them to him, hairs and all."

Walter B. Barrows (1912) says that this cuckoo feeds freely on elderberries and mulberries and that "large quantities of beetles and bugs also are consumed, and both species of cuckoo seem to be very fond of grasshoppers, eating especially such forms as frequent shrubbery and trees, among these the destructive tree crickets (*Oecanthus*). Ten specimens examined by Professor Aughey, in Nebraska, contained 416 locusts and grasshoppers, and 152 other insects."

Audubon (1842) writes: "In autumn they eat many grapes, and I have seen them supporting themselves by a momentary motion of their wings opposite a bunch, as if selecting the ripest, when they would seize it and return to a branch, repeating their visits in this manner until satiated."

In addition to those mentioned above, yellow-billed cuckoos have been known to eat many other insects, such as armyworms, ants, wasps, flies, and dragonflies. Several of the earlier ornithologists accused this cuckoo of eating the eggs of other small birds and produced some evidence of the bad habit, but some modern observers seem to think that they do very little, if any, nest robbing. C. J. Maynard (1896) writes:

This species in company with the former [black-billed cuckoo] are the terror of other small birds during the nesting season for they will constantly rob their nests. I have frequently seen a Cuckoo enter a thicket in which a Robin or a Cat Bird had built a home and in a moment the air would resound with the shrill cries of distress given by the parents, causing all the small birds in the immediate vicinity to rush to the spot and as each joins in the outcry, the noise produced is apparently enough to frighten away a bolder bird than a Cuckoo.

But in spite of all this din, the glossy thief nearly always succeeds in accomplishing his purpose and emerges from the thicket, carrying an egg impaled on his beak. He does not always escape unscathed, however, for he is pursued by a motley crowd consisting of Robins, Cat Birds, Thrushes, Warblers, etc. that follow him closely, harassing him on all sides, and some of the more courageous will even assault him with blows from their beaks so that he frequently leaves some of his feathers floating in the wind behind him. As the long and broad tail of the Cuckoo is a prominent object and as it is also a portion of the bird which its enemies can seize with comparative safety to themselves, this member often suffers in these forays, in so much, that by the middle of summer, it is quite difficult to find a Cuckoo of either species which has a full complement of tail feathers.

On the other hand, Major Bendire (1895) says: "I am aware that this species has been accused of destroying the eggs and even of eating the young of smaller birds, but I am strongly inclined to believe that this accusation is unjust, and in my opinion requires more substantial confirmation. I have never yet had any reason to suspect their robbing smaller birds' nests, and the very fact that they live in apparent harmony with such neighbors, who do not protest against their presence, as they are in the habit of doing should a Blue Jay, Grackle, or Crow come too close to their nests, seems to confirm this view."

But then he goes on to quote from a letter from William Brewster, who says: "While I have never seen either of our Cuckoos destroy the eggs of other birds, nevertheless I think they do it occasionally. One of my reasons for this belief is that many of our small birds, Warblers, Sparrows, etc., show great anxiety whenever the Cuckoos approach their nests, and they pursue and peck at them when they take wing, behaving toward them, in fact, exactly as they do toward the Crows, Jays, and Grackles, which we *know* eat eggs whenever they can get a chance. My other reason is that one of my friends once shot a Cuckoo (*C. americanus*, I think it was) whose bill was smeared all over with the fresh yolk of an egg."

Yellow-billed cuckoos sometimes eat tree frogs and other small frogs, and, in the Southern States, an occasional small lizard. Marcia B. Clay (1929) relates the following incident: "For an hour a Cuckoo searched about the dead under limbs of a huge untrimmed apple tree, peering and gliding noiselessly around and around. At last, after long and patient search, it dashed to the ground and began to walk directly toward me through the scant grass and weeds, and only then did I see a frog trying to slip away unseen. The bird followed the frog a rod, pecking its victim and gloating softly *Cuk*, *Cuk*. Having vanquished its prey, the Cuckoo deftly gathered it into its bill and flew away, the frog's legs sticking out stiff and straight together, exactly like the dead twigs which the Cuckoo carries to its nest."

Behavior.—Mr. Forbush (1927) has described the quiet, retiring behavior of the yellow-billed cuckoo very well as follows:

The cuckoo is a graceful, elegant bird, calm and unperturbed; it slips quietly and rather furtively through its favorite tangles and flies easily from tree to tree in the orchard, keeping for the most part under protection of the leaves, which furnish excellent cover for its bronzy, upper plumage, while the shadows of the foliage tend to conceal the whiteness of its under parts. It has a way also of keeping its back with its greenish satiny reflections toward the intruder in its solitudes, and while holding an attitude of readiness for flight it sits motionless, and its plumage so blends with its leafy environment that it does not ordinarily catch the eye. In the meantime it turns its head and regards the disturber with a cool, reserved, direct gaze, looking back over its shoulder, apparently unafraid and giving no indication of nervousness or even undue curiosity; but if the observer approaches too closely, the elegant bird slips quietly away, vanishing into some leafy, cool retreat where it may enjoy the silence and solitude, dear to the woodland recluse.

The flight of the cuckoo is rather swift, easy and graceful, exceedingly direct and horizontal, but turning frequently from side to side as it threads its way through the branches of the trees, giving occasional glimpses of its white under parts and the telltale black-and-white markings in its tail; it is stream-lined to perfection and glides noiselessly through the air with its long tail streaming out behind. It is very quiet in its movements in its shady retreats; it seldom perches in a conspicuous place but sits motionless for long periods in the dense foliage, watching, or moves about stealthily in search of its prey. It might easily be overlooked, were it not for its characteristic notes, which lead the observer to look for it.

About its nest it is rather shy, while incubating on its eggs, slipping away cautiously when approached, but when there are young in the nest its behavior is quite different. It then becomes quite solicitous and will often remain on the nest until almost touched, and then perhaps throw itself down to the ground, fluttering and tumbling along, feigning lameness, after the manner of many ground-nesting birds, uttering loud, guttural cries of distress.

Voice.—We hear the voice of the cuckoo much oftener than we see the bird; the well-known sound comes to us, like a wandering voice, from the depths of some shady retreat, but we cannot see the hidden author. We can recognize it easily as the voice of a cuckoo, but it is not always so easy to identify the species by its notes, though some keen observers claim that they can do so. Certain songs are characteristic of each of the two species, but both have a great variety of notes and many notes that are much alike in both. The notes of the yellow-billed cuckoo may be a trifle harsher and a little louder, but they are not always recognizable. The characteristic note of the yellow-billed cuckoo is well described by Charles J. Spiker (1935) as follows: "What may be considered the song of this species is a series of rapid, wooden-sounding syllables resembling the following: *Kuk-kuk-kuk-kuk-kuk-ceaow-ceaow-ceaow-ceaow;* the *kuks* being given rapidly, the *ceaows* more deliberately and with longer intervals."

Bendire (1895) writes:

One of their commonest notes is a low "noo-coo-coo-coo;" another sounds more like "cow-cow-cow" or "kow kow kow," several times repeated; others resemble the syllables of "ough, ough, ough," slowly and softly uttered; some remind me of the "kloop-kloop" of the Bittern; occasionally a note something like the "kiuh-kiuh-kiuh" of the Flicker is also uttered; a low sharp "touwity-whit" and "hweet hwee" is also heard during the nesting season. Though ordinarily not what might be called a social bird, I have sometimes during the mating season seen as many as eight in the same tree, and on such occasions they indulge in quite a number of calls, and if the listener can only keep still long enough he has an excellent opportunity to hear a regular Cuckoo concert.

Various other interpretations of the different notes have been given by other writers, but the above quotations cover fairly well the ordinary variations. The song, as given by Mr. Spiker above, is sometimes more prolonged by lengthening the series of *kuks*, with increasing speed of utterance and adding to the series of *ceaows*, with slowly decreasing speed. I believe that the black-billed cuckoo never gives this prolonged song, accelerated during the first half and retarded during the last half; its song is given in more even time, and is generally shorter. The song of the yellow-billed cuckoo is often heard during the night, and its notes are often uttered while flying.

Field marks.—A cuckoo may be easily recognized as a cuckoo by its size, shape, and color—a long, slender bird, longer than a robin, with a long tail, olive-brown above and white below; but the two species look very much alike unless the distinctive markings can be clearly seen. The yellow lower mandible of this species can be seen only at short range. But the rufous in the wing feathers is evident in flight, and the lateral tail feathers are conspicuously black, with large terminal white areas clearly defined. At very close range the yellow eyelids of this species may be seen.

Range.—Temperate North America, the Caribbean region, South and Central America; casual on Bermuda and accidental in western Europe.

Breeding range.—The breeding range of the yellow-billed cuckoo extends **north** to southern British Columbia (Kamloops); northeastern Oregon (Keenys Ferry); northern Utah (Salt Lake City); northern Colorado (Loveland, Greeley, and Fort Morgan); South Dakota (White River, Yankton, and Sioux Falls); Minnesota (Fosston and St. Paul); Wisconsin (Ladysmith, Waupaca, and New London); northern Michigan (Blaney and Sault Ste. Marie); southern Ontario (Listowel, Rosseau, and Ottawa); northern New York (Watertown and Plattsburg); and southern Maine (Auburn). From this point the breeding range extends southward along the Atlantic coast to Florida (New Smyrna and Kissimmee); the Bahama Islands Inagua Island); probably the Dominican Republic (Dajabon); and the Virgin Islands (St. Croix). **South** to the Virgin Islands (St. Croix); Jamaica (Port Henderson); Coahuila (Sabinas River); southern Sonora (Guaymas); and southern Baja California (San Jose del Rancho). **West** to Baja California (San Jose del Rancho and Cerro Prieto); California (Wilmington, Watsonville, Santa Clara, and Redding); Oregon (Salem); Washington (Grays Harbor, Tacoma, and Seattle); and British Columbia (Victoria, Chilliwack, and Kamloops).

The range as outlined is for the entire species, which has been separated into two geographic races. The yellow-billed cuckoo (*C. a. americanus*) occupies the eastern part of the range west to South Dakota, Nebraska, eastern Colorado, and Oklahoma, while the California cuckoo (*C. a. occidentalis*) is found over the rest of the country to the Pacific coast.

Winter range.—The winter home of this species has not been accurately determined, but it extends **north** to northern Colombia (Santa Marta, Bonda, Medellin, and Antioquia); and Venezuela (San Cristobal, Altagracia, the Orinoco River region, and Nericagua). It has been found at this season **east** to southeastern Brazil (São Paulo); Uruguay (Rio Negro); and eastern Argentina (Buenos Aires and Lomas de Zamora). **South,** probably only casually to central Argentina (Lomas de Zamora and Saladillo). **West** to Argentina (Saladillo and La Riojo); Ecuador (Nono, Chimbo, Cumbaya, and Guapulo); and Colombia (Cienaga and Santa Marta).

Spring migration.—Early dates of spring arrival are: Florida—Melrose, March 12; Daytona Beach, April 9; Pensacola, April 13. Alabama—Autaugaville, April 16. Georgia—Savannah, March 24; Kirkwood, April 7. South Carolina—Charleston, April 14. North Carolina—Raleigh, April 25; Weaverville, May 1. Virginia—Lawrenceville, April 23; New Market, April 26. District of Columbia—Washington, April 27. Pennsylvania—Philadelphia, April 20; Beaver, May 6; Renovo, May 11. New Jersey—Morristown, April 7; Elizabeth, May 9. New York—Shelter Island, May 2; Rhinebeck, May 3; Watertown, May 12. Connecticut—Hartford, May 9; Jewett City, May 10. Rhode Island—Providence, May 11. Massachusetts—Boston, May 4; Beverly, May 15. New Hampshire—Milford, May 11. Vermont—St. Johnsbury, May 27. Maine—Lewiston, May 6; Fryeburg, May 19. Mississippi—Biloxi, April 6; Rodney, April 8; Oakvale, April 10. Arkansas—Helena, April 19; Delight, April 24. Tennessee—Chattanooga, April 10; Knoxville, April 27. Kentucky—Eubank, April 22; Bowling Green, April 24. Missouri—St. Louis, April 28; Kansas City, April 30; Concordia, May 1. Illinois—Rantoul, May 2; Chicago, May 4; Olney, May 5. Indiana—Terre Haute, April 17; Fort Wayne, April 29; Waterloo, May 4. Ohio—Oberlin, April 26; Columbus, April 29; Youngstown, May 7. Michigan—Detroit, May 4; Battle Creek, May 11. Ontario—London, May 8; Guelph, May 12. Iowa—Sioux City, April 30; Grinnell, May 9. Wisconsin—Madison, May 10; Racine, May 10; La Crosse, May 12. Minnesota—Minneapolis, May 6; Winona, May 8. Texas—Fredericksburg, April 1; Kerrville, April 7; San Antonio, April 14. Oklahoma—Skiatook, April 20; Oklahoma City, May 3. Kansas—Ottawa, April 25; Onaga, April 28. Nebraska—Red Cloud, April 29; Lincoln, May 7. South Dakota—Vermillion, May 17. New Mexico—State College, May 25. Arizona—Phoenix, May 1; Tombstone, May 20. Colorado—Longmont, May 20; Denver, May 28. California—Petaluma, April 18; Pico, May 5; Berryessa, May 13. Oregon—Sauvies Island, April 24. Washington—Tacoma, May 3.

Fall migration.—Late dates of fall departure are: California—Murphys, September 1; Vineland, September 22. Colorado—Yuma, September 3; Clear Creek, September 8. Arizona—Tucson, September 8. New Mexico—Mesilla Park, September 7; State College September 18. North Dakota—Grafton, September 4. South Dakota—Lennox, September 15; Yankton, September 24. Nebraska—Dunbar, September 27; Lincoln, October 5. Kansas—Onaga, October 1. Oklahoma—Copan, September 23; Kenton, September 30. Texas—Bonham, September 25; Swan, September 28; Kerrville, October 19. Minnesota—Minneapolis, October 1; Hastings, October 20.

Wisconsin—Madison, September 27; Racine, October 6. Iowa—Grinnell, October 22. Ontario—Galt, October 2; London, October 11; Point Pelee, October 16. Michigan—Detroit, October 8. Ohio—Youngstown, October 12; Columbus, October 19; Oberlin, October 21. Indiana—Sedan, October 13. Illinois—Chicago, October 18; Rantoul, October 24. Missouri—Concordia, October 10. Kentucky—Lexington, October 10. Tennessee—Nashville, October 11. Arkansas—Delight, October 20. Mississippi—Biloxi, October 11. Maine—Fryeburg, September 1. Vermont—St. Johnsbury, September 12. Massachusetts—Marthas Vineyard, September 24; Lanesborough, September 29; Hadley, October 18. Connecticut—Meriden, October 12; New Haven, October 16; Portland, October 17. New York—Rhinebeck, October 1; New York City, October 12. New Jersey—Morristown, October 9; Elizabeth, October 12. Pennsylvania—Beaver, September 27; Philadelphia, October 17; Renovo, November 12. District of Columbia—Washington, October 13. Virginia—Lawrenceville, October 12. North Carolina—Raleigh, October 17. South Carolina—Mount Pleasant, November 7. Georgia—Savannah, October 19. Florida—Pensacola, November 2.

Casual records.—While the yellow-billed cuckoo may be considered only as a casual visitor to Bermuda, an extraordinary invasion was recorded on October 9, 1849, when thousands of individuals suddenly appeared in all parts of the island; a few more have been subsequently reported. During the period from 1825 to 1921 it was recorded fully a dozen times from England, Scotland, Ireland, and Wales, all these occurrences being in fall and mostly during October. One was taken at Bois de Lessines, Belgium, in October 1874, and one was collected at Turin, Italy, on October 28, 1883. Two occurrences have been recorded from the southern part of France, but there is some question that they were correctly identified.

Egg dates.—Arizona: 13 records, June 28 to August 24; 7 records, July 19 to August 22.

California: 55 records, May 15 to August 20; 28 records, June 17 to July 10, indicating the height of the season.

Florida: 19 records, April 12 to August 25; 10 records, April 16 to May 16.

Illinois: 39 records, May 20 to July 19; 20 records, June 4 to 26.

New York: 23 records, May 24 to August 19; 12 records, June 4 to 11.

Pennsylvania: 13 records, June 6 to July 29.

Texas: 34 records, March 22 to June 30; 17 records, May 6 to June 5.

COCCYZUS AMERICANUS OCCIDENTALIS Ridgway

CALIFORNIA CUCKOO

PLATE 6

HABITS

This western race of our common yellow-billed cuckoo has been separated on very slight average characters, hardly worthy of recognition in nomenclature. I am inclined to agree with Harry S. Swarth (1929), who says:

Between the eastern and western races of the Yellow-billed Cuckoo there is a slight average difference in size, the western bird being the larger and with a somewhat heavier bill. There is a rather wide range of variation in specimens from any one locality, * * * and the largest eastern birds do not fall far short of the maximum measurements of western specimens. Birds from the Pacific coast are the largest, those from central Arizona near the type locality of *occidentalis* (the Santa Rita Mountains) are intermediate in size. The subspecies would have a better claim to recognition if restricted to the Pacific coast. * * * The subspecies is certainly as slightly differentiated as any in our *Check-list*, and I feel that no violence to the facts would result from suppression of the name.

The California cuckoo is nowhere abundant but seems to be generally distributed, in suitable localities, throughout its range from British Columbia to Lower California and other parts of Mexico. In southern California, its favorite haunts seem to be the willow thickets and groves along the beds of streams, or in willow-bottom sloughs, such as the famous Nigger Slough, which formerly existed near Los Angeles. Alfred C. Shelton (1911) describes a favorite haunt in Sonoma County, Calif., as follows: "In the locality of which I write, about five miles southeast of Sabastopol, this stream, known locally as the 'Lagoon', becomes, after some winter storm, a turbulent river, flooding acres upon acres of bottom land. In summer its course is marked by a chain of long, rather narrow ponds, many of which are deep. The banks, and much of the intervening space between these ponds, are covered with a thick growth of willow, small ash and scrub oak, while the whole is tangled together with an undergrowth of poison oak, wild blackberry and various creepers, forming, as it were, an impenetrable jungle, hanging far out over the water."

Spring.—Mr. Shelton (1911) has this to say about the spring movements of the California cuckoo:

Of all migratory birds breeding in this vicinity, the Cuckoo is the last to arrive in the spring, usually appearing during the latter part of May or the first week of June. Upon its arrival, this bird keeps to the higher land, among the oaks and other timber, for a period of two or three weeks before retiring to the willow bottoms to breed. During this period it is wild and shy and difficult to approach. Most active in the early morning, its characteristic note, a loud, clear "kow-kow-kow," may be heard coming from some tree or group of trees, and perchance an answering "kow-kow-kow," may come from another tree, some distance away. * * *

After the birds retire to the willow bottoms to breed, their entire attitude changes. When watched and studied in the seclusion of their brush grown haunts, while engrossed with the cares of their domestic duties, the Cuckoos cease to be the wild, shy birds of the upland timber. The familiar "kow-kow-kow" is now forsaken for another note, a low guttural note, "kuk-kuk-kuk," always uttered by a brooding bird and is the most common call of the cuckoo during the breeding season.

Courtship.—J. H. Bowles (Dawson and Bowles, 1909) writes: "While standing in an open woodland listening to a pair of Cuckoos calling to each other, I saw the male suddenly fly past with a large green worm in his bill. He flew directly to the female, who was perched in a tree a few yards distant, and for a moment or two they sat motionless a few inches apart looking at each other. The male then hovered lightly over his mate and, settling gently upon her shoulders, gracefully bent over and placed the worm in her bill. It was a pretty and daintily performed piece of love-making."

Nesting.—The nesting habits of the California cuckoo are much like those of its eastern relative. In California its favorite nesting sites are in willow thickets in the river bottoms, or in such swampy lowlands as those referred to above. D. E. Brown writes to me that it is a rare bird in western Washington, and says: "It is found mostly in willow swamps, on the shores of fresh-water lakes, and along streams where the underbrush is thick. I have seldom seen it very far away from fresh water and never in real thick woods. It is a late arrival and does not begin nest building until about the fourth of July. I have found about a dozen occupied nests and only one of these was earlier than the above date; this one was on June 19. All these nests were in willow or wild-rose bushes, except one which was in a spirea bush. All nests were 2 to 8 feet from the ground, or water when built in swamps. The nest is a very frail, small affair composed of twigs loosely put together and lined with finer twigs and sometimes a few leaves. Most of the nests that I have seen have been so very flat and small that they would be exceedingly hard to find if the birds were not on them."

A nest in the Thayer collection, taken near Kirkland, Wash., on July 7, 1909, was found in an open space in a fir forest in low ground, which was dotted with a second growth of fir and some *Osmaronia* and *Spiraea;* it was placed on a branch of a fir on the exposed side of the tree, 9 feet from the ground; it was made of old fir twigs and lined with fresh fir twigs. I have heard of other Washington nests in fir trees.

Major Bendire (1895) says:

The nests here [Arizona] were placed in willow or mesquite thickets, from 10 to 15 feet from the ground, and they were usually fairly well concealed by the surrounding foliage. * * * If the California Cuckoo showed the same parasitic habit of occasionally depositing one or more of its eggs in the nests of other birds, as its eastern relatives are now and then known to do, I believe that I should have observed the fact in southern Arizona. Here I found eight of their nests with eggs, and fully five hundred nests of smaller birds, which nested in similar localities among the willow thickets and mesquite bushes, overrun with vines, in the creek bottoms, but not a single instance of parasitism came under my observation.

Wilson C. Hanna (1937) has published an interesting paper on the nesting habits of the California cuckoo in the San Bernardino Valley, Calif., with a photograph of a nest containing the unusual number of seven eggs; he writes:

I have rather complete notes on twenty-four nests that I have examined in the field, six along Warm Creek and eighteen along the Santa Ana River, and with two exceptions all were in willow trees. In one case the nest was 11 feet up in an alder tree next to the trunk, and in the other case 30 feet up in a cottonwood tree on top of a bare limb partly supported by a few twigs and therefore conspicuous. The last mentioned nest was ten feet higher than any other nest I have seen. Six of the nests in willows were either partly supported by or covered with wild grape vines, another nest was well concealed in the center of live mistletoe, while still another was well hidden in poison oak that was growning over the dead willow tree. A few nests were placed next to the trunks of trees, but by far the most common location was well out on a horizontal or leaning limb. The average height above ground or water was less than thirteen feet and two were only four feet up. A good supply of rope and a ladder were necessary for examining some of the nests without disturbing them or the surroundings.

Nests were always loose structures, of coarse twigs for a foundation, sometimes with a little superimposed grape-vine bark, cottonwood bark, or rootlets. In some cases there was no other lining and eggs could be seen through the bottom of the nest; but usually there were fresh or old leaves, bark strips, or willow cotton. In only one nest was there a feather in the lining. Often the nests were much longer in one dimension than the other, in one case four inches wide and twelve inches long.

Eggs.—The California cuckoo lays usually three or four eggs, occasionally only two. These are indistinguishable from those of the eastern yellow-billed cuckoo and average only slightly larger. The measurements of 43 eggs average 31.1 by 23.1 millimeters; the eggs showing the four extremes measure 35.5 by 23.5, 33.5 by 25, and 27.5 by 21 millimeters.

Food.—Bendire (1895) says that in a brood that he watched, the young were fed "always with a large black cricket (*Anabus simplex* or *purpuratus*) * * *. They picked most of these repulsive-looking creatures from grass stalks and low shrubs on which they were feeding, and although there were numbers of them to be found all around, as well as in camp, they generally went off some little distance to get them."

Mr. Swarth (1929) says that a female, collected in Arizona, "contained in its stomach two green caterpillars and a lizard 100 millimeters long, the latter swallowed entire and rolled into a coil. This seems a startling diet for a tree-dwelling cuckoo, but there is at least one other instance reported, also from the vicinity of Tucson, of a lizard being taken by one of these birds."

COCCYZUS ERYTHROPTHALMUS (Wilson)

BLACK-BILLED CUCKOO

PLATES 8–11

HABITS

The black-billed cuckoo is not so widely distributed as the yellow-billed, being confined in the breeding season to practically the northern half of the United States and southern Canada east of the Rocky Mountains. Within this range it seems to be commoner northward and rarer southward than the other species, ranging farther north and not so far south.

In appearance and habits our two cuckoos are very much alike, and their haunts are similar; both are often found together, or in similar places, though the black-billed is rather more of a woodland bird and rather more retiring than the yellow-billed. William Brewster (1906) says that in the Cambridge region it is "more given to haunting extensive tracts of dry upland woods and to nesting in wild apple trees, Virginia junipers and barberry bushes in remote rocky pastures such as those which lie scattered along the crest and sides of the high ridge between Arlington and Waverley."

Courtship.—William Brewster (1937a) writes: "On July 15, 1908, I witnessed the coition of two Black-billed Cuckoos in woods near Bethel, Maine. It took place on a branch only three or four feet above the ground. Although performed listlessly and intermittently, it was singularly protracted, for the two birds remained together at least four or five minutes, and did not finally separate until disturbed by my approach, when the male flew away and presently sang once. The female stayed quietly on her perch until I got near enough to see that she was a fully adult bird."

Nesting.—Most of the New England nests on which I have data were placed at low elevations, 2 to 4 feet above ground, in various small trees, bushes, or thickets. My first nest was the highest, 10 feet up, in the top of a leaning black birch in a strip of swampy woods and brushy thickets along a small brook. Another was 8 feet from the ground in a dense thicket of shrubbery and black-berry vines. Three nests were in small white pines, 3 to 4 feet up, in rather open spaces overgrown with various shrubs and small trees near the edges of the woods; the nests were placed on horizontal branches, against the trunk, and well concealed among the dense branches. Near Asquam Lake in New Hampshire I saw two nests in thick clumps of mountain-laurel in some dense and heavy deciduous woods, where the land sloped down to the lake; the mountain-laurel grew here in extensive patches, but not very high, seldom over 3 or 4 feet; the large and well-made nests were only 2 and 3 feet from the ground, but fairly well concealed.

Some nests of the black-billed cuckoo are very flimsy affairs, but often they are much more substantially built than the nests of the yellow-billed cuckoo. Owen Durfee describes in his notes a well-made nest that he found in a clump of chinquapin oaks near a road in Rehoboth, Mass. It was made of oak twigs and dry fern stalks, many of the twigs being fresh, with leaves attached; it was lined with dry oak leaves and a few fresh ones. It measured 8 inches in outside diameter and 3 by 3½ inches in inside diameter, being hollowed to a depth of 1 inch. There is a beautiful nest in the Thayer collection, taken from a thicket in Lancaster, Mass., 7 feet from the ground; it has a well-made foundation of coarse twigs, tufts of grass, and burs; and it is profusely lined with the green leaves and the cottony catkins of the poplar. S. F. Rathbun writes to me of an interesting nest that he found: "The nest was a saucer-shaped affair made entirely of the burs from the burdock plant, simply stuck together so as to form a shallow receptacle for the eggs. As a lining for the nest a few dry grasses were used, and the burs with the grasses represented the entire structure. The cuckoo certainly showed ingenuity when it made this nest, for it could not have been more simply or easily constructed."

Dr. T. C. Stephens has sent me some fine photographs (pl. 8) of a black-billed cuckoo's nest taken at the base of a willow sapling, near the shore of Lake Goodenough, in Union County, S. Dak., and says: "I have observed a rather marked tendency for the black-billed cuckoo in this region to build its nest within a very few inches of the ground or on the ground. This nest in the photograph was several inches above the ground outside the clump, but it might be regarded as a ground nest, because there was quite an accumulation of dirt and weed growth immediately below it. Of course, I have found nests of this species at heights about level with a man's eyes, also."

A. Dawes DuBois has sent me the data for eight nests of this cuckoo, as found by him in Tompkins County, N. Y., and Hennepin County, Minn. Two of them were 5 feet above ground, one in the top of a bush covered with grape vines on the steep slope of a ravine and the other in a small larch, in the midst of an extensive willow thicket, half a foot from the trunk of the tree on a branch where two branchlets were attached. One of the lowest two was not over a foot above ground, among weeds 2 feet high; the nest was supported by a small dead branch that had fallen from a tree and lay hidden in the weeds. Others were at intermediate heights in more normal situations. The nest in the small larch tree he describes as made first of some cottony seed pods (ripened willow catkins), then a main structure of woody twigs, and lined with finer twigs, a few grasses and bits of the cottony seed pods; two tufts of dry grass, with roots attached, were at opposite sides of the rim.

Major Bendire (1895) says:

The nests of the Black-billed Cuckoo appear to be slightly better built than those of the Yellow-billed species; the platform is usually constructed of finer twigs, the soft inner bark of cedar, fine rootlets, weed stems, etc., and there is generally more lining. This consists of the aments of oak, white and black ash, and maple, willow catkins, and the flowers of the cudweed or everlasting (*Gnaphalium*), dried leaves, and similar materials. The majority of the nests are placed in rather low situations, mostly not over 6 feet from the ground, on horizontal limbs of bushy evergreens, pines, cedars, and hemlocks, or in deciduous trees and shrubs, such as the box elder, chestnut, thorn apple, and beech trees; also in hedges, briar and kalmia patches, occasionally on old logs, and now and then even on the ground.

A rather high nest was found by P. G. Howes (1908) near Stamford, Conn. It was about 15 feet from the ground, at the extremity of a limb of "a scrubby apple tree at the foot of a hay-covered field." He says that, in his experience, the nest "has always been lined with maiden-hair ferns."

H. W. Flint, of Stamford, Conn., in a letter to Major Bendire (1895), mentions a still higher nest, and says: "I know of one spot in this vicinity where the Black-billed Cuckoo might almost be said to breed in colonies—a sloping hillside near a traveled road. Here I have found seven nests of this species within an hour, none of them placed over 3 feet from the ground. I have also frequently found their nest on a fallen limb, the top of which was resting upon underbrush. As an exception to their low nesting, I once found a nest containing two well-feathered young and two fresh eggs over 18 feet from the ground, placed in the top of a cedar tree, in a dense thicket of other cedars."

As already mentioned under the preceding species, both cuckoos often lay their eggs in each other's nests. Thomas McIlwraith (1894) mentions three cases of parasitism on the part of the black-billed cuckoo, as observed by Dr. C. K. Clarke, of Kingston, Ontario; he says:

The first birds Dr. Clarke observed being imposed upon were a pair of chipping sparrows, who raised the young cuckoo at the expense of the family.

Next came a pair of yellow warblers, whose *protégé* soon crowded out the legitimate occupants of the nest. They were raised from the ground and placed within reach, but the big boy required all the attention of the foster-parents, and the others died. During the whole period, the old cuckoo was always to be found flitting about in a restless manner, as if she had some doubt in regard to the ability of the warblers to take care of her child.

The third case was another pair of chipping sparrows, in whose nest the cuckoo was observed sitting, and from which she did not move till the observers almost touched her. The result was the same as in the other cases. The young cuckoo threw the sparrows out as soon as he had strength to do so.

Eggs of the black-billed cuckoo have also been found in nests of the wood pewee, cardinal, cedar waxwing, catbird, and wood thrush. Under the preceding species will be found a note, published by J. L. Davison (1887), describing the finding of a nest occupied by a robin, a yellow-billed cuckoo, and a mourning dove. Bendire (1895) published an almost identical account of such a remarkable occurrence, on the authority of the same observer, but with the black-billed substituted for the yellow-billed cuckoo. It seems hardly likely that such an unusual happening could occur with both species in exactly the same way, and leaves us in doubt as to which species of cuckoo was involved.

Eggs.—The black-billed cuckoo commonly lays 2 or 3 eggs; sets of 4 or 5 may sometimes be the product of a single pair; but the larger numbers that have been found in their nests, 6, 7, or even 8 eggs, were probably laid by two or perhaps three females, as these birds are notoriously careless about laying in each other's nests. Bendire (1895) says: "The eggs of the Black-billed Cuckoo are more nearly oval than elliptical oval, and shorter and rounder than those of the Yellow-billed Cuckoo, and much more deeply colored. Like these, they are unspotted; the shell is thin and fine grained, with little or no gloss. Their color is difficult to describe exactly, varying from nile blue to pale beryl green, and occasionally the shell shows a decidedly marbled appearance, caused by different shades running into each other. * * * Aside from their deeper color, they are also readily distinguished from eggs of the Yellow-billed Cuckoo by their smaller size."

Eggs that I have seen in collections I should describe as "pale glaucous green," "dull opaline green," or "microline green" and varying from oval to elliptical-oval. Some of these, as well as some of those included in the following measurements, may be yellow-billed cuckoos' eggs, as the two are probably not always recognizable with certainty. The measurements of 54 eggs, presumably of this species, average 27.18 by 20.57 millimeters; the eggs showing the four extremes measure **30.48** by **22.86, 22.61** by 18.80, and 25.40 by **18.29** millimeters.

Young.—Incubation is shared by both sexes and lasts for about 14 days. As the eggs are often laid at infrequent intervals, it is not unusual to find young birds of different ages, or even eggs and young, in the same nest. Both sexes assist in the care of the young and are devoted parents; even when an egg is hatched by a foster parent, the mother cuckoo does not seem entirely to lose interest in her youngster, as related above. On the other hand, William H. Moore (1902a), of Scotch Lake, New Brunswick, says: "I have known this bird to desert its young when the nest was molested, and after the young died they were covered with leaves by the adults." Cuckoos are careless about removing the cast-off shells, which are often found in the nest after the young have hatched. The young remain in the nest 7 to 9 days after hatching and then become quite precocial. While in the nest the young are fed by their parents in a rather peculiar manner, of which Dr. Thomas S. Roberts (1932) writes:

When the old bird returns, the food, which is very likely to be *live* caterpillars, is concealed in the throat. As a nestling raises its head with open mouth and rapidly vibrating wings, the parent thrusts its bill deeply into the open maw and the young bird grasps securely the smooth bill of the old bird, in which action it is greatly aided by several soft papillae or disks in the roof of the mouth. Then, with a slow, pumping motion, the squirming caterpillars are transferred with some difficulty from one mouth to another. The process is a slow one, the birds being attached a minute or more and the transfer aided, apparently, by a sucking effort on the part of the nestling.

When a young Cuckoo opens its mouth widely there are visible, in the roof of the mouth, a number of large, flat-topped, white papillae or tubercles, arranged symmetrically, the function of which is plainly to make it possible for the nestling to maintain its hold on the parent's bill, which is smooth and tapering. A small finger-tip inserted well down into the open, upturned mouth of a nestling is seized tightly and a sucking motion is distinctly perceptible. [Pl. 10.]

Prof. Francis H. Herrick (1935) has made a thorough study of the home life of the black-billed cuckoo, and I cannot do better than to quote a few of his remarks on the behavior of the young. After describing the peculiar appearance of the newly hatched young, he says:

More remarkable than anything about its appearance, however, is the muscular vigor and endurance the cuckoo displays at this tender age, for it seems to be able to withstand heat, hunger, and general neglect that would be fatal to the young of most wild birds. I soon found by experiment that when barely three hours out of its shell this little cuckoo could hang suspended by a leg or even by a single toe for upwards of a quarter of a minute, and that it could raise itself up until its bill was well over the twig that it grasped with both feet; and in a short time it was able to raise itself on to the twig, or even to draw itself up with the power of one leg, which implies an extraordinary muscular development. * * * Though born blind and essentially naked, the young black-bill is neither deaf nor dumb, and in proportion to its size it is probably the strongest and most enterprising altricial nestling on the North American continent. * * *

Like other nestlings, the cuckoo lies flat, with toes clenched, and holds to its fragile nest with a firm grip. Attempt to remove it, and it is likely to pull its nest to pieces rather than loose its hold; or it may even drag out a fellow-nestling, reminding one of crayfishes or lobsters, in the handling of which one may also get a living chain. Should you succeed in displacing a bird, its claws will rapidly open and close in its desperate search for any object to clasp, for a contact stimulus afforded by any solid body can alone satisfy this strong reflex. * * *

At the age of about six days the nestling cuckoo has reached that peculiar transitory state which we may call the "quill" or feather-tube stage. * * *

Towards the end of this brief and unique stage the behavior of the young bird changes in marked and rapid fashion. It indulges in new attitudes, acquires new call and alarm-notes, shows fear, and begins those preening or combing movements which are to effect a relatively sudden and altogether surprising change in its appearance. * * *

In one instance the first preening action was noticed on the sixth day; thereafter this kind of activity became frequent, and the bird would comb every "quill" within reach, drawing the mandibles over it from base to apex. Then, with apparent suddenness, at the close of the seventh day the transparent horny sheaths began to give way at their base—instead of wearing off gradually from apex to base in the usual fashion—and were raked off by the mouthful. * * *

Fear may become manifest as early as the sixth day, when a frightened bird will sometimes clear the nest at a bound and, seizing a branch with both feet, hold firmly to it. Should it drop to the ground, it can make off with surprising speed. If captured and held, it will emit loud, explosive squeals, than which nothing seems to arouse its parents to quicker attack or bolder measures. Replace it in the nest, and it spreads its wings, stiffens, and lies flat with every feather-tube on end; and it will repeat these defensive measures as often as it is touched or disturbed. * * *

When from seven to nine days old, with half of its feathers unsheathed, the cuckoo suddenly leaves its nest and enters upon a climbing period, which lasts about a fortnight or until it is able to fly. At one of my observation stations I saw three young birds leave their nest in succession, and the procedure in the case of the oldest one was particularly interesting. This bird, which had been sitting in the bright sunshine, for the day was not uncomfortably warm, of a sudden moved to one side of its platform. After having combed off several mouthfuls of feather-sheaths, it sat upright for some minutes and gazed into its outer world. Then, directing its attention to a small branch and ducking its head as if contemplating flight, with a leap it cleared the nest, and, catching hold of a twig, with both feet, it swung free with acrobatic dexterity. In another moment it had pulled itself up and was comfortably perched. If such a first perch is placed in the shade and the young bird is promptly fed, it may keep to it for a long time; but it can move about, and should it drop to the ground, it can mount to safety again.

The vertical position assumed by young cuckoos, probably as a hiding pose, has been noted by several observers, but the following incident reported to me in a letter from Frederic H. Kennard, is quite unusual; he says: "I had just been investigating a big highbush blueberry bush, looking for a nest, when I discovered, to my surprise, a fledgling black-billed cuckoo, squatting on a twig about 6 feet from the ground. The little bird, which really was not able to fly, was squatting on a limb, just as little birds ordinarily do; his wing feathers were fairly well developed, but his tail was only about a quarter of an inch long. When I parted the branches a trifle, so that we could see him better, and finding out that he was discovered, he promptly assumed an almost perpendicular position, with his neck stretched out almost unbelievably and his bill almost straight in the air; and there he sat, immovable, with his bill in the air like a bittern, only oscillating a trifle when the branch on which he was sitting was disturbed a little by the breeze.

"My youngest son, Jack, being interested in the peculiarities of cuckoos' feet, attempted to pick him off the limb; the little bird fluttered to the ground, where he picked him up. When we had duly examined and discussed the arrangement of his toes, Jack endeavored to put the little fellow back exactly where he had been when we first disturbed him. Then, as he endeavored to replace him on the limb, he suddenly went limp and, apparently, passed out in his hand, frightened to death, as I supposed. He was perfectly limp and my impression is that his eyes were closed. Jack finally, in trying to get him to stay on the limb, hung him across the limb by the neck, with his head across one side and his body down the other side. Just then there came a little breeze, the body dropped, and that little bird simply scuttled in under the ferns. It was the most astonishing performance that I ever witnessed, first the stake-driver attitude, as a protective position, and then playing dead."

Plumages.—Professor Herrick (1935) says of the newly-hatched young cuckoo: "Although most birds emerge from the shell wet with the amniotic fluid, the cuckoo just mentioned came out quite dry. It was two and one-half inches long and weighed less than a quarter of an ounce (or 7.4 grams). Its skin was coal-black, sparsely sprinkled with sharply contrasting snow-white 'hairs'—in reality the feather-tubes of a rudimentary down which never unfolds. These primitive feather-tubes are later pushed out by those of the juvenal contour feathers and for about a week are borne upon their tips, thus giving them a peculiar flagellate appearance."

When about six days old, the young cuckoo "bristles like the fretful porcupine in every feather-tract"; these bristles are the feather-tubes of the juvenal plumage, referred to above. At about this age, the young bird begins the "combing" process, by which the sheaths of these feather tubes are removed, as described above, and a marvelous change begins to take place in a remarkably short time, as the sheaths are removed and fall in a shower in and about the nest. Professor Herrick (1935) says: "Thus at one stroke one or more of the juvenal contour feathers are exposed and quickly fluff out in all their shapely proportions. * * * The change actually occupies about twelve hours, and it is really not complete, since the sheaths of the wing- and tail-quills flake off gradually, as in other birds, and those feathers of head and neck out of reach of the 'comb' remain sheathed for a considerable time longer."

By the time that the young bird leaves the nest, at the age of 8 or 9 days, it is in nearly full juvenal plumage; the wings are fairly well grown, but the tail is still very short. In this plumage the soft plumage above is "buffy brown," each feather tipped with white; the under parts are silvery white, tinged with pale gray on the belly and with pale buff on the breast and throat. During late summer and early fall, most, if not all, of this juvenal contour plumage is molted and replaced by the first winter plumage, but the flight feathers of the wings and tail are retained until spring. This first winter plumage is much like that of the adult, but it is more brownish on the head and back and more greenish olive on the scapulars than in adults; the throat is more buffy and the upper breast more grayish buff than in the adult; the young bird's tail is quite different, the grayish white tips are smaller and are not bordered inwardly with the dusky space, which is clearly visible in the adult tail. The molts are apparently the same as in the yellow-billed cuckoo; the adult plumage seems to be acquired before the young birds return from their first winter in the south, but we have no specimens showing a spring molt.

Food.—The black-billed cuckoo is just as good a caterpillar destroyer as the yellow-billed; in fact the food habits of the two species are almost identical in all respects. An abundance of caterpillars in a locality is very likely to bring with it an invasion of cuckoos. Frank L. Farley writes to me: "As far as I am aware, the black-billed cuckoo was unknown in central Alberta until the summer of 1923. That year the central portion of the Province was infested with tent caterpillars, which, in 1924–25, assumed plague proportions. Entire bluffs of poplar trees, several acres in extent, were entirely denuded of their leaves, while houses and other buildings were overrun with the pests." In June 1924 the cuckoos began to appear for the first time, birds entirely unknown to the residents. "Although caterpillars gradually disappeared after 1925, cuckoos were reported from widely separated parts of central Alberta, the most northerly one being about 150 miles north of Camrose, which is in latitude 53° N. The presence of cuckoos and caterpillars in the same territory during these years would tend to bear out the claims of other observers, that the insects are particularly relished by these birds, which, in some uncanny manner, are able to locate infested territory far removed from their usual place of residence."

Forbush (1927) says:

In seasons when caterpillars of any species are abundant, cuckoos usually become common in the infested localities. They follow the caterpillars, and where such food is plentiful, the size of their broods seems to increase. During an invasion of forest tent caterpillars in Stoneham, Massachusetts, in May, 1898, Mr. Frank H. Mosher watched one of these birds that caught and ate 36 of these insects inside of five minutes. He saw another in Malden eat 29, rest a few minutes and then eat 14 more. In July, 1899, he reported a family of these birds in a locality infested with the gipsy moth, and said that they were eating large quantities of gipsy caterpillars. In June, 1895, Mr. Henry Shaw reported great numbers of these cuckoos in Dorchester feeding on the same pests. The late Professor Walter B. Barrows, of Michigan, an extremely conservative ornithologist, is responsible for the statement that in several instances remains of over 100 tent caterpillars have been taken from a single cuckoo's stomach. The Black-billed Cuckoo, because more common than the Yellow-billed, is the species that most commonly attacks this insect in New England orchards. During an invasion of army worms, Professor S. A. Forbes found that 95 per cent of the food of this species consisted of that caterpillar.

F. H. King (1883), writing of the food of the black-billed cuckoo in Wisconsin, says: "Of thirteen specimens examined, nine had eaten caterpillars—among them were eight of the fall web-worms (*Hyphantria textor*), thirty-three of the oak caterpillars (*Dryocampa senatoria*), one of the Io caterpillars (*Saturnia io*), six of the antiopa caterpillars (*Vanessa antiopa*), and one of the caterpillars of the archippus butterfly (*Danais archippus*). One contained five larvae of the large saw-fly (*Cymbex americana*); six, twenty-five grasshoppers; one, a cricket; two, ten beetles; and two, two harvest-men."

Other authors have charged this cuckoo with eating minute mollusks and other small animals, fishes and aquatic larvae, fruits and berries, and even the eggs and young of small birds. On the latter point, Henry D. Minot (1877) says that "they do great mischief in destroying the eggs of other useful birds. Like arrant cowards, as they are, they take opportunities to approach stealthily the nests of many birds, whom they would be afraid to encounter, and then feast on the eggs of the absent parents, after which they hurry away. They are scarcely less destructive in this way than the black snakes, though I have never known them to kill young birds."

Behavior.—The two cuckoos are so much alike in haunts, habits, and behavior that most of what I have said about the yellow-billed would apply equally well to this species. The black-billed is rather more swift on the wing than the other, but it flies in the same graceful manner. It is the same shy recluse of the shady retreats, among the dense foliage of the woods and shade trees, unafraid to frequent the orchards and gardens in search for its food, but shunning any intimacy with human beings; we hear its wandering voice but seldom see more than a fleeting glimpse of its graceful form as it fades away into the shadows.

In defense of its eggs or young the black-billed cuckoo is often quite courageous. Olive Thorne Miller (1892) writes charmingly of her experiences with an incubating pair of these cuckoos; she watched them change places on the nest, and found the female quite confiding, but the male never became reconciled to her presence:

It happened that I arrived when the mother was away, and the head of the household in charge. No sooner did I appear on the path than he flew off the nest with great bustle, thus betraying himself at once; but he did not desert his post of protector. He perched on a branch somewhat higher than my head, and five or six feet away, and began calling, a low "coo-oo." With every cry he opened his mouth very wide, as though to shriek at the top of his voice, and the low cry that came out was so ludicrously inadequate to his apparent effort that it was very droll. In this performance he made fine display of the inside of his mouth and throat, which looked, from where I stood, like black satin. * * *

Finding that his voice did not drive me away, the bird resorted to another method; he tried intimidation. First he threw himself into a most curious attitude, humping his shoulders and opening his tail like a fan, then spreading his wings and resting the upper end of them on his tail, which made at the back a sort of scoop effect. Every time he uttered the cry he lifted wings and tail together, and let them fall slowly back to their natural position. It was the queerest bird performance I ever saw.

On another day, she says: "We had not waited long when the head of the cuckoo family appeared. He saw us instantly, and, I regret to say, was no more reconciled to our presence than he had been on the previous occasion; but he showed his displeasure in a different way. He rushed about in the trees, crying, 'cuck-a-ruck, cuck-a-ruck,' running out even to the tip of slender branches that seemed too slight to bear his weight. When his feelings entirely overcame him he flew away, and though we remained fifteen minutes, no one came to the nest."

E. A. Samuels (1883) writes:

Like the other, the Black-billed Cuckoo is very cowardly, and is quickly driven from the neighborhood of the nest of almost any of the other birds. If a robin, or other bird of equal size, discover one of these, to him pirates, in the vicinity of his nest, he immediately assaults the intruder, with loud outcries, pouncing upon him, and pecking with great ferocity. Others of his neighbors, who are near, join in the attack; the Cuckoo, in retreating, dives into the recesses of a stone wall, or the first secure retreat available; very seldom taking to his wings, as another bird would do. I have known of a cuckoo being driven into a barn by a Blue-bird (S. sialis), who sat perching on a fence outside for several minutes, keeping his enemy prisoner; and the latter, when pursued and captured by myself, preferred being my prisoner to facing his enemy outside.

Voice.—One cannot always distinguish with certainty *all* the notes of the black-billed cuckoo from *all* those of the yellow-billed. Many of the notes are much alike in both species. The notes of the black-billed are, as a rule, softer and more liquid than those of the yellow-billed and not so deep-toned.

The ordinary "song" of the black-billed is preceded by a gurgling note, and the rest of the long song is uttered in regularly measured time, not retarded at the end, as is that of the yellow-billed, and the notes are given in couplets or triplets, one syllable in each set being accented. Dr. Charles W. Townsend (1920a) describes it very well as follows: "The full song may be described as a preliminary harsh clearing of the throat followed by from six to twelve short coughs which in turn are succeeded by the more pleasing doublets and triplets of *cows*. The Yellow-billed Cuckoo repeats his *cows* or *cowks* in regular order without dividing them into sets and they sound as woodeny as if he were striking a plank with a mallet."

Aretas A. Saunders (1929) says: "The bird has a variety of calls. One consists of a gurgling note followed by single notes in even time, 'krak-ika kuh kuh kuh kuh kuh kuh kuh kuh'. Another is a series of groups consisting of two to six notes repeated many times, with one of the notes strongly accented, such as '*kuk*a *kuk*a *kuk*a,' or '*kakuk*aka ka*kuk*aka ka*kuk*aka.' I have known a bird to repeat such phrases over a hundred times without stopping."

The notes of the black-billed cuckoo are often given on the nest or while the bird is in flight, and they may be heard at all hours of the day or night. Both cuckoos are said to be more noisy just before a rain, hence the name "rain crow."

Mr. Brewster (1937a) says that "both species coo in the same subdued, mournful, dovelike tones, but when so engaged, the Yellowbill always utters only a single note at a time, and then waits at least a second or two before following it with another precisely similar; whereas the cooing notes of the Black-bill are invariably doubled or trebled or quadrupled, or perhaps even quintupled, yet separated from one another within such grouping by scarcely appreciable pauses."

Gerald H. Thayer (1903) has given an interesting account of what he calls "the mid-summer, mid-night, mid-sky gyrations of the Black-billed Cuckoo, as noted by my father and me for three consecutive seasons in the southwestern corner of New Hampshire":

Several years before we discovered the nocturnal-flight phenomenon, we began to be puzzled by the extreme frequency of Cuckoo calls on summer nights. * * * They uttered both the *cow-cow* notes and the rolling guttural call; but the guttural was much the commoner of the two, except on dark, foggy nights, when the case was usually reversed. * * * The birds were often so far up as to be only faintly audible when directly overhead, with no obstructions interposed; and this on a still night would seem to mean an elevation of at least a hundred and fifty yards. They sometimes flew lower, however, and on cloudy nights often moved about barely above the tree-tops.

* * * On the evening of July 11—a pitch-dark evening with a thunder-shower lowering,—they were remarkably noisy, both sitting in trees and flying high in air. The seated ones, of which I heard only two, made the *cow-cow* notes, while all the flying ones made the liquid gurgle. I heard this note overhead between thirty and forty times in the course of about three hours, during half of which time I was afoot on the road.

Field marks.—This bird may be recognized as a cuckoo by its size, shape, and general coloration. It can be distinguished from the yellow-billed cuckoo by the absence of the distinguishing marks of the latter, the cinnamon-rufous in the wings, and the conspicuously black-and-white lateral tail feathers.

The wings of the black-billed cuckoo are practically uniform in color with its back; and the lateral tail feathers are dark gray, with inconspicuous, grayish-white, smaller tips, bordered inwardly with a dusky spot. The wholly black bill and the red eyelids can be seen only at short range.

DISTRIBUTION

Range.—Southern Canada and the United States east of the Rocky Mountains, south in winter to northwestern South America. Accidental in Italy, the Azores, and Ireland.

Breeding range.—The breeding range of the black-billed cuckoo extends **north** to southern Saskatchewan (Johnstone Lake, Muscow, and Indian Head); southern Manitoba (Carberry, Portage la Prairie, and Shoal Lake); northern Minnesota (Crooked Lake); southern Ontario (probably Goulais Bay, Toronto, and Stirling); Quebec (Hull, Montreal, probably Quebec, and probably Kamouraska); New Brunswick (Scotch Lake); probably Prince Edward Island (North River); and Nova Scotia (Wolfville and Pictou). From this point the range extends **south** along the seaboard to North Carolina (Raleigh and Winston-Salem); Tennessee (Beersheba Springs and Nashville); northwestern Arkansas (Rogers); eastern Kansas (Lawrence and Clearwater); Nebraska (Red Cloud, Kearney, and Antioch); and southeastern Wyoming (Wheatland). **West** to eastern Wyoming (Wheatland and Dayton); eastern Montana (Terry); and Saskatchewan (Johnstone Lake).

The species has been detected in summer on several occasions west of its breeding range. Among these are: Colorado (Fort Morgan, Clear Creek, Fort Collins, and Wray); Wyoming (Laramie); Montana (Fort Keogh, Knowlton, and Billings); and western Saskatchewan (Eastend, Skull Creek, Medicine Hat, and Big Stick Lake). On June 23, 1924, a partially completed nest was found near Camrose, Alberta, a range extension that for the time being must be considered unusual (see remarks under "Food"). The species also was recorded at Godbout, Quebec, on August 11, 1885.

Winter range.—Available information indicates that in winter this species is concentrated in northwestern South America: Colombia (Antroquia, Medellin, and Bogota); Ecuador (Guapulo, La Carolina, Daule, Puna Lake, and Lechugal); and northern Peru (Huamachuco).

Spring migration.—Early dates of spring arrival are: Florida—Hastings, April 13; Eau Gallie, April 27; Pensacola, May 2. Alabama—Scottsboro, April 18; Barachias, April 22. Georgia—Atlanta, April 24; Athens, April 27. South Carolina—Frogmore, April 24; Spartanburg, April 29. North Carolina—Raleigh, April 15; Piney Creek, May 4. Virginia—Blacksburg, April 26; Lynchburg, May 8. District of Columbia—Washington, April 30. Maryland—Baltimore, April 20. Pennsylvania—Jeffersonville, April 30; Ridgway, May 6; Doylestown, May 9. New Jersey—Milltown, May 2; Passaic, May 7. New York—Medina, May 3; New York City, May 9; Rochester, May 15. Connecticut—Fairfield, May 1; Hadlyme, May 4; New Haven, May 7. Rhode Island—Block Island, May 6. Massachusetts—Belmont, May 4; Marlboro, May 6; North Amherst, May 12; Danvers, May 12. Vermont—Clarendon, May 12; St. Johnsbury, May 13; Wells River, May 18. New Hampshire—East Westmoreland, May 16; South Hooksett, May 16; Concord, May 21. Maine—South Portland, May 11; Winthrop, May 15; Waterville, May 20. Quebec—Montreal, May 10; Hatley, May 28. New Brunswick—Scotch Lake, May 27. Nova Scotia—Halifax, May 12; Wolfville, May 18. Louisiana—Avery Island, April 12. Mississippi—Bay St. Louis, April 14. Arkansas—Fayetteville, April 30; Broma Towns, May 2. Tennessee—Knoxville, April 12; Tate, April 26. Kentucky—Lexington, May 1; Bowling Green, May 6. Missouri—Jonesburg, May 3; Montgomery City, May 4; Columbia, May 7. Illinois—Rantoul, April 17; Elgin, May 5; Glen Ellyn, May 7. Indiana—Bloomington, April 26; Richmond, April 27; Vincennes, May 7. Ohio—Oberlin, May 1; Columbia, May 2; Upper Sandusky, May 3. Michigan—Detroit, May 1; Brant, May 3; Sault Ste. Marie, May 11. Ontario—Guelph, April 19; Ottawa, May 7; London, May 9. Iowa—McGregor, April 24; Mason City, April 30; Wall Lake, May 3. Wisconsin—Racine, May 8; Beloit, May 10; Whitewater, May 11. Minnesota—Montevideo, April 13; Anoka County, May 5; Excelsior, May 13. Oklahoma—Tulsa, May 3; Norman, May 5. Kansas—Fort Leavenworth, May 6; Bendena, May 8; Clearwater, May 9. Nebraska—Valentine, May 1; Red Cloud, May 11; Omaha, May 13. South Dakota—Yankton, May 1; Huron, May 13; Forestburg, May 15. North Dakota—Grafton, April 25; Antler, May 3; Jamestown, May

23. Manitoba—Aweme, May 20; Pilot Mound, May 24; Reaburn, May 26. Saskatchewan—Muscow, May 12; Indian Head, May 20, *Fall migration.*—Late dates of fall departure are: Manitoba—Margaret, September 3; Aweme, September 14. North Dakota—Fargo, September 13; Cando, September 18; Argusville, September 22. South Dakota—Forestburg, September 6; Sioux Falls, September 22; Lennox, October 14. Kansas—Cimarron, September 2; Osawatomie, September 22. Minnesota—Elk River, September 27; Red Wing, October 2. Wisconsin—New London, September 24; Racine, September 24; Madison, September 26. Iowa—Wall Lake, September 28; Osage, October 10; McGregor, October 20. Ontario—Ottawa, September 16; Point Pelee, October 18. Michigan—Charity Island, September 20; Grand Rapids, September 26, Detroit, October 9. Ohio—Saybrook, October 1; Berlin Center, October 12; Columbus, October 15. Indiana—Indianapolis, October 2; Fort Wayne, October 12; Bicknell, October 18. Illinois—Rantoul, October 4; La Grange, October 7; Glen Ellyn, October 21. Missouri—Columbia, October 4; St. Louis, October 16. Kentucky—Danville, October 5; Bowling Green, October 18. Mississippi—Bay St. Louis, October 11. Nova Scotia—Sable Island, September 25. Quebec—Montreal, September 5. Maine—Orono, September 21; Winthrop, October 20. New Hampshire—Jefferson, October 3; Durham, October 5. Vermont—Wells River, September 14; Woodstock, September 18. Massachusetts—West Groton, September 30; North Truro, October 13; Harvard, October 16. Rhode Island—Providence, October 23. Connecticut—New Haven, September 28; East Portland, October 3; Meriden, October 8. New York—Hyde Park, October 6; New York City, October 10. New Jersey—Elizabeth, October 3; Sandy Hook, October 5; Milltown, October 24. Pennsylvania—McKeesport, October 11; Jeffersonville, October 13; Pittsburgh, October 16. District of Columbia—Washington, October 28. Virginia—Naruna, October 18. North Carolina—Chapel Hill, October 3; Raleigh, October 10; Hendersonville, October 12. Georgia—Atlanta, October 14; Thomasville, October 21. Alabama—Autauga County, October 16. Florida—College Point, September 28; Pensacola, October 23.

Casual records.—While the black-billed cuckoo does not migrate regularly through the Caribbean region it has been recorded on Dominica (September 30, 1904), Tobago, and Trinidad. Gundlach is alleged to have taken a specimen in May (year?) near Cardenas, Cuba, and there is a somewhat doubtful record from the Isle of Pines on May 11, 1909. Specimens were taken in Bermuda in October 1874 and also in April and May 1875. The Ponta Delgada Museum has an undated specimen taken at San Miguel, Ponta Delgada, Azores; a specimen taken in 1858 near Lucca, Italy, is preserved in the Museum of the University of Pisa; and one was taken on September 25, 1871, at Killead, County Antrim, Ireland.

Egg dates.—Illinois: 13 records, May 7 to July 20; 7 records, June 1 to 26, indicating the height of the season.

Massachusetts: 20 records, May 19 to June 20; 10 records, May 30 to June 10.

Michigan: 14 records, May 25 to September 14; 7 records, June 21 to July 20.

New York: 23 records, May 11 to July 18; 12 records, May 29 to June 9.

CUCULUS OPTATUS OPTATUS Gould

HIMALAYAN CUCKOO

CONTRIBUTED BY EDWARD CHARLES STUART BAKER

HABITS

The Himalayan cuckoo very closely resembles the various races of the common cuckoo (*Cuculus canorus*) in its general habits, but it is, I think, a more secretive bird, keeping closely to tall trees with dense foliage, so that although one may hear its very distinctive call on many occasions quite close by it is often very difficult to see until it takes to wing. In Kashmir and the northwest Himalayas it is found in summer at all elevations between 5,000 and 10,000 feet and occasionally to some 2,000 feet higher but, never, I believe, above the forest line. In Sikkim it is common in well-forested land between 4,000 and 9,000 feet, while Stevens (1925) records having heard it calling at an elevation of 3,500 feet on May 25, so that it may breed as low down as this in that part of the Himalayas. In Assam it is very common between the same elevations as in Sikkim, there also keeping closely to forest, either deciduous, pine, or evergreen with dense undergrowth. All ornithologists seem to agree as to the nature of the country frequented by this cuckoo. In letters to me A. E. Jones mentions "dense forest," "dense deodar forest" as the breeding haunts of birds whose eggs he has found; B. B. Osmaston (MS.) found it in "open, well-wooded forest." Mackenzie and Hopwood (MS.) took eggs in the nests of *Acanthopneuste davisoni* in the Chin Hills, in "heavy evergreen forest." The only exception to this of which I am aware is an egg taken by T. R. Livesey (MS.) found in Kashmir in a nest of *Emberiza cia stracheyi* in a "well-wooded glade in forest."

At all seasons of the year it keeps almost entirely to branches of high trees, some 40 or 50 feet or more from the ground, descending to the undergrowth only when hunting for nests in which to deposit its eggs or for the actual deposition of the egg. When so employed it is, I believe, always silent and, even in its movements, very quiet and secretive unless it is being harassed by small birds who hunt it just as they do the common cuckoo. I have not seen this bird feeding in bushes or on the ground even when there are numerous caterpillars or a flight of termites to tempt it.

When on migration also this cuckoo seems to keep to forest or to exceptionally well-wooded country, and I have no record of its having been found in the open in India, though obviously it must sometimes pass over such country in its movements from one district to another, more especially in the northwest.

Spring.—In Kashmir and the northwest Himalayas the birds arrive from the lower hills and the plains adjoining them in April, a few apparently in the first fortnight, but the majority not until the last week or so. In Sikkim they arrive a good deal earlier, and Stevens (1925) records them as *seen* at Gopaldhara in the Rambong Valley about the middle of March "when it ascends to an elevation of 7,000 feet," while he *heard* them calling at the same place as early as March 12. Farther east in Assam it does not arrive at its breeding quarters in the higher hills until about the first week in April and then only in small numbers. In Burma at elevations of about 4,000 feet and over it breeds about a fortnight earlier and is in full call by the last week in March.

This cuckoo is possibly only a partial migrant in India, leaving the higher hills for the broken foothills, where it may be found more or less throughout the winter, as well as in the plains immediately adjoining them. To the east, however, as I show under the fall migration notes, it is a true migrant. According to La Touche (1931–1936), during the spring migration north the Himalayan cuckoo "appears in China from about the 10th April to the end of May," and he records three cuckoos taken at Shaweishan on May 1, 16, and 17. These birds were presumably on their way north to eastern Siberia or Manchuria.

La Touche does not think that this bird breeds anywhere in the Chinese Hills, its place being taken by the local breeding race *kelungensis*.

The 38 eggs in my collection were taken as follows: Three in April, 14 in May, 20 in June, none in July, and 1 in August. The earliest date was April 25, 1915, and the latest August 20, 1914. At the same time an egg taken in the Chin Hills on April 30 was on the point of hatching, so, in the Burmese Hills, some eggs must be laid in the middle of that month, birds arriving in their breeding haunts at least a fortnight earlier. Other eggs that have passed through my hands were all taken within these dates so far as I have recorded them, so they may be accepted as confirming my dates for migration.

Courtship.—There is nothing recorded upon this subject but, so far as I know, it differs in no way from that of the Khasia Hills cuckoo, and both sexes seem to be equally promiscuous in their sexual relations.

Nesting.—This cuckoo is parasitic principally on the small warblers of the *Phylloscopus* and *Acanthopneuste* group, which lay white eggs, either immaculate or speckled slightly with various tints of reddish brown or red, or the *Seicercus* group, which lay glossy pure white eggs.

In my own collection I have eggs taken from the nests of 16 species and subspecies of fosterers (see the following list); of these the first 10 may be considered to be normal fosterers and the latter abnormal.

The Himalayan cuckoo does adopt a certain territory but hardly in the restricted sense that *Cuculus canorus* and its various races do. The principal reason for this is the comparative rarity of the birds that she selects as foster parents to her eggs. For instance, although the little *Acanthopneuste* breeding in the Khasia Hills is a common bird, it nowhere breeds in the numbers in which birds of the *Suya* and *Cisticola* genera are found. Perhaps half a dozen pairs may be found in one big forest of many square miles, and to find even these six is very hard work. In the same forest another half dozen birds of the genus *Seicercus* of various species may be found. These little warblers of the two genera *Acanthopneuste* and *Seicercus* make very similar nests, balls of moss, quite green and fresh, which are placed in hollows in banks and generally among the same kind of moss as that of which the nests are built. They are exceedingly hard to find by human beings and, unless the birds are watched on to the nest, are generally located only when the female is disturbed from it by accident and doubtless the cuckoo also finds they are difficult to mark down.

LIST OF FOSTER PARENTS

Phylloscopus inornatus humei	2	eggs
Phylloscopus proregulus simlaae	1	"
Acanthopneuste reguloides harterti	13	"
Acanthopneuste reguloides davisoni	3	"
Acanthopneuste reguloides reguloides	1	"
Acanthopneuste occipitatis occipitatis	4	"
Seicercus cantator	3	"
Seicercus burkii	2	"
Seicercus xanthoschista xanthoschista	1	"
Seicercus castaneiceps castaneiceps	2	"
Ianthia rufilata	1	"
Niltava sundara sundara	1	"
Suya crinigera assamica	1	"
Orthotomus atrogularis nitidus	1	"
Napothera brevicaudata striata	1	"
Emberiza cia stracheyi	1	"

I have only two small series of three eggs, each of which I believe to have been laid by one cuckoo, one of these being taken in 1909 by myself. Of this latter the first two eggs were found on June 16 and 18 in a patch of forest in which we marked down three nests of the Khasia crowned willow warbler, one of which contained no cuckoo's egg. On June 13 we found that the pair of warblers first seen on May 16 had again built close by their original nest and the new one contained a third egg, apparently of the same cuckoo, and three of their own. The nests found on May 16 and 18 were between a quarter and a half of a mile apart.

On another occasion, June 27, 1935, three eggs were taken, one in the nest of the willow warbler and two others in nests of *Seicercus*. These were all in the same forest, but only two close together and the third nearly half a mile away. The eggs, however, appeared obviously to have been laid by the same bird.

Eggs.—The eggs of this species of cuckoo are all of the same type, white eggs sparsely marked with tiny black specks, sometimes confined to the larger end only. Several oviduct eggs have been taken, the first by Brooks from the oviduct of a female he shot in Kashmir on June 17, and three others by Rattray in 1903 on June 10, 15, and 17, respectively. All these were exactly alike and similar to the description given above.

The only two exceptions in coloration I have seen are eggs one of which has a faintly green tinge while the other has an equally faint pink tinge. The first of these was taken from a forktail's (*Enicurus maculatus guttatus*) nest and the second from that of a tailorbird (*Orthotomus atrogularis nitidus*).

In shape the eggs are rather long ellipses, and the shell is thin and rather fragile for a cuckoo's.

Forty-one eggs average in size 20.11 by 14.28 millimeters; maxima 25.3 by 16.2; minima 19.0 by 13.0 millimeters; the same number average in weight 141.4 milligrams; maximum 178; minimum 117 milligrams.

A large double-yolked egg weighs 222 milligrams, while two very small, almost pygmy eggs, weigh only 105 and 112 milligrams.

The method of the deposition of the eggs is not known, but in many cases they could not possibly be laid direct into the nest. The crowned willow warbler makes a nest in a hole in among the roots of trees with so small an entrance and so far in that the cuckoo could not possibly get in to lay her egg nor could she eject it from the cloaca sufficiently far to reach the egg chamber and, if she did, it would certainly break. Nests of the genus *Seicercus* and of *Acanthopneuste reguloides* are so shaped and situated that though the cuckoo could not enter them she could very often eject the eggs into them without much difficulty by clinging to their tops or sides during the operation.

Young.—Nothing is recorded, as to incubation, but I believe it to take only 10 or 11 days, i. e., much the same period as for the eggs of the small warblers the cuckoo selects to cuckold.

Ejection of young undoubtedly takes place in the same manner as that by which it is effected by the common cuckoo, the young cuckoo hoisting the other occupants of the nest, either eggs or young birds, onto its shoulder and then pushing them over the edge of the nest. I have seen several young birds from two days to a week old in the nests of various warblers, and they have always been alone. The young cuckoo has the same dorsal interscapular arrangement as that found in the nestling *canorus* to assist it in carrying out the fratricide.

Plumages.—Male: Similar to the male of *Cuculus c. canorus* and *C. c. bakeri* but less dark on the upper parts than the latter and always to be distinguished from all races of the *canorus* group by having the edge of the wing pure white and not barred. On the lower surface the white bars are broader and the black bars in consequence wider apart, while they are blacker and bolder in appearance.

Female: Similar to the male but generally with a more rufous tinge on the breast and abdomen; the under tail coverts are often pale fulvous with black crossbars.

The female has a hepatic phase like that of *C. c. canorus.*

Juvenile: In first plumage blackish brown above, the feathers all broadly edged with white; the wing quills are barred with rufous on the outer webs; the chin, throat, and breast are blackish, the feathers narrowly fringed with white and the rest of the lower parts white, or faintly fulvous-white, heavily barred with strong bands of black.

In intermediate stage between juvenile and adult the plumage is slaty, the feathers very narrowly edged with white; below, the chin, throat, and upper breast are blackish, the feathers broadly fringed with white and the remainder of the lower parts like the adult.

Hepatic young are like the hepatic female adult but less richly colored and more heavily banded below with blackish, especially on the chin, throat, and breast. Some specimens of young birds in the British Museum collection seem to be changing from a juvenile hepatic plumage into a normal adult plumage.

The white nuchal spot is very seldom seen in the young of this cuckoo but is occasionally present.

Measurements.—Wing 208 to 226; tail 151 to 176; tarsus about 20 or 21; culmen 20 to 22 millimeters. The female is little, if any, smaller than the male in Indian birds, but of Chinese birds La Touche gives the following measurements: Male, 23 (2 examples), wing 200 to 226; female, 22 (1 example), 190–200; culmen, male, 20–22; female, 19 millimeters.

Colors of soft parts.—Iris yellow or "grey with brown inner circle" (La Touche) ; bill dark horny green, the base of the upper, and most of the lower, mandible yellowish horny, the gape still more yellow; legs and feet wax-yellow to rather bright yellow.

Food.—This also is the same in character as that of *Cuculus canorus*, but *C. optatus* also devours more hard-bodied insects such as Cicadae and many small and some quite large beetles, while it feeds rather more exclusively on food obtained near the tops of high trees. I have never seen it feeding on the ground, nor have I noticed it in scrub or bushes except when it was probably hunting for a nest in which to deposit its egg.

Behavior.—I do not think that this bird could be distinguished from *Cuculus canorus*, except by its voice, by any field naturalist until the bird was actually in his hand. In flight, perching position, and general action I have been able to discern no difference of any kind between the two birds unless it is that when the two were seen together *optatus* looks a smaller, slighter bird than *canorus* and may fly a trifle faster with quicker wing beats.

Both sexes have the habit, as *canorus* has, of sitting, almost motionless, for a very long time in one position, possibly in the case of the female while she is watching certain birds and waiting for them to give away the site of their nest, or when she is waiting for the precise moment at which to fly down and place her egg in the nest of the foster parent selected to receive it.

Voice.—The call of the male consists of four notes, two rapid, then a pause, and then two more, all of the same cadence, sounding like *hoo-hoo hoo-hoo*. When one is close to the bird a fifth note can be heard preceding these, much higher pitched and far less resounding so that at a little distance only the four notes are heard. The call is a typical cuckoo note, and hearing it one would expect to find that a cuckoo had uttered it. There is also a sweet trilling note that is rarely heard, and I cannot say whether it is uttered by one sex or both, but I suspect it to correspond to the bubbling note uttered by the female *canorus*. Although occasionally this cuckoo calls on moonlight nights it does not do so with anything like the perseverance of the common cuckoo, nor is it so incessantly vocal during the day.

Enemies.—The same as those of the common cuckoo, but the young do not suffer so much from exposure by falling out of nests too small or too weak to hold them. In the case, however, of eggs laid in holes occupied by the nests of the crowned willow warbler the young birds have to vacate them at a very early stage or they would be unable to do so when full grown and would be incarcerated in them for life. As these cuckoos select ground nests so largely in which to deposit their eggs, these and the young birds when hatched do not suffer so greatly from the crows and magpies who hunt the hedges and bushes, but, on the other hand, they are easier for snakes and lizards to get at.

Fall.—Migration from the breeding grounds in northwest India apparently commences in the end of August and continues to the end of September or early October. From northeast India they would seem to migrate later by about a month, birds continuing to call up to the beginning of August, while in 1914 an egg was taken as late as August 20. It is a curious fact that in the continent of India birds do not seem to move far south and have only been recorded in winter from many places in the plains of the northwest and Punjab and from Lucknow, Jodhpore, Fategarh, Bihar, Dibrugarh and Cachar, in the United Provinces, Bengal, and Assam. Farther east it migrates much farther south and has been recorded from all over Burma to the extreme south, and from the Andamans and Nicobars, while it also ranges throughout the Malay Peninsula and the Austro-Malaysian islands to New Guinea and Australia. Birds found in winter east of Burma are certainly those that breed north of China and probably migrate, more or less, due north and south, and I am inclined to think it is possible that birds from the Himalayas migrate almost entirely to the east in India and then southeast through Burma and the Malay States. Otherwise it seems incredible that no specimens should ever be obtained, in south India or even central India, of a migrant which in and from China wanders so very far south in the winter months.

DISTRIBUTION

The Himalyan cuckoo is found throughout the Himalayas and central Asia from the extreme west of India and Baluchistan, while in central Siberia it extends from Dauria and Lake Baikal to the extreme east of the northern Chinese mountains and, possibly, to Japan. In China La Touche (1931) summarizes its distribution as follows: "China generally, Szechuen, Kwangsi, Fohkien, Lower Yangtse, Shaweishan, Shantung, Chihli (migrant)." To this he adds, "On the whole this Cuckoo is not common in North China, and very few have been noted by Dr. Wilder," and, again, noting on my distribution of the summer range he adds, "Corea and Manchuria should probably be added."

It certainly occurs and breeds in all the higher hills in Burma; quite commonly in the Chin Hills and rarely to the east in the Ruby Mines district and the Shan States.

Its appearance on the American list is due to a specimen obtained on St. Paul Island, Pribilof Islands, Alaska, on July 4, 1890 (W. Palmer, 1894).

CUCULUS CANORUS BAKERI Hartert

KHASIA HILLS CUCKOO

CONTRIBUTED BY EDWARD CHARLES STUART BAKER

HABITS

This most interesting race of the common European cuckoo was given a name in 1912 by Dr. Hartert (1912), no museum possessing sufficient material until 1911 to substantiate the differences that both Dr. Hartert and I believed to distinguish this subspecies from those others already accepted.

The Khasia Hills cuckoo is a race that breeds at considerably lower elevations than do either *C. c. canorus* or *C. c. telephonus* and, speaking generally, haunts during the breeding season more densely forested areas in much hotter and far more humid climates. Thus in the Khasia Hills of Assam, where it is extraordinarily common, it may be found in all the higher ranges at and about Sherraponji between 3,500 and 6,500 feet frequenting forest that is always lush and green, with luxuriant undergrowth and with an almost impenetrable tangle of creepers, beautiful orchids, ferns, and parasites growing on every tree. Here the rainfall averages about 550 inches in the year, while as much as 72 inches have fallen in 24 hours and over 700 inches in the 12 months. They are, however, equally numerous, between 4,000 and 6,000 feet around Shillong, where the rainfall is less than 150 inches in the year and where, in many parts, pine woods take the place of the wet evergreen forests.

Although on the whole this race of the cuckoo certainly frequents denser and thicker forest than do the other forms, individuals vary greatly in their tastes and those parasitic on pipits and other species of birds, which breed in the open grass plains, also haunt the same kind of country as that in which these birds breed. At the same time even in these places they always select those that contain a certain number of trees on which they can perch and from which they can survey the surrounding area and watch the fosterers to their nests. In the Khasia Hills many cuckoos are parasitic on the common Indian and Blyth's pipits, which are to be found nesting on the wide stretches of open grassland above Shillong, the former on ridges and plateaus up to some 5,500 feet and the latter on those above that altitude. Intermediate in habits between the evergreen forest cuckoos and the open country cuckoos there are others that haunt the more open pine forests, especially those that have brooks and small rivers running through them, or are broken up by ravines in which small deciduous trees, bushes, and brambles grow freely to the exclusion of the somber pine trees.

In Burma this cuckoo is commoner in the Ruby Mines district and in the Southern Shan States than anywhere else. T. R. Livesey, who has had a wonderful experience with them in the latter country, informs me that in these districts they frequent both the open deciduous forests as well as the open country of scrub and grass land around towns and villages, even depositing their eggs in the nests of birds breeding in and close to the gardens of houses occupied by Europeans or by Shans.

After the breeding season this cuckoo may be found in almost any kind of country that is fairly well wooded, while in the plains of Bengal and Lower Assam it seems to have a special liking for mango orchards and patches of jungles in tea plantations.

Spring.—In Assam those individuals that have migrated into the plains and lower hills the preceding autumn return to their breeding quarters in the end of March or early April, their numbers increasing rapidly up to the end of that month, when their mellow call may be heard almost continually in every direction at all elevations between 3,500 and 6,500 feet. Exact dates of arrival are recorded nowhere that I can trace, but I have eggs taken on April 14, odd eggs taken in the third week in April, and many after the 25th of that month.

In the Chin Hills, between Assam and the Ruby Mines district and Shan States, most cuckoos commence breeding about the middle of April, arriving in their breeding haunts nearly a month earlier. Here they are common at about 4,000 feet upward and haunt much the same kinds of country as they do in Assam, certainly breeding up to 7,000 feet, or a little over, as eggs have been taken on Mount Victoria and the hills above Fort White.

In the Shan States Mr. Livesey informs me that few if any birds remain above 4,000 feet in winter, in the end of August and early September the great majority moving into the lower hills and adjoining plains. The first birds returning to the higher hills put in an appearance early in March and commence to lay the last of that month, March 27 being the earliest date on which he has taken eggs and July 1 the latest.

The length of the breeding season is much more extended than is that of the European cuckoo (*C. c. canorus*) or the central Asian bird (*C. c. telephonus*), doubtless owing to the same factors of cold, food supply, etc., that compel the more northern birds of all families to compress their breeding arrangements into a far shorter time than that occupied by the southern birds, for whom temperature, food supply, and other factors are more or less favorable almost throughout the year.

The individual cuckoo, however, is governed in her time of egg-laying by the habits of the foster parent that she selects to bring up her young, while all cuckoos, as well as the foster parents, are affected more or less in their spring migration and breeding time by the late or early arrival of the rains and the consequent shortage or abundance of insect life. In Assam, where the rainy season is long and the rainfall heavy, eggs may be found in some numbers from April 20 to the middle of June and, then, in decreasing numbers, to the end of June, after which they further decrease in number until, after the middle of July, few will be taken, though my latest recorded date for a cuckoo's egg is August 24. In Burma, as already noted, birds commence laying about a month earlier, and few eggs are found after early June.

The 1,366 eggs in my collection were taken as follows: One in March (taken in Burma), 104 in April, 608 in May, 527 in June, 114 in July, and 12 in August. It may, I think, be accepted that migrating birds arrive on their breeding ground some two to three weeks before commencing to lay and leave again about one to two months after the deposition of their last eggs.

In Burma the peak of laying is reached in early May; in Assam not until the end of that month.

Courtship.—I can find nothing recorded as to the conduct of courtship between males and females during the breeding season and have, therefore, only my own observations to guide me. There appears to be no true courtship, and I have no doubt that, except in very rare instances, cuckoos do not pair, though in certain areas, where the bird is uncommon, a male and female may possibly mate and remain together throughout the breeding season. This is probably the case in North Cachar, where the bird is rare, breeding in deeper forest than I have seen anywhere else, and where I have seldom heard more than one male calling in any one particular area or found more than one type of egg deposited therein. In the Khasia Hills, in which district the birds swarm in incredible numbers, both sexes were undoubtedly promiscuous in their sexual relations. I have personally seen a female accept the attentions of one male and then fly off to a tree close by and accept another pursuing male within a few minutes. On this occasion several, I think four, males were pursuing the one female, who flew slowly from one tree to another on a roadside. Settling on one of these she crouched on a large bough, half lying there with both wings hanging slightly lowered and quivering, while her head was held quite low, her whole attitude expressing invitation. The first male, of those following her, at once accepted this after which he settled on a branch close by while the female flew away to a tree about 50 paces distant followed by the other three males, one of whom was again accepted by the female who, after the completion of the act flew off accompanied by the remaining two males to a tree beyond my view.

Among the Khasias, certain classes of whom are very intelligent observers, it appears to be well known that both sexes of cuckoo exercise no discretion in their love affairs.

Nesting.—The female cuckoo is, of course, parasitic in her habits, and I have personally taken eggs in the nests of no less than 103 species and subspecies of fosterer (see following list), the very great majority of which are, however, undoubtedly abnormal or casual only, for I feel satisfied that when the usual foster parent has no nest available the cuckoo will eventually deposit her egg in that of any other bird that may be convenient. Repeated instances have come within my own experience in which a cuckoo normally parasitic on one bird deposits one or more of a series of eggs in a nest utterly unlike those of the usual fosterer, merely because she has already exhausted all the nests known to her of the latter.

LIST OF FOSTER PARENTS

Suya crinigera (subspecies 6)	215	eggs
Cisticola jundicis cursitans	276	"
Cisticola exilis tytleri (generally with *C. j. c.* series)	7	"
Tribura luteiventris	32	"
Orthotomus (species and subspecies 2)	27	"
Acanthopneuste reguloides harterti	9	"
Megalurus palustris	7	"
Miscellaneous warblers (abnormal fosterers, 9)	25	"
Anthus (various species and subspecies, 8)	199	"
Rhodophila ferrea haringtoni	18	"
Saxicola caprata burmanica	55	"
Rhyacornis fuliginosus	25	"
Enicurus (species 2)	25	"
Petrophila (*Monticola*) (species 2)	21	"
Turdidae (abnormal fosterers, species 8)	15	"
Cyanosylvia leucura	13	"
Eumyias thalassina thalassina	63	"
Niltava (species 3)	43	"
Muscicapidae (abnormal fosterers, species 12)	22	"
Lanius nigriceps nigriceps	35	"
Laniidae (abnormal fosterers, species 2)	2	"
Troglodytidae (species 3)	21	"
Mesia agentauris	46	"
Leiothrix calypyga	33	"
Timaliidae (abnormal fosterers, species 32)	92	"
Other abnormal fosterers, *Passer, Sitta, Parus,* etc. (7 species)	8	"

Total Fosterers: Normal 23, abnormal 80 (=103).

Like the English cuckoo, as Chance (1922) has proved, the Khasia Hills female cuckoo sometimes adopts a certain area of country as its own breeding territory into which it will allow no other female, parasitic on the same foster parent, to enter, though it seems to have no objection to the entry of any number of males or of another female parasitic on a different species. Thus in a certain area close to the house in which I lived in Shillong I found three cuckoos breeding; one depositing its eggs in the nests of the little fantail warbler (*Cisticola jundicis cursitans*), the second in the nests of the verditer flycatcher (*Eumyias thalassina thalassina*), and the third in the nests of the black-headed shrike (*Lanius nigriceps nigriceps*). On another occasion I took eggs of three different cuckoos from nests of *Cisticola, Niltava,* and *Leiothrix* in the same strip of jungle and not 50 yards from one another. Yet another instance of shared territory was a grass-covered hillside occupied by two female cuckoos, the one parasitic on the same little fantail warbler and the other on pipits (species various). Other similar instances were quite common in this district.

My personal experience confirms what those interested in cuckoo-work have for some time maintained in regard to cuckoos being consistently parasitic on one selected foster parent. A good example of this constancy is a series, collected for me by a family of four men trained by myself in cuckoo-work in the Khasia Hills. From 1925 to 1935 these men obtained for me no less than 132 eggs of one cuckoo parasitic on the fantail warbler, all collected in the same area of grass and scrub surrounded by pine forest. Of these 132 eggs only 4 were taken from nests other than those of the little fantail and of these 4, 3 were placed in the nests of another little warbler (*Orthotomus sutorius patia*) and the other in the nest of the Assam brown hill warbler (*Suya crinigera assamica*), both, of course, in the same territory.

In addition to the above I have many series of eggs, numbering 3 to 15, from individual cuckoos, occasionally taken in two or more consecutive years, all placed in nests of the same warbler. Again I have other series of cuckoos' eggs, some taken from nests of *Suya* (various species); others from those of *Eumyias*, pipits (various species), the silver-eared mesia (*Mesia a. argentauris*), the Pekin robin (*Leiothrix lutea calypyga*), and other fosterers. As a rule the cuckoo also shows equal constancy to its chosen breeding area, returning year after year to it and leaving it only when the supply of fosterers is exhausted or the nature of the country has been altered by man or some other agency. Where the normal foster parent is exceptionally common, such as are the warblers of the genera *Cisticola* and *Suya*, the cuckoo often has ample nests in a compact area to act as hosts to her whole series of eggs, and we have found as many as 18 eggs laid by the same individual within such an area. Where, however, the fosterers such as pipits or mesia are less numerous or are breeding in comparatively small areas, some 4 to 10 eggs are laid in the one area and then, when the available nests have all been made use of, the cuckoo removes to another area, generally close by, eventually often returning to the original one later in the season and again cuckolding other nests of the same fosterer.

There can, I think, be no doubt that a cuckoo brought up in a nest of a certain fosterer will deposit its own eggs in nests of the same bird. This theory seems now to be one generally accepted, and certainly my experience goes to confirm this, and in my own collection I have eggs of a very definite type taken for over 30 years in the nests of the same species of fosterer in the same district.

Eggs.—The eggs of the Khasia Hills cuckoo are of very many and beautiful types of color and character of markings, while the eggs of each individual cuckoo, though varying slightly *inter se*, do not show so great a variation as is found in the eggs of single clutches laid by many species of Passeres or other orders.

Among the most common types of eggs are, naturally, those that have been evolved to assimilate with the eggs of the birds most frequently employed as foster parents. Among these may be mentioned the following:

An egg with a white ground lightly marked, chiefly at the larger end, with specks, spots, or small blotches of red, reddish brown, or brown. These eggs are excellent counterparts in all but size of the eggs of the fantail warbler, in whose tiny nest they are usually deposited.

The next commonest type has the ground color more or less distinctly tinged with reddish and is rather more profusely marked with larger blotches of various shades of red-brown. These are normally deposited in the nests of various species of *Suya*, or brown hill warbler, the most common types of whose eggs agree well with those of the cuckoo.

A third and common type of cuckoo's egg has the ground color a beautiful salmon-pink or buff-pink and has the surface freckled with deeper reddish; in some cases so finely and thickly that the eggs appear at first glance to be unicolored; in other cases more or less boldly, though sparsely, covered with reddish brown and underlying faint marks of gray or pale purple. These eggs agree well with various types of eggs laid by the verditer flycatcher and, even still more so, with those of the beautiful niltava (*Niltava sundara*), while it is in the nests of these birds we find them deposited. Cuckoos, however, that normally deposit their eggs in the nest of these birds seem regularly also to cuckold the large niltava (*N. grandis*) and the white-tailed chat (*Muscisylvia notodela*), which lay the same colored eggs and make similar cup-shaped nests of living moss, built in exactly similar positions in holes in banks and among boulders.

Another beautiful type is bright pale blue, often immaculate but sometimes faintly flecked with primary reddish and secondary gray blotches. In the Khasia Hills these are almost invariably deposited in the nests of the silver-eared *Mesia* or the red-billed *Leiothrix* (*L. lutea calypga*), two species that lay exactly the same type of egg to that of the cuckoo, though more boldly blotched, while the two species also make similar nests, which they place in somewhat similar positions in bushes, etc.

In Burma, more especially in the Ruby Mines district and in the Shan States, we have two dominant types of eggs: One blue, much darker in tint than those referred to as being deposited in *Leiothrix* nests, laid with the similar eggs of the Burmese dark gray bushchat (*Rhodophila ferrea haringtoni*), and the other having a pale pink ground, freely blotched all over with reddish, deposited in the nests of the Burmese stonechat (*Saxicola caprata burmanica*), which also lays eggs of this color and character. In connection with these two types of egg an interesting state of affairs has now been arrived at in parts of the Shan States. Thirty years ago the bushchat was extremely common in certain districts in hills between 4,000 and 5,000 feet, and the great majority of cuckoos found there were those laying blue eggs. Cultivation has now wiped out the scrub and bush jungle, beloved by the bushchat, and fields of rice, gardens, and the vegetation surrounding villages have taken its place. With this change in the character of the jungle growth has also come a change in the birds frequenting it, the bushchat has almost disappeared, and the little stonechat has taken its place, breeding everywhere in gardens, village grounds, and cultivated fields. The elimination of the bushchat, although so recent, has already gone far to eliminate also the cuckoo that lays blue eggs, while the one that lays eggs like those of the stonechat has become much more numerous and has become the common form. Even now, however, an occasional blue egg of a cuckoo will be found in the stonechats' nests, the latter similar in every respect to the nests of the bushchat and therefore cuckolded, *faute de mieux*, by the cuckoo.

It is impossible here to deal with the problem of the evolution of the various types of cuckoos' eggs, but the facts recorded above seem to go far toward proving that cuckoo eggs, to assimilate with those of their fosterers, have been evolved by discrimination among the foster parents leading to the slow but sure destruction of the unfit, i. e., Darwin's doctrine of the survival of the fittest in its crudest form.

In shape the eggs are rather broader ovals than those of the European cuckoo, and they also average larger and heavier. It is indeed much easier to separate the various subspecies of cuckoo by the eggs they lay than by the plumage of the birds that lay them.

The number of eggs laid by the Khasia Hills cuckoo probably varies somewhat individually, though I believe it generally to be 12 to 20. It is, however, very difficult to decide this definitely, as it is impossible to be satisfied that every nest of the selected fosterer in any given area has without doubt been marked down. It was not until 1907 that I concentrated on the attempt to solve any one of the numerous cuckoo problems, and it was some years after this before satisfactory evidence had accumulated on this particular point. My different series of eggs of individual cuckoos vary greatly in number, being, I believe, governed entirely by the number of nests of the foster parent available in the area searched over. In 1908, on May 25, in one small grass glade surrounded by pine forest I found five nests of *Cisticola*, three containing young cuckoos or eggs of the cuckoo, and I am practically sure that I missed no *Cisticola* or *Suya* nests. One of these nests had in it a young cuckoo about 2 days old, another nest had a young cuckoo just hatching, while a third had a slightly incubated cuckoo's egg. The two other nests of the *Cisticola* were unfinished and empty, but on June 1 one of these contained a slightly incubated cuckoo's egg and three of the foster parent, while, finally, on June 4 the last nest contained a fresh egg of the cuckoo and four of the warbler. As the egg from which the older of the nestling cuckoos had been hatched must have been laid about May 13, while the last egg was laid on June 3 or 4, we have only five eggs laid in 21 days, whereas we know now that the larger cuckoos lay every second day, so the five eggs and the two young found cannot possibly include all then laid. A series of 14 eggs, all found between May 19 and June 10, 1910, in a similar but much larger area, were probably laid between May 16 and June 10 and represent a complete series laid every alternate day. In another small series of five eggs of one and the same cuckoo found in a narrow strip of grassland three eggs were deposited in Cisticola's nests on May 16, 18, and 20, this exhausting all the nests then available. After this she apparently departed, but on July 5 and 7 the same cuckoo returned and placed two more eggs, one each in two new nests of Cisticolas. Another series of 14 eggs, of which 12 were placed in nests of *Cisticola jundicis cursitans*, one in a nest of *C. exilis tytleri*, and one in a nest of *Suya atrogularis khasiana*, were laid in two periods: The first from May 15 to 23 occupying each of the five nests of the fantail warbler available between these dates, and, then, from June 1 to 18 in all the nests then available in that particular area. Finally a series of eggs of one cuckoo that were taken from 1925 to 1935 consisted of the following numbers: 6, 8, 14, 9, 10, 12, 15, 18, 14, 11, 15. In 1925 and 1926 woodcutters were working in the pinewoods surrounding the open patch in which the fantail warblers were breeding and doubtless drove these little birds away and so deprived the cuckoo of foster parents during the latter period of her laying, or probably larger series would have been obtained in that particular patch of grassland. The various series prove satisfactorily that eggs are normally deposited every alternate day and, also, that there is no interval in the laying period dividing it into two.

The weights of 1,368 eggs of the Khasia Hills cuckoo are as follows: Average weight 231; maximum 307; minimum 153 milligrams; this latter is, however, an abnormally small light egg and very few will be found less than 180 milligrams.

The same number of eggs measure: Average 23.76 by 17.43; maxima, 28.5 by 18.0 and 27.1 by 20.0; minima 20.9 by 16.3 and 23.4 by 15.0 millimeters.

I should, perhaps, not omit to say that though the generally accepted idea that cuckoos' eggs can be distinguished by their weight is in most cases correct, it is not always so. For instance, I have 37 eggs of this cuckoo taken in shrikes' nests, and a comparison of weights and measures of the eggs of the two species is as follows:

C. c. bakeri, 37 eggs	*Lanius n. nigriceps, 100 eggs*
Average size: 23.56 by 17.50 mm.	23.60 by 17.9 mm.
Average weight: 232 mg.	215 mg.
Maximum weight: 266 mg.	249 mg.
Minimum weight: 190 mg.	185 mg.

The comparative weight of the eggs of different species of birds varies greatly. Thus *Anthus* eggs are normally very light while the eggs of *Passer* are very heavy, two of the former about equaling three of the latter of the same size and, in a few cases, otherwise indistinguishable in coloring, shape, etc. Hoopoes' and spine-tailed swifts' eggs are very heavy, far more so in comparison with their size than those of cuckoos.

This shows that weight alone in some cases does not suffice to distinguish cuckoos' eggs from their fosterers' eggs, and other comparisons of cuckoos' eggs with those of other species could be quoted to confirm this. The hard *gritty* shell with fine pits at wide intervals is a further good distinguishing feature of cuckoos' eggs, while when blowing it is noticeable that most cuckoos' eggs have the yolks tinged with flesh color and very pale, while the white is rather more opaque, like the white of a duck's egg when compared with that of a fowl.

In Europe it is very rare to find two eggs of cuckoos in a nest laid by the same female; in India this is not so rare, and I have on three occasions found three eggs of the same cuckoo in one nest.

It is not possible here to go fully into the fascinating subject of the method of deposition of eggs, but briefly it may be said that it has been fully proved that in many cases cuckoos lay their eggs directly into open nests, an act that has been witnessed by myself, Whitehead, and others in India and proved by Chance (1922) to be the case in England.

There are, however, any number of eggs deposited by cuckoos in nests into which it is utterly impossible for the cuckoo to gain an entrance. Into many of these the cuckoo projects her egg from the cloaca by pressing herself up against the entrance to the nest and ejecting her egg with sufficient force to propel it the 2 or 3 inches that may be necessary for it to reach the nest (Livesey, 1936; A. E. Jones, 1937).

On the other hand, there are many nests to which this method also would not apply, such as nests of small birds, more than 2 or 3 inches inside holes of various character, in some cases a corner having to be turned before the nest is reached. Into these I believe the cuckoo places her egg with her bill, and there is some evidence to support this which I hope to give in my proposed book on "Cuckoo Problems."

Young.—Incubation, I think, takes usually 12 or 13 days, rarely only 11 days but occasionally extending to 14. The period the nestling remains in the nest is 4 to 6 weeks, but in many cases the nest is far too small to retain the young cuckoo until it is full grown. Thus when the eggs are deposited in the nests of birds such as *Cisticola* and, to a lesser degree, *Suya*, the young bird when a quarter grown fills the small egg-shaped nest, sitting in it with its head projecting from the entrance at the top side. Gradually, as the young cuckoo grows, the nest is expanded until it looks like basketwork around it, which finally bursts, depositing him or her on the ground. This generally occurs when the cuckoo has fair feathering and is about half grown or a little later.

The young Khasia Hills cuckoo ejects the fosterer's eggs or young from the nest in the same way as its English cousin does, possessing the same curious interscapulary pit to assist it in doing so. This structural aid to ejection is found in all such genera as *Cuculus*, *Cacomantis*, *Penthoceryx*, and others that eject their foster brothers and sisters, but not in the young of *Clamator*, *Eudynamis*, and those cuckoos that do not commit such murders. In the cuckoos that possess it, the pit soon fills in and young cuckoos lose the impulse to eject after a very short time, sometimes within 4 days and almost invariably within a week of being hatched.

Plumages.—Male: Whole upper plumage and wing coverts a dark slaty-gray or blackish slate, decidedly darker than the same parts in the European cuckoo; the lower back, rump, and upper tail coverts are a purer and somewhat lighter gray; the wing quills and concealed portions of greater coverts more brown, the quills slightly glossed and barred with white on the inner webs of the outer primaries, turning to rufous on the inner primaries; tail ashy black tipped with white and with white notches along the sides of the shafts, the white increasing in extent on the lateral tail feathers; chin, throat, sides of head and neck, and the upper breast ashy gray, not so dark as the back; remainder of lower parts, axillaries, and under wing coverts white with rather irregular bands of black, broader and farther apart than in *C. c. canorus.* Under tail coverts the same but with the dark bars still farther apart.

Female: Differs in having a rufous tinge on the upper breast and sometimes on the throat and sides of the neck.

Nestling: Naked when hatched.

Juvenile: First plumage; whole plumage brownish gray or slate, obsoletely barred with buffish white; a patch of white on the nape or hind neck; whole lower plumage barred white or rufescent white and dark brown, very heavily on the chin, throat, and breast, and less so on the under tail coverts.

The young male after the first molt is like the adult but nearly always retains traces of the juvenile barring, more especially so on the wings.

Hepatic females have the whole upper parts barred chestnut and blackish slate or blackish brown; the lower plumage has the chin, throat, and breast barred pale chestnut and blackish and generally with a strong rufous tinge on the breast and abdomen.

Young hepatic females are duller in color than the adults and have the feathers of the upper part fringed with white.

Colors of soft parts.—Iris pale to deep yellow, sometimes brownish in young birds of the year; bill dark horny brown, or very dark horny green, paler and yellowish at the base and on the commissure and orange-yellow on the gape; legs and feet wax-yellow.

Measurements.—Wing 220 to 227; tail 155 to 178; tarsus 18 (La Touche) to 19; culmen from feathers of forehead 20 to 22 millimeters (24 La Touche).

Food.—The principal food of this, as of other cuckoos, consists of caterpillars, pupae, chrysalides, and soft insects of any kind. During flights of termites cuckoos may be seen both catching them on the wing and eating them on the ground as they emerge from it. I have also taken Cicadae from their stomachs, and occasionally quite hard beetles of considerable size.

The actions of this bird when attempting, and indeed succeeding in, the catching of termites in flight are very clumsy and labored and their progress on the ground very slow, similar to the progress of certain woodpeckers when hunting a lawn for ants and other prey.

As a rule they feed in trees at some height from the ground, but any plague of caterpillars will tempt them down to quite low undergrowth or even onto low grass in the open, and I once saw four cuckoos all feeding on small green caterpillars on the ground in an open glade in pine forest.

Behavior.—Normally cuckoos are seldom found on any but high trees, often resting in one position for a long time on some lofty branch and then flying to another tree with strong, easy beats of the wing, at a considerable speed. In the breeding season the females undoubtedly mark down the nests in which they intend to deposit their eggs, and they may be seen perched in a tree, watching their victims until these latter give away the position of the nest. While thus engaged the patience of the cuckoo seems inexhaustible, and it will sit for hours in one position, hardly moving, yet obviously watching the intended fosterers, which may be loath to return to their nests though they may come and perch on the same tree as that occupied by the cuckoo, sometimes within a few feet of her. Apparently they not only mark down nests for immediate victimization, but others to be made use of when later eggs are to be laid. At other times they seem to be able to ascertain the approximate, yet not the exact, position of a nest. (Livesey (MS.) gives me a most interesting example of this. He writes:

"Yesterday, May 19, 1937, I was out for a walk with my wife about 5 p. m. at Taungyi, which has an elevation of some 5,000 feet. Close to my cottage the dogs chased a bird off a ploughed field, which I recognized as a cuckoo. The cuckoo returned with two chats after her and perched on some bamboo rails, so, suspecting that the chats had a nest somewhere near in which the cuckoo was going to lay, I sat down to wait and watch with my glasses. Back came the cuckoo and flew low over the field almost settling on a place some 50 yards in front of us. Twice she flew backward and forward, chased by the chats, finally settling where I expected the nest to be. I could see her very plainly through the glasses as with throat feathers puffed out and crest feathers sometimes raised she jumped clumsily from clod to clod searching for the nest, straining her neck up and looking everywhere. The chats were now mobbing her furiously and in retaliation she only opened her beak and made faces at them. She did not appear to know where the nest was and began a systematic search for it in an area about 5 by 3 yards. The clods in the field were very large and lumpy with all sorts of holes which might have held a nest, and from time to time she disappeared from sight as she hopped into the various depressions, going backward and forward in the most persistent manner, mobbed all the time by the chats.

"She was, I think, a full 10 minutes searching for the nest, but, at last she dipped out of sight and a flutter of her wings suggested she had found the nest and was in the act of laying. She was out of my sight for about 4 seconds and then sped away in a great hurry.

"We climbed the fence and walking up to the place whence she had flown found a very well-concealed chats' nest in which by stooping down to the ground I could see that the nest contained two eggs, the cuckoo's and one of the chat's; by using the tips of my two fingers I was just able to draw the eggs out, one at a time with considerable difficulty."

Voice.—The call of the male during the breeding season is exactly the same as that of the European cuckoo, but in winter it also has a single note sounding like *chuck* softly repeated two or three times. At the beginning of the season the bisyllabic note, from which the bird derives its name, is not perfect and the imperfections cover quite a wide range of variations. Sometimes the note is single instead of double; often it is preceded by a rather hoarse note of the same character as the call, while sometimes the *cuck-oo* is followed by another hoarser note. The female has the summer bubbling note of its cousin and also certain chuckling notes, very seldom uttered, while in winter it gives vent to the same soft *chucks* as the male. Whether the female ever calls *cuckoo* is disputed, but, personally, I am fairly certain that she does, although it may be but seldom. The bubbling note is the call to the male and is also repeated after she has met her mate, but it is then, I think, lower and softer, perhaps an expression of satisfaction.

During the daytime the calling of the male is almost continuous, but that of the female far less so as the former calls in the presence of a female, while the latter does not "bubble" before the male except at the moment she takes to flight and invites him to follow her.

On moonlight nights the male often calls with as much persistency as during the day, but I have never heard it calling on dark nights until dawn is advanced.

Enemies.—Cuckoos have the usual enemies of all bird life, vermin of every kind, which during the breeding season hunt for and devour all the eggs and young they can find. All the civet-cat tribe, snakes, lizards, and iguanas are inveterate thieves of eggs and young, while even more destructive than these are the birds of the crow and magpie tribe, which systematically hunt out the nests and devour their contents. I have often watched the birds of the genus *Den-drocitta* and *Cissa* beating over an area in search of nests, quartering it with the care and energy of a spaniel after game. The young birds suffer also very greatly from being too large for the nests in which they are hatched. Half grown they fall out on to the ground, and many, which escape death from vermin, are killed by exposure to heavy rain.

The older birds seem to have no special enemies, their swift flight and comparatively large size saving them from the sudden death so often the fate of smaller, slower birds. At the same time birds of prey undoubtedly attack and kill them just as they would any other bird of similar size and their superficial resemblance— in human eyes—to a sparrow hawk, would certainly not deceive their would-be destroyers even if these were sparrow hawks. Nor do the small birds attack cuckoos because they *believe* them to be hawks, but because they *know* them to be cuckoos and, in their own way as objectionable as hawks.

Fall.—The Khasia Hills cuckoo is far more sedentary in character than its nearest relations and, possibly, is originally a sedentary race from which the migratory forms have sprung. I have seen the bird in the Khasia Hills in every month of the year except February and, as it is silent in the winter months and does not call attention to its presence, it is probably even more numerous in its breeding range at this time than has hitherto been supposed, while some individuals may be resident in the same locality all the year round. At the same time migration does take place in some degree and this dark race has been found in winter, certainly, in Bengal, more especially in the eastern districts on the Bay, in Orissa, once by Annandale (MS.), while it extends through Burma, south to Prome (Mackenzie and Hopwood, MS.); south Siam (E. G. Herbert, MS.) and finally, almost certainly, to southwestern China. I have no proof that in the Indian Empire adult cuckoos migrate any earlier than the birds of the year. About September the pleasant call, which has been heard continually up to the end of July and casually up to the end of August, ceases entirely, and the birds are also far less frequently seen on the higher ranges of hills and, by October, nearly all the birds, old and young, have left these and have taken to the lower hills and the broken country at their bases, thence slowly and gradually extending into the plains in the districts already mentioned. It is also possible, of course, that this cuckoo may range farther south in winter than stated above, as records of *Cuculus canorus* (subspecies?) have been recorded from Madras and from the islands of the Austro-Malayan region, between October and March, some of which almost certainly refer to this form. At present, from the evidence at my disposal, I can neither substantiate nor refute this suggestion, as it is quite impossible to recognize one subspecies from another in the field unless a particularly bright light shows up the comparative slaty darkness of this bird, to an observer with some experience of cuckoos.

DISTRIBUTION

Exact details as to the distribution of the Khasia Hills cuckoo are still wanting as so many records of cuckoos refer merely to the species, *Cuculus canorus*, while the subspecies is not given or, indeed, in many cases distinguished. The breeding area has been *proved* to extend throughout the hills of Assam and Burma as far south as Karen-nee and as far east as Yunnan, while Bangs and Peters (1928) consider it is this form that is found and breeds in eastern Tibet and Szechwan. To the west the breeding cuckoo in the Bhutan Hills is undoubtedly of this race, but how much farther west it may extend is not known though, almost certainly, it may be found breeding in the lower Himalayas below Sikkim. Stevens informs me that he believes it does.

A fine series of breeding specimens in the Stevens collection, collected by him in the Sikkim Hills, indicates that the range of *bakeri* is below 7,000 or 8,000 feet, and that above that, up to 12,000 feet, *telephonus* is the breeding form.

In the cold weather it extends to the countries mentioned above in this article as being visited on migration. To these may be added that it occurs in Siam, as far south as Bangkok and the Siamese peninsula west of Tenasserim. Finally, extraordinary as it may seem, it has been recorded by Friedmann (Friedmann and Riley, 1931) as having once been obtained in St. Lawrence Island, Bering Sea, an occurrence that entitles it to a place in the American avifauna. This specimen was originally described as belonging to the central and northeastern Asiatic race *telephonus*, which one might expect would occur at long intervals in Alaska.

Order TROGONIFORMES

Family TROGONIDAE: Trogons

TROGON AMBIGUUS AMBIGUUS Gould

COPPERY-TAILED TROGON

HABITS

This gorgeous Mexican species brings color from the Tropics, all too rarely, across our borders in extreme southern Texas and southern Arizona. Ever since Lieutenant Benson shot an immature male in the Huachuca Mountains on August 24, 1885, it has been known to occur there and in other neighboring localities in Arizona as one of our rarest birds. Specimens have been taken there under circumstances that would indicate that sometime its nest will be found within our borders. An adult female was shot by F. H. Fowler (1903) in the Huachucas during August 1892. Major Bendire (1895) writes: "Another adult female, which evidently had a nest close by, was obtained by Dr. Edgar A. Mearns, United States Army, on June 23, 1892, on the east side of the San Luis Mountains, close to the Mexican boundary line. The long tail feathers in this specimen are much worn and abraded, and look as if the bird had passed considerable time in very limited quarters. Its mate was also seen, but not secured. Judging from the character of the country this species inhabits in southern Arizona, that is pine forest regions, it is probably only a straggler in the lower Rio Grande Valley in Texas, and does not breed there."

Mrs. Florence M. Bailey (1923) reports that A. B. Howell discovered a pair of these trogons in the Santa Rita Mountains in southern Arizona in 1918, of which he writes: "While wrapping two birds which I had shot at 6,000 feet in a canyon, on August 4, I looked up and saw a pair of these birds watching me from live oak branches at perhaps a hundred yards. I had an unobstructed view of their bright underparts and characteristic form and flight, and identification was sure. They were very 'wise,' and as I carefully approached, they as slowly receded, flying from oak to oak until they separated and I lost them in the denser growth. The trees were almost entirely live oaks here with a very occasional pine."

Herbert W. Brandt has sent me the following notes on the status of this beautiful bird on the western slopes of the Huachuca Mountains, Ariz.: "The turkeylike call of this rare, semitropical visitor is a common bird note in Sunnyside Canyon and in the lower reaches of Bear Canyon. There are at least three pairs of birds in each of these valleys; and in the morning they noisily call back and forth to one another. These valley floors are usually densely wooded and would make this bird difficult to study were it not for its inquisitive nature, for it is usually easily lured by the 'squeech.' One lavishly garbed male and his more modest mate repeatedly allowed me to walk up to within about 20 feet of them before they would fly a short distance and then allow me to approach them again. Each time they both called their hen-turkey-like notes, *kum-kum-kum*, ever answering my squeeches of a like count and inflection. That this bird breeds in the vicinity there is little doubt, but we did not spend time seeking its home, as Arizona has wisely put it on the permanently protected list, and in consequence this mountain-loving species is becoming common again in its densely tangled retreats."

A. J. van Rossem (1936) adds the following news:

Regardless of its status in former years, this trogon may now be counted a fairly common summer visitant in the Santa Ritas. Possibly it has always been more numerous than was supposed, for one of the rangers, who has been stationed for many years in the Santa Ritas, knew the bird well and told me of having seen as many as five or six feeding together at a single patch of manzanita. At any rate there were several pairs in Madera Cañon in the summers of 1931 and 1932. * * *

On June 27 [1931], Mr. Gorsuch and I saw or heard eight birds between the forks of the cañon at 6000 feet, and Littleshot Cabin at 7000. On that date a fully adult male was collected by Mr. Gorsuch for the museum at the University of Arizona. On June 28, a very young trogon, about two-thirds grown and evidently just out of the nest, was shot, quite unintentionally, in a patch of oaks at 6000 feet.

At least two pairs were noted on May 30, 1931; "the association in which they were noted was the oak-sycamore growth near the juncture of Upper Sonoran and Transition. Two males (both of which presumably had mates) were heard in the left (north) fork— one at 7000, the other at 8000 feet altitude. These altitudes are in the pine-oak association in the Transition Zone."

Col. A. J. Grayson (Lawrence, 1874) says that, in western Mexico, "it is to be met with only in the dark forests of the *tierra caliente.*"

Nesting.—Colonel Grayson says that "it breeds in the hollows of trees like the parrots." According to Mrs. Bailey (1928), the nest is "reported in cavities in large trees, generally in large deserted woodpecker holes, but also in holes in banks." There are ten sets of eggs of the coppery-tailed trogon in the Thayer collection in Cambridge, all collected by, or for, Frank B. Armstrong near Ciudad Victoria, Tamaulipas, Mexico, between March 29 and April 27, 1908. If these dates are all correctly recorded, these trogons must breed very plentifully in that region, or Mr. Armstrong's collectors must have been very industrious. There are a number of sets in other collections from the same locality, all taken by the same collectors. These eggs were all taken from nests in holes in trees, apparently natural cavities; the holes were at various heights, ranging from 12 to 40 feet above the ground; some of the trees were in a river bottom and others in "big woods near town." The nests were made of various materials, such as hay, straw, trash, moss, wool, down, feathers, vines, and thistledown.

Eggs.—The coppery-tailed trogon lays ordinarily three or four eggs but probably sometimes only two. These are rounded-ovate to nearly oval in shape; and the shell is smooth but not glossy. The color is dull white or faintly bluish white and entirely unmarked. The measurements of 55 eggs average 28.50 by 23.18 millimeters; the eggs showing the four extremes measure **30.7** by 24.6, 29 by 25, **26** by 22.8, and 29.5 by **22.1** millimeters.

Plumages.—I have not seen any nestlings or very young birds. Ridgway (1911) gives very full and accurate descriptions of all the known plumages of both sexes of this trogon; but his accounts are too long to be quoted in full here, so I shall mention only the most conspicuous features of the different plumages, by which the reader may recognize them.

In the juvenal plumage, in July, the sexes are alike, or nearly so, and closely resemble, on the upper parts, the adult female, except that the central pair of tail feathers have very narrow black tips, instead of broad ones; the next three pairs of rectrices are black, and the two lateral pairs are mostly white, barred with black, except for a large terminal white area; the lesser, median, and to a lesser degree the greater wing coverts are tipped with a large spot of pale buff or buffy white, bordered with black; chin and throat grayish brown above a quite distinct white pectoral band; below this band the under parts are indistinctly barred, or mottled, with grayish brown and grayish white.

This unadulterated juvenal plumage is apparently worn through the first summer and early fall; I have seen it in its purity in birds collected at various dates between July 23 and September 20; but, on the other hand, some specimens show the beginning of a molt before the end of August. During all the remainder of their first year, young birds show more or less continuous progress toward maturity by a gradual and irregular molt. At an early age, between August and November, young males begin to show metallic green feathers in the back and throat, and metallic blue feathers in the rump and upper tail coverts; during winter and spring these metallic colors gradually increase; and on the under parts, below the white band, there is a gradual decrease in the brown and white and a corresponding increase in the "geranium red" of the adult plumage. At the same time, young females are acquiring more and more of the "peach red" of the adult female on the posterior under parts.

These transition plumages may be seen, in the series I have studied, in birds collected in November, December, February, March, April, May, June, and July, during all of which time the juvenal wings and tail are retained. From this I infer that the annual molt occurs in summer and fall and that young birds do not acquire the fully adult plumage until they are at least 15 months old, or perhaps much older.

Food.—Some coppery-tailed trogons that E. C. Jacot collected for me were feeding on wild grapes. Dr. A. K. Fisher wrote to Major Bendire (1895) that "a rancher who raises fruit in Ramsay Canyon stated that the species visited the gardens in considerable numbers, especially during the period when cherries were ripe." Major Bendire (1895) says of other members of the trogon family: "Their food consists of fruit, grasshoppers, and other insects, and in their actions while catching the latter they are said to resemble a Flycatcher, starting and returning from a perch like these birds, and often sitting for hours in the same place."

Cottam and Knappen (1939) state that a bird, collected by Dr. Fisher in the Huachuca Mountains in June, "had fed exclusively on the adults and larvae of lepidopterous insects." They examined the stomach of another bird, collected in October in Mexico, that contained 68 percent insects and 32 percent fruits. The insect food included one grasshopper nymph, long-horned grasshopper eggs, three Mantidae, three stink bugs, other Heteroptera, one leaf beetle, one very large larva of a hawk moth, larvae of undetermined Lepidoptera, and two sawfly larvae. The vegetable food consisted of fruits of cut-leaved cissus, fruit of red pepper, and undetermined plant fiber.

Behavior.—F. H. Fowler (1903) writes:

On June 9, 1892, my father and I accompanied Dr. A. K. Fisher to Garden Canyon seven miles south of the post. We reached the canyon and were riding up the narrow trail bordered with pines and live oaks, when suddenly a beautiful male trogon flew across the path just ahead of us, and perched on a live oak bush on the other side of the small stream which flows through the canyon. The Doctor tried to approach it, but the noise caused by his passage through the thick brush and over the sliding rocks on the hill side alarmed the bird, which from the first had seemed a trifle uneasy, and it was soon lost to view among the trees down the canyon. Higher up among the pines, on the same day, we heard the calls of another which sounded much like those of a hen turkey. While we were eating lunch on the way down, we heard still another calling from the hillside above us, and the Doctor, who found it perched on the lower limb of a pine after a short search, watched its actions for a few moments and then shot at it. It sat erect, the tail hanging straight down, and when uttering the call threw its head back until its beak pointed nearly straight up.

On August 14 of the same year I again found the trogon in Garden Canyon, this time higher up however at the Picture Rocks. A beautiful pair flew up from a fallen pine to the lower limb of a tree, and sat there quietly watching me. I dismounted and fired a reduced charge at the male, but the only effect was that he flew off through the trees unhurt, while the female flew up to a small tree on the hill, where she sat, looking at me until I loaded my gun, when I shot her. At the second shot the male flew up the canyon his beautiful carmine breast gleaming in the sunlight like a streak of flame. Both birds sat nearly erect when at rest, with their long tails hanging nearly straight down. Their flight was nearly like the slow flight of a magpie, until startled, when they flew like a dove and nearly as fast.

Voice.—Mr. Jacot says, in his letter, that the young birds were silent but that the adults had many notes, one of which was "almost like the chattering of our gray squirrel." A note referred to above was like that of a hen turkey. Dr. William Beebe (1905) says: "The call of the trogon, uttered especially toward evening when it came to drink, was a soft series of melodious notes, reminding one somewhat of the content-call of a hen with chickens. Regularly at dusk two of these birds went to roost in a dense tangle of wild clematis." Mr. van Rossem (1936) refers to the note of the male trogon as a "loud, hoarse, 'kóà-kóa-kóa'." Evidently the bird has a variety of notes.

Field marks.—The shape and posture, referred to above, as well as its brilliant colors, would mark this beautiful bird definitely as a trogon. The only other trogon likely to be met with anywhere within the range of this species is the Mexican trogon, found on the highlands of Mexico. The two species can be recognized in life by the color patterns of the outer tail feathers; in *ambiguus* these feathers are largely white, barred or vermiculated with black; in *mexicanus* they are largely black, broadly tipped with white.

DISTRIBUTION

Range.—Southern Arizona, south to central Mexico; accidental in the lower Rio Grande Valley of Texas.

The range of the coppery-tailed trogon extends **north** casually to Arizona (possibly Santa Catalina Mountains, Huachuca Mountains, and possibly Tombstone); northern Chihuahua (San Luis Mountains and the Sierra de la Campana); Nuevo Leon (Monterey and Montemorelos); and central Tamaulipas (Ciudad Victoria and Soto la Marina). **East** to Tamaulipas (Soto la Marina, Xicotencatl, Altamira, and Tampico); central Veracruz (Orizaba); and central Oaxaca (Talca and Juchatengo). **South** to Oaxaca (Juchatengo); Oaxaca (Omilteme and Amula); Michoacan (Tancitaro); and Jalisco (Zapotlan). **West** to Jalisco (Zapotlan, Ameca, and San Marcos); Nayarit (Mazatlan, Tres Marias Islands, and Mexcatitlan); Sinaloa (Escuinapa, El Limon, Angostura, and San Javier); eastern Sonora (Alamos, Chinobampo, and Guiracoba); and southeastern Arizona (Huachuca Mountains and possibly the Santa Catalina Mountains).

Casual records.—Although this bird can only be considered as rare anywhere in the United States, it appears to be fairly regular in the Huachuca Mountains, Ariz. During the summer of 1877 a trogon was killed near Ringgold Barracks and another at Las Cuevas, Tex. Although not preserved they were fully described, by the persons who shot them, to Dr. James C. Merrill, and were undoubtedly this species.

Egg dates.—Mexico: 23 records, March 29 to June 30; 12 records, April 15 to May 13, indicating the height of the season.

Order CORACIIFORMES

Family ALCEDINIDAE: Kingfishers

MEGACERYLE ALCYON ALCYON (Linnaeus)

EASTERN BELTED KINGFISHER

PLATES 12–14

HABITS

Our North American representative of the large and interesting kingfisher family is not so gaudily colored as some of the foreign species and is intermediate in size between the largest and the smallest members of the family, but it is an interesting bird, striking in appearance and voice, and unique in form. Its long, heavy bill and its large head with its prominent crest, contrasting with its diminutive feet and its short tail, seem entirely out of balance and give it a top-heavy appearance. But its peculiar proportions and structure are beautifully adapted for the life it leads; its large beak and head form an effective spearhead for use in its deep plunges, and they are well built to stand the shocks of frequent diving. Unlike the osprey, it does not need to use its feet in fishing; but the short legs and shovellike feet are most useful in shoveling the loose soil from its nesting burrows, after it has been loosened by the powerful beak.

The belted kingfisher, as a species, covers nearly all the North American Continent, breeding from northern Alaska and central Labrador southward to the southern border of the United States. Being essentially a fish-eating bird, its haunts are naturally near large or small bodies of water. It is common on the seacoast and estuaries, where it may be seen perched on some stake or pier, watching for its prey; or along the shore of a lake or pond, its favorite outlook may be the branch of a tree overhanging the water; I believe that it prefers to perch on a dead or leafless branch, where its view is unobstructed. Trout brooks, especially swift and rocky mountain streams, are favorite resorts, where its loud, rattling cry is often heard, as it flies up and down, patrolling its chosen fishing ground and driving away any intruders of its own species; it prefers to play the role of the lone fisherman.

Courtship.—Very little seems to be known about the kingfisher's courtship. Laurence B. Potter says in his notes: "Sometimes I have watched as many as five or six high up in the air, tumbling and wheeling about, uttering their harsh rattle; they appear to be doing it merely for the joy of flying, or it may be their courtship antics." Francis H. Allen writes to me: "From courting birds—a group of them—I have heard a mewing note uttered in rapid succession, almost if not quite as loud as the familiar rattle of the species. These same birds—or two of them at least—also kept up a continual, prolonged rattle."

Nesting.—The nest of the belted kingfisher is almost invariably in a burrow in a sandy, clay, or gravelly bank, excavated by the birds themselves. The site chosen is preferably near water and as near the favorite fishing grounds of the birds as a suitable bank can be found. But such banks are not always to be found in the most convenient places, so the birds are forced to nest in any bank they can find, often at a long distance from any water, such as the embankment of a railroad cut, the cliff of a sand dune, or a bank by a roadside where sand or gravel has been taken out for grading. On Cape Cod, the sandpits made while sanding cranberry bogs are favorite sites. The burrow may be at any height from the base of the cliff, depending on the height of the cliff, but it is usually not more than 2 or 3 feet from the top, though Major Bendire (1895) says that it is sometimes as much as 20 feet below the top of the cliff. The burrow extends inward, sloping slightly upward, for varying distances, usually from 3 to 6 feet, but sometimes as much as 10 or even 15 feet; as kingfishers sometimes use the same burrow for several years in succession, it may be that the deepest burrows are the oldest and have been extended from year to year to provide a fresh, clean nest. The burrow is usually straight, or nearly so, but often it curves somewhat, or makes a more or less abrupt turn to the right or left. One that I dug out ran straight in for 3 feet, made an abrupt turn to the left, and then made a reverse curve, so that the nest was only about 2 feet from the face of the cliff. The entrance and the tunnel itself are not quite circular, being usually about 3½ to 4 inches wide and 3 to 3½ inches high; an occupied burrow can generally be recognized by the footmarks of the bird, a central ridge with a furrow on each side of it, made by the bird as it enters or leaves the nest. The nest is placed in an enlarged chamber, which may be directly at the end of the tunnel, or a little to one side of it, and usually a little above the level of the tunnel. The chamber varies considerably in size and shape but is approximately circular and dome-shaped; it is usually 10 to 12 inches in diameter and 6 to 7 inches in height. Often the eggs are laid on the bare sand or gravel which probably indicates that the nest is a new one, or that the eggs are fresh; oftener, perhaps, the nesting chamber is lined with bits of clean, white fish bones, fish scales, or fragments of the shells of crustaceans; these, I believe, are the remains of ejected pellets and indicate that the nest has been previously occupied by young birds or that the female has been fed on the nest for some time;

there is no evidence to indicate that the birds ever bring in such material intentionally.

Bendire (1895) writes:

The time required to dig out a burrow depends largely on the nature of the soil to be removed, taking sometimes two or three weeks, but generally much less. I have personally seen an instance where a pair of these birds excavated a new burrow in a rather friable clay bank near Fort Lapwai, Idaho, to a depth of 5 feet (estimated measurement) in a little over three days. How they managed to dig so rapidly, considering their short and weak-looking feet, with which they must remove the greater part of the material, has always been a mystery to me, and I would not believe them capable of accomplishing such an amount of work had I not seen it done. When not disturbed the same nesting site is resorted to from year to year. Sometimes the male burrows an additional hole near the occupied nesting site, usually not over 3 feet deep, to which it retires to feed and to pass the night.

Dr. Thomas S. Roberts (1932) published the following account on the authority of Miss Frances Densmore, of Red Wing, Minn.:

On April 25, 1928, I found a pair of Kingfishers digging their tunnel at the top of a high cut about a foot below the surface, just where the black loam met the under sand, some one hundred feet, or thereabouts, above the water. They both dug, taking turn and turn about, except when she thought he hadn't stayed in long enough and sent him back. After watching them for an hour or more I formed a theory as to how they managed it. One would go in and work for two or three minutes and then push the dirt ahead of it to the entrance and fly out over it. No dirt ever came out with the bird that had been digging, but when the other went in there was a veritable fountain spurting out for nearly a minute after it entered. Then this subsided and more digging was done by the bird that had cleared the hole. They kept very close to their schedule of two or three minutes each. On this day the dirt they brought out was sand, but on the 27th it was black loam from above, and I decided that they had got back to their "sitting room." On May 1 they weren't working and, as both were in and out at the same time, I judged that there was room to turn and that they would call it done.

Dr. A. K. Fisher wrote to Major Bendire (1895) as follows:

On June 6, 1882, the writer found two nests of the Kingfisher in the side of a railroad cut near Croton Lake, Westchester County, New York. The burrows were placed in a bank not over 7 feet above the roadbed and within 18 inches of the top. That of the first one ran in about 7 feet and turned to the right as it entered the nesting chamber. The seven fresh eggs were placed in a nest of coarse grass, which, although rather scanty, covered the floor of the cavity on all sides. The burrow of the second one extended in about 4½ feet, and, like the other previously mentioned, turned toward the right as the expanded nesting cavity was reached. The nest, which was quite elaborate, was composed wholly of fish scales and bones, arranged in a compact, saucer-shaped mass. The writer made a tunnel from the top of the bank so as to intercept the burrow as it entered the nesting cavity. Viewed through this hole, the nest was a beautiful affair. The scales, which looked as if made of frosted silver, formed a delicate setting for the six pure-white eggs lying in the center, and by the projected light made a most effective picture. On two occasions, near Sing Sing, New York, the writer found the Kingfisher and

Rough-winged Swallow using burrows having a common entrance. It is probable in each case that the swallow had commenced its diverging burrow after the larger bird completed its work.

A few cases have been recorded of the kingfisher nesting in other cavities, where suitable sandbanks were not available. Mr. Forbush (1927) says: "Mr. Herbert F. Moulton of Ware, Massachusetts, tells me that he found a kingfisher's nest in a plowed field on a hillside. The entrance was made in a 'dead furrow.'" Arthur H. Howell (1932) says: "Baynard (1913) writes that in Alachua County [Florida] the Kingfisher nests early in April in holes in dead trees or stubs over water. He states, also (verbally), that he once found a nest at Clearwater, 4 feet above water in a leaning stub, the entrance hole being on the under side; this nest contained 4 eggs on May 6."

Beyer, Allison, and Kopman (1908), referring to Louisiana, say:

The character of the nest varies greatly with different conditions of soil: On the coast it is content with such elevations as can be found on the shores, and the burrow is sometimes scarcely more than a pocket in the clayey banks; in the upper districts, the site is often far from water, and the soft, coarse-grained soil renders easy the excavation of a burrow five or six feet deep, enlarged at the end, and often partly lined with leaves and pine straw; and finally, a unique condition exists in the extensive gum-swamps in the lake region of the southeast, where the land—always submerged—is perfectly flat, and nothing stands above water except innumerable trees and stumps of Nyssa; the nest is placed in the top of a decaying stump, with no attempt at excavation.

But tree-nesting is not wholly confined to the southern swamps, for Dr. George M. Sutton (1928) writes:

On May 27th, 1927, while observing Chimney Swifts at Bethany, Brooke County, West Virginia, I saw a Kingfisher fly rapidly across an open field from a near-by deep pool in Buffalo Creek. Wondering that it should thus cross overland, I watched it as it flew to a large, dead sycamore, not far from me, and disappeared in a hole at the end of a short, thick, horizontal stub. Upon going to the tree I heard the buzzing cries of the young birds. Shortly thereafter the male parent flew away as the female came in. The nest was located about ten feet from the ground in a large cavity near the juncture of the bough and the main trunk. The young birds were lying about seven feet from the entrance. The cavity was almost as dark as a bank burrow would have been. It is odd that the Kingfishers chose such a site for their nest, since earthen banks admirably suited to their needs were available along the creek.

Eggs.—The number of eggs laid by the eastern belted kingfisher varies ordinarily from five to eight, the commonest numbers being 6 and 7; on rare occasions as many as 11 or 14 eggs or young have been found in a nest. If the first set of eggs is taken, the birds will dig another burrow, often within a few feet of the first, and lay a second set; sometimes a third, or even a fourth, attempt will be made. But only one brood is raised in a season. The eggs are short-ovate or rounded-ovate in shape; the shell is smooth and rather glossy; they are pure white in color. The measurements of 54 eggs average 33.9 by 26.7 millimeters, the eggs showing the four extremes measure 36.8 by 27.9, 30.8 by 26.4, and 33 by 25.4 millimeters.

Young.—The incubation period is said to be about 23 or 24 days. Bendire (1895) says:

> The male does not assist in incubation, but supplies his mate with food while so engaged, and she rarely leaves the nest after the first egg has been laid; at any rate I have invariably found the bird at home if there were any eggs in the nest. Incubation lasts about sixteen days. The young when first hatched are blind, perfectly naked, helpless, and, in a word, very unprepossessing. They scarcely look like birds while crawling about in the nest, where they remain several weeks, their growth being very slow. The excrement of the young is promptly removed and the burrow is kept rather clean. They utter a low, puffing sound when disturbed, and frequently vary considerably in size, as if incubation, in some instances at least, began with the first egg laid. The young, even after they have left the nest for some time, require the attendance of their parents before they are able to secure subsistence for themselves.

I believe that Bendire's statement above, that the male does not incubate, is incorrect; perhaps he may not do so regularly, or to the same extent that the female does, but several observers have reported finding the male on the eggs, or at least in the nest. The young remain in the nest for about 4 weeks or more, and do not leave it until they are able to fly.

William L. Bailey (1900) made an interesting study of a family of young kingfishers, by digging a hole in the rear of the nesting cavity on four different occasions, taking photographs of the young at four different ages, and filling up the hole each time, so as not to disturb the birds too much. He says that when the young were about two days old they "were not only found wrapped together in the nest, but the moment they were put on the ground, one at a time, though their eyes were still sealed, they immediately covered one another with their wings and wide bills, making such a tight ball that when one shifted a leg, the whole mass would move like a single bird. This is a most sensible method of keeping warm, since the mother bird's legs are so short that she could not stand over them, but as they are protected from the wind and weather they have no need of her. Their appearance is comical in the extreme, and all out of proportion. This clinging to one another is apparently kept up for at least ten days, for a week later, when nine days old, they were found in exactly a similar position."

On his last visit, when the young birds were 23 days old, he made an interesting discovery, of which he says: "Taking the precaution to stop the hole with a good-sized stone, I proceeded to my digging for the last time on the top of the bank. This time I found the chamber had been moved, and I had some difficulty in locating it about a foot higher up and about the same distance to one side. The old birds had evidently discovered my imperfectly closed back door, and either mistrusted its security, or else a heavy rain had soaked down into the loosened earth and caused them to make alterations. They had completely closed up the old chamber and packed it tightly with earth and disgorged fish bones."

Mrs. Florence M. Bailey (1928) makes the following apt quotation from the writings of Professor Herrick:

From the time of birth the young lie huddled in a cluster in their dark underground chamber . . . As they grow in size and strength the monotony of sitting still, often with legs and wings interlocked, must become very great, and . . . they soon begin to bite and tease one another like young puppies. Should one be hard pressed, the only way of escape lies along the narrow passage, which they naturally traverse head first; but the instinct to return to the warm family cluster is strong, and to do this they are obliged to walk backwards. Again when the rattle of the *alma mater* announcing the capture of another fish is heard, each struggles to get down the narrow passage-way first, but when the parent enters the hole she hustles them all back.

The young are fed by their two parents while they remain in the nest, and for some time afterward while they are learning to fish for themselves. Mrs. Irene G. Wheelock (1905) made the following observations:

By care in concealment we were able to discover that the adult came to the nest on the first day with no visible supply of food in the bill but with a gullet conspicuously swollen. We had previously excavated the nest from the rear making a false back to it so that it would be protected from the weather and at the same time open easily. As soon as feeding was completed and the adult out of sight, we opened the nest at the false back, took out the young, then one day old, and examined the crops. They contained a dark gray, oily mass, nearly fluid and very ill smelling, but with no bones or scales in it. If fish they were very small and digested. Returning the young fishers to the tunnel, we closed it. Two days later the experiment was repeated with the same results. Four days later, or the seventh day after hatching, we examined again. This time one of the nestlings had swallowed several small fish about one and one half inches long and the others were still hungry. As yet we had not seen either of the adults bring visible food and the most frequent feedings had been forty minutes apart, I believe all by regurgitation. No record was kept from the seventh to the fourteenth day when an examination was made for the third time. We now found the young showing well developed pin feathers, and there were traces of disgorged fish bones and scales in the nest which had not been there before. The crops examined showed fish only slightly digested and regurgitative feeding had evidently given place wholly or in part to fresh food. On this day one of the adults brought several fish, possibly four inches long to the nest in different journeys. Examinations made on the twenty-first day revealed the same food conditions as the fourteenth. The pile of fish bones and scales was a trifle larger but was partially buried in the earth. There was surprisingly little of this debris in the nest or tunnel but the ground seemed to be saturated with fishy oil. On the twenty-eighth day the young kingfishers resented being examined or photographed, and made good their escape when taken from the nest.

Henry R. Carey (1909) writes:

The food brought to the nest-hole consists of various kinds of small fish. It not infrequently happens that one of these fish is too large to be carried by the parent bird into the narrow passage; it is then dropped upon the sand and is allowed to rot. * * * I once found a common salt-water flounder, four and one-half inches long and proportionately wide, which, being rather unwieldy for the parent bird to handle, had been left in this way. Another time I found a young Sculpin (*Callionymus aeneus*) in the same condition, and, yet again, a live minnow, which, in spite of a great patch on its side devoid of scales, was finally freed in perfect health. * * *

The young birds leave the earth about July 25 [in New Hampshire]. They are a sombre-looking lot, as for several days they sit tamely about the wharfs or venture on short, erratic flights, which makes one feel that they have not yet got used to the light after their long imprisonment underground. It is at this time that both parents and young, somewhat crowded in the vicinity of the home nest by their sudden increase in population, begin to seek out new fishing-stubs, or to use old ones for the first time in the year. When the young are able to care for themselves, the old birds leave them and lead once more the single life which they seem to enjoy most.

At this time of year, frequent quarrels occur among them, mostly about the best fishing spots, and now that strange, whining note, which Herrick describes as resembling the grating of two tree boughs in the wind, is often heard. It appears to be a note of anger; I have heard it when one bird, wanting the perch of another, hovered menacingly over him. Once I saw two birds dive simultaneously for the same spot in the water, the same note escaping them as each reluctantly swerved aside.

Floyd Bralliar (1922) writes interestingly of how the young learn to catch their own fish:

The young birds did not remain in the neighborhood of the nest more than a few days, but those few days were busy ones, for in that brief time the mother was teaching her children how to earn a living. She would perch by their side on an overhanging limb and patiently wait for the glimmer of a fish below. The first day or two she usually caught the fish, beat it into partial insensibility and then dropped it again into the water. The young were persistent in their plea for food, but the mother was as insistent that they catch their living if they got any. There was very little current where they hunted, and a fish did not float out of sight quickly. The young birds would crane their necks and look hungrily at the fish below until finally one more hungry or more bold than the rest would make a dive for it. At first the aim was not good, and the bird would miss even a dead fish more often than he succeeded in catching it. Usually, however, he fluttered about the surface of the water until he got his fish, even tho he had missed it when he made his plunge. * * * During the first few days when the young birds became too hungry, the mother would occasionally relent and feed them, but before the week was over, no matter how hungry they became, no food was coming until they caught it. Within ten days the young birds were catching live fish instead of half dead ones.

Then a young bird would catch his fish, carry it to his perch, whack it over the limb a few times, toss it in the air, catch it by the head as it came down and swallow it with as much skill as his mother. As soon as she was convinced of the skill of each of her brood, she forsook them entirely. I do not know whether she ultimately drove them from the neighborhood or whether they left voluntarily, but when July was past only the old birds were to be seen in the neighborhood.

Henry Mousley (1938), who made a prolonged study of a family of belted kingfishers, estimated the period of incubation to be about 24 days. His report says, in conclusion:

On summing up I find forty-two hours were spent with the birds (May 11–July 24), during which time the young were fed one hundred times, or at an average rate of once in every 25.2 minutes. Of course there were periods when the feeding was much faster, as for instance, once in every 8, 9, 13, 20, and 21 minutes respectively. Sometimes the parents were absent from the nest for long periods of time, such as, 150, 120, 105, 97, 93, 90, 85, 75, 70, and 60 minutes at a time, when of course the young were without food. It was after these long spells that the more rapid feedings generally took place. As already remarked, the male seemed to pay the most attention to this part of the business, for I find of those times when I was perfectly sure of the sex of the parent, the male fed twenty-eight times to his partner's fourteen, or just double. It was the male parent which was the last seen at the nest previous to the departure of the one surviving young—a male. The food for the most part consisted of small fish, crawfish, minnows, tadpoles, and probably beetles.

Plumages.—The young kingfisher is hatched naked, blind, and helpless, a shapeless mass of reddish flesh, looking much like a very young puppy with a huge conical bill. Its eyes do not open for about two weeks. Within a week, or less, the pinfeathers or feather-sheaths appear, and soon the young bird bristles in all the feather tracts with quills like a young porcupine, which grow to varying lengths and show, before they burst, the pectoral band and the general color pattern of the adult. When the young bird is 17 or 18 days old, a remarkable change takes places within the short space of 24 hours, for the sheaths rapidly burst and the juvenal plumage blossoms out all over the body.

In this plumage the young bird looks strikingly like the adult with only minor differences, and the sexes are alike. Young birds of both sexes, when fully fledged, have the pectoral band more or less heavily tipped or mixed with cinnamon, rufous or dull brown; this usually consists of narrow edgings in young males, but in young females many feathers are half or more brown; the rufous band of the female adult is only partially shown in the young female, mainly on the flanks, and it shows to some extent in nearly all young males, some having nearly as much as young females; the crest is darker than in adults, there is more white in the wing coverts, the white tips of the secondaries are more extensive, and the central tail feathers are spotted, as in the adult female. This juvenal plumage is also a first winter plumage, for it is worn without much change until spring. Young birds have a first, prenuptial molt early in spring, which involves most of the body plumage, perhaps all of it, the tail, and apparently the wings also; this takes place between

February and April. Adults have a complete postnuptial molt in August, September, and October.

Mr. Brewster (1937a) made some observations on the roosting habits of kingfishers at Umbagog Lake, Maine, of which he says: "Every evening, a little after sunset, two or three Kingfishers resort to Pine Point to spend the night. They fly directly into the forest and go to roost among the densest foliage, often that of spruces and arbor vitaes, growing anywhere from four to ten rods back from the nearest shore." One that he watched "flew up into a tall, slender Paper Birch, and alighted near the end of a long branch, about thirty feet above the ground. * * * As darkness gathered, the bird settled lower and lower on the branch, and drew in its neck without, however, burying its head in its plumage, for I could still see its bill pointing outward over the breast. At 9 P. M. I went under the tree, and by the light of a lantern dimly made out the Kingfisher, crouching in the same attitude, in exactly the same place."

Food.—The kingfisher is a fish eater and an expert fisherman, well deserving its name. It evidently prefers fish to any other food and would probably live on fish exclusively, if it were always able to secure all it needed. It catches mainly small fish, preferably not over 6 inches long, and mostly those species that are of little use, or even harmful, economically as far as human interests are concerned. The kingfisher has been condemned by trout fisherman as a great destroyer of trout, but in a large measure unjustly. Kingfishers undoubtedly visit trout hatcheries frequently and can easily catch plenty of trout in the open pools, where the trout have no place to hide and where they are congregated in large numbers; they can do considerable damage in such places, but the trout can be easily protected by placing wire screens over the pools. In the trout streams wild trout are not so easily caught, for, as every trout fisherman knows, the trout are seldom seen in the open places except when darting swiftly across them, but spend their time hiding under overhanging banks, or under logs or stones, and only dashing out occasionally to capture their prey. On the other hand, chubs, dace, suckers, and sometimes sculpins are very common in most trout streams, generally in larger numbers than the trout; they frequent the open spaces, are much slower in their movements than the swiftly moving trout, and consequently are more easily caught. The records show that these neutral or harmful fishes make up the greater part, or nearly all, of the kingfisher's catch in trout streams. Chub and sculpins are very destructive to small trout fry; and suckers eat quantities of trout spawn; consequently the kingfishers are really doing the trout fisherman a favor by reducing the numbers of these fishes in the streams and should be protected rather than persecuted.

The kingfisher must of necessity do its fishing in clear water, so is seldom seen on muddy streams or ponds, or on those that are choked or overgrown with thick vegetation, such as is often found along trout streams. It usually perches on some stake, snag, or pier standing in the water, or on some bare overhanging branch, where it can watch patiently for some passing fish. Favorite perches of this sort in good fishing spots are resorted to regularly and rival kingfishers are driven away, for the kingfisher is a solitary bird except during the nesting season or while training its young. From such a perch the bird may dive obliquely into the water to seize the fish in its powerful bill; or, rising 30 or 40 feet into the air and scanning the water below it in more active pursuit of its prey, it may stop and hover for a few seconds, with rapidly vibrating wings, and then make a straight or spiral dive directly downward, disappearing beneath the water sometimes for several seconds. It is not always successful in its plunges, as the fish may move and cause a sudden change of direction in the bird's rapid dive either above or below the surface; but it is not easily discouraged and is always ready to try again. Having secured the fish, it flies with it to some favorite perch, where it beats the fish into insensibility, tosses it into the air, or otherwise adjusts it, so that it can swallow it head first and thus avoid any injury to its throat from the sharp spiny fins. Sometimes the fish is too large to be swallowed completely, in which case the tail must be left protruding from the mouth until the rapid process of digestion enables the bird to gradually work it down. Manly Hardy wrote to Major Bendire (1895) of such a case, and says: "I shot a Kingfisher last spring that had swallowed a pickerel considerably longer than the bird from the end of the bill to the tip of the tail, and the tail of the fish protruding from the throat, while the head was partly doubled back, causing a large protuberance near the vent."

Where fish are not readily obtainable, especially in the arid regions of the Southwest where the streams largely disappear during the dry season, the kingfisher seems able to make a good living on various other kinds of food. The list includes crabs, crayfishes, mussels, lizards, frogs, toads, small snakes, turtles, grasshoppers, locusts, crickets, salamanders, newts, butterflies, moths, beetles and other insects, young birds, mice, and even berries. On the seacoast, it has been known to feed on clams and oysters, which sometimes results disastrously for the bird. H. C. Hopkins (1892) reports finding a kingfisher with "its bill held fast between the shells of an oyster." The bird had evidently inserted its bill into the open shell of the oyster, which had closed upon it; "the tongue [was] quite black from non-circulation of the blood, which showed that it must have been held prisoner for some time." The bird would probably have drowned at the next high tide. Dr. B. H. Warren (1890) reports that a friend of his once caught one of these birds on a hook and line while fishing with a live minnow for bait. He also says: "One day B. M. Everhart found a kingfisher lying on the bank of a small stream. On making an investigation, Mr. Everhart ascertained that the bird was unable to fly, as its bill was tightly clasped in the grasp of a large fresh-water mussel. I have heard of several instances where kingfishers have been captured under similar circumstances, which could naturally lead one to suppose that they feed to a limited degree on the flesh of these bivalves."

In the Bermudas, kingfishers are said to feed on squids. Walter B. Barrows (1912) quotes Professor Aughey, of Nebraska, as follows: "One that was sent to me to identify in September, 1874, had 18 locusts, in addition to portions of some fish, in its stomach. One that I opened in September, 1876, had mingled at least 14 locusts with its fish diet." Bendire (1895) caught a kingfisher in a trap baited with a mouse, and believed "that not a few mice, and possibly small birds also, are caught by them during their nocturnal rambles, and they are certainly fully as active throughout the night as in the daytime."

Kingfishers disgorge as pellets the indigestible portions of their food, such as fish bones and scales, the shells of crutaceans and the seeds of berries; the bones and scales found in the nests are the remains of such pellets. Henry R. Carey (1909) writes:

Only once have I seen a pellet of fishbones and scales being disgorged from the bird's beak, as he sat on his hunting perch. These pellets are found wherever the birds are accustomed to sit for any length of time. I once found one completely composed of various parts of the shell of a small crab. Only a few days later I had the pleasure of seeing a crab actually caught. The bird captured him by diving in the usual way and took him to a low rock where he proceeded to bang him just as he would have done to a minnow. During this process the crab, which measured an inch and a half sideways across the shell, lost several legs and was dropped upon the rock, from which by a considerable effort he managed to fall by scrambling to the edge with his remaining legs. The bird, perhaps seeing that he was rather a large morsel to swallow whole, then forgot him completely and went on with his fishing.

Ora W. Knight (1908) has seen kingfishers chase and capture moths and butterflies, taking them on the wing. Dr. Thomas S. Roberts (1932) says that they have been known to eat young sparrows; also that "crawfish are pounded and crushed before swallowing, and fish that are too large may be divided into pieces by the powerful bill. Miss Densmore, of Red Wing, once saw a Kingfisher that was making unsuccessful attempts to handle a small turtle. This was thoroughly pounded and variously manipulated but had to be discarded in the end."

Dr. Charles W. Townsend (1918) writes: "Early in August, 1917, Mr. John Hair, gamekeeper of Mr. R. T. Crane at Ipswich, missed six of a four days old brood of Bob-whites. He had seen a King-fisher nearby and later the same day saw it perched on the gable end of the little house where the Bob-whites had been hatched, and from there pounce on the young birds as they ran in and out. He shot the Kingfisher, and, on opening the bird, a female, found the legs and feathers of the young Bob-whites in its crop."

When hard pressed for animal food the kingfisher has been known to eat wild cherries and probably other wild fruits. Dr. Elliott Coues (1878) published the following note from Mrs. Mary Treat about a kingfisher that fished regularly from a private wharf in front of her house in Florida: "When the water is so rough that it is difficult for him to procure fish, instead of seeking some seques-tered pool he remains at his usual post, occasionally making an ineffectual effort to secure his customary prey, until, nearly starved, he resorts to a sour-gum tree (*Nyssa aquatica*, L.) in the vicinity, and greedily devours the berries. Returning to his post, he soon ejects a pellet of the large seeds and skins of the fruit."

Behavior.—The belted kingfisher is a striking and picturesque feature in the landscape whether in action or at rest. The mountain trout stream would lose much of its charm without the rattling call of the lone fisherman and the flash of his broad, blue wings, as he follows the course of the stream, flying well below the treetops until he glides upward to alight on his accustomed perch, there to tilt his short tail nervously up and down and raise and lower his long crest a few times, as he sounds his battle cry again. At the seashore, too, his trim, unique figure and his conspicuous color pattern, as he perches day after day on his favorite stake or goes rattling along the shore, add color and a tinge of wildness to the scene.

The flight of the kingfisher is strong, swift, and graceful, usually low, but high above the treetops when traveling; often there are five or six rapid strokes followed by a long glide on half-closed wings. Mr. Carey (1909) writes of it:

The Kingfisher's flight is remarkable for its beauty. How easily those long wings carry him about, as he skims so close over the water that their tips are sometimes wetted, or, as he hovers, his body appearing absolutely motionless, in that wonderful way which few birds can equal, for indefinite periods of time. Sometimes, especially in water half a foot or less in depth, he dives while flying nearly parallel to its surface. Sometimes, in his journeys from perch to perch when fish are plentiful, he dips again and again into the water in this way, reminding one of the Swallow as he gracefully touches the water here and there in his flight over the mill-pond. Again, he drops like a falling stone in a nearly perpendicular line upon his fishy prey.

Again he writes, referring to times of keen competition over good fishing grounds:

On such occasions one bird is often angrily pursued by another. These pursuits are most reckless and enduring in character. One sees the two birds swirl by like two blue flashes of light, to disappear in an instant of time on perfectly controlled wings perhaps far away in the pine woods, almost grazing the tough trunk of some mighty tree, or heading straight for a sheer cliff and rising fifteen feet or more to clear it when it seems that they must be dashed to pieces on the rock. I once saw a Kingfisher, hard-pressed in such a pursuit, adopt a clever means of escape. His pursuer was close upon him—about five feet behind. On they came down the creek, neither bird seeming to gain upon the other. Both were flying at top speed low over the water. Suddenly there was a splash, and the foremost Kingfisher disappeared under the water. The bird behind swept on and lit on a nearby stub, not attempting to renew the chase when his enemy reappeared.

The above was probably a case of one bird defending its territory against the invasion of it by another kingfisher. Frederick C. Lincoln (1924) saw a striking example of this during his field work in the marshes of the Illinois River; he says: "During the period of greatest abundance, practically every channel had its quota of birds, each of which appeared to patrol or to hold dominion over a certain well-defined section." As many as 8 or 10 birds were encountered, each always confined to its own limited section. One of the boatmen told him that "he took much pleasure in informing club members and others who might be with him in the club launch, just how far the kingfisher then in sight would go and where the next one would be met."

William Brewster (1937a) watched a kingfisher at Lake Umbagog that "plunged into the water, striking a fish so large, that he had to let it go after a brief struggle, during which he failed to bring it to the surface, although evidently trying his best to do so."

Voice.—There is not much beauty in the voice of the kingfisher, but the loud rattling call always produces a thrill in the listener; it is a wild, weird, wilderness call that enlivens the solitudes and punctuates the stillness of lonely shores or forest streams; it seems to fit in well with the active vigor of this aggressive guardian of his domain, as a warning to his rivals. It consists of a series of harsh, wooden, rattling notes of great carrying power. It has been likened to the sound made by an old-fashioned policeman's or watchman's rattle, a very good description for those of us who are old enough to remember such out-of-date sounds; but it may remind the younger generation of the sound made by certain noise-making instruments used at get-together dinners, political rallies, or other joyous gatherings.

It is not easily expressed in syllables, but Mr. Bralliar (1922) has written it fairly well as *rickety, crick, crick, crick.* The call varies some under different circumstances, sometimes being quite soft and low, as if in a conversational tone with its mate. The courtship note, referred to above by Mr. Allen, was "a mewing note uttered in rapid succession, almost if not quite as loud as the familiar rattle." Then there is the whining note, referred to by Mr. Carey above, "resembling the grating of two tree boughs in the wind," which seems to be a note of anger while quarreling over fishing rights. Brewster (1937a) says that "on such occasions they often utter a harsh *cah–car–car–car*, quite unlike the usual volley of watchman's rattle-like notes."

Field marks.—The kingfisher could hardly be mistaken for anything else. Its shape is distinctive, its large head and crest and its long, heavy bill are all out of proportion to its small body, short tail, and tiny feet. As it flies its great blue wings, its white collar, and its banded breast are unique. Its loud, rattling note proclaims it beyond doubt.

Enemies.—The most serious enemies of the kingfisher are the selfish fisherman, who wants all the fish for himself and begrudges the poor bird an honest living, and the proprietor of a trout hatchery, who is unwilling to go to the trouble and expense of screening his pools to protect his fish. The former shoots every kingfisher he can with misguided satisfaction; the latter either shoots or traps any that visit his pools. A small, unbaited, steel trap is set and fastened to the top of a stake or post near the bird's favorite fishing pool; if the trap is so set that the pan is at the highest point, the bird is almost sure to alight on it and is caught. Hundreds of kingfishers are caught and killed in this way along private trout streams, or about trout hatcheries, every year.

The natural enemies of the kingfisher are of no great menace to its welfare. The Cooper's and the sharp-shinned hawks often pursue it, perhaps largely for sport; under the accounts of these two hawks, in a previous volume, will be found references to these attacks and the successful attempts of the kingfisher to escape by diving; it even seems as if the kingfisher enjoyed the sport, judged by its derisive "laughter" at the defeat of the hawk.

The remains of a kingfisher have been found in the stomach of a red-tailed hawk; the former must have been caught unaware, for the hawk is no match for it in flight. The kingbird sometimes makes life miserable for the kingfisher; Fred T. Jencks (1881) writes:

The Kingfisher had poised himself several times to look for fish, and was just moving to do so again as the Kingbird approached and attacked him. The Kingfisher is not a troublesome bird, and always minds his own business. He was entirely unprepared, and acted as though he could not believe that the other had any evil intentions, for he tried to poise again. The second attack seemed to undeceive him, and show him his enemy was in earnest. He vaulted and turned, vainly endeavoring to rid himself of his persecutor. He soon saw he could not save himself by flight and tried diving. As soon, however, as he appeared at the surface he attempted to fly, but the Kingbird, keeping up an incessant twittering, forced him to dive again. Two or three times this was repeated, both birds making considerable noise, until the Kingfisher seemed convinced that escape in that direction was impossible, so he sat like a duck upon the surface, and as his persecutor would swoop at him he would go under. This lasted for some little time, until even the Kingbird seemed wearied and flew away.

Snakes and perhaps skunks or minks may crawl into the nesting holes, while the parent birds are away, and destroy the eggs or young; but it would seem that the formidable beak of the kingfisher, if at home, would prove to be an effective weapon of defense. H. H. Bailey (1907) says: "While digging out some Kingfishers' nests this season I was surprised to find a dead bird in about every fourth or fifth hole. This I was at loss to account for, as the birds showed no signs of combat or disease, while the plumage was not even disarranged. The bodies, though, seemed to be dried up, with no signs of blood in them, so I presumed that something had crawled into the holes and sucked the blood from them, leaving the carcass intact. This surmise proved correct, as the last hole I dug out contained a large black snake, and a dead kingfisher still warm."

I quote the above for what it is worth, but cannot agree with Mr. Bailey's conclusion. I have never heard that the black snake is a blood-sucker and doubt if it would attack a bird as big as a kingfisher. If such well-known blood-suckers as minks or weasels had attacked the bird, there would have been evidences of a struggle. I believe that the snake was looking for eggs. The kingfishers may have died from an epidemic of roundworms or ringworms, which have often proved fatal to these birds.

Frederic H. Kennard told me that while he was fishing on Grand Lake, Maine, he and his daughter heard a splash behind them and their guide saw a kingfisher dive, disappear beneath the surface and not come up. Although they all watched for some time, the bird never appeared. They paddled over to the place where the kingfisher dived but could see no trace of the bird in the water or in the air. They suspected that some of the large fish, pickerel, salmon, or togue, that abound in that lake, may have caught the kingfisher.

Arthur W. Brockway tells me of a nest that was dug into by a skunk and the young devoured, the excavation being made from above the nest.

Winter.—The belted kingfisher is a hardy bird, and remains as far north in fall and winter as it can find open water in which to catch a fair supply of fish. A few kingfishers remain all winter, especially during mild winters, in southern New England, frequenting to some extent the open inland streams, but more regularly along the southern coast from Cape Cod to Long Island Sound.

There, Mr. Forbush (1927) says, "they go into winter quarters in December, especially about river mouths where at that time the little frost-fish come in, and there they remain, unless extreme cold locks rivers and shores in ice."

They are occasionally seen in winter in the northern tier of States. Dr. L. H. Walkinshaw writes to me from Battle Creek, Mich.: "Along open stretches of water, a few kingfishers can be found during the entire winter. I have several dates for southern Michigan for December, January and February. I have watched them on zero, or near zero, days dive from some dead branch after minnows in the open stream."

Mr. Skinner says in his notes from Yellowstone Park: "Ordinarily this is a migratory bird, but here a few remain all winter along the streams kept open by hot water. During cold winds and storms, they are often seen in the most protected places, but with feathers all fluffed out. The winter birds noticed have been males, the females not appearing until March 17. In winter, I believe they roost in the tops of the thick cedars in the Gardiner Canyon, but I have no data about the other localities."

Most of the kingfishers migrate to the more southern States during the late fall, where they find open water and plenty of fish. There they establish regular fishing stations and live their solitary lives, each in its own territory. We often saw one in Florida perched day after day in practically the same spot, presumably the same bird in each case.

DISTRIBUTION

Range.—North America south to northern South America; accidental in the Azores, Ireland, and the Netherlands.

Breeding range.—The breeding range of the belted kingfisher extends **north** to central Alaska (Kowak River, Fairbanks, and probably Fort Yukon); Mackenzie (Fort McPherson, Fort Wrigley, Fort Providence, and Fort Smith); central Saskatchewan (Knee Lake and Pelican Lake); central Manitoba (Oxford Lake); Ontario (Rossport and North Abitibi River); Quebec (Lake Mistassini, Godbout, and Romaine River); and east-central Labrador (Grand Falls). From this northeastern station the range extends southward through Newfoundland and along the coasts of Nova Scotia and the Eastern United States to central Florida (Micanopy and Clearwater). **South** to Florida (Clearwater, probably St. Marks, and Chipley); southern Louisiana (Bird Island and Bayou Sara); Texas (Giddings, Corpus Christi, Kerrville, and Pecos); southern New Mexico (Carlsbad and Chloride); and southern California (Escondido). The western limits extend northward through California, Oregon, Washington, and

British Columbia (sometimes along the coast) to Alaska (Sitka, Hope, Mount McKinley, and Kowak River).

There are a few records north and west of the range as outlined that may possibly represent occasional nesting. One was seen August 5 and 6, 1915, at a point 100 miles above Bethel, Alaska, and another was seen on July 6, 1917, at Iditerod. MacFarlane (1891) reported seeing several birds in the Fort Anderson region of Mackenzie, but he states that no nests were found. An adult female was taken at Churchill, Manitoba, previous to 1845; one was seen at Fort Du Brochet on September 22, 1920, while the species also has been reported from York Factory.

Winter range.—In winter the species is found **north** with fair regularity to southeastern Alaska (Sitka and Wrangell); southeastern British Columbia (Okanagan Landing); Wyoming (Yellowstone Park and rarely Wheatland); rarely central Missouri (Marionville); rarely central Indiana (Crawfordsville and Richmond); Ohio (Canton); and southern New Jersey (Cape May). From this point the eastern boundary of the winter range extends **south** along the coast to southern Florida (Royal Palm Hammock and Key West); the Bahama Islands (Nassau); the Dominican Republic (Sanchez); Puerto Rico (Fortuna); the Lesser Antilles (Anguilla, Antigua, St. Lucia, Carriacou Island, and Los Testigos); and northeastern Venezuela (Cariaco). South to Venezuela (Cariaco, Guarico, and Apure); rarely northern Colombia (Santa Marta); Panama (Barro Colorado Island); and Costa Rica (San Jose). **West** to Costa Rica (San Jose and Rio Frio) and northward along the west coast of Nicaragua, Guatemala, Mexico, the United States, and British Columbia, to southeastern Alaska (Craig, Ketchikan, and Sitka). Occasionally kingfishers will be recorded in winter from points in the northern United States (Montana, Iowa, Wisconsin, Michigan, New York, Vermont, and Massachusetts), as well as from northern Ontario (London, Guelph, and Toronto). It also is a winter resident on Bermuda.

The range as outlined is for the entire species, of which two subspecies are currently recognized. The eastern belted kingfisher (*Megaceryle alcyon alcyon*) occupies all the range east of the Rocky Mountains and north to Quebec and Mackenzie; the western belted kingfisher (*M. a. caurina*) is found west of the Rocky Mountains and north to Alaska and Yukon.

Spring migration.—Early dates of spring arrival are: Pennsylvania—Renovo, February 22; Oil City, March 3; Beaver, March 22. New York—Ballston Spa, March 19; Rochester, March 21; Watertown, March 27. Connecticut—Hartford, March 16. Rhode Island—Providence, February 23. Massachusetts—Boston, March 19; Har-

vard, March 25. Vermont—St. Johnsbury, March 26; Rutland, April
4; Wells River, April 12. New Hampshire—Tilton, March 28.
Maine—Orono, April 6; Portland, April 7; Machias, April 18. New
Brunswick—Scotch Lake, April 22. Nova Scotia—Picton, April 6.
Prince Edward Island—Alberton, April 17. Quebec—Montreal,
April 21; Quebec City, April 24; Godbout, May 5. Missouri—
St. Louis, February 25; Kansas City, March 10; Concordia, March
17. Illinois—Chicago, March 11; Odin, March 13. Northern
Ohio—Oberlin, February 13. Michigan—Vicksburg, March 8; De-
troit, March 20; Sault Ste. Marie, April 11. Ontario—Toronto,
March 6; Ottawa, April 5. Iowa—Iowa City, March 7; Sioux
City, March 18. Wisconsin—La Crosse, March 11; Madison, March
16; Stevens Point, April 1. Minnesota—St. Cloud, March 23; Minneapolis, March 24. Kansas—Hays, February 7. Nebraska—Valentine, March 3. South Dakota—Vermillion, March 22; Dell Rapids,
March 23. North Dakota—Charlson, April 5. Manitoba—Margaret, April 1; Aweme, April 11; Reaburn, April 22. Saskatchewan—Indian Head, April 22; Eastend, April 23. Idaho—
Rathdrum, April 9. Montana—Bozeman, March 26; Great Falls,
April 13, Alberta—Banff, April 25; Stony Plain, May 12. Northwestern Alaska—Kowak River, May 21.

Fall migration.—Late dates of fall departure are: Alberta—Lac
la Biche, September 27; Banff, September 30; Camrose, October 24.
Montana—Great Falls, October 1; Big Sandy, October 9; Fortine,
October 31 (winters rarely). Saskatchewan—Indian Head, September 20; Eastend, October 5. Manitoba—Killarney, October 15;
Aweme, October 25. North Dakota—Rice Lake, October 2; Kindred,
October 22. South Dakota—Yankton, October 16; Sioux Falls, November 11. Nebraska—Valentine, October 24; Lincoln, October 30;
Red Cloud, November 10. Kansas (sometimes winters)—Hays, November 21; Wallace, November 24; Harper, November 30. Minnesota—Lanesboro, November 16 (sometimes winters); Minneapolis,
November 25. Wisconsin—Madison, November 12. Illinois—Rantoul, October 27; Chicago, November 20. Ontario—Toronto, November 3; Ottawa, November 26. Michigan, Sault Ste. Marie, October
16; Detroit, December 4. Quebec—Montreal, October 23. Prince
Edward Island—Alberton, October 10. New Brunswick—Scotch
Lake, November 5. Maine—Portland, October 13; Phillips, October
17. Vermont—St. Johnsbury, November 9; Wells River, November
23. Massachusetts—Boston, December 13. Rhode Island—Providence, December 2. Connecticut—Hartford, December 26. New
York—Watertown, October 31; Rochester, November 13. Northern
New Jersey—Elizabeth, December 15. Pennsylvania—Beaver, November 28; Renovo, November 30.

Further insight into the migratory flights of individual kingfishers is provided by banding records. One banded as a nestling at Noblesville, Ind., on June 21, 1924, was killed in the Naches River Valley, Tex., on November 19, 1924, while another, banded on June 30, 1937, at Waukesha, Wis., was retaken at Society Hill, S. C., on November 22, 1937.

Casual records.—At least a part of the reported occurrences of the belted kingfisher in the Old World are unsatisfactory. Two cases, wherein specimens were alleged to have been taken in Meath and Wicklow, Ireland, in the autumn of 1845 are now believed to be based upon fraud. A specimen is supposed to have been taken on the island of Flores in the Azores, but neither its disposition nor the details of collection are known. A male bird was taken, however, in Holland on December 17, 1899, and another was collected on Westmann Island, off the south coast of Iceland, in September 1901.

Egg dates.—California: 16 records, April 7 to June 24; 8 records, April 21 to May 17, indicating the height of the season.

Illinois: 5 records, May 10 to June 8.

Massachusetts: 8 records, May 11 to June 6.

New York: 27 records, April 10 to July 15; 14 records, May 10 to 29.

Ontario: 7 records, May 24 to June 28.

MEGACERYLE ALCYON CAURINA (Grinnell)

WESTERN BELTED KINGFISHER

PLATE 15

HABITS

It has long been known that the kingfishers of the Pacific coast are appreciably larger than eastern birds, but Dr. Joseph Grinnell (1910) was the first to give the western race a name. He characterizes it as "similar to the *Ceryle alcyon* of eastern and southern North America, but size throughout greater, especially measurements of flight-feathers," and goes on to say that "the secondary wing quills are *proportionally* longer in the northwestern birds. This means that in addition to its greater expanse of wing and generally larger size, the wing of *caurina* is *broader*. In the closed wing this difference presents itself conspicuously in the interval between the end of the longest secondary and the tip of the longest primary. In the northwestern birds this interval averages only 27.3 mm., while in the eastern birds it averages 33.7 mm. This is in spite of the larger size of the former. The ratio to total wing length in the two cases is 17 and 22 per cent., respectively."

The nesting habits of the western belted kingfisher seem to be very similar to those of the eastern bird; I find no record of its nesting anywhere but in sand, clay, or gravel banks; such banks are often much higher than those in the East, so the nesting burrow is often at a considerable height from the base, but usually near the top of the cliff.

In all other respects its habits are not materially different from those of the species elsewhere. Grinnell and Storer (1924) say: "This bird's wing-beat is characteristic, three quick beats followed by two executed in a more leisurely manner, like this: one, two, three; four; five.

"A Western Belted Kingfisher watched by Mr. Walter P. Taylor came to a perch on a bare limb overhanging some rapids in the river, and sat there motionless. The outline of the bird's body at once became indistinguishable from the light and shade of its background; in other words it was obliterated because of the disruptive pattern of its coloration, white and slate areas alternating. If the fishes in the water beneath got the same impression as did the human observer, the kingfisher must have become invisible to them, remaining so until the moment of its headlong plunge in their pursuit."

The eggs of the western belted kingfisher are similar to those of the eastern bird and average only slightly larger. The measurements of 38 eggs average 34.78 by 26.89 millimeters; the eggs showing the four extremes measure **36.6** by 27.4, 35.7 by **28, 31.6** by 27, and 33 by **25.4** millimeters.

MEGACERYLE TORQUATA TORQUATA (Linnaeus)

RINGED KINGFISHER

PLATE 17

HABITS

This handsome bird is the largest of the three species of kingfisher found on the American Continent. Its claim to a place on our list is based on the capture of a single specimen, an adult female, by George B. Benners, on June 2, 1888, about a mile below Laredo, Tex., on the United States side of the Rio Grande. The specimen was presented to the Academy of Natural Sciences, in Philadelphia, of which Dr. Witmer Stone (1894) says: "It was sitting on some old roots which had been washed up into a heap by the current of the river. and was shot immediately, so that he did not see it fly or hear its call. Mr. Benners further states that he never saw one of these birds in the vicinity either before or since. Upon the strength of the evidence just given this species seems entitled to a place in the fauna of the United States, along with several other tropical birds which occasionally reach the Rio Grande valley."

Col. A. J. Grayson, in his notes from western Mexico, sent to George N. Lawrence (1874), says:

I have seen the largest kingfisher only near the sea coast, in the vicinity of Mazatlan River, but not on that stream. They seem to prefer the stagnant pools and lagoons, whose waters are murky and densely shaded with over-hanging trees; here upon some dried branch it sits quietly watching the opaque water for whatever finny creature may make its appearance upon the surface, when if not too large, it instantly darts or plunges headlong upon it; after securing the prey in its powerful bill, it bears it to the perch, and beating it a few times upon the perch swallows it entire. Small fishes constitute almost its principal food, but frogs and small water reptiles are often struck and devoured by it. This species does not seem to be so wary as its near congener, the Belted. I have approached it quite near, in order to observe its habits, and it appeared to be very little concerned at my presence. In examining the stomach of one shot by me, I found it crammed with the small fry peculiar to muddy pools, among which was a mud catfish of considerable size. It doubtless breeds in holes scratched in sand cliffs, like the other members of this family, but I have never encountered the nest.

Dickey and van Rossem (1938) say that in El Salvador—

the ringed kingfisher is of general distribution along the coast where it shows decided preference for mangrove lagoons. Locally, the species is almost equally common on fresh water wherever there is a plentiful supply of small fish. It is notable, though, that the species attains its upward limit at Lake Guija at 1,450 feet, and seems to be absent from the higher lakes such as Ilopango. It is customarily solitary, although local conditions such as a very favorable stream may result in a number being found at one point. A great deal of ter-ritory may be covered by individual birds, for they seem to have regular routes along lake borders and rivers with lookout perches at intervals of every few hundred yards. In activity this species is far ahead of any of the other resident kingfishers and evidently prefers to range widely for its prey rather than to stake out a limited, private preserve.

Alexander F. Skutch tells me that in the Caribbean lowlands of Guatemala and Honduras they are partial to the larger, more open streams and lagoons, and avoid the narrow, tree-shaded waterways that the smaller species of kingfisher sometimes frequent.

Nesting.—Major Bendire (1895) quotes Dr. Herman Burmeister (1856) as saying that "it nests in perpendicular banks, occasionally quite a distance from water, in burrows from 5 to 6 feet deep, and lays two white eggs."

There are two sets of eggs, one of five and one of six eggs, in the Thayer collection, taken for Frank B. Armstrong, on March 21 and 30, 1910, near Ciudad Victoria, Tamaulipas, Mexico. One of the nests is described as a hole in the bank of a river, 8 feet deep and 10 feet above water.

Dickey and van Rossem (1938) state that "at San Sebastián in late July, 1912, nest holes were occasionally noted in vertical sandy banks. In size these holes were on an average four inches wide and three inches high at the entrance. Those investigated went straight back into the bank, in one case as far as six feet. This particular burrow then may have made a turn, but it was not dug out."

Alexander F. Skutch has very kindly lent me his unpublished manuscript for a proposed work on the birds of the Caribbean lowlands of Central America, which contains much interesting information on this species, from which I shall quote freely. He says that, in that region, these kingfishers "begin the excavation of their burrows in February, if not earlier. Their nesting is of necessity limited to the drier season when the rivers are lowest, which in this region extends from February to the end of May. The flood waters of June often undermine and eat away the banks in which they nest, if they do not actually rise high enough to flood their tunnels. Since they begin the excavation of their burrows early and raise a single brood each year, they proceed with their task in a leisurely fashion, and one may watch long and in vain for them to return to their work.

"One morning toward the end of February I concealed myself in a blind before a burrow in a bank of sandy loam beside the Rio Morja, near the boundary between Guatemala and Honduras. The tunnel was already well advanced and went far beneath the banana plants at the top of the bank, which had been freshly cut when the river ate into the plantation at the last high water. Although I began the watch early in the morning, it was 11 o'clock before I heard the measured *kleck kleck kleck*, and turning saw one of the pair approaching from upstream. It soon entered the burrow and remained within several minutes, appearing not to notice the rough-winged swallow that fluttered before the tunnel and several times rested in the entrance while it was busy inside. On emerging, the kingfisher perched atop a banana leaf and kept up a running conversation in low rattles with its mate, out of sight around the bend up-river. In five minutes it flew upstream to join the other, calling with a loud *kleck kleck kleck*.

"Soon the pair returned together and began to work in earnest. Each time one entered the burrow there was a jet of earth thrown out behind. As the bird moved inward the jet fell short of the entrance until it could be seen no more. Doubtless the bird continued to kick the earth back until it reached the head of the excavation, and so the material loosened by the bill was gradually pushed out of the tunnel. The kingfishers invariably emerged head first, indicating that the burrow had reached its final length and had begun to widen at the far end into the nesting chamber. The bird inside called in low *klecks*, which were answered by the mate perched on a rusty tram rail, washed out by the flood, which leaned against the bank just below the burrow. They seemed to encourage each other in their dark subterranean labors. Both sexes shared equally in the toil, and as soon as one emerged and flew up beside the other on the rail, the latter went into the burrow, throwing out a jet of earth as he disappeared into the darkness. Four or five minutes was the usual period spent in the earthwork. On one occasion both were together in the burrow for a few minutes. Just after noon, while one bird was working inside, its mate became tired of waiting on the rail and flew upstream. The other, when it emerged and found itself alone, followed in this direction. Although I remained until the middle of the afternoon, the birds did not return, having worked less than an hour that day.

"I waited almost a month before daring to open the nest. I probed the length of the burrow with a slender vine, repeating the measurement several times to make sure I had reached the back. I found the burrow to be 7 feet 3 inches long, measured back this distance from the top of the bank, and tried to calculate the position of the nesting chamber from the direction of the portion of the tunnel I could see from the front. Experience with Amazon kingfishers and motmots had taught me that by far the safest way to open a burrow is to dig down behind it and make an opening in the back of the nesting chamber just large enough to reach the eggs, afterward closing it with a stone or a board and carefully covering over the excavation.

"As I began to dig almost above it, the incubating bird, who had stood its ground in face of the thrusts with the vine, flew out, uttered a few *klecks* and headed upstream, where it perched on a giant cane leaning over the current and soon plunged for a fish. I now saw for the first time that it was the male. Like other burrow-nesting birds under the same circumstances, it seemed rather unconcerned, and this despite the fact that I afterward found it the most devoted of parents."

Because he "had faith that the activities of birds, including their periods on the nest during incubation, are rhythmic and more or less constant for the species, rather than irregular and arbitrary," Mr. Skutch was determined to learn how these kingfishers arranged their shifts on the nest. In his efforts to solve this problem, he was at "first baffled, next challenged, and finally surprised." For many weary hours, during nearly two weeks, and at various hours from dawn to sunset, he patiently watched that hole in the bank, mostly with little or no results. The use of what he called a "silent monitor," a small stick stuck upright and loosely in the entrance of the burrow, enabled him to tell that a bird had either entered or left the nest, but did not tell him the hour or the sex of the bird. His account of how he accomplished this and finally learned the secret is too long a story to be told here. But he did finally discover "that there is a single nest relief each day, early in the morning. This is comparatively easy to observe, for the bird coming to take its place in the burrow usually flies downstream sounding his powerful, metallic *kleck kleck* at measured intervals, and so heralds his own arrival." After three or four false starts he finally gathers courage to enter the burrow; and, after a minute and a half or two minutes, his mate launches forth and flies off upstream. The times at which the relief took place varied from 7:05 to 10:01 a. m., most of the shifts being made between seven and nine o'clock. He says, further: "After I learned what precautions were necessary in order to determine the sexes of the birds, I found that on some mornings it was the male who entered and the female who departed, while on other mornings the reverse was true. There was a regular alternation, the male entering one morning and the female the next.

"Each afternoon the incubating partner took a single recess, for food or exercise, from its long 24-hour turn on the eggs. It emerged suddenly and without warning, at some time between 1 and 4 o'clock, flew upstream to the feeding ground, leaving the nest unoccupied, and returned in half an hour to an hour. On returning, it flew downstream low above the water and entered the nest directly, without perching or calling, in a manner very different from the morning entry, since there was no mate on the nest to be advised of its arrival. Then it remained until relieved by the mate the following morning.

"Few birds incubate so continuously as the ringed kingfishers. One day the female took her afternoon recess early, and on returning remained on the nest more than 19 hours, for her mate was very late in relieving her the next morning, and did not appear until 10 o'clock. The usual period between their return in the afternoon and their relief the following morning is 16 or 17 hours."

Mr. Skutch found another nest of this kingfisher "400 feet downstream in the same bank. I opened it only two days before the eggs hatched. The bird on the nest, with a degree of attachment I have rarely seen equaled, remained bravely in the tunnel while I probed its length, dug in the rear, took out the eggs for measurement, fitted a stone in the aperture I had made, and tamped the soil above it. All this occupied well over an hour. This burrow was 7 feet 9 inches in length and the nesting chamber, 22 inches below the surface, contained, like the last, four white eggs. The territories of these two pairs extended in opposite directions from their burrows, the birds from the upper nest always entering it from upstream and returning thither when relieved, those in the lower nest fishing in the river below it."

Eggs.—The ringed kingfisher apparently lays three to six eggs to a set; probably four and five are the commonest numbers. What few eggs I have seen are pure white; they vary in shape from ovate to short-ovate; and the shells are smooth and quite glossy. The measurements of 19 eggs average 43.72 by 34.52 millimeters; the eggs showing the four extremes measure 46.8 by 35, 43.7 by 35.6, and 39.7 by 32.5 millimeters.

Young.—On the morning of March 28, the female arrived, at the first burrow examined by Mr. Skutch, at sunrise, an unusually early hour for her to appear, and seemed to be excited. He opened the burrow and found that two of the eggs had hatched. The nestlings were "pink skinned and were without the least vestige of feathers. They could already stand upright, supporting themselves on their feet and belly, and attempted to walk, which they did in a weak and tottering fashion." Three of the eggs in the other nest hatched the same day; as he removed the stone from the rear, "a sizzling noise arose from the earth," and two of the nestlings retreated into the tunnel with their mother, where they could not be reached.

Soon after the young in the first nest had hatched, some malicious person dug into the burrow at both ends but could not reach the young in the tunnel. Three of these nestlings eventually died, but the parents continued to feed and brood the fourth in the exposed and gaping burrow. Then, Mr. Skutch continues: "Stuffed with whole fish to the bursting point, the single nestling grew at a tremendous rate. Its eyes opened by the tenth day, when it uttered a high-pitched, trilling sound in response to its parents' rattle. It was 14 days before the upper mandible caught up to the lower in length. The young kingfisher was beginning to defend itself with energy and bit hard with its great mandibles whenever I picked it up. A few days later it squealed and fought like a fury. When 4 weeks old it was fully feathered except for the naked belly, which rested upon the sandy floor of the foul burrow. To its biting and squealing it now added an alarm rattle almost as loud as that of the parents, which at length drew one of them, who answered in kind. Still it did not attempt to flutter, and when I placed it on the ground it could do no more than hop along with outstretched wings. It remained in the burrow a full week after it was completely feathered, and finally departed at the age of 34 or 35 days.

"Although this nestling was one of the most vociferous I ever encountered, its struggles and cries were very mild in comparison with those of the single youngster who survived in the burrow down stream." When about 4 weeks old, it was almost as big as its parents. When he attempted to reach it from the back of the nest, "it fled through the tunnel and jumped into the river, where it spread its wings, turned upstream, and flapped its way slowly against the current. When it encountered obstacles of stranded brush it hooked its bill over them and scrambled across. Thus it led me a merry chase, wading in the muddy shallows, until a fallen banana plant stopped its wayward progress and I seized it. Unlike its neighbor of the same age upstream, it had not become accustomed to being taken in hands; its deafening screams and fierce attempts to bite made, for duration and intensity, the best efforts of the other pale to insignificance. It was ten agonized minutes before it became reconciled to me, and I let it perch on my hand until its feathers dried before returning it to the burrow. This bird left its burrow between its thirty-fifth and thirty-seventh day."

Plumages.—I have seen no very young birds. In immature birds, probably birds of the first year, the sexes are distinguishable. In the young male, the jugular area is dull gray washed with "cinnamon," and the under tail coverts are pale cinnamon, both of which parts are pure white in the adult male, though some adults have the under tail coverts barred with bluish gray; the brown areas on the under parts are paler than in the adult, "ochraceous-tawny" to "cinnamon," more or less mixed with white; these parts in the adult are rich browns, "Sanford's brown" to "cinnamon-rufous"; the upper parts and wing coverts are dotted with small white spots, and many of the feathers have shaft streaks or median wedges of black; these parts are clear, grayish blue, or "delft blue," in adults, without streaks; young birds also have broad, median, black streaks in the crest. Young females are similar to the young males but may be readily recognized by the broad pectoral band, which is never present in the male at any age; in the adult female this is clear bluish gray, but in the young bird it is broadly edged with rufous, or dull brown, and sometimes mainly rufous; in the young female the under wing coverts are wholly "cinnamon-rufous," whereas in the young male these are partly white.

I have not seen enough material to determine how long these immature plumages are worn, or to learn much about the molts.

Food.—Mr. Skutch (MS.) says on this subject: "The ringed kingfisher's diet is rather monotonous. They live almost entirely, if not exclusively on fish, often of large size, which they catch in the regular manner of kingfishers, but being larger birds their plunges are more spectacular than those of the others."

One day "a female flew into a balsa tree, growing beside a small stream, with a fish fully half as long as herself dangling crosswise in her bill. For more than two and a half hours by the watch she held it thus, changing her position only from one branch to another of the same tree. I was at the time watching a green kingfisher's nest, and I could keep her in sight without additional effort. When at length I was ready to leave, she had begun to beat her fish against the limb, although it must have been dead long since. After this exhibition of stolidity, I no longer felt sorry for the ringed kingfishers because the customs of their race obliged them to sit on the nest for such long periods."

Behavior.—Dr. Charles W. Richmond (1893) found this species very common in Nicaragua and Costa Rica, and he writes of its habits:

One morning a pair of these birds went through a very curious performance. Attention was first called to them by their loud rattling cry, which was kept up almost constantly as they circled and gyrated about over the water, occasionally dropping—not diving—into the water, and sinking below the surface for a moment. This maneuvering lasted some minutes, after which both birds flew upstream uttering their ordinary note.

Two or three individuals were in the habit of passing the night at some point on the creek back of the "I. P." plantation, and came over just about dusk every evening. I noticed them for several months, and was struck with the regularity of their coming, and the course taken by each on its way to the roost. The birds could be heard a considerable distance away, just before dusk, uttering their loud single "chuck" at every few beats of the wings. They appeared to come from their feeding grounds, often passing over the plantation opposite, probably to cut off a bend in the river. One of the birds invariably passed close to the corner of the laborers' quarters, though at considerable height, and the other near a trumpet tree some distance away. The third bird was only a casual visitor. At times the birds came together, but usually there was an interval of several minutes. Their routes met at a turn of the creek a few rods back of the house, where they usually sounded their rattling notes and dropped down close to the water, which they followed to the roost. This was a huge spreading tree, covered with parasitic plants and numerous vines, which hung in loops and festoons from the limbs. On one occasion I shot at one of the birds as it came clucking overhead, and caused it to drop several small fish. A female nearly ready to deposit eggs was shot October 9.

Referring to the behavior of ringed kingfishers, Mr. Skutch (MS.) writes: "Watercourses are their highways, and, like men, they are frequently reluctant to leave them. One day, ascending in a motor launch the Toloa Creek in Honduras, we drove a ringed kingfisher before us for possibly a mile. Each time the boat approached he would leave his perch, fly a few hundred feet ahead, and finally alight in a branch overhanging the stream. Here he would wait until the launch was almost opposite him, then fly ahead of it a few hundred feet more. Only after this procedure had been repeated many times did he finally double over the bank and return downstream."

He noticed, while studying the program of nest relief, that these kingfishers "showed a certain amount of formalism in their natures." One morning while he was on watch, "at 7:30 the male emerged from the burrow without warning [and without waiting to be relieved by the female in the usual way] and flew upstream as usual. I was surprised at this unexpected behavior, but probably no more than his mate. Five minutes later she appeared from the direction of his departure and perched in a trumpet tree growing on the bank a few rods from the burrow, where she often rested before going to relieve the male on the nest. Soon he reappeared and the female, who had not moved, greeted him with a rapid, low rattle, which was evidently a scolding. A minute later he flew upstream again. I thought now the female would certainly enter, it was her day upon the nest, but such an unwelcomed entry would have been a breach in formality, beneath the dignity of a well-bred kingfisher matron. She delayed another minute, as though considering what course to follow, then flew off after the delinquent. Soon they both returned, but separately, and there was a rather lengthy conversation between the pair as they perched on the banana leaves near the entrance of the burrow. Finally, after flying back and forth several times before it, the male entered, rather sheepishly we may suppose, while his mate continued to *kleck* from her perch in a low voice.

"Mrs. kingfisher had won her point. She delayed a seemly interval for him to compose himself for her reception, then entered herself with the usual warning. I shall probably never know what passes between them in the fraction of a minute they must be together in the nesting chamber, but whatever form of greeting they indulge in, we may well suppose it was not as cordial as usual. The male came out in record time, about one minute after his mate's entry, and turned upstream, klecking loudly, a free bird at last."

A change in the behavior of the two males was noted after the young had hatched in the two nests, of which Mr. Skutch (MS.) writes: "The males of both nests, both of whom happened to be free that day, behaved differently than on previous mornings. After being relieved, they had gone off as usual to their respective territories up and down the stream; but instead of remaining there, as they had always done before the eggs hatched, they soon returned to perch at no great distance from their nests, and loudly protested my presence. In their excitement, both perched at the same time in the trumpet tree which grew on the bank of the river between the two nests, and was apparently the boundary between their territories. They stood side by side on a branch, their beautiful, white-barred, slate-colored wings spread until they almost touched. One raised his crest, but the other laid his flat, and, with open bills and angry *klecks*, each defied the other to cross the accepted frontier."

Voice.—The same patient observer says: "Now that there were nestlings, I heard an utterance from the kingfishers that I had never heard before. It was really not so much a new note as a different manner of using the old familiar one, for their entire vocabulary consists of a sound that to our ears is suggested by the syllable *kleck*, but they employ their single word in a great variety of ways to express different meanings and emotions. A single loud *kleck*, uttered at measured intervals, punctuates their flight; a softer, rapidly repeated *kleck* is the signal that a bird wishes to relieve his mate on the nest; and now there were nestlings to guard they expressed their anxiety by a very loud, rapid, mechanical klecking, continued with momentary pauses so long as danger seemed to threaten. This harsh, deafening rattle was uttered while the bird perched with the bill open, the mandibles held motionless, and the tail vibrating rapidly up and down. I never heard another bird make more noise when its nestlings seemed to be in danger, nor give more evident signs of distress, yet, in common with other birds which nest underground, they never darted at me nor made any demonstration. They merely perched in full sight and rattled interminably."

DISTRIBUTION

Range.—Mexico, the Lesser Antilles, Central and South America; casual in the lower Rio Grande Valley, Texas; nonmigratory.

The range of the ringed kingfisher extends **north** to Nayarit (Tres Marias Islands and San Blas); Tamaulipas (Rio Cruz and Tampico); Honduras (Toloa and Lancetilla); northern Colombia (Cartagena, Sabanilla, and Santa Marta); northern Venezuela (Lake Valencia); the Lesser Antilles (Goyave); British Guiana (Georgetown and Blairmont); Surinam (Paramaribo); and northern Brazil (Santarem and Capim River). **East** to Brazil (Capim River and Cantagalla); Uruguay (Rio Negro); and Argentina (Villegas, Puerto Santa Elena, and Tierra del Fuego). **South** to southern Argentina (Tierra del Fuego); and southern Chile (Chonos Archipelago). **West** to Chile (Chonos Archipelago and Chiloe Island); western Peru (Huachos and Lima); western Ecuador (Tumbez, Bucay, Babahoyo, and Vinces); western Colombia (Cali and Honda); Panama (San Miguel and Alminante Bay); Costa Rica (Pozo Azul and Bolson); western Guatemala (Rio Morja); Jalisco (Las Penas Island); and Nayarit (Tres Marias Islands).

Casual records.—The only United States record of this species is a specimen in the Academy of Natural Sciences of Philadelphia that was collected on the American side of the Rio Grande, near Laredo, Texas, on June 2, 1888.

Egg dates.—Guatemala: March.

Mexico: March 21 and 30.

Peru: May 29.

CHLOROCERYLE AMERICANA SEPTENTRIONALIS (Sharpe)

TEXAS KINGFISHER

PLATE 16

HABITS

I made the acquaintance of this pretty little kingfisher when I made a short visit to Cameron County, Tex., as the guest of George Finlay Simmons, in May 1923. This is a most interesting bird country, rich in the number of Mexican species that reach their northern limits here and the only region in which some of them can be found within the limits of the United States. About Brownsville the chaparral, the open prairies, the tree claims, the ponds, and the swamps were all teeming with bird life of many species; but perhaps the most interesting of all were the dense forests along the resacas or stagnant watercourses, the old beds of rivers; these often contained large trees, mesquite, huisache, ebony, palms, etc., with a thick undergrowth of many shrubs and small trees, such as granjena, persimmons, coffee bean, and bush morning-glory. Here we found the characteristic birds of the region in abundance, such as the chachalaca, the red-billed pigeon, the noisy derby flycatcher, the brilliant green jay, and Audubon's oriole. Here, too, I was delighted to see my first Texas kingfisher, as it sat on a dead fallen tree over the water and then went flying away upstream, uttering its rattling twitter, suggestive of but different from that of the belted kingfisher.

Mr. Simmons (1925) says that it is "resident along clearer mountain streams of southwest-central Texas, from Comal County southward. * * * Occurrence depends largely on its habitat, the bird requiring the clearest of waters, particularly the crystal-clear rivers and brooks of the central Texas hill area; dislikes water the least bit muddy; larger, clearer streams and rarely smaller ones," as well as "shady little brooks," are mentioned as its favorite haunts.

Dickey and van Rossem (1938) record this kingfisher as a "common resident throughout the arid Lower Tropical Zone on all freshwater lakes, streams, and marshes below 2,300 feet, and also coastwise in the mangrove belt," in El Salvador. Of its haunts they say: "A favorite environment is along small, rocky streams of the uplands, and in such places the population averages about a pair to the mile. When the young of the year are on the wing, this average is considerably increased for a time. Probably the section of stream inhabited by any individual pair has pretty definite limits, for although individual birds or pairs show no hesitancy in keeping well ahead of a person for a time, sooner or later they will make

every effort to break back along the route to the places from where
they were first started. Salt water is apparently not greatly to
their liking, and in the mangrove lagoons they were decidedly uncommon. Scarcity of suitable nesting sites may, however, be in part
responsible for this condition."

Alexander F. Skutch found this kingfisher on small streams as
high as 7,000 feet above sea level in the highlands of Guatemala,
and writes (MS.) of its haunts: "While toiling over the rocky bed
of some narrow torrent rushing down a mountain valley, where the
huge trees arch overhead and shut out the sky, I have often heard a
pleasant *cheep* and turned to watch the solitary figure of a green
kingfisher fly swiftly past, low above the water and following all
the twistings of the channel, until lost in the depth of the forest.
While his larger relatives require deeper water and a longer drop,
he is often content to plunge from the top of a boulder projecting a
foot or so above a shallow channel, and fishes on the smaller streams
from which they are absent; but he joins them on the broader and
more sluggish waterways. He rarely hovers above the water in the
manner of the larger kingfishers."

Nesting.—The first account of the nesting of the Texas kingfisher
is by William Brewster (1879), who writes: "This beautiful little
Kingfisher was found by Mr. Werner in comparative abundance at
several points in Comal County, notably about some of the springs
that empty into the Guadaloupe River. A set of six eggs, taken
April 25, 1878, was authenticated by the capture of both parent birds,
the female being caught on the nest. * * * The nesting cavity
was in a sandy bank near the water's edge. The eggs were laid on the
bare sand, no fish bones or other extraneous material being near.
The entrance was not quite 1¾ inches in diameter, and the hole
extended inward from the face of the bank about 3½ feet."

Bendire (1895) says:

The nests of many of these little Kingfishers are yearly destroyed by high
water flooding their burrows, caused by heavy rains and cloud-bursts, which
are more or less prevalent in southern and western Texas. It is not uncommon
on both the Medina and San Antonio rivers, and a nesting site on the last-
mentioned stream found by Mr. C. H. Kearny, in the spring of 1892, containing
six fresh eggs, is described by him as being located in a bank about 15 feet high
and about 5 feet above the water level. The nesting chamber, which was slightly
larger than the tunnel leading to it, was placed about 2 feet from the mouth of
the hole. There was no nest proper, but a few fish bones and scales were
scattered about the eggs. In the same bank a number of Bank Swallows
(*Clivicola riparia*) had taken up temporary homes, and one of their holes was
located within a foot of that of the Kingfishers. They are devoted parents,
and these birds will usually allow themselves to be caught rather than forsake
their eggs.

There are four sets of eggs of this kingfisher in the Thayer collection and one in the writer's collection, all taken by, or for, Frank B. Armstrong, near Ciudad Victoria, Tamaulipas, Mexico, between March 12 and 28, 1908. The nests were all in holes in banks, about 3 feet deep and 6 to 8 feet above the water.

Mr. Skutch says (MS.) that this kingfisher, which he calls the green kingfisher, is one of the five species of birds that nest most commonly in the banks of the streams in the Caribbean lowlands of Central America. "The burrows of the ringed kingfisher are distinguished at once by the large diameter of the tunnel, 6 inches in width. Next in size are those of the Amazon kingfisher, 3¾ inches wide. Then come those of the turquoise-browed motmot, about 3½ inches in width; and finally those of the green kingfisher, only 2 or 2¼ inches in horizontal diameter.

"While the burrows of the larger kingfishers and the motmot are placed in plain sight in the bare and exposed banks, so that he who runs may see them, those of the green kingfisher I have found concealed by the fringe of vines and dead vegetation draping the top of the bank, or else behind exposed roots, and I discovered them only by seeing a bird enter or leave. Theirs were the last of the three kingfishers' nests I encountered, and I found only two, late in the season, although the species is equally abundant with the Amazon kingfisher. As befits the smaller bird, their burrows are far shorter than those of the larger species. The two I measured were only 22 and 25 inches in length.

"One morning at the end of April, I sat down to eat my breakfast upon a fallen log beside the Quebrada de Arena, a little brook so narrow that one can easily jump across it, flowing through a pasture grown up with low bushes and thorny vine tangles. Presently a male green kingfisher flew downstream, perched on a branch ahead of me, *ticked* a great deal and seemed excited about my presence. The bird's persistence in remaining in that stretch of the river and his evident excitement renewed my conviction [on a previous visit] that his burrow was not far distant. I removed my shoes and waded up and down, examining every likely bit of bank, while the bird flew back and forth to keep out of my way. I discovered only old burrows whose lack of fresh foot-furrows proclaimed clearly enough they were not in use. Quite baffled, I paused beneath the shelter of some overhanging bushes to watch the bird, and in a few minutes, after calling again *tick tick tick*, he flew up beneath the exposed roots of a dead stump, half washed out, and disappeared. This was almost the exact spot whence I had seen him or his mate emerge three weeks before, but the entrance to the burrow was so well concealed by the overhang of the top of the bank, the projecting roots and the vines which draped over them, that it had completely escaped me.

"I lost no time in opening the burrow. The male flew out with the second push I gave the machete which I used to dig, for the tunnel sloped upward so sharply that the nesting chamber was less than three inches below the surface of the ground, and I broke through into the rear of it before I supposed I had well started to dig. There were three white eggs, well advanced in incubation, to judge from their opacity. The male fluttered several times in front of the burrow, eager to enter before it had been closed again. I fitted a stone over the small aperture I had made, covered it with earth, and placed logs across the roof of the nesting chamber, to prevent the mules' stepping upon it and possibly breaking through. The birds continued to incubate.

"The pair arranged their turns on the eggs in much the same manner as the Amazon kingfishers. The female spent each night on the nest. Soon after 6 a. m. the male flew downstream, low above the water, uttering at intervals the high-pitched *cheep*, which is his flight call. He perched on one of the roots of the old stump projecting in front of the nest and called *tick tick tick* in a low voice, which his mate heard in the burrow. She came forth, greeting him with a single *cheep*, as she flew swiftly past and turned down the brook to her feeding grounds. Her behavior was rather erratic.

"One morning she could not await his arrival, although he was hardly late. She popped out of the nest without warning and flew off, but a minute later the pair returned together. The male went to the root in front of the burrow, *ticked* just as much as he was accustomed to do to call off his mate, although he could certainly see she was not inside, then entered the empty burrow. The following morning she acted in quite another manner. Just after 6, on a cloudy morning after a night of hard rain, the male flew downstream, perched in front of the burrow, and *ticked* for her to come forth, but she paid no heed to his repeated calls. He flew a few rods downstream, then returned to call *tick tick tick* again. Still no response, so he flew away out of sight. Ten minutes later he reappeared and perched again on the root in front of the burrow, where he called at intervals for two minutes before at length she darted forth. Then he entered for the morning. The male incubated until the female returned from her breakfast to relieve him. One morning she left him on the nest less than two hours, but the next it was nearly three. She covered the eggs for the remainder of the morning. The male was chiefly responsible for keeping them warm during the afternoon, until his mate called him from the nest and entered for the night at some time between 5 and 6 o'clock."

Eggs.—The Texas kingfisher lays three to six eggs, but five seems to be the commonest number. These vary in shape from oval to elliptical-oval; the shell is smooth and thin; some show little or no gloss and others are quite glossy; the color is pure white. The measurements of 64 eggs average 24.36 by 19.23 millimeters; the eggs showing the four extreme measures **26.4** by 20.3, 24.1 by **20.7, 22.3** by 19.3, and 23.8 by **17.5** millimeters.

Young.—The second nest that Mr. Skutch found contained five "pink-skinned, blind, and totally naked nestlings," which "like those of the larger species, had undershot bills and heel callosities." He visited this nest 18 days later and found that the young, which were not more than 25 days old, "could flutter just a few feet. One flew into the river, where she spread her wings on the surface and headed for the shore. I threw her into the shallow water again, and again she turned unerringly toward the marginal rocks, beating her wings on the surface until she gained a footing. The following morning I placed them on the shore for a photograph, but two found their wings and easily traversed the 50-foot channel, flying low above the surface. The power of flight had come to them almost overnight.

"One evening early in June, after the sun had fallen behind the bordering fringe of willow trees, I was resting on a log stranded on the flood plain of the river, when a young green kingfisher flew upstream, calling *cheep* at intervals, and perched on a pile of brushwood almost in front of the burrow in which it was hatched. Presently its father came flying downstream, with a small minnow in his bill, and perched on the same pile of brushwood, not far from the other. The young bird came toward him, as if to receive the fish, but the other raised his wings above his back to forfend it. The youngster took this as a hint to remain aloof and perched at a little distance. Not satisfied with the interval that remained between them, the male darted at the young bird, which retreated a few feet. Several times it started to approach its father, but each time was warned to remain away by the spread wings, a very picturesque attitude. Several times, too, the bird with the fish drove at the applicant for it and finally, still holding the fish in his bill, chased it down the stream and out of sight. The young kingfisher had been out of the nest 29 days and must now at least learn to dive for its own fish."

Plumages.—The young kingfishers are hatched naked and blind, as described above, but the juvenal plumage is acquired before the young leave the nest. A young male, taken on August 21, fully grown and fully fledged in juvenal plumage, is much like the adult female; the rich brown pectoral band of the adult male is only faintly indicated but is replaced by a band of greenish-black spots; and there is more black spotting on the flanks than in the adult male. Apparently there is a gradual change toward maturity during the first year, for October, February, and April birds show a gradual increase in the rufous band.

The youngest female I have seen, taken on June 8, is much like the adult female, but the pectoral band of greenish black spots is lacking, or nearly so, the under parts being nearly immaculate. These spots, which are more in the form of broad streaks than in transverse spots, increase with age to form one complete and one nearly complete band in the oldest birds. The observations made by Mr. Skutch on the brood of young that he studied agree substantially with the above.

I have no data on the molts, but Mr. van Rossem (1938) says that "the annual molt * * * takes place in the fall, but the definite time is not known."

Food.—The food mentioned by Mr. Skutch (MS.) consisted of small minnows. Mr. Simmons (1925) says that this kingfisher is a "business-like little fisherman, perching atop a stick or stake in the water or on a low branch overhanging low water"; it "frequently flies back and forth over the water, hunting for small fish." It is "often driven off feeding-grounds by the larger Belted Kingfisher, with which it is sometimes found."

Voice.—Mr. Simmons (1925) says that the voice of the Texas kingfisher is a "rather sharp, rattling twitter, uttered on the wing; quite different from and shriller than the loud, harsh rattle of the Belted Kingfisher." Mr. Skutch refers to the flight note as *cheep*, and the call or alarm note as *tick tick tick*.

Field marks.—This is such a small kingfisher that it could hardly be mistaken for anything else within its range. Its upper parts are dark, glossy green, and spotted with white, and it has no occipital crest. The under parts are white, with a rufous pectoral band on the male and a ring of black spots across the breast of the female.

Enemies.—The first set of eggs that Mr. Skutch found failed to hatch, as they were destroyed by ants. He writes (MS.) : "Opening the burrow, I found it swarming with myriads of small, amber 'fire ants,' a scourge to man and beast alike. Invading the nest, they had worried the birds until they fidgeted on their eggs and cracked them; then they had worked into the cracks and begun to eat the embryos. I had cleaned them out the previous evening, but all to no avail. The nest was completely ruined. That same morning they had attacked and killed three young woodpeckers in their nest in a dead stub standing a few paces from the kingfishers' burrow. In the humid coastal regions, ants are one of the principal enemies, if not actually the chief enemy, of nesting birds. I have found more eggs and nestlings destroyed by them than by all other known agents combined."

DISTRIBUTION

Range.—Southern Texas, Mexico, and Central and South America; casual in southern Arizona; apparently a nonmigratory species.

The range of the green kingfisher extends **north** to Sinaloa (Mazatlan); Durango (Rio Sestin); southern Texas (Turtle Creek and New Braunfels); Quintana Roo (Xcopan); eastern Nicaragua (Pis Pis River); northern Colombia (Santa Marta and Bonda); northern Venezuela (La Guaira); British Guiana (Potaro Landing and Bartica); Surinam (Paramaribo); and northern Brazil (Quixada). **East** to Brazil (Quixada, Rio Taquarussu, and Goyaz); and Uruguay (Santa Elena). **South** to southern Uruguay (Santa Elena); and central Argentina (Santa Elena, San Jose, and Tucuman). **West** to northwestern Argentina (Tucuman); Bolivia (San Jose); Peru (La Merced and the Ucayale River); Ecuador (Vinces); western Colombia (Tumaco, Cali, and Rio Frio); Panama (Sapo Mountains, Gatun, and the Chagres River); western Guatemala (Duenas, and Lake Atitlan); Oaxaca (Juchatengo); Nayarit (San Blas); and Sinaloa (Escuinapa, and Mazatlan).

The subspecies, known as *Chloroceryle americanus septentrionalis*, is the only form to enter the United States. It ranges southward from Texas to Yucatan.

Casual records.—A specimen was taken at Decatur, Tex., north of the normal range in this State, on January 3, 1889. Dr. Elliott Coues reported seeing this species in September 1865 at points on the Colorado River, Ariz., between Forts Mohave and Yuma, and one was taken on the San Pedro River near Fairbanks on February 13, 1910. One was collected on September 8, 1893, at Cajon Bonito Creek, Sonora, a few miles south of the New Mexico line. One was taken on the Santa Cruz River, Ariz., on October 1, 1938.

Egg dates.—Mexico: 24 records, March 5 to June 13; 12 records, March 12 to April 19, indicating the height of the season.

Texas: 4 records, April 11 to June 15.

Order CAPRIMULGIFORMES

Family CAPRIMULGIDAE: Goatsuckers

ANTROSTOMUS CAROLINENSIS (Gmelin)

CHUCK-WILL'S-WIDOW

PLATES 18–20

HABITS

CONTRIBUTED BY ALEXANDER SPRUNT, JR.

Dusk falls gently over the salt marshes, which reach out from a shoreline where moss-bannered live oaks and stately pines rustle softly in the late March breeze. A faint fragrance of jessamine hangs in the air; the sleepy note of a cardinal echoes from a cassina thicket, while atop a tall palmetto a mockingbird salutes the coming night with a burst of melody. Silence comes and the stars appear, glinting in golden splendor through the purple gloom.

Suddenly through the air comes another sound, a sharp, clear-cut, insistent chant. Splitting the silences, it strikes clappingly upon one's ears, ringing with startling emphasis, unmistakable, thrilling and welcome. The first chuck-will's-widow has returned to the Carolina low country, and spring is definitely back again!

There is something about nocturnal birds that fascinate one strangely. Doubtless the cloak of darkness that shrouds their movements and activities has a great deal to do with it. One cannot but wonder at their comings and goings; how they pursue their hunting amid the gloom. Their voices too lend much to the fascination, for the notes seem a part of the night itself, just as the bodies of the birds themselves seem more like detached and living particles of darkness than of flesh and feathers.

All my life I have lived amid the haunts of some of these furtive kindred of the dusk, but the chuck-will's-widow above all seems to typify the mystery of the night and invests it with a sense of intangible yet satisfying tranquillity. It has always seemed to me that those beautiful lines, written of the cuckoo, might be even more applicable to the chuck-will's-widow, for, in truth, much of the time it does not seem a bird at all, but simply "a wandering voice." Without brilliant plumage or grace of form, it nevertheless possesses undoubted character, and long acquaintance with the bird only increases the interest that is bound to be aroused in any study of its life and habits.

Spring.—Generally speaking, the chuck-will's-widow arrives in the South in March. There is some indication that a few birds spend the winter in southern Florida for C. J. Pennock (MS.) has stated that "in the Charlotte Harbor district a few at least appear to winter. February 26, 1926, one heard calling; February 24, 1927, while camping, we heard one." Arthur H. Howell (1932) states that it "winters in small numbers" and gives December and February dates. R. J. Longstreet's opinion (1930) is that "the chuck-will's-widow is a summer resident in north Florida and a permanent resident in south Florida." Audubon considered the species a permanent resident in the State, and his idea was, according to Allen (1871), confirmed by "old residents," though he himself states it "is not observed till about the first of March." I am obliged to spend portions of every winter month in Florida, being constantly in the field throughout the southern Everglades and the Keys, but it so happens that I have yet to find the chuck-will's-widow during this season. The wintering population is undoubtedly small and scattered.

It reaches north-central Florida about March 18 (D. J. Nicholson, MS.) and appears in the coastal districts of southern Georgia a few days later (T. D. Perry, MS.). In South Carolina, about Charleston, it arrives anywhere from the third week in March to the first week of April. The males always arrive first, followed in a few days by the females.

Courtship.—Little time is lost by the chuck-will's-widow, after its arrival from its winter home, in seeking a mate. Almost at once it undertakes the search, and it is at such times that the observer has an opportunity to see them actively in daylight. The courtship performance is an interesting one and, all things considered, is not difficult to observe. The outstanding characteristic is the strutting pomposity of the male. He sidles up to the watching female, his wings droop, the tail is widely spread, and he swells and swells until it really seems that the limit of inflation is reached and another fraction of distention would cause him to disintegrate like a bursting bomb. Various vocal efforts are indulged in meanwhile, accompanied by quick, jerky motions. Audubon (1840) has compared this phase of the proceedings to that of the domestic cock pigeon, while Arthur T. Wayne (1910) likened it to a turkey gobbler's antics. This latter has always seemed to me most apt, for not only does the seemingly endless inflation remind one vividly of the turkey, but the motions also suggest this bird.

After this period of intense and apparently exhausting display, a space of calm and quiet pervades the pair should the male have been successful in his suit, and he perches placidly beside her.

Nesting.—No semblance of a nest is constructed. The eggs are placed on the ground upon a carpet of dead leaves, and the sitting bird constitutes one of the finest examples of protective coloration that nature affords. Such dependence is placed in it that the closest approach is possible, and the bird flushes only when nearly trodden on. The mottling of the plumage is exactly like that of the variegated background of leaves, sun splashes, and shadow, and one may look directly at the bird without seeing it. Once the bird is flushed, however, it is perfectly easy to see the eggs, for they then stand out like huge pearls against the leaves, not having the similarity to the ground that characterizes the eggs of the nighthawk.

Mixed oak and pine woods are usually the nesting haunt of the chuck. In the large live-oak groves, which occur over so much of the plantation country of the South, the species is abundant and shows a remarkable tendency to place the eggs in nearly the same spot year after year. As a rule there is little if any undergrowth about the eggs. When under the pines, this would not be expected, and in the oak groves the ground is always covered by a veritable carpet of leaves, through which no undergrowth appears. Thus the eggs can be seen from a considerable distance should the bird be off them.

On May 8, 1926, I found two eggs on Folly Island, S. C., lying upon pine needles. Marking the spot accurately I returned the next year and on May 12, 1927, found two eggs within 5 feet of the spot used previously.

M. G. Vaiden (MS.) writes from Rosedale, Miss., that he discovered a set of eggs on May 1, 1911. *Twelve years later*, on April 27, 1923, he returned to the same locality and found two eggs within 10 feet of the same spot! He states that the "trees were larger, the hillside washed into gullies, but otherwise about as formerly."

Walter Colvin (MS.), of Arkansas City, Kans., reports the first nesting of the species in that State, two eggs having been found in May 1923, near Arkansas City, Cowley County. Another nest was discovered the following year (1924) also in May. Probably the chuck had been nesting there for some time previous and was also discovered in Miami County, by Mr. Colvin's son John, in 1929.

Nesting observations from a variety of sources indicate that the chuck raises but one brood. However, if the eggs are taken, the bird will lay again and again until young are hatched. The late Arthur T. Wayne, of Mount Pleasant, S. C., once took in succession three sets from a pair near his home, and a fourth was laid, incubated, and hatched.

The chuck brooks no tampering with the eggs whatever. If they are handled, or as much as touched in some cases, the bird removes them to what is considered a safer locality. This habit was noted long ago and gave rise to much dispute and speculation as to the method employed in the transportation. It has been definitely proved that the bird takes them in the mouth. Audubon (1840) describes it so well that his account is given herewith:

When the Chuck-wills-widow, either male or female (for each sits alternately) has discovered that the eggs have been touched, it ruffles its feathers and appears extremely dejected for a minute or two, after which it emits a low murmuring cry, scarcely audible at a distance of more than eighteen or twenty yards. At this time the other parent reaches the spot, flying so low over the ground that I thought its little feet must have touched it, as it skimmed along, and after a few low notes and some gesticulations, all indicative of great distress, takes an egg in its large mouth, the other bird doing the same, when they would fly off together, skimming closely over the ground, until they disappeared among the branches and trees. But to what distance they remove the eggs, I have never been able to ascertain; nor have I ever had an opportunity of witnessing the removal of the young. Should a person, coming upon the nest when the bird is sitting, refrain from touching the eggs, the bird returns to them and sits as before. This fact I have also ascertained by observations.

The first "apparent" recorded instance of the occurrence and nesting of the chuck in Ohio is recorded by E. S. Thomas (1932) and dated May 14, 1932. On May 21, 1932, the nest and two eggs were found and the female, with two eggs, was collected for the Ohio State Museum.

My earliest nesting record for South Carolina was made on April 13, this being nearly two weeks in advance of the next nearest date. The eggs are laid somewhat sooner than usual in forward seasons, the above record being an illustration of such an instance.

Eggs.—[AUTHOR'S NOTE: The chuck-will's-widow regularly lays two eggs, which are between oval and elliptical-oval and usually moderately glossy. Major Bendire (1895) considered these eggs as "among the handsomest found in the United States." I cannot do better than to quote his description of them, as follows:

The ground color of these eggs is of such a subtle tint that it is almost impossible to describe it accurately; it varies from a rich cream, with a faint pinkish suffusion, to a pale cream, and more rarely to pure white. They are in most cases more or less profusely blotched, marbled, and spotted with different shades of brown, tawny, fawn, and Isabel-color, underlaid and mixed with lighter shades of ecru drab, lavender, pearl gray, and pale heliotrope purple. In an occasional specimen some of the markings take the shape of irregular lines and tracings, like those of the Grackles; in others they are fine and minute, obscuring the ground color to some extent. In some specimens the darker shades predominate; in others, the lighter; in fact, there is an endless variation in the style of markings, but in the entire series there is not a single specimen which is not perceptibly marked.

The measurements of 54 eggs average 35.56 by 25.57 millimeters; the eggs showing the four extremes measure 40 by 27.5, 38.1 by 28.2, 32.9 by 25.1, and 36.2 by 23.1 millimeters].

Young.—Some notes of unusual interest in regard to the behavior of the adult at the nest, as well as the actions of the young birds, have been sent me by Herbert L. Stoddard, of Thomasville, Ga. These are transcribed herewith, and in the general lack of such knowledge they serve to illuminate something of the home life of this interesting species:

"April 30 (1928), 7 a. m.: One egg has hatched and the chick is a queer little mite covered with a yellow-ochre down, and hops about like a frog in a very lively manner. When he is uncomfortably hot or chilled he gives a plaintive little pipe that can be heard *about 20 feet.*

"May 1: Other chick hatched out this morning or during the night and eggshells were gone.

"May 3: Chicks growing fast but still being brooded in same spot. Mother goes to sleep on a fence post after flushing, but as soon as chicks start to squeal from the heat, she becomes frantic and will nearly fly into my face. I bother her a few minutes at 3 p. m. each day, as I chase her well away, then duck into the blind and take a few feet of film as she comes back to the nest. Not much action, however, and she is a *wise fowl.* She knows perfectly when I am in the blind!

"May 6: Found the nest spot empty today at noon but finally located the old bird (she has two patches of albinistic feathers in center of upper breast, so I know it's the same individual that performed the incubation) brooding her two chicks about 30 feet south. Their eyes have been open from the first but are now a little deeper in color and are always half closed like those of the adult in daytime.

"May 13: Have kept in rather close touch with the chuck-will's-widow family recently. They are living under a growth of sparkle-berry shrubs and have lived here within a radius of 6 feet for the last ten days.

"The place is pretty well marked by their mourning-dovelike excrement. When disturbed, the chicks hop off with elevated wings in a 'mechanical toy' sort of way. That is, their progress is marked by a series of rapid, toadlike hops until they are 'run down' (usually in 30 or 40 feet). The wings serve as balances.

"The chicks have a little complaining whine that brings the mother in frantic haste. She flies noiselessly about, every now and then lying on the ground with her wings *widely spread and reached forward,* with the primaries pressed to the ground. In this queer position, she beats them a bit and opens and shuts her huge mouth, exhaling air audibly as she does so and occasionally uttering the queer, froglike croak. Altogether an odd performance. No evidence of a mate has been seen about this location."

Plumages.—[AUTHOR'S NOTE: The young chick is completely covered with long, soft, silky down; on the upper parts the color varies from "ochraceous-tawny" or "light ochraceous-buff" on the head to "tawny" on the back; on the lower surface the color grades from "ochraceous-tawny" on the chest to "light ochraceous-buff" on the throat and belly.

The growth of the juvenal plumage, in which the sexes are alike, is rapid. Ridgway (1914) describes it very well as follows: "Similar to the adult female in 'pattern' and coloration of tail, primaries, and primary coverts, but otherwise different; scapulars and middle wing-coverts ochraceous-buff, irregularly barred with black; pileum more grayish, with small spots, instead of streaks, of black; under parts barred with black on a light brownish buffy ground, without vermiculations, mottling, or spots, and band across lower throat indistinct or obsolete."

This plumage is worn but a short time, as a partial molt into a first winter plumage begins in July; I have seen a specimen that had nearly completed this molt on August 2; this plumage closely resembles that of the adult female, as the juvenal wings and tail are retained; I can find no evidence of a spring molt. Young birds apparently retain the first winter plumage, including the juvenal wings and tail, until the following summer; I have seen birds in this plumage during winter and as late as May in spring.

Both adults and young have a complete annual molt, mainly in July and August. At this first postnuptial molt young birds become practically indistinguishable from adults, and the sexes become differentiated. Young birds in fresh fall plumage are darker and more richly colored than adults, with more "ochraceous-tawny"; the colors have faded some by spring.

Adults have two recognizable color phases, a tawny phase, in which the ground color of the two central rectrices varies from "ochraceous-buff" to "ochraceous-tawny", with deeper ochraceous or buffy colors in the scapulars and wing coverts; and a gray phase, in which the ground color of the two central rectrices is pale buff, or pale grayish buff, and the scapulars and wing coverts are paler and grayer.]

Food.—The chuck-will's-widow, like its family relatives, is an insect eater par excellence. The semitropical nature of much of its range is highly conducive to an abundance of insects and other night-flying creatures that are the bulk and mainstay of its diet. The mouth of the chuck is enormous, a characteristic of the goatsucker tribe, and is provided with bristles that act as a sort of additional trap. The widely open mouth is as much as 2 inches at the greatest breadth.

Prey is secured at low elevations, often only a few feet from the ground. The bird works the edges of woodlands bordering open fields and often makes sallies over the latter. The flight is silent, and the birds seem to be no more than gigantic moths. Beetles, "flying ants," and moths make up a large bulk of the food in many localities. Small birds have frequently been found in the stomachs of this species. While seemingly incongruous, this is, after all, not difficult to understand when the conditions are considered. Many observers have concluded that this type of stomach content is taken by mistake; that the small, fluttering bird, confused by the darkness, is taken for a moth and snapped up by the cruising chuck, of course being swallowed whole.

An alternative theory exists, however, and, if true, the bird-taking habit would be removed from the realm of the accidental and fall into purposeful, predatory effort. The late Edward H. Forbush pointed out that the "goatsuckers show an anatomical affinity to the owls. They have similar, soft plumage, noiseless flight, large eyes and nocturnal vision." It is possible that, with this structural relationship, there are other phases of likeness between the chuck and the owls. It is the largest of the goatsuckers that occur in this country, and the other representatives of the family do not seem to indulge in small bird prey. Doubtless this is because of their considerably smaller mouths, but whatever the reason the chuck remains as the outstanding example of this procedure.

That this habit is certainly not accidental sometimes is definitely proved by the observation recorded by Gerald Thayer (1899) in which he relates the instance of a chuck-will's-widow pursuing and catching warblers near a ship off the Carolina coast. Hummingbirds, swallows, sparrows, and warblers have been among those birds found in the stomachs of the chuck, and the frequency with which this occurs lends color to the supposition that it is more intentional than accidental. More research is necessary on this subject.

Even granting the truth of it, the economic status of the chuck is on the right side of the ledger and the great percentage of its activities are beneficial, for the noxious insects which it destroys are numerous. Miss Phoebe Knappen, of the United States Biological Survey, in answer to a request of the writer has very kindly furnished a summary of specific results in the stomach analysis carried out on this species in the laboratories of that Bureau. A full stomach from Oklahoma, without date and therefore not included in the tabulation below, contained the following: *Dendroica* (sp.), 70 percent; Coleoptera (*Calasoma*, *Harpalus*, Carabidae, *Ligyrus*, *Strategus*, Scarabaeidae), 22 percent; Orthoptera (*Schistocerca*, *Nesconocephalus*), 8 percent.

The remarkable percentage of bird remains shown by this stomach would seem a great argument for the support of predation by purpose.

Seventy percent of the total food among the wood warblers! However, it seems also to be a most exceptional case, for nothing that even approaches it is found in the list below, which embraces a range of 45 stomachs from five States and one Canadian Province. The entire amount of the stomachs listed contained the remains of but *two* birds!

With reference to the Oklahoma stomach, I wonder whether there might be a seasonal variation in the bird-taking propensities of the chuck-will's-widow in relation to migration. It would appear reasonable to believe that when there is high activity among birds traveling through a given area, such as would take place in the spring migration, the chucks of that locality would have greater opportunity in securing them. One would not have to incline to the predatory theory to accept this, for if there are a great many small birds passing through an area for a few weeks, the chucks in their night hunting would blunder across more birds than would be the case later in the season. If the take *is* accidental, a higher percentage of accidents would then occur. If, on the other hand, the take is deliberate, then the chances of indulging that habit would be greater and would fall off later in the season. So, whatever impulse governs the matter, the migrations would result in more birds appearing in the diet. Unfortunately, the Oklahoma stomach was undated, so it is impossible to ascertain whether the bird secured its high percentage during a migration or not, but I incline to the belief that it was a spring specimen.

To return to the analysis, Miss Knappen states: "The other 45 stomachs taken in March (2), April (31), May (11), and November (1) were collected in Florida (37), Georgia (1), Mississippi (2), North Carolina (1), Ontario (1), and Texas (3). The annual percentages of different items in the food, which was entirely animal, equal: Carabidae, 3.64; *Phyllophaga*, 32.98; other Scarabaeidae, 25.28; Cerambycidae, 4.49; Elateridae, 1.34; other Coleoptera, 5.13; Lepidoptera (moths), 12.36; Odonata, 4.63; Aves, 7.21; and miscellaneous animals, 2.85.

"The genera most persistently eaten were *Phyllophaga* (May beetles) and *Anomala*. The birds consumed were 1 *Dendroica palmarum* and 1 *Helminthophila* sp., while the miscellaneous bracket includes various bugs, flies, a bivalve, and other animal material."

The insect content of these 45 stomachs totals more than 70 percent in but three classes (*Phyllophaga*, Scarabaeidae, and Lepidoptera) and other kinds make up considerably more than that. Birds are represented by only 7.21 percent, and both victims were warblers. One cannot but wonder at the single "bivalve," an item that would certainly not occur to most students as being connected with a chuck's diet.

Behavior.—Being as close kin to the whippoorwill as the chuck is, it cannot be expected that its habits will vary extensively. Inactive by day and a persistent hunter by night, it fulfills the usual characteristics pertaining to the family. Sitting motionless on a mossy log, a branch of some forest tree, or ensconced within a natural cavity, it dozes away the daylight hours. Some observers have found it sleeping in company with bats, in an obscure hollow. I have never found the chuck among such company, all my daylight observations being connected with the bird's occupancy of some low limb, or on the ground itself.

When flushed, it rises with easy, fitful wafts of silent wings, alternating the beats with periods of sailing. Frequently it describes a curve and swings back near the spot from which it was flushed. Fairly close approach is allowed, even after the bird has been disturbed and alighted again. Doubtless it puts a great deal of dependence upon the wonderfully protective coloration of the plumage.

In the Carolina low country the chuck is very fond of roosting in the sandy roads so characteristic of the rural districts. Passing along at dusk, one may see the reflection of the eyes plainly in the glare of a car's headlights. At times a roosting bird is disturbed under these conditions by day, and I have had them flush and come directly at the car, swerving only slightly aside to pass. One bird on Bulls Island, S. C., was flushed two or three times in an hour, as we had occasion to pass the same spot often, and once it flew by so closely that an extended arm might have touched it. This habit of frequenting the sand roads is shared by the whippoorwill when it is present in coastal Carolina during the winter months.

Little or no distinction is made between these two birds in much of their range. The uninformed observer takes it for granted that any night bird that calls, except an owl, is a whippoorwill, and this seems the more strange in a section where the chuck is abundant and the whippoorwill comparatively uncommon, as in coastal Carolina. The latter calls but rarely during its winter sojourn in the Charleston area; indeed, I have heard it but twice in all my years of ornithological study. One of these instances was in January, the other early in March. When the whippoorwill is present in this area, the chuck is not, for the former leaves before the latter appears from the south. In spite of this fact and the overwhelming evidence of the chuck's presence and comparative absence of that of the whippoorwill, the people of the low-country are far more familiar with the name of the latter and credit the call of the chuck to the other bird.

The eyes of the chuck-will's-widow reflect light admirably. Some years ago E. B. Chamberlain, of the Charleston Museum, and I carried out a series of experiments in "jack-lighting" amid the woods of Cumberland Island, Ga. It was a revelation in many ways. The night woods were literally twinkling and sparkling with eyes! The ground and low bushes gleamed with hundreds of points of light from the eyes of spiders; the lagoons reflected the ruby-red of many alligators, while here and there along the bank a wandering raccoon stared into the light beam or a trotting gray fox paused to sniff, one foreleg upraised like a pointer. Florida screech owls were seen perched atop low stumps, hunched and motionless, and although we could work up to within 3 feet of them, the take-off when it occurred was so utterly noiseless that not a whisper of sound ensued at even that close range. Dozens of deer were seen, their eyes, of course, reflecting the light perfectly, and even grazing horses and cows along the edges of the lagoons were as plainly noted.

Now and then a very large pair of eyes close to the ground shone out. Coming closer, we could see a chuck, sitting like a stone, staring rigidly into the light. While one of us held the light, the other worked around to the side and came up on the bird from behind, and reaching out could pick up the staring bird with ease. We examined several in this way, while they uttered a hissing note of fear or anger. The birds struggled strongly while held and were very difficult to quiet.

Though sharing with the other goatsuckers the characteristic habit of perching lengthwise, the chuck occasionally departs from custom and proves the ancient adage that exceptions make the rule. N. B. Moore (MS.) writes that he has seen it perch directly across a branch when the latter is an inch or more in diameter. He once "saw one perch on a greenbrier one-quarter inch in diameter as cleverly as any bird, though it sank suddenly under its weight for 7 or 8 inches. The bird remained on it for 10 or 15 minutes." It is likely that the chuck indulges in this more than one would ordinarily suppose. I have seen it but once, when a bird was flushed in daylight and flew to a small, gnarled oak, where it alighted among the outer twigs, perching distinctly crosswise. It had two young in the near vicinity.

In the reference already made above to Thayer's (1899) account of this species capturing warblers on a ship off the South Carolina coast, he noted that, on shipboard, the bird perched crosswise on the rigging at times. Another remarkable character was that this bird was seen, on flights out from the ship, actually to alight on the surface of the ocean! This is certainly phenomenal and constitutes behavior that is utterly at variance with the bird's ordinary habits. One more instance of crosswise perching is noted by W. S. Long (1935) ; he saw a specimen near Lawrence, Kans., that indulged in this posture.

The chuck-will's-widow frequently roosts in the same spot day after day, and one may be fairly certain of surprising a bird regularly when once the roosting area is located. During migrations it occasionally is found in rather extraordinary situations, one of the most striking of these being noted by J. M. McBride (1933), of New Orleans. He writes that he watched one for a week, September 14 to 21, 1933, occupy an unprotected branch of a hackberry tree just even with his second-floor window. It was to be seen daily on this branch from 6 a. m. to 6 p. m. His house was in the heart of the residential district of New Orleans.

Voice.—There is no doubt that the voice of the chuck-will's-widow is its most interesting and outstanding characteristic. Indeed, it is the one thing that many ever know of the species. It is a bird easily heard but comparatively seldom seen; therefore, though the call may be a nightly sound throughout the summer, the author may be utterly unknown to many by sight. However, no one who lives within the range of the chuck can have failed to listen to the notes perforce, and only a deaf person can fail to be aware of its presence. Though the specific name of "vociferous" has been applied to the whippoorwill, it is equally true of the chuck-will's-widow, if not more so, but the generic name of the latter is well chosen, for the mouth is certainly "cavelike."

The call of this species is well deserving of comment, particularly in view of the fact that there seems to be so much confusion about it in the recent literature. Why this difference of opinion should exist, and why certain positive statements have been made, are sources of wonder to me and to others who know the voice of the chuck intimately. How anyone could listen for only a few minutes to the call and then say that "the song of the chuck-will's-widow is less vigorous than that of the whippoorwill; it consists of *three* notes . . . . with a slight accent on the *first* syllable" is beyond my comprehension. And yet more than one ornithologist has so stated. It seems significant that all those so describing it are northerners, that they know the chuck only by reason of short southern trips of a few days or weeks. Or, perhaps, they take the opinion of others who have as little information as themselves. If their experience with this bird covered any extended period, they could hardly fall into such error.

The call of the chuck-will's-widow is distinctly 4-syllabled (some observers say five at times), and therein lies one of the marked differences between it and the whippoorwill, which does have a 3-syllabled call. The accent is not on the first but on the third syllable; in other words, on the "wid" of widow. Few birds "say" their names as plainly. The *chuck* is uttered on a lower tone than the rest but is distinctly audible at 300 yards or more. At some distance one might be excused for thinking the call 3-syllabled, for it may sound like *will's-widow*, but on still nights the first syllable is plainly heard even across broad bodies of water, as occur over much of the southern coast region.

The notes are not limited entirely to the dusk of evening or night. The bird sometimes calls in full daylight, either on cloudy or bright days, and sometimes during rains. I have heard it at 1 p. m. on a bright, clear day. It is, of course, not the rule any more than is the cross perching sometimes indulged in, but it certainly occurs. However, it is during late evening and all through the night that the chuck really performs, and it sometimes calls through the entire period. In localities favored by the species, several birds may be calling at once, which results in a jumble and overlapping of notes. Herbert L. Stoddard writes that, never having heard a chuck-will's-widow calling in the daytime, he was "greatly surprised to hear two calling back and forth at 11:30 a. m. today (May 25, 1928). It was crystal clear and the sun was *hot*, but these two called over 5 minutes, exactly as they do in the nighttime."

In rapidity and frequency, there is much variation. A bird may utter a very few calls or very many. I have counted individual calls many times, and there seems to be no established custom or sequence. The usual interval between the notes is about 2½ seconds, when the bird is doing a string of them. I counted the calls of a bird just outside my window one night and it ran off 111 without "drawing breath" other than the short spacing between each, 2½ seconds. The calls were uttered at the rate of 25 a minute, this series taking about 4½ minutes. One of my longest counts is 176 calls successively uttered without a break. E. S. Dingle tells me that he has counted 300 consecutive calls. On the night of June 2, 1939, at my home in St. Andrews Parish, Charleston, I heard a chuck that beat anything I have encountered yet. I had gone to bed; the night was warm and I was lying near a window, when a chuck started up about 50 yards away in one of the live oaks in my yard. I began counting almost automatically, and kept it up, idly wondering whether it would reach my former record. It did, and then some. I continued to count, and count. Finally, I got up and sat by the window, in order not to miss any of it. The calls were perfectly continuous, and uttered at the usual rate, although twice there was a slight break in perhaps as much as a second's lateness between them. The bird shifted its perch twice, moving perhaps a few yards each time, but did not stop calling. The total was *eight hundred and thirty-four calls* (834).

The notes are clear-cut, insistent, and sharply enunciated with the exception of the first syllable. There is a ringing quality about them that is very striking, and one gets the impression of full-voiced effort. The head is moved noticeably when the call is uttered, and doubtless considerable muscular effort is put forth. Some writers have termed the notes "doleful," "monotonous," and "melancholy," but to me they have never seemed anything but sooth-ing and dreamily satisfying. Charles Torrey Simpson (1920) says that the chucks "make night hideous" with their "terrible chatter." Thus do tastes differ!

When it arrives from its winter quarters the chuck is particularly vociferous, and keeps this up until after the eggs are hatched. There is then a cessation followed by some renewed activity before de-parting for the south on the approach of fall. It must be very susceptible to cool weather, for it does not remain even as far south as Charleston until early in fall. The first part of September usually sees it gone, although individuals linger longer than that.

Besides the regular, self-naming call, the chuck has another note, which is not well known and is very difficult to describe. It is not the hissing sound uttered when the bird is caught or handled but is given occasionally when about its hunting. Almost entirely, if not entirely, it is a *flight* note; at least I have never heard it when the bird is sitting. It is inadequate to describe it as a "growl," and yet that is the only word that seems to approach it. As one flies by in the gloom, this note is heard, and it is an eerie, utterly indefi-nite sound, possessing a strangely unearthly quality which impres-ses one with wonder that it comes from a bird.

It is seldom if ever referred to in the literature but some have remarked upon it in correspondence to the writer. The late James Henry Rice, Jr., of Brick House Plantation, Wiggins, S. C., once had an army officer visiting him who remarked on this note, but Mr. Rice himself, being very deaf, was not aware of it, though he knew the chuck well. He asks, in a letter to Mr. Bent, whether anyone has noted what he termed "that clucking sound." I should hardly describe it as a "cluck" but it may impress some as such.

One other note has been commented on by those thoroughly familiar with the chuck. It is often given just as the bird is *flushed* and, like the one above, is very difficult to describe. It can be interpreted as a "croak" perhaps, and Dr. Eugene E. Murphey (MS.), of Augusta, Ga., calls it "froglike." His allusion to it, as well as the utterances of the regular call as given in fall, is given in a communication as follows:

"I imagine most field ornithologists are familiar with the frog-like croak that the bird makes when flushed, and I am inclined to believe that this note is much more apt to be sounded when the bird has been flushed from the nest. One observation may be worthy of note, namely, that I have heard the chuck-will's-widow singing as late as September 12 in Edgefield County, S. C. When it comes to interpreting the quality of a bird's song, it is impossible to get away from a personal construction, which, of course, is invalid in a scientific observation, but it seemed to me that on this occasion the song was very definitely less vehement and forceful, certainly less frequently reiterated than is the case in spring; in fact, the whole thing seemed to have a querulous and uncertain character, somewhat as if he were wondering why he should be singing at this particular time of year. I endeavored to collect the bird, but the rapidly gathering darkness made it impossible for me to secure it, although I was very close to it several times and saw it take flight. Unfortunately, it chose to fly toward the darkening east rather than the west where there was still an afterglow."

In commenting generally upon the continuity of the chuck's calls during the early part of the season, Herbert L. Stoddard, of Thomasville, Ga., has sent me the following notes:

"Spent the entire night of April 14, 1927, on the alert in the observatory at the quail pens on lookout for an owl which has been killing quail . . . a brilliant moonlight night. Chuck-will's-widows called *all night*, no 5-minute period between 9 p. m. and 5 a. m. elapsing without one to eight or ten calling. They have many guttural notes of different inflection, as well as the beautiful call note, a guttural, low-toned *waugh* given in questioning tones being common. These notes are most frequently uttered when a pair of the birds are together."

Fall.—The latest record in fall for the chuck-will's-widow in lower South Carolina is September 28 (Wayne, 1910). The great majority of the birds have left some time before this date. Indeed, Dr. Murphey's record mentioned above was a late one and impressed him markedly, as his account shows.

The earliest arrival record for the whippoorwill for the same locality is September 15, 1928 (Edward S. Dingle, MS.). The latest whippoorwill record is for April 1, 1911 (Wayne, 1910). Thus, in some exceptional years there may be the slightest overlapping of the arrival and departure of the chuck and the whippoorwill, but in the main the one has gone when the other appears, and there is usually some little interval between the sojourns of the two.

Referring to the fall migration in El Salvador, Dickey and van Rossem (1938) say: "Chuck-will's-widows were seen as late as October 29 at Rio Goascorán, where they were more common than in any other locality. * * * Most were found well up in trees, once as high as a hundred feet above the ground, and so wild that collecting them was usually impossible. At Lake Alomega one flew from tree to tree through the high forest and at no time permitted an approach closer than about a hundred yards. * * *

"The usual daytime locations were large, horizontal branches twenty feet or so from the ground and in rather heavy woods."

DISTRIBUTION

Range.—Southeastern United States, the Caribbean region, Central America, and northern South America; casual north to Ontario and Nova Scotia.

Breeding range.—The chuck-will's-widow breeds **north** to southeastern Kansas (Arkansas City and Independence); Missouri (Willard, Springfield, and Sulphur Spring); southern Illinois (Olney); southern Ohio (West Union); and southern Maryland (Point Lookout). **South** along the Atlantic coast to Florida (St. Augustine, Daytona Beach, Royal Palm Hammock, and Man-o-war Key). **South** to Florida (Man-o-war Key, Fort Myers, St. Marks, Lynn Haven, and Pensacola); southern Alabama (Spring Hill); southern Louisiana (St. Francisville and Urania); and southern Texas (Houston, San Antonio, and Kerrville). **West** to central Texas (Kerrville, Waco, and Commerce); eastern Oklahoma (probably rarely Norman and Copan); and southeastern Kansas (Arkansas City).

Winter range.—The winter range is not clearly defined, but at this season it has been found **north** to Cuba (Isle of Pines and San Pablo); the Bahama Islands (Andros Island and Nassau); the Dominican Republic (Catarrey and Samana); and Puerto Rico (Arecibo, San Piedras, and Vieques Island). **East** to Puerto Rico (Vieques Island); and northern Colombia (Medellin). **South** to northern Colombia (Medellin and Antioquia); Panama (Panama City and Divala); Costa Rica (Rio Sicsola and Candelaria); Nicaragua (San Juan del Sur); El Salvador (Lake Olomega and probably Barra de Santiago); and Guatemala (Guatemala City). **West** to Guatemala (Guatemala City); and western Cuba (Isle of Pines). It appears that occasionally individuals may spend the winter in Florida, as one was recorded from Orlando on December 1, 1885; one from Lake Jackson on December 5, 1911; and another from the same general area on December 28, 1903. One also was seen at Chenier au Tigre, La., on January 2, 1934.

Spring migration.—Early dates of arrival are: Florida—Orlando, February 17; Melrose, March 3; Palma Sola, March 5; Daytona Beach, March 9; Merritts Island, March 12. Alabama—Prattville, April 2; Barachias, April 3; Greensboro, April 5; Montgomery, April 6. Georgia—Savannah, March 15; Cumberland, March 25;

St. Marys, March 28, South Carolina—Charleston, March 12; Frogmore, March 31; Columbia, April 6. North Carolina—Raleigh, April 10; Louisburg, April 17. Virginia—Lawrenceville, April 12; Bowers Hill, April 26. Louisiana—Bains, April 2; Bayou Sara, April 11; Baton Rouge, April 18; New Orleans, April 28. Mississippi—Biloxi, April 9; Jackson, April 10. Arkansas—Delight, April 10; Monticello, April 10; Fayetteville, April 14. Tennessee—Chattanooga, April 10; Knoxville, April 12; Belfast, April 18. Kentucky—Covington, April 7; Bowling Green, April 25. Missouri—Valley Park, April 18; Monteer, April 23. Texas—Refugio County, March 17; Corpus Christi, March 18; Austin, March 21; Kerrville, April 8. Oklahoma—Tulsa, April 20. Kansas—Manhattan, April 26; Elmdale, April 29.

Fall migration—Data on the autumn movement are not plentiful, but late dates of departure are: Oklahoma—Canadian River, September 5. Texas—Grapevine, September 20; Brownsville, October 1; Corpus Christi, October 22. Akansas—London, September 1; Delight, October 7. Mississippi—Bay St. Louis, September 25. Louisiana—New Orleans, September 21. Virginia—Lawrenceville, August 24. North Carolina—Louisburg, September 19; Raleigh, September 21. South Carolina—Summerton, September 23; Charleston, September 28. Georgia—Athens, September 6; Savannah, September 23. Florida—College Point, October 19; Pensacola, October 21; Punta Rossa, October 30.

Casual records.—Among records of this species north of its known breeding range are several for Maryland—one heard at North Beach on June 28, 1930; one heard at Clements on August 14, 1932; a mounted specimen in the collection of the Cambridge High School, taken at Fishing Creek sometime prior to 1933; and one recorded at Laurel on May 12, 1935. A specimen was taken at New Haven, Conn., on May 17, 1889; another was captured at East Boston, Mass., on October 13, 1915; one was killed at Pictou, Nova Scotia, on October 22, 1890; one was taken at Dayton, Ohio, on May 1, 1933, one was collected on Point Pelee, Ontario, on May 19, 1906; one was taken at Indianapolis, Ind., during April or May 1908; and one was obtained at Sugar Creek, in southeastern Iowa, on June 17, 1933. There are several records for Kansas north of areas where it is known to breed, among them being a specimen collected at Wichita on June 12, 1898; one taken at Hamilton on April 30, 1912; and one obtained at Lawrence on May 4, 1935.

Egg dates.—Arkansas: 11 records, May 15 to June 26.

Florida: 53 records, March 7 to June 30; 27 records, March 20 to May 13, indicating the height of the season.

Georgia: 28 records, April 25 to June 18; 14 records, May 7 to 24.

Texas: 17 records, April 4 to June 16; 9 records, May 2 to June 5.

ANTROSTOMUS VOCIFERUS VOCIFERUS (Wilson)

EASTERN WHIPPOORWILL

PLATES 21–23

HABITS

CONTRIBUTED BY WINSOR MARRETT TYLER

Almost every man, woman, and child living in the wide breeding range of the whippoorwill knows the bird by name. Those who once hear it singing, reiterating its name perhaps a hundred times or more without a pause, cannot fail to realize that they are listening to a whippoorwill, but how many of this multitude who know the whippoorwill's name ever saw the bird, or would recognize it if they did see it? Not, it may be presumed, one-tenth of 1 percent.

Yet the whippoorwill lived many long years in denser obscurity still, for, playing a part behind the scenes, so to speak, its lines were ascribed to another actor in the play; it was not recognized as a bird at all until the early part of the last century. Prior to this time the whippoorwill was supposed to be nothing more than the voice of the nighthawk, and even now in many rural districts the two birds are not clearly distinguished from each other. William Brewster (1895) says: "They are still very generally regarded by country people throughout New England as one and the same bird."

Spring.—The whippoorwill starts northward from central Florida in the latter part of March. This northerly movement evidently represents a general migration from the southern and eastern Gulf States, and through them from points farther south. The bird arrives in the latitude of Boston, Mass., late in April or early in May, thus flying a distance of a thousand miles or more in 35 or 40 days— a migration that corresponds closely, both in time of year and in speed of travel, with that of the chimney swift. Of this journey Wilson (1831) says:

In their migrations north, and on their return, they probably stop a day or two at some of their former stages, and do not advance in one continued flight. The whip-poor-will was first heard this season [1811] on the 2d day of May, in a corner of Mr. Bartram's woods, not far from the house, and for two or three mornings after in the same place, where I also saw it. From this time until the beginning of September, there were none of these birds to be found within at least one mile of the place; though I frequently made search for them. On the 4th of September, the whip-poor-will was again heard for two evenings successively in the same part of the woods. I also heard several of them passing, within the same week, between dusk and nine o'clock at night, it being then clear moonlight. These repeated their notes three or four times, and were heard no more. It is highly probable that they migrate during the evening and night.

F. Seymour Hersey (1923) tells of a striking instance of nocturnal migration when a multitude of whippoorwills arrived suddenly at Lakeville, Mass., in the middle of the night.

In 1901 [he says], on the evening of May 4, about eight o'clock, a single bird was heard singing. This was the first arrival noted and no others were heard that evening. At two o'clock the following morning, six hours later, I was awakened by birds singing loudly everywhere. I dressed and went out and for more than an hour the chorus continued. There were numbers of birds about the house, on the door-step and ridge-pole, others singing in the road or from the stone walls along the road side, while still others could be heard down in the pastures,—often eight or ten were singing at the same instant. I walked down the road for half a mile and the birds seemed equally as abundant on neighbors' farms. It seems probable that the migration takes place at night as these birds had just arrived.

Courtship.—Few observers have had the good fortune to watch the sexual activities of the whippoorwill. One must be very near the birds to see, in the semidarkness, the courtship in detail, and even should we catch sight of a courting pair—a rare happening— we may get but a glimpse of their actions, because, if they flit only a little way back into the gloom, they are lost to view, fading into the shadows.

Frank Bolles (1912) tells of the following experience. He was hidden under a "narrow fringe of spirea bushes, 2½ ft. high only 3 ft. from the stone"—a stone on which a whippoorwill sang every evening. He says:

It uttered its note about twenty or thirty times when to my astonishment another whip. alighted near it, on the left (W.) end of the boulder. One or two sounds like the soft popping of corn came from the new arrival, and the first bird, which had ceased its call, faced west and began a strange, slow dance, advancing a step at a time towards its mate, raising its body to the full length of its legs at each step, thus making a sort of undulating approach. The other bird remained where it alit, but seemed to be moving its body up and down or else slowly pulsating its wings. The first bird, which I think was the male, seemed to continue its dance entirely around the female. As he passed her, indescribable purring and popping sounds were made and one of the birds flew lightly away—the ♀ I think. The male resumed his first position, and remained silent. Then he rose and circled in the air, catching an insect I thought, for he came back at once to the spot on the rock which he always covers. A moment later his mate seemed to call from below the house, near the lake, and he flew, his white feathers flashing as he spread his tail, and the strokes of his wings making a distinct and quite loud sound as he passed close above my head.

Henry K. Coale (1920) reporting the observation of his neighbor, Moritz Boehm, says:

On different occasions, while the male was calling, he saw the female going through some peculiar antics, but in the dusk could not make out just what she was doing. One evening, when he was sitting on the lower step, the birds came up and performed within ten feet of him. He kept perfectly quiet. The male called from a low branch overhead, while the female strutted on the gravel path below, with wings and tail outspread and head lowered, and side-stepped back and forth, half way around to the right, then to the left, all the time uttering a curious guttural chuckle. This performance was kept up for ten or fifteen minutes.

Bendire's (1895) account of the whippoorwill's courtship is the best in the literature; it has become almost a classic, and ornithologists still deplore the regrettable incident that interrupted the observation.

While on a collecting trip in Herkimer County, New York, with Dr. William L. Ralph, in June, 1893, I witnessed a most amusing performance, which one may see perhaps once in a lifetime. I happened to be in a little outbuilding, some 20 feet in the rear of the house at which we were stopping, early on the evening of the 24th, about half an hour after sundown, when I heard a peculiar, low, clucking noise outside, which was directly followed by the familiar call of "whip-poor-will." * * * Directly alongside of the small outbuilding previously referred to, a barrel of sand and lime had been spilled, and from the numerous tracks of these birds, made by them nightly afterwards, it was evident that this spot was visited regularly, and was the trysting place of at least one pair. Looking through a small aperture, I saw one of the birds waddling about in a very excited manner over the sand-covered space, which was perhaps 2 by 3 feet square, and it was so much interested in its own performance that it did not notice me, although I made some noise trying to fight off a swarm of mosquitoes which assailed me from all sides. Its head appeared to be all mouth, and its notes were uttered so rapidly that, close as I was to the bird, they sounded like one long, continuous roll.

A few seconds after his first effort (it was the male) he was joined by his mate, and she at once commenced to respond with a peculiar, low, buzzing or grunting note, like "gaw-gaw-gaw," undoubtedly a note of approval or endearment. This evidently cost her considerable effort; her head almost touched the ground while uttering it, her plumage was relaxed, and her whole body seemed to be in a violent tremble. The male in the meantime had sidled up to her and touched her bill with his, which made her move slightly to one side, but so slowly that he easily kept close alongside of her. These sidling movements were kept up for a minute or more each time; first one would move away, followed by the other, and then it was reversed; both were about equally bold and coy at the same time. Their entire love making looked exceedingly human, and the female acted as timid and bashful as many young maidens would when receiving the first declarations of their would-be lovers, while the lowering of her head might easily be interpreted as being done to hide her blushes. Just about the time I thought this courtship would reach its climax, a dog ran out of the house and caused both to take flight.

Nesting.—The whippoorwill lays its two eggs on dry, well-drained ground, generally near the edge of a wood of small mixed growth—oak, beech, pine—where the floor of the wood is clear of dense underbrush and where the trees are not crowded together, but spaced far enough apart to cast an uneven shade. The eggs may lie on the open floor or under a small bush—not tucked away near the stems, but out in the shadow of its branches. The bird builds no nest, although a slight depression about the eggs may result from the presence of the parent there during incubation; for concealment it relies solely on the soft colors of the fallen leaves and the flickering light of the woodland.

It is rare to find the eggs laid in a more open situation.

Lewis McI. Terrill, in a letter to Mr. Bent, gives in detail the results of remarkably close observations on the home life of a pair of whippoorwills and their brood. His observations were made near St. Lambert, Quebec, in 1933.

On May 14 Mr. Terrill came upon a pair of whippoorwills in a patch of deciduous trees, mainly young maple and birch. A week later he flushed the female "from a single egg lying on a bed of old leaves in a small glade" near the spot where he first saw the birds. "There was no depression whatever, and the egg appeared as if it had been casually dropped there." The second egg was not laid until the 23d, indicating "that egg deposition takes place on alternate days."

Invariably at his subsequent visits Mr. Terrill found the female incubating or brooding, but while the young birds remained in the vicinity of the nest he saw the male near it only once (June 20).

He says: "The male spent the day in a thicket over 400 yards away. I usually heard him singing from this direction in the early part of the evening; later he sang from a point nearer the nest; and finally from its immediate vicinity. I gather from this that he visited his family regularly at night.

"On May 27 the eggs were resting in a noticeable depression made by the pressure of the bird's body. One might almost call it a nest although no extraneous nesting material whatever had been added. The female was very consistent in her behavior, usually leaving the eggs when I was 10–15 feet away and flying to a dead branch 2 feet from the ground where she uttered a few protesting chucks, which resembled a call of the catbird and to a lesser extent the *chuck* of the hermit thrush.

"On the occasion of the male's visit (June 20) both birds were very worried, and their calls, especially that of the male, resembled the *whip* note of his song, although much subdued. He sometimes called *whip-will* when excited by the distress calls of the young.

"When returning to the nest the female frequently hovered before alighting, often dropping to the ground a few feet from the nest. Even at that short distance she would not attempt to walk onto the eggs, but would fly up again, hover, and then alight directly on the nest.

"The nighthawk, we may note, progresses differently. To be sure, it occasionally flies short distances when approaching the nest, but the final approach is by walking, or perhaps I should say creeping in a

Charlie Chaplin-like' shuffle. The different methods of approach to the nest are, I think, indicative of the different habitats of two very similar birds. The woodland whippoorwill hops or flies to avoid obstructions, whereas the nighthawk can gain its objective without leaving the ground.

"The female whippoorwill was still incubating on June 10, but on the 11th there were two young in the nest. The incubation period for the last egg laid was, therefore, at least 19 days, and possibly nearer 20.

"The first definite movement away from the nest was noted on June 18, when the female was brooding the young 50 feet away. On the 19th and 20th she was respectively 70 and 85 feet from the nest. The female often alighted crosswise on a limb when excited, or for the purpose of facing me, but quickly assumed the lengthwise position.

"June 21–22—Female brooding young 100 feet from nest.

"June 25—One young bird flew 15 feet.

"June 26—Older chick flew 25 feet when female was flushed. Younger bird still jumped, then squatted, but when I placed it on a branch, it flew 15 feet. Both young always alighted on the ground, but perched readily. This was the last I saw of the family."

Mr. Terrill's report of this family of whippoorwills makes it clear that the male parent very rarely came near the nest at the times he was watching it. This accords with the experience of many observers at other nests. For example, H. E. Tuttle (1911) says: "The male Whip-poor-will I saw only once, and that was after the young were fully grown. He was very conspicuous in the dusk as he sat on a log, uttering rasping sounds in his throat and opening and shutting his tail, brilliantly marked with white at the edges. It was only a day or so after seeing the male bird that I lost sight of the young birds altogether."

But why should we expect the male whippoorwill to come to the nest in the middle of the night—the whippoorwill's day? There is nothing to do there at night except to keep the eggs warm, or, after they hatch, to brood the young, and his mate can do that while she sleeps on the nest. So he sleeps a little way off. But when the dark comes—when his morning breaks—when the night insects begin to fly, and food abounds, and his hungry children cry, where is the male parent then? We do not know, but we may assume, as Mr. Terrill suggests, that he joins his family and aids in feeding the young.

When a female bird is approached while she is incubating (Bendire says: "I believe the female attends to this duty almost exclusively") the behavior varies a good deal in different individuals. In many accounts of her actions, she is reported to flop about on the ground, seemingly trying to lead the intruder away. Wilson (1831) reports that "in traversing the woods one day in the early part of June, along the brow of a rocky declivity, a whippoorwill rose from my feet, and fluttered along, sometimes prostrating herself, and beating the ground with her wings, as if just expiring." On the other hand, H. E. Tuttle (1911) speaks of a bird, brooding young, which was "very fearless, allowing me to touch her back and making it necessary for me to shove her gently off the young when I wanted a glimpse of them."

Arthur C. Bent, in his notes, says that late in May he "flushed a whippoorwill from near a woodland path, where it apparently had been roosting regularly as evidenced by its droppings." A few days later, not 25 yards from the path, he "flushed the whippoorwill from the ground and saw its single egg lying on the flat, bare oak leaves."

C. H. D. Clarke, writing to Mr. Bent from Ontario, Canada, points out how changes in the topography of a region may affect the local whippoorwills. He says: "The common denominator explaining the local distribution of this species is, I believe, to be found in its feeding and egg-laying habits. The whippoorwill feeds in the open, like the nighthawk, but unlike it, fairly near the ground. Although both birds lay their eggs on the ground, the nighthawk nests in the open, whereas the whippoorwill always nests among trees. Hence, as a breeding bird, it is found in glades and around the edges of woodlots. Many of the woodlots, however, in this vicinity are closely grazed by cattle at the present time, a condition that prevailed less commonly in the semipioneering stage of our country. The whippoorwill does not tolerate this change; it will not breed in the grazed woodlots and, as a consequence, has been reduced in numbers here. It also seems to avoid extensive areas of conifers, possibly because of the absence of hardwood litter on which to lay its eggs. The area at Frank's Bay, in which the bird breeds very commonly, is a sand plain that was burned over about 25 years ago and has since grown up in many places to dense stands of poplar from 15 to 20 feet high. Here the whippoorwill has plenty of shelter in the dense poplar woods, an abundance of hardwood litter, and may cruise about over the treetops not far above ground."

Eggs.—[AUTHOR'S NOTE: The two eggs of the whippoorwill are between oval and elliptical-oval in shape and become somewhat glossy when incubated. The ground color is usually pure white, but occasionally a faint creamy tint is perceptible. The markings consist of spots or small blotches of "pale Quaker drab" or "pallid Quaker drab," scattered over the eggs more or less irregularly; an occasional egg has large, irregular blotches of this color. Overlying these pale gray markings, or scattered among them, are often many small spots or fine dots of various browns, such as "cinnamon-brown," "tawny," or "tawny-olive." An occasional egg is almost immaculate.

The measurements of 50 eggs average 29.0 by 21.3 millimeters; the eggs showing the four extremes measure **31.5** by 21.0, 30.48 by **22.86, 20.48** by 21.34, and 28.45 by **20.07** millimeters.]

Young.—The little whippoorwill chick, hatching out from an invisible egg, finds itself lying on the ground, with dead leaves all about. The dead leaves look like the chick, and the chick looks like the dead leaves; no one can tell them apart; practically the chick *is* a dead leaf, and, although hatched, it is still invisible, just as it was when hidden in the egg.

Some birds depend on speed for safety, or on agility or strength, but the whippoorwill relies chiefly on not being seen. Safety comes to the whippoorwill in dim light, half shadows, and the faint, confusing obscurity of dusk, and among these, on the borderland of invisibility, the whippoorwill lives all its days.

Nests of the whippoorwill are found almost always by accident. The old bird starts up from near the observer's feet, and a search—sometimes a long one—reveals the eggs or the young birds. For example, A. Dawes DuBois (1911) says:

The first nest was found on May 16, 1908, in a strip of woods of medium size trees, thickly undergrown, on a high bank of the Sangamon River [Illinois]. The ground was well carpeted with dried oak leaves. Our first intimation of Whippoorwills in this place was the sudden appearance of an adult bird fluttering along the ground in front of us, apparently with a broken wing. We stopped at once and while my companion stood to mark the place, I followed the bird a short distance. She fluttered along noiselessly, feigning serious injury and leading me away from the nest as rapidly as I could be induced to follow.

A search revealed the nest within a pace of the spot we had marked. It contained one egg and the broken shell of another which gave evidence of having hatched. Although I stooped to examine the broken shell I did not see the bird that had hatched from it until my companion called my attention to it. The little fellow was crouched, motionless, upon the brown leaves not six inches from the broken egg-shell.

H. E. Tuttle (1911) speaks thus of the young birds: "The newly hatched birds were very attractive-looking little chicks so long as they kept their mouths shut. They were a uniform buff color, which matched well with the leaves, and the instant their mother left them they each ran in opposite directions and squatted. In this maneuver the old bird seemed to aid them materially by the vigorous flip which she gave them as she rose, often tumbling them over on their backs."

J. G. Suthard writes to Mr. Bent from Muskegon, Mich., as follows: "On June 14, 1936, I flushed a whippoorwill from an oakleafed spot on a steep hillside overlooking a large timbered swamp. I shortly discovered two downy young with their eyes only partly opened. They made no effort to escape and were silent when handled. The parent flew around several times, uttering a *whup-whup-whur* note, and then perched on a dead limb of a nearby tree. One of the eggshells was about 6 feet below the nest on the hillside, and the feces of the young had not been moved by the parents. As this nest was only about 30 yards from the main highway, I returned several times between this date and June 24 to see if, owing to my disturbance of the young, the parents would move them. Each time I visited the nest the parent was brooding the young in practically the same spot."

Lewis McI. Terrill, in his study of nest life, quoted under "Nesting," says that on June 12, before the young birds were two days old, "whenever the female was flushed, the nestlings hopped or jumped several inches with the suddenness and unexpected agility of 'jumping beans,' then squatted in hiding posture in the manner of woodcock chicks. The entire movement was so rapid that it almost escaped notice." He continues:

"From the 13th to the 16th the female was brooding the young either in the nest or in the shade 2 or 3 feet away. On the latter date I heard one of the nestlings give a weak, complaining *whip*, which was answered by the mother 20 feet away. It attempted to follow her, progressing by little hops, but was in difficulty when it encountered heavy undergrowth where it was unable to hop. The smaller of the nestlings remained in the nest.

"June 26—The older bird when placed lengthwise on a limb quickly turned about and perched crosswise, demonstrating youth's objection to slavish custom! The older bird now frequently used the *whip* note, which appears to be the chief motif in the whippoorwill vocabulary. The younger bird still called in wheezy tones that I readily imitated by sucking my finger—so well that the mother bird frequently responded by flying to me and fluttering at my feet. The young at this date, nearly 16 days old, closely resembled their parents."

Terrill definitely established the incubation period of one of the eggs in the nest he observed as not less than 19 days, "and possibly nearer 20." Burns (1915) gives the incubation period as 17 days, and Audubon (1840) gives it as 14 days.

Plumages.—[AUTHOR'S NOTE: The downy young whippoorwill is thickly covered with long, soft, silky down, shading in color from "cinnamon" on the back to "pinkish cinnamon" on the chest, and to "light pinkish cinnamon" on the crown and abdomen; it matches the dead leaves on which it is hatched.

The juvenal plumage begins to grow at an early age. Ridgway (1914) says that the young male is "similar to the adult male in 'pattern' and coloration of lateral rectrices, as well as of primaries and primary coverts, but rest of plumage quite different, the wing-coverts and scapulars deep brownish buff or clay color, the former with coarse and irregular small spots of black, the latter with very large irregular spots of balck, the under parts barred with dusky on a brownish buffy ground and, like most of the upper parts, without fine vermiculations, the pileum spotted instead of streaked with black, and the band across lower throat indistinct, more or less broken by dusky barring, and buffy instead of white." The young female, he says, is "similar to the young male, but three lateral rectrices broadly tipped with ochraceous-buffy instead of having a large white distal area."

A young bird in juvenal plumage, nearly grown, collected in Massachusetts in July, is like the young male described above, except that the feathers of the interscapular region and the median wing coverts are from "ochraceous-buff" to "light ochraceous-bluff," with a narrow shaft streak and a conspicuous subterminal small spot of black.

During July and August the juvenal contour plumage is shed, the juvenal wings and tail being retained, and a first winter plumage is acquired, in which the contour plumage closely resembles that of the adult. This is worn until the following summer, when a complete molt produces the fully adult plumage. Both young and old birds have a complete annual molt between July and September.]

Food.—The earliest report on the food of the whippoorwill is that of Wilson (1831), who was the first writer to show that the whippoorwill and the nighthawk are different birds. He says: "Their food appears to be large moths, grasshoppers, pismires, and such insects as frequent the bark of old rotten and decaying timber. They are also expert in darting after winged insects."

Knight (1908) puts the following items on the whippoorwill's bill of fare: "Their diet," he says, "would seem to be entirely insectivorous and among the various things I have known them to eat are Sphinx moths of various species, *Actias luna, Samia cecropia, Samia columbia, Telea polyphemus,* and a great variety of species of Noctuidae, also grasshoppers, crickets, mosquitoes, caddis flies, and in fact almost any sort of insect available."

Bendire (1895) reports that "in the Western States, which are sometimes overrun by swarms of Rocky Mountain Locusts, it also feeds largely on these when abundant."

Forbush (1927) tells of the whippoorwill the following story which will endear the bird to all mosquito-haters. He says: "While I slept unsheltered nightly for a week in the Concord woods, rolled in my blanket, with only a head-net hung to a branch overhead to protect me from mosquitoes, I noticed each morning upon awaking just before daylight that something fluttered softly about my head. The sound was like that produced by a large night-moth, but soon I heard something strike the ground a few feet away, and then a well-known cluck convinced me that my visitor was a Whip-poor-will. The bird came nightly while I remained in the woods, and each morning before daylight it flew around my head-net until it had caught all the mosquitoes there."

Eaton (1914) says: "I have taken 36 full-grown moths from the stomach of a single Whippoorwill which was killed early in the evening, indicating that within an hour and a half he had killed and devoured these full-grown moths, each one of which contained hundreds of eggs."

Whippoorwills secure a large part of their food by capturing night-flying insects on the wing, but Ernest Ingersoll (1920) states that they also "have a way of balancing themselves near a tree-trunk or barn-wall, picking ants and other small provender off the bark; and even hunt for worms and beetles on the ground, turning over the leaves to root them out."

Francis H. Allen (MS.) says: "One evening I saw one take off from the branch of an oak for what was probably its first feeding flight of the night. It opened its mouth wide *before* launching into the air."

Behavior.—In order to study the whippoorwill at short range it is well to visit its haunts for a few evenings and learn how the bird we are to watch behaves when it wakes from its day's sleep. Whippoorwills move about over a considerable territory when they come into the open for their daily session of singing and feeding, they follow a route, evening after evening, that varies little, and on the circuit there are stations—a stone wall, a low branch, or a certain spot on the ground—where they are almost sure to stop and sing for a while.

If we seat ourselves near one of these stations where the light, which will be almost gone when the bird arrives, will favor our view, and where a dark background will obscure us from the bird, we shall be able to see the whippoorwill at short range, for if we sit motionless (no easy task, for mosquitoes will torture us) the bird will pay little attention to us. We must sit quiet and wait, following the song as it swings around the circuit, and we must watch the spot where the bird is about to alight, for, although in flight it looms big even in the dusk, when it comes to rest, with a

flip of wings it becomes a bit of dead wood, a clod of earth, or van-
ishes altogether.

On several evenings late in May 1914, at Wilton, N. H., I visited
what appeared to be the whippoorwill headquarters—a dry wood
of small deciduous growth bordering a sloping field, on one of
which was a moist alder run that ran down to the edge of the wood.
When I arrived, between sunset and dark, wood thrushes and
veeries were singing, but before they quieted down for the night,
the whippoorwills (from one bird to two or three) began to sing,
always from the dry wood. They sang intermittently, and generally after each series of *whip-poor-wills* their voices came from a
different part of the wood. By the time the light was becoming
uncertain (when one would have difficulty in reading print) one
bird, leaving the wood, worked up the slope, passing the field either
by way of the alder run or by a wood of larger growth and an
apple orchard that bordered the higher sides of the field.

On each of the first evenings when I visited the ground, one bird
paused in the corner of the field where it joined the alder run, and
sang a few times, and on two of these evenings I was able to approach
the bird but not near enough to see it. The next evening, therefore,
as soon as the bird that was singing in the wood began to change his
position, I retired to this corner of the field to await him and sat down
on a bank where my figure would not show against the sky. That
evening was unusually dark and cloudy. The bird left the wood by
the lower side, and at 7:50 I heard the song coming nearer and
nearer through the alders behind me. Then, two minutes later, it
came with startling suddenness from almost at my side. The bird
sat on the bare ground at the foot of the bank not 6 yards from where
I sat. In bringing my glass to bear upon him, I disturbed him, I
think, for he flew silently away. He alighted, however, on a rock and
began to sing. He was now 12 yards from me and on a level with
my eyes. His side was toward me, and he faced nearly in the direction from which he had just flown. He sat flat on the stone with
his head thrown slightly backward and upward and, on alighting,
immediately began to sing.

The song at close range sounded like *cuck-rhip-oor-ree*, the final
note accented and held longer than the other three, although the *rhip*
was louder and longer than the *oor*. The song was remarkably
regular; twice, however, the bird increased the tempo, and once he
doubled one note—either the *rhip* or the *oor*. After a pause the
cuck was invariably the first note given when he continued his song.

Even in the dim light the band of white across the throat was
clearly visible, and twice during each repetition of the *cuck-rhip-
oor-ree* this band was drawn backward—slightly at the *cuck*, mark-

edly during the final *ree*, when, I think, the beak was open wide. Later, when the bird more nearly faced me, these movements of the white band were less noticeable. The bird sat on the rock for three or four minutes, singing almost continuously. He sat absolutely still for the most part, but twice he moved backward about an inch, as if each time he took a single backward step. His departure, with no apparent cause, was noiseless and abrupt, breaking the song at *oor*.

F. Seymour Hersey (1923), who watched with great care a whippoorwill making its nightly round, says: "The time taken to make this circuit varied from 25 to 30 minutes. I watched this bird from several places of concealment and ascertained to my satisfaction that it was the same individual that visited each of these places and that the order given above was not varied. The spot from which he sang was, in all cases, nearly the same, i. e., within a very few feet of the place where he was seen on a previous evening."

Frank Bolles (1912) gives a remarkable picture, seen from almost within arm's reach, of a singing whippoorwill. Mr. Bolles, who was hidden near a stone to which the whippoorwill came nightly, says:

Suddenly I hear a rather feeble whip, 12 times S. of me, then silence and then a bird flies to the stone in front of my face, coming low over the bushes and alighting with its tail towards me. It squeaks or clicks three times, and I fear it suspects me and is giving a slight alarm note, but the next moment it begins the piercing *quip o'rip* slightly raising its head and dipping its tail each time it makes the sound. The head rises on the *quip* and falls on the *rip*. The wings do not move, nor the body save by a slight tipping. I could see the bird's outline perfectly against the white background of the shingled barn on which the moonlight fell fully.

When the whippoorwill comes out in the dusk for its evening round, alighting on a stone wall, on the ground, or on a big horizontal branch high in a tall tree, we may sometimes catch sight of it against the sky, as it flies from one station to another. In the air the whippoorwill does not resemble the nighthawk at all. Its wings are broad and, compared to those of the nighthawk, short, and it moves them with an easy sweep, with none of the nighthawk's jerkiness. When we see it flying steadily across an open field, it suggests an owl moving through the gloom on its broad, silent wings.

Taverner and Swales (1907) give a remarkable description of the flight of a whippoorwill seen under such circumstances at Point Pelee, Ontario. They say:

One evening, just as the dusk was darkening into night, a Whip-poor-will was heard near the camp. We stole out, and the bird was located in a large bare walnut tree in the open bush where, looking up against the still faintly illuminated sky, it could be plainly made out, sitting lengthwise, as is their fashion, on a rather large and almost horizontal branch. It remained perfectly motionless except for an occasional jerk of its white blotched tail, when it gave vent intermittently to a guttural "gluck." These notes were repeated at irregular intervals of perhaps half a minute, several times and then, without start or warning, it launched away into the air, starting off immediately at full speed, with a drop that carried it in a large, even circle half way to the ground, and then up on the same curve, to vanish in the gloom of the trees. Then it appeared on the other side, swinging down on fixed wings in great elliptical curves as though whirled from the end of a cord, perfectly silent in flight and threading the dusky mazes of the tree tops with the utmost confidence and precision. Here and there it rapidly wheeled, without an apparent stroke of the wing, now coming into view in the lower arc of its great circling, and then vanishing silently again on the upward sweep on the other side. As suddenly as it started, it ceased in the middle of a swing and, while the eyes vainly searched for the dark object along the continuation of its course, it was seated again on the branch from which it first sprang, silent and still. This was repeated several times, and then it was joined by another, and the two circled about like great soft, gliding bats until the sky above grew so dark that their movements could no longer be watched.

Several writers mention the fearlessness of the whippoorwill, or perhaps its failure to recognize man as a danger. For example, Bendire (1895) quotes E. A. McIlhenny, who says: "These birds are very tame, for on two occasions, while sitting still in the twilight to observe the movements of some Owls, I have had them come so close that I could have caught them. On one occasion one lit on my knee, and another on my foot as it was extended before me." And H. E. Tuttle (1911) says: "Once I watched two males fighting and singing at intervals on a fallen birch sapling. I was quite close to them,—within a yard—but they did not seem to regard me as dangerous, and when I tried to imitate the guttural noises they were making, they circled round my head so closely that one touched me with his wings. In the darkness I was probably no more than a charred stump."

C. W. G. Eifrig (1919) mentions "a unique experience" with a whippoorwill, which, displaying unexpected aggressiveness, darted repeatedly at his head.

It has been surmised that the whippoorwill uses its capacious mouth to carry its eggs, and even its young, out of danger when its nest has been discovered. There is no satisfactory evidence that the bird employs its mouth in this way, but it has been seen, on two occasions at least, carrying a young bird through the air held between its legs. J. H. Bowles (1895) says: "I flushed a whippoorwill that rose with a baby bird clutched firmly *between her thighs*," and Bendire (1895) quotes H. W. Flint as follows: "I once, and once only, saw a female (the male is never present at the nest) carry a young bird about a rod, but can not say she used her bill, and don't think she did, but I am almost sure the claws and legs only were used, as the young was hugged close to the body."

The whippoorwill is fond of taking dust baths. When driving after dark we sometimes catch sight of one as it starts up from its bath on a country road, and, as it flies off and our headlights pick it up, the white tail feathers, if the bird is a male, shine out for an instant. Forbush (1927) says: "Mr. Stanley H. Bromley of South-bridge, Massachusetts, tells me that a farmer there placed a large tray of dry wood ashes on the ground, and whippoorwills came there at night to dust in it."

Wilson (1831) states: "The inner edge of the middle claw is pecti-nated, and, from the circumstances of its being frequently found with small portions of down adhering to the teeth, is probably employed as a comb to rid the plumage of its head of vermin."

Voice.—If the whippoorwill "should sing by day, when every goose is cackling," the song might lose some of its witchery; we do not know; the bird sings in the dark, or when darkness is coming on fast, and the singer is invisible or almost invisible among the shadows. The song at a little distance comes to the ear as a pene-trating whisper of the bird's name, repeated perfectly regularly, time after time with scarcely a pause between, at a rather rapid rate—about once a second. The fourth note, a *cluck* before the *whip-poor-will*, is heard usually only when the bird is fairly near us, although we may hear it at a distance of 200 yards under favorable circumstances. The syllable *will* carries farthest of all the syllables.

It is rare to hear any material variation in the song, but there are individual birds that regularly sing an unusual form, and some-times a bird will introduce occassionally one abnormal phrase into his singing.

Simeon Pease Cheney (1891), speaking from the point of view of music, says: "In the courageous repetition of his name he accents the first and last syllables, the last most; always measuring his song with the same rhythm, while very considerably varying the melody— which latter fact is discovered only by most careful attention. Plain, simple, and stereotyped as his song appears, marked variations are introduced in the course of it. The whippoorwill uses nearly all the intervals in the natural scale, even the octave. I have never detected a chromatic tone." Describing altercations between two or more birds, he says:

These altercations are sometimes very amusing. Three whippoorwills, two males and a female, indulged in them for several evenings one season, in my garden. They came just at dark, and very soon a spirited contest began. Frequently they flew directly upward, one at a time. Occasionally one flew down into the patch near me, put out his wings, opened his big mouth, and hissed like a goose disturbed in the dark. But, the most peculiar, the astonish-ing feature of the contention was the *finale*. Toward the close of the trial of speed and power, the unwieldy name was dropped, and they rattled on freely with the same rhythm that the name would have required, alternating in their rushing triplets, going faster and faster, louder and louder, to the end.

The bird is remarkable on account of the regularity of its song and the great number of times it repeats the *whip-poor-will* without a pause. From 50 to 100 repetitions are not uncommon. Forbush (1927) says: "John Burroughs, however, made a count which so far as I know exceeds all others. He records that he heard a bird 'lay upon the back of poor will' 1088 blows with only a rarely perceptible pause here and there, as if to take breath."

F. Seymour Hersey (1923) writes: "The Whip-poor-will sings most continuously from dusk till about 9.30 p. m. and from 2.00 a. m. till dawn. During the intervening hours only an occasional song is heard. The song season lasts from their arrival in spring until late July or early August. Then there is a marked falling off in the number of singing birds heard until toward the end of August or early in September an increase in the number of singers is again noted. The songs of these late birds often lack the energy that characterizes the spring performance but a good many continue to sing until they leave for the south. My latest singing bird was noted September 24, 1901." These dates refer to eastern Massachusetts.

Of the possibility of the female singing, he says: "June 15 a Whip-poor-will alighted on the fence and uttered its 'chuck' note, which usually precedes the regular song, repeating it a number of times but not giving a note of the usual 'Whip-poor-will' call. It also did the same while on the wing. This bird was supposed to be a female as no conspicuous light area was visible on the tail. If so, she was capable of singing the same as the male for I later heard and saw her sing, both from the fence and while on the ground in the middle of the road. She finally flew and was followed by another bird which may have been her mate."

Of the whippoorwill's minor notes, we have seen above that the growling *gr-gr-gr* or *gaw-gaw-gaw* is presumably associated with courtship. I have never heard the note except when two (or more) birds were together, on or near the ground. This note suggests a little a note of the female woodcock, which is used under similar circumstances. The whirring *whup-whup-whirr* is evidently an alarm note.

A. Dawes DuBois (1911) mentions two other notes, evidently of alarm. He says: "She fluttered from the spot as she had done the previous day, but this time uttering a very low hissing or 'soughing' sound," and again, "She kept vigilant watch, however, at a short distance, moving about near the ground with a remarkably noiseless flight but uttering a 'chip' or 'whit' similar to that of a domestic chick."

If we are outdoors at the end of the day, when the sun has gone down and all the ways are darkened, if we are walking along a quiet country road fringed by woods and open fields, or, in a canoe, are drifting down a stream flowing slowly past farmland—pastures, stone walls, orchards—and if we listen, what do we hear? If it is summer, the bird songs are gradually fading away as the birds fall asleep, the robin chorus lessens when the light grows dim, and when it is almost dark a field sparrow may sing for the last time before night comes. If it is autumn we hear little bird song, only a short period of chipping and clucking before the birds settle for the night, and after that only the insects that will sing the night through. But let us listen. Was that a whippoorwill? Do we hear a whippoorwill, or do we imagine we hear one because the scene has changed to a world of shadows—the whippoorwill's world—and association has brought the bird to our mind, and its song has come to our ears? The song is faint and comes from far away. Perhaps we did not hear it; perhaps there was no song to hear.

This is a peculiarity of the whippoorwill's song; it is so bound up with association that we are sometimes misled. It is the same with the bluebird when we listen for its song over the brown fields of March.

Field marks.—The whippoorwill and the nighthawk appear very much alike when sitting either on the ground or along a horizontal branch of a tree, for in such situations it is difficult to see the points where the two birds differ. The whippoorwill is bristly about the mouth; the nighthawk is not. The tips of the whippoorwill's folded wings do not come to the end of the rounded tail, whereas the nighthawk's wings project beyond the forked tail. The whippoorwill has a narrow line of white on the upper breast. The corresponding mark on the nighthawk is broader and includes the throat. Perhaps the best mark for diagnosis is the pale, barred sides of the nighthawk. For purposes of field identification this part of the whippoorwill may be said to be unbarred.

In the air the distinguishing mark of the nighthawk is a conspicuous spot of white in the wing. The whippoorwill lacks this mark. The flight of the two birds (see above) is very different and identifies them at a glance.

The chuck-will's-widow, although similar to the whippoorwill in plumage, is a much larger bird.

Enemies.—The clearing away of a large part of the North American wilderness during the past two centuries or so has not materially affected the whippoorwill; it drove the bird back from the settlements a little way, farther and farther as the towns grew in extent and became the great cities of today, but at the present time, not far beyond the city limits, whippoorwills find miles and miles of country wild and secluded enough for their breeding purposes. Fifteen miles from the city of Boston, Mass., for example, as well as within a mile or two of many small towns in the State, the bird is still abundant, nesting on the dry wooded ridges and eskers.

This ability to flourish as man advanced into the country, when so many birds failed to hold their own, may be accounted for by the habits and equipment of the whippoorwill, which, when it moves about, is "bescreened in night" and is so obscurely colored that we may say "the mask of night is on its face" even in the daytime, as it lies motionless on a carpet of dead leaves.

If the bird should be discovered and attacked, we may imagine how often the whippoorwill, with its marvelous powers of flight, may escape hawk, owl, or fox.

Fall.—We rarely see whippoorwills in autumn, but as we hear them sing not infrequently at this season we know that they sometimes linger in New England almost to the end of September, a time when hard frosts are at hand, which will either kill the insects or hasten them into retirement.

Taverner and Swales (1907) report an unusual gathering of whippoorwills on Point Pelee, Ontario. They say: "In our various September visits we have usually found them more or less common, but at that season they are much quieter, and seldom do more than call a few times in the early evening and then cease. Sometimes one will be heard again through the night, but more often not. September, 1905, beginning the 4th, we saw from one to six until the 13th, when a great flight of them appeared on the Point. That day, in the red cedar thickets near the extremity of the Point, we flushed thirty between twelve and half-past one in the afternoon."

Winter.—George Nelson, who has known the whippoorwill for years in its winter quarters on the east coast of Florida, tells me that the bird is pretty evenly distributed in the country about Sebastian, frequenting chiefly the ridges and hammocks where, during the day, it rests on the ground or on the trunk of a fallen tree. Not infrequently, as Mr. Nelson has been driving after dark along U. S. Route 1, a bird has started up from almost beneath the wheels of his car and has flown off in the glare of the headlights. He says that the bird is not in song during winter, but just before it starts northward, late in March, it sings for a few evenings, and that its departure invariably coincides with the arrival of the chuck-will's-widow.

Each evening during my stay at Sebastian with Mr. Nelson in mid-February 1931, just as it was beginning to grow dark, a whippoorwill appeared in the dooryard, a clearing in a dense hammock on the shore of the Indian River. The bird perched lengthwise here and there on the thick limbs of a live oak, well up in the big tree, but clearly visible from the ground, and made frequent sallies out into the air, sometimes sweeping clear away from the tree, sometimes only flitting among its branches, returning either to the perch from which it had flown, or to another one. Presumably these sallies were made in pursuit of flying insects—there was a businesslike air in the bird's behavior—but there was no sound of any snapping of the beak audible to me as I stood near the foot of the tree. Our first intimation that the bird had arrived from its day's seclusion was the sound of a low *chuck* repeated at short intervals. The bird gave this note from its perch and from the air; it was very similar to the introductory note in the whippoorwill song, but a little sharper. As the bird flew about, it sailed a good deal, wheeling around with some tilting from one side to the other, the wings held out straight and flat from the body with no, or very little, bend at the wrist joint. I was strangely reminded of the flight of a shearwater—the whippoorwill seeming to avoid the branches as the shearwater avoids the tops of the waves, tilting over them as it sails.

This was when the bird was moving slowly, but at times it increased its speed and executed the most intricate maneuvers, appearing and disappearing among the branches, ever changing its direction, either sailing or flapping its wings, swerving sharply from side to side, heeling over till one wing pointed nearly to the zenith and the other to the earth, then snapping back to an even keel. It shot straight upward, dived head downward, and doubled back, twisting and gyrating with such rapidity that it seemed to be tumbling about in the air. The turns were so quick and the pace so reckless that the bird appeared in a frenzy and in danger of dashing itself against a limb of the tree, yet from the midst of these complicated evolutions it instantly righted itself and, with a flash of wings, settled flat and motionless on its perch.

Although there was the appearance of a lack of caution in these mad dashes among the network of branches, we were convinced, as we watched, that the bird governed its movements with perfect precision, with the acme of coordination.

The flight seemed silent; even when the bird passed within a few feet of my head, I heard no sound. It appeared to be alone, and after remaining for ten minutes or so, it flew off, and we heard or saw no more of it until the next evening.

When we flashed a light on it, the eye gleamed back a bright orange.

Mr. Nelson said that earlier in the winter the behavior of the bird had been different. It came about the house every evening for a while, visiting a small tree (*Assonia*) to which insects were attracted by big clusters of open flowers. This tree was about 10 feet tall, with large leaves but plenty of open space between the branches. The bird went to the ground after each flight into the tree, and it appeared to Mr. Nelson that the insects, as they flew among the flowers, could best be seen against the sky from this point. The bird did not return to this tree after the flowers had faded.

During a second visit to Florida, more than a month later, I saw, presumably, the same bird again. It acted exactly as it had before, perching, indeed, on the identical spot on the limb of the live oak that had been a favorite perch in February. On this occasion also only one bird visited the tree, and while feeding was silent except for the low chuck. On March 24, after the bird had been to the tree and had gone away, I heard him singing off in the hammock. This singing on his winter quarters indicated that he felt spring was here, and it was time to leave for his summer home in the north.

DISTRIBUTION

Range.—United States and southern Canada east of the Rocky Mountains, south in winter to El Salvador.

Breeding range.—The breeding range of the eastern whippoorwill extends **north** rarely to central Saskatchewan (Prince Albert); southern Manitoba (Gypsumville, Lake St. Martin, Shoal Lake, and Winnipeg); northern Michigan (McMillan and Sault Ste. Marie); southern Ontario (Sudbury, Algonquin Park, and Ottawa); southern Quebec (Montreal and Sherbrooke); rarely northern Maine (Presque Isle); and rarely southern New Brunswick (Scotch Lake). The **eastern** limits extend southward from this point along the Atlantic coast to eastern Virginia (Ashland and Lawrenceville); hence southwest through the interior to North Carolina (Raleigh and Highrock); and Georgia (Young Harris and Atlanta). **South** to northern Georgia (Atlanta); northern Alabama (Lookout Mountain and Sand Mountain); central Arkansas (Clinto and Big Piney Creek); and Texas (Troup). **West** to eastern Texas (Troup); northwestern Arkansas (Rogers and Pearidge); eastern Kansas (Ottawa and Topeka); eastern Nebraska (Peru, Omaha, and Neligh); southeastern South Dakota (Vermillion); Minnesota (St. Cloud, Fosston, and Williams); southwestern Manitoba (Treesbank); and rarely central Saskatchewan (Prince Albert).

Closely related subspecies, Stephens's whippoorwill (*A. v. arizonae*), is found chiefly in Mexico, but in summer it has been recorded **north** to Arizona (Bradshaw Mountains, Sierra Ancha, Mount Graham, and the Chiricahua Mountains); New Mexico (Turkey Creek, Blank Range, and Fort Bayard); and southwestern Texas (Chisos Mountains).

Winter range.—The winter range of the *entire* species is **north** to southern Sonora (Alamos); southern Texas (San Patricio and Port Arthur); rarely Louisiana (Baton Rouge); southern Alabama (Fairhope); northwestern Florida (Pensacola and St. Marks); and east-central South Carolina (Mount Pleasant). **East** to east-central South Carolina (Mount Pleasant); Georgia (Savannah); eastern Florida (Amelia Island, Orlando, Lake Worth, and Royal Palm Hammock); British Honduras (Toledo District); and Costa Rica (probably San Jose). **South** to Costa Rica (probably San Jose and Puntarenas); El Salvador (Rio San Miguel, Puerto del Triunfo, and La Libertad); Oaxaca (Tehuantepec); and southern Jalisco (Colima Volcano). **West** to Jalisco (Colima Volcano and Bolanos Volcano); probably western Durango (Salto); and southern Sonora (Alamos).

Spring migration.—Early dates of spring arrival are: North Carolina—Louisburg, March 19; Weaverville, March 23; Raleigh, March 28. Virginia—Variety Mills, March 29; Lawrenceville, March 30. District of Columbia—Washington, April 1. Maryland—Mardela Springs, March 29; Cambridge, April 12. Pennsylvania—Williamsport, April 21; Berwyn, April 22; Philadelphia, April 22. New Jersey—Vineland, April 11; Morristown, April 23. New York—Jay, April 14; Geneva, April 25; Rochester, April 29. Connecticut—Jewett City, April 23; Hartford, April 23. Massachusetts—Boston, April 13; Taunton, April 20; Wilmington, April 26. Vermont—Wells River, April 25; St. Johnsbury, May 5; Rutland, May 7. New Hampshire—Charlestown, April 26; Tilton, May 2. Maine—Portland, April 26; Phillips, May 2. Quebec—Montreal, April 25. New Brunswick—Scotch Lake, May 7. Mississippi—Suffolk, March 22. Arkansas—Delight, March 29; Clinton, March 30. Tennessee—Athens, March 24. Kentucky—Eubank, April 2; Bowling Green, April 6. Missouri—Palmyra, April 9; St. Louis, April 13. Illinois—Chicago, April 13; Port Byron, April 23. Indiana—Fort Wayne, April 11; Bicknell, April 12; Lafayette, April 16. Ohio—Columbus, April 13; Wauseon, April 16; Youngstown, April 18. Michigan—Detroit, April 15; Sault Ste. Marie, May 3. Ontario—Ottawa, April 25; Toronto, April 28. Iowa—Keokuk, April 11; Sabula, April 16; Iowa City, April 18. Wisconsin—Milwaukee, April 21; Madison, April 26. Minnesota—Lanesboro, April 17; Elk River, April 24; St. Vincent, May 11. Texas—Grapevine, April 7. Kansas—Onaga, April 19; Topeka, April 20. North Dakota—Larimore, May 20. Manitoba—Aweme, May 1; Raeburn, May 1.

Fall migration.—Late dates of fall departure are: Manitoba—Aweme, September 27. Minnesota—Elk River, September 23; Lanesboro, October 2. Iowa—Keokuk, October 2; Sabula, October 4. Missouri—Concordia, October 3; Palmyra, October 12. Ontario—Ottawa, October 16; Point Pelee, October 17. Michigan—Sault Ste. Marie, September 23; Detroit, October 6. Ohio—Wauseon, September 20. Indiana—Bicknell, September 21; Fort Wayne, September 22. Illinois—Port Byron, September 19. Kentucky—Eubank, October 4. Tennessee—Athens, October 3. Arkansas—Delight, October 4. New Brunswick—Scotch Lake, September 8. Maine—Phillips, October 6. New Hampshire—Ossipee, October 2. Vermont—Wells River, September 14; Rutland, September 21. Massachusetts—Harvard October 10. Conecticut—Hartford, October 18. New Jersey—Morristown, October 10. Pennsylvania—Berwyn, October 5; Philadelphia, October 11. District of Columbia—Washington, October 13. West Virginia—French Creek, October 2. North Carolina—Raleigh, November 6.

Casual records.—The whippoorwill has been recorded, either by its call or by the collection of specimens, at several points outside its normal range. One was taken at Port Collins, Colo., on September 14, 1903, and one was heard at Eastend, in southwestern Saskatchewan, on August 29, 1919. In North Dakota, two specimens have been obtained at Grafton, one on October 9, 1923, and the other on May 24, 1924, while it was recorded at Stump Lake in the spring of 1910 and also at Cando. It has been noted occasionally near Wichita, Kans., and one was noted at Harper, Kans., on May 1, 1936. During the period July 5 to September 22, 1905, one was heard calling on Isle Royale, Mich., and in the summer of 1922 one was heard on the Cascapedia River, Gaspe Peninsula, Quebec. In Puerto Rico a specimen was collected for Cory, probably in 1888, and Wetmore reported seeing a bird that he felt certain was this species on December 23, 1911, near the experimental station at Rio Picdras.

Egg dates.—Arizona: 12 records, May 3 to August 8; 6 records, May 22 to June 12, indicating the height of the season.

Connecticut: 9 records, May 20 to June 18.

Illinois: 39 records, May 9 to July 26; 20 records, May 18 to June 17.

West Virginia: 40 records, May 6 to July 7; 20 records, May 15 to June 3.

ANTROSTOMUS VOCIFERUS ARIZONAE Brewster

STEPHENS'S WHIPPOORWILL

PLATE 24

HABITS

This southwestern race of the whippoorwill is found in southern Arizona and New Mexico, in southwestern Texas, and southward through the mountains of northern Mexico, being replaced by another subspecies farther south. Although it is common enough in some of the Arizona mountain ranges, it is oftener heard than seen. It sits so closely, is so inactive during the day, and is so protectively colored that it is easily overlooked. The use of a flashlight at night will often enable one to locate one of these birds by the "eye-shine," even at considerable distance.

William Brewster (1881), in naming this subspecies, described it as "generally similar to A. *vociferus* but much larger; with the rictal bristles considerably longer; the gular crescent and a pretty well defined superciliary stripe, ochraceous; the lores and auriculars tawny ochraceous. The white of the tail barely tipping the outer web of the lateral tail feathers and on the others confined to a narrow apical space; the under tail-coverts nearly without barring."

Mr. Brewster's type came from the Chiricahua Mountains, Ariz., where they were evidently common, for Frank Stephens, the collector, wrote to him: "I have heard several of these Whip-poor-wills singing at one time and am told that they were heard here last year. I hear A. *nuttalli* every evening. They keep high up the mountain sides, while A. *vociferus* affects the lower part of the cañons."

Harry S. Swarth (1904) says that this whippoorwill is a "fairly abundant summer resident" in the Huachuca Mountains, Ariz., "occurring principally between 5000 and 8000 feet; they may occasionally occur at a little higher elevation, but I have never seen any below the lowest altitude given."

A. J. van Rossem (1936) writes:

The vertical range of Stephens's Whip-poor-will is not limited to the higher mountains. Above 6000 feet in the Santa Ritas many birds were heard on every occasion that we stayed out after dark, but I also heard a whip-poor-will several times at 5000 feet in the Atascos and Dr. Miller collected a specimen at Peña Blanca Spring, Pajarito Mountains, in June, 1931. These two localities are well down in the Upper Sonora Zone.

I took, all told, six specimens of this common, though seldom collected, whip-poor-will and saw or heard several times that number. In the Santa Ritas they showed a decided preference for groves of oaks and sycamores in the cañon bottoms, and nearly all of those which were found at night were feeding in the immediate vicinity of running water. A pair to the mile seemed to be normal in most cañons which contained water and it was obvious that each pair had its own territory.

Spring.—Mr. Swarth (1904) saw the first arrival in 1903 "on April 28, and soon after their notes could be heard every evening, usually from some thickly wooded hillside, near the bottom of the canyon." But Mr. Stephens wrote to Mr. Brewster (1881): "I heard the first Whip-poor-will about the middle of May. By June 1, they were as common as I ever knew them to be in the East. Sometimes I could hear three or four whistling at once."

Nesting.—We did not succeed in finding a nest of Stephens's whippoorwill in the Huachuca Mountains, but my companion, Frank C.

Willard, had previously found one there on May 24, 1899; the nest
was on the ground at the base of a bush, and the eggs were lying
on a few dead leaves; it was at an elevation of about 6,000 feet.

Mr. Stephens wrote to Major Bendire (1895) : "The locality where
I found the egg was a gulch near the summit of the Chiricahua
Mountains, in a thick forest of yellow pine. The nest, if it can be
called so, was a slight depression scratched in the ground, under the
edge of a bowlder."

Dr. A. K. Fisher sent Bendire the following notes:

The Whip-poor-will's note was not heard at Fort Bowie, Arizona, during the
last three weeks of May, 1894. When we made camp at the mouth of Rucker
Canyon, some forty miles south of the Post, in the Chiricahua Mountains,
on the last day of the month, we heard a few, and a couple of days later
found the species abundant higher up in the same canyon, among the pines
(*P. ponderosa*). Here at early dusk and at dawn their notes were heard almost
continuously, and numbers of birds were seen. On June 5 Mr. Fred. Hall
Fowler found a nest, if the slight depression in the ground can be so desig-
nated, on a steep side hill about 50 feet above the stream. It was situated
under an overhanging bush at the edge of a flat rock, and contained two young,
recently hatched, and the fragments of egg shells from which they had
emerged.

Mr. Fowler wrote to Bendire concerning the same nest: "The eggs
were deposited on a bed of oak leaves by the side of a large rock;
there was no nest excepting the bare leaves, which had been hollowed
out slightly."

Mr. van Rossem (1936) found this whippoorwill nesting in the
Santa Rita Mountains, Ariz., of which he writes:

Though males, and sometimes, before eggs were laid, mated pairs, were
invariably found in the cañon beds, the two nests discovered were on hillsides at least a quarter of a mile from water. On the night of June 6, 1931, I
caught the red eye-shine of a whippoorwill some distance away (estimated by
daylight at 150 yards) and across a steep-banked cañon. With no expectation
of collecting anything I followed the trail to a point where I estimated the
shine to have been, but could locate nothing and supposed that the bird had
gone. On my return to the original spot the eye was seen in the same location as before, and this time, after a little search, I found a female sitting
under the protection of a fallen spray of leafless twigs which lay on a steep
bank beside the trail. Three of us had passed within five or six feet of this
sitting bird on two occasions the day before. The sitting bird made no effort
to escape and was picked up by hand. There was one nearly fresh egg in
the shallow depression in the gravelly soil which served as a nest, and stuck
to the ventral plumage of the incubating female were several small pieces of
shell, showing that another egg had been laid and somehow broken.

Eggs.—The two eggs laid by Stephens's whippoorwill have been
said to be pure, immaculate white, but this is not always the case.
Mr. Brewster (1882) says of the egg sent to him by Mr. Stephens:
"The egg is white with a dull gloss. At first sight it appears to be

immaculate, but a closer inspection reveals a few faint blotches of the palest possible purple, so faint indeed that they might pass for superficial stains were it not for the fact that they underlie the external polish." This egg measures 29.72 by 22.10 millimeters.

Mr. van Rossem (1936) says of the egg referred to above: "This single egg was by no means immaculate white, but was clouded and mottled with brown and lilac, mostly in the nature of semi-concealed shell markings. It was similar to but very much less highly colored than eggs of the eastern *vociferus*, however." Another nest, found by him later, "contained one pure white egg and a newly hatched chick."

Philo W. Smith, Jr. (1900), received two sets of eggs, taken by O. C. Poling in the Huachuca Mountains, which "very much resemble in shape and color sets of the common Poor Will in his collection, being possibly a trifle larger, and one egg of each set has a few almost imperceptible pinkish spots on one end, the other egg in each set being unspotted."

There is a set of two eggs in the Thayer collection, taken in the Chiricahua Mountains, Ariz., on June 6, 1904, by Virgil W. Owen, that are decidedly spotted. These eggs are oval and only moderately glossy. The ground color is pure white, and both eggs are finely and irregularly marked with small spots and minute dots of "pale Quaker drab," "pallid Quaker drab," and very pale "clay color."

The measurements of 29 eggs average 28.8 by 20.8 millimeters; the eggs showing the four extremes measure 30.9 by 21.8, 29.0 by 22.6, 25.8 by 20.1, and 28.9 by 19.9 millimeters.

Plumages.—I have not seen the downy young of this subspecies, but the two newly hatched chicks, taken by Mr. Fowler, are described as "covered with light brown down, and were not more than 1½ inches long." Mr. van Rossem (1936) describes a newly hatched chick as "clothed with a very respectable covering of down—in color between 'cinnamon' and 'orange-cinnamon' of Ridgway."

I have not seen enough material to work out the molts of this race, but I suppose that they are not very different from those of the eastern whippoorwill. Mr. Brewster's type was a male, which is described above. He later received an adult female from Mr. Stephens, of which he says (1882): "This specimen differs even more widely from the female, than does my type from the male of *A. vociferus*. The ochraceous of the lores, superciliary-stripe, and neck-collar, spreads over the entire plumage both above and beneath, giving it a tawny tinge which overlies and obscures the usual dark markings. On the shoulders, breast, lores and throat this color deepens to a fine reddish-chestnut, and elsewhere it replaces the ashy, dirty white and other light tints of the eastern birds. In its general coloring the plumage strikingly resembles that of the brown phase of *Scops asio kennicotti.*"

Mrs. Florence M. Bailey (1928) says that the young male is "similar to adult male but top of head spotted instead of streaked with black, throat band indistinct, wing coverts and scapulars broadly barred with dusky, and irregularly marked with black; underparts barred with dusky on a brownish buffy ground. *Young female:* Similar to young male but outer tail feathers tipped with brownish buff instead of white."

Behavior.—The food, feeding habits, and general behavior of Stephens's whippoorwill are apparently similar to those of its eastern relative. Mr. van Rossem noticed a peculiarity that I have not seen in the eastern bird, of which he writes: "A, to me, surprising circumstance, was the marked erectability of the feathers above the eyes. Both of the sitting females carried these tufts constantly erect the entire time they were under observation. A male seen from directly in front alternately raised and flattened them. On one previous occasion, when night hunting in El Salvador, I had observed the eastern subspecies (*vociferus*) to have markedly erectile tufts; in fact until I picked the bird up I was certain that I had shot some small 'eared' owl. About 45% from the horizontal was the maximum elevation, though when viewed from directly in front the tufts appear nearly vertical."

Fall.—Mr. Swarth (1904) says that, in the Huachucas, "they seem to remain rather late in the fall, as at the end of August their notes were heard as frequently as ever, and I have a female taken by H. Kimball on September 29, 1895. An adult male secured on August 29, 1902, had not yet quite completed its moult."

PHALAENOPTILUS NUTTALLI NUTTALLI (Audubon)

NUTTALL'S POORWILL

HABITS

Nuttall's poorwill is the best known and the most widely distributed race of this species, occupying a wide range in western North America, from southern Canada to Mexico and from the Great Plains to eastern California. Major Bendire (1895) says of its haunts:

In some of its habits it differs considerably from the preceding species of this family which are almost entirely confined to the denser woodlands; the Poor-will, however, although frequently found in similar localities, is apparently equally as much at home on the open prairie and the almost barren and arid regions of the interior, which are covered only here and there with stunted patches of sage (*Artemisia*) and other desert plants. The climate does not seem to affect it much, as it inhabits some of the hottest regions of the continent, like Death Valley, in southeastern California, as well as the slopes of the Rocky and Blue mountains, in Oregon, where it reaches altitudes of from 6,000 to 8,000 feet. I have heard the Poor-will in Bear Valley, Oregon, in a locality where frost could be found every month in the year.

Dr. Alexander Wetmore (1932) writes: "At times poorwills are found in growths of low forests, but they are more often encountered in regions where dense clumps of brush are scattered over otherwise open ground, as is common in desert and semiarid localities, or in brush-grown, rocky canyons, where the ground is rough and strewn with bowlders."

Referring to the Huachuca Mountains, in Arizona, Harry S. Swarth (1904) says: "I found the Poor-will quite abundant during the summer months in the foothill region and in the lower parts of the canyons; but though most numerous below 5000 feet they were by no means restricted to these parts, for I saw or heard some in all parts of the mountains occasionally up to an altitude of nearly 10,000 feet."

George F. Simmons (1925) designates its haunts in Texas as "high, gravelly flats or bits of plateau grown with post oak timber and with occasional moist spots; gravel patches dotted with catsclaw bushes, located in post oak growth on slopes and flat tops of hills; high prairies on rough ground along the terraces of valleys; bare ground on rocky hillsides; among shrubbery or on semi-arid flats."

Nesting.—The nesting of the poorwill is a very simple affair. The two eggs are laid on the bare ground, without any semblance of nest building; a slight hollow may be scraped in the bare earth, or the eggs may be laid on hard gravelly ground, or even on a flat rock. The exact spot chosen for a nest site may be in full sunlight, but oftener it is at least partially shaded by some bush, often a greasewood bush or a bunch of sagebrush, or some other bunch of vegetation. The only eggs taken by Major Bendire (1895) were "laid on the bare ground under a small grease-wood bush (*Obione*) and were fully exposed to the sun," near Tucson, Ariz. Prof. D. E. Lantz wrote to him from Kansas, regarding the nesting habits of the poorwill in that region, that "with one exception the eggs taken were laid upon bare patches of gravel or on low, flat rocks, and placed usually near a bunch of weeds or a tuft of grass. The exception was a set found on the bare ground in an alley in Manhattan City. This alley was in constant use and it was strange that the eggs remained for so long a time undisturbed, for when taken incubation had begun in both eggs. The Poor-wills usually keep to the vicinity of steep hills and old dead grass. They seem to return to the same locality from year to year to breed."

E. S. Cameron (1907), reporting from Montana, says: "On June 26, 1907, Mr. M. M. Archdale flushed a Poor-will from her two white eggs on a steep hillside in some rough pine brakes at his ranch near Knowlton. In this unfrequented place the eggs were fully exposed on the bare earth amidst the pines. On June 28, we went together to the place intending to photograph the eggs, but they had been already removed by the bird."

Eggs.—The two eggs of the poorwill are generally said to be pure white, but Bendire (1895) says that the color is not pure white and that "on close inspection it can readily be seen that it is a delicate cream, with a faint pinkish tint which does not perceptibly fade. Eggs in the collection taken more than twenty years ago still plainly show this peculiar tint. The eggs are unspotted as a rule, but an occasional specimen shows a few faint, darker shell markings around one end, which are barely perceptible to the naked eye, and which fade considerably in time."

In shape the eggs vary from oval to elliptical-oval; and they are only moderately glossy. The measurements of 50 eggs average 26.3 by 19.9 millimeters; the eggs showing the four extremes measure 28.9 by 19.8, 27.5 by 21.6, 22.1 by 19.3, and 24.6 by 18.1 millimeters.

Young.—The period of incubation does not seem to be definitely known. Dr. Wetmore (1932) says: "Both birds are said to assist in incubation. When disturbed about the nest, they tumble about and with widely opened mouths make a loud hissing sound terrifyingly like the hissing of a snake."

Robert B. Rockwell writes to me that he found a female with two young "as large as an ordinary week or ten days old chick. They were squatting perfectly motionless on the ground, about a foot apart, each in the shadow of something. Their feathers were quite well developed. They made no move when I picked them up, but opened their eyes when I put them down again."

Plumages.—Elmer C. Aldrich (1935) describes the downy young of the dusky poorwill, less than a day old and about 2½ inches long, as covered with a rich buff down. Ridgway (1914) describes the downy covering of a young *nuttalli* as "vinaceous-buff, paler on underparts." Two small partially downy young in my collection are showing the growth of the first plumage on the forehead, crown, nape, back, and scapulars; these feathers are dull buffy white, minutely sprinkled with grayish, and have small spots and narrow bars of black; the new feathers on the underparts and flanks are dull white, indistinctly barred with dusky; the wings are less than one-third grown, and the tail is just sprouting.

Ridgway (1914) says of the young in juvenal plumage: "Not essentially different from adults, but markings in general less sharply defined, especially on underparts, and throat patch buff instead of white."

I have been unable to learn anything about the molts of either young or adults, but Dr. Joseph Grinnell (1908) says that a specimen in juvenal plumage, "taken August 22, shows many feathers of the full adult plumage in the throat and breast. The juvenal plumage is characterized by having the throat patch buff and the back conspicuously mixed with cinnamon-rufus."

A young male, collected by Van Tyne and Sutton (1937) in Brewster County, Tex., on May 25, was in the midst of the postjuvenal molt; "the crown is uniform gray, without any suggestion of a dark central patch, the feathers being only lightly speckled with black. * * * The chest lacks entirely the black patch and band, the feathers being lightly and indistinctly tipped with tawny and whitish."

The so-called frosted poorwill (*nitidus*) is now regarded as merely a color phase of *nuttalli*.

Food.—The food of the poorwill consists, so far as it appears by the data available, entirely of insects, mostly the smaller, night-flying species, such as moths, beetles, chinch bugs, and locusts. Mrs. Bailey (1928) says that "in one stomach, 80 per cent of the contents was grasshoppers and locusts." Many of these insects are caught on the wing in the capacious mouths of these birds, but many are also picked up on the ground.

Dr. R. W. Shufeldt (1885) noticed a poorwill "apparently amusing himself by making short jumps of two feet or more up in the air, then resting on the road to repeat the performance in a moment or so. Another was going through similar capers on the broad walk. They seemed to be perfectly oblivious to my presence, and, indeed, some children further along were trying to catch them with their hands." He shot one of the birds, and "was much surprised to find in its mouth some four or five quite sizable moths, and the upper portion of the oesophagus was filled with a wad of a dozen or fifteen more. Fully half of these were yet alive, and two or three managed to fly away when freed from the bodies of their more disabled companions. This, then, is what the bird was up to; instead of flying about as a Nighthawk does, taking his insect prey in a conspicuous manner upon the wing, he captures it in the way I have described above."

A. Brazier Howell (1927) writes:

August 28, 1926, I was sitting near midnight, on the observation platform of the California Limited as it stopped at Needles, California. It was with much interest that I then noted at least three poorwills (*Phalaenoptilus nuttalli nitidus?*) hawking about a powerful arc light in the railway yards close by. The observation point of one of these was upon the top of a board fence well within the circle of illumination; of the others, some point out of my direct vision and just beyond the fence. One after the other, until my train left ten minutes later, they would flutter up in their quest for insects, not just somewhere near the light but apparently right against the glass globe which inclosed the arc, returning each time to their respective stations for observation.

Mrs. Bailey (1928) says: "When hunting for food the Poor-will skims swiftly and noiselessly close over the ground with irregular turnings and windings and rests between, and when its catch contains hard indigestible parts like the wing coverts of beetles, ejects them in the form of pellets, as do the hawks and owls, kingfishers, and others of similar food habits. A road through a forest with its abundant flies and insects is said to be one of its favorite hunting grounds."

The stomach of one taken by Van Tyne and Sutton (1937) on May 25 in Brewster County, Tex., was crammed with four large June beetles (*Phyllophaga* sp.) and a large army ant (male *Eciton* sp.).

Behavior.—Mrs. Bailey (1928) says that a poorwill, wounded by Mr. Bailey, exhibited a surprising method of defense; he "opened his mouth wide and hissed and blew and flopped about on the ground, always facing the enemy. Blowing like a blow snake and opening and shutting his mouth, he was enough to terrify all minor enemies."

Referring to the eye-shine, common among the Caprimulgidae, Mrs. Bailey quotes Dr. Bergtold as saying: "While motoring at night through a particularly dark canyon, I noticed far ahead in the illuminated road, two small glowing pink spots which were extinguished when a bird flew from the road on the near approach of the car. The bird alighted again, some distance ahead in the road, when the pink spots reappeared and were identified as the bird's eyes; it was shot and proved to be a Poor-will."

Dr. Wetmore (1932) says that poorwills "rest during the day on the ground, though after night, when feeding or calling, may seek higher perches on stones or posts or on low branches. On one occasion I saw one by bright moonlight calling from a bush, where it perched crosswise on a small limb, like any ordinary bird, though ordinarily they rest lengthwise of branches, like others of their family."

Dr. Elliott Coues (1874) says: "Like others of its family, Nuttall's Whippoorwill is oftener heard than seen. When flushed from its retreat in the daytime, among the shrubbery or tall weeds, it rises hurriedly with wayward flight, dashes a few yards, and realights. There is something about it at such times that strongly recalls the Woodcock, and the bird is quite as difficult to shoot on the wing."

Voice.—The call of the poorwill is generally recorded as a clear pronunciation of its name, but many observers have noted a third syllable, audible at only a short distance, making the complete song sound like *poor-will-low*, or *poor-will-ee*, when the bird is near, or

poor-will when farther away, or even *p'-will* when still farther away.
Mr. Simmons (1925) writes it *puih-whee-ee*.

Dr. Coues (1874) says: "This cry is very lugubrious, and in places
where the birds are numerous the wailing chorus is enough to excite
vague apprehensions on the part of the lonely traveler, as he lies
down to rest by his camp-fire, or to break his sleep with fitful dreams,
in which lost spirits appear to bemoan their fate and implore his
intercession."

Some other writers give a less unpleasant impression of the song;
for instance, Dr. Wetmore (1932) says: "Near at hand these calls are
harsh, but with distance the first two assume a pleasant, somewhat
melancholy cadence." And Mrs. Bailey (1928) writes: "When we
were camped on the edge of a canyon in the Guadalupe Mountains,
at dusk while the bats were flying down in the canyon, up along the
edge came the Poor-wills so near that we could hear their syllables
distinctly—*poor-will'-uck, poor-will'-uck*. Sometimes two would call
antiphonally, faster and faster till they fairly tripped over each
other. The call as it is often given is a delightfully soft, *poor-will',
poor-will', poor-will'-uck*, which like the delicious aromatic smell of
the sagebrush clings long to the memory of the lover of the west."

Henry W. Henshaw (1875) says that "their notes are most
often noticed in early evening, and again just before dawn, but not
infrequently their song is heard through the entire night. * * *
When flying, they emit a constantly repeated clucking note, which
is, I think, common to both sexes. * * * The males continue their
notes till very late in the season; for I frequently heard them during
the first part of October, and even as late as the 17th."

Field marks.—In superficial appearance the poorwill looks very
much like a small whippoorwill, and its behavior is similar. It also
somewhat resembles a partly grown young nighthawk, but its behavior is different; whereas the nighthawk flies about high in the air
in pursuit of its prey, the poorwill hunts on or near the ground,
flitting about like a large moth on silent wings; the poorwill is more
strictly nocturnal in its activities than the nighthawk; furthermore,
it exhibits no white patch in the wing, while flying, but shows white
tips on the lateral tail feathers. Its note is, of course, characteristic.

Winter.—The poorwill retires from the northern portions of its
range late in fall and spends the winter near, or beyond, our southern
borders. Dr. Coues (1874) reports, in some notes from Ogden,
Utah, that "it lingers at its summer home till the autumn is far advanced, as we found it at Ogden as late as October 6, quite far up
the slope of the mountains, in the midst of a driving snow-storm—
the first of the season—the snow having then already accumulated to
the depth of several inches."

In Arizona, New Mexico, and central Texas it is usually absent from late in October to early in April. It apparently winters more or less regularly in southern Texas, though its main winter range is in Mexico.

DISTRIBUTION

Range.—Central and western United States, and southern British Columbia, south to central Mexico.

Breeding range.—The breeding range of the poorwill extends **north** to southern British Columbia (Kamloops and Okanagan Landing); Montana (Billings and Terry); northwestern South Dakota (Slim Buttes); north-central Nebraska (Long Pine Canyon); and southwestern Iowa (Pottawattamie County). **East** to southwestern Iowa (Pottawattamie County); eastern Kansas (Blue Rapids, Onaga, Lawrence, and Clearwater); central Texas (Kerrville, San Antonio, and Somerset); eastern Coahuila (Sabinas and Saltillo); and probably Morelos (Cuernavaca). **South** to probably Morelos (Cuernavaca); southern Sonora (Alamos); and southern Baja California (San Jose del Cabo). **West** to Baja California (San Jose del Cabo, Miraflores, Triunfo, Pozo Grande, San Fernando, Santo Domingo, La Joya, San Telmo, and probably Todos Santos Islands); California (San Diego, Escondido, Ojai Valley, Santa Cruz Mountain, San Geronimo, Covel, and probably Yreka); Oregon (Brownsboro, Bridge Creek, and probably Netarts); eastern Washington (Crab Creek and Cheney); and British Columbia (Summerland and Kamloops).

Winter range.—The species is probably resident in the southern part of its range and during the winter season is found **north** to southern California (Berryessa Station, Paicines, Death Valley, and Laguna); rarely southern Arizona (Tucson); and southern Texas (El Paso, rarely Kerrville, Laredo, and Falfurrias).

The range as outlined is for the entire species, which has been separated into four currently recognized geographic races. The typical subspecies, Nuttall's poorwill (*P. n. nuttalli*) occupies all the United States portion of the range except that part of California west of the Sierra Nevada. The dusky poorwill (*P. n. californicus*) is found in western California from the northern part of the Sacramento Valley south to northwestern Baja California; the desert poorwill (*P. n. hueyi*) is restricted to the lower Colorado River Valley, southwestern Arizona, and northeastern Baja California; and the San Ignacio poorwill (*P. n. dickeyi*) is found in Baja California south of latitude 30° N.

Spring migration.—Early dates of spring arrival are: Texas—Kerrville, February 4; San Antonio, February 27. Kansas—Manhattan, April 7; Onaga, April 7. New Mexico—Chloride, March 31;

State College, April 7; Rinconada, April 10. Colorado—Beulah, April 29; Denver, May 9. Wyoming—Laramie Peak, May 2; Lingle, May 3. Montana—Terry, May 16. Arizona—Tombstone, March 20. Utah—Kobe Valley, May 23. California—Piedra, March 5; Daggett, March 12; San Clemente Island, March 30; Lassen Peak, April 16. British Columbia—Okanagan Landing, April 22.

Fall migration.—Late dates of fall departure are: British Columbia—Okanagan Landing, September 20. California—Daggett, October 21; Los Angeles, October 25; La Verne, October 28; Garnsey, November 2. Arizona—San Francisco Mountain, September 29. Montana—Big Sandy, September 4; Bighorn River, September 19. Wyoming—Powder River, September 9; Clear Fork, September 19. Colorado—Beulah, October 8. New Mexico—State College, October 30; Sierra Hachita, November 24. South Dakota—White River, September 27. Kansas—Onaga, September 27. Oklahoma—Kenton, September 26.

Egg dates—Arizona: 5 records, May 2 to August 2.

California: 42 records, March 22 to August 8; 21 records, May 6 to June 25, indicating the height of the season.

Colorado: 5 records, May 26 to July 27.

Texas: 11 records, April 29 to June 20.

PHALAENOPTILUS NUTTALLI CALIFORNICUS Ridgway

DUSKY POORWILL

PLATES 25-27

HABITS

The goatsuckers are now in their proper place in the A. O. U. Check-list, showing their relationship to the owls, which they strikingly resemble in several characters. The poorwills are conspicuous in this respect; they are more strictly nocturnal in their activities than some of the owls, for which they are well adapted; the eyes are very large, suggesting those of owls; the mouth is very broad, but some of the owls have broad mouths also; the plumage is fully as soft as that of the owls; and their flight is noiseless, like that of most night-flying birds. The Caprimulgidae are not predators on vertebrate animals, although the chuck-will's-widow has been known to eat birds; but they all live on animal food; and many owls live largely on insects.

The dusky poorwill does not enjoy so extensive a distribution as its inland relative, *nuttalli*, but perhaps it is equally as well known throughout its range in California.

Nesting.—The steep slopes and ridges of the foothills and the sides of canyons seem to form the favorite nesting haunts of this, as well as other poorwills. Elmer C. Aldrich (1935) gives a very good description of a locality in Tuolumne County, Calif., where a nest was found on July 5, 1934:

The altitude was about 5600 feet, and the general vegetation of the area consisted of yellow pines, incense cedars, white firs, black oak islands, a few species of ceanothus, and a little manzanita, with mountain misery covering most of the open hillside. The immediate location of the nest was in a little circular clearing about fifteen yards in diameter, surrounded by young yellow pines closely knit together by small, interwoven branches. The clearing contained three manzanita bushes and one ceanothus bush. The greater part of it was strewn with long dead pole-like logs, which appeared to be one of the basic requirements for the Poor-will's protection. The entire north side of the opening was bordered by a large decayed log of a diameter of three feet, which, because of the common use by the Poor-will, came to be called "the log."

The nest was found when we were coming from the north and upon advancing four yards after stepping over this log. When the adult flushed from the nest the observer's foot was but eighteen inches from the site. The bird flew across the clearing into the edge of the dense forest, where it lit on a small log and watched without movement for fifteen minutes while pictures of the two light buff eggs were obtained.

Dr. William L. Holt writes to me that he found a nest near Banning, Calif., on June 13, 1909, on the bare ground on the north side of a sandy hill, nearly bare of vegetation. J. E. Patterson has sent me two excellent photographs (pls. 25, 26) of poorwills' nests. The one taken in Stanislaus County, Calif., on June 23, 1934, was on the ground in open timber; the other, taken in Mariposa County, Calif., on June 21, 1933, was on the ground in a fire deadening on a hillside; both were in the Transition Zone.

A. J. van Rossem (1920) found a nest on April 18, 1919, a very early date, on the side of a canyon, where there was a heavy growth of wild lilac and white sage; "no attempt whatever seemed to have been made at constructing a nest, the eggs lying on the bare ground among pebbles, etc., in the shade of some dense brush that bordered upon a small open space." The nest has also been found on bare rock, but is usually, at least partially, shaded by some bush, loose brush, brakes, or weeds. The birds are very apt to return to the exact spot to nest each year.

Eggs.—As a rule the eggs of the dusky poorwill, two in number, are similar to the eggs of other poorwills, but van Rossem and Bowles (1920) write:

In a majority of the descriptions that are given for eggs of the various forms of the Poor-will, the color is stated as white, without markings, sometimes with a pinkish tinge. However, such was by no means the case with the set of eggs under discussion. Before blowing, the ground color was a strong salmon pink; but this, after blowing, turned to a clear, glossy, pinkish white, strongly suggesting eggs of the Merrill Parauque (*Nyctidromus albi-collis merrilli*), although the pink of the Poor-will eggs showed a closer approach to salmon. Around the larger ends was a rather dense wreath of lavender and dusky spots and dots, making the eggs look exceedingly like the marked eggs of some small petrel. * * * In the course of time many of the smaller dots have faded out, leaving only a comparatively few spots and dots to show where the heavy wreath was once located. The strong pinkish tinge has also very largely gone, in spite of the fact that the eggs have been carefully kept from exposure to the light.

The measurements of 40 eggs average 26.3 by 19.4 millimeters; the eggs showing the four extremes measure 28.4 by 20.0, 27.7 by 21.1, 24.2 by 18.2, and 24.9 by 17.0 millimeters.

Behavior.—Poorwills are notoriously close sitters, but the pair studied by Mr. Aldrich (1935) were unusually tame. He was repeatedly able to approach cautiously to within 3 or 4 feet of the incubating bird; once, at night, eight observers managed to approach within 2 feet, while the bird sat tight all the time. The next morning, "when we were but three feet from the nest, the bird's large clear white spots on the tail identified it to be the male that was doing the incubating. Many pictures were taken, some as close as ten inches, without the slightest sign of fear on the part of the sitting bird. * * * Experiments were made to find the extent of his 'bravery' by touching him. While touching the head the first time he flattened out his wings and spread the fan-like tail over the tips of them showing all the tail spots. The large head was then brought far back on the shoulders, the cavernous mouth opened extremely wide showing the pink interior, and a low guttural hiss was emitted at short intervals."

Later in the same day, at 2 p. m., he flushed the female from the nest and sat down 5 yards away to watch her return; "exactly ten and one-half minutes marked the reappearance of the same bird. She had flown from behind the log nearly to the top where she could barely look over and observe the surroundings. Immediately she started swaying from side to side very slowly and rhythmically for about five seconds before walking to the top of the log, each step in synchronization with the swaying. Here she paused for about twenty seconds, and then flew a few yards, within two and one-half feet of the nest, where she began swaying again. The rest of the distance to the nest was accomplished by this slow walking-swaying process, and she did not seem to get anxious and speed up as she came closer. Two short stops were made on the way."

The dusky poorwill is tame and unsuspicious at other times also. Rollo H. Beck (1897) watched one at short range while it was catching insects on a road and finally succeeded in putting his hat over it, though it escaped; he says: "After watching it a while I crawled up within four feet and had a chance to watch it in the bright moonlight. It would fly perhaps twenty or thirty feet into the air after insects and return again within four or five feet of me. One time it flew up and evidently picked an insect off the leaf of a wild cherry tree, fluttering for several seconds in its endeavor to do so. It several times flew by me after food and returning would fly within a foot or so of my head and alight just in front of me."

Voice.—H. Gordon Heggeness writes to me of the song of the dusky poorwill as he heard it in the Sequoia National Park: "Sometimes early in the morning the poorwill would be heard—the calm, liquid notes carrying far on the cool air. On August 12, 1935, a poorwill began singing back of my cabin at 2:30 a. m. His most pleasing notes were heard continuously for the next half hour."

Grinnell and Storer (1924) write: "It is heard most persistently at dusk of evening or in the early morning; but near Pleasant Valley on the morning of May 23, 1915, one of these birds suddenly broke out at 10 o'clock and uttered its *poor-will-o* 85 times (by count, within 2 or 3) at intervals of two or three seconds."

R. H. Lawrence wrote to Major Bendire (1895) that, according to his hearing, "the words 'Pearl-rab-it' give a fair idea of its call"; and that "when startled it gave quickly, two or three times in succession, a low, soft note, like 'pweek, pweek, pweek,' which could only be heard a few yards away."

PHALAENOPTILUS NUTTALLI HUEYI Dickey

DESERT POORWILL

HABITS

Donald R. Dickey (1928) described and named this pale race of the poorwill from a fine series of specimens collected in the valley of the Colorado River by Mrs. May Canfield and Laurence M. Huey. As to its subspecific characters, he says that it is "nearest in color to the light type of *Phalaenoptilus nuttalli nuttalli* (Audubon), which Brewster named *nitidus* and to which he gave the eminently fitting vernacular of the Frosted Poor-will, but averaging very much lighter. The backs of *hueyi* are pinkish tan, almost devoid of the silver frosting characteristic of more eastern birds, and with the size of the dark dorsal 'owl's eye' marking greatly reduced, in many cases practically obsolete; under parts lighter throughout, with the dark band below the white collar narrower and of lighter tone, and with narrower barring of sides and flanks. Tail lighter and less contrastingly barred above and below."

The 1931 Check-list gives the range of this race as the valley of the lower Colorado River, in southeastern California, southwestern Arizona, and extreme northeastern Baja California.

A. J. van Rossem (1936) took four poorwills near Bates Well, in south-central Arizona, that were somewhat intermediate between *hueyi* and *nuttalli*, though nearer the latter; this locality probably indicates the approximate area of intergradation between the two races. "All were collected in an arrowweed-mesquite association along the borders of the dry stream bed. Conditions, both as to habitat and temperatures, closely approximated those found along the Lower Colorado River Valley, beyond the confines of which *hueyi* has not been detected."

This poorwill probably does not differ materially in its habits from neighboring races of the species.

PHALAENOPTILUS NUTTALLI DICKEYI Grinnell

SAN IGNATIO POORWILL

HABITS

Three races of the poorwill are found on the peninsula of Baja California. The present form ranges from about latitude 30° southward to the Cape region; the dusky poorwill (*californicus*) extends its range southward in the northwestern portion to about latitude 30°, chiefly on the Pacific slope; and the desert poorwill (*hueyi*) is found in the extreme northeastern portion.

The San Ignatio poorwill is a small, dark race. Dr. Joseph Grinnell, who described and named it, says (1928) that it is "similar to *Ph. n. californicus* in degree of general darkness but decidedly smaller, and with black areas on the individual feathers of scapulars, top of head and chest greatly reduced, in this respect resembling *hueyi;* terminal white of lateral rectrices greater in amount than in *californicus;* light portions of general color scheme much darker than in *hueyi* or *nuttallii*, tinged with clay color rather than 'frosted'—in this respect darker even than in average *californicus;* dark barring on posterior lower surface much more extensive and heavier than in *hueyi* or *nuttalli*."

William Brewster (1902) referred the poorwills of the Cape region to the race he named the frosted poorwill (*Ph. n. nitidus*), based on a pair collected by M. A. Frazar in the Sierra de la Laguna. Mr. Frazar said that on the mountains the poorwills did not begin singing until about the middle of May. "Their note is a *pow-wè-hoo*, the first syllable given long, the accent on the second, and the last little more than a retraction of the breath. They were almost invariably in large oaks and very seldom on the ground. A female shot June 6 was undoubtedly mated and would have laid soon."

Nothing seems to be known about the nesting or other habits of this poorwill.

NYCTIDROMUS ALBICOLLIS MERRILLI Sennett

MERRILL'S PAURAQUE

PLATE 28

HABITS

Merrill's pauraque is the largest subspecies of a widely distributed species of goatsucker that ranges throughout Mexico, Central America, and northern South America, and that has been divided into six subspecies. Our pauraque extends its range from northern Mexico into the valley of the Rio Grande and northward through the Gulf coast of Texas to Nueces, Aransas, and Refugio Counties. The vernacular name, pauraque, pronounced "pou-rä'-kā," is derived from a fancied resemblance to one of its notes. The Mexican name, cuiejo, pronounced "coo-ya-ho," has a similar origin.

This bird was first introduced to our fauna by Dr. J. C. Merrill, who took the first specimen at Fort Brown, Tex., on April 1, 1876. The subspecies was first described and named by George B. Sennett (1888), who gives a full account of its plumages at different ages and says of its relation to other races of the species: "This form, when compared with others of the species from Southern Mexico, Costa Rica, Panama, Guiana, and Brazil, can be distinguished, first by the prevailing gray color on upper parts, where the others have brown, rufous or cinnamon; second, by its large size, exceeding the large southern Brazilian form in length of wing and equalling it in length of tail; third, by the males having the outer tail-feather generally without white, and the white when it does occur being much restricted, while in more tropical and South American forms the rule is that males have much white on inner web of outer tail-feather." This third point seems open to question, as this character seems to be very variable, possibly owing to age.

D. B. Burrows, in some notes sent to Major Bendire (1895) says: "During the winter the birds may be flushed from the dense thickets in the bottom lands, but as the nesting season approaches they leave these close retreats and seek more open ground."

Mr. Sennett (1878) says of their haunts: "I saw them occasionally, singly and in pairs, about the thickets and open chaparral, and once in the canebrakes close to the woods." Again (1879) he says: "They breed in the more open places among the cactus and scattered bushes along with *C. texensis*—Texas Nighthawk. On dark days I flushed them from thickets in the chaparral, or from copses near the bottom-lands on the edges of the woods."

Nesting.—Mr. Sennett's nests "were found in open brush, on the bare ground. One of them was partly concealed by the branches of a low bush 6 or 8 inches from the ground."

Mr. Burrows wrote to Major Bendire (1895) : "I have never found the Parauque nesting in the dense thickets, where they hide during the winter. They seek the more open ground, the high, level spots near the river, or up some arroya, among scattering bushes and pear cactus, but never on the rocky hills, where the Texan Nighthawk is frequently found. In one instance a nest was found at the edge of a cultivated field. The eggs are placed on the bare ground, with no attempt at nest building, and usually at the foot of a clump of bushes. The bird, when flushed from the nest, quietly darts off and drops to the ground but a short distance away."

Dr. James C. Merrill (1878) writes: "On the 15th of May, 1876, I found a set of eggs near camp at Hidalgo, and on returning in about fifteen minutes to secure the parent, who had disappeared among the thickets, I found that she had removed the eggs, although they had not been touched."

Eggs.—The pauraque lays two very handsome eggs, quite unlike the eggs of any other species in the family. They vary in shape between oval and elliptical-oval, with a decided tendency toward ovate or elliptical-ovate, one end often being slightly more pointed than the other. The shell is smooth, with little or no gloss. The ground color varies from "light ochraceous-salmon" to "pinkish buff". Some eggs appear to be nearly immaculate, but in most cases they are more or less evenly covered, some sparingly and some profusely, with small blotches, spots, or dots of pale "clay color," pale "cinnamon," or, more rarely, with deeper shades of "cinnamon-rufous"; often there are underlying blotches or spots of "ecru-drab" or "light cinnamon-drab." Occasionally the markings are concentrated around the larger end, but usually they are quite evenly distributed.

The measurements of 50 eggs average 29.80 by 22.36 millimeters; the eggs showing the four extremes measure **35.10** by 23.10, 31.50 by **24.64**, **27.18** by 20.57, and 28.96 by **20.32** millimeters.

Young.—In his unpublished manuscript on the birds of the Caribbean lowlands of Central America, kindly lent me, Alexander F. Skutch devotes considerable space to his studies of the care and feeding of the young of the local race of the pauraque (*Nyctidromus albicollis albicollis*). As the habits of the different races of this species probably do not differ materially, it seems pertinent to include here some of his remarks on this subject. He says that "during the day male and female take turns on the eggs, relieving each other every two or three hours. The male is usually found incubating in the early morning. At night, I have found only the female covering the eggs." Other species of goatsuckers have been reported as moving their eggs to a place of safety after being disturbed, but he found no evidence that this species does so, saying: "I have given pauraques all kinds of incentives to move their eggs to a safer place, but they have never shifted their positions even a few inches as a result of my interference. The case was quite different when I moved the eggs from the spot which the birds had selected as their nest." In this case, he had moved the eggs twice, once only a few inches and once a foot away from an area infested by fire ants; but each time the parents moved them back again to their chosen spot; the result was that, as soon as the eggs began to hatch, the chicks were destroyed by the ants. He did not see how the eggs were moved; probably they were pushed along with the feet and body, as the nighthawk has been seen to do.

Both parents took turns in brooding the young throughout the day, relieving each other at intervals of two or three hours, as they did on the eggs. As the young were fed in the dusk or deeper darkness of evening, it was only after several trials that he was able to see the performance clearly. He writes: "It was dark now, but at the critical moment I pushed the button of a powerful flashlight. The mother was resting on the ground in her customary position, looking toward me with eyes that shone like rubies in the beam of light. The little ones stood on tiptoe in front of her, their necks stretched up, bringing their heads on a level with her mouth. One was being fed while the other waited impatiently for its turn. Though her *mouth* was so big she could easily have swallowed her nestling whole, her little *bill* was inserted into its widely open mouth, just as with a hummingbird, and with distended throat and convulsive movements of the body she regurgitated into it the insects she had captured. When she had given sufficient to the first one, she paused with head erect, clearly much alarmed by the light, but the second continued its silent importunities and the parent yielded despite her fears, feeding it in the same manner. Then she went off to hunt more insects.

"Presently one of the parents entered the thicket again, but instead of going to the youngsters it settled on the ground behind the blind, fully 20 feet from them, and began the low croaking-clucking call, which draws them as the magnet draws the floating needle. The two- and three-day-old bantlings drew themselves up and began hopping bravely toward the voice, peeping as they went through the darkness. Directly in their path was a young banana plant, which I had felled in clearing a place for the blind. The large, slippery leaves lay in a tangled mass that loomed above them; the Alps formed no more insurmountable obstacle to the advance of Hannibal's army than this confusing barrier to the young pauraques. Dauntless as the renowned Carthaginian, they pushed resolutely onward, lured by the continued calls. I completely lost sight of them in the obscurity, but for many minutes their weak cries emerged from the dark mass. At length they descended victorious into the plains of Italy, and henceforth their path, although not free from obstacles, was comparatively easy. Finally they found a haven beneath their parent's sheltering wings."

On this and previous occasions Mr. Skutch discovered that the young pauraques were perfectly capable of locomotion, even at an early age, in response to warning calls from their parents. He saw no evidence that the adults ever carried them in their capacious mouths, as other species of the Caprimulgidae have been reported to do, or assisted them to move in any other way. He says that "during the day male and female take turns on the eggs, relieving each other every two or three hours. The male is usually found incubating in the early morning. At night, I have found only the female covering the eggs."

Plumages.—The downy young pauraque is as unique among the Caprimulgidae as are the eggs. It is completely covered with fine, soft down, leaving nothing exposed but the tip of the bill and the feet. The colors are rich and contrasting; the forehead, crown, and nape are "pinkish buff"; the lores, cheeks, and auriculars are "mikado brown"; the back and rump are "sayal brown," with a central band of pinkish buff"; the chin and throat are pale "pinkish cinnamon," and the remainder of the under parts are "pinkish buff."

Ridgway (1914) describes a female nestling, not yet fully grown, as follows: "General color of upper parts pale brownish gray, very minutely vermiculated or stippled with darker; pileum and scapulars with scattered roundish and subtriangular small spots of black; interscapular region clouded or blotched with black; under parts light grayish buff, narrowly barred with dusky on chest, more broadly barred with the same on throat, breast, and sides, the abdomen and under tail-coverts immaculate; thighs uniform light fawn color; remiges and rectrices (not fully grown) apparently as in adult female."   Of a young female, fully grown, he says: "Primaries and rectrices as in adult female; pileum spotted, instead of streaked, with black, the spots mostly of broadly triangular form; back also heavily spotted, or blotched, instead of streaked, with black; scapulars without buff margins; barring of under parts much less sharply defined, less dark in color; throat band light dull buff, barred with blackish."

Mr. Sennett (1888) says of the young male: "White wing-patch of male mixed with buff; white on tail not so sharply defined, nor does it extend so near to base as in mature birds. The outer tail-feathers are barred and streaked with brown and buff. White throat-patch smaller and barred sparingly with black and buff. In this immature stage the sexes are not easily determined aside from the difference in the white tail-patches; in the males the white on second feather from outside is never less than 2.5 inches long, while in the females the corresponding patch is about one inch in length."

The above descriptions evidently refer to the juvenal, or first plumage, which is largely replaced in summer, July and August, by a first winter plumage. In this the contour plumage is much like that of the adult, the spots on the crown and back being replaced by streaks; but the juvenal wings and tail are retained; the sexes are much alike in this plumage but can always be distinguished by the amount of white in the tail.

I have seen birds in this plumage in October, December, and March, from which I infer that it is worn until the first postnuptial molt the following summer. Mr. Sennett (1888) thought that "at least two years must elapse before the perfect plumage is attained"; but it seems more likely that the first postnuptial molt produces a plumage that is practically adult, except for some dusky mottling on the tips and edges of the white tail feathers, and some buffy intrusion of the white wing patch, which may indicate that the full purity of these white areas is not attained at the first postnuptial molt.

Dickey and van Rossem (1938) say: "Young birds which have assumed the postjuvenal plumage may be distinguished from adults by the narrower, more pointed, and usually impurely colored tail feathers and by the buffy edgings and mottlings on the tips of the primaries. The juvenal primaries which are worn until the bird enters the second fall (first annual) molt, are from 5 to 10 mm. shorter than those of adults. Males, at least, breed the first spring as shown by dissection of several specimens. The annual molt of adults takes place in August and September."

There are two distinct color phases in the adult plumage, a gray-brown phase and a tawny phase, mainly recognizable in the coloration of the upper surface. Ridgway (1914) says of the former, "pileum, hindneck, and interscapular region grayish brown," and of the tawny phase, "general coloration of upper parts much more tawny or ochraceous, the general color of the pileum varying from fawn color to mars brown or russet."

Food.—Bendire (1895) says that "the food of Merrill's Parauque, like that of the rest of the *Caprimulgidae*, consists mainly of night-flying insects, such as moths, beetles, etc. The crop of a specimen shot by Mr. H. P. Attwater, near Rockport, Texas, was filled with fireflies, *Photinus pyralis* ?"

On several occasions, Mr. Burrows (Bendire, 1895) observed a pauraque "perched upon the extremity of a low, dead limb, or on the top of a bush. At these times I found that the bird was watching for food, and at intervals would leave the perch, dart off a short distance as if in pursuit of an insect, and as quickly return, in very much the same manner that the Whip-poor-will is accustomed to do. I believe that these birds are strictly insectivorous; but I have never made an examination of the stomach except in one instance. The stomach of this bird, killed in January, showed parts of the feet and wings of beetles and other insects."

Three stomachs examined by Cottam and Knappen (1939) contained parts of ant lions, stink bugs, soldier bugs, locusts, click beetles, tiger beetles, ostomid beetles, twig borer, carrot muck beetle, long-horned beetles, and traces of butterflies, moths, bees, or wasps. Beetles made up 89 percent of the whole food.

Behavior.—Mr. Burrows (Bendire, 1895) writes:

During the daytime the birds were commonly found on the ground at the foot of a growth of bushes or among fallen branches, and I have occasionally found them perched, nighthawk-fashion, upon a low branch not more than a foot from the ground. When closely approached, they dart quickly forward in a zigzag course, dropping as suddenly to the ground. This flight is short, usually not more than 50 or 60 feet, and when settled they commonly remain perfectly quiet until again flushed. They have a peculiar way of turning or facing about as they strike the ground, so that they can better watch the approaching danger. They lie so close that it is with great difficulty that they can be detected, unless the spot is carefully marked. In a number of instances, where the bird seemed to feel that it was observed, I have had them go through a peculiar bowing movement, resembling that of the Burrowing Owl, except that the body is raised from its completely prostrate condition.

The pauraque has a relatively longer tarsus than our other members of the goatsucker family; hence it is more active on its feet. Dr. Frank M. Chapman (1896) observes: "I was surprised to learn how rapidly these birds can run. On one occasion two lit within a few feet of me when it was light enough to distinguish their movements. They crouched close to the earth, sometimes running quickly and with unexpected ease for a few steps, then turned their heads sharply from side to side as though looking for insects. They would also spring suddenly fifteen feet into the air to catch a passing insect."

Voice.—Dr. Merrill (1878) writes: "Their notes are among the most characteristic night sounds of the Lower Rio Grande, and are constantly heard at evening during the summer months. They consist of a repeated whistle resembling the syllables *whew-whew-whew-whew-whe-e-e-e-w*, much stress being laid upon the last, which is prolonged. The whole is soft and mellow, yet can be heard at a great distance. The preliminary *whews* vary somewhat in number, and late in the season are often omitted altogether."

Mr. Burrows wrote to Major Bendire (1895) : "At the approach of the breeding season and as early as the middle of March the peculiar whistle of the Parauque becomes general, and along the lower Rio Grande, where they are common, it may be heard on all sides. * * * The birds begin to call as the dusk of evening comes on. The commonest call is a long-drawn 'ko, whe-e-e-e-e-w', much prolonged, and raised to a high pitch toward the last. This is repeated often and with great energy, and on a still night may be heard at a long distance. At other times the first syllable is omitted. Again it is varied by a repetition of the first syllable, as 'ko, ko, ko, ko-whe-e-e,' the first syllables repeated deliberately, and the last not so long-drawn and suddenly cut short." He also refers to a short *put, put* note, resembling one of the notes of a wild turkey.

The name of the pauraque is said to have been derived from a fancied resemblance to one of its notes; the same is true of its Mexican name, cuiejo.

Winter.—The pauraque is a permanent resident in southern Texas and farther south, and even as far north as the Nueces River Mr. Burrows found it "to be fairly common" during the winter and spring of 1894. He met with it during the winter in Starr County, southern Texas, and says: "When the nesting season is over the birds remain quiet, and their peculiar whistling note is not heard with regularity, and yet, on very warm nights during each of the winter months, I have occasionally heard them. During the winter the birds may be flushed from the dense thickets in the bottom lands."

DISTRIBUTION

Range.—Southern Texas and northeastern Mexico; not regularly migratory.

The range of Merrill's pauraque extends **north** to southern Texas (Refugio County and Aransas County). **East** to Texas (Aransas County, Corpus Christi, Rio Hondo, and Brownsville); eastern Tamaulipas (Aldama, Altamira, and Tampico) ; and Veracruz (Mirador and Jalapa). **South** to central Veracruz (Jalapa) ; and Puebla (Metlaltoyuca and Tehuacan). **West** to southeastern Puebla Tehuacan) ; western Tamaulipas (Santa Leonor and Rio Cruz) ; and Texas Lomita, Neuces County, San Patricio County, and Refugio County).

Closely allied races of this bird are found in Central and South America.

Egg dates.—Mexico : 9 records, March 22 to June 22.

Texas : 66 records, March 5 to June 26 ; 33 records, April 15 to May 16, indicating the height of the season.

CHORDEILES MINOR MINOR (Forster)

EASTERN NIGHTHAWK

PLATES 29–33

CONTRIBUTED BY ALFRED OTTO GROSS

HABITS

The nighthawk, because of its piercing calls and the extraordinary evolutions and gyrations of its flight, attracts many persons, even the casual observers who ordinarily pay no special attention to birds. A bird so unique and striking, one that during its breeding season plays such an important role in our experiences out of doors, is destined to be the recipient of many common names.

Long before the white man came to America the nighthawk was well known to the Indians, and we find it taking a prominent place in their myths and traditions. Apparently the notes of this bird appealed most, since the names chosen by the various tribes were usually graphic allusions to the calls or to the characteristic booming noise heard during the courtship season. To the tribes along the Connecticut River this booming was the sound of the Shad Spirit announcing to the shoals of shad, about to ascend the river, of their impending fate. The nighthawk was known to the Seminoles of Florida as "Ho-pil-car." In the Milicite Indian Natural History there is the name "Pik-teis-k wes," and according to W. W. Cooke (1884) the Chippewas not only had the name "Besh-que" for the nighthawk but recognized it as a species distinct from the whippoorwill, to which they gave the name "Gwen-go-wi-a." That the Chippewa Indians differentiated these two species is all the more remarkable when we recall that this distinction was confused by Catesby and the American ornithologists of the next 50 years who followed him. It was Alexander Wilson who first noted that they were distinct species.

When the first European settlers came to our coast they compared the nighthawk and the whippoorwill with the nightjar of their old homes, and hence we find this name in the earlier ornithological writings used as a synonym for the American bird. In certain districts of England and Scotland the nightjar is called the goatsucker, a name that originated from the queer superstition that this bird with its enormous mouth sucked the teats of goats. Like the name nightjar the name goatsucker also crossed the Atlantic, as is manifested by such names as long-winged goatsucker and Virginia goatsucker to be found in the older books and papers dealing with American birds. The name goatsucker is still applied to the order and family but is seldom used today in designating the species.

In parts of the United States, especially in the South, nighthawks are known as bats, since the birds are usually seen at dusk when their erratic flight resembles somewhat that of the common mammal. This resemblance linked with the bellowing or booming sound produced by the wing feathers during the courtship plunge has given source to the commonly used name bullbat. Audubon (1840) used the synonym Virginia bat and stated that the French Creoles of Louisana knew the nighthawk by the metaphorical French name "crapau volans," or flying toad. In the Bahamas, as well as in certain localities of America, a common local name is "pick-a-me-dick" a crude imitation of one of its notes. The name mosquito hawk was well earned by one individual that, according to the Biological Survey, had eaten 300 mosquitoes. Other names sometimes applied to the nighthawk but less frequently than some of those previously mentioned are pisk, pork and beans, will-o'-wisp, burnt-land bird, and bird hawk.

The commonly accepted name nighthawk probably originated because of the bird's resemblance to the smaller hawks when observed in flight. However, it has sometimes proved to be an unfortunate choice, since to the layman it suggests a bird of the true hawk type. This name on occasions has been a source of trouble to an innocent bird as illustrated in the following cases. According to B. H. Warren (1890) the Pennsylvania Game Commissioners, in their interpretation of the Scalp Act of 1885, took the stand that they were obliged to allow bounty on all nighthawks because they were known as hawks. Mr. Warren also states that there is a somewhat prevalent idea that nighthawks are destroyers of young poultry, the name doubtless having given origin to the absurdity. The following clipping taken from the Portland (Maine) Press is another example of the way the name has misled well-meaning persons. "The Press building acquired a new claim to distinction yesterday as the haunt of wild fowl when janitor Phillip Ward, upon making an ascent to the roof, discovered two hen hawk's eggs there. Apparently some bird of the genus so despised by farmers had found the top of Portland's skyscrapers the right kind of a nesting place, and had laid her plans to hatch a few juvenile hen hawks up there. Janitor Ward's unexpected arrival put an end to such plans, however, and farmers may rest assured that the breed of distasteful birds who pillage their chicken yards is two the less." Arthur H. Norton, director of the Portland Society of Natural History, investigated the story and found the victim to be an innocent nighthawk. Adverse criticisms of the name nighthawk have been numerous but the name although inappropriate is destined to persist.

Spring.—The vanguard of the nighthawks in the spring migration reaches Florida and the Gulf States about the middle of April.

There have been March arrivals reported, but these are exceptional. Large flocks, some of them numbering thousands of individuals, have been seen during May. Many of these southern records may be representatives of the southern form, *Chordeiles minor chapmani*.

It is not necessary to search the isolated retreats away from the habitations of man for the first nighthawk arrivals. In fact, they are more likely to appear in the midst of our populous cities and towns, where they may be seen flying high above the graveled roofs that later are to be the scene of their nesting activities.

Courtship.—The courtship of the nighthawk is an ardent and amorous performance on the part of the male. He may be seen at twilight or early dawn uttering his sharp *peent* calls as he flies in wide circles sometimes hovering or soaring in the air high above the proposed nesting site. At more or less regular intervals he swoops down often within a few yards of his mate. Just as he seems about to dash into the ground he makes an abrupt upward turn, the vibrating primaries producing the well-known boom. After these preliminary aerial performances the male alights on the ground or graveled roof near the resting passive female. He now stands on his feet instead of resting his body on the ground. His tail is widely spread like a fan and wagged from side to side while the body is given a peculiar rocking motion. The throat is frequently puffed out, displaying a large white patch, which is ordinarily concealed when he is at rest. Synchronized with the throat distension is the uttering of guttural croaking notes. In producing these notes the bird holds the beak tightly closed, so that the throat membrane is distended by the pressure of the air emitted from the lungs. Under these conditions the sound waves originating at the syrinx beat against the tense membrane, producing notes of a striking and peculiar resonant quality. These notes are not uttered under ordinary conditions and constitute a very important part of the courtship.

The female, as far as outward manifestations are concerned, does not seem to be at all impressed by these extraordinary antics. The male at times in seeming desperation flies directly over the female uttering a sharp *peent*. He may then circle the female several times but even to this she seems unmoved. At times, when he approaches too near, the female will take a short flight, alighting a few yards away. The male follows and the performance described above is repeated. Eventually the courtship terminates in copulation.

The aerial evolutions of the male, including the downward plunges and "booming," are continued throughout the nesting period, but after the young are hatched his effervescent energies are directed in part to securing food for his offspring. With regard to the courtship of the nighthawk, Charles W. Townsend (1920b), who gave the subject of the courtship of birds careful study, stated: "The rapid headlong plunges of the nighthawk may be classed as a display of motion, a form of the dance. Incidentally, and perhaps accidentally at first, a loud booming sound is produced by the rush of air through the wing feathers. This instrumental music is now the important feature, although the dance is by no means a negligible one."

Nesting.—The nesting site, according to the procedure of a pair of nighthawks studied by me at Brunswick, Maine, is chosen by the female. A banded female returned to the same nesting site on the graveled roof of the high school building for four successive years, although the males, during at least two seasons, were different individuals.

The nighthawk is solitary in its nesting habits, though there have been instances where the nests of this species have been placed very near together, approaching a gregarious tendency. For example, E. A. Samuels (1872) states that on "a ledge of rocks back of the settlement known as Wilson's Mills, which seemed a favorite breeding-place for these birds, and, in the space of every four or five rods, a female was sitting on her eggs." B. H. Warren (1890) writes that he has found several nighthawks breeding within a few yards of each other. A similar case of this kind was noted at Gardner, Maine, where five pairs of birds nested in a very restricted area of an old deserted dock. I am inclined to believe that the existence of a good nesting site rather than a social tendency is the more important factor in causing these birds to nest in proximity. In general, each pair of birds has a relatively large nesting territory, which is vigilantly guarded. I have never noted any marked tendency of the birds to flock together until after the nesting season prior to and during the migrations.

The nests of the nighthawk located on the ground are found in a diversity of situations as far as the surroundings are concerned. It prefers gravel beaches or open barren areas of rock or soil unobstructed by tall shrubbery or trees. It never builds a nest in the seclusion of a forest. In regions where forests abound it nests in places where vegetation is sparse or preferably where forest fires have left a barren waste. C. F. Batchelder (1882) found the nighthawk frequenting burnt lands in the region of the upper St. John River near Fort Fairfield, Maine, and it has also been found to be common in the burnt lands of the Restigouche Valley, New Brunswick. R. W. Chaney (1910) found a nest in a burnt-over area near a partly burned log in Mason County, Mich. I found three nests of the nighthawk in a burnt-over area near the Biological Station, Douglas Lake, northern Michigan, and C. E. Johnson (1920) saw two young on a scantily moss-covered and stick-strewn rock outcrop in Lake County, Minn., in a district previously burnt over. It has been noted that in regions that have been burnt over the nighthawk population increases; hence the burning of timber land, which is so destructive to many species of birds, is not a hindrance but possibly an aid to the general welfare of the nighthawk.

The nighthawk has also been found to breed in cultivated areas. I. E. Hess (1910) noted its nesting in plowed fields in central Illinois, and T. G. Gentry (1877) states that old stubble fields are frequently selected as nesting sites. H. J. Rust (1911) has reported the western nighthawk in cornfields in Idaho and California. The Texas nighthawk, according to Sharp (1907), is a common inhabitant of the vineyards of San Diego, Calif., where the eggs are placed on the ground under or near the vines. Nests have also been found in potato fields and even in gardens near the houses of man. C. B. Ressel (1889) reported the eggs of the nighthawk placed upon the loose soil thrown up by the woodchuck (*Marmota monax*), indicating that barren places even though they are composed of loose soil may be preferred to sites covered with vegetation, twigs, or other debris.

In Virginia, according to H. H. Bailey (1913), the nighthawk often departs from its usual ground nest to a place on a stump, fence rail, or tops of drifts formed on the islands off the Virginia coast. Nests on stumps have been reported from various localities. I have found nests on the flat surface of top rails of fences in central Illinois; one of these nests was 8 feet from the ground. V. Max Kemery (1925) reports an unusual nesting site between the rails on a railroad track that was in daily use. The bird would fly when the cars or engine approached but returned as soon as the train had passed. Another unique nesting place that has come to my attention is an old robin's nest located in a tree near Farmington, Maine. This nighthawk, according to Mr. Jewell (1908), nested in this unusual site for five successive years, the tree being destroyed by fire at the end of that time.

The nighthawk in increasing numbers is availing itself of nesting sites provided by the graveled roofs of our cities and towns. In certain sections of the country this tendency is so marked that nighthawks are now seldom seen remote from graveled roofs during the nesting season, according to Lynds Jones (1909). The chimney swift, a not distant relative of the nighthawk, long ago forsook its primitive nesting sites in hollow trees, and today we no longer associate them with such places. Occurring simultaneously with the destruction of the giant forest trees was the erection of chimneys in connection with the homes of civilized races. The chimney swift, deprived of its original nesting site, was quick to make the radical but necessary change. Doubtless this adaptability to a changing environment has been an important factor in the preservation of the species. Chimneys have been used in America for centuries, but the graveled roof on which the nighthawk builds its nest is a comparatively recent development. It was not until the middle of the nineteenth century that the mansard and the flat type of graveled roofs were introduced. It was not long after these first roofs were built that the nighthawks discovered the possibilities of a new and admirable type of nesting site. As early as 1869 W. P. Turnbull wrote that the nighthawk was often seen high in the air above the streets of Philadelphia and that their nests were frequently found on the roofs of the warehouses of the city. Louis A. Zarega (1882) reported finding them breeding on a roof on the north side of 71st street, Philadelphia, in June 1882. In 1870 and 1871 Dr. T. M. Brewer (1874) found a number of instances of this bird nesting on the flat mansard roofs of Boston, and a few years later it was discovered nesting on the flat roofs of Montreal, Canada, by William Couper (1876). In 1879 a pair of the birds built a nest on a roof in the heart of the city of Cleveland, Ohio, and a few years later E. Sterling (1885) observed three pairs nesting on a slate roof of a large building near his study. Since 1880 there are innumerable records of nighthawks that have deserted the rural districts to take up their residence in the city. Today roof-nesting sites of the nighthawk seem no more unusual than the nests of the chimney swift built in our sooty chimneys. It is difficult to determine the factors that have been instrumental in this radical change, for unlike the case of the swift's hollow trees, there are just as many rocky knolls, pebbly beaches, and barren fields as there were prior to the appearance of the flat-roofed buildings. Although certain insects such as flies and mosquitoes are abundant about our cities I do not believe that the food supply has an important bearing on this question, as has been maintained by certain observers. Even in the small country villages, wherever there are graveled roofs there is the usual quota of nighthawks. In these villages the environment, as far as food for the nighthawk is concerned, is not different from regions isolated from civilization.

W. E. Saunders (1917) states that the young after their first flight often land on the ground and he asks the question: "What chance of survival is there for a young nighthawk on a city street or vacant lot?" Mr. Saunders believes that the nighthawk has steadily decreased in numbers since the bird has taken up its abode in the city and states further that immigration is the only thing that keeps up the city population. To the contrary my observations of the past 25 years in Maine indicate that the birds are not only maintaining but are increasing their numbers. Furthermore, the mortality of the birds that nest on roofs is much less than among those that choose nesting sites on the ground. In the latter place the birds are constantly exposed to the ravages of predatory animals including the cat. In the country hundreds of young birds meet with a tragic end without any of us being the wiser, while in the city such cases are more likely to be brought to our attention. On the city roof there is freedom from natural enemies. In the study of a large number of nighthawk families I have noted relatively few young that left the nesting roof prematurely, and it has been a common experience to see them return to the roof many times after the initial flight. One bird, the account of which is related in a subsequent division of this paper returned to the roof every day until it went south on its migration at the age of 52 days. Many of the birds that nest on the roofs are never disturbed by human beings during the entire nesting period, and under such circumstances the young do not leave the security of the roof until they are able to fly well. It is obvious that the young of parents that nest on roofs are the ones most likely to survive, and they in turn will nest in similar situations the following seasons. It seems reasonable to suppose that after the habit is established natural selection and heredity play an important part in the general departure from the old to the new nesting environment.

No attempt is made by the nighthawk to construct a nest, and no materials are added to those already present on the nesting site chosen by the birds. The eggs may be in a slight depression, but no material is excavated or removed by the bird except that incidentally shoved aside by the incubating bird.

Eggs.—Normally two eggs are laid, and there is seldom a departure from this number. In a letter dated January 20, 1936, F. W. Rapp, of Vicksburg, Mich., writes that he found a nest of the nighthawk containing three eggs on May 22, 1889.

The eggs are elliptical-ovate or elliptical-oval, one end being slightly smaller than the other. The shell is strong, closed grained and moderately glossy. The ground color varies from pale creamy white to shades of cream olive-buff and olive-gray. The eggs are marked and speckled with shades of slate, black, drab, smoke and lilac gray, and tawny-olive, and some of the eggs have shades of pearly gray, lavender, and plumbeous. In some eggs the markings are fine and uniform in size, almost obscuring the ground color; in others they are less numerous but larger and more prominent. There is an endless variation in the details of the markings and colors, but the eggs in general exhibit a coloring that blends effectively with their surroundings.

The average measurements of 81 eggs in the United States National Museum are long diameter 29.97, short diameter 21.84

millimeters. The largest egg of the series measured 33.53 by 22.86 and the smallest 27.68 by 20.57 millimeters. The average capacity of nighthawk eggs, according to Walter Hoxie (1887), is 0.448 cubic inch.

The eggs do not necessarily remain in the position in which they are first laid, especially when the nesting site is on a comparatively level surface such as that provided by graveled roofs. During the period of incubation of two nests under daily observation, the eggs were gradually moved for a distance of 5 to 6 feet. This shift in position comes about by the habit of the female pulling or pushing the eggs under her breast, thus moving them a short distance each time she settled on the eggs. As the direction of the bird's approach was more or less constant, the eggs were moved in the same general direction. This resulted in a distinct trail being formed, giving an appearance that one would expect to see if a giant snail had traveled over the graveled surface and forced the larger pebbles to one side. B. H. Warren (1890) writes that the eggs of a nighthawk in one instance were moved 200 feet by the bird, which carried them in her mouth. I have never been able to verify this extraordinary behavior of a nighthawk transporting an object as large as an egg in its mouth.

The following experiment is of interest as it suggests an interpretation of the manner in which a nighthawk locates its eggs. One evening when the female nighthawk was away feeding I moved the eggs to a place on the graveled roof about 6 feet from their original position. When the bird returned she alighted in the accustomed place and waddled up to the spot where she had left the eggs. No eggs being there, she went by a few inches, turned around, and recrossed the spot. This was repeated several times, and finally much bewildered she flew away. The eggs were in plain view yet were not discovered. Fearing she might desert her nest, I returned the eggs. In about 10 minutes the female returned, alighted in the usual position and without hesitation went directly to the eggs. This experiment was repeated on this and other birds with essentially the same results. It is evident that some factor such as a hypothetical sense of location or orientation is important, whereas sight plays a minor role for the nighthawk in locating its eggs. The same factor is probably important to the nighthawk in finding its way over thousands of miles during migration and its ability to arrive punctually not only in the same State and the same town but to the identical nesting site.

Incubation.—Both the male and female have been reported as sharing the duties of incubation. George H. Selleck (1916) states that the male nighthawk incubated the eggs during the daytime, whereas the female took charge of the nest at night in the case of a pair of birds he observed at Exeter, N. H. Dr. A. A. Allen (1933) states that the male takes his place on the eggs in the evening while the female is away feeding. Forbush (1927) states that both male and female share in incubation. On the other hand, J. H. Bowles (1921), who made an intensive study of the nighthawk, records only the female incubating the eggs. T. G. Gentry (1887) states that incubation "is the exclusive labor of the female" but that the young are cared for by both parents. It is evident, if the above statements are all true observations, that there is considerable individual variation in the behavior of the male in regard to incubation. In my own intensive studies of several pairs of nighthawks that nested on graveled roofs at Brunswick, Maine, I have never seen the male incubating the eggs. In the case of one nest under daily observation the birds were subject to study day and night by a relay of observers for a considerable part of the incubation period. The same held true for a pair of nighthawks studied in northern Michigan. Furthermore, visits made to numerous nests revealed in those cases that only the female was incubating the eggs, although the male was often very near to the female or to the eggs. My observations agree with the statement of Gentry that the female does all the incubating, but the male in most instances assists in caring for the young.

The behavior of the birds in relation to the nest and eggs and correlated with the time of day, the weather, environmental conditions, and the activities of other birds can be illustrated by field notes taken on June 20, 1921. These notes are representative of observations taken throughout the nesting season. The nest under consideration was located on the graveled roof of a two-story highschool building at Brunswick, Maine, a village of about 7,000 inhabitants located on the Androscoggin River. There are numerous giant elms and other shade trees along its streets, and the spacious yards and gardens present an environment attractive to a large number of birds. The times given throughout the following notes are eastern daylight saving:

June 20, 1921. 2:50 a. m. Cloudy, moon hidden by clouds, clear near the eastern horizon where the stars shine brightly. Entered the blind on the roof at 3 a. m. Female incubating the eggs. Her eyes were wide open when viewed with the flash light.

3:20 a. m. The female has been quiet during the past 20 minutes but has now shifted her position and is facing northeastward directly toward the first faint light of dawn. (Daily observations revealed that the nesting bird usually faced the sunrise in the morning and the sunset in the evening. In other words, she oriented herself toward the source of light preceding the times she anticipated leaving the nest to feed. It became evident through repeated experimental tests that her leaving the nest was considerably influenced by the factor of the intensity of light.)

3:24 a. m. The male gives a loud *peent* call as he awakens on his perch in the elm tree. (The elm stands in the school yard and some of its branches extend over the roof wall. The male's favorite perch was on a large horizontal limb just above the level of the roof. When he was through with his activities in the morning or evening he usually retired to this limb. He generally perched lengthwise on this limb, but it was not rare for him to depart from the conventional nighthawk position and perch crosswise to the limb.)

3:40 a. m. Light growing brighter in the east, the female can be seen without the use of the flashlight. She sits with her eyes closed, but from time to time she opens them, then raises her head and peers around, as if testing the intensity of the light prior to her leaving the nest.

3:42 a. m. The male nighthawk alights on the roof and gives a sharp *peent* call, followed by a series of guttural *awk-awk-awk* notes.

3:44 a. m. The male shifts his position to the roof wall but continues the guttural calls, each time displaying his conspicuous white throat patch.

4:04 a. m. The male leaves the roof wall and alights on the graveled surface within 8 inches of the female. He utters a single sharp *peent* note, then continues with the striking guttural *awk* calls. The female shows no outward signs of being impressed by the ardent attentions of her mate.

4:08 a. m. The male leaves the roof but soon returns and is joined by a second male. Female leaves her nest and flies toward the males, and all leave under great excitement, uttering sharp, piercing calls. The female lent a hand in driving away the strange male.

4:10 a. m. The female returns and pulls her eggs beneath her in the usual manner.

4:14 a. m. The male alights on the roof about 30 feet from the nest and utters a series of *awk* calls in rapid succession, as if much excited as the result of his combat.

4:30 a. m. The male is chasing a strange nighthawk and, as he pursues he utters a series of *yap-yap-yap-yap* calls in rapid fire succession, a note I have not heard before.

4:33 a. m. The male is now going through his hair-raising dives and producing the so-called boom notes, which to me resemble *swo-o-o-onk*, with the accent on the last syllable.

4:46 a. m. The sun has not yet risen. The male nighthawk flies to his perch in his favorite elm tree, and thus end his activities for the morning.

9:00 a. m. The nighthawks have been quiet since 4:46 a. m. For the greater part of the time the female has been motionless, with her eyes closed, but at intervals she opens her eyes wide in response to some unusual disturbance. She did not leave to feed, as is usual for her to do each morning.

9:10 a. m. The female shifted her position and turned her eggs. I left the blind at 9:15 a. m. and my place was taken by student observers, who took notes in relays until my return in the evening. They reported no activity on the part of the male. He remained on his perch in the elm throughout the day. The female did not leave the nest but merely shifted her position slightly from time to time in adjusting her eggs. When the heat was excessive she panted vigorously in order to adjust her body temperature.

7:30 p. m. When I arrived at the roof the sun was shining on the nesting female. Her eyes were opened as I approached the nest but were again closed after I had entered the blind.

8:05 p. m. The first *peent* call of the nighthawk is heard from the male nighthawk, perched in the elm tree near the school building, where he had retired at 4:46 a. m.

8:09 p. m. Male leaves his perch in the elm. Simultaneously another nighthawk appears from the elms farther down the street.

8:46 p. m. The male alights near the nesting female.

8:47 p. m. The female, facing toward the western sky, opens her eyes wide and turns from side to side. With this preliminary action repeated several times, she leaves the nest. The male remains within a few inches of the nest but makes no attempt to incubate the eggs. He merely serves as a guard while the female is away.

8:48 p. m. The male leaves the roof for a moment, uttering the sharp *peent* calls, and then returns to take up his position near to the nest.

8:50 p. m. The female returns to the nest after being away only three minutes. The male was quiet while on the roof alone, but as soon as the female returned he started his guttural notes.

8:58 p. m. The male takes leave without any ceremony and flies to his perch in the elm tree.

9:01 p. m. The female leaves the nest quietly.

9:22 p. m. No nighthawks have been seen or heard during the past 20 minutes. The female unannounced returns, after her quest for food, to brood her eggs for the remainder of the night.

Activities began again at 3:14 a. m. the next day, and the program was in all essentials similar to that recorded for June 20. Although a large series of such observations were made the male never was seen to incubate the eggs, but he regularly visited the nesting female each morning and evening. Sometimes, especially in very cloudy weather, the male left the elm tree during the day and flew about uttering the usual *peent* calls. He was never seen on the roof during the middle of the day.

The female was always faithful to her task regardless of a parching sun or torrential downpours of rain. At one time the thermometer placed on the graveled roof reached 130° F., although it was only 98° F. in the shade on the street level. At such times her enormous mouth was wide open, and she panted incessantly. The female's presence was needed to protect the eggs from the excessive heat fully as much as it was to supply warmth during the cool evenings when the temperature sometimes dropped as low as 45° F. If the female should leave her eggs when the temperature rises as high as 130° F. the embryos inside of the eggs would be killed in a few minutes.

It was common for the heat to melt the tar beneath the gravel so that it oozed to the surface of the pebbles. Milton Goff (1932) relates an interesting experience of a nighthawk that nested on a school roof at Rockford, Ill. One of the two eggs became firmly embedded in some tar melted by the sun. The female was unable to move the egg after nine desperate attempts made during the course of two hours.

Young.—In 1922 the nighthawks arrived at Brunswick, Maine, on May 15. On June 3 the first egg was laid and was marked No. 1. It was not incubated the first day. On June 4 the second egg was laid at 11:05 a. m. and marked No. 2. The laying of the second egg was observed. It was seen when it first appeared and watched until it emerged from the cloaca two minutes later. The egg was moist at first but quickly dried in the warm air, after which the female turned around and tucked it under her breast. Incubation began immediately after the second egg was laid.

On June 23, 1922, egg No. 1 was pipped at 8:30 a. m. and at this time the peeps of the confined embryo could be heard distinctly. At 11:00 a. m. the chick had emerged. The egg shells of the first egg were removed about noon. The female took them in her beak and dropped them during flight at a point about a hundred yards from the building. Egg No. 2 was pipped at 2 p. m., and at 3 p. m. portions of the shell were broken away. The female seemed little concerned about the first chick but lavished all her attentions on the unhatched bird. At times she elevated her body, peered at the egg, and responded to the calls of the embryo with an assuring note. She frequently rocked her body over the egg as if to assist in removing the shell. At 6 p. m. the shell was cracked latitudinally and soon thereafter the cup of the larger end was slightly lifted. At 6:30 p. m. the young was completely freed from the shell, which broke away in two parts. As the shell membrane dried the two cups closed again forming a complete empty shell case. At this time the first young was being brooded while the second, in a wet bedraggled condition, awkwardly and weakly wavered its head beneath the bill of the female. The faint peeping notes uttered by the youngster were answered with guttural purring notes of the proud and triumphant mother. After the down of the second youngster was dry it joined its fellow under the breast of the mother. The egg shell was not removed until the following morning. The incubation period for this set of eggs was definitely established to be 19 days.

The next day the female attempted to brood the young continuously. One of the young, however, persisted in its attempts to break away from parental care in spite of the warning notes of its mother. In one instance the mother dragged the one young under her body until within reach of the unruly youngster, which was quickly and violently tucked under her breast with something of an attitude of rebuff.

On the second day the young frequently appeared in the open and at such times often pecked at the mother's beak as if recognizing it to be the door of a well-filled cupboard. The young had not yet been fed, as they were still dependent on the yolk provided by the egg and stored in their bodies at the time of hatching. The female remained with the young throughout the day, whereas the male did not make his appearance until 8:50 in the evening. He announced his arrival with a sharp call as he landed on the roof. His call was immediately answered by the female, whereupon he made his way to the nest and without ceremony or delay delivered the first food received by the young.

I was not prepared to see the male feed the young because the male of the preceding summer (another individual) never assisted in the care of the young. This striking difference in individual behavior emphasizes the point that it is not safe to generalize on observations of a single individual.

The next morning the female was brooding her young, and being accustomed to my daily presence she allowed me to reach under her breast to remove the young without exhibiting the least bit of fear. A female nesting on another roof when visited for the first time scooted away hurriedly, fluttered helplessly on the roof, enacting a perfect imitation of a crippled bird, a ruse to attract my attention away from her young. When I followed her she quickly flew away. On subsequent visits this bird stood her ground, elevated her wings in an upright position, and hissed at me in defiance of my approach.

The following notes are from observations made of the young that were hatched on the high-school roof the preceding year (1921).

The female of that year was the same bird that nested there in 1922. The identity of the female was established by banding and also by a slight deformity of the maxilla, the tip of which was broken off. The males of the two broods were different individuals.

The young were fed during the early morning before sunrise and again in the evening after sunset. During the heat of the day, when the temperature frequently went soaring above 110° F., the young kept well concealed under the breast of the brooding bird in close contact to her abdominal air sacs. When the temperature was less torrid the young peeked their heads through the feathers and often came out entirely. At such times they sometimes amused themselves by picking at the mother's beak and rectal bristles. If the annoyance became too great the female would thrust her head beneath her breast. The young then proceeded to pick at the feathers of her crown and nape.

The female left the nest regularly about 8:30 p. m. (daylight saving time) to obtain food for herself and young. In the case of this brood the female delivered all the food required by the young. The food was delivered by the process of regurgitation. The beak of the female was thrust well into the large and widely distended mouth of the young when the transfer of food was made. After feeding, the adult brooded her young in the earlier stages of their development.

For the first three days the young remained near the spot where they had been hatched, but on the fourth day after a heavy rain they had moved to a slightly raised portion of the roof, which was free from excessive dampness. The female never left the young during a rain at this stage of their growth, even if it meant depriving them of food. The male regularly visited the roof early in the morning and again in the evening throughout the breeding season, but he was never seen to deliver food to the young. The male was usually stationed on the roof when the female was away and thus served as a watchdog in her absence. More than once he was called upon to chase away a strange nighthawk that had inadvertently alighted in his territory on the high-school roof.

On the fifth day (June 29) the young had wandered to the southern end of the building where the shadow of the roof wall protected them from the direct rays of the burning sun. The heat during the middle of the day was frequently excessive. On July 7, when the young were 13 days old, a thermometer placed on the gravel of the roof registered 140° F. The heat was too much for one of the young, which succumbed and was found dead near the middle of the roof. Its fellow nestling, hidden in the shadow of the roof wall and behind a clay ventilating pipe, escaped death but was in a serious condition. A sponge soaked with cold water was placed near the youngster, whereupon it ignored its parent to enjoy the comfort provided by the cool sponge.   This act probably aided the survival of the young nighthawk through the remainder of the record-breaking hot day.

As the nighthawk grew older he became very aggressive and pugnacious and never hesitated to pester his mother whenever he was hungry.   At times he seemed mischievous.   It was not a rare experience to see him crouch under his mother's breast and then by standing up quickly and rigidly topple his mother so that she was forced to extend her wings to keep from falling over.   During the period of the rapid growth of the wing feathers the youngster was continually extending and stretching his wings as if to relieve the uncomfortable feeling caused by growing pains.

When the young nighthawk was three weeks old he was able to make short flights from one place to another on the gravel roof.   At this stage of his growth he had become so large that it was difficult for the female to cover him adequately while brooding.   This was strikingly demonstrated on the evening of July 17, when he was 23 days old.   The mother had left him alone on the roof while she was away on her regular evening search for food.   It was so cool and damp that the young bird uttered notes that clearly indicated discomfort.   I placed him in a woolen bag, and this, combined with the warmth of my hands, was very satisfying, as indicated by his change to notes of contentment.   He remained there in comfort until his mother alighted on the roof and gave the characteristic call note, announcing supper.   The little nighthawk struggled out of my bag and ran directly to his mother to be fed.   After he was gorged with insects, the female attempted to brood him, but to her apparent dismay he rushed back to the woolen bag, clearly recognizing that I could do a much better job at brooding.

On July 19, when the nighthawk was 25 days old, I discovered that he was no longer solely dependent on his parent for food.   I found him busily engaged catching some white moths that had collected about a drain pipe of the roof.   He was flying this way and that, catching the moths with great delight.   As I sat there watching I chanced to pull a small handkerchief from my pocket, whereupon he dashed at the white object with the ferociousness of a tiger.   Evidently to the nighthawk this was some giant moth large enough to provide for an entire meal.

The female now made frequent attempts to entice the young bird away from the roof by first offering food but flying away before it was delivered.   The youngster would follow her in extended flights but invariably returned to the roof.

On July 24, when the bird was 30 days old, the female was photographed with the young for the last time.   Thereafter she forsook her offspring for a roost in the nearby elm tree. She then visited the roof only for short intervals at feeding times. On each successive day the young bird took longer and longer flights, and each day I anticipated it would be my last opportunity to photograph and to observe him. Much to my delight he continued to return, seeming to enjoy my companionship.

On August 15 he left with the other nighthawks of the vicinity on their migration to the south. This unusual experience of having the bird return to the roof gave me an unprecedented opportunity to make a continuous set of daily observations and measurements of a nighthawk living under normal natural conditions up to the time it was 52 days of age. By this time the growth of the juvenal plumage was completed and exchanged in part for the first winter plumage.

Plumages.—On the first day the young are able to stand upright and are very active from the time of hatching. The eyes are open, iris bluish black; skin darkly pigmented darker above than below; bill "pale mouse gray"; tarsus and toes brownish drab. Down present on both dorsal and ventral parts of the body. Down of the ventral tracts pale gray shading to "pallid neutral gray" on the belly; chin gray, malar stripes and patch on the throat "dark mouse gray," approaching black. Upper parts mottled and marbled, made up of patches of pale gray and "dark mouse gray." In the region of the nape and scapulars the down has a distinct "pale olive-buff" tint. At the base of the beak the down has a tinge of buff. A circular area about the anus, the outer part of the shanks, and fore arm have patches of darker colored down. Patterns of dark and white vary considerably in different young. The average length of the down on the various parts of the body varies as follows: Crown 9, base of bill 4, region over eye 6, throat 12, belly 15, wing 11, and region of anus 8 millimeters.

On the third day the color of the bill has changed to a "deep neutral gray," and the tarsus and toes become a dusky drab. Down at the base of the beak, scapular region, and irregular patches of the back has faded from the colors present in the day-old chick to a "tilleul buff." Iris is now a clear brown instead of the bluish black of the freshly hatched chick.

At the age of 10 days the tarsus and toes are "deep Quaker drab," bill "dark neutral gray," eyelids "light neutral gray." Exposed portions of the eyes are noticeably greater. Down of the back much worn and matted down, the feather papillae in the region of the crown, wing coverts, scapulars, and rump now more conspicuous than the down. The tips of the feathers of the back are unsheathed and exhibit a black and cinnamon color. The color pattern of the back is completely lost since the appearance of the feather papillae and their unsheathed tips. The papillae of the tail feathers are only 8 millimeters long and as yet do not show through the down. The feather papillae of the head and tail are the last to unsheath.

In chicks 13 days old the "pinkish cinnamon" of the tips of the feathers of the dorsal tracts has faded to a "pinkish buff," and some of the feathers approach a "tilleul buff." Freshly unsheathed feathers of the crown are "pinkish cinnamon." Black markings have faded to a "fuscous-black" or "dusky neutral gray"; yellowish color of the breast feathers of the younger stages now faded to gray tinged with yellow. The juvenal plumage is rapidly replacing the natal down in all parts of the body. The yellowish-gray breast feathers are barred with "dusky neutral gray." As previously noted, one of the two birds died from exposure to great heat at this time and the remaining descriptions are based on one bird.

At the age of 15 days the down is ragged in appearance but is still prominent on the breast, sides of the head, wing coverts, and region of the tail. The down is worn off the feathers in the region of the crown and scapulars. Feathers of all tracts of the juvenal plumage are partially unsheathed. When the young are handled there are numerous particles of the feather sheaths that scale off. The wings exhibit a marked development. The tips of the under tail coverts recently unsheathed are ivory colored. The down persisting at the tips of the feathers comes off with the slightest pull. The pupil of the eye appears bluish black and the iris has changed to a "Van Dyke brown."

When 17 days old the sixth primary has now proceeded with unsheathing so that the white patch is 13 millimeters in extent. Tarsus and toes are "blackish plumbeous," bill is a "dusky purplish gray," eyelids are "dark olive-gray"; otherwise the markings are similar to those of the 15-day-old bird.

When 20 days old a relatively small amount of down remains, but a few filaments can be seen on the tips of some of the crown feathers, sides of neck, and breast. Feathers of the wings are growing fast and are so heavy from the large amount of blood and large sheaths that the wings rest on the surface of the roof, the bird being unable to support them. The wings are frequently outstretched, apparently to relieve the uncomfortable sensation produced by rapid growth of the feathers. Bristlelike feathers now appear around the base of the beak. The fifth primary is grown so that the white patch is beginning to unsheath, and the base of the fourth primary shows white area on sheath, which is destined to form part of the white patch on the wing of the fully grown young. The white on the sixth primary made its first appearance in the 17-day-old chick.

At this age the crown is "dusky neutral gray" or black, the feathers tipped, barred, and spotted with "vinaceous-buff"; some of the tips approach "avellaneous." The feathers of the upper parts are dark, or dusky, neutral gray variously mottled with shades of gray and "avellaneous" many of the feathers tipped with "pinkish buff." Auriculars "light cinnamon-buff" and black, tipped with lighter shades. Primaries and secondaries blackish warm gray, some of the feathers having an olivaceous-black appearance. All the remiges are tipped with "tilleul buff" or "vinaceous-buff." Some of the secondaries and inner primaries spotted with "vinaceous-buff." Coverts of primaries unspotted "blackish mouse gray" or black. Coverts of secondaries spotted with "tilleul buff" and "vinaceous-buff." Lesser wing coverts variously mottled with colors mentioned above. Feathers of the breast barred with "dark mouse gray" and shades of gray and white. Throat and chin with a crescentic band of feathers, which are barred with dark gray and white, the white predominating. Band of feathers along the edge of mandible extending below the eyes to the auriculars "neutral gray" and marked with "vinaceous-buff." Under tail coverts "cartridge buff," narrowly barred with black. Middle of the belly a heavy mat of down. Eyelids "light olive-gray," tarsus deep metal gray.

At 25 days the down has been lost, except that of the middle of the belly and small patches on the legs above the heels.

At 28 days the colorings are about as described for the 20-day-old chick, but the colors are subdued and faded because of exposure to the intense sunlight. The down is now entirely replaced by the feathers of the juvenal plumage. Although the outer primaries are only partially unsheathed, the young bird is capable of long flights and frequently leaves the roof, but invariably returns.

At 30 days the secondaries and the primaries, except the outer ones, are now unsheathed. The barred feathers lining the wings are now in process of unsheathing.

At 35 days the prevailing color of the upper parts is olivaceous-black, glossed with greenish, but this base color is very much broken by irregular markings, spotting, and marbling of buffy gray and whitish; many of the larger spots approach a light vinaceous-buff, which is especially evident on the crown. Spots of the crown are larger than those of the back. The throat patch now is clear white, an indication of its sex.

At 40 days, all the primaries except the outer two are completely unsheathed. The white patch of the second to fifth unsheathed, that of the first is 11 millimeters.

The bird, although able to fly as well as an adult, returned to the roof each day and allowed me to make daily measurements and weighings without the least resistance. It never attempted to run or fly away when I approached to pick it up. When I arrived on the roof wall it gave a series of calls, which seems to be a sign of recognition. The bird placed before me in a natural sitting pose measured 187 millimeters from the tip of the bill to the tip of the wings. Distance from level of the crown to the board on which it is seated is 90 millimeters. Tip of tail to front of toe in natural position 150, and tip of folded wing to toe 165 millimeters.

The bird at this age is very active and vivacious and captures all its own food. It offers no difficulty for me to capture it for measurements and poses perfectly for photographs.

On Monday, August 15, there was a great flight and departure of nighthawks, and after that date the nighthawk was seen no more. Presumably it went southward on its migration. The bird was 52 days old, and I had an unexcelled opportunity to observe the bird up to the time of the completion of its growth.

The completed juvenal plumages of both sexes is similar to that of the adult female except that the throat patch is not so well defined; in some it is replaced by blackish and buffy bars. The barring of the underparts is more extensive and the coloration in general is paler than that of the adults. There are whitish tips on all the primaries.

The postnatal molt has already been described in detail under the account of the young. There is a partial molt that does not include the wings and tail in September. There is a partial or complete prenuptial molt in spring when the young attain the plumage of the adult. The adults have a complete postnuptial molt before they return for their nesting activities the following year. I have not been able to ascertain the time of the postnuptial molt.

Albinistic phases of plumage, in which there is an absence of dark pigment, may appear in any species of birds. W. A. Strother (1886) reports a perfect albino taken at Lynchburg, Va.

Food.—The nighthawk is insectivorous in its eating habits. Since the major part of the insects it destroys are destructive to useful vegetation or are otherwise adverse to human welfare, the nighthawk ranks high in the list of birds beneficial to man.

The nighthawk captures the insects chiefly during its flight. The birds sweep up in their capacious mouths all types of insects from the large moths and beetles to the tiniest of flies and mosquitoes. Some of the stomachs examined have contained no less than 50 different species of insects, and some of the smaller insects are at times represented by thousands of individuals.

One of the most conspicuous elements of the food is flying ants. In the examination of 87 nighthawk stomachs, the United States Biological Survey reports that ants comprised nearly one-fourth of the total food eaten by the birds. In 24 of the stomachs the number of ants ranged from 200 to 1,800, and in all the stomachs examined there were not less than 20,000 ants (Beal, 1897). In the stomach of a nighthawk that met with accidental death at Brunswick, Maine, on August 20, 1925, there were 2,175 ants. The mass and weight of these insects were so great that they constituted a serious handicap and probably a factor in the bird's untimely ending. Charles Drury (1887) obtained a specimen in August that contained 320 insects, chiefly winged ants. W. L. McAtee (1926) found more than one hundred carpenter ants (*Camponotus herculeanus*) in one nighthawk stomach. In most all instances the ants captured are the mating winged individuals, which fly in immense swarms during the late summer. These ants are killed at a time when they are preparing to propagate their kind, and hence the death of every female means the destruction of thousands of the next generation.

According to examinations of the United States Biological Survey (Beal, McAtee, and Kalmbach, 1916) beetles comprised one-fifth of the food eaten by 87 nighthawks examined. May beetles, dung beetles, and others of the leaf-chafer family were in greatest numbers. Beal (1897) reported finding the remains of 34 May beetles (*Phyllophaga*) in a single nighthawk stomach, in another 23, and in a third 17. In the stomach contents of one specimen no less than 17 species of beetles were identified. Chester Lamb (1912) reports that all nighthawks collected by him had eaten enormous quantities of beetles. Thomas G. Gentry (1877) reports eight species of beetles in food examined by him. McAtee (1926) reports various leaf chafers, sawyers, wood borers, bark beetles, weevils, and plant lice in the food eaten by nighthawks in the course of his study of the relation of birds to woodlots in New York State. In the examination of hundreds of droppings of nighthawks obtained from various nesting sites chiefly at Brunswick, Maine, a large percentage of the identifiable remains consisted of parts of various species of beetles.

Nighthawks, especially in the Middle West, have been known to eat a considerable number of grasshoppers and locusts. According to Ernest Harold Baynes (1915) seven Nebraska specimens were found to have eaten 348 Rocky Mountain locusts; five specimens collected in Indiana reported by A. W. Butler (1898) had eaten 9 grasshoppers, 19 beetles, 23 Heteroptera, and 4 Neuroptera. B. H. Warren (1890) reported that grasshoppers were an important element of the food eaten by nighthawks collected in Pennsylvania. F. E. L. Beal (1897) states that one nighthawk contained the remains of 60 grasshoppers. A male killed on July 7, 1882, was reported by Everett Smith (1883) to have "an ichneumon fly, a black cricket, about twenty small grasshoppers, and many small, hard insects" in its crop.

Flies, plant lice, and mosquitoes frequently form an important element of the food of the nighthawk. A nighthawk examined by the Biological Survey had eaten more than 300 mosquitoes, and E. H. Forbush (1907) reports finding 500 mosquitoes in the stomach of one bird. McAtee (1926) reports that he found 650 plant lice in the stomach of a single nighthawk. Phoebe Knappen (1934) found stone flies in 21 nighthawks. The insects were chiefly adults but also a few larvae, nymphs, and eggs were present.

In the South various observers have noted that the nighthawk is an important factor in the control of the cotton-boll weevil. F. H. Herrick (1901) writes of a nighthawk that had been feeding on fireflies; the wide open mouth of an adult observed feeding its young was brilliantly illuminated like a spacious apartment all aglow with electricity. F. H. Carpenter (1886) relates a unique experience with nighthawks that darted at the artificial flies on his line when he was casting for trout. It is not an unusual experience to see nighthawks after dusk flying about electric lights of city streets (Knowlton, 1896) or about campfires of remote districts where they capture myriads of insects attracted by the lights.

During the migration nighthawks frequently fly near the ground and at such times may take advantage of any insects that appear in their path. During an afternoon late in August I observed a flight of several hundred nighthawks near Urbana, Ill. As I sat in a car alongside a large meadow I noticed that the birds were ravenously feasting on grasshoppers. Some of the birds lingered long enough to capture half a dozen of the insects before passing on to make place for other nighthawks in the migrating procession. A. Dawes DuBois, of Excelsior, Minn., relates a similar experience he had in the vicinity of Salt Creek, Logan County, Ill., as follows: "At dusk on the evening of May 22, 1913, as I walked along a cloverfield, we witnessed an assemblage of nighthawks in pursuit of low-flying insects. They skimmed over the clover like swallows; and their dusky forms were so numerous that they seemed to be weaving an intricate pattern in the gray twilight. They were so intent on their bountiful repast that they paid no heed to our presence, but sometimes darted past us only a few feet away."

Nighthawks not only capture food on the wing, but they also have been observed to drink, in the manner of swallows, as they skim near the surface of the water of lakes and streams. F. Stephens (1913) observed a nighthawk drinking from a watering trough. This bird dropped its lower mandible into the water, rippling the surface of the water as it passed along. A. Dawes DuBois writes of the following experience he had at Springfield, Ill., on July 29, 1923: "Mr. R. B. Horsfall and I were walking along the margin of a small pond when a nighthawk swooped down, touched the surface of the water and rose again; but we could not tell whether it was scooping up a floating insect or a drink of water."

Voice.—The nighthawk has no claim as a singer, but nevertheless its notes are of great interest and attract fully as much attention as the voices of our more gifted songsters.

The loud piercing calls uttered by the nighthawk during flight are simple yet, like all bird notes, extremely difficult to represent in written words so as to enable a reader unfamiliar with them to gain a clear conception of their character and quality. This fact is at once emphasized if we compare the interpretations of a few of the many authors who have attempted a written version of its calls. For example to C. G. Abbott (1914) it sounds like a "grating 'beedz, beedz,'" and to Charles Bendire (1895) it is a querulous and a squeaky note resembling "aek-aek, aek-aek" or "speek-speek, speek-speek." W. E. Grover describes this note as a sharp "mueike"; and E. H. Forbush (1907) states that "the note is s-k-i-r-k or s-c-a-i-p-e, a little like the call of Wilson's snipe,—rather a startling squeak when heard close at hand." W. L. Dawson (1903) interprets the note as "mizard, mizard," and E. H. Eaton (1914) describes it as a "loud nasal 'peent, peent.'" N. S. Goss (1891) writes that its voice is a "squeak" or a "pe-up" note, and Arkansas Hoosier (1890) states that "the note is best produced by speaking the word 'beard' in a whisper." To G. R. Mayfield (1921) the call is a shrill "B-e-e-r-b" and to H. Nehrling it is "Brirrr-brirrr." H. Tullsen (1911) interprets it as a sharp penetrating "Spe-eak," and H. H. Bailey (1913) thinks it sounds like "Queek-queek."

There was probably only the slightest variation in the notes of the different nighthawks as heard by the authors mentioned above, yet how strikingly different are the interpretations as represented in the written or printed words. The note described above is the one most frequently heard, and it is uttered independently of the seasons. It is the note that announces the arrival of the nighthawk in spring, and it is the call uttered at the time the nighthawks are congregating in fall in preparation for their departure to the south. I have been unable to ascertain whether this call is heard at their winter home in South America.

Frequently, during the courtship season, the males in their competition for a mate vigorously pursue each other. At such times both birds utter a series of sharply accented calls recorded in my field notes as resembling *Dick-a-dick-a-dick-dick-dick-dick-dick*, given in rapid succession.

There is another note of the nighthawk very different in character, an aeolian sound, produced by the rush of air through the primaries of the wings at the termination of the extraordinary downward plunge executed during the courtship season. In order to see this performance and to hear this peculiar and unique note to the best advantage it is necessary to visit the vicinity of the nesting site. Alexander Wilson (1828) described this note as a "loud booming sound very much resembling that produced by blowing strongly into the bunghole of an empty hogshead." E. H. Eaton (1914) offers a modification of Wilson's description in stating that the note is like that produced "by blowing across an empty bottle." T. G. Gentry (1877) describes it as a sound resembling that "produced by a tense cord set in vibration by a sudden gust of wind." T. Jasper (1878) states that it is a hollow whir like the rapid turning of a spinning wheel, and F. A. Hartman (1914) describes it as a "guttural 'woof.'" The note reminds W. A. Stearns (1883) of the sound produced by a bellowing bull. In my field notes I have described this note as a muffled *wr-r,r,r,r-oonk*, but sometimes more nearly approaching *sw-r,r,r,r-ooonk*, the last syllable decidedly accented and produced with great resonance. There is nothing about this note suggesting an explosive boom or bellowing.

It has long ago been well established that this peculiar note is not a vocal sound but one produced by the vibration of the primaries. As keen an observer as Alexander Wilson (1828) stated that it is "produced by the sudden expansion of his capacious mouth." Others shared Wilson's view or thought that it was a sound produced by the syrinx. After one has observed the performance it can be readily understood how such an erroneous interpretation was made by the earlier observers. The plunge takes place so quickly that it is only by repeated observations made under the most favorable conditions that the observer is convinced that the primaries are involved. Audubon (1840) was the first to arrive at a correct explanation. He writes that the source of the singular noise is "the concussion caused, at the time the bird passes the centre of its plunge by the new position of its wings, which are now brought almost instantly to the wind, like the sails of a ship suddenly thrown back." This observation with variation of its details has been made by numerous subsequent observers. J. B. Canfield (1902) gives a description of the performance as follows: "He suddenly paused and came soaring toward me like an arrow. About fifty feet in front of me his wings were lowered below his body, throwing them forward with the flight feathers spread wide apart * * * His speed was so great that the flight feathers vibrated like a loosely-stretched rubber band when snapped with the fingers. This performance was repeated in front, back, and beside me twelve times in all, never more than fifty feet away, and as near as fifteen. In all cases the wings were in the same position, and his mouth never open." F. A. Hartman (1914) writes, "It is very evident that the mouth plays no part, otherwise the sound would be produced at other times [than on the downward glide]. * * * The bird threw its wings far to the front at the end of his downward glide, so that the uppermost quill feathers were pointed exactly in the direction of his glide. Going at such head-long speed, these quill feathers when thrown edgewise to the air vibrated strongly, causing the 'woof'." Alden H. Miller (1925) while at Camp Lewis, Wash., during June and July succeeded in attracting nighthawks within 10 feet of himself by merely waving his hat in the air. He noticed that if the wings, during the down-ward plunge, were held in the upturned V-shaped position, a normal pose when soaring, no boom was heard, but when the wings were bent downward near the end of the dive the boom sound was pro-duced. The intensity of the sound, according to Mr. Miller, is more or less proportional to the speed attained. The main explosive boom seems to be preceded by a brief, lesser vibrating sound, which bursts forth into the full bellow. Both parts seem to have a distinct element of pitch, but the latter part is lower, with greater reso-nance and depth of quality.

The sound produced by the wings described above is a part of the courtship performance and is usually produced near the nesting site. After the young no longer require the constant attention of both parents, the male loses the glamour of romance and performs less frequently and soon after ceases almost entirely until the court-ship season of another year. However, birds migrating in August sometimes "boom."

Another note associated with the courtship season is a guttural call uttered only when the male is at rest and in the presence of the female. It may be described as an oft repeated *auk, auk, auk* or *awk, awk, awk*. This note is produced by the syrinx, but as it is uttered the bill is tightly closed and the gular membrane is tightly distended each time the note is produced. The distension is caused by the expulsion of air from the respiratory system. The distended membrane, although feathered, acts as a resonator and modifies the note, giving it a peculiar quality. Such a mechanism is present in other birds. It is especially highly developed in the prairie chicken, in which large lateral vocal sacs are present that give the "booming" notes of this grouse great carrying power.

The notes of the female nighthawk are simple calls uttered in response to the those of the male or of the young. She may utter a purring, pacifying note when brooding the young, but often these notes are so weak that they cannot be heard by the observer unless he is stationed very near in a blind.

Game.—Today we do not think of the nighthawk as a game bird, yet 60 years ago large numbers of them were killed by gunners and sportsmen, especially in the Southern States. M. G. Elzey, writing on September 18, 1876, stated: "Bull-bats (nighthawks) are the best of the minor game of this country for sport or table; have been very abundant and in superb condition here (Blacksburg, Virginia) for the past two weeks. I have killed several hundred. On one occasion took out 28 cartridges and brought in 23 birds besides 2 which fell out of bounds and were recovered by boys. Killed 17 in succession. The bats are quite as fat and better game than the reed birds." Dr. E. Sterling (1885) wrote: "Their rapid and irregular flight makes them a difficult mark for the young sportsman to practice on, as he never fails to make a target of them when the opportunity offers. I can now understand the object for which this bird was created." Dr. F. M. Chapman (1888), writing of conditions at Gainesville, Fla., stated, " 'Bat' shooting is here a popular pastime, great numbers being killed for food, and in August, when the birds have gathered in flocks, favorite fields may be occupied at nightfall by as many as a dozen shooters." Stockard (1905) lamented the fact that the birds "are foolishly slaughtered by pseudo-sportsmen who shoot them merely to watch the bird's graceful fall or to improve their skill as marksmen."

The practice of killing nighthawks was stopped through laws and by educational methods initiated by the National Association of Audubon Societies. William Dutcher (1902), in writing of conditions in Florida, stated, "It is believed, on very satisfactory evidence that the new law has stopped to a large degree the disgraceful practice of shooting 'bull-bats' or Nighthawks (*Chordeiles virginianus*) for sport." Bird-Lore for September-October 1903 published the following note: "The Night-hawk, or Bullbat, has been so long considered a legitimate target for shotgun practice, in the south, that a report of prosecution for killing these birds at Greensboro, North Carolina, marks a new era of bird protection in our southern states."

Enemies.—The greatest enemy of the nighthawk has been man. In the past great numbers of the birds were killed for food and often for mere sport or for satisfying a lust for killing. This was especially true in the Southern States, where the birds were slaughtered during the great flights of the annual migrations.

Nighthawks nesting on the ground are subject to the same enemies experienced by other species of ground-nesting birds. Night hawks nesting on roofs are usually free from such molestation, but Albert F. Ganier informs me that he has known of sparrow hawks invading the cities and preying upon the nighthawks, especially the young.

Cats and dogs become enemies of the city dwellers in the event the young leave the nest prematurely and land on the streets below.

Nighthawks have a remarkable protective coloration and have developed methods of deception such as imitating a wounded individual when an enemy approaches the nesting site. At times they assume an attitude of aggression; i. e., raising their elongated wings in a vertical position and hissing in defiance at an intruder.

DISTRIBUTION

Range.—The Western Hemisphere generally, from Yukon to Patagonia.

Breeding range.—The breeding range of the nighthawk extends **north** to Yukon (Sixty-mile River and probably Lapierres House); Mackenzie probably Fort Goodhope, probably Fort Franklin, Fort Resolution, and Hill Island Lake); northern Saskatchewan (Methye Portage, Stanley, and Reindeer River); northern Manitoba (probably Du Brochet Lake, Grand Rapids, and probably Churchill); northern Ontario (Martin Falls, probably Fort Albany, and probably Moose Factory); and Quebec (Lake Mistassini, Godbout, and Mingan Island). The **eastern** boundary of the range extends from this point southward through the coastal regions of the Maritime Provinces, the Eastern United States, the Bahama Islands (Nassau), to Puerto Rico (Mayaguez). **South** to Puerto Rico (Mayaguez); Haiti (Hinche and Jean Rubel); Jamaica (Port Henderson and Grand Cayman); Cuba (Isle of Pines); southern Texas (Brownsville, San Antonio, Kerrville, and Pecos); Chihuahua (Babicora); Sonora (Oposura and Los Nogales); and southern California (San Bernardino Mountains and Pine Knot). **West** to California (Pine Knot, Mono Lake, Grass Valley, and Eureka); western Oregon (Medford, Eugene, Corvallis, Portland, and St. Helen); western Washington (Bumping Lake, Gig Harbor, Seattle, and Blaine); British Columbia (Errington, Courtenay, Fort St. James, and Hazleton); southeastern Alaska (Wrangell); and western Yukon (Carcross, Whitehorse, and Sixty-mile River).

Winter range.—When the numerical abundance and extensive breeding range of this species are considered, it is surprising that knowledge concerning the winter range should be extremely limited. It seems certain, however, that it is entirely in South America **north** to Colombia (Antioquia); Venezuela (Orinoco Valley); and central Brazil (Matto Grosso). **East** to southeastern Brazil (Matto Grosso, São Paulo, and Rio de Janeiro); Uruguay (Concepcion); and Argentina (Barracas and La Plata). **South** to central Argentina (La Plata and Cordova). **West** to Argentina (Cordova, Santiago, Tucuman, and the Gran Chaco); western Paraguay (Asuncion); western Brazil

(Chapada); western Ecuador (Portoviejo); and western Colombia (Bogota and Antioquia).

The outline presented is for the entire species, which has, however, been separated into seven subspecies, or geographic races. The typical eastern nighthawk (*C. m. minor*) breeds in the eastern part of the continent west to the edge of the Great Plains from Oklahoma to Minnesota and in Canada to British Columbia and southern Yukon; the Florida nighthawk (*C. m. chapmani*) nests in the Gulf and South Atlantic States north to Arkansas, southern Illinois, central Alabama, and central North Carolina and west to eastern Texas; Howell's nighthawk (*C. m. howelli*) breeds in the southern part of the Great Plains region from northeastern Utah and western Kansas south to Oklahoma, central Texas, and New Mexico; Cherrie's nighthawk (*C. m. aserriensis*) is found in south-central Texas and the Mexican state of Tamaulipas; Sennett's nighthawk (*C. m. sennetti*) occupies a breeding range in the northern Great Plains from northeastern Montana and North Dakota south to eastern Wyoming, Nebraska, and northwestern Iowa; the western nighthawk (*C. m. henryi*) breeds in southwestern Colorado, eastern Arizona, New Mexico, Chihuahua, and Sonora; and the Pacific nighthawk (*C. m. hesperis*) nests in the western part of the continent from southeastern British Columbia and California east to southwestern Saskatchewan, northwestern Wyoming, and central Utah. In no case is it possible to indicate subspecific winter ranges, but it appears that all forms winter together in South America.

Spring migration.—Early dates of spring arrival in North America are: Florida—Orlando, March 20; Palma Sola, March 29; Pensacola, April 8. Georgia—Savannah, April 1; Kirkwood, April 19. South Carolina—Frogmore, April 12; Columbia, April 17. North Carolina—Hendersonville, April 13; Raleigh, April 15. Virginia—Variety Mills, April 10; New Market, April 24. District of Columbia—Washington, April 18. Maryland—Mardela Springs, April 19. Pennsylvania—Philadelphia, April 23; Beaver, April 27. New Jersey—Morristown, May 7. New York—New York City, April 20; Ballston Spa, April 29; Rochester, May 7. Connecticut—Hartford, April 24; Jewett City, May 6. Massachusetts—Harvard, April 19; Amherst, May 10. Vermont—St. Johnsbury, May 6; Rutland, May 12. New Hampshire—South Manchester, May 2; Concord, May 14. Maine—Dover-Foxcroft, April 29; South Portland, May 1. New Brunswick—St. Johns, May 13. Quebec—Quebec City, May 4; Montreal, May 9. Louisiana—New Orleans, April 8. Mississippi—Biloxi, April 8; Rodney, April 19. Arkansas—Monticello, April 11. Tennessee—Athens, April 20. Kentucky—Lexington, April 19;

Eubank, April 23. Missouri—St. Louis, April 22; Kansas City, May 2. Illinois—Chicago, April 21; Odin, April 27. Indiana—La Fayette, May 1; Fort Wayne, May 6. Ohio—Cleveland, April 20; Oberlin, April 21. Michigan—Sault Ste. Marie, April 30; Detroit, May 1. Ontario—Toronto, April 30; Ottawa, May 9. Iowa— Keokuk, April 23; National, May 6. Wisconsin—Madison, May 2; Milwaukee, May 3. Minnesota—Minneapolis, April 26; Lanesboro, May 7. Kansas—Onaga, April 30; Manhattan, May 1. Nebraska— Omaha, May 8; Red Cloud, May 3. South Dakota—Vermillion, May 10; Forestburg, May 16. North Dakota—Grand Forks, May 1; Argusville, May 18. Manitoba—Margaret, May 10; Aweme, May 12. Texas—San Antonio, April 2; Kerrville, April 22. Colorado—Denver, May 4; Yuma, May 9. Wyoming—Cheyenne, May 8; Torrington, May 24. Montana—Great Falls, May 15; Columbia Falls, May 29. Saskatchewan—Indian Head, May 18; Eastend, May 26. Arizona—Oracle, April 20; Santa Rita Mountains, May 1. Utah—Kobe Valley, May 24. Idaho—Ruper, May 18; Meridian, May 20. Alberta—Flagstaff, May 27; Banff, May 28. California—Red Bluff, April 1; San Diego, April 22; Eureka, May 7. Oregon—Coos Bay, May 1; Klamath Lake, May 26. Washington—Tacoma, May 22. British Columbia—Burrard Inlet, May 26; Okanagan Landing, June 1.

Fall migration.—Late dates of fall departure are: British Columbia—Okanagan Landing, September 15. Washington—Tacoma, September 11. Oregon—Weston, September 9. California—San Francisco, September 21. Los Angeles County, October 27. Alberta— Banff, September 17. Idaho—Meridian, September 15; Rupert, September 16. Arizona—Chin Lee, September 25. Saskatchewan—Eastend, September 15. Montana—Columbia Falls, September 28; Great Falls, October 6. Wyoming—Yellowstone Park, September 15. Colorado—Yuma, September 25; Denver, October 14. Texas—Taylor, October 2; Palo Pinto, October 21; Corpus Christi, November 6. Manitoba—Winnipeg, September 19; Aweme, September 24. North Dakota—Charlson, September 22. South Dakota—Forestburg, September 21; Sioux Falls, October 1. Nebraska—Blue Springs, October 5; Red Cloud, October 10. Kansas—Topeka, October 6; Onaga, October 22. Minnesota—Minneapolis, September 15; Lanesboro, September 30. Wisconsin—Madison, October 6. Iowa— National, September 30; Keokuk, October 8. Ontario—Ottawa, September 23; Toronto, October 11. Michigan—Detroit, September 17. Ohio—Wauseon, September 30; Cleveland, October 8. Illinois— Chicago, October 7; Odin, October 14. Missouri—Concordia, October 18. Kentucky—Eubank, October 9. Tennessee—Athens, October 5. Arkansas—Rogers, October 4; Dardanelle, October 25. Louisiana—New Orleans, November 3. Quebec—Montreal, September 17. New Brunswick—St. Johns, September 27. Maine—Portland, September 26; Livermore Falls, October 2; Vermont—Rutland, September 12; St. Johnsbury, September 13. Massachusetts—Amherst, September 27; Harvard, October 3. Connecticut—Hartford, September 26. New York—Rochester, September 28; New York City, October 1. New Jersey—Morristown, October 11. Pennsylvania—Renovo, September 23; Philadelphia, October 15. District of Columbia—Washington, October 11. North Carolina—Raleigh, October 6; Hendersonville, October 13. South Carolina—Columbia, October 22; Mount Pleasant, November 9. Alabama—Autaugaville, October 11. Florida—Orlando, October 13; Pensacola, October 20.

Casual records.—With a range that covers most of the Western Hemisphere, it is not surprising that comparatively few nighthawks should be recorded beyond the known normal limits. A specimen was taken by an Eskimo at Allakaket, on the Koyukuk River in northern Alaska, late in September or early in October 1923. One was seen at Grand Falls, Labrador, on May 31, 1895, and a specimen was collected at Makkovik in June 1929. The species is a fairly regular visitor at Bermuda during migration, sometimes being very common.

Egg dates.—California: 36 records, March 20 to July 26; 18 records, June 18 to July 1, indicating the height of the season.

Colorado: 11 records, May 31 to July 18.

Florida: 40 records, April 7 to July 17; 20 records, May 15 to June 3.

Georgia: 16 records, May 17 to July 13; 8 records, May 24 to June 10.

Kansas: 28 records, May 31 to July 7; 14 records, June 13 to 28.

Maine: 30 records, May 24 to July 3.

Michigan: 13 records, May 15 to July 19; 7 records, June 2 to July 3.

New York: 9 records, May 29 to July 8.

South Dakota: 9 records, June 10 to July 1.

Texas (Brownsville region): 28 records, April 5 to June 28; 14 records, May 10 to June 5.

Texas (elsewhere): 62 records, April 11 to July 29; 31 records, May 15 to June 1.

CHORDEILES MINOR HENRYI Cassin

WESTERN NIGHTHAWK

HABITS

Dr. Gross has contributed such a full life history of the eastern nighthawk that it hardly seems necessary to say much about the other subspecies, as they are all much alike in general habits.

The above name formerly covered most of the western races that are now recognized as subspecifically distinct. This race is now supposed to be confined to the southern Rocky Mountains and adjacent high plains, from Colorado southward into Mexico, Chihuahua, and Sonora. Other races are recognized in the more lowland plains.

Cassin (1862), in his original description of this bird, named it as a species in honor of Dr. T. Charlton Henry and said of it: "This bird may be distinguished from other American species by its color, which is lighter and of a different style of variegation, the prevailing tone being a dull, pale reddish and yellowish, somewhat approaching what is called buff or drab color. It is larger than *Chordeiles virginianus.*"

Dr. Harry C. Oberholser (1914), in comparing it with some more recently described races, says that it is "similar to *Chordeiles virginianus howelli*, but upper surface, both ground color and markings, much darker, the latter more tawny and also coarser; lower parts posteriorly more buffy, anteriorly more rufescent." It is lighter and more brownish than *hesperis*, darker and more rufescent than *sennetti*, and lighter and more brownish than *virginianus*.

Nesting.—The nesting habits of the western nighthawk are very similar to those of the eastern bird. Dr. Edgar A. Mearns (1890) says of his experience with it in the mountains of Arizona: "I have never known this species to infringe on the territory of the Texan Nighthawk during the breeding season; each keeps to its own ground, the latter being confined to the region below the pines, and the former residing in the pines and spruces, breeding in great numbers in these limited areas. * * * Two fresh eggs were taken at Flagstaff on June 18, 1887, in a level place, bestrewn with volcanic scoria, beneath the pines."

We found only the western nighthawk in the mountains and only the Texas nighthawk in the lower valleys. After I left, Mr. Willard found a nest on July 9, 1922, at an elevation of 5,200 feet in the Huachuca Mountains, Arizona. The eggs were lying in the open on gravelly soil; just before the eggs were taken, a heavy hailstorm occurred, during which nearly 6 inches of hail fell; evidently the female had covered the eggs during the storm, or the eggs might have been broken.

Eggs.—The two eggs of the western nighthawk are indistinguishable from those of other nighthawks, showing the same variations. In shape they are between oval and elliptical-oval, usually with little or no gloss, though some incubated eggs are quite glossy. The ground color is dull white, or grayish white, rarely "dark" or "deep olive-buff". Usually they are quite evenly marked; some are closely sprinkled with fine dots, but oftener they are covered with small spots, streaks, or small blotches of "olive-brown," "sepia," or "mummy brown"; occasional eggs are marked with brighter browns, such as "russet" or "hazel"; very often there are underlying spots or blotches of "pale Quaker drab." The measurements of 19 eggs average 30.2 by 21.6 millimeters; the eggs showing the four extremes measure 33.0 by 21.1, 30.0 by 23.1, 27.3 by 21.5, and 27.5 by 19.7 millimeters.

Food.—Mrs. Bailey (1928) says of the food of the western nighthawk in New Mexico: "Ants in large proportion and also beetles which are the adult forms of noted pests. Specimens taken at Fort Stanton—caddice flies and gnats, together with injurious insects, including ants, plant bugs, leaf hoppers, crane flies, click beetles, wood-boring and engraver beetles, clover root weevils, and nut weevils."

Beal, McAtee, and Kalmbach (1916) say that these birds are "so expert in flight that no insects can escape them. They sweep up in their capacious mouths everything from the largest moths and dragon flies to the tiniest ants and gnats, and in this way sometimes gather most remarkable collections of insects. Several stomachs have contained fifty or more different kinds, and the number of individuals may run into the thousands."

Dr. Mearns (1890) writes:

In our summer camp, near the summit of the Mogollon Mountains, a small beetle was annoyingly abundant, flying into our tents in great numbers during the day, and at night swarming around our log fires. As the twilight gathered, hundreds of these Nighthawks appeared upon the scene, preying upon the troublesome insects. Careless of our presence at the fires and of the noisy hilarity of camp, they flitted through the smoke with astonishing freedom from diffidence, capturing myriads of the hated beetles, as they passed and repassed above, between, and around us, until their flickering forms were as familiar as the stirring of the pine boughs overhead, and the fanning of their wings almost as little heeded.

Field marks.—There are two other races of this species, *hesperis* and *howelli*, that are likely to be seen within the range of the western nighthawk on migrations; these three races are not easy to recognize in life, though *henryi* is lighter than *hesperis* and darker than *howelli.*

The western nighthawk can be distinguished in flight from the Texas nighthawk by the position of the white wing band; in the western nighthawk this band is about halfway between the bend of the wing and the tip; in the Texas nighthawk the white wing band is nearer the tip than the bend of the wing.

Fall.—Mrs. Bailey (1928) says that after the breeding season and in the fall the western nighthawks range up to higher altitudes in the mountains, even as high as 12,600 feet. "They all desert the State for the winter, beginning their southward journey soon after the middle of summer. They are most numerous in migration during August and have nearly all left [New Mexico] by the end of September. * * * On the return journey in the spring they are among the very latest migrants, seldom reaching northern New Mexico before May 10."

CHORDEILES MINOR CHAPMANI Coues

FLORIDA NIGHTHAWK

HABITS

This small race occupies the southern Atlantic and Gulf States, from North Carolina to eastern Texas. In general appearance it differs but little from the eastern nighthawk, except in size. Dr. H. C. Oberholser (1914) characterizes it as "like *Chordeiles virginianus virginianus*, but decidedly smaller; upper parts averaging a little more mottled and spotted with whitish and buffy, particularly on back, wings, and scapulars, and the ground color averaging slightly less deeply blackish (more grayish or brownish); posterior lower parts usually more purely white."

Nighthawks are tender birds and spend their winters in South America, from Colombia to northern Argentina. Even in Florida they usually do not arrive until some time in April. Arthur H. Howell (1932) says of the haunts of the Florida race: "The Florida Nighthawk frequents open pine forests, old fields, pastures, prairies, cultivated lands, marshes, and ocean beaches. Although most active early in the morning and late in the evening, the birds frequently may be seen flying about in search of food in bright sunshine."

Nesting.—Mr. Howell (1932) says on this subject: "The two eggs are deposited on the ground, with no semblance of a nest, in an open situation, often in a pasture, broomsedge field, or wood lot, or in palmetto scrub in open forest or on the prairie, or sometimes among sparse grasses on or near the ocean beaches."

Major Bendire (1895) says that Dr. William L. Ralph took several sets of eggs in Putnam County, Fla., and that here "during the breeding season at least, the Florida Nighthawk frequents mainly low, flat pine woods, especially such as have recently been burnt over, the eggs generally lying on the bare ground. Sandy soil seems to be preferred for nesting places. One set of eggs was found by him under a small orange tree in an orange grove on the side of a sandy hill; three others were taken in flat pine woods, and in one instance the eggs laid on a few fragments of charcoal left where a fallen tree had been partly burnt, between the remaining part of the tree and the stump, about 3 feet from each."

On Cat Island, off the coast of Mississippi, I found the Florida nighthawk very common in the extensive forest of tall, long-leaf pines, with which the island is largely covered. Here, on June 16, 1910, I saw two pairs with young, the old birds fluttering along the ground to toll us away from their little ones; and I found one nest with two eggs on the bare, sandy ground among the pines.

The only other nests of this subspecies that I have seen were on some low, sandy islands in Galveston Bay, Tex., where several pairs were breeding on May 4, 1923; two nests were seen, the eggs lying in slight hollows in the bare sand, in such situations as might be chosen by least terns. In some of the southern cities this nighthawk has developed the habit of nesting on the flat, gravel roofs of buildings, after the manner of the species elsewhere.

Eggs.—The eggs of the Florida nighthawk are similar to those of the eastern nighthawk but will average somewhat more heavily marked with darker colors and are somewhat smaller. The measurements of 38 eggs average 28.86 by 21.23 millimeters; the eggs showing the four extremes measure **31.75** by 21.59, 31.59 by **22.61, 26.42** by 20.32, and 28.20 by **20.10** millimeters.

The habits of the Florida nighthawk are not essentially different from those of its northern relative; the two are not easily recognizable in life; and the two forms are seen on migrations all through the Southern States, where heavy flights often occur. R. J. Longstreet noted an unusually heavy flight at Daytona Beach on May 11, 1926; "in about an hour, from 6 to 7 p. m., he estimated that about 3,000 birds passed north over the beach" (Howell, 1932).

Heavy flights also occur on the fall migration, mainly during August, when formerly large numbers of "bullbats," as they were locally called, were shot for food or sport. Dr. Chapman (1888), writing of Gainesville, Fla., in 1888, said: " 'Bullbat,' or as it is more frequently termed, 'Bat,' shooting is here a popular pastime, great numbers being killed for food, and in August, when the birds have gathered in flocks, favorite fields may be occupied at nightfall by as many as a dozen shooters." This bad practice is now outlawed, and very wisely, as the small bodies of the nighthawks have very little food value, and the nighthawk is one of our most useful birds; it has no objectionable food habits and is so valuable as a destroyer of troublesome and injurious insects, such as grasshoppers, beetles, gnats, mosquitoes, and the destructive cotton-boll weevil, that it ought to be rigidly protected.

CHORDEILES MINOR SENNETTI Coues

SENNETT'S NIGHTHAWK

HABITS

The nighthawks of the northern plains were given the above name by Dr. Elliott Coues (1888), who gave as the characters of the subspecies "silvery grayish-white predominating above, the white below greatly in excess of the narrow, irregular or broken, dark bars, and little or no rufous anywhere." It is a bird of the treeless plains and prairies, ranging from northern North Dakota and northeastern Montana south to eastern Wyoming, northwestern Iowa, and northern Nebraska. It migrates southward through Oklahoma and Texas, and probably to South America.

F. A. Patton (1924) says of its haunts in South Dakota: "The Sennetts Night Hawk, is a bird of a barren, isolated region, moving ahead and away from settlements, to a thinly settled section, preferring a dry, almost a desert region.

"Through the eighties and up until about 1890 this bird could be found much over the entire State of South Dakota. At present its range is confined to that part of the state from the Missouri River to the Black Hills, frequenting the Bad Lands section, well up in the foot hills, preferring barren knolls and stony places. Never have I seen the bird or its eggs in any way concealed by grass or vegetation."

Nesting.—The same observer writes: "A favorite nesting place is in a cattle or horse trail over a stony knoll destitute of vegetation and what sets I find are found mostly by the bird flying from beneath my saddle horse. * * *

"The eggs are laid on a rock or stones. No depression or formation towards a nest whatever, the eggs are plain gray in color and no blend with the rock that though they may be almost at one's feet are difficult to see."

Eggs.—The Sennett's nighthawk lays two eggs, the usual number for the species, which are practically indistinguishable from those of the eastern nighthawk, though they may average a trifle paler with somewhat smaller markings. The measurements of 9 eggs average 31.1 by 22.3 millimeters; the eggs showing the four extremes measure 33.8 by 21.6, 31.5 by **23.3, 29.3** by 23.1, and 29.6 by **21.5** millimeters.

Young.—Ernest T. Seton (1890) made an interesting observation on two young nighthawks, which were apparently about three days old and still retained the shell tooth on the tip of the bill; he says:

I gently touched one of them, whereupon it crouched down more closely to the ground; but its companion, rising, hissed with open beak and snapped savagely at my fingers. On being further teased they ran off, exactly in the manner of young ducks, with outstretched wings and with neck and body at an angle of 45 degrees. After running a few feet they stopped, squatted as before, and closed their eyes. This they repeated several times, but at best they only made little progress, and each time on being overtaken the bold one was always ready to fight. * * *.

In the light of these observations it seems likely that in some of the cases in which the Night-hawks are supposed to have carried off their young, the latter had really run from danger, or were led away by the parent birds.

Plumages.—Dr. Louis B. Bishop (1896) has called attention to the fact that the females of this race do not show the characters of the race as well as the males. He collected a series of 13 birds in North Dakota, of which he writes: "Three females from the same locality taken in June and July—one of them a breeding bird taken with a typical male and two eggs—are similar but with the upper parts darker and the entire lower parts tinged with buff, which becomes ochraceous-buff on the throat. Two other female Nighthawks from the same region, one taken on June 11, and the other with two eggs on June 24, are quite different, the prevailing tint of the entire plumage, except the greater wing-coverts, wings and tail, being ochraceous-buff. These birds might readily be referred to *henryi*, but all the males taken or seen during the breeding season were unmistakably *sennetti*."

He says further: "The pale colors of the male protect him admirably, harmonizing with the dull gray of the fences and rocks, perched on which he passes the day, while the darker colors of the female render her less conspicuous when seated over her eggs on the black soil."

Behavior.—F. A. Patton (1924) says that "these birds will perch on a hot rock in the blazing sun the hottest summer day, the rock so hot one cannot hold a hand on it. You would think they would cook, they however seem stupid, they seem to lack the pep of other Night Hawks, to get out and soar at twilight, but are a quiet retiring bird, and I have known them on a hot day to let one approach close enough to strike them with a stick."

CHORDEILES MINOR HESPERIS Grinnell

PACIFIC NIGHTHAWK

PLATES 34, 35

HABITS

What was formerly part of the range of the western nighthawk (*henryi*) is now assigned to this more recently described race. According to the 1931 Check-list, it "breeds from southeastern British Columbia to southwestern Saskatchewan, central Montana, central Utah, and northwestern Wyoming south along the Pacific coast to northern California and in the Sierra Nevada south to the San Bernardino Mountains, southern California."

Dr. Joseph Grinnell (1905a) named this race and described it as "most nearly resembling *Ch. v. virginianus*, but:—outer surface of closed wing grayer toned; lower tail-coverts and feathers of belly region more narrowly and sparsely dark-barred; and, in the male, white patches on throat, wings, and tail more extensive." He remarks further:

In tone of coloration the male is much darker than in either *Ch. v. sennetti* or *Ch. v. henryi.* Altho somewhat lighter than *virginianus*, this is in the direction of pale gray and white rather than ochraceous. The extended mottling of the otherwise blackish feathers dorsally is responsible for this lighter tone, and especially notable is the extensive silvery gray mottling on the wing coverts. Yet this dorsal tone does not nearly reach the paleness of *sennetti.* * * * The [white] patch on the outer primary invades across the shaft to include the outer web; and the same is observable of the patches on the tail-feathers. * * * The female of *hesperis* is gray rather than tawny, and is thus at once distinguishable from the female of *henryi.*

Nesting.—Major Bendire (1895) writes:

A set of eggs of this subspecies was found by me on July 3, 1875, in the foothills of the Blue Mountains, some 6 miles northeast of Camp Harney, Oregon, laid among some pebbles on the bare ground under a little sage bush. The sitting bird allowed me almost to touch it, and was very reluctant to abandon its eggs, which were but slightly incubated. On my approach, it ruffled its feathers and emitted a hissing sound, resembling somewhat the spitting of a cat when mad. Their favorite nesting places in that vicinity were the crests of gravelly ridges, always selecting a well-drained spot, where the rains could not chill the young or eggs. Bare, rocky table-lands are also frequently resorted to for similar purposes, and less often the flat tops of bowlders. Extensive burnt tracts also furnish favorite abiding places for them in the more northern portions of their range; in fact, in such localities they are fully as abundant as on the more open sagebrush plains.

Henry J. Rust (1911) tells of a nest that he found near Coeur d'Alene, Idaho, in an open space in a cornfield, where the scattered cornstalks and a few weeds furnished scanty shade for the young. D. E. Brown tells me that "on the prairies of Pierce County [Washington] the bird nests on small patches of gravel, where the two eggs blend perfectly and the bird itself is hard to see. In King County, I find most of the nests in burnt-over sections. The eggs are usually placed among the remains of a rotten and charred log, where both egg and bird blend with the surroundings."

A. Dawes DuBois has sent me some notes on three nests found by him in Flathead County, Mont.; in one of these the eggs lay on a thick bed of coarse moss which covered the rocky ground for some distance around it; this was on the top of a high foothill. Of this nest he says: "The bird was sitting when I approached, July 16. When she saw me coming she closed her eyes and appeared to be asleep. By covering the large shiny eyeballs with the lusterless lids the nighthawk makes herself much more a part of her surroundings. The eyes are not shut tight; a narrow slit is left through which to peek. While I was in the tent blind, placed near the nest, her eyes were usually wide open; but if I slipped out at the rear and looked around the corner of the tent she slowly closed her eyes until only a narrow slit remained."

Dr. Grinnell (1908) found the Pacific nighthawk "to be a common species of the Boreal and upper Transition zones" in the San Bernardino Mountains. On June 18 he flushed a female from her two eggs at an altitude of about 9,000 feet. "These were laid on the bare ground in an open place among the pines. Nothing but a few pine needles separated them from the granite gravel."

Eggs.—The eggs of the Pacific nighthawk are similar to those of the eastern nighthawk, but will average somewhat paler. The measurements of 38 eggs average 30.23 by 21.6 millimeters; the eggs showing the four extremes measure 32.5 by 21.8, 31.5 by 23.1, and 24.6 by 19.0 millimeters.

Food.—Dr. Grinnell (1908) says: "A specimen shot at dusk, July 4, 1906, was skinned at 11 o'clock the next day. The capacious throat and gullet were found to be crammed with large winged white ants. By actual count there were forty-three of these and many of them were still alive, although it was at least fifteen hours since they had been captured by the nighthawk."

Like other nighthawks this subspecies feeds mainly during the dusk of early morning and evening, but all observers seem to agree that it hunts largely during the day, even in bright sunlight. Its food consists of a great variety of insects, such as beetles, moths, ants, grasshoppers, and other flying insects.

Voice.—This nighthawk indulges in all the characteristic notes of the species, but Mr. DuBois mentions a note that he heard on August 20, which is somewhat different; he writes: "For two weeks or more some of the nighthawks flying over the hill by the ranger station have been uttering a *click-click-click-click*—rapidly repeated and continued at considerable length. It is somewhat like a series of high-pitched quacks. Other nighthawks, flying with these birds, are calling the characteristic *peënk* at the usual intervals. I suppose the rapidly uttered quacks to be the notes of the young."

CHORDEILES MINOR HOWELLI Oberholser

HOWELL'S NIGHTHAWK

PLATE 36

HABITS

The 1931 Check-list gives the range of this subspecies as "southern Great Plains and central Rocky Mountain regions; from Wyoming to middle Texas, Colorado, Oklahoma, middle and western Kansas, northeastern Utah, northeastern New Mexico, and southwestern Nebraska, casually to North Dakota."

In naming this bird in honor of his friend Arthur H. Howell, Dr. Harry C. Oberholser (1914) characterized it as "somewhat like *Chordeiles virginianus sennetti*, but male with upper parts more rufescent and somewhat paler, the dark brown color more rufescent, less grayish, and the light markings much more buffy or ochraceous; posterior lower parts more buffy, and the anterior dark brown areas more rufescent."

Robert B. Rockwell writes to me that this nighthawk is common in the region about Colorado Springs and that he has seen it in various other parts of Colorado, on the plains, in the valleys, and in the mountains up to 10,000 feet altitude.

George Finlay Simmons (1925) says that it reaches about its southern limit in the vicinity of Austin, Tex., and that its habitat includes "the plains; barren fields; cowtrails in pastures; roadsides and along railroad tracks; barren gravelly ridges, and gravelly surfaces in the open, barren hills; backland plowed fields; rocky hillsides; edges of woodlands; flat, gravelly roofs of office buildings in town."

I cannot find anything to indicate that the habits of Howell's nighthawk differ essentially from those of the other neighboring subspecies. Mr. Simmons (1925) says of the fall migration in Texas: "Gathers in flocks in late summer, mid-July to third week in August; migration begins early in August, and by the end of that month the local breeding birds have departed; hundreds pass through, August 10 to August 30, but the last have not gone until late in October. During one fall migration flocks containing as many as 200 to 300 birds were observed on the open prairies northeast of Austin. During both migration seasons the various subspecies of nighthawks mix up on their way to and from South America, so that identification of migrants is hopeless without a specimen in hand."

The eggs are similar to those of other nighthawks. The measurements of 26 eggs average 30.2 by 21.7 millimeters; the eggs showing the four extremes measure 33.0 by 21.9, 31.7 by 23.4, and 26.3 by 20.2 millimeters.

CHORDEILES MINOR ASERRIENSIS Cherrie

CHERRIE'S NIGHTHAWK

HABITS

George K. Cherrie (1896) described this race from a bird collected on November 2, 1893, in the valley of the River Aserri, Costa Rica. It is a small, pale race, about the size of *chapmani*. Nothing was known about its distribution at that time, but it has since been found to be the breeding form of southern Texas, from San Antonio southward and into Tamaulipas.

Dr. H. C. Oberholser (1914) describes it as "resembling *Chordeiles virginianus sennetti*, but decidedly smaller; general tone of upper parts lighter and more ochraceous, the light areas more buffy or ochraceous (less grayish or whitish) and somewhat more extensive; and the dark brown areas of anterior lower surface less grayish." He remarks further: "This heretofore unrecognized race seems to be in color most nearly like *Chordeiles virginianus sennetti*, though in this respect also near *Chordeiles virginianus howelli* and probably in reality most closely resembling this form, which it adjoins geographically."

Mr. Cherrie's type specimen seems to have been lost; at least, neither he nor Dr. Oberholser have been able to locate it, but the full description of the type convinced Dr. Oberholser that "there is no doubt that Mr. Cherrie had in hand a male nighthawk of the *virginianus* style in fully grown juvenal or first autumn plumage, not adult, as he supposed. Allowing for this immaturity, the characters that Mr. Cherrie gives are just those distinguishing the small, pale race which summers in southern Texas."

The nesting habits, eggs, food, and behavior of this nighthawk probably do not differ materially from those of other races living in similar environment. The measurements of 43 eggs average 29.3 by 21.4 millimeters; the eggs showing the four extremes measure 32.5 by 22.5, 27.1 by 21.3, and 28.4 by 20.6 millimeters.

Plates

PLATE 1

Tela, Honduras, July 5, 1930. A. F. Skutch.

Female on nest.

Ulua Valley, Honduras, August 5, 1930. A. F. Skutch.

Nest of two pairs.

GROOVE-BILLED ANI.

PLATE 2

Tela, Honduras, August 15, 1930.   A. F. Skutch.

Young about 6 days old.

GROOVE-BILLED ANI.

Tela, Honduras, July 21, 1930.   A. F. Skutch.

Young 11 days old.

PLATE 3

Fairbank, Ariz., May 18, 1922.   A. C. Bent.

Nest in a willow.

San Diego County, Calif., April 9, 1929.   A. C. Bent.

Nest in a pricklypear.

ROADRUNNER.

PLATE 4

Adult taking lizard to feed young.

Arizona.

W. L. and Irene Finley.

Small young in nest.

ROADRUNNERS.

PLATE 5

Mojave Desert, Calif., May 28, 1916.   W. M. Pierce.

Young nearly grown.

Arizona.   W. L. and Irene Finley.

Adult on nest.

ROADRUNNERS.

PLATE 6

Logan County, Ill., June 21, 1913. A. D. DuBois.

NEST OF YELLOW-BILLED CUCKOO

Arizona. F. C. Willard.

NEST OF CALIFORNIA CUCKOO.

PLATE 7

Battle Creek, Mich., August 30, 1936.   L. H. Walkinshaw.

Ithaca, N. Y.   A. A. Allen.

YELLOW-BILLED CUCKOOS AND YOUNG

PLATE 8

Sioux City, Iowa.   T. C. Stephens.

NEST OF BLACK-BILLED CUCKOO.

PLATE 9

Omaha, Nebr., July 1, 1901.   F. H. Shoemaker.

Young in juvenal plumage.

Hennepin County, Minn., June 11, 1935.   A. D. DuBois.

A well-made nest.

BLACK-BILLED CUCKOO.

PLATE 10

Showing the sucking pads.

Ithaca, N. Y.   A. A. Allen.

Showing the unopened feather sheaths.

YOUNG BLACK-BILLED CUCKOOS.

PLATE 11

Allen Frost.

ADULT BLACK-BILLED CUCKOO ON NEST.

PLATE 12

Carver County, Minn., June 29, 1936.   A. D. DuBois.

Feeding young at entrance.

Ithaca, N. Y.   A. A. Allen.

Brooding newly hatched young.

EASTERN BELTED KINGFISHERS.

PLATE 13

Young just hatched.

Ithaca, N. Y.

A. A. Allen.

Older young.

EASTERN BELTED KINGFISHERS.

PLATE 14

Ann Arbor, Mich.

F. N. Wilson.

EASTERN BELTED KINGFISHER.

PLATE 15

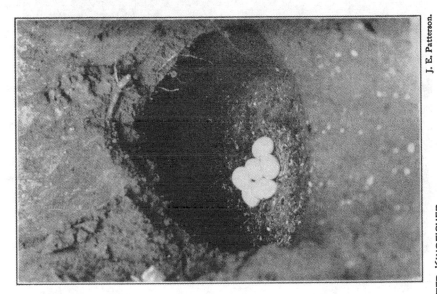

J. E. Patterson.

Jackson County, Oreg., May 24, 1931.

NESTING OF WESTERN BELTED KINGFISHER.

PLATE 16

Copana Bay, Tex.   G. F. Simmons.

Nesting site.

Near Los Amates, Guatemala, May 5, 1932.   A. F. Skutch.

Young ready to leave nest.

TEXAS KINGFISHERS.

PLATE 17

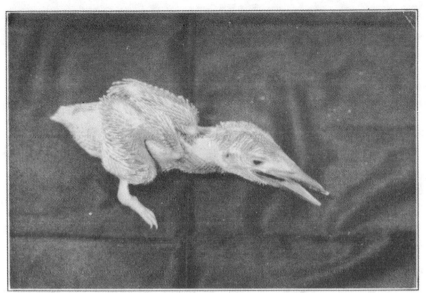

April 10, 1932.

Nestling 2 weeks old.

Near Los Amates, Guatemala, April 26, 1932.

A. F. Skutch.

Juvenal 29 days old.

YOUNG RINGED KINGFISHERS.

PLATE 18

Near Dania, Fla., April 14, 1927.   D. J. Nicholson.

NESTING OF CHUCK-WILL'S-WIDOW.

PLATE 19

Plant City, Fla., May 1934.   A. M. Bailey.
                    Courtesy of Chicago Academy of Sciences.
Female and young.

Miami County, Kans., May 24, 1929.   Walter Colvin.
Eggs in nest.
CHUCK-WILL'S-WIDOW.

PLATE 20

Duval County, Fla., May 22, 1932. S. A. Grimes.

Dade County, Fla., F. N. Irving.

YOUNG CHUCK-WILL'S-WIDOWS.

PLATE 21

Raynham, Mass., June 5, 1903.   A. C. Bent.

NESTING OF EASTERN WHIPPOORWILL.

PLATE 22

Sangamon County, Ill., May 17, 1908.   A. D. DuBois.

Downy young.

St. Lambert, Quebec.   L. M. Terrill.

Young 16 days old.

EASTERN WHIPPOORWILLS

PLATE 23

L. M. Terrill.

Female brooding young.

EASTERN WHIPPOORWILL.

PLATE 24

Huachuca Mountains, Ariz.   F. C. Willard.

Santa Rita Mountains, Ariz., June 27, 1932.   A. J. van Rossem.

NESTS OF STEPHENS'S WHIPPOORWILL.

PLATE 25

J. E. Patterson.

Stanislaus County, Calif., June 23, 1934.

J. E. Patterson.

Mariposa County, Calif., June 21, 1933.

NESTS OF DUSKY POORWILLS.

PLATE 26

Stanislaus County, Calif., June 23, 1934.   J. E. Patterson.

DUSKY POORWILL ON NEST.

PLATE 27

San Bernardino County, Calif.   W. M. Pierce.

Longbard, Calif.   E. C. Aldrich.

EGGS AND YOUNG OF DUSKY POORWILL.

PLATE 28

May 20, 1930.

Nest and eggs.

Lancetilla Valley, Honduras, May 22, 1930.   A. F. Skutch.

Young 1 and 2 days old.

PAURAQUE (NYCTIDROMUS ALBICOLLIS ALBICOLLIS).

PLATE 29

Michigan, June 18, 1924.   K. Christofferson.

Roof nest.

Near Church Creek, Md.   F. R. Smith.

Ground nest.

EASTERN NIGHTHAWK.

PLATE 30

Roosting poses.

Charlevoix, Mich., June 20, 1925.   W. E. Hastings.

A well-made ground nest.

EASTERN NIGHTHAWK

PLATE 31

Brunswick, Maine, June 25, 1921.   A. O. Gross.

Young 1 day old.

Brunswick, Maine, June 27, 1922.   A. O. Gross.

Young 12 days old.

EASTERN NIGHTHAWKS.

PLATE 32

Brunswick, Maine, July 11, 1921.   A. O. Gross.

Young 17 days old.

Brunswick, Maine, July 18, 1921.   A. O. Gross.

Young 24 days old.

EASTERN NIGHTHAWKS.

PLATE 33

Brunswick, Maine, June 16, 1922.   A. O. Gross

Adult male roosting.

Brunswick, Maine, June 16, 1921.   A. O. Gross.

Adult female incubating.

EASTERN NIGHTHAWKS.

PLATE 34

A. D. DuBois.

Flathead County, Mont., June 30, 1914.

J. E. Patterson.

Jackson County, Oreg., June 22, 1924

NESTING SITES OF PACIFIC NIGHTHAWKS.

PLATE 35

A. D. DuBois.

PACIFIC NIGHTHAWK.

Flathead County, Mont., July 12, 1914.

PLATE 36

July 4, 1911.

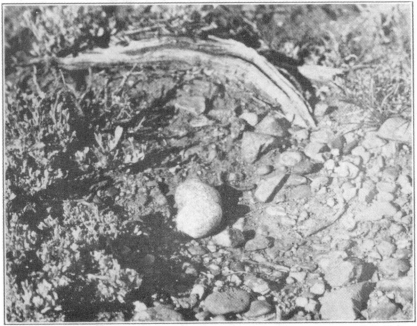

North Park, Colo., June 28, 1911.   E. R. Warren.

NESTING OF HOWELL'S NIGHTHAWK.

PART TWO

CONTENTS

*Life Histories of North American
Cuckoos, Goatsuckers, Hummingbirds,
and Their Allies*

LIFE HISTORIES OF NORTH AMERICAN CUCKOOS, GOATSUCKERS, HUMMINGBIRDS, AND THEIR ALLIES.

ORDERS PSITTACIFORMES, CUCULIFORMES, TROGONIFORMES, CORACIIFORMES, CAPRIMULGIFORMES, AND MICROPODIIFORMES

By Arthur Cleveland Bent

Taunton, Mass.

CHORDEILES ACUTIPENNIS TEXENSIS Lawrence

TEXAS NIGHTHAWK

PLATES 37–39

HABITS

The Texas nighthawk is a large, pale race of the species *Chordeiles acutipennis*, which is divided into additional races in Central and South America. Our 1931 Check-list states that it "breeds in the Lower Austral Zone from north-central California, southern Nevada, southern Utah, and central Texas south to about lat. 30° in Lower California, and to south-central Mexico."

The Texas nighthawk is a common summer resident in the warmer portions of the Southwestern United States; we found it generally distributed throughout the arid desert regions of Arizona, along the river bottoms and dry washes, and, in the more fertile regions, about the sloughs and coursing over the alfalfa fields. H. S. Swarth (1920) writes: "In all the valley towns of southern Arizona the Texas nighthawk is a familiar sight. It has not, as yet, acquired the habit of its eastern relative of nesting upon the flat roofs of buildings, but throughout the summer the birds may be seen in numbers at dusk, hawking about, low over the houses. In walking about on the desert one is sure to flush Texas nighthawks from their resting places under the bushes, where they usually remain during the daytime."

In Texas Dr. J. C. Merrill (1878) found it most plentiful just outside of Brownsville, and he discovered several sets of eggs within the fort. In the San Bernardino Mountains, Calif., according to Dr. Grinnell (1908), "the Texas nighthawk is a characteristic breeding bird of the Lower Sonoran zone, but like several other species of the same zone wanders up even into Transition during the late summer." And farther north, "in the Yosemite section it was observed only at our lowest stations, west of the foothills" (Grinnell and Storer, 1924).

Courtship.—Mr. Swarth (1920) says: "The male Texas nighthawk performs no such spectacular evolutions as the eastern nighthawk does in the breeding season, but he has a comparable, though lesser performance, usually given when in pursuit of the female. Both birds flying low over the bushes, the male repeatedly utters a low, chuckling sound, 'tuc-tuc-tuc-a-tuc-tuc—c-r-rooo,' a rolling note, the finale very dove-like in effect. While uttering this call the wings are held stiffly extended downward. Then, in ordinary flight, there is repeatedly given a long drawn, nasal 'w-a-ng.' "

Grinnell and Storer (1924) give the following account of it:

It was the height of the nesting season [May 5] and the birds were courting actively. A male, distinguished by the larger and whiter bands on his wings and the more conspicuously white chin patch, was pursuing a female. The male always followed, but at close range, rarely more than two lengths behind the female. Occasionally a second male joined in the pursuit, but evidently with only partial interest, for he frequently circled off by himself. Less often the two male birds pursued one another, weaving an irregular course up and down, in and out, but never rising much if any over 50 feet above the ground. The progress through the air was easy yet swift, a few strokes of the long wings sufficing to carry the birds through a long glide. Often as they passed close over the observer the barred pattern of the under surface was clearly visible, as was also the broad subterminal band of white on the lower side of the tail. While the males were on the wing their low crooning trills were heard almost continually, swelling and diminishing as the birds approached or departed. When they rested on the ground between flights they gave the same notes, prolonged but also with longer intervals of quiet. One trill lasted 25 seconds and another fully a minute. These notes remind one of the quavering call of the Screech Owl save that they are longer continued, on one key, and uttered in almost the same cadence throughout.

Alden H. Miller (1937) adds the following observation: "The contrast in degree of whiteness in wing and throat patches of males and females was at once evident. That this sexual difference apparently was recognized by the birds and that it was specifically accentuated by the actions of the male were facts new to me. As a male swung into line behind a female, his white throat was displayed so that, as the pair flew toward me, the brownish white throat of the female was scarcely noticeable, whereas that of the male was a conspicuous white beard. The impression was gained that the feathers of the throat of the male were lifted and that the whole throat area was expanded. Usually, perhaps always, this 'flashing' of the throat patch was accompanied by vocal notes."

Nesting.—The nesting habits of the Texas nighthawk are no more elaborate than are those of its relatives in the *minor* group; the eggs are laid on the bare ground, without any attempt at nest building or even scooping out a hollow, in some open sandy or gravelly spot, and usually with little or no cover to shade them from the full glare of the sun. We were too early for eggs while I was in Arizona, but. after I left, my companion, Frank Willard, found two nests in Pima County on June 10, 1922; each was on the ground at the foot of a greasewood bush; he says that after the female had been flushed from one of the nests the male attempted to drive her back onto the eggs.

Bendire (1895) says that he has "found its eggs on the parched gravelly mesas of southern Arizona, miles from the nearest water. Their favorite breeding resorts here are dry, barren table-lands, the sides of canyons, and the crests of rocky hills." Dr. Merrill (1878) says that in Texas the eggs "are usually deposited in exposed situations, among sparse chaparral, on ground baked almost as hard as brick by the intense heat of the sun. One set of eggs was placed on a small piece of tin, within a foot or two of a frequented path. The female sits close, and when flushed flies a few feet and speedily returns to its eggs. They make no attempt to decoy an intruder away. I have ridden up to within five feet of a female on her eggs, dismounted, tied my horse, and put my hand on the bird before she would move."

Robert S. Woods has sent me some photographs (pls. 38, 39) of a nest that he found on April 27, 1923, in the San Gabriel Wash, in Los Angeles County, Calif., where he says this nighthawk is a common summer resident; the eggs, he says (Woods, 1924b)—

were deposited in a gravelly area covered with low second growth, mostly deer-weed or wild broom (*Syrmatium glabrum*). It may be observed in the photograph that the gravel, which was here loose because of previous leveling of the ground, had been smoothed by the removal of the larger pebbles over a space such as would be covered by the body of the nighthawk. The few stones scattered over it were probably rolled there by the movements of the bird in rising or alighting after the eggs had been laid. * * * On one hot day the eggs were moved back several inches into the partial shade of the nearest shrub, being restored to the original position after the warm weather had passed. The mother would remain on her eggs until approached within perhaps ten feet, but after being once disturbed she would not return as long as any person or suspicious object remained anywhere in the vicinity. The other parent, if present in the neighborhood, showed no interest in the family affairs.

In the Fresno district, according to John G. Tyler (1913), the great majority of the Texas nighthawks nest in the vineyards; four of the five nests observed by him were in vineyards, either at the base of a vine or on bare ground between the vines; the fifth was "on soft ground at base of a sunflower growing in a field of melons."

Mrs. Bailey (1928) says that "at Brownsville, Texas, hundreds of Texas Nighthawks are said to be found in the city nearly throughout the year nesting on the flat roofs of the adobe houses."

Eggs.—I cannot do better than to quote Bendire's (1895) description of the eggs, as follows:

They are exceedingly difficult to detect on account of their similarity in color to their general surroundings, which usually harmonize very closely. The shell is strong, close grained, and rather glossy, while in shape the eggs are more variable than those of other Nighthawks, ranging from oval to elliptical oval, and again to elliptical ovate. The ground color varies from pale gray (a sort of clay color) to pale creamy white, with a faint pinkish tint. This latter phase of coloration is rather unusual however. The whole surface is minutely marbled, speckled, or rather peppered, with fine dots of different shades of grays, lilac, and a few darker and coarser markings of fawn color, slate, and drab. Occasionally a specimen is found which, to the naked eye, appears entirely unmarked; but on more careful examination a few dark spots, mere pin points, can readily be noticed. They are much lighter colored than the average eggs of our other Nighthawks, and readily distinguished from these on this account, as well as from their smaller size.

The measurements of 52 eggs in the United States National Museum average 27.05 by 19.53 millimeters; the eggs showing the four extremes measure 29.72 by 21.08, 27.18 by 21.59, 24.89 by 19.05, and 25.65 by 18.29 millimeters.

Young.—Carroll D. Scott writes to me that one of the favorite pastimes of his childhood was playing hide and seek with young Texas nighthawks: "The sport on our part was to find the baby birds squatting on the ground, almost invisible, and to see the mother trail away, endeavoring to decoy us by the broken-wing ruse. The next day we were faced with the same puzzle—Where were the nestlings? For they were always somewhere else. We always found them again, 20, 50, or 100 feet away. We wondered if the parents carried them in their wide mouths, or shoved them over the ground, inch by inch, or flew with them on their backs."

Several other observers have noticed this same behavior; young nighthawks have moved, or been moved, for greater or lesser distances, either because they had been disturbed or to take advantage of some slight shade from the hot sun. Mr. Woods (1924b) found that young birds less than three days old "could open their

eyes and crawl over the ground at a very fair rate of speed." Dr.
Gayle Pickwell and Miss Emily Smith (1938), who made extensive
studies of several nests of this nighthawk, found that the young
could move by crawling haltingly, to the call of the female, as much
as 6 or 8 inches when not over 48 hours old; these young birds were
hatched between May 25 and 27; on May 29 they had moved 8 feet
more, and on June 2, when about 8 days old, they were found 56
yards from the nesting site.

The same observers learned that the period of incubation was 18
days in one case and 19 days in another. Incubation was performed,
during the daytime at least, by the female alone, but both sexes did
their share in feeding the young.

All feedings were by means of regurgitation, wherein the bill of the parent
was thrust into the open mouth of the young, the food brought forth by
peristalsis in the regurgitation. Each feeding was terminated by a violent
agitation of the heads of both the bird supplying the food and the one being
fed. * * * Feedings noted were all crepuscular, at 9 p. m. or earlier, or
again at 4:30 a. m. or later. * * *

The protective behavior of the young had the following elements: (1) as
long as the young were brooded, concealment by the parent bird sufficed as
protection for them: (2) flushing the parent would leave the young in
crouch-concealment wherein they supplied their own self-concealment through
coloration, which became strikingly protective as their feathers advanced;
(3) almost from the beginning these precocial young were able to run to cover,
however haltingly, though this cover consisted of the female bird who caused
them to run to her by her calling; (4) not until they were about three weeks
old were they able to substitute flying for running; (5) the astonishing method
of protective behavior presented by the nighthawks was their intimidation
display which was first presented when they were approximately 12 days old.

Plumages.—Dr. Oberholser (1914) has given us full descriptions
of the various plumages of this species; of the downy young nestling,
he says: "Upper surface fawn color, clouded or obscurely mottled
with mars brown; lower parts fawn color, unmarked, but paling on
the median portion of breast and abdomen. Very young birds, both
male and female, before they are full grown, are above very pale
buff, finely and sparingly spotted with black, and vermiculated with
silvery gray; and below, pale buff, with narrow widely spaced bars
of dusky or blackish."

In the juvenal plumage, the sexes are unlike; he describes them
as follows:

In this plumage both sexes are decidedly lighter and more closely and evenly
mottled than in the adult, particularly above. In the male the upper parts
are also more uniform, with more ochraceous or gray and less black; the tail
and wing-quills are broadly tipped with buff; the light bars of the tail are
more deeply buff; the white throat-patch is more buffy; the lower surface
duller, more ochraceous, more uniform, less distinctly and less broadly barred.
The subterminal bar on the tail is white, about as in the adult.

The juvenal female differs from the adult female much as above detailed for the male, but somewhat less so. She is similar to the juvenal male, but has the light spot on the primaries smaller and more deeply buff or ochraceous buff, instead of white or slightly buffy; the light throat-patch more deeply buff, never whitish; and she lacks the subterminal white bar on the tail.

What he calls a first autumn plumage, which is also the plumage of the first winter, "is practically the same in both male and female as that of the adults so far as the contour feathers are concerned, and otherwise differs only in having whitish or buffy tips on the primaries, secondaries, and rectrices. These light tips mostly wear off before the next molt, but usually persist sufficiently, at least on the shortest secondaries, to serve for the discrimination of year-old birds." He says of the molts:

From the fugitive natal plumage the young bird molts directly into the juvenal plumage, growing the while, so that at least by the time, often before, it has attained full size of body and wings, the juvenal plumage is complete. Then by a practically continuous molt, usually in September, it again changes its contour feathers, but retains the remiges and rectrices. The combination plumage of the first autumn is worn apparently until the following summer, when the regular sequence of adult molt is begun. The adult of this species molts but once a year, usually between the last of July and the middle of September, most individuals chiefly in August, during which period all of the feathers, including remiges and rectrices, undergo a renewal.

Food.—The food of the Texas nighthawk consists of a variety of flying insects, which it scoops up in its capacious mouth while on the wing; almost anything in this line seems to be acceptable. Mrs. Bailey (1928) writes: "Their food consists of almost any insects that may be out when they are. The stomach of one had a mass of mosquitoes and a small bug. Another contained one or more ground beetles, injurious click beetles, large leaf chafers, leaf hoppers, and green plant bugs, together with 150 winged ants (Merrill MS)." Dr. Grinnell (1908) says that one collected in the San Bernardino Mountains "contained in its stomach four of the immense seven-lined June beetles." A. J. van Rossem (1927) made the following observations on the feeding habits of this species in Salvador:

The Texas Nighthawks were more varied in feeding habits than any of the others. During the winter they were very common in favorable lowland localities, and shortly after sundown would appear in hundreds, flying high and toward the sunset. A little later in the short interval of dusk, they flew much lower and the general direction was opposite to that taken at first. We supposed them to be working back to the localities from which they first started, feeding as they went. It was some time before we found out anything of their nocturnal activities, for their eyes gave only a pale green reflection, which was easily overlooked and not visible beyond a few feet. Many spiders gave a much brighter glow than these nighthawks, and only by careful search in suitable places, could we find them. All the individuals which we found after dark were on the ground in the open. *Chordeiles acutipennis* therefore hunts through three air levels, high in the air at sundown, closer to the ground at dusk, and on the ground after dark. Because of this versatility, its food must necessarily be more varied, and, because obtained from three strata of insect life instead of one or two, must be more regularly plentiful.

A. W. Anthony (1892) says that "a large part of his bill of fare is obtained by jumping up from the ground and catching passing insects, without taking wing—a habit also noticed in *Phalaenoptilus*."

Behavior.—Robert S. Woods (1924b) writes:

The flight of the Texas Nighthawk gives the impression of ease to a greater degree than that of any other of our smaller birds. While not slow, it appears leisurely and is frequently varied by periods of gliding. The large expanse of wing gives great buoyancy and the bird seems to float through the air almost without effort, while a turn of the wing serves to change its course at an abrupt angle. The Texas Nighthawk flies at a much lower altitude than is the usual habit of swallows and swifts. While hunting it never ascends to any great height, and often skims close to the ground, passing among the vegetation. In the evening its activities begin about sunset or earlier, usually ceasing before dark, and in the morning it is apt to remain in the air for some time after sunrise. It may sometimes be seen hunting at mid-day, especially in cloudy weather. The nighthawk displays some curiosity and often swoops down within a few feet of one's head. Even at that distance the flight is entirely inaudible.

Major Bendire (1895) says: "Its flight is equally as graceful as that of the other Nighthawks, but it rarely soars as high as the former, and generally skims just over the tops of the bushes or close to the surface of the water. In fact, I have repeatedly seen them touch the surface, as if drinking or catching insects, probably the latter." Mr. Dawson (1923) has seen them drinking "hen-fashion" from a waterhole or dipping on the wing to drink from a larger body of water.

Texas nighthawks have favorite roosting places, to which they return regularly for their daytime rest. Near our camp in the valley of the San Pedro River, Ariz., one roosted regularly, apparently sound asleep all day, sitting lengthwise on a horizontal limb of a large willow. Ned Hollister (1908) says that about Needles, Calif., "the nighthawks here spend the day in the thickets of arrow-weed from which I frequently flushed them." Grinnell and Storer (1924), referring to the Yosemite region, write: "Each individual nighthawk seemed to have a favorite resting place to which it returned regularly. This was on the gravel, at the side of, and partially shaded by, a lupine or other bush. The male bird of the pair mentioned was seen to return to the neighborhood of such a spot time and time again, and upon flushing him directly and thus ascertaining its exact location, the site was found to be marked by an accumulation of droppings of characteristic form—each a small spiralled mass composed chiefly of finely triturated insect remains."

Voice.—Mr. Woods (1924b) writes:

In general the vocal utterances of the Texas Nighthawk are of three kinds: first a low soft cluck, repeated slowly; second, a louder, querulous, nasal cry, repeated more rapidly and used when two or more of the birds are together; third, a series of throaty staccato notes delivered in monotone so rapidly as to be almost continuous, sustained for several seconds at a time and resumed after a short pause as if for breath. This trill is usually given from the ground, but sometimes also while flying. [The foregoing sentence was incorrectly printed and was revised in a letter to the author.] It is used only when the birds are undisturbed and is not ordinarily heard at close range. While the tone is soft, the carrying power is great, and sometimes on summer evenings when several of the nighthawks are about, the air seems filled with an indefinable vibration.

Alden H. Miller (1937) recognizes four main types of vocal notes: (1) Long-continued guttural trills, well characterized by Dawson as amphibian-like, but also remindful of the sound of a motor at a distance; (2) a twing like the picking of a banjo (Dawson) or, more prosaically, like the twang of a jew's-harp; (3) staccato clucks; and (4) melodious trills of varying intensity, similar to those of western screech owls (Grinnell and Storer), except for cadence. The twang and melodious trill may follow one another in rapid succession. The guttural trill seemed not to enter into the courtship on the wing. I could not be certain that this note was given on the wing at all; its source always seemed stationary. The melodious trill was occasionally given by birds perched in mesquite trees in the heat of midday.

M. W. deLaubenfels (1925) heard an unusual note, both in Arizona and again in Texas, which he described as "a loud ringing whistle— whee-*eep*-poor-will. The notes were not at all like those of the Whip-poor-will, which are repressed and muffled by comparison."

Dr. Merrill (1878) says: "The notes are a mewing call, and a very curious call that is with difficulty described. It is somewhat like the distant and very rapid tapping of a large woodpecker, accompanied by a humming sound, and it is almost impossible to tell in what direction or at what distance the bird is that makes the noise. Both these notes are uttered on the wing or on the ground, and by both sexes."

Field marks.—The most conspicuous character by which the Texas nighthawk can be distinguished from the nighthawks of the *minor* group is the position of the white band (buffy in the female) in the wing; in *minor* this is about midway between the bend of the wing and the tip; in *acutipennis* it is nearer the tip than the bend. The Texas nighthawk is also somewhat smaller, rather browner, and has a somewhat shorter and broader wing. But perhaps the most satisfactory means of identifying the two species in the field is the decided difference in the notes, as described under each; from the Texas nighthawk one never hears the harsh, rasping *peënt* note or sees the plunging "booming" flight.

Winter.—Dickey and van Rossem (1938) record this nighthawk as an—

abundant winter visitant and migrant in the Arid Lower Tropical and locally in the Arid Upper Tropical Zones [in El Salvador]. Although observed as high as 3,600 feet, its metropolis is along the seacoast. * * *

At Puerto del Triunfo hundreds of these nighthawks appeared shortly after sundown over the tide flats in front of the town, on first appearance flying at some height toward the sunset and later, in the dusk, flying in the opposite direction and close to the water and mud. After real darkness had set in they were found on the ground, most frequently in open, sandy places such as corn-fields. The visibility on sandy ground is, of course, much better than on leaf mold or similar dark surfaces, and it may well be that this species has not so good a nocturnal vision as have some of the other Caprimulgidae. The eyes of *texensis* reflect pale, dull green and not the bright red of most members of the family.

DISTRIBUTION

Range.—Southwestern United States, Mexico, and Central and South America; casual in Colorado.

Breeding range.—The breeding range of the Texas nighthawk extends **north** to central California (Red Bluff, Dales, and Grass Valley); southern Nevada (Fish Lake and Oasis Valley); southern Utah (St. George); east-central Arizona (Fort Verde and the Salt River Reservation); southern New Mexico (Cuchillo, Socorro, and Lakewood); and southern **Texas** (Pecos, probably **Kerrville**, and Somerset). **East** to Texas (Somerset, probably Corpus Christi, and Brownsville); Tamaulipas (Jaumave); Campeche (Campeche); northeastern Colombia (Turbaco and Rio Hacha); Venezuela (Alta-gracia and Guarico); French Guiana (Cayenne); and eastern Brazil (Banaos, Barra, and Rio de Janerio). **South** to southeastern Brazil (Rio de Janeiro); and southern Peru (Santa Lucia). **West** to Peru (Santa Lucia and Tumbez); western Colombia (Rio San Juan); Guerrero (Chilpancingo and Coyoca); Nayarit (Acaponeta); southern Sinaloa (Rosario); Baja California (Triunfo, Espirito Santo Island, and Santo Tomas); and California (Santa Barbara Island, Winslow, Paicines, Gilroy, Coyote, and Red Bluff).

The range as above outlined is for the entire species, which has been separated into several subspecies, all but one of which are found south of the Mexican border. This race, the Texas nighthawk (*C. a. texensis*), breeds south to south-central Mexico and winters from that point south to Panama and Colombia. The San Lucas nighthawk (*C. a. inferior*) is found in the southern part of the peninsula of Baja California.

Winter range.—It appears that at least some of the Central and South American races are nonmigratory, which, without extensive collections, makes it difficult to outline the winter range of the form occurring in the United States. Nevertheless, the winter range of *texensis* may be said to extend north to southern Sinaloa (Escuin-apa); Michoacan (Lake Patzcuaro); and southern Veracruz (Orizaba). South at least to Panama (Colon and Veragua); and Colombia (Noanama).

Spring migration.—Early dates of spring arrival in the United States are: Texas—Brownsville, March 8; northwestern Atascosa County, March 29; Refugio County, April 11. New Mexico—State College, April 20; Apache, May 6; Deming, May 17. Arizona—Gadsden, March 6; Tucson, April 7; Fort Mojave, April 17. California—Mecca, March 20; Buena Park, March 22; Pasadena, March 31; Azusa, April 2.

Fall migration.—Late dates of fall departure are: California—Clovis, September 18; Buena Park, November 1. Nevada—Charleston Mountains, September 14. Arizona—Paradise, September 25; Yuma, October 5; Boundary, October 5. New Mexico—Apache, August 11; State College, September 21. Texas—Atascosa County, October 4; Corpus Christi, October 22.

Casual records.—A specimen was collected at Hoehne, near Trinidad, Colorado, on June 11, 1908. A winter record for Arizona is a specimen collected at Phoenix on December 27, 1897, and a similar case for California is the observation of one near Calexico on January 23, 1922.

Egg dates.—California: 60 records, April 21 to July 11; 30 records, May 11 to June 12, indicating the height of the season.

Baja California: 3 records, May 12 and July 22.

Mexico: 7 records, May 20 to July 6.

Texas: 60 records, April 16 to June 29; 30 records, May 8 to June 3.

CHORDEILES ACUTIPENNIS INFERIOR Oberholser

SAN LUCAS NIGHTHAWK

HABITS

The San Lucas nighthawk is apparently a permanent resident on the peninsula of Baja California, breeding north to about latitude 30° and wintering in the extreme southern part. It is a smaller edition of the Texas nighthawk, which it closely resembles in general appearance except in size. It is larger and and somewhat lighter in coloration than the other Central American races of the species. William Brewster (1902) observed that his specimens from Lower California "average a trifle smaller and, as a rule, are somewhat lighter colored than a number of Texas specimens," but evidently did not think that the difference was worth recognizing in nomenclature. He writes:

At Triunfo the birds were abundant during the last three weeks of June, appearing regularly every evening near the ranch, and skimming back and forth close over a large wood pile, which evidently harbored insects on which

they were feeding. After a succession of heavy showers which occurred at
this place early in July they suddenly and wholly disappeared. At San José
del Cabo a few were seen at intervals through the autumn up to November
11, and several were observed near Santiago on December 3. * * * It seems
fair to assume that the December instance * * * was not exceptional, and
that at least a few birds regularly winter in the Cape Region. Mr. Frazar
obtained a set of two eggs, slightly incubated, at Pierce's Ranch, on July 20.

We have no reason to think that the habits of the San Lucas nighthawk differ materially from those of the closely related form found
farther north.

The measurements of 9 eggs average 25.6 by 18.8 millimeters; the
eggs showing the four extremes measure 27.4 by 18.8, 26.0 by 19.8,
23.1 by 18.1, and 25.6 by 18.0 millimeters.

Order MICROPODIIFORMES

Family MICROPODIDAE: Swifts

NEPHOECETES NIGER BOREALIS (Kennerly)

NORTHERN BLACK SWIFT

PLATES 40–43

HABITS

I prefer to follow Ridgway (1911) in the use of the above common name. The name black swift properly belongs to the type race,
Nephoecetes niger niger (Gmelin), which is found in the West Indies. Moreover, Baird (1858) and some other early writers called
it the northern swift. The range of the northern black swift, as
now understood, extends from southeastern Alaska to southern Mexico,
including much of the Rocky Mountain region, Colorado, New
Mexico, Nevada, and California. It breeds wherever it can find suitable rocky cliffs in which to nest, but as these are widely scattered
its distribution is naturally spotty; however, its marvelous powers
of flight carry it over a large expanse of country, far from its nesting area.

The northern black swift is somewhat larger than the type race,
but it is apparently similar to it in coloration.

Baird (1858) states: "This remarkable swift was first indicated
as North American by Dr. Kennerly (1857), in the proceedings of
the Philadelphia Academy, where it is described as *Cypselus borealis*.
It was obtained in the northern part of Puget's Sound, at Simiahmoo
bay, the locality of the main camp of the Northwest Boundary Survey. A large flock was seen one day sailing about the camp, but,
owing to the height at which the birds flew, only one specimen
could be procured.

"It seems very remarkable that so large a swift could have remained unnoticed in North America until the present day."

J. K. Lord (1866) next reported it from British Columbia, saying: "Amongst the earliest of these visitors I noticed the Northern Swift (*Nephocaetes Niger*, Baird). It was a foggy day early in June, and, the insects being low, the birds were hovering close to the ground. I shot four. The next day I searched in vain, but never saw the birds again until the fall of the year, when they a second time made their appearance in large numbers—birds of the year as well as old ones."

On June 23, 1868, Ridgway (1877) "found it abundant" in the valley of the Carson River, Nev.; "they were observed early in the morning, hovering over the cotton-wood groves in a large swarm, after the manner of Night-Hawks. * * * They were evidently breeding in the locality, but whether their nests were in the hollow cotton-wood trees of the extensive groves along the river, or in crevices on the face of a high cliff which fronted the river nearby, we were unable to determine on account of the shortness of our stay."

Frank M. Drew (1882) discovered this swift at Howardsville, Colo., and collected a series of ten birds in 1880 and 1881; he says that "they always hunt in flocks, range far above 13,000 feet and breed up to at least 11,000 feet." During the next two decades it was noted as a migrant in New Mexico and in California; but the mystery of its nesting habits was not solved until 1901, nearly 45 years after its discovery as a North American bird.

Spring.—It is as a spring and fall migrant that the northern black swift is usually observed, as it covers a wide expanse of territory in its movements to and from its more restricted breeding grounds, often occurring in large scattered blocks, feeding more or less on the way, and giving an interesting exhibition of its great powers of flight. Samuel F. Rathbun (1925) has published in detail his numerous observations on the migrations of this swift in the vicinity of Seattle, Wash., to which excellent paper the reader is referred. He writes:

During the vernal migration in the region about the Sound the first Black Swifts will be seen sometime between the fifteenth and the twenty-fifth of May. Quite frequently during the latter half of this month there will occur a spell of foul weather, and the arrival of the birds seems to be coincident. When this fact was first noticed it was regarded as incidental, but as it occurred with a degree of regularity our attention became attracted to it and we then gave the matter especial attention. Soon after the first of May we began to closely follow the weather conditions of this region and also those existing far southward, and after a time a good idea was obtained as to when to expect the arrival of the Swifts. In fact, on several occasions our expectations were confirmed almost to a day. * * * From what we have seen of this spring movement it appears to be soon completed, not lasting much more than ten days.

Courtship.—The courtship of the black swift and apparently copulation also are accomplished on the wing. Mr. Rathbun (1925) says:

Black Swifts appear to mate in June. There is no sign that this has taken place when they arrive in May, as then the birds are always seen in companies and not in pairs as is subsequently often the case. But soon after they have become distributed in colonies about the region and begin to make the daily flight to and from the lower country, indications of mating are seen. All may be gliding about when suddenly—perhaps from a far height, a Swift will dash at one beneath, this followed by erratic flight actions on the part of both and their disappearance in the distance. This dive I have seen made with such speed that the eye could scarcely follow it, and during the time that the birds are darting and twisting about it is a common thing for them to descend almost to the ground.

He says, in some notes sent to me: "On one occasion the latter part of June, I saw a pursuit by one black swift after another that lasted a full 15 minutes. This was the longest of any we ever observed, and we have seen many of them."

Nesting.—The honor of discovering the first nest of the northern black swift belongs to A. G. Vrooman (1901), who relates the historic incident as follows:

On the morning of June 16, 1901, I, with a companion, started out with the intention of taking a few sets of Cormorants' eggs on the cliffs a few miles west of Santa Cruz, California. On reaching the locality, I noticed a pair of Black Swifts flying about over the cliffs, much lower than they usually fly. One bird rose high in the air and struck off in a bee line, at the rate of a mile a minute. I then resumed my search for the Cormorants, which I found on the face of the cliff, where shore line turns sharply inland and about where the Swifts had been seen. * * *

After moving my ladder a little, I proceeded to reach out and down for a more distant set of Baird's Cormorant eggs when suddenly, right from under the pole and not more than three or four feet from my hand, a Black Swift flew out and down toward the water and passed around the angle toward the ocean. It did not rise above the cliff, in the immediate vicinity, as my companion above the cliffs did not see it at all, though I called to him to watch if it came above.

I then moved my ladder a little closer and went down farther so that my face was about a foot and a half from the egg which the Swift had just left. It was placed on a shelf or crevice in the lower edge of a projection standing out perhaps four or five feet from the main wall and about ninety feet from the breakers below. This crevice was four or five inches high, five or six inches deep, and about twenty inches long, very narrow at one end, and about thirty feet from the top of the cliff, twenty feet of which is earth sloping back to the level land above. This portion of the cliff was wet and dripping constantly, causing tufts of grass to grow here and there, where there was earth enough to support the roots. It was just behind one of these tufts of grass, in a slight depression in the mud, formed no doubt by the bird, that the egg was laid. I did not disturb the egg or nest, not going nearer than a foot and a half, intending to return a week later to get possibly a full set, which I did, but found things just as I had left them a week before and no Swifts were in sight. I took the egg, and pealed off the nest, grass and all, and have it in my collection.

Mr. Vrooman's report of finding the black swift nesting in crevices in sea cliffs and laying only one large egg was received with incredulity by many ornithologists. The generally accepted theory was that the bird would be found nesting in cliffs in the mountains, as indicated by Major Bendire's observations on the upper Columbia River in 1879; here, he reported (1895) "quite a colony nested in a high perpendicular cliff," which "was utterly inaccessible, being fully 300 feet high." Others had seen the swifts in similar localities elsewhere, where they were doubtless breeding, but no one had ever actually seen a nest. The incredulous ones thought that Mr. Vrooman must have found an egg of some small petrel, rather than that of the swift. Mr. Vrooman remained silent over the skepticism but kept steadily at work every season, sometimes without success, and eventually collected enough eggs to convince his critics. There are six eggs and one nest of this swift in the Thayer collection in Cambridge, all from Mr. Vrooman, including the type egg and nest; the latter is a clod of mud, rather deeply hollowed, and now dry and hard, with the tuft of dried grass in front of and partly surrounding it.

Many years passed before we learned anything about the inland nesting habits of the northern black swift, and, strangely enough, the first report came from a locality that is not included in the Check-list range of the species. This report came to me in a letter from Clarence E. Chapman, who discovered a nest in Johnson Canyon, near Banff, Alberta, on September 2, 1919. He describes the incident so clearly and convincingly that there can be no doubt about it. His letter states: "A walk of a mile brought us up through a lovely, small canyon to the falls; the upper canyon, just below the falls, was crossed by a high footbridge. While I was standing on this bridge, my attention was attracted by a bird flapping its wings under and against the overhanging rock wall. Mrs. Chapman and I each had high-power glasses (8 diameters). We saw a young black swift, not quite ready to fly, and close watching showed that it was exercising and strengthening its very long wings; it could not fly, as its feathers near the base were still covered with the scaly sheaths. The nest was built in a niche in the overhanging wall; the niche was about 18 inches long, 18 inches high, and 8 inches deep at the lower part; it was evidently made by a bit of rock being broken out by frost; the bottom of the niche sloped downward. The nest was a semicircle, not much more than a dam to prevent the egg from rolling out; we could not determine what the nest was made of, but considerable mud was used."

The nest was within 20 feet of Mr. Chapman's face, and within 30 feet of the fall, close enough to have the spray blow over it in certain winds. The single black young, clinging to the rock wall and to the edge of the nest, and flapping its long wings, which projected well beyond the end of its tail, could hardly be anything but a black swift.

The next account comes from Charles W. Michael (1927), who, on July 6, 1926, discovered a colony of northern black swifts, containing at least six pairs, nesting in a canyon in the Yosemite Valley, Calif. He writes:

In the inner chasm of the Tenaya Gorge a hundred paces beyond the "wedged boulder", where vertical walls rise two hundred feet or more, the swifts had chosen a nesting site. The nest was placed on a bit of projecting rock which presented a level space of perhaps four by six inches. The projection was located within the shelter of an overhung wall, thirty feet directly above a deep pool in the creek. Towering above the nest the cliff rose sheer for a distance close to two hundred feet. The inner chasm is here very narrow; the vertical walls stand not fifty feet apart. The channel is dark and cool; in the long summer days the sun lights its depth for but a brief hour. And at no time or season does the sun ever play on the nest of the swift—cramped quarters, I should say, for birds of the wide skies.

It was the wild, erratic wingings of a lone Black Swift, as he whizzed back and forth through this narrow flight lane, that first attracted my attention. * * * While I watched, the bird suddenly swooped and fairly seemed to plaster himself to the wall not fifty feet from where I stood. Then, with fluttering wings the bird moved upward—not straight upward, however, but in an angling course across the face of the cliff. As I followed the movements of the swift the nest was suddenly descried. The swift paused, clinging to the projection that held the nest, and I thought at first that he was feeding young. After a moment he scurried on upward a few feet, fell backward, and then twinkling wings carried him away down the channel. * * *

As for the nest itself, as best I could see it, it resembled in form and construction that of the Western Wood Pewee; but in size it appeared larger. Also it reminded me of certain cormorant nests I have seen plastered to the ledges above the sea. The general appearance of the structure, its apparent adhesion to the shelf, and the droppings plastered to the granite immediately below, led me to suspect that the nest may have been occupied through several nesting seasons. The rock wall roundabout was absolutely bare and dry. There was not a growing plant within ten feet of it.

Of a later visit, July 11, he says:

Beyond the "wedged boulder" I moved cautiously, but before I had come within sight of the nest a swift was seen to leave the wall and dash down the canyon. I was afraid that I was not to find the swift at home, but as I came opposite the site, there was the bird in plain sight. She sat on the nest with her tail appressed against the wall and with one long wing drooping over the side. Her body rested in a horizontal position and she appeared much too large for the nest.

While I was watching the bird a second nest was discovered. The second one was tucked away in a niche and, but for the droppings below, it would hardly have been noticed. The nest was a little round cup, shallow, and composed, apparently, of some soft, brown material like dry leaves; the rim was tinted slightly green. On a later visit, with assistance and encouragement from "Big" Con Burns, I managed to climb to a point within eight feet of the nest. And then it was learned that the nest was composed of the delicate pinnae of the five-fingered fern. Great banks of these ferns hung from neighboring walls, and it would be quite possible for the swifts to procure material while on the wing. Perhaps, though, the swifts may gather nesting material while clinging to a wall, as I have often seen swifts alight on a ferny ledge above Vernal Fall. In any event, this nest was rimmed with fresh green leaves.

Another nest was later discovered near these two, all three within a radius of three feet. Three other nests were discovered later in the same canyon. Summing up his experiences, he says:

I now feel that I have the system for locating Black Swifts' nests. Knowing the precise requirements demanded by a nesting swift, the thing to do is to find the locality that approximates these requirements. * * * What really simplifies the problem is the scarcity of suitable nesting localities for Black Swifts. There must be cozy niches in which to place the nests, and these niches must be so situated as to afford complete protection against rain, wind, and sunshine. Perhaps, too, there should be many of these niches, that nesting swifts may have nesting neighbors.

Then comes Emily Smith (1928) with her report of finding three nests of black swifts close to and behind Berry Creek Falls in a not very remote canyon in Redwood Park, Santa Cruz Mountains, Calif. The first nest seen "was not behind the falls, but a little to one side in a niche twenty feet above the pool which lies at the base of the sheer seventy-foot cliff. * * * I could not get closer than the edge of the pool, but from there the nest thirty feet away was in plain view, a thick, round mat of moss and possibly some mud, set in an almost square little niche in the rock wall. The wall roundabout, covered with mosses, five-finger ferns, and other moisture-loving plants, was dripping wet."

The other two nests were behind the falls, one only 8 feet above the pool, and the other much higher up and "hardly more than ten inches back from the main stream of the falling water. Some of the moss of which the nest was constructed appeared green and living, giving the nest a cushiony look."

Joseph S. Dixon (1935) records the first nests found in the southern Sierra Nevada:

We found three nests, but there probably were others in the vicinity, since over a dozen Black Swifts were seen. The three nests were located within a linear distance of twenty feet, so that the species might reasonably be said to have colonial nesting habits, at least in this instance. The nest site was located in the deep granite gorge of the Marble Fork of the Kaweah River. All three nests were located in a shallow cave that had been formed by the falling of a section of the cliff, leaving a broad arch about thirty feet in height. The bare, wet, dark granite wall rose precipitously above a deep pool beside a waterfall, spray from which kept the entire surroundings drenched with mist.

In all three instances the swift nests were made of green resurrection moss pressed down but not stuck together with saliva, and were placed on and supported by a clump of fragile five-fingered ferns. The first nest was a firm, mossy cup placed about eighteen feet above the water. This nest measured outside 3 by 4 inches in diameter and was 3 inches high. The trampled-down shallow cup was empty, the young bird evidently had just left the nest [August 7].

The latest nesting record comes from Albert Ervin Thompson (1937), who found a nest "near the western boundary of General Grant National Park in Fresno County, California, in the Transition Life Zone at an elevation of five thousand two hundred feet above sea level in the Sierra Nevada Mountains." He says further:

The narrow mountain gorge in which the nest was found is forested with tall sugar and yellow pines, white fir, incense cedar, and giant sequoia, and, because of a steep slope to the northwest, receives very little direct sunlight except during a brief portion of the afternoon. At other times only random shafts of light find their way among the trees.

The nest was built in a hollow of a granite wall, sheltered by an overhanging projection of rock. It was about six feet above the bed of a mountain brook and not more than twelve feet removed from a rushing cascade that boiled down a chute from a cliff above. Because of the smoothness of the sheer face of the rock, the situation was inaccessible to snakes and small mammals. The nest was formed by moist mossy material, imbedded in a natural growth of the same plant. Seeping water and spray from the waterfall kept the site continually moist. For this reason the nest was at first mistaken for that of a water ousel. One egg was laid, but after it hatched the young bird mysteriously disappeared, perhaps devoured by an enemy.

Eggs.—The single egg of the northern black swift is usually, in the six specimens that I have examined, elliptical-ovate in shape, though some are nearly elliptical-oval. The shell is smooth but without gloss. They are dull, pure white in color, but one is somewhat nest-stained. The measurements of 34 eggs average 28.6 by 19.0 millimeters; the eggs showing the four extremes measure **31.5** by 18.3, 28.0 by **20.6**, **24.5** by 19.5, and 28.5 by **17.8** millimeters.

Young.—Nothing seems to be known about the period of incubation or to what extent the two sexes assist in incubation and the feeding of the young, though it seems to be assumed that the female does most of the brooding and feeding. All observers seem to agree that the young swift is fed at infrequent intervals, mainly early in the morning and late at night. Mr. Michael (1927) says: "Most young birds receive food every few minutes, but here we find young birds that go for hours without food. Raking the skies all day long, the old swifts probably return in the evening to pump their young full of concentrated nourishment." Many hours of patient watching yielded very little information on this point, but on August 15—

at 12:30 an old bird arrived. She flew up the canyon and alighted directly on the edge of the nest. Clinging here with her tail appressed and one long wing spread out across the surface of the wall she apparently pumped food into the young bird. She appeared to fairly stuff the young one, pumping food into him ten times in twenty seconds with but slight pauses between times. At first the young one was very eager and squirmed with delight while being fed. Soon, however, he was full and had to be coaxed to take the last two or three helpings.

When through feeding her young one, the mother bird crawled up onto the nest and the young one squirmed and twisted until his head was quite snuggled under his mother's breast. Not an audible sound was uttered during the meal. but just before the parent bird departed she uttered two sharp, squeal-like notes; and then three more as she tumbled backward into space to speed off down the canyon. The young bird stretched and preened and once more settled down. * * * I believe that the female takes upon herself all the duties of incubation and of the feeding of the young.

Miss Smith's (1928) observations at Berry Creek Falls corroborated Mr. Michael's statement that the young birds can, and do, go long hours without food. She writes:

On each visit my chief interest was in finding out how often and when the young birds were fed. Unfortunately, I was not able to spend a whole day with the swifts until August 25, and then the youngest bird was more than two weeks old. I had not seen Primus (so named because he was first discovered) fed during my four previous visits with him. I had, however, seen Secundus fed at about four o'clock in the afternoon, and again the next morning at half past nine. I suppose being a very young bird he was fed more than once on each of these two days. But August 25 they all were fed only at nightfall. That day my sister and I managed to cover the four and one half miles from camp to the falls before a quarter past five o'clock in the morning. As we approached we heard soft, low cheeping notes, and then in the dim light saw birds circling and darting about in the small amphitheatre in front of the falls. It was impossible for the eye to follow them or count them, they flew so swiftly and the light was so faint. One could be seen chasing another, and then we could see several fluttering up the cliff and disappearing behind a log, and almost immediately half a dozen swept by us. By half past five, before it was light enough to see clearly, every bird had left. From then until sunset not one of the swifts returned.

Just before sunset Primus backed out of his nest, and clinging to the threshold of the niche, exercised his long wings. Seven times he vibrated them, with short intervals of rest during which his wonderful wings were stretched wide against the rock. Suddenly, a swift, surprisingly light gray in color, "plastered" itself against the wall below Primus, and motionless watched us for fifteen minutes. Primus, seeing no reason for concern about us, scrambled back onto the nest and waited patiently for his meal. Finally the old bird fluttered up and for two minutes in the fading light we could see it feeding the young one by regurgitation. Then the other parent arrived, darker and seemingly larger, and immediately we guessed it was the mother. She fed the young bird for four minutes with only very short pauses, while the father looked on.

Mr. Dixon (1935) says of the young swift that he observed in Sequoia National Park: "The outstanding feature of the young swift was his aversion to light. He always turned around in the nest so as to face the darkest corner. Another feature was the ease and tenacity with which he clung to the nest with his sharp, strongly-curved claws. When placed against a vertical granite cliff, he had no trouble clinging by one foot, but tucked his head down to avoid the bright light."

Plumages.—Mr. Dixon (1935) says that a recently hatched chick was "bluish black in color. Its eyes were closed, and there was not a bit of natal down on its body." An older young bird, found dead in a nest on July 25, 1912, and now in the Thayer collection, is completely covered with long, soft down, "dusky drab" to "blackish brown"; the down is longest on the back and rump and shortest on the head; the wing coverts are growing, and the primaries have burst their sheaths for over a quarter of an inch.

Frank M. Drew (1882) estimates that four years are necessary for the black swift to acquire its fully adult plumage, which hardly seems likely. Based on a study of ten specimens, collected in Colorado, he describes the succession of plumages as follows:

A young male of the year, taken Sept. 17, was marked as follows. General color dull black, every feather tipped with white, scarcely appreciable on upper back and throat, broader on upper tail coverts and rump. Crissum almost pure white. In birds of the second year the general plumage has a brownish cast; feathers of back tipped with brown, the head whitish, belly feathers yet broadly tipped with white. The third year the color is black, with a very faint edging of white on under tail coverts. In the fourth year pure black, forehead hoary, neck with a brownish wash.

Tail in young of first year, rounded; in second year, slightly rounded; in third year slightly emarginate, feathers becoming more acute. In adult, forked, outer feathers three-eighths of an inch longer than inner.

I have never seen a young black swift, with "every feather tipped with white," but I am inclined to believe that Mr. Drew is correct in describing this as the juvenal plumage. The juvenal plumage apparently has never been described in the manuals, and probably there are no specimens in young juvenal plumage in collections. The downy young, described above, has the incoming feathers of the wing coverts, and the remiges tipped with white. Enid Michael (1933) had a young black swift brought to her on August 10, 1932, that had fallen out of a nest and was unable to fly; from what she had previously learned from her study of young swifts in their nests, she estimated that this bird was about five weeks old; and she says: "Every feather on its back, tail, wings and crown was daintily tipped with white. The tiny feathers of its crown and forehead, being fringed with white, gave its crown, and especially its forehead, a frosted appearance." Mr. Rathbun has sent me the following description of a young black swift picked up dead in the Willamette Valley, Oreg., September 20, 1924: "Seemingly an immature bird—not in good condition of preservation. Back and abdominal feathers tipped with grayish white. Head from bill to crown also with grayish-white-tipped feathers. Primary wing feathers edged in grayish white. Length 7 inches." From the above descriptions, and from what shows in the few published photographs of the young swifts in the nests, it seems fair to assume that the juvenal or first plumage is characterized by the white tips of the body plumage, above and below, and by the white-tipped primaries. How long this plumage is worn, or how soon the white tips wear away, we do not know; but evidently this plumage is worn until after the birds leave for the south.

Considerable discussion has occurred and much has been published on the plumages of the black swift, particularly on the significance of the white spots on the under parts, as sex characters or age characters.

Mr. Ridgway (1911) evidently considered this a sex character, for he says: "All the sexed specimens examined by me, from whatever locality, show that all those with white-tipped feathers on posterior under parts are females and all those without these white-tipped feathers are males." This is not so in a series of 42 specimens, of various ages and sexes, that I have examined. More than one-third of all the birds that showed conspicuous white spots, or more or less white tips, on the feathers of the abdomen and under tail coverts are sexed as males, and less than two-thirds are sexed as females. Perhaps this character is more persistent in females than in males.

Mr. Drew (1882) implies that the sexes are alike in all plumages, and says: "In birds of the second year the general plumage has a brownish cast; feathers of back tipped with brown, the head whitish, belly feathers yet broadly tipped with white." He seems to be substantially correct on both of these points. The white-spotted birds that I examined were collected mainly in June, though two were taken in May, two in July, and one in August. All these birds have square, or slightly emarginate, tails; and none of them white-tipped remiges, which are characteristic of the juvenal plumage, as indicated above. They could not be young birds of the year, for the young birds of the year were still in the nests at the time nearly all of these birds were collected. They agree perfectly with Mr. Drew's description of the second-year bird, and I am inclined to think that that is what they are. They are numerous in collections, as perhaps immature birds may be easier to collect than adults. If this assumption is correct, then the conspicuous characters of the second-year plumage are the absence of white tips on the remiges and the presence, in varying degrees, of white spots or tips on the feathers of the abdomen and under tail coverts. This assumption has been made after giving due consideration to all that has been published on the subject and a lot of data from and correspondence with my friend S. F. Rathbun; he has made an extensive study of the black swift for many years and is inclined to agree with Mr. Ridgway; but it seems to me that all the evidence fits into the theory advanced above and agrees with Mr. Drew's (1882) idea of a second-year plumage.

Mr. Drew's statement, that "four years are necessary for them to acquire their complete plumage," seems open to question. He says that in "the third year the color is black, with a very faint edging of white on under tail coverts." There is great individual variation in the amount of white on the under parts of immature birds, probably due to wear or earlier or later molting in different individuals. It seems fair to assume that the "very faint edging" referred to by Mr. Drew may be only evidence of further advance in second-year birds. Apparently these swifts molt their contour plumage, perhaps their wings and tails, during the early summer. Mr. Rathbun tells me that he has always noticed that summer specimens "appear to have almost fresh plumage"; and Harry S. Swarth (1922) says that the birds he collected in the Stikine region, between August 19 and 30, "had entirely finished the annual molt and were all in the new plumage."

In the adult plumage the sexes are very much alike in coloration, though females average somewhat paler and browner on the under parts, and the female tail is not so deeply emarginate as that of the male. Mr. Drew (1882) says that in the adult the outer tail feathers are three-eighths of an inch longer than the inner feathers, giving the tail a forked appearance; this is undoubtedly true of fully adult males, and perhaps of some very old females. Mr. Rathbun tells me that he can usually distinguish the two sexes in flight by the extent to which the tail is emarginated. In the series that I have examined all the young white-spotted birds have square or slightly emarginate tails, all the adult males have deeply emarginate tails, and all the adult females have only slightly emarginate tails. Major Brooks, who probably has handled more black swifts than anyone in North America, wrote to Mr. Rathbun: "Swarth and myself, together with another observer in the last century, have carefully recorded that some females, probably about 10 percent, are absolutely indistinguishable from the adult male in every external character, emargination of tail, absence of white spots, etc." In a series of black swifts, collected by Mr. Swarth (1912) in southeastern Alaska in June and July 1909, "there is one female that in color and markings is indistinguishable from the males. * * * Like the others, however, it differs from the males in having a square, rather than a forked tail." This particular female contained an egg, almost ready to be laid, so that there was no doubt about the sex.

Mr. Rathbun (1925) writes: "The males are larger and darker than the females. As a rule their sooty underparts from the breast down lack any trace of light tipping on the feathers, and when this does occur the tips are of a brownish tint and very faint. In all our males the under tail coverts are tipped with brownish, rather well defined though much obscured in some individuals. There is a large variation in the amount of hoariness on the forehead."

He tells me that this swift has a complete molt during summer and is in full fresh plumage before leaving in fall.

Food.—The northern black swift feeds entirely on the wing, where it is very successful in catching the flying insects, on which it feeds exclusively; it captures a great variety of insects, and anything in the way of aerial insect life seems to be acceptable to it. Mr. Rathbun (1925) publishes a detailed list of the contents of six stomachs, collected by him near Seattle between June 22 and September 7 and reported on by the Biological Survey. The list is too long to be included here. The stomachs were reported as all full and all containing 100 percent animal matter. Prominent among the contents were caddisflies, Mayflies, crane flies and various other flies, a variety of beetles, many termites and flying ants, numerous plant lice, leafhoppers, treehoppers, wasps, and a few moths and spiders.

Clarence Cottam has sent me the following notes on the contents of 36 stomachs of this swift, as analyzed in the laboratory of the Biological Survey:

"Both in frequency of occurrence and in total percentages of volume, ants, bees, and wasps (Hymenoptera) appear to be the dominant food items taken by the black swift. Ants of the genus *Lasius* were consumed by 6 of the 36 birds here considered and comprised 90 to 100 percent of the total content, averaging about 150 individuals per stomach. The paper wasps (*Vespula*) were ingested by one-sixth of the birds and formed 51 to 87 percent of the food. Traces or small percentages of the Ichneumonidae, or parasitic wasps, occurred in the majority of the stomachs.

"Flies (Diptera) were a close second in importance and formed at least a trace in most of the stomachs; in many they made up 70 to 95 percent of the total content. The principal types met with were the long-legged flies (Dolichipodidae), flesh flies (Sarcophagidae), root maggots (Anthomyiidae), crane flies (Tipulidae), midges (Chironomidae), Ephydridae, and the grass-stem maggots (Chloropoidae). In a series of six birds from King County, Wash., flies of nine genera made up 100 percent of the contents.

"Many species of beetles (Coleoptera) were encountered in the food items, but most of them made up only minor percentages or traces, and in only a few cases did they amount to as much as 6 percent of the total. The chief families of Coleoptera taken were the ground beetles (Carabidae), rove beetles (Staphylinidae), weevils (Curculionidae), leaf beetles (Chrysomelidae), click beetles or wireworms (Elateridae), and scarab beetles (Scarabaeidae).

"Large termites, or white ants (*Thermopsis angusticollis*), also known as Isoptera, were the principal items consumed by four of the 36 swifts and comprised 70 to 99 percent of the contents, with numbers per stomach varying from 15 to 90 individuals. Mayflies (Ephemeridae) and caddiceflies (Trichoptera) were also taken at times and formed 5 to 35 percent of the content."

Behavior.—Mr. Rathbun (1925) writes admiringly of the powers of flight exhibited by the northern black swift:

In all its flight actions this Swift shows a power and an easy grace that win our admiration. It seems to live upon the wing, and to restrict its flight most of the time to a considerable elevation, the height being seemingly influenced by the character of the weather. It is generally the case that during the continuance of a low atmospheric pressure the Swifts will not fly very high, but when this condition ceases they then ascend. At the time of high pressure the Swifts are often at a great height and it is not uncommon to see them gliding at the very limit of vision. At such times so high are some of them that even with the aid of field glasses they show but faintly against the sky. It would be mere surmise as to the height that they attain, several thousand feet certainly, and as some have even disappeared from view, when the glasses were in use, one has no knowledge of the height to which they go. On a bright summer day to see these dark birds circling far above is always captivating. Should the sky happen to have clouds some of which are white and shining, the Swifts as they wheel across their glistening surfaces, are plainly outlined, but seem to fade insensibly from view when in turn they cross the open spaces of the sky. At such times it is the constant shifting view with the seeming change in distance of the gliding Swifts that adds to our interest when watching them. * * *

But this bird has also the power of very rapid flight. Infrequently it happens near the close of day that some will be seen hastening to their mountain retreats, at such times being widely scattered and flying rather low. With strong and rapid wing beats an almost direct course is followed, and but a few seconds elapse from the time one is first seen until after passing it fades from sight in the distance. And when thus observed in full flight, the power shown for fast flying never fails to impress the beholder.

The position of the Black Swift's wings as it glides or circles is dihedrally down. We have never seen any variation from this, and in this respect a contrast is shown by our *Chaetura*, whose wings are often highly elevated when sailing short distances or on entering their nesting places or roosting resorts. This wing position of the Black Swift seems worthy of mention, although it may be possible that it varies at times under conditions with which we are not familiar.

He mentions in his notes an occasion on which the swifts were flying low; he was crossing Lake Washington in a row boat on a rainy day in June: "While crossing, we noticed very many of these birds flying about at quite a low height above the water. Two were taken, and then we proceeded on our way. It was not long before a heavy rain began to fall and this hastened our return; but, when we reached the spot where first the swifts had been observed, suddenly on all sides of the boat were numbers of the birds hawking about quite close to the water's surface, some flying past not more than fifteen or twenty feet away."

Referring to the summer movements of the swifts, about Seattle, Wash., he writes (1925):

The Swifts that remain in this region undoubtedly nest far within the Cascade range, and each morning from their chosen retreats make a trip to the lowlands where they seem to stay most of the day. * * *

By the middle of June, the Swifts instead of associating in such large numbers seemed to have separated into colonies of varying sizes, each of which, during the summer months, appears to follow a certain more or less defined route every day, which the birds used each morning when flying from their mountain resort to the lower country, returning over it with equal regularity as the evening drew near.

These journeys have the appearance of being long excursions, but the wide distances mean little to this Swift with a power of flight to which there seems but little limitation. The valley of the Middle Fork of the Snoqualmie River, some thirty miles almost due east of Seattle, is one such route that we have noticed the Swifts following; and here at various times during several summers we have watched the daily flight of a colony of these birds that numbered nearly one hundred and fifty.

In a valley of one of the mountain rivers, on an afternoon in June, Mr. Rathbun observed a flight behavior, which he describes in his notes as follows: "No swifts were seen until about 5:30 p. m., when a few flew by widely scattered. At 6:30 p. m., more swifts began to straggle past. While watching them, I noticed a dark, dense cloud moving slowly toward where I stood. I expected to see some swifts in company with it. I was not disappointed. There were about 50, and it was of interest to see them gliding around in advance of and below the cloud. By their actions it looked as if they were feeding, and all kept pace with the slow movement of the cloud. None of the swifts were below 400 feet, some much higher. As the cloud passed the swifts kept company with it; and then followed an interval when none were seen. Half an hour or so later another of the heavy clouds rolled up from the west. Only a short distance in front of it were more swifts circling, these soon followed by others gliding about beneath the cloud. In this flight were at least 60 of the birds, and, as in the first instance, they moved along with the cloud until lost to our sight."

M. P. Skinner has sent me the following notes on a flock of swifts that he watched at the Vernal Falls in the Yosemite Valley: "After circling once or twice around at the falls, they flew down the canyon below for half a mile with great swiftness, then whirled in a circle and came back. They repeated this over and over again. They kept in the early morning shade as long as I watched them. Periods of wing beating alternated with gliding on set wings, and both periods varied very much in length."

Ralph Hoffmann (1927) says: "The flight of the Black Swift is amazingly swift; it includes sudden sharp turns, steep downward plunges and hurried upward flights. The long, narrow wings at times 'twinkle' rapidly, or when the bird is sailing, are either held uplifted over the back or curved downward with the tips well below the body. The tail is very slightly forked but in flight it is constantly spread and appears fan-shaped when the bird makes a sudden turn."

I can find no evidence that the northern black swift has ever been seen perching on a tree or wire, or resting on the ground; its regular resting places seem to be the steep, rocky walls, often dripping with moisture, such as they choose for nesting sites. Though their feet are small and light, they have very sharp claws, and are able to cling to the rough surface for long periods. Mrs. Michael (1926) has seen them clinging to the wet walls behind the Vernal Falls and near it. "From the distance of fifty yards the birds appeared to stick as limpets do to the wet rocks of a sea shore." But, on closer examination, she found that "they were not sticking to the wall as limpets, but their bodies were held slightly away from the wall, with not even their tails touching." With one bird, she noted that "his strong toe nails were hooked to some tiny support and his entire tarsus rested firmly against the wall, thus holding his body and tail free." Later (1933) she says of a young black swift that she had in captivity: "When climbing up a sheer surface the swift used its wings, feet, tail and sharply hooked bill. When in repose it lay flat on its belly in the manner of a poor-will. * * * The legs seemed to have swivel joints, and it was strange to see the bird reach up its foot between the body and wing to comb its back and crown feathers."

Voice.—There is not much to be said about the voice of the black swift. All observers agree that it is generally a silent species; its note is seldom heard, except during the mating season and on its breeding grounds. Mr. Rathbun (1925) writes:

During its spring migration and shortly following, a period when the birds are associated in numbers, we have watched them for long spaces of time and always a perfect silence seemed to prevail among them. And this apparently is the case until the time comes when by their actions they show that they are mating. Even now their chatter-like note is but seldom heard, although invariably it is given at the time when one dashes at another, and this often proves the case when a pair may happen to fly in close company. During the midsummer we have heard their rapid notes as the birds passed in flight near the close of day, and in the autumnal migration when rarely one would make a quick dash at another. But these instances are uncommon and the species can properly be regarded as quite silent, being very different in this respect from the Chaeturine Swifts whose shrill twitterings are so frequent as they fly about. And the chatter of the Black Swift somewhat resembles that of the smaller ones; it being as rapid, but smoother in quality and more rolling, in fact rather pleasing to hear.

Grinnell and Storer (1924) describe its note as "a high-pitched twitter, not so shrill or long-continued as that of the White-throated Swift."

Field marks.—The black swift can be recognized by its size and coloration. It is the largest of the three western swifts. The white-throated swift, which most nearly approaches it in size, differs from it in having a well-marked and conspicuous pattern of black and white on the under parts, as well as the white rump patches, which show from above. The black swift appears wholly dark, except under certain conditions of reflected sunlight; the white markings on the immature bird are not conspicuous, except at close range. Vaux's swift is the smallest of the three and does not show in flight the slightly forked and fan-shaped tail of the black swift. Mr. Hoffmann (1927) suggests that "the beginner may take the much commoner Purple Martin for a Black Swift; the deeply notched tail, never spread like a fan, the habit of perching on stubs, the loud, musical notes and the difference in the sexes should readily identify the Martin." Grinnell and Storer (1924) state that, in the black swift, "the fore margin of the two wings as viewed from below is a double convex, and not a single continuous arc as in the White-throated Swift; moreover, the movements of the wings are more deliberate than in that species."

Fall.—Mr. Rathbun says in his notes: "The autumnal migration straggles over a more or less extended period. In the Puget Sound region it begins to take place soon after September 1, and it lasts three weeks or slightly more. I have observed this for many years, and the swifts do not pass by in the large groups that one will see in spring. Day after day in fall they straggle by in small numbers. Very often we have noticed that these groups were in multiples of three, which in our opinion would represent the parent birds with their single young. Invariably associated with the black swifts were the Vaux's swift, and if either was seen you could expect to see the other. And quite often, in company with both species of swifts, would be violet-green and barn swallows, all straggling past at odd times throughout the day."

In the Stikine region Mr. Swarth (1922) observed: "At Sergief Island, August 17 to September 7, black swifts were abundant, though seen only in cloudy or rainy weather. Then large flocks appeared, as many as seventy-five or a hundred being in sight at once flying over the marshes, the individuals moving about in wide circles, and the flock as a whole moving in a definite path. The birds sometimes flew very low, occasionally skimming along just over the tall grass. A flock would appear, circle about overhead awhile, and then vanish. About fifteen or twenty minutes later, others, or perhaps the same flock, would come in sight again."

DISTRIBUTION

Range.—Western North America; closely related nonmigratory races are found in southern Central America and in the West Indies.

Breeding range.—The breeding range of the black swift extends **north** to southeastern Alaska (Portage Cove); and northwestern British Columbia (Telegraph Creek). **East** to British Columbia (Telegraph Creek, Hazelton, and 158-mile House); southwestern Alberta (Banff); probably western Montana (Libby, Glacier National Park, and Stryker); and southwestern Colorado (Howardsville). **South** to southwestern Colorado (Howardsville); and southern California (Cerro Gordo, Sequoia National Park, and Santa Cruz). **West** to California (Santa Cruz, Berry Creek, and Yosemite Valley); western Washington (Seattle and Bellingham); British Columbia (Chilliwack and Okanagan Landing); and southeastern Alaska (Boca de Quadra and Portage Cove).

Winter range.—Unknown. Despite repeated statements that this species spends the winter season in southern Mexico, an examination of the available data fails to substantiate the assertion, the dates of observation or collection being entirely within the seasons of migration. Accordingly, while it is possible that these birds do winter with the resident form in southern Central America, factual evidence is at present lacking.

Spring migration.—Early dates of spring arrival are: Baja California—San Telmo, April 30. California—Haywards, April 19; Grapevine, April 24; Yosemite Valley, May 11. Washington—Seattle, May 16; Simialmoo, May 27. British Columbia—Chilliwack, May 8; Courtenay, May 15; Lulu Island, May 25; Alberni, June 9.

Fall migration.—Late dates of fall departure are: Alaska—Sergief Island, September 7. British Columbia—Hazelton, August 29; Errington, September 20; Okanagan Landing, September 26; Courtenay, September 29. Washington—Bellingham, September 1; Seattle, October 7. Oregon—Albany, September 22. California—Santa Cruz County, September 13; Haywards, October 1.

Casual records.—Among the records of occurrence of the black swift outside the range as above outlined are the following cases: New Mexico, reported from Willis in September 1883 and noted at Lake Burford, on September 28, 1904; Arizona, seen at Flagstaff on August 18, 1920; eastern Colorado, two seen on July 8 and three on July 10, 1910, in Estes Park, several seen near Trinidad, July 8–14, 1892, while a specimen in the collection of George B. Sennett was labeled as taken at Denver on June 26, 1884; and Idaho, taken or observed on the Malade River on August 13, 1834. A specimen came

on board the S. S. *Antigua* on September 20, 1933, while the vessel
was 84 miles off the coast of Guatemala.

Egg dates.—California: 27 records, June 16 to July 29; 14 records,
June 24 to July 9, indicating the height of the season.

CHAETURA PELAGICA (Linnaeus)

CHIMNEY SWIFT

PLATES 44–46

HABITS

CONTRIBUTED BY WINSOR MARRETT TYLER

From its unknown winter quarters, somewhere in Central America
or on the South American Continent, the chimney swift comes northward in spring and spreads out over a wide area, which includes a
large part of the United States and southern Canada.

Individually the swift is an obscure little bird, with a stumpy, dull-
colored body, short bristly tail, and stiff, sharp wings, but it is such
a common bird over the greater part of its breeding range and col-
lects in such enormous flocks, notably when it gathers for its autumnal
migration, that as a species it is widely known.

The birds also have the habit of continual flight during the hours
of daylight throughout the summer, and therefore keep always before
our eyes when we look up at the sky. They exemplify speed and tireless energy; they sail and circle on set wings, then with flickering
wing beats they are off in a burst of speed, shooting like an arrow
through the air, chattering their bright notes as they race along—
little arrows "cutting the clouds" over country, town, and woodland.

Spring.—Swifts move up into the northern latitudes only when
spring is rather far advanced, not until their aerial insect food is
plentiful well above the ground. Therefore their arrival varies a
good deal from year to year.

Kopman (1915) reports that the average date of appearance in New
Orleans is about March 18. In New England, in an average year,
we do not expect the birds for fully 30 days after this date; hence
we may infer that they spend a month in moving across a dozen
degrees of latitude.

A daylight migrant, solely, so far as is known, we see the first
arrivals of this swift commonly in the afternoon, sailing in small
companies—perhaps only a single bird—often high in the air. As
they fly along, they give an occasional chatter, or a few rather feeble
chips, but with none of the energy and volubility characteristic of the
breeding season. On cloudy days in spring, when the swifts dip down

over the surface of a pond and feed among the twittering swallows—a common habit of theirs—they are apt to be silent.

When the birds appear, leisurely drifting up from the south, they often fly in great loops. They turn slowly aside from their northerly course, swinging farther and farther around until they are moving for a time toward the south, then, veering gradually, they resume their journey, but soon turn again and make another sweeping curve, each loop carrying them nearer their destination.

An hour before dark, in the lengthening evenings of early May, we often see a little gathering of New England swifts that have settled on their nesting grounds but are not occupied as yet with breeding activities, flying about in company, high over their chosen chimney, chattering together. The birds may be so high in the air that the sound of their voices barely reaches our ears. These newly arrived birds pay little attention to each other and do not approach near or chase one another as they will in June, yet they keep in a loose flock, sailing and flickering in a somewhat circular path and sometimes coast down from their high elevation, and climb up to it again. Then, as dusk deepens, at about the time the bat appears, they gather around their chimney and drop into it.

Although swifts, during their spring migration, often collect, before going to roost, in flocks of considerable numbers, they are less conspicuous at this season than during their impressive gatherings in autumn. These are described under "Fall."

Courtship.—In June, here in New England, the swifts become very noisy. Even from within doors we hear their voices as the birds hurry past not far from our roof. As we listen their chips appear sharper and faster than they did the week before, more clearly enunciated, and they run in a long series that seems to grow in intensity as the birds come nearer, reaches a maximum when they pass overhead, and dies away as they rush on.

When we watch the birds at this season we notice also a difference in their behavior. There is little of the slow, apparently aimless circling of early spring, when, although the birds gather in small companies and follow similar paths in the air, they are seemingly indifferent to one another's presence.

The breeding season is here. Purpose has come into the swift's brain, and purpose has brought intensity and speed, and concentration on a mate. Now they fly close together, two birds, three birds, sometimes four in a little bunch. The length of a swift's body scarcely separates them as they tear along, ripping through space, following the twists and turns of the bird in the lead.

Soon two birds are left alone, the others circling off for a time. Both of these birds are chipping sharply, flying fast, close together, and during their mad dash, one, if not both, uses a peculiar note—a line of chips, a chatter, then the chips again. This combination of notes accompanies the height of the pursuit, and the swifter and closer the chase the sharper and quicker the notes. It seems also that the nearer the birds are to one another, the faster they fly. They may fly sometimes, their wings almost touching, at a pace that seems reckless; then the notes spatter out as if self control were lost, and at last, as the pursuer overtakes his goal, he rises a little above her and lifts up his wings, and there appears to be a moment of contact.

The probability that the nuptial flight leads, at least sometimes, to sexual contact in the air is increased by Sutton's (1928) careful study of the swift. He says: "In this courtship flight, the pair of birds may fly rapidly about, twittering loudly; suddenly the upper bird will lift its wings very high above the back and coast through the air, sometimes for several seconds, while the bird beneath may soar with its wings held in a fixed position below the plane of the body. It may be that this graceful and interesting display is at the culmination of courtship activity."

From the fact that swifts in the courting season so often fly three together when engaged in their pursuits—in the initial part at least, for at the culmination the pair find themselves alone—a surmise has arisen that one male and two females make up the trio and that the swift is polygamous. This surmise, however, is not yet attested by any conclusive evidence.

Nesting.—Of the few North American birds—and they are very few—that were influenced favorably by civilized man when he settled on this continent, the chimney swift received the greatest benefit. Before the coming of man, the swifts had been building their nests for thousands of years in hollow trees, here and there in the American wilderness. Then man came, and unwittingly supplied, within his chimneys, exactly the situation the swift required for nesting, an upright surface inside a cavity, protected from the weather—the equivalent of a hollow tree. Thus the birds' nesting sites were increased a millionfold.

Nowadays the typical site is in a chimney, "from near top to 22 feet below it," Forbush (1927) says. Yet, as the following quotations show, the swift occasionally avails itself for nesting purposes of some other of man's works; also from time to time it is found breeding in its ancestral manner.

The nest itself is a little hammock—half-saucer-shaped—composed solely of dead twigs, which the bird breaks off as it flies past a tree. The twigs are attached to the wall, and the twigs themselves are fastened to one another by the glutinous saliva of the bird, which hardens and fixes the structure so firmly to its support that it withstands, as a rule, the rain of summer storms.

Lewis (1927) reports that "a pair of Chimney Swifts built a nest and hatched a brood of young in an open well near an old deserted farm-house in the southern part of the county [Lawrenceville, Va.]. The nest was typical for the species and was stuck just above a bulge in a rock in the well wall, just as they are stuck to the rocks in a chimney. It was located about 7 feet below the surface of the ground, and 10 feet above the water."

Hyde (1924) found an occupied nest "in an abandoned cistern about one mile east of the town of Magnolia, Putnam County, Ill." He says: "The cistern was half hidden by vegetation. The diameter at the aperture was three feet and at the bottom nine feet. There was water nine feet below the aperture. The nest was in an entirely sheltered position four feet above the water. All these figures being approximate."

Kennard (1895), speaking of a nest in New York State, says: "I found a Chimney Swift's nest placed just under the ridge pole of an old log barn and against the side of one of the logs of which it was constructed. * * * It was within a foot of an enormous hornet's nest. The five young birds which were nearly fledged were clinging to the bark of the logs in the immediate vicinity and seemed to get on much better with the hornets than I did."

Evermann (1889) describes a "peculiar nidification of this species" as follows: "A pair fastened their nest in 1884 upon the inside of the door of an out-house at the Vandalia depot in Camden [Indiana]. The birds entered the building through small holes made in the gables. This building was in daily use, but those who visited it were cautioned by the railroad agent to open the door with care so as not to jar the eggs from the nest. Four eggs were laid, one of which was jostled from the nest, the other three hatched, and the young were reared in safety. The nest was repaired and used again in 1885, and again in 1886, a brood being reared each season."

Most astonishing records of nesting are reported by Moore (1902b) thus: "In this locality [Scotch Lake, New Brunswick], more nests are built inside buildings than there are inside chimneys. The nests are usually glued to the gable end of the building—sometimes barns, sometimes old uninhabited houses are chosen—and one nest, the past summer, was built in a blacksmith shop within fifteen feet of the forge. A number of years ago a pair nested in the upper part of a house in which a family lived, and near to a bed in which children slept every night. In this case the birds entered through a broken window."

Daniel (1902) gives an instance of the nesting of swifts in hollow cypress trees in the Great Dismal Swamp. He says:

Along the southeastern shore, growing in the lake some distance out from the shore line, are a number of large hollow cypresses. The roots or "knees" of these trees extend upward and outward from the surface of the water, curving inward some distance up, and in most of them, between the water and base of the tree proper, there are openings large enough for a canoe to enter. By pushing our canoe in these intervals between the roots, we were able to examine the interiors of the hollow trees. In these we found the swifts nesting in their primitive fashion, the nests being fastened to the interior walls about midway down.

T. E. Musselman wrote me in 1935 that he has noted that swifts are beginning to use silos as nesting sites in the Middle West.

Eggs.—[AUTHOR'S NOTE: The chimney swift lays three to six eggs, more commonly four or five. These are pure white and only moderately glossy. In shape they vary from elliptical-ovate to cylindrical-ovate. The measurements of 56 eggs average 20.10 by 13.24 millimeters; the eggs showing the four extremes measure **21.59** by 13.46, 21.34 by **13.72,** **17.53** by 13.72, and 18.29 by **12.70** millimeters.]

Young.—The young swift starts life in a world of danger. It comes from the egg a blind little naked thing, no bigger than your fingernail, lying in a frail cradle of sticks that overhangs a black "drop into nothing." The little swift, however, is equipped to deal with the dangers of its birthplace. Very early in its life it can cling and crawl; it can hide under its nest; it can move about over the walls of the abyss in which it lives; and, when the time for flying comes, it can clamber toward the free air, taking, perhaps, the longest and last walk of its career.

Frederic H. Kennard illustrates in his notes the hardiness of the young swift when it comes from the egg. He says: "On July 15, 1918, somewhere between 9 and 10 a. m. at Duck Lake, Maine, I found among the ashes of the fireplace, in a friend's unoccupied camp, a chimney swift's nest which I had been watching and which, when I had last seen it, the previous noon, in the chimney, had contained two eggs. It had evidently been dislodged from its proper place by a thunderstorm and torrential rain of the night before.

"The nest and both eggshells lay among the ashes, close together, at the back of the large fireplace. Both eggs were broken, and the shells lay just where they had fallen. One of them was evidently addled, while the content of the other was apparently missing.

"Imagine my surprise, when after hunting for some time, I discovered that the content of the other egg was a tiny swiftlet, which, blind and with the back of its skull badly bruised and suffused with blood from its fall down the chimney, had nevertheless made its way out through the ashes, dropping down the thickness of a brick from the fire place proper to the hearth beyond, then across the hearth; and had climbed, in a style worthy of a young hoatzin, and was still clinging in an upright position to the finely woven wire fender that had enclosed the fireplace, but which I had moved aside in order to facilitate inspection.

"Of course this bird might have been hatched the day before, some-time between noon and the time of the storm, which occurred about 10 p. m., but my impression was, from the position of the eggshell as it lay broken in halves among the ashes, that the little fellow ready to hatch had come down either in the shell or in the act of emerging from it. There were no signs of any yolk to be seen. Judged from his size and development he must have been less than a day old. There had been but one nest in the chimney; and there was no possibility of any outside intermeddling, as the camp was kept locked and I had been the only one to enter it in weeks."

Of the young when nearly ready to fly he says: "Found a swift's nest down in Charlie Boyce's boat house on the wall about 5′ 9″ above the floor, and the four nearly fledged young clinging to the pretty smoothly sawed board wall from 18″ to 24″ away from the nest. Upon investigating I found that their toenails were long and sharp and that they could flutter up or across the wall at will, though when undisturbed they kept well together in a compact little group, propped up on their tails. When disturbed the young birds squealed loudly something like an exaggerated rattlesnake."

Burns (1921) states that the eyes of the young swift become wide open on the fourteenth day. This accords with the observation of Mary F. Day (1899), who watched at close range the development of a brood of swifts and noted that the incubation period was 19 days; that "even at the tender age that must be reckoned by minutes, these young birds were fed, seemingly, by regurgitation"; that the "two first ventured from home when nineteen days old"; and that they flew from the chimney four weeks after hatching. Speaking of the exercising of the nestlings, she says: "The young aspirants would stand in the nest and for a time vibrate the wings rapidly, so rapidly that the identity of wing was lost." And of the fledglings 26 days after leaving the egg she says: "They take flying exercises up and down the chimney, but I believe have not yet left it."

Carter (1924) studied the feeding of five fledgling swifts at a nest built on the wall of an abandoned cabin in Ontario. He says:

The old birds gained access to the interior of the building through a broken window and were remarkably tame, feeding the young within three feet of the observers, thus giving an excellent opportunity to observe the process of feeding. The parent, with greatly extended cheeks and throat, alighted upon the wall among the young. Immediately there was a great commotion. After a short hesitation a young bird would be fed by forcing some of the food from the mouth of the parent into that of the offspring. After a moment's feeding there was a pause and then the process was repeated, either to the same young or another. As many as three were served at a single visit.

Lewis (1929) describes thus the feeding of a brood of young birds that had fallen when their nest had been dislodged by rain but were clinging to the wall of the chimney:

From the start the old birds did not see me sitting on the hearth, or, seeing they paid little attention. I was much surprized to see that they always fluttered down and lit on the wall a little below the young birds, bracing themselves in the same manner as the young and reaching up to feed them. The young would turn their necks down as far as possible without changing the position of their bodies. The old birds would stretch up, putting the bill inside the gaping mouths of the young, and seemingly feed by regurgitation. This was invariable during the time I spent watching them, which amounted to a number of hours.

The four young clung to the wall without moving noticeably, always side by side, and were fed from daylight until dark at intervals of from 1 to 28 minutes until July 31, when I was obliged to leave home. [The nest had been dislodged on June 25.]

After the nest had fallen, but before the parents came down into the lower part of the chimney to feed their young, the little birds gave a note that Mr. Lewis describes as "a loud, harsh squeal, quite unlike the chattering they always make when being fed."

Townsend (1906) comments on the noisiness of a nestful of chattering swifts he found inside "a small hay barn" at Cape Breton. He says: "The shrill twittering of the young was almost deafening in the small hay loft."

Guy A. Bailey (1905), in a study of a swift's nest built inside a barn near Syracuse, N. Y., shows that the parent bird urges the young to leave the nest even before (according to his photographs) the flight feathers are more than half released from their sheaths. He says:

Generally, after feeding the young, the old bird crawled over to one side of the nest and cautiously insinuated its body behind the young birds. The adult bird kept crowding until all but one or two of the brood of five were forced out of the nest and took up positions on the vertical roost. The remaining birds would sometimes leave the nest of their own accord and follow their mates. This was noticed especially after those clinging to the boards had been fed.

It often happened that the adult birds would remain away from the young as long as twenty minutes, during which time the little ones would return to the nest. Usually, however, one parent would remain with the brood until relieved by the mate. On such occasions there was a period of several minutes when both parents were present.

Plumages.—[AUTHOR'S NOTE: The young swift is hatched naked and blind, but the spinelike quills soon begin to appear, and these develop into a juvenal, or first-winter, plumage, which is much like that of the adult; there are some light edgings on the scapulars and rump, which soon wear away, and the under parts are somewhat darker than in adults, especially on the throat. I have seen young birds acquiring the first winter plumage as early as August 10 and others still in the postnatal molt as late as September 25. This plumage is probably worn through the winter, though no winter specimens have been available for study. Forbush (1927) says that a "complete prenuptial molt beginning in late winter or early spring is followed by a plumage as adult; adults apparently molt twice a year, a complete postnuptial molt in autumn and a partial (possibly complete) molt in spring."]

Food.—Pearson (1911) quotes a letter from W. L. McAtee of the United States Biological Survey: "The bird's food consists almost wholly of insects, and beetles, flies and ants are the principal items. It gets many beetles (Scolytidae), the most serious enemies of our forests, when they are swarming, and takes also the old-fashioned potato beetle (*Lema trilineata*), the tarnished plant-bug (*Lygus pratensis*), and other injurious insects. The bird is, of course, largely beneficial to the agricultural interests of the country."

Knight (1908) says: "The food of the Chimney Swallow consists of almost any of the smaller insects which fill the air of a summer's day."

Behavior.—The relationship between man and the chimney swift is a rather curious one. Although the species spends the summer scattered over a large part of the North American Continent, it never, except by accident, sets foot upon one inch of this vast land. The birds build their "procreant cradle" in the chimneys of thousands of our homes and crisscross for weeks above our gardens and over the streets of our towns and cities, yet, wholly engrossed in their own activities far overhead, they do not appear to notice man at all. Indeed, it is easy to believe that the swift is no more aware of man during the summer, even when it is a denizen of our largest cities, than when in winter it is soaring over the impenetrable jungles of Central America.

How do we regard this bird that does not know we are on earth? We are glad to have swifts breed in our chimney; we like to see them shooting about over our heads, and we enjoy their bright voices, yet, do we feel such friendship for them as we feel for a chipping sparrow, for example, which builds sociably in the vines of our piazza? The little sparrow may be wary, and may fly away if we come too near, but at least it pays us the compliment of recognizing our existence. The swift, however, is not even a semitrustful neighbor; it is a guest that does not know we are its host. We may almost think of it as a machine for catching insects, a mechanical toy, clicking out its sharp notes.

But let us note this fact. Every ten years or so the swifts do not appear about our house in the spring. Something has gone wrong on their journey northward. Our chimney will be empty this year; there will be no dark bows and arrows dashing back and forth above our roof, no quick pursuits and chattering in the evening. All summer something is lacking because there are no swifts to enliven the season. We realize, now that they are gone, how we should miss their active, cheerful presence, if they never came back again. But we may be sure they will come back—next year perhaps—to visit us again, this most welcome "guest of summer."

Bird banding has brought man and the chimney swift for the first time into close association. During the past few years, swifts have been banded in very large numbers. At daybreak, as the birds pour out of the chimneys where they have roosted during their autumnal migration, they are captured in traps placed over the chimney and so ingeniously devised that the outward flow of hundreds of birds is not interrupted. The banders who have handled the birds report that they show little or no fear (or consciousness) of man and appear tame to an extraordinary degree.

The following quotations from Constance and E. A. Everett (1927) illustrate their behavior after being caught. These authors state that: "In less than five minutes, with but one casualty, one hundred sixty-four Chimney Swifts were inside of that cage ['a six-foot house trap'], clinging to its walls of wire mesh like a swarm of bees, except that though densely massed, they were clinging to the wire and not to each other. A few were at all times on the wing, as they changed from one group to another, bewildered, perhaps, but not in the least frightened. Most of them, however, promptly alighted and tucked their heads under the wings and tails of those birds above them, until the inner walls of the cage took on the appearance of being shingled with birds."

When removed from the cage, "these swifts were very quiet, and apparently comfortable at all stages of the game. When held in the hands they would snuggle between the fingers confidingly; and when held against the clothes they would wriggle under the folds of the garments and contentedly go to sleep."

Of the next morning's work they say: "Since there were so few birds, we took the time to enjoy playing with them. Miss Constance and the boys tried wearing them either singly as a brooch, or collectively as a breast plate; and always the birds snuggled down as though perfectly willing to join the game, provided their naps were not interfered with. Finally some passing school girls were adorned with live breast pins to take home for show, while several birds, clinging to Constance's coat rode many blocks in the car, and, scolding, had to be dragged off to their liberty."

These observations were made at Waseca, Minn., on September 8 and 9, 1926.

In flight, the swift, perhaps from necessity because the bird spends so much of the day in the air, relieves its wings from time to time from their quick flickering and sails—the wings held motionless, fully extended from the body. When beating its wings, the bird appears always in a hurry; it seems to be moving them up and down as fast as it can; it often rocks from side to side, as it turns this way and that, and ever seems to be trying to fly a little faster.

Sutton (1928), in an able study of the swift's flight, aided by examination of captive birds, states that "no intermediate, half-spread position [of the wing] was ever maintained in healthy individuals. In fact, such an intermediate position seemed impossible [on account of anatomical structure]. * * *

"It may be stated broadly, therefore, that the Chimney Swift wing, so far as its spreading is concerned, has but two normal positions; one, folded at rest, the other, open for flight, whether that flight be rapid forward flapping, soaring, coasting, or even sudden descent."

One evening Dr. Sutton, standing at the mouth of a chimney while swifts were going to roost, watched the birds enter, within arm's reach. Describing this experience, he says:

I was amazed at their precision and speed. As a rule, they slowed up abruptly just before making the final plunge, this being accomplished by a spreading and lowering of the tail, and by rapid, vigorous, downward and forward strokes of the wings, during which the loosely and widely spread primaries seemed to aid in checking the speed. When a proper point above the mouth of the chimney was reached the birds suddenly pressed the spread tail downward as far as possible, and with outstretched wings high above the back, still loosely fluttering, through an arc of about forty-five degrees, either dropped directly, turned jerkily from side to side, or twirled gracefully downward into the chimney.

Again, in the morning, peering down the chimney as the birds emerged, he says: "I was surprised to see that the birds were flying almost directly forward, but in an upward direction. Their bodies were not in a horizontal position; they were almost vertical, and the whole spectacle gave the impression that the birds were crawling up invisible wires."

For years there has been a controversy concerning the swift's flight. Some observers held that the swift moved its wings simultaneously, like other birds; others believed that the wing beats were alternate, like the strokes of a double-bladed paddle. It is easy to see how confusion between fact and appearance might arise. Swifts *do* appear to fly with alternate wing beats, but chiefly, if not wholly, when the birds tilt to one side in making their quick turns. Then one wing appears to be up and the other down, and as a matter of fact such is the case in reference to an imaginary line drawn across the swift parallel to the ground—one wing is above the line, and the other is below it. But the bird being tilted to one side, in order to show the relative position of one wing to the other, we must allow for the tilting, and we must draw the imaginary line, not parallel to the ground, but through the short axis of the *bird's body*. The observer, standing on the ground, does not make this adjustment, for he does not take into account the instantaneous tilting of the bird.

The question was definitely settled by Myron F. Westover (1932), who demonstrated by motion photography that *"there was no instance where there was any alternation of wing-movement;* the wings move in unison as do those of other species of birds." Dr. Chapman appends an editorial note to the article: "Mr. Westover's film was shown in the American Museum to the members of the Bird Department who agree that it demonstrates beyond question the truth of his conclusions."

There is a difference of opinion also among observers as to whether the swift, when collecting nesting material, breaks off dead twigs with its feet or with its beak. Coues (1897), questioning the correctness of a drawing by Fuertes representing the bird snapping off a twig with its feet, says: "We have always supposed the bird secured the object with its beak, as it dashed past on wing at full speed; or at any rate that has been my own belief for more years than I can remember. But Mr. Fuertes vouched for the correctness of his representation from actual observation. The question being thus raised, I set it forth recently in a query inserted in one of our popular periodicals, asking for information."

There are six replies to Coues' query printed in The Nidologist (vol. 4, pp. 80, 81), five of which are in accord with his opinion, while one is against it, as is one more reply published in The Osprey (vol. 1, p. 122). Dr. Coues declares that "these leave the case still open!"

More recently Shelley (1929), from an ample experience of 13 uninterrupted years of observation of swifts at close range, states unequivocally that they "gather their nesting material * * * *with their feet.*" He adds: "I never yet observed a Swift grasp or carry a twig in its beak."

Mr. Shelley's well-weighed opinion added to that of Mr. Fuertes, whose accuracy and skill in observing birds have never been surpassed, should be accepted with confidence until motion photography shall prove or disprove the correctness of their view, although the swift may adopt both methods of collecting nesting material.

We may recall that Audubon (1840) appears to have had no doubt upon the question, for he says: "They throw their body suddenly against the twig, grapple it with their feet, and by an instantaneous jerk, snap it off short, and proceed with it to the place intended for the nest."

Although without much doubt swifts pluck off twigs with their feet, they may find it convenient to arrive at the nest site with their feet free to grasp the wall of the chimney. To gain this end, it is possible that on the way to the nest, the birds may transfer the twig to their beak, for William Brewster (1937b) in his Concord journal says that on June 15, 1905, he saw one "drop into the chimney this evening carrying a short twig held crossways in its *bill*."

An entry in Brewster's Concord journal also indicates that the swift may be more nocturnal in its habits than is commonly believed. He writes under the date August 5, 1893: "At about 2 A. M. I was surprised to hear Chimney Swifts twittering outside the window. There seemed to be a good many of them and the sound of their voices indicated that they first circled about the house several times and then went off towards the South. When I first heard the twittering, there were also several birds making their peculiar rumbling in the chimney, but this soon ceased and was not again repeated. The night was dark and still at the time, with rain falling gently and steadily."

We must remember also that Wilson (1832) states that "the young are fed at intervals during the greater part of the night," and Henry C. Denslow writes to Mr. Bent of "the vivid memory" of an observation of the birds' nocturnal activities. He says that "the chimney swift feeds its young in the middle of the night, going out and in the chimney several times with the usual rumbling of wing beats and the usual chirring sound of the young birds while being fed. I chanced to sleep in a small room with a chimney, near Rochester, N. Y., for several years, and so became familiar with this habit of the bird."

Frederic H. Kennard, in his notes, describes an interesting habit that he observed at very close range at a nest containing young built on the inner wall of a boathouse. He says: "She(?) [a parent bird] sat very close, moving her head only occasionally, panting with the heat, and did not appear to mind me much until her mate flew in, lit on the wall nearby, when she got off the nest and fluttered up and down the wall beside or below the nest, snapping her wings together (apparently behind her), a note of warning or anger, or something of the sort, perhaps to scare me away or to show her displeasure. She would raise her wings slowly until they stood out straight behind her back, parallel and almost touching." And later he adds: "They do not seem to snap their wings except when disturbed by me. There is no snapping when they ordinarily leave their nests. When they do snap they slowly raise their wings until they are straight up from their backs and then snap them a couple of times."

At the same boathouse he "saw one of the swifts fly through a crack in the door just after I had come out and closed it. He didn't slow down at all, never missed a beat, but merely turned on one side and went through, full speed."

Voice.—The notes of the swift remind us of the bird itself—energetic and quick; sharp and hard like the bird's stiff wings. The note most commonly heard as the birds shoot about over our heads is a bright, clear, staccato *chip* or *tsik*—whichever suggests the sharper sound—often repeated in a series and sometimes running off into a rapid chatter. The chip note varies little, if at all, except for the quickness of the notes, and seems to punctuate the bird's ceaseless rush through the air. Sometimes, when the birds are very high in the air, the chattering call comes down to our ears, softened by distance—like sparks slowly falling to the earth after a rocket has burst.

Simple as these notes are, the birds introduce a good deal of variety into them by modifying the interval between them, thereby changing the expression of their lively theme.

One modification, which I have mentioned under "Courtship," having heard it only in the breeding season and only when the birds were under stress of excitement, serves to illustrate this ability and may be regarded as representing the song of the swift. It is made up of a long series of notes in which the birds, after giving several isolated chips, change abruptly to a series of very rapid notes, a sort of chatter, then, with no pause between, change back to the chips, then back again—chips–chatter–chips, and so on. We may term it the "chips and chatter call."

Another modification of the chip note, often heard in summer when the birds are in a comparatively quiet mood, is a long chatter in which the volume increases and lessens, suggesting the sounding of a minute watchman's rattle.

There is one note quite different in quality from the above notes and less frequently heard than any of the variations of the chip. This is a musical monosyllable—sometimes divided into two syllables—a squeal, almost a high whistle with a slight upward inflection, like *eeip*, sometimes repeated once or twice. I have heard it both in spring and fall; hence it cannot be, as I once thought it was, a note of immature birds.

Field marks.—The swift may be distinguished readily from any of the swallows by the shape of its wings and the manner in which it moves them. Swallows' wings are roughly triangular, the triangle seeming to join the bird's body by a fairly wide base, whereas the swift's wings are narrow at the base—they are pointed, and slightly curved like the terminal part of a sickle's blade—and appear to be set on well forward.

The stroke of the swift's wing gives a jerky, hurried effect compared with the more leisurely movement of a swallow, and the tips of the wings are not swept backward, even when the birds are sailing, as they are, in varying degree, in the flight of all the swallows.

The swift has been likened to a winged cigar, tapered at both ends, flying through the air. The resemblance is very close, except when the bird fans out its stumpy tail, as it does from time to time.

The nearly uniform dull color of the swift's under parts and its very short, square tail, combined with its characteristic flight, serve to identify the bird even at a considerable distance.

Enemies.—Because the swift spends a large part of its life moving rapidly through the air, almost never coming to rest except at its nest or when roosting in a chimney or a hollow tree, it is practically out of reach of any mammal that otherwise might prey upon it. And while flying its speed and its erratic course render it almost immune from attack by hawks.

In his notes T. E. Musselman cites an exception to this immunity. He says: "I was watching a flock of about 1,500 swifts circling about a chimney in Quincy, Ill., forming an avian funnel which was dropping into its black depths. It was almost dusk when a sharp-shinned hawk flew from a neighboring sycamore tree to the top of the chimney and seized one of the swifts as it was poised with upturned wings and was just about to drop into its night's sanctuary. The swift squealed as it was being carried away, so I was able to follow the course of the tiny hawk as it flew through the semidarkness back to the tree."

Musselman (1931) also reports an occasion when swifts were overcome by gas while roosting in the chimney of a church in Quincy, Ill. He says: "One cold October night it was necessary to turn on the fire, which resulted in the killing of between 3000 and 5000 Chimney Swifts that had harbored there. Three bushel baskets of dead birds were taken from the flue."

Julian Burroughs (1922) tells of an instance in which a large number of swifts, taking refuge in a chimney, dislodged the soot. Many were smothered in the chimney, while others, several hundred, evidently confused by the soot, continued down into the house where they were found "on all the mouldings and pictures." These were released apparently unharmed. "There were about fifty live ones and fifty dead in the furnace—also ten water-pails full of dead ones in the pipes and bottom of chimney."

The greatest hazard of the swift's life, perhaps, comes in the spring or early summer when, once in a dozen years or so, a prolonged, drenching downpour of rain clears the air of insects, and threatens the local birds with starvation. Brewster (1906), referring to such a storm, says: "The Swifts * * * were seriously reduced in numbers, throughout eastern Massachusetts, during the cold, rainy weather of June, 1903, and the losses which they suffered that season have not as yet been made good." Since 1903 the birds here in New England have been decimated by several minor storms but have quickly recovered their loss.

Fall.—Fall comes early in the yearly cycle of the swift's life. At the end of the summer there is a long journey before the birds, old and young, to the warm air of the Tropics where they can find food throughout the winter months.

Late in July and early in August we often see small groups of swifts in the air, evidently preparing for migration. These flocks are doubtless made up of our local birds, those that have spent the summer in our vicinity, and they are accompanied, presumably, by as many of their young as are on the wing. They travel such long distances through the air, often curving round and round a chimney or church tower, that they derive a good deal of exercise from the flights—exercise that must serve to strengthen the wings of the young birds.

Under date of August 7, 1917, my notes mention this habit. "In these exercising flights, as I take them to be, the birds fly mostly in long curves; they are really circling, although they may turn at any time to either side. The birds, a dozen or more of them, are sailing in a great ring; they suggest bits of wood floating in an eddy of a slow-moving stream. They are far from one another, flying silently, mainly on set wings. One veers toward another, which quickens its pace by rapid, flickering wing beats. A chase is on. One or more birds join in, giving the long chatter. Now they hurry through the air, close together. When one comes near another, it may raise its wings in a V above its back, soaring for a moment. The chases are soon over, however; the birds seem to lose interest in speed and resume their circular, soaring flight. They often turn out from the circle, tilting to one side, the outer wing uppermost.

"During the middle of the day I do not see the swifts gathered about the house; it is chiefly in the morning and evening that they are most active. This evening two birds, close together, flew slowly over my head at a low elevation. One gave the long chatter and chips alternately, but in a quiet way with little staccato quality."

It is at about this time, the first two weeks of August, that we see evidence of molting in our local swifts. As they fly overhead we notice a narrow gap in their wings where a flight feather or two is missing, and in every case the little gap in one wing corresponds almost exactly with the gap in the other, but this slight bilateral loss of wing surface seems to hinder the birds' flight little, if at all. Apparently molting does not cripple them, as it does many woodland birds; indeed, the swift, spending the hours of daylight in the sky, must not be disabled for even a single day.

The most spectacular event in the swift's life, from our point of view, occurs during the autumnal migration when the birds, late in the afternoon, congregate in a large, wheel-shaped flock and circle about the chimney they have selected as their roosting place for the night. The following quotations describe in detail such gatherings.

Townsend (1912), writing of the bird in the St. John Valley, New Brunswick, says:

At Fredericton, on July 25, I watched a large flock of Swifts enter for the night a chimney on the southwest corner of the Parliament Building. Sun set at about 8 P. M. At 8.24 P. M. one bird set its wings and dropped into the chimney and soon they began dropping in fast, while the flock circled first one way then another or crowded together in a confused mass, twittering loudly all the time. Owing to the proximity of the dome regular circling was somewhat interfered with, but as a rule the birds circled in the direction of the hands of a clock, and individuals would drop out and into the chimney in dozens when the circle passed over it. Occasionally they would all swoop off to the other side of the building, soon to return. At 8.45 P. M. practically all the birds had entered the chimney and I had counted roughly,—at first singly and later by tens,—2200 birds.

The setting of the wings, which Dr. Townsend speaks of, takes place just over the mouth of the chimney. The bird raises its wings above its back and drops into the chimney or very often shies off, like a horse refusing to take a fence and, after making another circuit, tries again.

Linton (1924) gives us a vivid picture of the Swifts "at bedtime," showing a spirit of play among the birds. He writes from Augusta, Ga.:

October 5, 6.5 P. M.: Sky overcast; large numbers of Swifts in the upper air; look like swarm of bees; general direction of flight in circle, counter-clockwise. 6.7: A few began to enter the chimney, when a passing auto frightened them for a short time. 6.8: Entering again, average probably not far from 15 per second, at times many more than this [the flue of this chimney was said to be 3 feet square]; circling continuously counter-clockwise. As the circle approaches the chimney, a column of Swifts, from a point 20 feet above the level of the top of the chimney descends to the chimney. The Swifts in this column which fail to enter continue the circle at a lower level, joining the higher level at the opposite side of the circle, and in a position which makes them contributing parts of the descending column, when they again come to that point. Great swarms of Swifts could be seen in the upper air, their paths apparently crossing and recrossing, but really all flying in circular paths at different levels. Many appeared as minute specks in the upper air. At 6.23 all were in, stopping abruptly; probably no more than a dozen stragglers in the last 5 seconds. It thus took the flock a little over 15 minutes to enter the chimney.

October 8, 6.12 P. M.: Sky clear; 3 or 4 Swifts seen from window. 6.13: 12 or more Swifts in sight. 6.15: 100, more or less, in sight. 6.15:20: 500, more or less, in sight. 6.16: Increasing in numbers rapidly; general course in wide circles, counter-clockwise. 6.17: Seem to be enjoying themselves too much to go to bed; immense numbers; upper air full of them. 6.19:20: Getting closer to chimney; some of them dipping down to within a foot or two of the top. 6.20: Changed their minds for a few seconds; again enjoying themselves in the air.

6.21: Getting closer again. 6.21:30: Changed minds again. 6.22:30: Look as if they were getting ready to go to bed. 6.23: Getting closer; circles variable, 150 to 200 feet in diameter nearest level of top of chimney, lower portion, at times, possibly no more than 50 feet in diameter. 6.23:30: Passing near top of chimney. 6.24: Passing very close to top of chimney. 6.24:30: A few going in. 6.24:40: Entering at rate of 15 or more per second. Same maneuvers as on previous evenings. 6.25:30: Going in very rapidly; 15 per second a very conservative estimate. 6.28: A second or two when they did not go in so rapidly, being disturbed by the puffing of a locomotive on the Georgia Railroad near by. 6.28:30: Going in as rapidly as ever. 6.30: All in; stopped suddenly.

Audubon (1840) gives an interesting account of a large number of swifts he found roosting in a hollow tree in Louisville, Ky. He says:

I found it to be a sycamore, nearly destitute of branches, sixty or seventy feet high, between seven and eight feet in diameter at the base, and about five for the distance of forty feet up, where the stump of a broken hollowed branch, about two feet in diameter, made out from the main stem. * * * Next morning I rose early enough to reach the place long before the least appearance of daylight, and placed my head against the tree. All was silent within. I remained in that posture probably twenty minutes, when suddenly I thought the great tree was giving way, and coming down upon me. Instinctively I sprung from it, but when I looked up to it again, what was my astonishment to see it standing as firm as ever. The Swallows were now pouring out in a black continued stream. I ran back to my post, and listened in amazement to the noise within, which I could compare to nothing else than the sound of a large wheel revolving under a powerful stream. It was yet dusky, so I could hardly see the hour on my watch, but I estimated the time which they took in getting out at more than thirty minutes. * * *

The next day I hired a man, who cut a hole at the base of the tree. * * * Knowing by experience that if the birds should notice the hole below, they would abandon the tree, I had it carefully closed. The Swallows came as usual that night, and I did not disturb them for several days. At last, provided with a dark lantern, I went with my companion about nine in the evening, determined to have a full view of the interior of the tree. The hole was opened with caution. I scrambled up the sides of the mass of exuviae, and my friend followed. All was perfectly silent. Slowly and gradually I brought the light of the lantern to bear on the sides of the hole above us, when we saw the Swallows clinging side by side, covering the whole surface of the excavation. In no instance did I see one above another. Satisfied with the sight, I closed the lantern. We then caught and killed with as much care as possible more than a hundred, stowing them away in our pockets and bosoms, and slid down into the open air. We observed that, while on this visit, not a bird had dropped its dung upon us. Closing the entrance, we marched towards Louisville perfectly elated. On examining the birds which we had procured, a hundred and fifteen in number, we found only six females. Eighty-seven were adult males; of the remaining twenty-two the sex could not be ascertained, and I had no doubt that they were the young of that year's first brood, the flesh and quill-feathers being tender and soft.

Audubon estimates that the number of birds "that roosted in this single tree was 9,000." This investigation took place "in the month of July." He visited the tree again on August 2, after the local young birds "had left their native recesses." Of this visit he says: "I concluded that the numbers resorting to it had not increased; but I found many more females and young than males, among upwards of fifty, which were caught and opened."

Musselman (1926), writing of swifts overtaken by wintry conditions with snow in Quincy, Ill., says: "I discovered that on days when the thermometer indicated an approach to the freezing point the birds remained in the chimneys until about nine o'clock in the morning. During the daytime the birds quickly returned from their feeding over the river, circled but a time or two, and dropped into the chimney until warm. * * *

"The most popular chimneys were those which connected below with the basement, and served, therefore, as warm air flues. In such chimneys the temperature reached 70°. Little wonder that the birds preferred these chimneys on damp and cold nights!"

The two following quotations describe very unusual departures from the swift's regular habit of roosting.

Latham (1920), writing from Orient, Long Island, N. Y., states:

About one P. M. August 17. 1919, while collecting insects near the eastern border of a broad brackish meadow, my attention was attracted to Chimney Swifts (*Chaetura pelagica*) frequently flying slowly in from the west and disappearing in the fringe of vines and shrubs that separated me from the extreme east boundary of the marsh. In this heavy growth, from waist to head high, were elderberry bushes (*Sambucus canadensis*) heavily hung with ripe fruit. I selected a bird for special study. It advanced on descending, hovering flight. About four feet above the tangle, near the farther side, it paused and dropped abruptly into a clump of elderberries. Carefully marking the locality, I worked my passage to a few feet of the spot. The swift was clinging to the cymoid head of the elder eating the fruit. The ease with which the bird took flight from its slender perch, rising directly upward several feet above the cover and dropping rail-like back into it, was interesting and worthy of note.

The cover harbored at the time not less than fifty swifts. Most of them were flushed with more or less difficulty, but some individuals took wing within arm-reach of the observer. No others were noted eating fruit. * * *

It is evident that the birds had established a roosting, or resting place out of the ordinary. It is not satisfactorily settled whether the birds sought the brush to feed on elder-berries or for shelter. The writer is of the opinion that the bird seen eating berries was only an exceptional case where the bird took a berry after alighting within reach of it.

E. K. and D. Campbell (1926) report from Cold Spring, N. Y., an astonishing roosting place for swifts, *the bark of an oak tree*. They state:

At 2.30 P. M. September 5, 1926, we observed an excited flock circling between the house-front and the adjacent oak trees, and above the house-top and back. Their flight seemed to focus at a point 25 feet up on the trunk of a tall oak. The day was dull and we judged there was some sort of food there. Really, however, they were gradually alighting on the bark, as we discovered at 4.30 P. M., when most of the flock was found to have grouped itself in close formation, as shown in the rough sketch. * * *

The birds seemed two or three deep, and several of us estimated well over a hundred of them. They were snuggled together, seemingly to keep warm, and the heads all concealed beneath the wings of those above. This patch of birds was of irregular shape, nearly 5 feet high and 7 to 8 inches wide at the widest part. It was constantly changing, as some birds seemed to lose their grip and fly off and return, so that a dozen or two were on the wing and seeking a place to work into the group. We saw some alight at the edge and work up close, while others lit in the middle of the group and must have reached through with claws to grasp bird or bark, those failing falling back and taking wing. All had their heads concealed but the few upper ones. Toward dusk the birds, matching the moist bark, were invisible, but we examined them again by flashlight after dark, and all was quiet.

Next morning, to our surprise, they were still there, in broad daylight, and some remained through to the afternoon.

Cottam (1932) describes in detail some remarkable gatherings of swifts "at night circling the great dome of our national capitol, feeding on the small insects attracted there by the powerful flood lights." He observed the birds on many evenings, both in spring and fall, once in a flock of "approximately 2,000," circling "the dome—the area of greatest light concentration—where they remained until the lights were turned off shortly after midnight." Of the bird's evolutions, he says:

On the nights when flocking occurred at the capitol, the birds began to arrive in small groups from all directions about sundown, and by the time they normally would have been going to roost they had formed into one great swarm. For the first fifteen or twenty minutes after sundown the birds foraged over the tree tops and flew in all directions without any apparent system to their movements, except that they remained in a rather restricted area. Gradually, as it grew darker, a greater number were seen to fly more or less in the same general circular direction; in other words, there was a distinct impression of group movement. About the time the lights came on or shortly thereafter, all were following a definite course. Each time flocks of incoming birds disrupted the rhythm and unison of the concentric flight there was a momentary disbanding. When they reformed, however, all seemed instinctively to fly in the same direction. Most often the flight was uniformly circular, but occasionally it took the form of a conical cloud somewhat resembling a cyclone funnel. On one occasion it was seen to form a great figure "8" with one loop at a lower elevation than the other.

Frederic H. Kennard (MS.) makes this note of an unusual roosting place at Duck, Maine: "In the evening [August 8, 1924] I was treated to a performance of flocking, roosting chimney swifts, which at sundown flocked up and, flying in circles about one end of the smaller of Charlie Boyce's barns, gradually dribbled into a little window up under the ridgepole of the gable end and there clinging by the hundreds in an almost solid sheet against the gable end of the barn. We climbed up into the hayloft and flashed a light onto them, and they gradually flew out until only perhaps 75 to 100 were left. There must have been 500 or 600 in all, though, of course, difficult to estimate."

Winter.—In 1886 all that was known of the chimney swift in winter was that it passed south of the United States (A. O. U. Check-list of North American Birds, ed. 1, 1886). The third edition, published in 1910, adds that the bird winters "at least to Vera Cruz and Cozumel Island [Yucatan] and probably in Central America." The fourth edition, 1931, extends the probable winter range to Amazonia.

Chapman (1931) cites two specimens of the chimney swift, taken late in autumn in West Panama at a time when many South American bound migrants were passing through this region. He says:

If we may assume that they [the chimney swifts] winter in a forested, rather than an arid region it is not improbable that they were bound for Amazonia, where the presence as permanent residents of five species of *Chaetura* shows that the region offers a favorable habitat for birds of this genus. From at least two of the Brazilian species, *pelagica* could not certainly be distinguished in the air. Sight identification, therefore, is out of the question, and until a specimen is secured we shall not know where the Chimney Swift winters. But, as every collector of birds in tropical America knows, to see a Swift is one thing, to get it quite another. Native collectors are not willing to expend the ammunition required to capture Swifts, and even visiting naturalists secure comparatively few. With our attention directed toward Amazonia as the possible winter quarters of the North American species it may be long, therefore, before our theory is confirmed by specimens.

DISTRIBUTION

Range.—Temperate North America east of the Rocky Mountains, wintering probably in northeastern South America.

Breeding range.—The breeding range of the chimney swift extends **north** to probably southeastern Saskatchewan (Indian Head); southern Manitoba (probably Carberry, Portage la Prairie, Winnipeg, and Indian Bay); southern Ontario (Goulais Bay, Sault Ste. Marie, Algonquin Park, Kirks Ferry, and Ottawa); and southern Quebec (Montreal, Quebec City, probably rarely Godbout, and Grande Greve). From this northeastern point the range extends southward along the coast of the Maritime Provinces of Canada and the United States to Florida (St. Augustine, Daytona Beach, and Orlando). **South** to Florida (Orlando, Tarpon Springs, St. Marks, Chipley, and Pensacola); southern Mississippi (Biloxi); southern Louisiana (New Orleans, Thibodaux, and New Iberia); and southeastern Texas (Houston). **West** to eastern Texas (Houston, Troup, and Commerce); Oklahoma (Norman, Oklahoma City, Tulsa, and Copan); eastern Kansas (Wichita, Topeka, and Onaga); Nebraska (Neligh and Cody); eastern South Dakota (Sioux Falls, Dell Rapids, and Fort Sisseton); central North Dakota (Bismarck and Devils Lake); and probably southeastern Saskatchewan (Indian Head).

Winter range.—Unknown, but probably over the dense rain forest of the Amazon Valley, in Brazil. During the winter of 1937–38, however, two of these birds remained on the campus of the Louisiana State University, at Baton Rouge.

Spring migration.—Early dates of spring arrival are: Florida— Pensacola, March 24; Orlando, March 30. Alabama—Autaugaville, March 28. Georgia—Savannah, March 19; Atlanta, April 4. South Carolina—Charleston, March 18; Columbia, March 26. North Carolina—April 4; Hendersonville, April 5. Virginia—New Market, April 7. District of Columbia—Washington, April 5. Maryland— Cambridge, April 15. West Virginia—White Sulphur Springs, April 20. Pennsylvania—Philadelphia, April 2; Beaver, April 14. New Jersey—Morristown, April 18; Vineland, April 22. New York— Geneva, April 19; New York City, April 20; Syracuse, April 23. Connecticut—Jewett City, April 19; Hartford, April 23. Massachusetts—Boston, April 21; Northampton, April 23. Vermont—Rutland, April 18; Wells River, April 26. New Hampshire—Hanover, April 20; Tilton, April 24. Maine—Portland, May 1; Phillips, May 3. Nova Scotia—Wolfville, May 4; Pictou, May 10. New Brunswick— Chatham, April 29; St. John, May 8. Prince Edward Island—North River, May 19. Quebec—Quebec City, April 25; Montreal, April 27. Louisiana—New Orleans, March 13. Mississippi—Biloxi, March 23. Arkansas—Monticello, March 17; Helena, March 21. Tennessee— Athens, March 29; Knoxville, April 10. Kentucky—Lexington, April 2. Missouri—Concordia, April 2; St. Louis, April 4. Illinois—Odin, April 8; Chicago, April 10. Indiana—Richmond, April 1; Fort Wayne, April 5. Ohio—Columbus, April 7; Youngstown, April 8. Michigan—Ann Arbor, April 9, Sault Ste. Marie, April 20. Ontario London, April 16; Ottawa, April 22. Iowa—Keokuk, April 7; Iowa City, April 17. Wisconsin—La Crosse, April 15; Madison, April 21. Minnesota—Minneapolis, April 26. Texas—Houston, March 24; Bonham, April 2. Kansas—Ottawa, April 3; Manhattan, April 10. Nebraska—Omaha, April 27. South Dakota—Vermillion, April 24. North Dakota—Fargo, May 6; Grafton, May 8. Manitoba—Pilot Mound, May 14.

A swift banded at Charlottesville, Va., on May 2 was found dead on May 19 at Cape May, N. J.; while two birds taken in eastern Massachusetts in May and July had been banded the preceding October at Tuskegee, Ala., and Hattiesburg, Miss., respectively.

Fall migration.—Late dates of fall departure are: Manitoba—Winnipeg, August 27. North Dakota—Grafton, September 5. South Dakota—Sioux Falls, September 11; Yankton, September 26. Nebraska—Dunbar, September 28; Omaha, October 15. Kansas—Lawrence, October 11; Ottawa, October 12. Texas—Bonham, October 20. Minnesota—Lanesboro, September 18. Wisconsin—Madison, October 12. Iowa—Keokuk, October 18. Ontario—Toronto, September 30; Ottawa, October 3. Michigan—Detroit, October 2. Ohio—Youngstown, October 17; Oberlin, October 23. Indiana—Fort Wayne, October 21; Richmond, November 13. Illinois—Chicago, October 6; Rantoul, October 11. Missouri—Concordia, October 11; St. Louis, October 19. Kentucky—Eubank, October 9; Lexington, October 19. Tennessee—Knoxville, October 23; Athens, October 29. Arkansas—Helena, October 19. Mississippi—Biloxi, October 20. Louisiana—New Orleans, November 4. Quebec—Montreal, September 10; Quebec City, September 30. Prince Edward Island—North River, September 11. New Brunswick—Scotch Lake, September 11; St. John, September 18. Nova Scotia—Wolfville, September 15; Sable Island, September 30. Maine—Phillips, September 11; Orono, September 17. New Hampshire—Tilton, September 10. Vermont—St. Johnsbury, September 1. Massachusetts—Boston, September 20; Harvard, September 28. Rhode Island—Providence, October 9. Connecticut—Hartford, October 19. New York—Ballston Spa, October 9; New York City, October 11. New Jersey—Morristown, October 17; Pennsylvania—Beaver, October 8; Philadelphia, October 29. District of Columbia—Washington, October 25. Maryland—Hagerstown, October 16. Virginia—Naruna, October 11; Newport News, October 14. North Carolina—Raleigh, October 4; Hendersonville, October 11. South Carolina—Columbia, October 28; Charleston, November 5. Georgia—Atlanta, October 12; Savannah, October 26. Alabama—Autaugaville, October 27. Florida—Orlando, October 23; Pensacola, November 2.

Further insight into the fall migration of the chimney swift is provided by the consideration of a few of the several hundred banding records that have been accumulated. One banded at Lexington, Mo., on September 23 was recaptured at Baton Rouge, La., on September 27; one banded at Newark, Ohio, on September 20 was retaken at Nashville, Tenn., on September 27; while a third, banded on August 23 at Kents Island, New Brunswick, was retrapped at Opelika, Ala., on September 20. A swift banded at 5:30 a. m. on September 22 at Glasgow, Ky., was taken that same evening in a chimney at Nashville, Tenn., 90 miles from the point of banding. Another record, which seems to indicate the direction of the movement along the Gulf coast, is of a bird banded at Sanford, Fla., on August 9 and found with a broken wing near Tallulah, La., on September 25.

Casual records.—Some of the following records in Latin America probably indicate the migration route of this species, but lack of intermediate data makes it appear desirable to list them under this heading.

Panama: Two specimens were obtained on the Caribbean coast near the Colombian border on April 24 and 25, 1934; a specimen was taken at Bocas del Toro on October 28, 1927; another was taken at Almirante Bay, on October 24, 1926; while Dr. Frank M. Chapman saw a flock of about 40 at sea, some 10 miles north of the mainland near Porto Bello, on April 18, 1937. Costa Rica: About 30 were seen and a specimen was obtained at Villa Quesada on October 24, 1933. Nicaragua: Two specimens were taken at Eden on April 1, 1922. Guatemala: There is said to be a specimen in the British Museum (Natural History) taken in this country, but details are lacking. British Honduras: A specimen was taken (accidentally destroyed) in March 1905. Mexico: A specimen was obtained at Presidio, Veracruz, on May 6, 1925, while another was obtained on April 4, 1902, at Pueblo Viejo in this State, the collector reporting that swifts were crossing the lagoon all day, headed north; one was obtained at Rio Givicia, Oaxaca, on March 21, 1906; one was taken in Nuevo Leon on April 24, 1911; and the species also is believed to have been taken on Cozumel Island, Quintana Roo. Haiti: Several were seen over Port-au-Prince on April 19, 1917; a specimen was taken at Tortue Island, on May 18, 1917; a flock of 40–50 was seen over Morne La Selle on April 15, 1927; it was noted at Hinche on April 23, 1927; and several were observed at Belladere, on April 30, 1927. Dominican Republic: Several were seen at Comendador on May 1, 1927.

A specimen was taken on September 13, 1849, in Bermuda; several others were seen in the same locality on the 24th of that month; and one was collected there in September 1874. There seems to be no authenticated record for Newfoundland, but one was taken at Sukkertoppen, Greenland, in 1863. One was collected at Anticosti Island on June 9, 1901; in western North Dakota two were seen at Sanish on July 27, 1918, and a pair were noted at Charlson during the summer of 1923; four were seen at Miles City, Mont., on May 20, 1917, and two specimens were collected in Custer County on July 17, and 27, 1919; a specimen was found dead at Indian Head, Saskatchewan, on October 11, 1905, and they were seen in that locality on September 2, 1897; two were noted at Edmonton, Alberta, on May 17, 1897; and in New Mexico a specimen was taken at Rinconada on March 1, 1904, and another on the Mimbres River on May 22, 1921.

Egg dates.—Illinois: 6 records, May 15 to July 3.
New York: 17 records, May 27 to July 5; 9 records, June 8 to 20, indicating the height of the season.
Quebec: 5 records, June 14 to July 3.
Virginia: 11 records, May 27 to July 13.

CHAETURA VAUXI (Townsend)

VAUX'S SWIFT

HABITS

This, the smallest of the North American swifts, replaces in the northwestern part of our continent the common chimney swift of the eastern States. It breeds from southeastern Alaska and central British Columbia southward to the Santa Cruz Mountains of California and eastward to Montana and Nevada; but it is rare east of the Cascades and the Sierra Nevada.

Throughout most of its range it is much less numerous than the chimney swift is in the East. Most observers speak of it as rare during the breeding season, but S. F. Rathbun tells me that in the vicinity of Seattle, Wash., "the little Vaux's swift is more or less a common bird. It arrives late in April and, though widely distributed, is more apt to be seen in the river valleys, somewhat open, in which are tall, dead trees; and quite likely one reason for this is that among such trees are some that are hollow and will afford nesting places for the birds."

Spring.—While migrating, or when preparing to migrate, this little swift often gathers into immense flocks. The following observation by H. H. Sheldon (1922b), made at Santa Barbara, Calif., illustrates this point: "On April 29, 1922, about 7 P. M., the largest flock of Vaux Swift (*Chaetura vauxi*) I have ever seen or, in fact, heard of, circled over my house several times. By careful estimate I judged the number to be very nearly six hundred individuals. My observations of the Vaux Swift have heretofore been made only within its breeding range; while this is my first observation of a migrating flock, such an immense gathering of this rather rare wilderness dweller is no doubt a most unusual occurrence."

Courtship.—Mr. Rathbun writes to me: "This swift does not appear to be mated when it comes, but after a short time some change is noted in its actions. As they fly about, suddenly with a shrill twitter one of the swifts makes a dash or a dive at another, and away both rush, each striving to out-fly or out-dodge the other, the chase brought to an end only when one escapes, or, as often is the case, both fly off in company. As it appears to be quite playful, these actions may be partly in sport, though at this particular time some must have an earnest intent, for the courtship of this little swift evidently takes place upon the wing."

Nesting.—He says in his notes: "It begins to nest quite soon after it has mated. Its nest is built inside a hollow tree, as in this respect the bird chiefly follows the ancient habit of its kind. But with the arrival of man changes have taken place in some of the primitive sections where this swift is found, and it seems to have begun to adapt itself to these, for on occasions it is known to build a nest in some disused chimney, a practice of its eastern relative, the chimney swift, which so commonly uses a like place in which to nest.

"The nest of Vaux's swift is a small, rather saucer-shaped affair. It is attached to the inner wall of a hollow tree, or on rare occasions in a chimney, and usually some distance from the top. It is made of small pieces of twigs stuck together with a gluey saliva of the bird, the twigs broken off from the tips of dead limbs of trees by the swift as in flight it passes the branches. It does not seem to be quickly made, as shown by an instance when we found a pair of these birds nesting in a chimney. A few years ago, on a day in early June, we went to a little schoolhouse near the Snoqualmie River in the foothills of the Cascade Mountains, to find out whether the chimney of the building was in use as a nesting place by Vaux's swift. This was about 40 miles east of Seattle. When we reached the spot no swifts were to be seen, but after a wait of a half hour or so a pair of the swifts appeared and flew in circles about the chimney. Without warning one of the birds dived into it so quickly the eye could scarcely follow it. After a brief stay within the swift came out of the chimney and was joined by its mate, and for a short time both flew around in the vicinity, then ascended very high to mingle with some swallows. Nearly an hour elapsed before one of the swifts returned. It circled the chimney several times, then dropped into it so quickly as to resemble a dark streak. This time it remained in the chimney at least ten minutes. After another long wait both of the swifts returned, one entered the chimney, and several minutes elapsed before it came out. From these actions we assumed that the one that went into the chimney was making a nest, and invariably each time it flew out it gave a sharp twitter. For some time thereafter we stayed in this locality, but although a number of these swifts were seen none entered the chimney.

"Eleven days later we once more visited the schoolhouse. It was about 10 o'clock in the morning when we reached the place, but no swifts were in the locality. After a short time a pair of the birds arrived, both circled the top of the chimney six times, and then one entered by a straight-down dive. The other, which had remained outside, flew away but returned five minutes later and twittered. Immediately the swift in the chimney came out, and in company both left the vicinity. Forty-five minutes elapsed before the pair came back. With rapid twittering notes they swiftly circled the chimney a number of times, then flew from sight. We went on the roof of the building and looked down the mouth of the chimney but could see no sign of any nest. Next we entered the schoolhouse and, as the large stovepipe hole in the side of the chimney was high above the floor, we stood upon a table, stuck our head through the hole, and carefully looked at the inside of the chimney. A good sight of its upper part was had because of the light, but its lower part was dim, and no nest could be seen. Then we went to the lower part of the building into which the chimney extended to the ground, and by the removal of a few loose bricks from one of its sides we had a good view of the lower part of the inside of the chimney. Here we found the nest. It was about 5 feet from the bottom of the chimney and firmly attached to the wall in the angle of the southeast corner, which might give some protection from the rain, as usually this comes with a wind from some point south. The nest was a small, slightly shallow structure, compact and well made, but it contained no eggs. We left the locality soon after but returned later in the day, and during our brief stay one of the swifts came back and went into the chimney.

"A few days later we again went to the schoolhouse to see if any eggs were in the swift's nest. In this we were disappointed, for since our preceding visit the building had become occupied by a family who, of course, made use of the chimney for its ordinary purposes; for, while we were there, smoke issued from it, and evidently the swifts had deserted their nest as it still lacked eggs. We remained some long time in the vicinity of the schoolhouse, but no signs of any swifts were seen at all."

D. E. Brown writes to me that "on July 8, 1924, a nest was found in an old chimney near Seattle that contained young birds. I could not tell whether there were four or five young birds. On June 30, 1925, a nest with four eggs was found in an unused chimney of a fireplace in Seattle. The nest was 6 feet from the bottom of the fireplace, and the female bird was on the nest. The eggs were slightly incubated at this date."

Although there are other records of nesting in chimneys, the great majority of Vaux's swifts apparently still cling to the ancestral habit of nesting in hollow trees. The trees chosen are usually tall, dead stubs, frequently charred by forest fires and often hollow nearly or quite down to the ground level, and the nest is generally well down from the top, or even near the ground level. W. L. Dawson (1923) says: "Almost invariably the birds nest within twenty inches or such a matter of the bottom of the cavity, no matter how elevated the orifice. * * * The Vaux Swift also nests, according to Mr. C. Irvin Clay, of Eureka, in the stumps of logged-off redwood lands. The birds enter by weather fissures, and since the stumps are almost always undermined by fire, it sometimes happens that the nest is found beneath the level of the ground."

There are four nests of this swift in the Thayer collection in Cambridge, all from Eureka, Calif. One nest is made of pine needles, glued together, and was fastened to the inner wall of a hollow stub and only 2 feet above the ground level. Another was made of spruce twigs and needles and was placed in a burnt redwood stub, 20 feet high; the nest was 12 feet down from the top on the inside. Three of these nests are very small and narrow, so that the eggs had to be laid in two parallel rows; and the bird must have incubated lengthwise of the nest, for two of the nests held six eggs each, one five and one four. One larger, well-made nest was constructed of spruce and fir twigs and was profusely lined with spruce and fir needles, smoothly laid; this nest was 3 feet from the ground inside a hollow redwood stub 18 feet high. The other nest was taken from a redwood stub 60 feet high and about 10 feet in diameter at the base; it was burned black on the outside, but the inside was smooth and unburned; a V-shaped break on one side afforded an entrance to the hollow 20 feet below the top of the stub; the cavity below this opening was 14 feet deep, and the nest was placed only 8 inches from the bottom of the cavity.

Some unusual nesting sites have been reported. Charles A. Allen (1880), of Nicasio, Calif., writes: "They are to be found only on the highest hills or mountains, where there are plenty of pines. In these trees they construct their nests, which they build in old holes excavated by the California Woodpecker. They invariably select old, decayed trees, and build at great heights, so that it is impossible to get their eggs." As Mr. Allen evidently did not actually see a nest in such a situation, his statement is subject to confirmation and is offered here only as a suggestion.

J. A. Munro (1918) says: "Mr. T. L. Thacker sent me a nestling in the flesh, from Yale, B. C. It had fallen from a nest that was built under the roof of the C. P. R. water tank. There are a number of small openings under the eaves, and Mr. Thacker tells me that several pairs breed there every year."

William L. Finley (1924) tells of a still more remarkable nesting site: "At Wiedemann Brothers' nursery, is an engine house with a metal smokestack sixty feet tall and thirty inches in diameter. The lower end of the flue broadens out and opens into the front of the boiler. A pair of Vaux Swifts dropped down the metal flue sixty-two feet and built their nest on the front of this metal boiler. * * *

"Mr. Wiedemann did not find the nest until he heard squeakings in the boiler and thought some bats had taken possession. Opening the metal doors of the boiler, there he saw the parent Vaux Swift with her four young birds. He saw her go and come and even caught her, but she did not object, for when she flew out of the door she was soon back through the top of the stack with more food."

Eggs.—Vaux's swift lays three to six eggs; four, five, and six seem to be the commonest numbers. The eggs are usually elliptical-ovate or elongate-ovate, rarely ovate. They are pure dead white, without gloss, or sometimes faintly creamy white in color. The measurements of 51 eggs average 18.5 by 12.4 millimeters; the eggs showing the four extremes measure 19.8 by 12.2, 18.5 by 13.5, 16.8 by 12.0, and 18.8 by 11.8 millimeters.

Young.—Mr. Finley (1924) watched the feeding of the young swifts in the nest described above, of which he writes:

I stood outside at twelve o'clock, noon, and saw one of the parent Swifts come flitting along just above the chimney top, suddenly swerve and drop in. He, or she, whichever it was, was feeding every fifteen or twenty minutes. I went below and with the aid of an electric light, I could see the bird feed her young. Sometimes she would light on one side of the nest and sometimes on the other, to feed. Once I saw her clutch the edge of the nest and brace herself with her tail underneath, and she jabbed her bill in the mouth of a young bird and fed by regurgitation. As she started up the long climb, she quivered her wings, hooked her sharp toes in the sooty side of the stack and walked right up as if she were going up a ladder.

William B. Davis (1937) made some observations on a nest located in a brick chimney, and about 12 inches below the roof of the building, in Bellingham, Wash.; on August 2, between 9:37 and 11:15 a. m., the parent, or parents, made eight trips to the nest to feed the young. He writes:

When I first looked into the chimney, I was greeted by the clamor of the young. Their calls consisted of series of rasping notes uttered in rapid succession. The young were perched on the edge of the nest, each with its posterior end projecting over the edge and with its head directed toward the corner of the chimney. Below the nest the chimney was streaked with excrement, a circumstance which indicated the young were not defecating in the nest. This probably explains the clean condition in which Edson found the empty nest when it was collected two days later. No evidence was obtained that the parent bird removed the fecal sacks of the young, although one can infer that it probably did when the young were smaller and unable to perch on the edge of the nest. Each time the parent returned from a trip afield, the young became vociferous, their calls lasting until the old bird left. By listening for the calls of the young, one could mark the coming and going of the adult.

After the parent had returned from its sixth trip, I moved close to the chimney and witnessed the feeding of the young. When first observed, the old bird was clinging to the chimney beside the nest, supported partly by the stiff tail feathers. The young were facing her (?), each with its mouth wide open clamoring for food and vying with its nest mates. I was led to wonder what relation existed between lustiness of voice and the chance of being fed at that particular visit. Later, after additional observations, I learned that proximity to the parent determined to a large extent which of the young was fed. At succeeding visits, the old bird alighted first at one side of the nest and then at the other, feeding the one, or ones, closest. The food, consisting of insects, largely leaf hoppers (as determined by gullet examination of the young), was placed far back in the open mouth of each young one. * * *

After the parent bird had fed one of the young, it caught sight of me and dropped to a lower level in the chimney where it alighted out of sight. I moved closer and placed my head directly over the opening to get a better view. As I did so, I heard the rapid beating of wings and, thinking the bird was coming out, I instinctively jerked my head to one side to avoid being hit. It did not appear, so I looked in a second time and again I heard wing beats. This time I kept my position, and after my eyes had become adjusted to the darkness, I observed its stunt several times. The bird would let go its hold on the wall, and, by rapidly beating its wings, suspend itself in the middle of the chimney and at the same time produce the br-r-r-r-ing sound. Apparently the sound was produced by the beating of the wings themselves, for I could not observe them touching the sides of the chimney. During these performances the young were quiet. I interpreted this behavior as a means employed to intimidate the intruder, much as does the hissing of the chickadee or the swooping dive of the Red-tailed Hawk.

Plumages.—As far as I can learn from the rather scanty material examined, the sequence of plumages and molts in Vaux's swift is about the same as in the closely related eastern chimney swift. The spiny quills of the nestling develop into a juvenal, or first winter, plumage that is much like that of the adult. The narrow whitish edgings on the scapulars of the young bird soon wear away; and adults will average paler on the throat and under parts.

I have seen adults molting the contour feathers and primaries in August, but the molt of the primaries must be very gradual in a bird that spends so much of its life on the wing. Mr. Rathbun tells me that this swift has a complete molt during summer.

Food.—Almost nothing has been published on the food of Vaux's swift, beyond the statement by Mr. Davis (1937) that the food fed to the young consisted of insects, largely leafhoppers. Probably its food consists wholly of small flying insects, such as mosquitoes, gnats, various flies, and perhaps small beetles. On dull, damp days much of its food is gathered at low levels, but on clear hot days, when the insects fly high, it ascends to great heights in pursuit. I can find no record of stomach contents.

Behavior.—Mr. Rathbun says in his notes that "Vaux's swift flies at all heights, at times just above the surface of the ground, and again it will be seen high against the sky. Its flight need not be mistaken for any swallow. It is fast, lacks a certain smoothness, and is apt to fly more directly, circle less; also, it has at times somewhat of a darting movement, erratic as it were, which brings to mind the actions of a bat. In fact, this bird is always in a hurry."

Ralph Hoffmann (1927) notes a marked difference in flight between this swift and the swallows: "A close observation of the tail shows that it never displays a forked tip; it either ends in a point like a cigar or is spread like a fan when the bird makes a sudden turn.

* * * The Swift takes a number of very rapid strokes, its wings fairly twinkling through the air, and then sails with the long narrow wings curved backward and slightly downward."

Vaux's swift shares with its eastern relative the social habit of roosting in chimneys in large numbers at certain seasons. Mr. Rathbun has described this very well in the following elaborate notes: "About the middle of August the actions of this swift show the time is near when it intends to leave the region for its winter home. Now the social trait of this bird is much in evidence. For late in each day the swifts begin to assemble in the vicinity of some hollow tree of size, or some good-sized chimney not in use, within which they aim to pass the night. We have watched this action on the part of the birds from its commencement to the close. In one case where a large, tall chimney was used, 25 days elapsed from the time when first they began to use it until the last of the swifts ceased to do so. The swifts began to resort to the chimney about the middle of August, and each evening thereafter for the next 10 days showed an increase in their number until at least 500 made use of it. Then for 16 days the number of birds steadily grew less until only three swifts entered the chimney to pass the night, and after this for several days no more were seen to use the place.

"The swifts began to come to the locality where the chimney stood an hour or two before sunset. Usually they flew about the chimney or quite close to it. From time to time there were arrivals, which mingled with those in flight, all forming a long and narrow flock of flying swifts that swept around the top of the chimney, their twittering so loud and ceaseless as to be heard some distance. At times a few would leave the flock and enter the chimney, but the constant arrival of others seemed to keep the flock entire. As they circled some made feints to enter, and this appeared to be a sign that soon an entrance would be made by all. Usually these actions lasted for more than half an hour, but ceased when the twilight reached a certain stage. For then the swifts would suddenly enter their retreat, and while this act was taking place, it bore a likeness to a long black rope one end of which dangled in the chimney's mouth.

"Each evening the performance was much the same, but sometimes an incident would be connected with it. Once when the swifts were racing, a pigeon hawk appeared and dashed at them. Instantly the birds scattered, with the hawk in chase of one it had singled from the flock, but as it made no capture it returned and perched for a short time in a tree not far distant from the chimney. But when it left the swifts at once returned in close formation, hung above the chimney for an instant, and then appeared to fall therein. Not one wavered in the act, all seemed to have a single aim—to get inside the chimney just as quickly as they could.

"But this we noticed: that the temperature and the amount of light prevailing each evening influenced the swifts as to the time they would enter the chimney. On the cooler and darker ones the entrance would be made much earlier, whereas on the warmer and fairer evenings they would enter it quite late."

Dr. S. A. Watson (1933) made the following observation on another method of roosting at Whittier, Calif., during the spring migration:

On the evening of May 12, 1933, large numbers of Vaux Swifts (*Chaetura vauxi*) were noticed circling around the barns of Mr. John Gregg near Whittier. As night came on they began flying into a hay loft where they would cling to the walls and to each other. At places they would cover large sections of the wall five or six deep. It was estimated that at least three thousand swifts found shelter in the barn that night.

Next morning the birds began leaving the barn at about eight o'clock. They would fly out, a few at a time, circle around a while and then fly off in groups. They returned again the next two nights in about the same numbers, and for the two nights following these the numbers decreased rapidly, and on the sixth night they failed to return. The birds were heavily parasitized with lice and seemed weak and emaciated. A dozen or more were found dead each morning during the period they were taking refuge in the barn.

Since there was considerable snow in the mountains when the swifts were staying over, it is assumed that the unfavorable weather barrier caused them to accumulate here until warmer days and better feeding conditions called them farther north.

Voice.—Mr. Rathbun tells me that "its note is a rapid twitter, given often as it dashes through the air with other swifts and sometimes with the swallows, for it is a bird fond of company, though at times only one or two are seen." Charles A. Allen (1880) says that the note is different from that of the chimney swift: "They do not utter the sharp, rattling chipper of that species, but have a weak, lisping note, which is, as near as I can imitate it, *chip-chip-chip-cheweet-cheweet*, and this is only to be heard during the pairing season, when two, probably the male and female, are chasing each other." Mr. Hoffmann (1927) says: "On the breeding ground pairs of Vaux Swifts pursue each other with a faint *chip-chip-chip*."

Field marks.—Vaux's swift looks and acts like a small chimney swift. It might be mistaken at a distance for the black swift, but it is much smaller and much lighter in coloration below. It can be easily distinguished from the white-throated swift, as it lacks the conspicuous white areas on the breast and the flanks. Its flight, as described above, is different from either of the other western swifts.

Fall.—Mr. Rathbun's notes from the vicinity of Seattle, Wash., containing the following observations on the migration through that

State: "Throughout the first three weeks in September we have observed Vaux's swift to pass by in its flight toward the south. The birds will be seen at intervals all day and at times even at twilight. They fly at all heights, singly or in groups, and as a rule quite rapidly. It is not uncommon to see them in the company of other birds: black swifts, nighthawks, and certain of the swallows, species that are on the wing southward at the same time. Even when migrating the playfulness of this little swift is seen, for often one will pursue another of its kind. And on occasions we have seen it make a dash at a black swift, or a nighthawk, though when this took place no notice was taken of the act by either of these birds.

"On one occasion in fall we observed a large number of Vaux's swifts in flight whose actions were quite different. It was at the west coast of this State, along the ocean beach. When first seen, the swifts were 'milling' in the air within a narrow limit, the sight bearing a resemblance to a swarm of bees about a hive. Again and again this action was repeated. At times the birds would suddenly scatter as if a wind had strewn them, but soon they reunited and once more began to mill, though meanwhile the flock slowly drifted southward and at last was lost to view. On this occasion in company with the Vaux's were a number of the black swifts. These were at some height above the smaller swifts, and their graceful circling flight was in marked contrast to that of the Vaux's."

Winter.—The winter range of Vaux's swift is imperfectly known but is supposed to be in Central America. An important addition to our knowledge has been recently made by George H. Lowery, Jr., who found this swift wintering on the campus of the Louisiana State University, East Baton Rouge Parish, La. He has kindly lent me his unpublished manuscript on the subject, from which I quote as follows:

"Swifts were first observed in Louisiana outside of the regular seasons of occurrence during the winter of 1937–38, when two individuals were recorded almost daily from November through February. One of them was captured and banded on February 16, 1938.

"During November 1938 swifts were again noted in the same chimney on the university campus. This time a larger number, 5 to 10, were found. They were observed almost daily from November through February. Six specimens were caught, five of which were banded and released; the sixth was prepared as a study skin. Only after being placed alongside specimens of *C. pelagica* in the Museum of Zoology collection was it noted that the bird differed from that species. Being smaller and paler, it was immediately suspected of being *C. vauxi*. The question arose as to whether the five birds banded and released were the same species as the one made into a skin. These were recaptured on February 15, along with four additional unbanded birds, and all proved to be of the smaller and paler variety. The four un-banded birds were retained as museum specimens, and the others were released.

"After careful comparison with material kindly lent by the Museum of Vertebrate Zoology of the University of California and by the Bureau of Biological Survey, it is obvious that the five specimens taken at Louisiana State University in February belong to *Chaetura vauxi*. Both Dr. H. C. Oberholser and George Willett have examined the specimens and confirmed this identification. It is therefore probable that the specimen captured and released in February 1938 was also of this species."

DISTRIBUTION

Range.—Western North America.

Breeding range.—The breeding range of Vaux's swift extends **north** to southeastern Alaska (probably Baranof Island and probably Thomas Bay); and northern British Columbia (probably Flood Glacier and probably Telegraph Creek). **East** to British Columbia (probably Telegraph Creek, Hazelton, Lac la Hache, Vernon, Edge-wood, and Newgate); western Montana (probably Glacier National Park, probably Kalispell, and Red Lodge); west-central Oregon (Fort Klamath and Mount McLoughton); and eastern California (Meadow Valley, probably Campbells Hot Springs, and probably Kenawyers). **South** to central California (probably Kenawyers, and Santa Cruz). **West** to the coastal regions of California (Santa Cruz, San Rafael, Sebastopol, and Eureka); Oregon (Tillamook and Beaverton); Washington (Tacoma, Seattle, Crescent Lake, and Bellingham); British Columbia (Chilliwack, Comox, and Courte-nay); and southeastern Alaska (Chickamin River and probably Baranof Island).

Winter range.—Imperfectly known. At this season the species has been detected north to East Baton Rouge Parish, La. (see above), Taxco, State of Guerrero, and Leguna del Rosario, State of Tlaxcala, Mexico; and south to San Lucas and Mazatenango, Guatemala.

Spring migration.—Early dates of spring arrival are: Arizona—Chiricahua Mountains, April 13; Agua Caliente, April 22. Cali-fornia—Eureka, April 10; Buena Park, April 14; Redwood City, April 16; Azusa, April 23. Oregon—Mercer, April 29; Beaverton, April 30; Fort Klamath, May 6. Washington—Nisqually, April 11; Tacoma, April 23; Clallam Bay, May 3. Idaho—Coeur d'Alene, May 6; Rose Lake, May 11. British Columbia—Chilliwack, April 26; Arrow Lakes, April 28; Revelstoke, May 12.

Fall migration.—Late dates of fall departure are: Alaska—Cas-cade Bay, September 9. British Columbia—Kispiox Valley, September 3; Errington, September 15; Okanagan Landing, September 15. Idaho—Priest River, September 10; Trestle Creek, September 11. Washington—Mount Rainier National Park, September 16; Seattle, September 25; Tacoma, October 1.   California—Nicasio, September 24; Buena Park, September 24; Santa Cruz, October 5; Los Angeles, October 14.   Arizona—Tombstone, September 20; Pima Indian Reservation, September 26; Santa Catalina Mountains, October 6.

Casual records.—Two individuals were recorded in Jasper National Park, Alberta, on July 6, 1918.   The British Museum (Natural History) has two specimens taken in Costa Rica, one at Los Cuadros de Laguna, in July 1898, and the other at Carrillo on November 7, 1898. This institution also lists a specimen from Honduras without exact locality or date of collection, but it seems probable that all three of these examples may be referable to the form resident in southern Central America.

Egg dates.—California: 44 records, May 7 to July 9; 22 records, June 12 to 30, indicating the height of the season.

MICROPUS PACIFICUS PACIFICUS (Latham)

WHITE-RUMPED SWIFT

CONTRIBUTED BY FRANCIS CHARLES ROBERT JOURDAIN

HABITS

The first and, up to the present, only record of this species within our limits is that of a female that was obtained on St. George Island, Alaska, on August 1, 1920.   It was observed flying over the tundra and along the cliffs by G. D. Hanna and was recorded by Mailliard and Hanna (1921).

Like most of the swifts, this is a bird of extremely powerful flight and has an enormous range, breeding in eastern Siberia west to the Altai range and east to the Pacific, as well as in the Japanese and other island groups of the northwest Pacific Ocean.   Southward its breeding range extends to the northwest Himalayas, where it is represented by a local race, *Micropus pacificus leuconyx*, and to Burma, where another form is found nesting, *M. p. cooki*.   In all probability these two races are resident, or at any rate do not migrate far, and have not been proved to leave the Asiatic Continent.   The typical race, with which we are concerned, on the other hand migrates by way of the Malay Archipelago to Australia.

The white-rumped swift was first described by Latham in 1801 under the name of *Hirundo pacifica*, not from the bird but from the celebrated Watling drawings, which were executed in Australia (New South Wales).   Nothing was known at that time as to its breeding grounds, but when Pallas' great work on the zoology of Asiatic Russia appeared in 1811, he described a variety of the common swift under the name of "*Hirundo apus*, var. B. *leucopyga*," which was subsequently proved to be the same species that Latham had described ten years previously. John Gould later named it *Cypselus australis*, and Jardine and Selby introduced a fourth name, *C. vittatus*, but finally it was recognized that Latham's name had priority, and it has been generally accepted ever since.

The Himalayan bird, *M. pacificus leuconyx*, was first described by Blyth in 1845. It is considerably smaller than the typical race and the feet are flesh-colored, instead of blackish, but it is treated as a subspecies of *M. pacificus* in the second edition of "The Fauna of British India." A third form, *M. pacificus cooki*, was described in 1918 from the northern Shan States in Burma by the late Maj. H. H. Harington. This is also a small race, with black feet and dark shaft stripes to the feathers of the chin and with dark mantle. More recently Domaniewski has suggested the separation of the northern birds into three more races—the typical form (*M. p. pacificus*) from Vladivostok; the Japanese race (*M. p. kurodae*), said to be much darker; and the Kamchatkan bird (*M. p. kamtschaticus*), from Petropaulovsk. It may prove to be necessary to accept some of these new forms, but without an adequate series of skins for comparison it seems at present desirable to let the matter remain as it is and to treat the Japanese, Chinese, and Siberian birds under one heading.

Spring.—In Japan and eastern Asia this species is a summer resident. As there is some doubt with regard to the Burmese and Himalayan subspecies as to whether they are partially migratory or not, it is best to confine our attention to the dates of arrival in the countries north of India and the Malay Peninsula. J. D. D. La Touche (1931), writing on the birds of eastern China, gives its distribution as follows: "China Coast, Shaweishan Is. (migrant). Islands off Fohkien coast, Shantung coast and Is. (summer). Chihli (summer and migrant). Yangtse Valley to Szechuen (summer and migrant)." He does not, however, give any data as to the time of arrival of the migrants from Australia, but the gap can be partially filled from other sources. The same writer, in an article on spring migration at Chinwangtao, on the coast of Chihli, quotes as the earliest date April 14 (2), 1913. Another was obtained in Fohkien on April 22. The next date is May 9, 1913, when two more were seen, and flocks were observed subsequently in May and June, the latter probably merely visits from adjoining breeding places. There are, moreover, earlier dates of specimens obtained, for there is a specimen in the Hume collection (British Museum) from Takow, China, dated March 22, obtained by Swinhoe, and he also states (1870) that he secured a specimen from

a large flock in Nychow Harbor, Hainan, apparently on March 19.
T. H. Shaw (1936), writing on Hopei Province, says that it is a regu-
lar migrant to the plains, arriving in April. R. E. Vaughan and
K. H. Jones (1913) record the first arrival on March 26, but most
come in April. In the Japanese Islands specimens in the British
Museum collection were obtained at Nagasaki on March 18 and May
30 by P. Ringer, and from "Japan" in May (Hume collection). In
Sakhalin, L. Munsterhjelm (1922) records the date of first arrival as
June 4, when three birds were seen.

C. Ingram (1908) saw one near Kioto, Japan, on May 4 and
several at Lake Kawaguchi on May 23. Blakiston and Pryer (1878)
also record it as present in May. The late Alan Owston noticed the
date of first arrival in Japan for two consecutive seasons on May 15.
In Siberia it is recorded as arriving in the second half of May; at
Darasun in Dauria it was first noted on May 24 by Dybowski, but
Przewalski records its arrival in southeast Mongolia on April 12,
1872, a very early date.

Nesting.—Accounts of the nesting of this species differ very considerably, and there is no doubt that the species adapts its habits to its
surroundings. R. Swinhoe's (1860) statement that these swifts were
breeding among the huts of a coastal village on Lamyit Island in the
Formosa Channel receives some confirmation from the accounts of
nesting in Siberia, but it does not seem to have been authenticated on
the spot. At Chefoo (Shantung Province), however, he (1874) obtained a dozen birds, caught on the nests on June 22 by his collector,
on a small rocky islet about 15 miles out to sea. Here the swifts were
breeding in numbers in crannies of the rocks, and out of the 12 birds
captured 5 were males and 7 were females, showing that both sexes
take part in incubation. A nest of the year was like a shallow saucer,
nearly 4 inches broad, thicker behind than in front, and constructed
of refuse straw and a few bits of catkins and feathers, all agglutinated
with the bird's saliva. In another case, six nests had been built in
successive years on top of one another and strongly glued together.
From the same coast, off the Shantung littoral, we have an excellent
account of a breeding colony by Capt. H. L. Cochrane (1914) near
Wei-Hai-Wei. After stating that one breeding colony on a rocky islet
had been destroyed by an army of hungry rats, he adds:

Nevertheless, it was a considerable surprise to find a small colony of *Micropus
pacificus* established on an unpretentious rock of the most modest dimensions,
both in length and height. This particular rock, much broken up, some 50 yards
long, and at its highest point 39 feet high, is situated 1400 yards from the
mainland, and 400 yards from a respectably sized island, which latter is un-
tenanted by Swifts of any description. Of limestone foundation, the rock is
seamed with deep fissures and long narrow crannies, and it is in these recesses
that the White-rumped Swift was found breeding in such elevated situations

that sea and spray, in their most angry moments, are ineffective to disturb the tranquility of the site chosen. On landing upon the rock and commencing to climb over it, not a sign of any bird life was visible, with the single exception of a solitary shag (*Phalacrocorax pelagicus*) which flew off hurriedly from the far side of the rock near the water's edge, where it had been dreaming away the hot summer afternoon. Altogether seven Swift's nests were found; of these two were in vertical crannies, the remainder in horizontal fissures, and all a full arm's length in. Only two nests contained eggs (June 6th), and only three Swifts were seen on the rock. The first nest found contained two eggs. The female bird was on the nest, and the male bird underneath the nest, clinging to it with both feet. So narrow was the cleft, that the birds were constrained to remain in one position, turning round being out of the question. The nest itself, wedged between the rock faces, was a small, perfectly round plate of straw, three and a half inches in extreme diameter, thickest at the rim and very slightly dished in the centre. A few feathers had been worked into the outer part of it, which was hardened with glutinous matter produced by the bird. The two birds at the first nest made no attempt to fly, and allowed themselves to be drawn out, a somewhat difficult operation. They clung very tenaciously to the fingers with exceedingly sharp claws, but when thrown into the air, immediately flew off with a strong swinging flight. A single bird flew from the second nest discovered, which was two feet down in a horizontal crack, and was similar in all respects to the first nest and contained three eggs. The eggs of the *Micropus pacificus* are typical Swift's eggs—pure white in colour and elongated in shape. Three apparently new nests were found close to each other in the same cranny, a long narrow aperture between two boulders. The remaining two nests were adjacent but separated, the whole area for the purpose being very restricted.

The rock was again visited five days later. All the nests now contained eggs, three of them one apiece only. No other nest beside that previously mentioned contained three eggs. One additional nest was discovered containing two eggs; this made eight nests in all. A Swift was found on each nest, but both birds at only two nests. Three Swifts made their appearance when the rock was approached on the latter occasion, and continued to fly around during the visit.

Captain Cochrane's excellent paper is illustrated by a plate showing the rocks, with deep fissures, and the nest and eggs in position within the cleft.

From Japan we have a few all too scanty notes from Alan Owston, who informed A. J. Campbell (1901) that on a yachting cruise he visited an island called Ukishima, about half a mile long, 200 feet high, and about 20 miles south of Yokohama. Here he explored some caves on the south side of the island, where he roughly estimated that there must have been not less than 2,000 of these birds nesting. There is also a well-known breeding place (which is shared with the spine-tailed swift, *Chaetura caudacuta*) behind the Kegon waterfall, near Nikko, Japan. Here the rocks consist of alternate hard and soft strata, making a series of shelves, and between these the swifts place their nests. Since the outer edges of the ledges are weathered and so rotten that they will not bear the weight of a man, the place is practically inaccessible.

In Sakhalin, Marquis Yamashima describes nests found on the rocky coast as being built of seaweeds, fallen leaves, and *Usnea longissima*, stuck together with saliva and forming a dish-shaped nest, 7 to 12 centimeters in outside diameter and 1 to 4 centimeters in depth.

In Siberia and Mongolia most of the breeding places appear to be in cavities and recesses among rocks, not only in the lower zones, but even at 12,000 feet or more. Madame Kozlova (1932) describes the nests as sometimes placed in cavities and at other times built openly under a prominent ridge. At Yakutsk, however, R. Hall (Hartert and Hall, 1904) states that these swifts nest on beams under the market-place verandas and among them but do not breed in close company. The inhabitants have a superstitious fear about disturbing them, so it was only through the good offices of the chief of police that Mr. Hall was able to secure two specimens of adults and two full-grown nestlings at dusk from a quiet corner of the market place by the help of a local youth. The nest consisted of a few straws and feathers cemented together by saliva, and the grasp of the bird's claws was strong enough to pierce the fingers and draw blood.

Eggs.—The clutch is composed of two or three eggs, which closely resemble those of other species of swift, being "cylindrical-ovate" and dull white without gloss. In the new work in course of publication on the eggs of Japanese birds, by K. Kobayashi and T. Ishizawa, two eggs of the Kobayashi collection are figured, taken on Mount Fuji, Hondo. It is here stated that in Japan the normal clutch is two, but that three have been recorded. The average of 17 Japanese eggs is given as 26.76 by 17.44; maxima, 29 by 17.7 and 28.7 by 18.4; minima, 25.2 by 18.2 and 25.5 by 17.6 millimeters. Twenty eggs from Siberia, China, and Formosa (14 measured by the writer and 6 by Dybowski) average 26.06 by 16.61; maxima, 28.1 by 17.1 and 26.1 by 17.5; minimum, 23.5 by 15.6 millimeters; Japanese eggs, therefore, seem to be slightly larger. The average weight of 10 Japanese eggs is 4.4 grams (Kobayashi).

Plumages.—R. Hall notes that in the two nestlings the feet were reddish brown, and E. Hartert (1904) states that the juvenile plumage is similar to that of the adult. T. H. Shaw (1936) says the upper parts are browner, feathers with whitish edges; wing coverts and inner webs of inner primaries bordered with white.

Adult: Upper parts blackish brown; back, upper tail coverts, almost black with faint gloss; chin, throat, and broad band across rump white, with narrow black shaft stripes to feathers; under parts otherwise dark brown, each feather with broad white tips and subterminal blackish band. Iris deep brown; bill black, feet purplish black. Weight, 32–39 grams (Shaw).

Measurements (in millimeters) : Exposed culmen, 6–7; tarsus, 10; wing, 166–173 (Shaw), 176–184.5 (Hartert). Tail deeply forked, 77–79 (Shaw), 72–84 (Hartert).

Food.—Entirely insects, taken on the wing, but little definitely recorded. J. C. Kershaw (1904), however, says that on the Kwangtung coast it feeds largely on a species of beetle that infests the "paddy" (rice).

Behavior.—All writers call attention to its extraordinary powers of flight, often at great heights, coming down to lower levels in thundery and stormy weather. Przewalski describes it as spending whole days on the wing, shooting through the air and among the rocks, but in morning and evening coursing low over the steppes and feeding.

Voice.—On the whole it is not a particularly noisy bird. Cochrane (1914) speaks of "a moderate amount of subdued screaming" while hunting. C. Ingram (1908) also, comparing it with *M. apus*, says it has very similar habits, but is a much more silent bird and more sparing of its screamlike cry; and La Touche (1931) also speaks of it as extremely silent, only a faint scream being now and then audible.

Field marks.—At close quarters the white rump, taken in connection with the large size, renders identification easy, as the white-rumped swifts of the *affinis* group are much smaller. It is frequently seen on the wing in company with the large spine-tailed swift (*Chaetura caudacuta*), from which it is readily distinguishable by the difference in the shape of the tail, square in *Chaetura* and deeply forked in *M. pacificus*.

Fall.—Toward the end of August the flocks disappear from Mongolia, but in Japan they seem to linger till October, and an extraordinary incident occurred in 1897, when Mr. Owston saw more than a dozen on December 26, when they should have been in Australia, as related in A. J. Campbell's work (1901). It may be a coincidence, but this was the year of the great bush fires in Tasmania and Australia, the smoke from which covered thousands of miles at land and also at sea. Swinhoe obtained a specimen at Amoy in November, now in the British Museum, and at Hongkong departure takes place early in September. It arrives in India about September, but the bulk of the migrant horde comes in October and November.

Winter.—From the Asiatic mainland and the islands of the North Pacific this species migrates across the Pacific Ocean to Australia and also in smaller numbers to Tasmania. On the way it has been recorded from Borneo by Salvadori; also from New Guinea by the same author, R. B. Sharpe, and O. Finsch; it winters in Australia, rarely visiting Tasmania. During its stay in Australia it is usually seen on the wing, coming down only in stormy weather.

A. J. Campbell (1901) states that he has only two records of this species perching; one a case of an apparently over-fatigued bird, which settled for a moment on the ground; the other, by Dr. W. Macgillivray, who reports a passage of thousands of these birds at Portland on February 14, 1899; he was informed that a flock took up their quarters for the night in a large gum tree, where their constant twittering could be heard till quite dark.

DISTRIBUTION

Breeding range.—In the North Pacific: Kurile Islands, Hokkaido, Seven Islands of Izu, Quelpart Island, Tanegashima, Yakushima, Tokuroshima, Loochoo (Riu-kiu) Isles, Botel Tobago, Sakhalin, and Formosa.

On the Asiatic mainland: Kamchatka, east Siberia west to the Altai, Manchuria, Mongolia, Korea, China, Kansu, and Tibet. Replaced in Burma by *M. p. cooki* and in the northwest Himalayas by *M. p. leuconyx.*

Migration range.—Southeastern Asiatic mainland, passing through India and Malay Peninsula, through the Malay Archipelago, Papua, etc., to Australia generally and occasionally also Tasmania.

Egg dates.—China, 8 nests with 1 to 3 eggs between June 6 and 11 (Weihai-Wei).

Japan, June and July; June 19 (Hondo, Kobayashi).

Siberia, fresh clutches in Dauria June 14 (Dybowski), also July 17; also Makutsk, June 19.

AERONAUTES SAXATALIS SAXATALIS (Woodhouse)

WHITE-THROATED SWIFT

PLATES 47, 48

HABITS

In the mountainous regions of the far west, especially where precipitous, rocky cliffs tower above deep canyons, one may catch a glimpse of these little winged meteors darting about far overhead. It was in the Huachuca Mountains in Arizona where I first saw this marvelous swift; a mountain brook flows swiftly over its rocky bed through a steep and narrow canyon, known as "the box," so narrow that in some places one can almost touch both sides of it at once; on each side the rocky cliffs rise to a height of 100 or 200 feet, almost shutting out the light of day; and far above us we could see these swifts darting in and out of crevices in the rocks, or cleaving the sky in their rapid gyrations. Swifts are well named, for, in proportion to their size, they are the swiftest birds that fly, and this species is one of the swiftest of them all. I am tempted to quote the following appreciation from the writings of Dr. George M. Sutton (1935) : "The White-throated Swift belongs to the heavens, not to earth. Beautiful as the creature is, when seen lying among the rocks where it has fallen, or on your hand, it somehow is no longer a White-throated Swift at all. Like a fish from the deep sea that has burst in shallow water, it is only a mass of flesh already starting to decay—of feathers that so recently had pushed aside the thin atmosphere of dizzy heights; feathers that twanged and rustled as the bird shot forward a hundred yards in a twinkling; feathers that knew nothing of the shadows of forests, that knew only the shadows of clouds, the full blaze of the sun, the coolness of clean unscaled pinnacles."

Courtship.—Courtship seems to be performed largely, if not wholly, on the wing. W. L. Dawson (1923) writes: "That most friendly of encounters, the nuptial embrace, appears to take place, also, in the air. In this the birds come together from opposite directions, engage with the axes of their bodies held at a decided angle laterally, and begin to tumble slowly downward, turning over and over the while for several seconds, or until earth impends, whereupon they separate without further ado."

Enid Michael (1926) says: "White-throated Swifts we have seen cling together and pin-wheel down through the air for a distance of five hundred feet."

Several others have noted a similar performance; and Frederick C. Lincoln has twice collected, with a single shot, two birds in the act, which in both cases proved to be a male and a female (Bradbury, 1918).

But coition may take place in the nesting crevices also, for James B. Dixon says in his notes: "The males are so amative that when we would take the females out of the cracks they would pounce onto them while in our hands; and we actually caught a pair in this way while hanging onto a ladder in front of the nest crack."

Nesting.—The white-throated swift nests in cracks and crevices in almost or quite inaccessible rocky cliffs on the sea coasts on rocky islands off the coast, and in the mountains up to elevations of 10,000 to 13,000 feet. Much has been written about the difficulties encountered in reaching the nests of these birds, for the nesting cliffs are difficult, or impossible, to scale, and when the nesting crevice is reached the nest is placed so far back in a narrow crack that it is often beyond reach and sometimes even out of sight. Some few nests have been found in niches at a comparatively low height in a cliff, but usually a climb on a rope for 75 or 100 feet from the top or the base of a cliff is necessary to reach the nests. This swift is evidently one of the most successful of birds in placing its nest beyond the reach of predatory animals and birds, not excepting the human egg collector.

James B. Dixon has sent me the following notes: "This bird is a common breeder in the rougher, more mountainous sections of the whole of southern California, as I have found them nesting in every county south of Tehacipi, and from the ocean cliffs to the highest peaks up to 6,500 feet above sea level. I have seen them nesting in the dug-out holes of rough-winged swallows and right in the middle of a large colony of swallows, where it was extremely difficult to tell which one of a myriad of holes the swifts were inhabiting.

"Usually the nests are very flimsily built of feathers glued together into one complete structure. The nest naturally takes the shape of the crack in which it is located and therefore takes all kinds of shapes; but where they have room they will build a nice, round, well-cupped nest that is so well stuck together that it can be dropped from the cliff and not a feather will be lost. Nest building begins very early in spring and continues for a long time. I have seen birds enter the cracks in a cliff early in March with feathers in their bills, which they must have carried for miles, as the feathers were chicken feathers and there were no poultry yards nearer than 6 or 8 miles in an air line.

"In 1915 I made a special effort to collect several sets of eggs. As we did not know when the eggs would be laid and had seen them building their nests so early, we started operations in April. At this time we found the females sitting on their nests and still building by adding occasional feathers. We inspected these locations week by week from early in April until the last of May before any eggs were laid. The females were in the nests the better part of the time, and the minute a female left a nest every male within sight would take after her.

"The main colony of about 12 pairs was located in the center of a 400-foot hard granite cliff. Here we located three nests that could be reached; the others were too far back to be seen, although the sitting birds could be heard twittering and giving their typical shrill calls."

There is a set of four eggs, with the nest, collected by J. B. Dixon and C. T. Schnack, in the Thayer collection in Cambridge, which came from the same nesting site. In the elaborate data that came with it they state that the nest was located on a large granite cliff in a steep, narrow canyon near San Pasqual, San Diego County, Calif. It was taken on May 25, 1913, from a diagonal crack on the face of the cliff, 175 feet from the top and on a projecting point of the cliff. The nest is a compact wad of white plant down, mixed with feathers, all securely glued together, and is lined with white, brown, buff, and black feathers, with a few small, bright-yellow feathers; it measures about 4 inches in longest diameter and is hollowed to a depth of about three-quarters of an inch; the eggs are badly "flyspected," as seems to be frequently the case in nests of this species.

There is another interesting nest of this species in the collection, perhaps a different subspecies, taken by Gerald B. Thomas in the Coxcomb Mountains of British Honduras on May 27, 1906. It was located in a cave, 50 feet from the ground, in a high cliff; it was glued to the wall of the cave 10 feet from its mouth. The nest resembles that of the chimney swift in shape and size, being almost too small for the five eggs it contained; it is made of weed stems glued together into a firm basket, and is profusely lined with small feathers, dark brown and white, which look as if they might have come from the parent bird.

Wilson C. Hanna has published two interesting accounts (1909 and 1917) of the nesting habits of the white-throated swift in a quarry on Slover Mountain in the San Bernardino Valley, Calif. He describes the difficulties involved in securing the eggs, shows photographs of the nests, and gives a series of measurements of both the nests and the eggs. In his second paper, he says of the nests:

Both the vertical and the horizontal cracks are used as nesting sites, but with the exception of set no. 5, all that I took were from vertical cracks. It is almost impossible to take nests from horizontal fissures without destruction of the eggs and in the exception noted, a rock weighing at least 35 tons was removed. * * * The location of nest no. 6 was rather unusual, being reached by going into a vertical crack about three feet, then up eighteen inches, then to the side about eight inches. * * *

Nests are constructed, for the most part, of chicken feathers and grasses cemented together and to the rocks, probably by saliva. They vary in size to suit the space between the walls of rock and are usually shallow and narrow. * * *

All nests that I have examined have been infested with numerous "bugs." In the two nests where birds could be seen while incubating, the insects could be observed crawling on the birds' heads. The eggs, in every case, were more or less spotted as a result of the insects, depending upon how long they had been in the nest.

William C. Bradbury (1918) made some elaborate preparations and, with the help of three young men, collected several sets of eggs near Hot Sulphur Springs in Grand County, Colo. He writes:

The cliffs where the birds were seen, bordering the Grand River, east of Sulphur Springs, are of a mixed lava formation, with some parts of hard, ringing material, and others of cracked, crumbling formation, intermixed with seams and deposits of soft lava ash, through which the river has cut its way in ages past. The visible base of the cliffs is at the top of a steep slope of debris, extending to the Grand River several hundred feet below. * * *

The first available prospect, located by Niedrach through the presence of excrement about eight feet up, and to which he was able to climb, was in a horizontal crevice about two and one-half inches in width, sloping slightly downward and partly filled, in places, with lava, sand and vegetable matter evidently deposited by the wind. Upon reaching the crevice a Swift darted forth nearly in his face, and he caught sight of its mate retreating back into the crevice, from which it was not seen to emerge. Less than an hour's work resulted in collecting, from a point about eighteen inches back, our first nest, containing four fresh eggs.

Florence Merriam Bailey (1907) made the interesting discovery that white-throated swifts were nesting in cracks in the walls of the old mission building at San Juan Capistrano, Calif. She located four nests by seeing the birds enter the cracks; but only one nest was actually seen, of which she says: "The nest behind the end of the stone arch was the only one seen and this—as it was ten feet from the ground—only by climbing and peering up the crack. The crack, as seen in the photograph, was behind the capitol of the pilaster on which one end of the arch rested, the capitol having been jarred away from the wall by an earthquake—doubtless that of 1812. About ten inches up this crack the nest could be seen tightly wedged in between walls less than two inches apart. As well as could be seen without destroying the nest, it was made of bark, feathers, grass, and wool."

Eggs.—The white-throated swift lays three to six eggs, oftenest four and frequently five. The eggs vary from elongate-ovate to cylindrical-ovate, or almost narrowly elliptical. They are dead white to pale creamy white and without gloss. As mentioned above, the eggs are often more or less spotted with the excrement of the insects with which the nests are often badly infested. The measurements of 50 eggs average 21.24 by 13.74 millimeters; the eggs showing the four extremes measure 25 by 15, 19.1 by 12.9, and 21.9 by 12.7 millimeters.

Young.—Enid Michael (1926) had a young swift in captivity that she kept alive for ten days.

This captive swift slept much of the time, but during his wakeful hours he was a very active bird; shoving and flopping along on his breast he could move rapidly. He was kept in a wooden box with a screened cover, where there were folded flannels into which he could snuggle away and sleep. When awakened he would set out at once to explore his box. He could crawl up the vertical wall of the box without the least difficulty, and one of his favorite stunts was to race about, back down, on the under side of the cover screen. This screen was ordinary mosquito-proof netting. When the screen cover was removed he would scurry up the wall of the box and topple headlong onto the floor. No sooner had he hit the floor than he would begin to skid about on his breast, using his feet as propellers. He had a fancy for dark cracks, and if he should find such a place he would surely disappear. Best of all, he loved to crawl up one's sleeve to snuggle warmly under one's arm. He had very strong feet and claws like a mammal. When attached to one's garments he clung tenaciously, and each hooked toe nail had to be pried loose before he could be removed.

Plumages.—I have seen no very young white-throated swifts, but birds in the juvenal plumage show the same color pattern as the adults, though the colors are duller and less clearly defined. The long, curved claws are highly developed for climbing.

Food.—As the food of this swift is obtained wholly on the wing, it probably feeds on whatever small flying insects it can capture. Mrs. Bailey (1928) lists "winged ants and other hymenoptera, bugs, flies, dung beetles, engraver beetles, clover root weevils, leafhoppers, etc."

Clarence Cottam contributes the following report on the stomach contents of white-throated swifts: "In 21 stomachs of the white-throated swift analyzed in the food-habits laboratory of the Biological Survey, the dominant food items appear to be flies (Diptera), the root maggots (Anthomyiidae) being the most important, with the long-legged flies (Dolichipodidae), the flesh flies (Sarcophagidae), and the March flies (Bibionidae) occurring in lesser numbers. March flies make up 100 percent of the food of a bird from Wyoming but did not occur in any of the remaining 20 stomachs. Flies were present in nearly every stomach and formed from 6 to 100 percent of the total contents.

"Beetles (Coleoptera) were well represented, especially the dung beetles (*Aphodius*), and entered into the diet of ten of the birds with amounts varying from 2 to 84 percent, although they averaged about 10 percent of the total content. Other Coleoptera identified were weevils (Curculionidae), hister beetles (Histeridae), leaf beetles (Chrysomelidae), rove beetles (Staphylinidae), skin or larder beetles (Dermestidae), bark beetles (Scolytidae), and the antlike flower beetles (Anthicidae).

"Bees, wasps, and ants (Hymenoptera) entered prominently into the bill of fare of about a fourth of the birds and were present as traces in three-fourths of stomachs examined. Bees were found to represent from 1 percent to as much as 86 percent of the total content, and ants in two cases formed over 90 percent of the food.

"The true bugs were moderately abundant, the most important being stink bugs (Pentatomidae), treehoppers (Membracidae), leaf-hoppers (Cicadellidae), and squash bugs (Coreidae); of the last named family, 50 specimens in one stomach formed 67 percent of the content."

Behavior.—The one striking characteristic of the white-throated swift is its dashing, exceedingly rapid, and erratic flight. Of the three western swifts, Vaux's may be swift, and the black swift swifter, but the white-throated is certainly the swiftest of the three. S. F. Rathbun writes to me: "If there is a faster-flying bird than the white-throated swift, I would like to see it. Always it appears to fly at top speed. At times the velocity of its flight seems beyond belief. The flight of this swift is often more or less direct, but it darts and swoops, and turns so quickly as it flies that the eye is not quick enough to see how the reversal in the direction of its flight takes place. You watch one as it passes, almost disappears, and in an instant it returns and flashes by. Its flight is so unpredictable that one never knows what next it will do. At rare times, we have seen the white-throated and the black swift in company, and this gave us an opportunity to compare the flight actions of the two. Always the flight of the former is dashing, whereas that of the latter is easy and graceful, as it glides around."

Mr. Hanna (1917) writes:

It is claimed by some that these birds do not use their wings in unison, but I am of the opinion that they do flap both wings at the same time, at least part of the time if not always. When flying about feeding upon insects, usually at several hundred feet elevation above the ground, they make a few rapid beats with the wings, then soar a little while, then beat their wings rapidly for a few moments and so on. They vary their flight by sharp darts in other directions, probably to catch insects. When returning to the cliffs they often keep their wings beating fairly steadily. Both when penetrating and leaving the crevices they seem to use both their wings and feet as aids to locomotion. * * *

During the heavy rains of January, 1916, quite a number of swifts were found on the ground in a helpless condition. It seems that some of the crevices had become flooded with water which had drenched the birds, causing them to attempt to escape, but it was impossible for them to fly with wet feathers. Several of these birds were kept in a warm place till their feathers were dry enough for them to fly away.

The white-throated swift has well been called the rock swift, for it lives its life in the rocky cliffs and in the air. So far as I know, no one has ever seen one alight on the ground, on a tree, or on any kind of perch. Its feet are not well formed for walking or perching, but they are well adapted, with long, strong claws, for climbing about in the caves and crevices in the cliffs. Mr. Dixon says in his notes: "Their legs are so malformed from nonuse as to be almost nothing but claws, to propel them through the cracks; and they can climb around much the same as bats or mice in such a location."

The photograph and the diagram published by Enid Michael (1926) illustrate this character.

Dr. Gayle Pickwell (1937) gives an interesting account of the roosting habits of this swift in Santa Clara County, Calif.:

The niche in which the swifts quartered themselves in 1931, and throughout the observations here reported upon, consists of a recess of unknown depth extending beneath a rock face that lies at an angle a little short of the vertical. It is about fifteen feet immediately above Sycamore Canyon Road. The crevice through which the swifts enter and leave measures, it is estimated, from two to three inches in width and about two and one-half feet in length. All the swifts noted, during the dates specified, used this aperture and this one only.

On August 3, the swifts were flying about in the canyon when first observed just at sunset. A crude estimate made of their numbers in the air gave from one hundred to two hundred individuals. Prior to entering the night roost the birds streamed in a procession into the shadows by it and then turned out into the light of the canyon. Shortly thereafter they entered the rock, streaming in with unbelievable rapidity. Three or four struck the crevice simultaneously, and now and then they struck one another. Twenty or more entered in an interval of one or two seconds. The entire flock was housed between 7:20 and 7:25 p. m., and a constant chattering thenceforth welled from the rock face. The sun had set some time previously, and deep shadows filled the gorge of the canyon.

On September 21, a similar performance was witnessed, but the number had decreased to approximately 49 birds; these all entered the rock in exactly two minutes, between 6:30 and 6:32 p. m. On October 24, "the birds went into the roosting niche as fast as shot poured through a funnel; faster than the tongue could waggle in an attempt to count." They all entered within a space of ten seconds. Later observations were made in November and in January; at the latter time only about a dozen swifts were seen to use the roost.

Voice.—Dr. Alexander Wetmore (1920) says: "The call note of this bird is a shrill laughing *he he he he* heard usually when two or three are coursing along together." Ralph Hoffmann (1927) writes: "In spring and during the breeding season while pursuing each other about the cliffs in which they nest they utter a shrill twitter, suggesting the syllables *tee-dee, dee, dee, dee.*" Mr. Hanna (1909) describes the vocal powers more fully, as follows: "The swifts do not seem to have any musical ability, but their notes or calls are pleasing, especially to one who is studying them. One series of peculiar shrieks is given while the bird is in rapid flight and is suggestive of joyous freedom. Another series of notes is given when the birds are in the crevices, which sound very much like the twitterings of small chickens as they cuddle under their mother's wings, only the swifts' notes are much louder. These twitterings are quite a contrast to the wild shrieks, and they cannot help but suggest comfort and satisfaction."

Field marks.—White-throated swifts are very apt to be associated with violet-green swallows, when insects are flying low and the birds are coursing about at no great height above the ground; at such times it is often confusing to try to pick out the swifts, as they dart about among the swallows. But the shape of the swift is very distinctive, with its long, narrow wings set, as it sails, in the form of a cross; and its wing strokes, as it flies, are much more rapid than those of the swallow. Moreover, the swallow is all white on the under parts, whereas the swift looks mainly black, except for the conspicuous white throat, a central streak of white on the breast, and a white patch on each side of the rump. These white markings will easily distinguish the white-throated from the other two western swifts.

Winter.—At least a few white-throated swifts attempt to spend the winter as far north as west-central California, although some of them evidently perish in the attempt, for lack of food or from the effects of the cold. Dr. Gayle Pickwell's (1937) observers reported that during January 1937 only about a dozen swifts were seen entering the roosting place in the rock in Santa Clara County, referred to above, and that two or three dead birds were found on the ground below the rock.

Mr. Hanna (1917) reports that "during the extremely cold wave of early January, 1913, eight, to me perfectly healthy, swifts were taken out of a crevice where they, with many others, seemed to be roosting in a dazed or numb state. They were kept in a room for about six hours and then turned loose, one at a time, a few hundred feet from the point where they were captured. All flew away in a dazed fashion and nearer the ground than usual and none were observed to return to the place where they were captured. * * * The facts are that these birds are not observed for many days in the coldest weather, yet are found to be plentiful within the rocks, in a dormant state."

DISTRIBUTION

Range.—Western North America north to southern British Columbia.

Breeding range.—The breeding range of the white-throated swift extends **north** to southern British Columbia (Vaseux Lake); Montana (Libby, Columbia Falls, Yogo Creek, and Billings); and northwestern South Dakota (Slim Buttes). **East** to western South Dakota (Slim Buttes, Elk Mountains, and Hot Springs); northwestern Nebraska (West Monroe Canyon); southeastern Wyoming (Goshen Hole Rim); eastern Colorado (Chimney Canyon, Golden, and Garden of the Gods); New Mexico (Lake Burford, Cañon el Diablo, Anton Chico, and Capitan Mountains); western Texas (Davis Mountains and Chisos Mountains); Tamaulipas (Jaumave); Hidalgo (Chico); and El Salvador (Los Esesmiles). **South** to El Salvador (Los Esesmiles); western Guatemala (Duenas); southwestern Chihuahua (Jesus Maria); and Baja California (Guadalupe Island). **West** to Baja California (Guadalupe Island, San Fernando, San Ysidro, and Los Coronados Islands); western California (Escondido, San Juan Capistrano, Santa Cruz Island, Santa Barbara, San Luis Obispo, Pine Canyon, and probably Mount Lassen); central Washington (Lake Chelan); and British Columbia (Fair View and Vaseux Lake).

The range above outlined is for the entire species, but a southern subspecies (*A. s. nigrior*), apparently resident in the southern part of the range, is now recognized.

Winter range.—In winter these swifts are found **north** to California (Alum Rock Canyon, Santa Clara County, Redlands, Indio, and Salton Sea); casually central Arizona (Big Sandy Creek and Phoenix); and southwestern New Mexico (15 miles southwest of Hachita and Chloride). From these northern limits the winter range extends southward, probably to Guatemala and El Salvador.

Spring migration.—Early dates of spring arrival are: New Mexico—Chloride, March 6. Colorado—Colorado Springs, March 20; Durango, April 4; Palisades, April 25. Wyoming—Laramie, April 24; Midwest, April 28. South Dakota—Sioux National Forest, May 12. Montana—Billings, April 23. Arizona—Tucson, March 9; Paradise, March 14; Grand Canyon, March 25. Utah—Salt Lake, May 1. Washington—Everett, May 10.

Fall migration.—Late dates of fall departure are: Utah—Willard, September 4. Arizona—Grand Canyon, October 6. South Dakota—Hot Springs, September 9. Wyoming—Laramie, September 9. Colorado—Boulder, October 2.

Casual records.—A specimen of this species was captured alive at Hillsdale, Mich., in August 1926; and another was obtained at Hot Springs National Park, Ark., on May 4, 1935.

Egg dates.—California: 86 records, May 8 to June 21; 43 records, May 21 to June 3, indicating the height of the season.

Family TROCHILIDAE: Hummingbirds

EUGENES FULGENS (Swainson)

RIVOLI'S HUMMINGBIRD

PLATES 49, 50

HABITS

This fine, large hummingbird is the largest of our North American hummingbirds, though the blue-throated hummingbird closely approaches it in size, the two appearing about equally large as seen in life. It is also one of the handsomest, although not so brilliantly colored as some of the smaller species. In the male the crown is a rich metallic violet-blue, and the throat a brilliant emerald-green, abruptly contrasted with the glossy-black breast and the bronzy green of the back; this color pattern is so arranged that every change in the bird's position brings a different color into view.

It is mainly a Central American species, ranging as far south as Nicaragua, through the tablelands of Guatemala and Mexico, and barely crossing our southern border into the mountains of southern Arizona and New Mexico. It was added to our fauna by Henry W. Henshaw (1875), who took the first specimen at Camp Grant, Ariz., in 1873. Since then, as he expected, it has been found to be a fairly common summer resident in various other mountain canyons.

We found it in the Huachuca Mountains, Ariz., in several of the canyons, where its favorite haunts seemed to be among the maples along the mountain streams, and where it ranges from 5,000 feet up to 7,500 feet on the slopes just below the main pine belt, where there were scattering yellow pines. Otho C. Poling (1890) says of its haunts in this same region:

It arrives in May, but is nowhere plentiful until the mescal shrubs begin to blossom, about the middle of June. From this time on during the entire summer one may observe on almost any hillside below the pine belt large clusters of bright red or yellow flowers spreading out from stalks ten or fifteen feet high. There are many varieties of this plant and all are favorite feeding resorts of the Rivoli Hummer. I have shot as many as a dozen in a day simply by sitting down and watching for them to come and feed. It is necessary to select a well-matured plant, and at the proper elevation, as well as in good surroundings of spruce pines. While feeding, these birds range from 4,500 to 8,000 feet altitude or up to the pine belt, their favorite grounds being where the pines end on the downward slope.

Bendire (1895) quotes from some notes given him by Dr. A. K. Fisher, as follows:

The Rivoli Hummer was not met with by us in the Chiricahua Mountains until we made camp in the upper part of Ruckers Canyon, among the yellow pines (*Pinus ponderosa*). On the morning of June 5, 1894, an adult male dashed through the camp, paused a moment over a flower spike of a scarlet *Pentstemon*, and then disappeared up the canyon as rapidly as it had come. No more were seen until we reached the high mountains at Fly Park. * * * They were usually found in the more open parts of the forest where fire had killed a portion of the evergreens, and a deciduous undergrowth of aspens and shrubs thrived about the cool springs and little rivulets. A boreal honeysuckle (*Lonicera involucrata*) was abundant and just coming into bloom. All the Hummers in the vicinity, the Rivoli Hummer among them, delighted to glean from the flowers and to sit half concealed among the large leaves of this shrub."

Dickey and van Rossem (1938) say of its haunts in El Salvador: "Rivoli's hummingbird was found only among the oaks and pines and among the scrubby, flowering growths between 7,000 and 8,000 feet on the south slope of Los Esesmiles, and about some flowering agave plants scattered over rocky portions of the summit of Volcán de Santa Ana at 7,200 feet."

Nesting.—Mr. Henshaw (1875) seems to have reported the first nest discovered, of which he says:

A very beautiful nest was discovered, which, save in its large size, resembles in its construction the best efforts of the little Eastern Rubythroat. It is composed of mosses nicely woven into an almost circular cup, the interior possessing a lining of the softest and downiest feathers, while the exterior is elaborately covered with lichens, which are securely bound on by a network of the finest silk from spiders' webs. It was saddled on the horizontal limb of an alder, about twenty feet above the bed of a running mountain stream, in a glen which was overarched and shadowed by several huge spruces, making it one of the most shady and retired little nooks that could be imagined. * * * The dimensions of the nest are as follows: depth, externally, 1.50; internally, 0.75; greatest external diameter, 2.25; internal diameter, 1.15.

Major Bendire (1895) received two nests from W. W. Price, taken in the Huachuca Mountains, Arizona: "The best preserved one of the two measures 2¼ inches in outer diameter by 2 inches in depth; its inner diameter is 1½ by 1¼ inches in depth. It is composed of soft, silky plant fibers, and is thickly coated exteriorly with small pieces of lichen, and lined with fine down and one or two soft, fluffy feathers, apparently those of a species of Titmouse. It resembles the nest of the Ruby-throated Hummingbird very closely in its general make up, but is naturally considerably larger. It was found by Mr. L. Miller on June 22, 1894, at an elevation of about 7,000 feet, saddled on a walnut branch about 10 feet from the ground, and contained one young nearly able to fly."

Apparently this hummingbird does not like to have its nest location observed, for, on May 28, 1922, as we were walking up through the narrow, rocky canyon known as "the box," we happened to see a partially built nest on a horizontal branch of a maple overhanging the stream. While we were watching it the female came to the nest with building material and evidently saw us. On our return, a few hours later, we were surprised to find that the nest had been entirely removed, and it was never again rebuilt in that same spot.

On the following day we found another nest in Miller Canyon, in the same general region in the Huachuca Mountains. It was about 30 feet from the ground, saddled on a horizontal branch of a maple over the trail, and so far out on the branch that it could be reached only with the aid of a rope. My companion, Frank C. Willard, succeeded in securing it for me, however. It was a beautiful nest, much like those described above, made of plant down and other soft substances, covered with lichens on the outside, and all bound together with cobwebs. This, and other nests that I have seen, though suggesting those of the rubythroat, are proportionately broader and not so high.

Mr. Willard records seven other nests in his notes, all found in the Huachuca Mountains. Five of these were in maples at heights ranging from 20 to 55 feet above ground; one was 40 feet up on a horizontal branch of a large pine and 20 feet out from the trunk; the other was placed 40 feet from the ground in a sycamore near the tip of a branch at the top of the tree. Of this last nest he says: "The nest appeared to be built in an old western wood pewee's nest, and was made of sycamore down, covered with lichens. The female sat in the nest until I reached the branch, and then flew, returning again almost immediately and sitting on the nest until I almost touched her with the net; she tried to get under the net while I was taking the eggs out, and finally settled right in the net. After the eggs were taken she returned and rearranged some of the lining while I was cutting off the branch." All these nests were found at altitudes ranging from 5,000 to 8,500 feet, mostly nearer the former level. Bendire (1895) says that they range up to 10,000 feet.

Mr. Willard, in his published article (1899), describes the bird's actions in building its nest:

Returning the next day, what looked like the beginning of a nest could be seen; so I sat down to watch. The bird soon came with something in her bill which she stopped just a second to place in position, then flew off through the branches of a large pine nearby. On her return I could see nothing in her beak, but she evidently had some spider web, for she laid something on one side of the nest and then, turning around, reached under the branch and took hold of it and pulled it under and up, fastening it in place by a stroking motion with the side of her bill. This work continued with great regularity during the hour spent in watching her, nearly every other trip seeming to be after spider web. Once a short stop for rest was made, and several expeditions against neighboring Wood Pewees or an inquisitive Jay relieved her labors. Just a week was required to build the nest and lay two eggs.

Of the behavior of the bird at another nest, he writes in the same paper: "While I was trying to get within reach the female made numerous dashes at me. She would fly from an oak a few rods distant, straight as an arrow right at my head, turning off and upward at a sharp angle when within two or three feet of me. I instinctively dodged several times, she came so close. During the last few feet of her flight the wings were held perfectly steady, not vibrating in the least until after she had turned. The humming of her wings was like that made by an immense beetle or a bumblebee, lacking the sharpness of that of small hummingbirds."

Eggs.—The Rivoli's hummingbird lays almost invariably two eggs. These are like other hummingbirds' eggs, pure white, without gloss, and varying from oval to elliptical-oval, sometimes slightly elliptical-ovate. The measurements of 43 eggs average 15.4 by 10.0 millimeters; the eggs showing the four extremes measure **16.5** by 10.4, 15.3 by **11.4**, **14.0** by 10.0, and 15.1 by **9.4** millimeters.

Plumages.—I have seen no nestlings and can find no description of them. Ridgway (1892) says that the immature male is "intermediate in coloration between the adult male and female, * * * the crown only partly violet, the throat only partly green, chest slightly mixed with black, etc., the tail exactly intermediate both in form and color." And that the young female is "similar to the adult female, but all the contour feathers of the upper parts margined with pale buffy-grayish, and under parts darker, with entire sides distinctly glossed with bronze-green." These characters are well shown in a large series that I have examined. Four young males, collected in July, all show more or less green in the throat, but only one, taken July 25, shows any violet in the crown. Others, taken in September and on November 1, show further progress toward maturity; and two young males, taken July 9 and 12, are still in first winter plumage.

Food.—Not much has been published on the food of Rivoli's hummingbird. Bendire (1895) mentions a boreal honeysuckle (*Lonicera involucrata*) as one of the plants from which Dr. Fisher saw them gleaning food, and says: "They are said to be especially fond of hovering about the blossoms of the mescal (*Agave americana*); these are generally infested by numerous small insects, on which they feed, and, like all our hummingbirds, they are exceedingly greedy and quarrelsome, chasing each other constantly from one flower stalk to another."

He quotes Mr. Price as saying that "during the flowering season it feeds extensively in the flowers of the *Agave parryi* in the Huachuca Mountains. In the Chiricahuas I have found it early in the mornings in open glades, feeding on the flowers of an iris." Mr. Poling (1890) mentions its fondness for the bright red and yellow flowers of the mescal on the slopes of the Huachucas.

Probably any brightly colored flowers, to which insects are attracted, are resorted to by this and other hummingbirds, the insects feeding on the nectar and the hummingbirds feeding on both insects and nectar. Mr. Fowler (1903) saw it feeding "among some scarlet geraniums in a large flower-bed."

Three stomachs examined by Cottam and Knappen (1939) contained leaf bugs, plant lice, leafhoppers, parasitic wasps, beetles, flies, fragments of a moth, and undetermined insects and spiders. "No fewer than eight species of insects and spiders were noted in one stomach." Spiders made up 31.66 percent and flies 26 percent of the whole food.

Behavior.—While I was collecting birds with Frank Willard in the Huachuca Mountains, he asked me not to shoot any blue-throated hummingbirds, as they were so rare, and I agreed to respect his wishes. One morning we were sitting on a steep hillside watching some large hummingbirds that were chasing each other about in the tops of some tall pine trees on the slope below us. I wanted a Rivoli very much, so he pointed out one that I could shoot, but, much to his disgust, when we picked it up, it proved to be a male bluethroat. This illustrates the similarity of the two species in general appearance.

The flight of Rivoli's hummingbird is somewhat different from that of the small hummers that I have seen. It is a large, heavily bodied bird, and its flight, though swift, is somewhat slower in proportion to its size than that of the smaller species; its wing strokes are less rapid, and it indulges in occasional periods of sailing on set wings, much after the manner of a swift.

F. H. Fowler (1903) writes of one that he saw: "Its motions are unlike any other hummer I have ever seen as its wings did not hum in the manner that has given this family its name, but cut the air with strong, firm, wing beats. Its flight was erratic, like that of the hummingbird moth, and at times like that of a bat. It would even soar, or sail for a few feet. It was not very shy, but when it made up its mind to go it would flit away on an erratic course without the slightest warning."

Mr. Poling (1890) observes that "their flight is exceedingly rapid at times but they often fly slowly so that the wings can be easily seen during the beats. The noise made by this bird's wings during a rapid flight is not like the buzzing of the small Hummer's wings, the beats being more slow and distinct, without any buzzing noise."

Like many other hummingbirds, the Rivoli is very quarrelsome; those that we watched, as mentioned above, were evidently quarreling with the bluethroats. And Mr. Ridgway (1892) quotes the following remarks of Mr. Salvin, who was trying to collect a specimen of this species: "Another Humming Bird rushes in, knocks the one I covet off his perch, and the two go fighting and screaming away at a pace hardly to be followed by the eye. Another time this flying fight is sustained in midair, the belligerents, mounting higher and higher till the one worsted in battle darts away seeking shelter, followed by the victor, who never relinquishes the pursuit till the vanquished, by doubling and hiding, succeeds in making his escape. These fierce raids are not waged alone between members of the same species. *Eugenes fulgens* attacks with equal ferocity *Amazilia dumerilii*, and, animated by no high-souled generosity, scruples not to tilt with the little *Trochilus colubris*."

Voice.—Mr. Poling (1890) says that their "note is a twittering sound, louder, not so shrill, and uttered more slowly than those of the small Hummers."

Field marks.—The large size of Rivoli's hummingbird and its manner of flight will distinguish it from all except the blue-throated hummingbird. The adult males of these two species may be easily distinguished by the different color patterns, if the bird is near enough; the bluish-purple crown, the brilliant green throat, and the glossy black breast of the Rivoli are very different from the greenish crown, dull blue throat, and grayish-brown breast of the blue-throated. More conspicuous at a greater distance are the broad white tips of the three outer tail feathers of the blue-throated, as compared with the uniformly dark, greenish-bronze tail of the male Rivoli. The females of the two species are more alike but can be recognized by the tails; the female Rivoli has the three outer feathers tipped with grayish, whereas in the blue-throated these tips are white.

DISTRIBUTION

Range.—Southern New Mexico and Arizona; south to Nicaragua.

Breeding range.—Rivoli's hummingbird breeds **north** to southeastern Arizona (Santa Catalina Mountains and Fort Huachuca); southwestern New Mexico (Chiricahua Mountains and San Luis Mountains); and Nuevo Leon (Bravo). **East** to Nuevo Leon (Bravo); western Tamaulipas (Rampahuilla); and Guatemala (Momostenango and Tecpam). **South** to Guatemala (Tecpam, San Lucas, and probably Santa Marta); and Guerrero (Omilteme). **West** to Guerrero (Omilteme); State of Mexico (Volcano of Toluca); Durango (Arroyo del Buey); western Chihuahua (Pinos Altos); eastern Sonora (Oposura); and southeastern Arizona (Huachuca Mountains, Santa Rita Mountains, and Santa Catalina Mountains).

Winter range.—Present information does not permit exact delineation of the winter range, but at this season it apparently is not found north of Guerrero (Taxco). From this point it occurs southward casually to Nicaragua (San Rafael).

Migration.—Early dates of spring arrival in Arizona are: Huachuca Mountains, April 24; Tombstone, May 9. No data are available for the fall migration.

Egg dates.—Arizona: 24 records, May 6 to July 28; 12 records, June 14 to July 14, indicating the height of the season.

LAMPORNIS CLEMENCIAE BESSOPHILUS (Oberholser)

ARIZONA BLUE-THROATED HUMMINGBIRD

PLATES 51–52

HABITS

Although the blue-throated hummingbird had been known for more than half a century, as a Mexican bird, it was not until 1884 that it was introduced to our fauna. William Brewster received the first specimen, which was taken by Frank Stephens's assistant in the Santa Catalina Mountains, Ariz., on May 14, 1884. Since then it has been found in the Huachuca, Chiricahua, and Santa Rita Mountains in Arizona and in the San Luis Mountains in New Mexico; it probably will be found to occur in summer in some of the other mountain ranges in that general region. This race of the species also is found in the Sierra Madre of western Mexico.

The species was split into two subspecies by Dr. H. C. Oberholser (1918), who named the northern race *Cyanolaemus clemenciae bessophilus* and described it as "similar to *Cyanolaemus clemenciae clemenciae*, but bill shorter; male with upper parts duller, particularly on the rump, which is more washed with grayish; lower surface decidedly paler; and throat duller. Female duller above and paler below than the female of *Cyanolaemus clemenciae clemenciae*." The difference in the length of the bill between the two races is not very impressive; in typical *clemenciae*, the average for eight males is 23.8, and for two females 26.7 millimeters; whereas in *bessophilus*, the average for ten males is 22.2, and for two females 24 millimeters; however, there seems to be no overlapping in the list of measurements given.

The Arizona blue-throated hummingbird will always be associated in my mind with Ramsay Canyon, that interesting bird paradise on the eastern slope of the Huachuca Mountains in southeastern Arizona. The approach to it lies across some gently sloping, grassy plains, which rise to an elevation of about 4,500 feet at the base of the mountains; from here the trail in the canyon slopes upward to a height of about 9,000 feet at the summit of the divide. Around the mouth of the canyon an open parklike grove of large black-jack oaks furnishes a congenial home for a number of noisy and conspicuous Arizona jays. The lower and wider portion of the canyon, along the bed of the stream, is heavily wooded with giant, picturesque sycamores and various oaks, maples, ashes, walnuts, alders, and locusts; while on the drier slopes are dense thickets of scrubby oaks and various thorny bushes, with scattered red-stemmed manzanitas and small alligator-bark cedars; and on the hillsides the rounded head of a handsome madrone towers occasionally above the forest.

The canyon is well watered by a clear, cool mountain stream that comes bounding down through a narrow, rocky gorge, furnishes the water supply for a summer colony, and finally disappears below ground in the washes out on the plains. We made our headquarters at Berner's place, at an elevation of about 5,000 feet, a cool and delightful place in the wider part of the canyon, where a number of neat cottages and small gardens are maintained for the summer colony. Here the stream ran almost under our cabin; and here we often heard the loud buzzing of the blue-throated hummingbird or observed its direct and rapid flight, as it whizzed by our doorway along the stream. It seemed never to wander far from the narrow confines of this mountain gorge and always seemed to feel perfectly at home and unafraid among the cottages and gardens.

Courtship.—Once we saw two males contending for the affections of an observant female; they were chasing each other about in the treetops and displaying their widespread, long tails, with the conspicuous white tips on the outer feathers; perhaps the bluethroats were more in evidence than they appeared to us. They saw us and departed before the ceremony was completed.

Nesting.—One of our main objectives in Arizona was to find the nest of the blue-throated hummingbird; but all our efforts were in vain, for we never succeeded in finding an occupied nest. We did, however, find some old nests in two entirely different situations. There was an open dancing pavilion, roofed over but open on all four sides, that stood close to the stream. My companion, Frank C. Willard, told me that this hummer had nested under the roof of this building in the past, and he pointed out to me the remains of two nests of previous seasons on a dead branch that extended under the eaves. We saw the hummer near this pavilion several times, but, up to the time that we left, she had not built another nest there.

We had been told that the blue-throated hummingbird had been known to build its nests on the stems of some flowering plants that grow in clusters on the rocks, above the pools or waterfalls, in a narrow rocky gorge, known as "the box," a short distance above our cabin. While passing through this gorge on several occasions we had heard or seen this hummer flying past us, and had looked for its nest in vain. But one day, while examining a large clump of cardinal monkeyflower (*Mimulus cardinalis*) growing on a sloping ledge near a little waterfall, we found a last year's nest of this hummer attached to the stem of one of these plants and not over a foot above the ledge.

George F. Breninger (Childs, 1906a) found and collected a nest and two eggs of this hummer, which came into the collection of John Lewis Childs, who published a colored plate of it in The Warbler. The nest was found on May 29, 1897, in the gorge where we found the nest referred to above. It was attached to some of the taller stems in a large clump of maidenhair ferns, "which grew in the side of a wall of rock in a cut worn by water." It was a large nest, apparently about three inches high and about two inches wide; it was "composed of oak catkins, green moss and spiders' webs."

Frank C. Willard (1911) has found several nests of the Arizona hummingbird, of which he writes:

In July, 1899, I located a nest built in an old Black Phoebe's nest on a rock overhanging a shallow pool. * * *

Although I made repeated efforts I failed to locate another nest until the season of 1910. I made my headquarters at Berner's ranch in Ramsay Canyon. He has a flower and fruit garden, with several small greenhouses for winter use. Hanging from a nail in the roof of one of these was the handle of a lard bucket, and built upon the lower crook was a many-storied hummer's nest, some four inches high. It contained one newly hatched young. The tell-tale "squeaks" of an unseen bird identified my find and by keeping out of sight, and quiet, I was able to get a good look at the female parent. Later I saw very frequently both parents feeding among the flowers and occasionally within arm's length of me. * * *

During the last few days of my previous visit, I had seen the female in a bunkhouse that had formerly been used as a greenhouse. A piece of baling wire was wound around a nail in a rafter and formed a sort of hook. When I found the young one gone, I went at once to this bunkhouse and found the female sitting on a completed nest. She flew as I entered the room. I secured a ladder and soon held the nest and two fresh eggs in my hand. Some children were occupying this room so I did not dare leave the nest for further notes. I put another wire up, however, to furnish another nesting site.

June 21, the nest where the young had been seemed to be receiving additions, and the sides were somewhat built up, but I could not see the birds around. June 25 the nest contained one egg and the next morning there were two. A visitor told me that it was liable to be taken by some small boys who were there, so again I was afraid to leave it for observation and collected the nest and set, first taking a picture of it, showing the eggs. * * *

The nest is made largely of oak blossom hulls, and stems of the same, with a small amount of plant down intermixed. The whole is well tied together with cobwebs. The nest cavity is shallow and the edges are not incurved, differing in both these respects from the nests of other hummingbirds with which I am familiar.

There is a nest, with a set of two eggs, of this hummer in the Thayer collection in Cambridge that was taken by Mr. Willard in the same locality on May 31, 1913. It was placed "on a wire hanging from the ceiling of an old barn; this pair had already raised one brood of young this season." It is a large and roughly made nest, nearly 3 inches high by 2½ inches in diameter and the inner cavity nearly an inch deep. It is made of a great variety of plant material, as described above, felted closely into a compact structure, reinforced with coarse straws and weed stems, bound together with fine fibers and cobwebs, and lined with finer pieces of similar material. The material used reminds me of the kind used in bushtits' nests. Similar materials were used in the nest we found in the *Mimulus cardinalis*, referred to above.

Milton S. and Rose Carolyn Ray (1925) found a nest in a narrow canyon in the Huachuca Mountains on May 28, 1924. It was "suspended on a wire hanging from one of the rafters" in a small deserted building. Mr. Ray says of it: "The nest is beautifully woven of moss, plant down and cottony fibers, webbed together on the exterior and decorated there with bits of very bright green moss and pale green lichens. The lining of the nest consists almost entirely of cottony fibers and down. It is unusually large for a hummingbird, measuring 3¼ inches high by 2⅜ across. The cavity is 1¾ across by 1⅛ deep."

Eggs.—The Arizona blue-throated hummingbird lays either one or two eggs, normally two. These are like other hummers' eggs, elliptical-oval, pure white, and without gloss. The measurements of eight eggs average 15.1 by 10.0 millimeters; the eggs showing the four extremes measure **16.8** by 10.0, 15.0 by **10.4**, and **13.8** by **9.7** millimeters.

Plumages.—I have seen no naked young and no partially fledged nestlings. In the young male the forehead and more or less of the crown are brownish gray, with no green feathers; the green feathers of the upper parts are margined with gray; the postocular and rictal stripes are less clearly defined than in adults; and the blue throat is only partially developed. I have seen birds in this plumage in July, August, and September. Probably the fully adult plumage is not assumed until the following summer, for I have seen birds in this plumage in March and April and as late as June 12.

Food.—In Ramsay Canyon, this hummingbird feeds regularly and fearlessly at the flowers in the gardens about the cottages and even in the greenhouses, where it doubtless secures small insects as well as the nectar from the flowers. Mrs. Bailey (1928) says that, in New Mexico, its food consists of "insects from flowers of the shrubby honeysuckle, gilia, agave, and other plants."

In the summary of the contents of three stomachs, Cottam and Knappen (1939) include fragments of true bugs (Hemiptera), small beetles, flies, wasps, spiders, daddy-longlegs, pollen grains, and plant fiber. In two stomachs 10 percent and 15 percent, respectively, of the food was pollen. "One bird had made 92 percent of its meal on seven specimens of a fly (*Hypocera johnsoni*), which is rare in collections."

Behavior.—The flight of the blue-throated hummingbird seemed to us to be exceedingly swift, as it whizzed by us up or down the stream, uttering at intervals its squeaking note. It always seemed to fly directly over or along the stream; and it was gone almost as soon as it appeared. It was not at all shy and seemed to pay little attention to human beings, coming into the gardens freely while people were about. It would often alight within a few feet of a quiet observer and seemed to spend much time perched quietly on some dead twig, treetop, or other open perch.

Voice.—The only note we heard was the squeaking note, which was repeated every few minutes; Mr. Willard (1911) noted that the second note is higher pitched than the first, and the third note lower than either of the other two. Mr. Ray (see Rose Carolyn Ray, 1925) refers to it as "a rather far-reaching but not overloud alarm note, 'seek'-'seek'-'seek'." Dr. Alexander Wetmore (1932) says: "The birds utter sharp, squeaking calls, and the male has a simple song of three or four notes, repeated at short intervals while the singer perches upright with head elevated."

Field marks.—This large hummer is not likely to be confused with any other hummingbird except the almost equally large Rivoli's. The most conspicuous field mark of the blue-throated is the long, broad tail, with the prominent white tips of the three outer rectrices, recognizable in both sexes and at all ages; only the female Rivoli's has light tipped outer rectrices, and these are gray rather than white. The blue throat of the male is not conspicuous, except at short range and in good light, but the white postocular and rictal stripes are more easily seen at short distances, especially the former.

DISTRIBUTION

Range.—Southern Arizona, New Mexico, and Texas south to southern Mexico.

Breeding range.—The blue-throated hummingbird breeds **north** to southeastern Arizona (Santa Catalina Mountains, Paradise, and the Chiricahua Mountains); southwestern New Mexico (San Luis Mountains); southwestern Texas (Chisos Mountains); and Nuevo Leon (Bravo). **East** to Nuevo Leon (Bravo and Galindo); and Veracruz (Las Minas, Las Vigas, and Huamantla). **South** to southern Veracruz (Huamantla); State of Mexico (Mexico and the Volcano of Toluca); and Guerrero (Omilteme). **West** to central Guerrero (Omilteme); Durango (Arroyo del Buey); western Chihuahua (Jesus Maria and Pinos Altos); eastern Sonora (Oposura); and southeastern Arizona (Ramsay Canyon, Tombstone, and Santa Catalina Mountains).

Winter range.—During the winter season the species is apparently concentrated in southern Mexico, chiefly in the States of Michoacan (Nahuatzen and Mount Tancitaro); and Guerrero (Taxco and Chilpancingo).

The range as outlined is for the entire species, which has been separated into two subspecies. The Texas blue-throated hummingbird (*L. c. clemenciae*) ranges from southern Mexico north to western Texas, while the Arizona blue-throated hummingbird (*L. c. bessophilus*) is found through the Sierra Madre of western Mexico north to Arizona and New Mexico.

Migration.—Very little is known about the migrations of these birds, but they have been observed to arrive in the spring at Tucson, Ariz., as early as April 21.

Egg dates.—Arizona: 7 records, May 14 to July 17.

Mexico: 2 records, February 17 and September 9.

LAMPORNIS CLEMENCIAE CLEMENCIAE (Lesson)

TEXAS BLUE-THROATED HUMMINGBIRD

HABITS

Since Dr. Oberholser (1918) has described the Arizona bird as subspecifically distinct from the Mexican bird of the earlier authors, this type race of the species has been restricted in its distribution to central and southern Mexico from Michoacan and Oaxaca northward to the Chisos Mountains in western Texas. It would seem as if this race might more properly be called the Mexican blue-throated hummingbird, as most of its range is in Mexico; furthermore the birds from the Chisos Mountains do not seem to be quite typical of the southern race; Dr. Oberholser (1918) remarks that these birds "show in some specimens a tendency toward typical *Cyanolaemus clemenciae clemenciae*, but are decidedly referable to *Cyanolaemus clemenciae bessophilus*." On the other hand, Van Tyne and Sutton (1937) refer the Chisos Mountains birds to the Mexican race, *Lampornis clemenciae clemenciae*.

Typical *clemenciae*, the subject of this sketch, has a somewhat longer bill, darker under parts, a slightly more brilliant blue throat, and more extensive as well as brighter green on the upper parts and flanks, than the Arizona bird.

Nesting.—Dr. E. W. Nelson wrote to Major Bendire (1895) as follows:

Coeligena clemenciae is a sparingly distributed summer resident of all the mountain regions of south central Mexico, between 7,500 and 12,000 feet. They are rather quiet birds, often found perched on the tips of large maguey leaves. In the forests of pines of the higher slopes they are not often seen except as they dash by among the trees. On the 9th of September, 1893, a nest containing two eggs was found at an altitude of 11,500 feet on the north slope of the volcano of Toluca, in the State of Mexico. At this time the nights had already become quite frosty here. The nest was built in the fork of a small shrub, growing out of the face of a cliff about 30 feet above its base, on the side of a canyon, in the pine and fir forest. The nest was discovered by seeing the parent approach its vicinity. She flew quietly close up to the nest, and then, turning so that she faced out from the cliff and away from the nest, she moved backward several inches and settled lightly on the eggs. She was easily alarmed, darting away through the forest, and was not seen again. The nest was nearly inaccessible, and one egg was thrown out and broken in securing it.

Major Bendire (1895) says of the nest:

This nest, No. 26332, United States National Museum collection, now before me, is a handsome and rather bulky structure, which is apparently composed entirely of fine mosses, the whole evenly quilted together into a smooth, homogeneous mass, and bound firmly together with silk from cocoons and spiders' webs. It is saddled in a tripronged fork of a small twig, the three stems being incorporated in the walls of the nest, holding it firmly in position, the main stem being only one-twelfth of an inch in diameter. It measures 2¾ inches in outer diameter by 3 inches in depth; the inner cup is 1¼ inches in diameter by three-fourths of an inch deep. The walls of the nest are three-fourths of an inch thick, and the inner cup appears very small for the large size of the nest. It looks like a warm and cozy structure, and it needs to be so. As the eggs were only slightly incubated when found, the young would probably have hatched by September 20, and would scarcely have been large enough to leave the nest before October 12, by which time one might reasonably look for snowstorms at such an altitude. There is but very little inner lining, not enough to hide the moss, which looks to me like the down from willow catkins.   Two eggs are laid to a set, and probably two broods are raised in a season.

At the other end of the breeding season, Josiah H. Clark (1900) found a nest on February 16, 1899, near Las Vigas, Veracruz, Mexico, in a canyon at an elevation of about 4,500 feet, of which he writes these interesting circumstances:

On February 12 we had snow, with the thermometer down to 32° F. at 4 p. m., and on February 13, at 7 a. m., down to 29° F. All the plants and trees were covered with ice, and the leaves of almost everything were killed; we found many frozen birds, and that was the fate of the owner of this nest. We only had two cold days, but that was enough to destroy many birds.

The nest was fastened to a vine one tenth of an inch in diameter and about three feet above a small stream of water. The vine hung from a large rock, and would have been sheltered from rain by the overhanging rock. The nest is of bulky structure, and is perhaps a new nest built on top of an old one. It is composed of fine moss massed together, and bound with spiders' webs or similar material. It measures, outer diameter, 2¾ inches, depth 4 inches; inside diameter, 1¼ inches, depth, ¾ inch. There is very little lining, only enough for the eggs to rest on, consisting of down from some fern.

Eggs.—The only two sets of eggs of this hummingbird of which I have any record consisted of two eggs each. The eggs are indistinguishable from those of the Arizona race, dull white and elliptical-oval. The measurements of the only egg I have been able to locate, in the United States National Museum, are 16.26 by 12.45 millimeters.

The food, behavior, voice, and general habits of this subspecies do not differ materially from those of the Arizona race.

ARCHILOCHUS COLUBRIS (Linnaeus)

RUBY-THROATED HUMMINGBIRD

PLATES 53–57

HABITS

CONTRIBUTED BY WINSOR MARRETT TYLER

The ruby-throated hummingbird is the only species of hummingbird that enters the eastern two-thirds of the United States. A minute spritelike bird, scarcely bigger than a good-sized insect, it is white below and burnished, sparkling green on the back. The adult male has a gorgeous flaming throat, which, when the sun strikes it, flashes back a deep, glowing orange or red.

The hummingbird moves its wings with such extraordinary rapidity that it seems to be moving through the air between two wisps of mist. Its buzzing wings hold it steady in the air. We see it poised before a flower, most often alone, its body motionless, its tail swaying, as firmly fixed in space as if it were standing on a perch. We see it dart adroitly from one blossom to another, and another—an inch away, six feet away—pausing exactly in front of each one, probing it with its beak, starting and stopping with a jerk, almost, turning at any angle with a sudden twist; or it may shoot off and away, bounding along at full speed. A remarkable power, unbirdlike, more like an overgrown bee.

Spring.—In spring the ruby-throated hummingbird leaves its tropical or semitropical winter quarters and presses northward, keeping pace as the season advances with the opening of its favorite flowers. The bird's preference for some of these is so marked that it seems oftentimes to regulate its migration so as to arrive on the very day of their blossoming. For example, Austin Paul Smith (1915), writing of the Boston Mountains, Ark., says: "The arrival of the 'ruby-throat' and the blossoming of the dwarf buckeye (*Aesculus parviflora*) were found to be coincident. For it is upon the flowers of this shrub that the ruby-throat finds most of its subsistence for the first two weeks after arrival."

At the start of the northward journey many of the tiny birds fly over a wide stretch of the Gulf of Mexico on their way to the southernmost States. They cross these dangerous waters with little concern, apparently, for W. E. D. Scott (1890) speaks of seeing them "at considerable distance from land" while he was fishing off the Dry Tortugas. "One morning" he says, "I counted six pass by the boat. * * * At such times their flight was direct and very rapid and all were going in a northerly direction. They flew about twenty-five feet above the water and did not appear in any way fatigued, nor show any desire to alight on the boat, as small birds crossing the water so frequently do."

Even in the Southern States hummingbirds run the danger of late, killing frosts. "Didymus" (1891) tells thus of the calamity that overcame them in Florida. "It was a warm winter and the early opening of spring brought out the flowers and started myriads of these little creatures on their journey toward the north. Then came that blighting frost—which they could stand, but the 'death of the flowers' was too much for them and they were picked up dead and dying everywhere. They came in unusual numbers and seemed to be nearly all males. After the frost but few were seen. * * *"

On the other hand, Charles B. Floyd (1937) describes an occasion in which some hummingbirds withstood prolonged low temperature and even snow:

The following observations with Hummingbirds * * * made in the Laurentian Mountains of Canada during the last two weeks of May, 1936, are of interest. * * *

On May 20th the temperature in the early morning was 22 degrees Fahrenheit above zero after a snowfall during the night of six inches. This snow did not completely melt until late in the afternoon. The temperature the following night was 28 degrees above zero. Early on the following morning the temperature was again 22 degrees. Ice formed in water-pails and a cold wind blew all day. * * *

During the morning of May 20th the ground and trees were covered with six inches of heavy, wet snow. I spent several hours paddling along the lake-shore on which our camp was located, observing the Hummingbirds and warblers that came there to feed. * * * All these appeared sluggish with the cold, and the Hummingbirds fluttered about on the underside of the snow-covered leaves, which were about half-developed, apparently capturing minute insects (probably aphids), on which they fed, occasionally dropping to the logs that floated along the shore to secure something so small that I could not determine what it was they were eating. * * *

All the birds permitted so close an approach that I could not use field-glasses during these observations. The last day of my stay the Hummingbirds were observed in their usual feeding places and apparently survived the cold weather unharmed.

Usually in spring we meet hummingbirds singly, or at most two or three together, but once in a while we come upon a gathering of migrating birds—almost always of one sex—collected sometimes in a single favored tree. About noon on May 22, 1936, I came upon such a gathering. The birds were in a good-sized red horse-chestnut tree in full flower. They must have numbered more than a dozen, perhaps twice this number. As I came near the tree there burst out a long series of short, sharp, high, jerky notes, the pitch rising and falling, the volume increasing and decreasing. The individual notes had a squeaky quality suggested by the letters *sk*, but in spite of this I was reminded of the house wren's chatter. By direct comparison, however, the wren's voice was much more mellow, and the delivery more indolent, if one may use the word in reference to that sprightly bird.

Looking in among the branches, I could see here and there two or three birds flying about, making darts at each other. Sometimes a bird or two birds, one chasing the other, flew out and, after flying around the tree a little way, shot in among the branches again. The tree seemed swarming with hummingbirds. Soon the activity calmed down, and the birds perched motionless on small branches, here and there.

The sound quieted also, but rose again energetically when the birds resumed their activity. They probed the blossoms, evidently feeding, but for the most part seemed interested in one another—playfully, or with little hostility. Once I saw two birds fly straight up in the air, close together like mating bees or a swallow feeding its young on the wing, strike at each other, I think, then turn and dive head-downward into the tree. Again a bird flies out from the tree at an approaching bird, utters *zzzt-zzz*, and drives it off.

The notes varied a good deal. Sometimes a note was so fine, high, and drawn out that it was only a hiss; generally they were very short and clearly cut, either single or double; sometimes they took on a rhythmic form and were repeated over and over, for example, *z, z, z, z, z, z, zzt,* the last note emphasized; and often they came in a long series—single, double, and triple notes all intermixed like a telegraph instrument in action.

It was difficult, owing to their activity among the dense branches, to see the birds clearly, and impossible to count them accurately, but I believe that most, if not all, of them were males, their throats in the dark shadow of the branches appearing black.

On the 24th there were fewer birds in the tree—the petals were falling to the ground—and on the 25th only two or three remained.

Jane L. Hine (1894) reports a similar gathering of female birds. She says: "About nine o'clock one spring morning, when lilacs were in bloom, we discovered that the old lilac bush by the well was 'swarming' with Hummingbirds—just come; we knew they were not there a few minutes before. There are five large lilacs on our premises and those of a near neighbor. On investigation I found four of these bushes alive, as it were, with Hummers—all females. The fifth bush, a Persian, they did not favor."

From these observations, and several more in the literature, we may infer that the sexes do not as a rule migrate together, and according to the opinion of many observers the males always precede the females.

Courtship.—In his courtship display the male rubythroat makes use of his marvelous proficiency in flight as well as of the brilliantly glowing feathers of his throat. As we watch him performing such flights as are described below, swinging back and forth along the arc of a wide circle, we get the impression of a bird upheld by a swaying wire; his swings are so accurate and precise that they suggest a geometric figure drawn in the air rather than the flight of a bird. Carl W. Schlag (1930), speaking of the courtship flight, says:

It is comparable to the strutting actions of various species of birds. It is performed several times daily during the breeding season. While the female is quietly feeding from flower to flower, the male will go through this performance, calculated no doubt to impress her more fully with all his charms. Rising up about eight or ten feet above and five or six to one side of her, he will suddenly swoop down, wings and tail outspread, right at her, passing within a few inches of her, the wings and tail making a terrific buzz for a bird so small. Passing her, he rises to an equal height on the opposite side, and turning comes down again in the same way, describing an inverted arc, with that surprisingly loud buzz just as he gets nearest to her. He keeps up this continuous swooping, as I term it, as long as half a minute, at times; at the conclusion of which he usually flies to some near-by perch and rests. During this performance the female feeds quietly at the same cluster of blossoms, not moving any distance away, and sometimes resting on a flower-stalk until he is through.

Mrs. Charles W. Melcher, of Homosassa Springs, Fla., describes a flight that, from its formal, regular character, was probably a variant of the usual courtship display, although there was no dipping—the bird progressing on a level line back and forth—and although Mrs. Melcher did not see a female bird in the vicinity. She writes to Mr. Bent: "Instead of the circular flight he flew in a straight line. Facing the north, he hovered, then moved eastward about 3 feet, then hovered, then moved eastward again for the same distance, continuing thus until he had covered perhaps 25 feet. Then, still facing north, he moved toward the west in the same manner, back to his starting point. I saw him cover the distance four times, twice east and twice west. The fact that he seemed to move sideways makes this a fantastic story, but I think that I have seen the birds that come to our feeders move in almost every direction.

"My attention was first attracted to this flight by the *regularity* of a humming sound out in the garden. There was a hum, then a second's pause, then another hum, each humming and each pause being of equal length. The humming was made, of course, while he hovered, and lasted perhaps three or four seconds. The pause was very short, just the time it took him to move 3 or 4 feet. The sounds of humming and twittering were so different from usual that I went to the door expecting to see some sort of flight that was out of the ordinary.

"Another performance we witnessed lasted two or three minutes. A male and a female were flying up and down. They were facing each other with tails spread, and there was much twittering. They covered a distance of 5 or 6 feet, and their flight was almost vertical. When he was at the top of his flight she was at the bottom of hers, and when she was at the top he was at the bottom. They were about 2½ feet apart. There was no thrusting at each other until, at the last, they came together for an instant on the windowsill. I was too far away to see if the contact was friendly."

Charles L. Whittle (1937) presents a full account of the actions of a male hummingbird during several weeks before egg-laying time— nine days of watching for a mate, weeks of courtship after she arrived, and after the culmination of his wooing, the almost immediate cessation of display. The bird came to his station in Peterboro, N. H., on May 21 "and began a long vigil lasting until May 30th, believed to be a search for a female." He continues:

This vigil took place from three observation posts overlooking a circular garden, one on an aerial, one on a dead branch of an elm, and a third on a dead twig at the top of an apple tree, all these perches being from fifteen to twenty feet from the ground. For the major portion of each day he occupied these perches, moving from one to another, and while perching he continually moved his head from side to side through an arc of 60–70 degrees. One cannot well escape the conclusion that he was searching for a female, since the habit was immediately discontinued upon the arrival of a female at the station on May 30th. Now, for a period of about a month, his attention was devoted to the female and consisted of the usual zooming before her whenever she appeared. * * * On July 2nd a male and a female were seen facing each other in the air about eight or ten inches apart, ascending and descending vertically to a height of about ten feet, and occasionally dropping to the ground for a moment. At other times their flights were more or less spiral in character, and such exhibitions were frequent up to July 7th, when Mrs. Whittle observed a pair drop to the ground beside our driveway, where copulation took place. From this time on the males were seen zooming only occasionally, and vertical flights ceased entirely after the first week in July. * * *

Mating, in the ordinary sense of the word, that is, pairing off well in advance of nest-building and continuing during nidification and raising of the young birds, as far as any evidence observable at this station is concerned, appears not to take place. No preference for a male on the part of a female is indicated until *just prior to egg-laying*, a period seemingly of three or four days. I have found no evidence that a male's interest in a female one day is manifested towards the same female the following day. All the pretty ways common among many species of mated pairs, often lasting two months at least, are entirely lacking among Hummingbirds. The male appears to be a free lance whose intimate interest in the female is confined to the short period just before and during egg-laying.

Nesting.—The hummingbird's nest, "a model of artistic workmanship," Torrey (1892) calls it, is a little compact mass about an inch deep and an inch across, firm in texture, lined with soft plant down, and covered over on the outside with tiny bits of lichen. It is commonly saddled on a limb, usually a small, down-sloping one, often near, and sometimes directly over, water. Wilson (1831) aptly describes the nest when viewed from below as "a mere mossy knot, or accidental protuberance."

Aretas A. Saunders (1936), who made an extensive study of the hummingbird in New York State, describes the situation of the nest thus:

In Allegany Park, the nesting site seems to be always along a brook valley, and in most cases the nest is on a limb that overhangs the brook. Eight nests that I have seen in Allegany Park were on limbs less than an inch in diameter, and one was on a limb a little more than a quarter of an inch through. The limb, in my experience, always slants a little downward from the tree. It is never so high in the tree that it is not sheltered above by other limbs or leafy branches. * * *

I do not suppose that the proximity of the brook has any particular significance in the Humming Bird's nesting except that its favorite flowers grow along the brook and the stream affords an open space. * * *

The [small] size of the limb and its downward slant seem to be aids in protection against possible tree-climbing enemies * * *

The protection from above is possibly to screen the nest from flying enemies, but chiefly to protect it against heavy storms * * *

Various kinds of trees are used for nesting, but in Allegany Park the majority of nests found have been in Hornbeams. Of the 11 nests I have observed, and one other reported to me, six were in Hornbeams, two in Yellow Birch, and one each in Sugar Maple, Red Maple and Beech. I have seen nests in Hemlocks in other regions * * *

The nests found have ranged from five to 18 feet from the ground or water, all but two of them being actually over water.

Saunders (1936) also points out that "the distribution of Humming Birds in Quaker Run valley is governed primarily by the occurrence of Bee Balm, *Monarda didyma*, the flower upon which they depend chiefly for nectar at the beginning of their breeding season in this region."

Bendire (1895) states that the height of the nest varies "from 6 to 50 feet high, usually from 10 to 20 feet from the ground." Of the nest itself Saunders (1936) says:

The nesting materials are of four kinds, bud scales, plant down, lichens and spider silk * * *. The bud scales make up the bulk of the nest, but by the time it is finished they are entirely covered by the lichens and plant down. * * *

Lichens * * * are put on the outside before the plant down is put in. The lining, in one case at least, was not put into the nest at all until some days after the eggs were laid and incubation begun. The bird continues adding lining material to the nest after the young are hatched, in one case gathering Fireweed down and taking it to the nest when the young were two weeks old. The plants from which down is gathered in Allegany Park are Fireweed, Canada Thistle, Orange Hawkweed and Rattlesnake Root. Possibly others such as Milkweed and various Composites are used also, but the Fireweed seems to be the most commonly used lining material. The bird gathers thistle down that is flying about in the air, but in the case of Fireweed gathers it directly from the plant * * *

I have never seen the Hummingbird gathering or working with the spider silk which holds the nest together and fastens it to its limb. The fastening of the nest to the limb is probably an early step in the nest building. But the spider silk is an important item, and in one nest I have seen, was run out and wrapped along two or three twigs that branched out from the point where the nest was fastened, to a distance of 15 inches.

A. Dawes DuBois, in a letter to Mr. Bent, describing the behavior of a female bird while weaving her nest, says: "I stationed myself close to the nest (which was 12 feet from the ground) and watched the bird come and go. She always flew off in the same direction and sometimes was away for five minutes or more. On returning with a tiny tuft of down in her bill, she alighted at once upon the nest and began to tuck the material into its walls on the inner side, using her delicate bill like a needle; then she vigorously worked her body up and down, and round-about thereby enlarging and shaping the cavity. Afterward she tucked or adjusted more securely the lichens on the outside. The male bird was not seen at any time."

H. E. Wheeler (1922) says that "the behavior of the female will invariably betray her home. It is easier still to locate the 'house' if the birds are building * * * for the birds keep their territory pretty well cleared of intruding visitors. On one occasion the female Ruby-throat left her nest repeatedly to torment a family of Carolina Wrens, and to pay her respects to a Tufted Titmouse. Otherwise I think I should have never located the tiny nest situated 50 feet above ground, and so thoroughly concealed from view."

In the experience of almost all observers the female parent builds the nest and rears the young unaided by her mate. Bradford Torrey (1892) long ago called attention to this habit in two delightful essays, and Saunders (1936) states in corroboration that "male Humming Birds do not seem to stay in the Quaker Run valley through the nesting season. They are rarely if ever seen after the middle of August."

It is very rare to find any deviation from this habit; hence the following is a very exceptional observation, and it may be that the male's attendance at this nest was merely perfunctory. W. A. Welter (1935), speaking of a nest found in Kentucky, says:

The entire nest, with the exception of bits of lichens that were added later, was built in one day. It is interesting to note that both birds, male and female, worked on this nest that first day. The male evidently was doing his share of the work. This seems to be an unusual circumstance, as ordinarily the male is supposed to scorn such menial duties. * * *

It would seem that the time consumed in nest building diminishes as the season progresses. Perhaps haste is necessary in order that the potential young may be completely developed by the time of fall migration. This need for haste may also have been the stimulant which caused the male in the last case to assist in nidification.

Bendire (1895) says: "I believe two broods are frequently raised in a season, occasionally three perhaps, as fresh eggs have been found as late as August 7. An old nest is sometimes occupied for several seasons and remodeled each year; and should the nest and eggs be taken or destroyed, a second and occasionally even a third and fourth attempt at nesting is made within about a week, and sometimes these subsequent nests are built in the same tree again, or in others close by."

Eggs.—[AUTHOR'S NOTE: Like other hummingbirds, the rubythroat regularly lays two eggs; I have no record of more or fewer. An interval of one day is said by Bendire (1895) to occur between the laying of the two eggs; he says also that the eggs are often laid before the nest is completed. The eggs are pure dead white without gloss and usually elliptical-oval in shape, though occasionally approaching elliptical-ovate, with one end slightly more pointed than the other. The measurements of 52 eggs average 12.9 by 8.5 millimeters; the eggs showing the four extremes measure 14.5 by 9.1, 11.5 by 8.2, and 12.7 by 7.8 millimeters.]

Young.—Bradford Torrey (1892) describing the young hummingbirds newly hatched from eggs no bigger than a pea, says: "Two lifeless-looking things lay in the bottom of the nest, their heads tucked out of sight, and their bodies almost or quite naked, except for a line of grayish down along the middle of the back." Isabella McC. Lemmon (1901) speaks of the young birds as "dark slate-color, with a little yellowish fuzz on the bodies, exceedingly thin necks, three-cornered heads and short yellow bills," and of birds slightly older, Brewster (1890) says: "Their bills were perhaps a quarter of an inch long, wide at the base, and in general shape not unlike the bill of a *Dendroica*, but more depressed."

Bendire (1895) states that the young "are born blind, and do not open their eyes until they are about a week old." These minute, naked, helpless bits of life grow, as Bendire (1895) says, "amazingly fast, and when about ten days old they are about as large as their parents." Torrey (1892), however, speaks of the brood which he watched closely until after they left the nest, as developing more slowly. He says: "Though at least eleven days old, the tiny birds * * * were still far from filling the cup." He describes thus the behavior of the parent as she brooded her young a few days after they had hatched: "It was noticeable that, while sitting upon the young, she kept up an almost incessant motion, as if seeking to warm them, or perhaps to develop their muscles by a kind of massage treatment. A measure of such hitchings and fidgetings might have meant nothing more than an attempt to secure for herself a comfortable seat; but when they were persisted in for fifteen minutes together, it was difficult not to believe that she had some different end in view. Possibly, as human infants get exercise by dandling on the mother's knee, the baby humming-bird gets his by this parental kneading process."

Torrey's birds were hatched on June 30. "On the 12th [of July]," he writes, "just after the little ones had been fed, one of them got his wings for the first time above the wall of the nest, and fluttered them with much spirit." On July 19 the first young bird left the nest. Mr. Torrey continues:

I was standing on the wall with my glass leveled upon the nest, when I saw him exercising his wings. The action was little more pronounced than had been noticed at intervals during the last three or four days, except that he was more decidedly on his feet. Suddenly, without making use of the rim of the nest, as I should have expected him to do, he was in the air, hovering in the prettiest fashion, and in a moment more had alighted on a leafless twig slightly above the level of the nest, and perhaps a yard from it * * * [Soon] the youngster was again on the wing. It was wonderful how much at home he seemed—poising, backing, soaring, and alighting with all the ease and grace of an old hand.

Illustrating the activity which precedes the flight from the nest, Mr. Torrey says of the other young bird: "He grew more and more restless; as my companion—a learned man—expressed it, he began to 'ramp around.' Once he actually mounted the rim of the nest, a thing which his more precocious brother had never been seen to do, * * * exercising his wings till they made a cloud about him."

C. J. Pennock, in a letter to Mr. Bent, describes a young bird "standing erect on the rim of the nest moving his wings *slowly*—so slowly that I could see the wings distinctly—then rapidly again."

Of the length of time the young birds remain in the nest Forbush (1927) says that it "has been given by different writers as from 6 to 18 days. It may be possible that in the south or during a hot wave in the north, when the female can safely leave her young without danger of chilling them, that she may procure enough food for them to develop wings to the flight stage in a short time; but my New England records of this period run from 14 to 28 days."

During this long period of time the young are fed by regurgitation. Torrey (1892) gives a vivid description of the operation, viewed from close at hand: "The feeding process, which I had been so desirous to see, was of a sort to make the spectator shiver. The mother, standing on the edge of the nest, with her tail braced against its side, like a woodpecker or a creeper, took a rigidly erect position, and craned her neck until her bill was in a perpendicular line above the short, wide-open, upraised beak of the little one, who, it must be remembered, was at this time hardly bigger than a humble-bee. Then she thrust her bill for its full length down into his throat, a frightful-looking act, followed by a series of murderous gesticulations, which fairly made one observer's blood run cold."

When the young bird grew larger, and its beak longer, the parent's beak, Mr. Torrey says, "was thrust into his mouth at right angles," and later, after the young had left the nest, she sometimes passed food directly from her beak to the young bird. "If she found a choice collection of spiders, for instance, she brought them in her throat (as cedar-birds carry cherries), to save trips; if she had only one or two, she retained them between her mandibles."

Carl W. Schlag (1930) says: "In cleaning the nest the hummingbird placed the droppings of the young in a line on the same branch, just above the nest."

Dr. Arthur A. Allen (1930) states that during the first few days after hatching the female feeds the young by merely inserting her tongue into the nestlings' throats and squirting them full of nectar and tiny insects.

Burns (1915) gives the period of incubation as 14 days. Wilbur F. Smith (1920), however, says of a closely watched nest: "On June 2 * * * the first egg was laid, and, after an interval of a day, the second was laid * * *. The young hatched on June 15, after eleven days' incubation, during which time the nest was built higher."

Plumages.—[AUTHOR'S NOTE: The young hummingbird is hatched naked, but pinfeathers soon appear, and the young bird is practically fully grown and fully feathered in the juvenal plumage before it leaves the nest. The sexes are unlike in the juvenal plumage. The young male closely resembles the adult female, with the white tips on the three outer tail feathers; but the feathers of the upper parts are narrowly edged with grayish buff, the throat is marked with narrow dusky streaks, and the sides and flanks are strongly tinged with brownish buff. The young female is like the young male but lacks the dusky streaks on the throat. Young males begin to acquire one or more ruby feathers on the throat in August and September, but no great progress in this direction is made before they leave for the south, and the adult plumage is assumed before they return in the spring. Dickey and van Rossem (1938) say: "In February and March both adults and young go through a complete molt, and at this time the young males acquire the red throat of maturity. Most individuals have completed this molt by the first week in March."]

Food.—The hummingbird is popularly regarded solely as a sipper of nectar, as it buzzes from flower to flower; as one who might say with Ariel, "Where the bee sucks, there suck I"; but when it comes down to the examination of stomach contents, it is proved that a considerable part of the bird's food consists of insects, chiefly those that come to the flowers the hummingbird visits. Frederic A. Lucas (1893), after examining the contents of 29 stomachs of several species of hummingbirds, comes to the following conclusion:

It would seem to be safe to assume that the main food of Hummingbirds is small insects, mainly diptera and hymenoptera. Homoptera are usually present, and small spiders form an important article of food, while hemiptera and coleoptera are now and then found. The small size of the insects may be inferred from the fact that one stomach contained remains of not less than fifty individuals, probably more.

Most of the insects found occur in or about flowers, and my own views agree with those of Mr. Clute, that it is usually insects, and not honey, that attract Hummingbirds to flowers * * *.

In view, however, of the testimony cited at the beginning of this paper, it would seem unquestionable that Hummingbirds do to some extent feed on the nectar of flowers and the sap of trees * * *.

I am much inclined to believe with Dr. Shufeldt that Hummingbirds first visited flowers for insects and that the taste for sweets has been incidentally acquired.

This taste for sweets is very well known to the many observers who have supplied hummingbirds with sugar and water placed about their gardens in artificial flowers. Miss Althea R. Sherman (1913), for example, who has experimented in feeding hummingbirds during seven summers, estimated that a single bird consumed "two teaspoonfuls of sugar daily."

Hummingbirds also avail themselves of the sap flowing from holes drilled by sapsuckers. In the article quoted under the yellow-bellied sapsucker, Frank Bolles (1894) speaks of the hummingbirds as constant and numerous visitors to the sapsucker's "orchards."

In order to attract hummingbirds to our gardens Dr. Arthur A. Allen (1930) suggests planting "caragana, pelargonium, tritoma; * * * tiger lilies, painted cups, bee-balms, scarlet salvias, azaleas, and gladiolus; * * * scarlet runners and trumpet vines; * * * horse-chestnuts and buckeyes."

Prof. O. A. Stevens writes to Mr. Bent from Fargo, N. Dak., as follows: "About the earliest flower that the hummingbirds visit here is *Ribes odoratum*, cultivated from the Missouri River region. The next one, and the one where I always watch for them about May 20–25, is *Caragana arborescens*, an introduced shrub that is much planted here. A little later the native *Aquilegia canadensis* and *Lonicera dioica* are available. On a specimen of the latter some of the flowers drooped to the ground, and, as I watched the bird at them, he rested on the ground for a few moments while he probed several flowers. Early in fall the cannas and gladioli are, of course, their favorites. The most natural summer flower seems to be the native *Impatiens*, and I believe that the hummingbirds' nesting grounds are closely associated with these plants."

Caroline G. Soule (1900) speaks of the activities of a male hummingbird about a bed of nasturtiums. She writes: "Most of his time was spent in slashing off the spurs of the nasturtiums to get at their nectar. We had hardly one perfect nasturtium flower all summer long, owing to his attacks."

Wilson (1831) charmingly notes his experience with the hummingbird as a flycatcher thus: "I have seen the humming bird, for half an hour at a time, darting at those little groups of insects that dance in the air in a fine summer evening, retiring to an adjoining twig to rest, and renewing the attack with a dexterity that sets all our other flycatchers at defiance."

Behavior.—The ruby-throated hummingbird gives the impression of being a nervous, high-strung, irritable little bird. It often resents the presence of other species of birds, however innocent their design may be. It is intolerant also to members of its own species to such a degree that, as a rule, the more hummingbirds there are together, the more excited and hostile they become.

I once saw a hummingbird attack a chimney swift—a strange bird to arouse the hummer's venom. My notes say: "August 2, 1909. This evening I saw Greek meet Greek—a hummingbird chasing a swift. The birds flew overhead rapidly, well above the treetops, the hummingbird a little behind and above. I saw it make a dive at the swift, who avoided the attack by a spurt that carried him well in advance. The hummingbird soon overtook his enemy and made a second swoop down toward him. By this time the birds were so far away that I lost sight of them."

Toward man, however, hummingbirds are usually complaisant, almost to the point of tameness. There are many instances recorded of their being attracted, sometimes in large numbers, to gardens where tubes of sugar and water are put out for their entertainment.

One of the most successful of these feeding stations is the garden of the late Mrs. Laurence J. Webster in Holderness, N. H. Here, for many years, Mrs. Webster studied the birds and provided them with such a bountiful supply of food that, apparently, all the hummingbirds in the vicinity resorted to her garden throughout the summer. She told me that she came to recognize some of the individual birds and, in a few instances, noticed that certain birds would take a long flight, always in the same direction, when they left her garden, and would not return for a long time—evidently visitors from a considerable distance—whereas other birds were in and out of the garden all day. She accustomed the birds to associate the sound of her voice with the presence of food and often called them to a vial she held in her hand by whistling the "phoebe" note of the chickadee.

Her garden on August 5, 1937, when Mr. Bent and I visited her, was whirring with hummingbirds—at least 40, we thought. Mrs. Webster covered the scattered feeding tubes and, seated at an open window beside Mr. Bent, who held a filled tube in his hand, gave the chickadee call. A bird came up out of the garden, poised a moment, then alighted on Mr. Bent's finger.

All day a deep hum sounds through her garden, rising or falling in intensity as birds come together or feed from the vials undisturbed, alone. At dusk, as one by one the birds leave the garden, the pitch of the whirring wings lowers, gradually dying down to a dull, tranquil sound, until "at twilight's hush" the last bird has gone.

It was in this garden that the motion pictures, described below, were taken.

The remarkable flight of the hummingbird, during which the wings move so rapidly that they are practically invisible, has attracted a great deal of interest and conjecture. Some observers maintained that the birds sometimes fly backward when leaving a flower—Bradford Torrey, for example, seemed to have had no doubt on the subject (see above); other observers, however, objected on mechanical grounds that no bird can fly backward. It remained for motion photography to settle the question.

That the hummingbird does fly backward has been definitely proved, and the manner in which backward flight is accomplished has been demonstrated by means of motion pictures taken in 1936 by a new application of photography. Dr. Harold E. Edgerton took advantage of the intermittent flashes in a low-pressure tube in which the flashes occur for 1/100,000 of a second with a period of darkness between them lasting 1/500 of a second. He used a constantly moving film, geared so that a new bit of film came opposite the lens of the camera at each flash, and thus secured about 540 pictures a second. Pictures of hummingbirds in flight taken in this way, when thrown on a screen, apparently reduce the speed of the birds' wing beats to that of a leisurely flying gull and make it possible to study the flight of the bird in detail.

Dr. Charles H. Blake examined with great care the films taken of hummingbirds in flight and found that the birds beat their wings 55 times (completed strokes) a second when hovering, 61 a second when backing, and as rapidly as 75 a second when progressing straightaway. Probably this last figure would be found to increase as the bird gained speed, if the camera could keep the bird in focus. Dr. Blake calculated that, during hovering, the wing tips moved at the rate of 20 miles an hour, and he also learned that the bird is in flight *before* it leaves its perch (the takeoff took 0.07 second) and pulls the perch after it a little way, a phenomenon that Mrs. Webster had suspected from feeling the birds leave her hand.

Dr. Blake kindly explained to me the mechanism of backward flying thus: In backing away from a flower or feeding tube the hummingbird stands almost vertically in the air with its tail pointing downward and a little forward. In this pose its wings beat horizontally, and what would be the downward half of each complete wing stroke if the bird's long axis were parallel to the ground forces the air forward, away from the bird's breast in its upright position, and *drives the bird backward.* Then, on the return half-stroke, the whole wing is rotated at the shoulder joint so that its *upper surface* strikes the air, and, driving it downward, balances the pull of gravity. Dr. Blake also points out that the distribution of weight in the hummingbird's wing is evidently favorable to a very low inertia upon which the quick reversal of motion depends, the weight being concentrated close to the body by reason of the short, heavy humerus.

The following quotation shows the high rate of speed the hummingbird may attain by the lightninglike strokes of its wings. H. A. Allard (1934), who was making a fast trip by auto out of Washington, D. C., says: "Not far out of Warrenton we had settled down to a speed of fifty miles per hour on highway 211, when a Ruby-throated Hummingbird (*Archilochus colubris*) suddenly paralleled our course along the side of the roadway as if deliberately racing with us. It actually passed us for a short distance keeping straight with our course, then swerved away. Its speed appeared to be somewhere between 55–60 miles per hour."

Hummingbirds have been seen so frequently hovering before the brilliant red flowers in our gardens—trumpet vines clambering over the porch, salvias gleaming scarlet in the flower beds—that it has been assumed the birds have a preference for the color red. However, the extensive investigations of Andrew L. Pickens (1930) bring out the fact that it is the brightness of color—its conspicuousness against the background—that draws the hummingbird to a flower. He says:

It is easy to perceive that Hummingbirds prefer the intensity of color shades rather than the paleness of color hues * * *

[But] the question is one that cannot be decided by mere rule of spectrum or pigments. There is so to speak a relativity of colors. * * *

Red being the complement of green is the most conspicuous color that a flower can show. * * *

Orange, while not so brilliant, is more showy in deeply shaded swamps and woods than is red * * *.

Green flowers are too inconspicuous among foliage. In certain contrasting desert backgrounds, or on the sere dry-season prairies it should have value. Thus, while no green Hummingbird flowers are known in the East, *Nicotiana paniculata* one of the greenest large flowers I know, is much frequented in the west during the dry season at least * * *.

Complete lists [of flowers] would probably show red, the sharpest contrast to green, a favorite everywhere, with orange in some favor in tree-shaded regions and a neglected color like green rising in sun-browned territory.

Experiments made by Miss Althea R. Sherman (1913) to test the "supposedly erroneous theory which had been published to the effect that Hummingbirds show a preference for red flowers" indicated conclusively that hummingbirds visited the bottles she placed about her garden *if they contained syrup*, whether or not they simulated a flower in shape or color. The birds associated even an untrimmed bottle with food, just as they soon came to recognize Miss Sherman herself as a supplier of food.

Speaking of pollination Saunders (1936) says that the bee balm "is the most important Humming Bird flower in Allegany Park. The anthers and stigma brush the crown of the Humming Bird's head as the bird probes the flower. The pollen is bright yellow, so that most summer Humming Birds appear to have yellow crowns."

Pickens (1927) points out in detail an interesting adaptation, insuring cross fertilization by the hummingbird, in the flower of *Macranthera lecontei*. He says: "Of all the forms that I have studied this is the most exclusively Hummingbird flower, and I recall seeing no other honey-gatherers in its vicinity."

Voice.—The notes that come from the hummingbird's tiny throat are high pitched and have a petulant quality, reflecting the bird's irritable nature. Sometimes the notes are angry-sounding, mouselike squeals; sometimes they are run into a nervous, fretful chattering, always very sharp and clear, though by no means loud, and delivered in a jerky, excited manner.

A lone hummingbird is usually silent, except for the buzzing of its wings, but when several birds are together they often become very voluble and quarrelsome and jerk out their notes, now arranged in emphatic phrases, squealing and chattering back and forth as if they were carrying on an animated controversy in a jabbering language.

Sometimes a single bird approaches another one poised before a flower and disputes its right to the place. Both then express their mutual hostility by beginning to jabber, and after a dart at each other and a fight, or at least a whirling about in the air, the winner of the encounter returns quietly to the flower. Thus when we stand close to a company of hummingbirds we hear the sound of their voices rising and falling in irregular waves—anger or resentment mounting up again and again and, in between, a short truce, marked by the peace of humming wings.

The pitch of the notes is invariably high, but it varies a good deal. Sometimes a note rises almost to a piercing whistle, and often the tone suggests the steely voice of the chimney swift.

In the phrases the notes are arranged in many ways; usually both squeals and short *chips* are combined, but either may be given alone, and the pitch of either one may run upward or downward. The short notes, when uttered alone are generally in series, repeated without change over and over, coming in twos, threes, or more again and again, the last note of each series commonly accented sharply. When the squeals and chattering are interspersed they often fall into a very pleasing rhythm. For example, a form often given when one bird joins another is a single sharp note followed by a long, descending chatter.

The chief characteristics of the hummingbird's voice are the sharply cut, emphatic enunciation and the attenuated quality.

Mary Pierson Allen (1908), speaking of a fledgling hummingbird that she fed with sweetened water, says: "He had his mother's *zip-zip*, which meant flowers or happiness, and a plaintive baby *peet, peet*, when he wanted food."

Field marks.—Audubon (1842) states: "If comparison might enable you, kind reader, to form some tolerably accurate idea of their peculiar mode of flight, and their appearance when on wing, I would say, that were both objects of the same colour, a large sphinx or moth, when moving from one flower to another, and in a direct line, comes nearer the Humming-bird in aspect than any other object with which I am acquainted."

It is true that the ruby-throated hummingbird bears not the slightest resemblance to any other bird occurring in the Eastern and Middle United States. It is sometimes mistaken, however, for the hawk moths, which hover about flowers in the manner of a hummingbird.

The adult male differs from the female and the immature bird in possessing a highly colored throat, which gleams in the sunlight like a glowing coal, oftentimes nearer coppery brass than true ruby. The male's tail is plainly forked and is not marked by the white spots that distinguish the rounded tail of the female and the young bird.

Enemies.—In addition to the dangers of migration, notably the occurrence of frost when the hummingbird overruns the advance of spring, there are other hazards, chiefly of an accidental nature, imperiling the life of the bird.

Ralph E. Danforth (1921) speaks of a bird caught in "a pendulous mass of cobweb" from which he freed it with some difficulty, and Bradford Torrey (1903) relates what he calls "a pretty story" told to him by an observer whom he describes as "a seeing man." The man, hearing "the familiar, squeaking notes of a hummer, and thinking that their persistency must be occasioned by some unusual trouble, went out to investigate. Sure enough, there hung the bird in a spider's web attached to a rosebush, while the owner of the web, a big yellow-and-brown, pot-bellied, bloodthirsty rascal, was turning its victim over and over, winding the web about it. Wings and legs were already fast, so that all the bird could do was to cry for help. And help had come. The man at once killed the spider, and then, little by little, for it was an operation of no small delicacy, unwound the mesh in which the bird was entangled."

Joseph Janiec sends the following story to Mr. Bent: "While I was wandering through a large hollow one June afternoon, my attention was attracted to the unusual waving of a pasture thistle. No air was stirring, and my curiosity prompted me to ascertain the cause of the movements. As I approached the thistle I noticed what I at first supposed to be a large dragonfly impaled on the prickly purple flower; closer examination, however, revealed a male ruby-throated hummingbird stuck to the flower, his wings not being involved in the contact but his stomach feathers adhering to the prickly, pointed stamens. Cutting off the flower, I carried it and the bird home and carefully removed the bird. Although it lost a few feathers in the operation, the little bird flew away unharmed."

There is a surprising record from California telling of the capture of an unidentified species of hummingbird by a fish. Mary E. Lockwood (1922) says, quoting from a letter: "We were seated by the lotus-pool when a hummingbird flew and hovered over the pool. Suddenly a bass jumped from the water and swallowed the hummingbird."

George H. Lowery, Jr. (1938), reports the following apparently unique record:

I shot a female Eastern Pigeon Hawk (*Falco columbarius columbarius*) on April 16, 1937, at Grand Isle, off the coast of Jefferson Parish, Louisiana. Upon examination of its stomach contents, I was surprised to find the identifiable remains of a Ruby-throated Hummingbird (*Archilochus colubris*). Later, on a visit to Washington, D. C., I discussed the matter with Mr. Clarence Cottam, Director of the Food Habits Division of the Bureau of Biological Survey. With his permission and the assistance of Mr. Robert McClanahan of the Food Habits offices, I went through the extensive records of that division and found that no species of hummingbird had ever heretofore been recorded from any bird stomach.

L. T. S. Norris-Elye writes to Mr. Bent: "During the summer of 1934, James Ashdown, Jr., and his mother were walking in the woods at Kenora, Ontario, and heard a continuous rattling. Investigation showed it to be a male ruby-throated hummingbird on the ground, with a huge dragonfly on the bird's back; it had seized the bird by the neck. They drove the dragonfly away, picked up the bird, and held it in the palm of the hand for several minutes, after which it flew away.

"We have had instances of frogs capturing and swallowing ruby-throats, one at Gull Harbor and one at Gimli, Lake Winnipeg. The Gimli case was observed by my friend Hugh Moncrieff, who captured the frog (leopard) and had some boys cut it open and recover the bird, while he took some good motion pictures of the operation."

Fall.—Taverner and Swales (1907) describe vividly a great concourse of migrating hummingbirds on Point Pelee, Ontario, Canada:

The first three days of September in 1906 were notable for the vast numbers of Hummers present. In certain low slashings in the open woods were luxuriant growths of Jewel Weed (*Impatiens* sp.?) standing nearly shoulder high and so dense that to enter it one had to force his way through. It was simply spangled with blossoms, and all about and over it hovered and darted hundreds of Hummingbirds. From some little distance, as we approached such clumps, we were aware of innumerable little twitterings that followed each other so rapidly as to scarce be separable, one from another, and so fine, sharp, and high in pitch that it took a little effort to realize that it was real sound and not imagination or a ringing in the ears. Underlying this was a low hum that arose from the vibrations of many little wings. Approaching closer, the pugnacious little mites were all about us, chasing each other over the smooth rounded surface of the jewel weed or darting angrily at us from this side or that, with furious chatterings that made one instinctively cover the eyes, or involuntarily flinch at the expected impact of their sharp, rapier-like, little bills. * * * All these birds were juveniles. * * *

Keays noted that in 1901 the Hummingbird was the only species that did not turn back when, in migrating out the Point, it reached the end. We verified this many times. The final end of the Point stretches out for a couple of hundred rods, in the form of a long, low, more or less winding and attenuated sand spit. Stationed about half way out on this, it was most amusing to watch the little mites come buzzing over the last half of the red-cedar bushes and then drop down towards the ground and, without pause or hesitation, follow every winding of the ever-changing sand to its extreme end, and then, with a sudden and resolute turn, square away for Pelee Island, just visible on the horizon. Dr. Jones was stationed on the opposite islands from August 26 to September 2, 1905, and makes the following statement as to the movements of the species over the waters of the lake: "Hummingbirds were passing during the daylight, and all those noted were flying very low. In fact they dropped down between the waves for protection from the wind, which was quartering, or at right angles to their line of flight and seemed to disturb them. I noticed that in the strong westerly wind, all birds headed southwest, but always drifted south."

I remember seeing, in Lexington, Mass., on two or three occasions in September, a single hummingbird, a dozen feet from the ground, bounding past me through open country, undulating in long, low waves as it held a rapid course toward the southwest—the line of migration in autumn through eastern Massachusetts. And again in May I once saw a lone bird steering due north, or a little east of north, flying, straight as an arrow, not 2 feet above the grass blades.

DISTRIBUTION

Range.—Eastern North America and Central America.

Breeding range.—The ruby-throated hummingbird breeds **north** to rarely southern Alberta (Camrose); southern Saskatchewan (Indian Head and Fish Lake); southern Manitoba (Aweme, Shoal Lake, and Big Island Lake); northeastern Minnesota (Rice Lake and Isle Royal); southern Ontario (Goulais Bay, Algonquin Park, Cobden, and Ottawa); southern Quebec (Montreal, Quebec City, Kamouraska, and Godbout); New Brunswick (Chatham); Prince Edward Island (Malpeaque Bay); and Nova Scotia (Pictou). From this northeastern point, the range extends southward along the Atlantic coast of the United States to Florida (St. Augustine, Daytona Beach, New Smyrna, and Princeton). **South** to Florida (Princeton, Fort Myers, St. Marks, and Pensacola); southern Louisiana (Thibodaux and New Iberia); and southern Texas (Houston, Victoria, and San Antonio). **West** to eastern Texas (San Antonio and Waco); Oklahoma (Norman, Oklahoma City, and Tulsa); Kansas (Clearwater, Wichita, and Hays); South Dakota (Vermillion, Arlington, and Faulkton); eastern North Dakota (Wahpeton, Fargo, and Argusville); and rarely Alberta (Camrose).

Winter range.—The normal winter range extends **north** to southern Sinaloa (Escuinapa); probably rarely southeastern Texas (Port Arthur); probably rarely southern Alabama (Fairhope); and Florida (Pensacola, Tallahassee, and Jacksonville). **East** to Florida (Jacksonville, St. Lucie, Miami, Royal Palm Hammock and Key

West); Quintana Roo (Cozumel Island); Honduras (Tela and Lancetilla); Nicaragua (Ometepe Island); Costa Rica (San Jose); and Panama (Volcano de Chiriqui). **South** to Panama (Volcano de Chiriqui); El Salvador (La Libertad); and Guatemala (San Lucas). **West** to Guatemala (San Lucas); Chiapas (Comitan); Oaxaca (Santa Efigenia, and Tonguia); Guerrero (Chilpancingo); western Jalisco (Volcano de Colima); and southern Sinaloa (Escuinapa).

Spring migration.—Early dates of spring arrival are: Alabama—Autaugaville, March 29; Long Island, April 13. Georgia—Savannah, March 15; Atlanta, April 3. North Carolina—Raleigh, April 11; Weaverville, April 17. Virginia—Variety Mills, April 10. District of Columbia—Washington, April 16. Maryland—Mardela Springs, April 20. Pennsylvania—Philadelphia, April 16. New York—Ballston Spa, April 20; Buffalo, May 2. Connecticut—Jewett City, May 5. Massachusetts—Pittsfield, May 6; Boston, May 8. Vermont—Wells River, April 24; St. Johnsbury, May 8. New Hampshire—Hanover, May 10. Maine—Portland, May 9. Nova Scotia—Pictou, May 7; Wolfville, May 15. New Brunswick—St. John, May 17; Chatham, May 20. Quebec—Quebec City, April 25; Montreal, May 9. Mississippi—Biloxi, March 3. Louisiana—New Orleans, March 7. Arkansas—Helena, March 24; Delight, April 4. Tennessee—Chattanooga, April 5. Kentucky—Eubank, April 13. Missouri—St. Louis, April 5. Illinois—Odin, April 27; Chicago, May 7. Indiana—Fort Wayne, April 14. Ohio—Oberlin, April 12; Youngstown, May 6. Michigan—Detroit, April 28; Sault Ste. Marie, May 21. Ontario—Toronto, April 12; Ottawa, May 5. Iowa—National, May 7; Sioux City, May 17. Wisconsin—Madison, May 4. Minnesota—Minneapolis, May 1; Lanesboro, May 9. Texas—Brownsville, March 18; Gainesville, April 5. Kansas—Onaga, May 15. North Dakota—Fargo, May 16. Manitoba—Pilot Mound, May 16; Aweme, May 17. Saskatchewan—Indian Head, May 24.

Fall migration.—Late dates of fall departure are: Manitoba—Aweme, September 12. Minnesota—Minneapolis, September 24; Lanesboro, October 8. Wisconsin—Madison, September 20. Iowa—National, October 4; Keokuk, October 23. Missouri—Concordia, October 12; St. Louis, October 25. Ontario—Toronto, September 29; Ottawa, October 16. Michigan—Detroit, October 7. Ohio—Youngstown, September 24; Oberlin, September 29. Indiana—Fort Wayne, October 9. Illinois—Rantoul, October 6; Chicago, October 13. Kentucky—Eubank, October 1. Tennessee—Athens, October 28. Arkansas—Helena, October 8; Delight, October 15. Louisiana—New Orleans, November 1. Texas—Bonham, October 18; Brownsville, November 5. Quebec—Montreal, September 17. Prince Edward Island—North River, September 5. New Brunswick—St. John, September 17. Maine—Phillips, September 16; Portland, September 24.

New Hampshire—Durham, September 25. Vermont, Wells River, September 16; St. Johnsbury, September 30. Massachusetts—Amherst, September 16; Boston, September 21. Connecticut—Hartford, September 27. New York—New York City, September 26; Rochester, October 1. New Jersey—Morristown, September 29. Pennsylvania—Philadelphia, October 12. Renovo, October 15. District of Columbia—Washington, October 20. North Carolina—Raleigh, October 7; Weaverville, October 15. Georgia—Atlanta, October 18.

Although the Biological Survey does not advocate the banding of hummingbirds, several have been successfully marked and a few have been recaptured at banding stations in Maine and Massachusetts in subsequent seasons.

Casual records.—Among the records of occurrence of the ruby-throated hummingbird outside its normal range, the following may be cited: A male was obtained at Casa Blanca, near Habana, Cuba, on April 4, 1937, and it is probable the species occurs in the western part of this island with fair regularity. To the north it was recorded on August 15, 1901, at Ellis Bay and on July 18, 1898, at English Bay, Anticosti Island; it was reported as seen at Grande Greve on July 6, 1919, and at Gaspé Basin, Quebec, on August 21, 1924; a specimen was obtained at Davis Inlet, Labrador, on July 17, 1882; one was seen at Red Deer River, Manitoba, on August 16, 1881; the Hudson's Bay agent at Lac La Ronge, Saskatchewan, has reported the species as of casual occurrence in his flower garden; and the United States National Museum has a mummified specimen picked up by a native on the beach at Klukatauck, near St. Michael, Alaska, probably during 1925.

Egg dates.—Florida: 23 records, March 25 to June 15; 12 records, May 10 to 20, indicating the height of the season.

Michigan: 8 records, June 1 to July 17.

New York: 30 records, May 23 to July 4; 15 records, June 13 to 26.

North Carolina: 25 records, May 2 to June 20; 13 seconds, May 11 to June 4.

ARCHILOCHUS ALEXANDRI (Bourcier and Mulsant)

BLACK-CHINNED HUMMINGBIRD

PLATE 58

PLATE 58

This active little hummer is accredited with a rather wide breeding range, from southern British Columbia and western Montana to northern Mexico and western Texas, but it is comparatively rare over much of this range. It is most abundant in the southern portions of the range, especially in southern California, southern Utah, Arizona, and portions of New Mexico. In the dry foothills and canyons of the Upper Austral Zone in this general region, it is one of the commonest of the hummingbirds. Dr. Joseph Grinnell (1898) says that in Los Angeles County it is a "summer resident from the lowlands to the summit of the mountains, but most abundant in the foothill regions, where it breeds in the cañons in some years by the thousands. * * * By the first of July, when the vegetation of the foothills becomes dry, and flowers cease to bloom, the Hummingbirds are found in countless thousands at higher elevations (6000 to 8500 feet) where summer is just dawning."

He says elsewhere (1914), referring to the Colorado Valley: "At Ehrenberg the last week of March and opposite Cibola the first week in April, the species was abundant in the desert washes, feeding about the profusely blossoming palo verdes. * * *

"The males were more seldom seen, and the females became closely restricted to the willow strip along the river, in which association we were convinced that this was the only species of hummingbird breeding. The males were not seen in the willows, but only in the mesquite association and up the desert washes. The females foraged everywhere except on the desert mesa, but nested exclusively in the willows."

In southern Arizona we found the black-chinned hummingbird to be the most abundant species of the family; its favorite haunts seemed to be about the mouths of the canyons, where a line of sycamores followed the underground course of a mountain stream out onto the plains; it was also commonly found in the small patches of willows along the dry washes, where water had formerly flowed, or where, probably, an underground supply still kept the trees and shrubs alive. It was not seen in the mountains above 6,000 feet.

Courtship.—The courtship flight of the black-chinned hummingbird is much like that of the closely related eastern ruby-throated hummer, consisting mainly of the long, swinging, pendulumlike swoops, with some variations. Laurence M. Huey (1924) describes it very well as follows:

The female was perched on a dead, horizontal limb about five feet from the ground and the male took flight from a position approximately twenty feet above her on the twig of a cottonwood, against the trunk of which I was quietly resting. With a bold sweep and a whizzing noise made by flight, which resembled that of the Costa Hummer except that the tone was not so intense, he passed very close to her and headed up to a point about fifteen feet above. There, while the upward motion died until a complete stop was reached, he seemed to pat his wings together underneath him, causing a sound much like that of a bathing bird flopping its wings in the water after they have become thoroughly saturated. After a second downward swing, with the whizzing noise, he rose to another point about fifteen feet up, where again the wing flopping performance was repeated. This U-shaped figure was repeated five different times, and, at each stop at the apex, the flopping of wings was indulged in, after which the bird again sought his perch on the cottonwood above his mate. I was close enough almost to hear his wing beats as he sped to and fro, and I watched the pair for three minutes, when they both flew off of their own will, without being disturbed. At no time during the minute and a half duration of the nuptial flight was there any vocal demonstration, though both birds were rather vociferous when perched.

Mrs. Bailey (1923) saw some "giving their aerial courtship dance from among the mesquites. One that I watched varied the usual triangulation by first flying back and forth horizontally across the face of a bush, then making narrow V's with the point at the bush, followed by wide-sweeping swings out over the mesquites as if from pure spirits."

Robert S. Woods (1927b) writes:

The shuttling of the Black-chinned Hummingbird, which follows a path like a narrow figure 8 lying on one side, has often been mentioned in accounts of the species. Its other form of nuptial flight most closely resembles that of the Rufous Hummingbird, just described [a swooping dive, punctuated at the bottom of its course by what might be described as a tremulant squeak or a rapid sucession of about four thin, vibrant notes], but the vocalization is more prolonged and of rather different character—a long-drawn, pulsating, plaintive, liquid note, probably the most pleasing utterance of any of our Hummingbirds. The heavy droning sound of its flight, so noticeable in the shuttling movement, is heard in this case only while momentum is first being gained on the downward swing. The shuttling flight, it may be noted, is practiced almost solely by those species in which the wings of the male are specially modified for noise-making purposes.

Nesting.—Major Bendire (1895) gives a rather comprehensive account of the nesting of black-chinned hummingbirds, and I cannot do better than to quote his remarks. He says:

Throughout the greater part of their range, it rarely begins laying before May 1, and the season is at its height through this month, while second or possibly third sets are found up to the latter part of July, and occasionally still later. The nest is readily distinguishable from that of the Ruby-throated Hummingbird by not being covered on the outside with lichens. It is composed of plant down, varying in color from white to buff; the latter is obtained from the under side of the young leaves of the sycamore, the former probably from willows, milkweed, or thistles. These materials are well worked together, and the outside of the nest is thickly coated with spider web. In an occasional specimen a small leaf or two, or a few flower blossoms of the oak are worked in the outer walls. In a specimen from Marfa, Texas, the outside is well covered with small flower spikes, the male aments of a species of oak, hiding the inner lining completely.

He mentions a beautiful nest that "is mainly composed of white willow down, mixed on the outside with a few small leaves and the scales from the willow buds."

These are firmly held in place by an abundance of spider web, with which it is also securely attached to the little fork in which it is saddled. The outer diameter of this nest is about 1⅜ inches by 1 inch in depth; the inner cup is 1 inch in diameter by five eighths of an inch deep; and while some specimens before me are a trifle larger, others are considerably smaller. Nests taken in the Sequoia National Park, in Tulare County, California, have perceptibly thicker walls than those from the warmer lowlands, and are also correspondingly larger. The nests are either saddled on a small, drooping branch or on a fork, one or two of the smaller twigs composing this usually being incorporated in the walls and holding it securely in place. Many of the nests resemble small, fine sponges, and are equally elastic, readily regaining their shape after being squeezed together. They are generally placed from 4 to 8 feet from the ground, mostly in the shrubbery found near small creeks or springs, and frequently their nests overhang the water or the dry creek bed. Alders, cottonwoods, oak, sycamore, laurel, and willows are most often selected for nesting sites, as well as young orchards, especially apple and orange trees, where they are available.

Frank Stephens wrote to Bendire that he "found a set of eggs of this species * * * laid in a nest of the House Finch, *Carpodacus mexicanus frontalis*. No lining had been added, or any other changes made; the bird evidently was in haste to lay, her nest, perhaps, having been suddenly destroyed."

Nests have also been found in a pear tree in an orchard, in a wild grape vine, in a tree-rose in a garden, and even on the stalks of various weeds; Dr. Grinnell (1914) mentions one that "was four feet above the ground on a slanting dead stalk of arrowweed beneath a large spreading willow." John McB. Robertson (1933) reports a nest in a most unusual location. It was built in the loop of a small rope that hung from a board in his garage. The nest rested on a knot at the bottom of the loop and was supported on opposite sides by the rope, to which it was securely tied with spider web; it was made of plant down and covered on the outside with stamens of eucalyptus blossoms. "Other objects to be seen in it are several tiny bits of eucalyptus bark, a scrap of dry leaf, several long human hairs, a small feather that is probably from a Linnet, a pair of bracts from a plant that furnished down, and a seed of alfilaria."

The nest of the black-chinned hummingbird is an exquisite structure, semiglobular in shape, or little more than half of a sphere, as if less than the upper half of the globe had been removed; it is deeply hollowed, and the rim is curved inward at the top, a wise provision of the builder to prevent the eggs or small young from falling out, as the supporting twig or weed stalk is swayed by the wind. It is firmly felted with plant down of various colors, mainly in different shades of buff, from "cartridge buff" to "pale pinkish buff" or "cinnamon-buff"; an occasional nest, in some 40 that I have examined, is made of the buffy-white or pure white down of the willow. The elastic, spongy structure is well reinforced and firmly bound to the supporting twigs with spider web, giving it much greater strength than it appears to have. Its durability is remarkable for such a frail-looking nest, as frequently a new nest is built on the well-preserved remains of a nest of the previous season.

The nest seems hardly large enough at first to contain even the small young, but, as the young increase in size, the elastic top expands, as Bayard H. Christy (1932) so gracefully portrays it: "As the young continue to grow a beautiful contrivance comes into play; the surrounding wall of the nest becomes as it were a living integument about the chicks; it expands with their growth; its rim yields to their little strugglings; its sphere opens like a flower-bud; until the little birds, all but ready to take flight, remain resting upon the full-blown corolla."

Mrs. Bailey (1896) gives the following account of the nest building: "The peculiar feature of the building was the quivering motion of the bird in moulding. When the material was placed she moulded the nest like a potter, twirling tremulously around against the sides, sometimes pressing so hard she ruffled up the feathers of her breast. She shaped the cup as if it were a piece of clay. To round the outside she would sit on the rim and lean over, smoothing the sides with her bill, often with the same tremulous motion. When she wanted to turn around in the nest she lifted herself by whirring her wings."

In southern Texas this hummingbird sometimes builds its nest at greater heights above the ground than mentioned above; Van Tyne and Sutton (1937) report two such nests found in Brewster County; one was "about twenty feet from the ground on a slender willow branch," and the other was "fully thirty feet from the ground in a gigantic cottonwood."

James B. Dixon writes to me from Escondido, Calif.: "Like most of the hummingbirds they are sometimes found nesting in very unexpected locations, such as on a porch where doors were swinging open at all hours of the day or night, on a steel rod poked into the roof of a blacksmith shop where men were busy at an anvil, and on an old piece of haywire stuck into a chink in the wall of a barn. Two locations seem to be preferred in the wilder places, the most popular being a long, meandering canyon filled with scrawny sycamores in the bottom and located where the surrounding hillsides are covered with flowering sage; the other location is in the dense willow thickets, locally known as willow montes, which border running streams or lakes. Here the black-chinned hummingbird is found breeding in large numbers, and it is not unusual to find a nest on the average of every hundred feet in such locations. I have found as high as three-storied nests of his bird, where apparently the bird had returned to the same nest for three successive seasons and built a new nest on the foundations of the previous year's home."

The nest shown on plate 58 illustrates the durability of the apparently fragile material used in its construction; it was composed exclusively of plant down firmly bound with cobwebs, and had served for the rearing of two young, meanwhile experiencing three 11-hour overhead irrigations.

Roy W. Quillin writes to me from Bexar County, Tex.: "All the nests I have seen were made of plant down of various colors and plastered on the outside with tiny lichens, very much like the nest of the rubythroat. They are totally different from nests of this species that I have examined from California. The fact that the nest of the blackchin, in this locality, is much like that of the rubythroat and the fact that the latter species is in migration here when the blackchin is nesting have caused records of the nesting of the rubythroat to be printed for Bexar County. I do not think it nests here."

Eggs.—The black-chinned hummingbird lays ordinarily two eggs, but several sets of three have been found, and occasionally a single egg is incubated. The eggs are much like those of the ruby-throated hummingbird but average a trifle smaller; they are about elliptical-oval, pure white, and without gloss. Often two and sometimes three broods are raised in a season. The measurements of 52 eggs average 12.51 by 8.30 millimeters; the eggs showing the four extremes measure 13.72 by 8.64, 13.21 by 8.89, 11.68 by 8.13, and 12.19 by 7.87 millimeters.

Young.—The period of incubation, performed by the female only, is said to be about 13 days. Mary Beal (1933) writes of the young:

At feeding-time they looked like pale yellow-brown caterpillars with widely gaping mouths, stretching up hungrily. Mother Hummer left the nest every fifteen minutes, and each alternate time on her return she fed the babies, thrusting her long bill down their throats until I held my breath lest she'd punch a hole through them, and every time I breathed a sigh of relief when it was safely over.

They grew amazingly fast. In a week they made quite a respectable appearance, and at the end of two weeks they were beautiful, shapely birdlings, completely filling the nest. * * *

On the nineteenth day, the babies perched on the edge of the nest and tried their wings with a quick humming motion just like Mother's, but they made no attempt to lift themselves into the air. They were still fed as regularly as clockwork, every half hour.

The day they were three weeks old, they left the nest, flying about with a smart little air of importance, giving thin squeaks of excitement.

The care and feeding of the young seem to depend entirely on the female, as well as the building of the nest. The male is seldom seen even in the vicinity of the nest.

Plumages.—The naked young soon begin to acquire a nestling, or juvenal, plumage and are fully fledged before they leave the nest at the age of about three weeks. The nestling has a much shorter bill than the adult; the crown is a mixture of grayish buff and dusky;

the back shows a mixture of dusky and glossy green, the latter feathers tipped with buffy; the throat and abdomen are dull white; the flanks are light drab; and the remiges, except the middle pair, are tipped with dull white. This plumage, which is much like that of the adult female, is apparently worn through most of or all the summer; I have seen it in its purity as late as August 24; but I have seen young males that were beginning to acquire a few violet feathers in the gorget as early as July 20. Progress toward maturity is rather slow and is prolonged through the winter; I have seen young males with imperfect gorgets in February and as late as May 15. As the ruby-throated hummingbird is said to have a complete molt in spring, this may also be the case with the black-chinned, which is so closely related; if this is so, the fully adult plumage must be acquired at this molt. Ridgway (1911) says that the young male is "similar to the adult female, but feathers of upper parts margined terminally with pale grayish buffy, under parts more or less strongly tinged or suffused with pale buffy brownish, and throat always (?) streaked or spotted with dusky"; and that the young female is "similar to the young male, but throat usually immaculate or with the dusky spots or streaks smaller and less distinct."

Adult females are considerably larger than adult males, the wing averaging nearly 10 percent longer. This seems to be more or less true of all the species of *Archilochus* and *Selasphorus*.

Food.—The black-chinned, like other hummingbirds, feeds on insects and sweets, mostly obtained from various flowers. It does not seem to be very particular in its choice of flowers in which to forage, though I was greatly impressed in California with the popularity of the "tree tobacco" (*Nicotiana glauca*) as a feeding ground for this and other hummingbirds. This is a small tree or large shrub that grows from 12 to 20 feet high and bears numerous clusters of slender, yellow, tubular flowers. The hummers frequent these little trees in large numbers; Major Bendire (1895) says that R. H. Lawrence saw some 70 or 80 hummingbirds in a patch of wild tobacco in less than two hours. The same observer noted that this and Anna's and Costa's hummingbirds "were attracted by a bright red flower (*Delphinium cardinalis*) growing on a clean, slender, juicy stalk, from 2 to 6 feet high."

In the Santa Rita Mountains, Arizona, Mrs. Bailey (1923) took one "feeding from the orange-colored tubes of honeysuckle (*Anisocanthus thurberi*)"; its throat was full of nectar; others were seen about the red terminal blossoms of ocotillo. In the Colorado Valley, Dr. Grinnell (1914) found it feeding about the flowering bushes of *Lycium andersoni*, about the profusely blossoming palo verdes, and about the lavender flowers of ironwoods. George Finlay Simmons (1925) says that, in Texas, it "hovers and feeds about the laterally-clustered pink flowers of the Texas buckeye, the pink flowers of the Texas redbud, and the rich purple and overpoweringly-perfumed flowers of the Texas mountain laurel on slopes and flattened valleys in the hills, largely on minute insects but also on nectar, pollen, and dew." Robert S. Woods (1927), at a time of unprecedented drought in southern Arizona, noted that "aside from a very few scattered mescals, there was an entire lack of flowers, in lieu of which the hummingbirds were systematically probing the clusters of leaves at the ends of the live oak twigs." The black-chinned hummingbird, like its eastern relative, has been known to feed on syrup made of sugar or honey and placed in artificial containers.

This hummer also poses as a flycatcher, as noted by several observers. Milton P. Skinner writes to me: "I saw one perched on a bush, 12 feet above ground on the edge of an open space. It was watching for insects. When one came within reach the humming-bird darted after it, sometimes going as much as 40 feet. It perched quietly and was quite hump-backed, but its head turned constantly from side to side. Generally its prey was not high up, but once the bird shot up into the air at least 50 feet. After watching it for half an hour I left it still looking for insects as at first. Later another one was seen buzzing about the bases of some willows. This one caught its insects as it came to them, but it did not perch and watch for them."

Behavior.—The flight of the black-chinned hummingbird when traveling from one place to another is swift and direct. While hovering about its feeding stations it has perfect control of its movements; it can remain stationary in the air, rise or fall at will, and even move backward with a downward thrust of its broad tail. The little wings vibrate with astonishing rapidity, as described more fully under the ruby-throated hummingbird; no ordinary camera shutter is quick enough to stop the motion. Mr. Skinner says in his notes: "Early in the morning these birds are rather quiet, but by 9 o'clock they become livelier and are really quite nervous. About 9 a. m. one was seen to fly to a small creek and have a good splatter bath in a shallow pool; then it flew up on a 12-foot willow to sun itself and preen. When they perch on willows and small limbs they alight both crosswise and lengthwise of the perch. As a rule they seem bold and unafraid of people."

W. L. Dawson (1923) relates the following:

Once, a hummer, finding itself entrapped in a porch by a wall of "chicken-wire" netting with meshes only an inch and a half in diameter, first passed slowly before the face of the screen, searching whether there might be any exception in his favor. Finding none, he made up his mind and darted through. So swiftly was the passage effected that the eye could detect no change in the position of the bird's wings. Only the ear noted an infinitesimal pause in their rhythm. Yet to accomplish this, the bird had been obliged to suspend the propeller motion of its winds, to furl them, to halve their normal spread, and to resume again upon the other side of the screen.

Voice.—Mr. Simmons (1925) tersely describes the vocal efforts of this bird as follows: "Song, by male, a sweet and low, though very high-pitched warble, like the sound produced as a result of whistling through the teeth; on still air, can be heard for 25 or 30 feet. Chase note, similar to song, but louder and chippering, like a light and rapid smacking of the lips together, uttered as one bird rapidly chases another hither and thither."

Mr. Woods (1927b) describes a courtship note as "a long-drawn, pulsating, plaintive, liquid note, probably the most pleasing utterance of any four Hummingbirds."

Field marks.—The male black-chinned hummingbird is easily recognized by the black chin and sides of the head and by the conspicuous white collar separating the square-cut gorget from the rather dark under parts; the violet gorget, just below the black chin, is not easily seen unless the light happens to strike it just right; there is a white spot behind the eye, which can be seen at short range. The female is not so easily recognized; it is much like the female Anna's hummingbird and is often seen with it, but it is decidedly smaller; the female Costa's and female black-chinned are so much alike that they can be distinguished only by a close view of the tail. In Costa's, according to Ridgway (1911), the middle pair of rectrices are bronze-green, the next pair similar, but with terminal portion black; third pair tipped with dull white or pale brownish gray, extensively black subterminally and dull brownish gray basally, the gray and black separated (at least on outer web) by more or less of metallic bronze-green; fourth and outermost pairs with whitish tip broader, basal grayish more extended, and with little if any metallic greenish between the gray and black. In the black-chinned, the three outer rectrices on each side are broadly tipped with white, the subterminal portion extensively black, the basal half (more or less) metallic bronze-green (sometimes grayish basally). Thus, the comparative amount of green on the two outer pairs of tail feathers determines the species.

DISTRIBUTION

Range.—Western North America.

Breeding range.—The breeding range of the black-chinned hummingbird extends **north** to southwestern British Columbia (probably Brentwood, Chilliwack, probably Vaseaux Lake, and probably Edgewood); and probably northwestern Montana (Columbia Falls). East to probably western Montana (Columbia Falls, Flathead Lake, Missoula, and Stevensville); south-central Idaho (Blue Lake); western Colorado (Glenwood Springs, Grand Junction, and Paradox); New Mexico (Espanola, Roswell, and Carlsbad); and western Texas (San

Angelo, Kerrville, San Antonio, and Losoya Crossing). **South** to southern Texas (Losoya Crossing, Somerset, and Chisos Mountains); southern Chihuahua (Rio Sestin); southern Sonora (San Javier and Guaymas); northeastern Baja California (Cerro Prieto); and southern California (Palo Verde and San Diego). **West** to California (San Diego, Escondido, Santa Barbara, Gilroy, Marysville, and Dales); Oregon (Prospect and Eugene); Washington (Prescott and Yakima); and southwestern British Columbia (probably Brentwood).

Winter range.—During the winter season this species is apparently concentrated in the region from extreme southern California (Palm Springs and San Diego); south to Guerrero (Venta de Zopilote and Chilpancingo); and the Federal District of Mexico (Mexico City).

One was seen at Marysville, Calif., on December 23, 1910, while another was noted at Fresno on January 8 and again on January 18, 1937.

Spring migration.—Early dates of spring arrival are: Texas— Kerrville, March 11; San Antonio, March 27. New Mexico—Rodeo, April 9. Colorado—Ouray, May 10; Fort Lewis, May 12; Grand Junction, May 20. Montana—Columbia Falls, May 17; Cornwallis, May 29. Arizona—Phoenix, February 10; Paradise, April 1; Tombstone, April 21. California—Santa Barbara, March 27; Los Angeles, April 3. Oregon—Prospect, April 10; Corvallis, April 15; Portland, April 22. Washington—Yakima, May 13; Pullman, May 28. British Columbia—Victoria, May 4; Agassiz, May 13.

Fall migration.—Very little information is available concerning the fall movement, but late dates of departure are: Washington— Yakima, September 18. Oregon—Coos Bay, August 10. California— Los Angeles, September 3. Texas—Somerset, November 4.

Casual records.—A specimen was collected at Kearney, Nebr., in August 1903.

Egg dates.—California: 105 records, April 3 to September 3; 53 records, May 8 to June 6, indicating the height of the season.

Texas: 20 records, April 4 to June 12; 10 records, April 12 to 21.

CALYPTE COSTAE (Bourcier)

COSTA'S HUMMINGBIRD

PLATES 59–61

HABITS

This little feathered gem is, to my mind, the prettiest of all the North American hummingbirds. The gorgeous, glowing colors of its brilliant helmet adorn, in the male, the top of the head, the throat, and the elongated feathers on the sides of the gorget; the burnished metallic violet of these feathers changes in certain lights to royal purple, magenta, blue, or even green, a beautiful display of colors at various angles.

Its breeding range in the United States is in the Lower Austral Zone in southern California, southwestern Utah, Arizona, and southern New Mexico; and it extends southward throughout the whole of Baja California. It winters mainly in southern Baja California and northwestern Mexico but has been seen casually in southern California in winter.

It is less dependent on the presence of water than some other hummers and seems to prefer the more arid regions in the deserts, the chaparral, the sagebrush plains, and the desert washes. Ralph Hoffmann (1927) describes these washes very well, as follows: "In the foothills of southern California the dark green belt of orange orchards is here and there interrupted by wide tongues of stones and gravel poured out by the canyon streams. These stony plains are overgrown by cactus, sumach, and occasional junipers, but in May and June are gay with scarlet larkspur, tall white yuccas and other humbler bloom. If one stands for a moment in the midst of this bee paradise, the tiny figure of a Hummingbird shoots past or stops to probe the tall spikes of the white ball-sage. After feeding, the little creature perches perhaps on a dead twig, and, protruding its long needle-like tongue, wipes off the last bit of honey against its slender bill."

Spring.—Costa's hummingbird is a summer resident in the United States, arriving during the latter half of March or early in April and making a rather short stay. Robert S. Woods, who has had considerable experience with this and other hummingbirds, says (1924a) that "the males arrive about the last of March, or later, according to the season, and leave early in June, females or young being seen for some time thereafter." He says elsewhere (1927b) that these hummingbirds, when they first arrive, "are almost constantly in a state of activity, so that it is often difficult to obtain more than a fleeting glimpse of them as they chase one another about. At these times there appears to be a great preponderance of males, which is partly accounted for, no doubt, by the quieter and more retiring habits of the females." Again (1922), he writes:

"In no case have I seen a male hummingbird in the vicinity of the nest or in any way showing interest in the matter. In fact, all the males had apparently started on their southward migration by the middle of June, 1922, or soon after the eggs had been laid in the last nest and while the young in the second nest were no more than half grown. None was seen earlier than May, probably on account of the lateness of the season, so their stay was very short this year. By July 1 the females and young were also noticeably scarcer. If the owner of the third nest had remained to hatch out and rear her young she would probably have been detained beyond the usual time for migrating."

Courtship.—The courtship performance of Costa's hummingbird follows the same general pattern of that of other hummingbirds, consisting of spectacular swoops, dives, and loops in the vicinity of its observing mate. James B. Dixon (1912) says that for a short time prior to the nesting season "they are quite noisy, chasing each other up, down and around through the surrounding bushes and trees." He continues:

Their note consists of a few sharp squeaks, given out more often when in very rapid flight than otherwise. During the breeding season the male has a very peculiar way of disporting himself before the female. When he locates his mate sitting on a tree, or more often on a low bush, he will ascend to an elevation of about one hundred feet and to one side of the female and will then turn and swoop down at a fearful speed, passing perhaps within a few inches of the watching female and ascending in the air to complete a half circle. This he keeps up until the female becomes impatient and endeavors to escape; then perhaps all that one will see is a streak, and a sharp squeak or two is heard as they flash up the hillside. The noise that the male makes in doing his fancy dive is easily heard at some distance and quite often heard when the bird himself is not visible on account of the extreme speed at which he travels on his downward plunge.

Mr. Woods (1927b), in comparing the performance of this hummer with that of the Anna's hummingbird, says: "The Costa's Hummingbird, instead of making a more or less abrupt turn, sweeps through a great arc to describe an immense letter **U**, then passes overhead to shoot downward again, either from the same direction or at a new angle. A continuous shrill whistle or miniature shriek accompanies most of the downward course and part of the upward—in other words, that part of the circuit in which the velocity is highest. This Hummingbird often ends his series of loops by darting away at high speed in an erratic, zigzagging flight."

W. L. Dawson (1923) says that the sound made by the male hummer in this flight is, he believes, "the very shrillest in the bird world, and one which is fairly terrifying in its intensity. This sound is generically like that produced by the Anna Hummer, but it is much more prolonged and more dramatic, more, in fact, like the shriek of a glancing bullet, or a bit of shrapnel."

Nesting.—Dr. T. S. Palmer (1918) has published an interesting paper on the early history of Costa's hummingbird, in which he makes the rather surprising statement, with the supporting facts, that "the first specimen, the first eggs, and the earliest nest of the season were all found in the southern part of Lower California at localities only a few miles apart. Twenty years elapsed after the species was first discovered before it was actually collected in California and nearly fifty years intervened before the eggs were found in the state."

Costa's hummingbird builds its nest in a great variety of situations and in many different kinds of trees, shrubs, and weedy plants. Among the trees recorded are various oaks, alders, bays, walnuts, willows, gums, sumacs, cypress, sycamore, hollyberry, hackberry, orange, lemon, olive, avocado, and Paraguay guava (*Feijoa sellowiana*). It has also been found nesting in sage and various other bushes, in dead yuccas, in *Opuntia echinocarpa*, *O. ramosissima*, and other branching cacti, and in various weeds, as well as in a hammock hook and a wire loop under a porch.

James B. Dixon writes to me: "Its range is in the more arid regions and the nesting locations are often a long way from known water. They often nest close by water also, and in favored locations are prone to colonize. I have found as many as six pairs nesting within a 100-foot radius in a dead cocklebur thicket near the edge of open water. One of their favorite nesting locations is the dead yucca stalks, where the nest is placed in the hard, dead framework of the last year's dead stalk, and usually some 4 or 5 feet from the ground. I have noted nest locations in dead trees, on top of thistle leaves, on clinging vines on cliff faces, and in citrus trees in open orchards, but not near houses. It does not seek nesting sites near habitations and seems to like the wild isolated areas the best."

Major Bendire (1895) says that "in the desert regions of southeastern California various cacti, the different species of sage (*Artemisia*) and greasewood bushes (*Larrea*), while in the canyons ash, sycamore, scrub oak, palo verde, cottonwoods, and willows, furnish their favorite nesting sites."

In the Thayer collection in Cambridge, there are 24 nests of this hummingbird, all of which I have examined. One of these was located in a sage over a stream, another in a weed over a road, and another over a stream in a white-alder bush, as well as many others in more usual locations. One nest was built on the top of an old nest of the previous season, the buffy color of the new nest contrasting with the dull, faded gray of the old one. The nests in this series show great variation in size and shape and in the material used in their construction. Most of them are rather shallow. The nests are not handsome or even neat in appearance, being rather loosely made, as a rule, of a great variety of materials, plant down of different colors giving a mottled appearance, shredded material from the sage, bits of gray lichens, scales of buds or flowers, thistledown, vegetable fibers, thin strips of bark, willow or yucca down, the whole tightly bound together with cobwebs or fine plant fibers. Many nests are more or less profusely lined with small, soft feathers of different colors, and some are decorated with these on the outside. Some nests are almost as simple as those of the black-chinned hummer, but even these show some mixture of some of the above materials. The outside diameter of the nests varies from 1¼ to nearly 2 inches, the average being about 1½; the height varies from about 1¼ to about 1½ inches.

Mr. Dixon says in his notes sent to me: "The nest of the Costa is very distinctive as to structure and material used, and I find this is true with all of the hummingbirds, it being easier to tell the nests apart than the female birds. The Costa uses dead weed leaves and cobwebs in building the outside of the nest and soft plant down and other soft materials for the lining. The general structure is of a grayish tone and very distinctive in this respect." This grayish tone of the nest helps to conceal it when it is built on a dead branch, a dead yucca stalk, a gray-toned cactus, or, especially, in a sagebush where the shreds of sage leaves with which it is decorated blend perfectly with its surroundings.

Griffing Bancroft (1930) says that in Baja California "they nest in the immediate proximity of surface water, sometimes snuggled into grapevine leaves, sometimes near the tips of fig branches, but most often on the leaf stems of the date palm. The birds obviously seek and usually obtain the protection of living foilage. The sites selected average, in height above the ground, at least twice that of northern breeders; roughly eight feet against three."

Mr. Woods (1927b) says: "At Azusa, California, the nests have been found at heights ranging from two to nine feet, but most commonly in the neighborhood of four feet. When a bush or small tree is selected, as is frequently the case, the nest is almost invariably located at a height of approximately one-half of the total height of the tree, but near the outside rather than the center, and in a position from which a reasonably clear outlook may be obtained. On this account, trees of dense, leafy growth, such as an orange tree in thrifty condition, are not favored. * * * If in a large tree, the nest is usually on a small twig near the end of a projecting lower limb."

Major Bendire (1895) says: "They are usually placed in low situations, from 1 to 6 feet from the ground, rarely higher, although Mr. W. E. D. Scott records one taken on May 5, 1882, near Riverside, in southern Arizona, from the extremity of a cottonwood branch 35 feet from the ground."

Mr. Woods (1922) writes:

On June 2, 1922, I found another Costa Hummingbird building a nest near the end of a long horizontal limb of a good-sized avocado tree, at a height of about five feet from the ground. Her method was first to alight in the nest, then place the material under her and compact it by treading with the feet and turning about. Material for the outside of the nest was placed while hovering or while perched on a branch. On one occasion after leaving the nest the bird flew up to a twig a few feet above, whereupon I was surprised to see another hummer alight in the nest and rearrange some of the material, afterwards sitting there for some time until the presumably rightful owner presently darted at the intruder and drove her away.   The nest was composed largely of small achenes bearing soft pappus.   Other items noticed were fibers, minute leaves, feathers and a short piece of string, the whole bound securely to the branch with cobwebs.

Eggs.—Costa's hummingbird lays almost invariably two eggs. Sidney B. Peyton has a set of three eggs, taken in Ventura County, Calif.; a third egg was laid to complete a set of two, now in the Thayer collection, after one egg had fallen from the nest. I have no record of a complete set of one. The eggs are like other hummingbirds' eggs, dead white, without gloss, and elliptical-oval with an occasional tendency toward elliptical-ovate. The measurements of 51 eggs average 12.4 by 8.2 millimeters; the eggs showing the four extremes measure **14.0** by 7.8, 12.7 by **9.4, 11.4** by 7.8, and 11.6 by **7.6** millimeters.

Young.—There seems to be considerable difference of opinion as to the period of incubation, which is performed by the female alone. Mr. Woods (1927b) writes:

An interval of about two days separates the laying of the eggs. Incubation, in every case that I have observed, has begun with the laying of the first egg, and the young are usually hatched out a day or more apart. If we are to accept the widely differing periods reported—from nine to eighteen days—the time of incubation must be regarded as extremely variable. On account of absences I have not succeeded in collecting as full information on this subject as could be desired, but data of varying accuracy obtained during five successive years indicate that the normal incubation period for Costa's Hummingbird in the San Gabriel Valley is about sixteen days, lengthening in certain instances to as much as eighteen days, but never falling below fifteen days. * * *

The growing period of the young is even more markedly prolonged than is the incubation. Some eight broods for which the time was determined with fair accuracy remained in the nest from twenty to twenty-three days after hatching, with all but two approximating the higher figure. * * *

Even more pronounced than in most other altricial birds is the contrast between the newly hatched Hummingbird and its parents. The minute grub-like creature is black above and brownish below, with the body entirely bare except for a row of yellowish filaments along each side of the median line of the back. The bill is yellow and triangular, its length being but slightly greater than its width at the base. The eye sockets project beyond the base of the bill. Until about the sixth day, when the pin-feathers begin to appear, the most notable change, aside from the increase in size, is the gradual lengthening and darkening of the bill. The first part of the young Hummingbirds' lives is spent stretched out on the bottom of the nest, but after a time they become longer than the interior of the nest, so that they are gradually forced to raise their heads against its sides until at one stage of their growth their bills are pointing directly upward. After this their development is more rapid, and when they begin habitually to hold up their heads and assume an alert appearance, they are nearly ready to fly. The last few days before leaving the nest, the young birds frequently exercise their wings, sometimes perching on the edge of the nest for freer action. Finally a time is reached when, contrary to their former indifference, they are likely to leave on very slight provocation. A person may be quietly standing and watching them when as with one impulse both spring from the nest and fly in different directions. It sometimes so happens that the younger of the two is thus induced to venture forth before its wings are capable of sustained flight or of enabling it to obtain a foothold in a tree. On two such occasions I found that the bird might readily be picked up and when restored to its nest gladly settled itself to await more adequate strength.

The young Hummingbirds are fed by regurgitation, of necessity, at intervals of about half an hour. The feeding requires perhaps half a minute in all and is accomplished by a violent pumping process, with the bill thrust deep into the open mouth of the young bird. One would not judge that the slow growth of the Hummingbird was due to inability to supply sufficient food, since the mother, though bearing the entire care of her offspring, does not seem overworked, but has plenty of time to rest, preen her plumage and engage in skirmishes with other Hummers. Her care of the young continues for some time after they have left the nest. Then their call for food may be heard at intervals, a shrill cheep resembling the cries of other young birds rather than the voice of the adult Hummingbird. After the young have attained their full growth in other respects, they may still be recognized by the comparative shortness and straight, subulate form of the bill.

Major Bendire (1895) quotes R. H. Lawrence, regarding the feeding of the young, as follows:

She fed the young by touching the point of her bill to the tips and sides of the bills of her youngsters, as if to urge or invite them to stir and open their mouths, not inserting her bill over one-fifth or one-fourth of its length. Once she thrust it down half its length into the throat of one nestling, who then clung to it to the very last moment of its withdrawal, apparently reluctant to let the very smallest particle of the regurgitated food miss its way or remain on the parent's bill. The performance was rather ludicrous, as both old and young, especially the youngsters, went through many wriggling and squirming motions. * * * Once, upon her return, settling down to brood the youngsters, she kept up for some moments a kind of paddling motion, as if she were giving them a little massage treatment. Her respiration was very rapid after this exertion. Life with these atoms of sensitiveness must be at a white heat always. The young were lying side by side, but headed in opposite directions. Both had voided excrement in one case, but the parent did not remove either deposit while I was there. Except for this and a piece of eggshell, the nest appeared clean.

Plumages.—The young Costa's hummingbird is hatched blind and nearly naked; at first there is only a narrow line of pale, yellowish down along each side of the back; this spreads within a few days to cover the back, wings, and top of the head, through which the juvenal plumage later appears; and at the end of twelve days, they are fairly well feathered (Wheelock, 1904).

In full juvenal plumage, the young male is much like the adult female, but the feathers of the upper parts are more or less margined with grayish buff; the tail is double rounded, instead of wholly rounded; the throat is spotted with dusky, most heavily on the sides; and there are usually some, often many, violet-purple feathers on the throat; in a considerable series of young males that I have examined, I have not seen any that did not have at least a few of these violet feathers on the throat; one had a little bunch of them in the elongated lateral extension of the gorget only. Later in the season these metallic feathers appear in the crown, but there is not very much progress toward the fully adult plumage until the complete prenuptial molt takes place late in winter or early in spring, when young birds become indistinguishable from adults.

The young female is similar to the adult female, except for the buffy margins on the feathers of the upper parts. Young females can be distinguished from young males by having immaculate, instead of spotted, throats. I have seen young females, probably very young birds, that were strongly washed with pinkish buff on the flanks, and more faintly tinged with buff on the throat; the feathers of the head and back in these birds were broadly tipped with grayish buff; probably the buff soon fades and the tips wear away.

Both adults and young apparently have a complete molt late in fall and early in winter; I have detected it in February.

Food.—The usual hummingbird food nourishes this species; probably it consists mainly of small Diptera, Hymenoptera, and other minute insects, sweetened with nectar or honey from various flowers; the amount of the latter is difficult to determine, as it is not easily detected in the stomach, where it is so soon digested. As to the flowers from which the food is obtained, Bendire (1895) says that "in Inyo County, California, Costa's Hummer seems to be very commonly found about the flowers of the squaw cabbage, a species of *Stanleya*, also about wild rose, plum, or cherry bushes (*Prunus*) growing in the canyons, as well as about other shrubs and plants found in these desert regions."

Mr. Woods (1927b) says: "During the nesting season it has seemed to me that the female Costa's Hummingbird visits the flowers much less than does the male. At such times the female may often be seen buzzing about inside non-flowering trees and shrubs. While the search may be primarily for cobwebs or other nesting material, numerous minute insects and spiders might incidentally be obtained. * * * Costa's Hummingbird, for some reason, seems less partial to the Tree Tobacco than do the larger species."

Dr. Grinnell (1914) says that, in the Colorado Valley, "they were feeding about the spiny bushes of *Lycium andersoni* which were at this time profusely laden with flowers. A tall-stalked milkweed (*Asclepias subulata*) growing high among the precipitous peaks was also an attraction; so, too, a sage (*Hyptis emoryi*)."

In probing into the flowers in search of food this and other hummingbirds serve a useful purpose for the plants in pollination, as do the bees, by helping to transfer the pollen from stamens to pistil; the bills and heads of hummingbirds are often smeared with pollen.

Behavior.—Quoting Mr. Woods (1924a) again:

As the male Hummingbird takes no part or interest in the nest-building or the rearing of the young, and a brief visit to any convenient flowers serves to satisfy his appetite, he has considerable spare time at his disposal. Most of this he spends on certain favorite observation posts, one of which is shown in the photograph, whence he sallies forth occasionally in pursuit of a trespassing Hummer or bird of some other sort. Even the Cliff Swallow is not immune from his attacks and seems quite unable to avoid his onslaughts. The Hummingbird frequently mounts vertically into the air until almost out of sight, then descends like a bullet directly at the object of his attention. If the other bird flies, the Hummingbird follows; if not, he passes within a few inches, sweeping through an arc which carries him upward again to repeat the process until tired. The downward swoop is accompanied by a long shrill whistle which is characteristic of the species and is often the first indication of its arrival in the spring.

Elsewhere (1927b) he writes: "There is a remarkable difference in the shyness of the various individuals when on the nest. Some will leave as soon as a person comes into sight, perhaps forty feet away; others will permit one to reach within a few inches, or possibly, with care, even to touch them, without leaving the nest. The shyer ones, however, are inclined to hold to the nest more closely as the incubation advances, and especially around the time of hatching. Most of them, though easily frightened from the nest, will soon return if one stands quietly a few feet away, a decided reversal of the tendencies of the majority of nesting birds."

A case of tameness, or curiosity, is reported by F. C. Lincoln (1917): "Mr. Figgins had an interesting experience with one of these birds while sketching under his umbrella. The bird, a female, was fearlessly curious and repeatedly came under the umbrella and perched on the ribs, or the canvas, once flying so close to his face that he (Mr. F.) forgetting the protection afforded by his glasses, shut his eyes for fear the bird would strike at them."

Hummingbirds seem to have few enemies. Perhaps they are too small to attract birds of prey, or too active to be easily caught. But accidents will happen occasionally. Mr. Woods (1934) reports finding a bird of this species hopelessly entangled in a coarse, heavy spider's web; it was released with some difficulty and was at first unable to fly away, but it finally recovered.

Voice.—Mr. Woods (1927b) remarks that "the presence of a Costa's Hummingbird is frequently announced by the two-or-three-syllabled whistling call with which he greets passing members of the tribe from his perch or salutes his mate as he hovers before her. The young males begin practicing on these whistling notes, which are doubtless among the highest-pitched sounds audible to the human ear, before they have yet attained their brilliant gorgets, with results that sometimes rather resemble the song of the Anna's Hummingbird, though much fainter and less sustained."

Field marks.—With the exception of the calliope, Costa's hummingbird is the smallest of the common North American species. The adult male should be easily recognized by its full helmet, crown, gorget, and elongated sides of the gorget, of brilliant amethyst, purple-violet, though these colors appear black in certain lights. The young male is like the female but usually shows some violet feathers about the head. The adult female is almost impossible to distinguish from the female black-chinned in the field; for the characters that distinguish these two females the reader is referred to the field marks of the black-chinned hummingbird.

DISTRIBUTION

Range.—Southwestern United States and Mexico; only slightly migratory.

Breeding range.—Costa's hummingbird breeds **north** to southern California (Fresno and Owens Valley); southern Nevada (Cave Spring and Bitter Springs); and probably southwestern Utah (Beaverdam Mountains). **East** to probably southwestern Utah (Beaverdam Mountains); east-central Arizona (Salt River Reservation); and rarely southwestern New Mexico (Cliff). **South** to rarely southwestern New Mexico (Cliff); southeastern Arizona (Tombstone and Huachuca Mountains), and southern Baja California (La Paz and Santa Margarita Island). **West** to Baja California (Margarita Island, Magdalena Bay, Cerros Island, San Benito Island, Todos Santos Island, and Los Coronados Islands); and California (El Cajon, Escondido, Santa Barbara Island, Glendale, and Fresno).

Winter range.—In the winter season this species is found **north** to southern California (Azusa, Riverside, Palm Springs, and rarely Amboy); and southwestern Arizona (Camp 117, Phoenix, and Tinaches). **East** to southern Arizona (Tinaches and Tucson); Sonora (Tiburon Island and Tesia); and southeastern Baja California (La Paz). **South** to southern Baja California (La Paz and Santa Margarita Island). **West** to Baja California (Santa Margarita Island, Magdalena Bay, Cerros Island, and Rosarito); and southwestern California (San Diego and Azusa).

Migration.—The only data available are applicable to the spring migration. The following are early dates of arrival: Arizona—Tombstone, March 5. California—Los Angeles, March 21.

Casual records.—A specimen was taken at Oakland, Calif., on May 8, 1890, well north of the normal range.

Egg dates.—California: 100 records, March 11 to June 29; 50 records, May 12 to June 10, indicating the height of the season.

Baja California: 14 records, February 24 to June 5; 7 records, May 26 to 30.

CALYPTE ANNA (Lesson)

ANNA'S HUMMINGBIRD

PLATE 62

HABITS

CONTRIBUTED BY ROBERT S. WOODS

In two respects Anna's hummingbird occupies a unique place among our hummingbirds. It is the only species the greater part of whose general range is included within a single State of the Union, and the only one that winters mainly within the United States. It is also the species most familiar to residents of California, since its territory includes all the more populous districts of the State, where it is a constant and by no means shy visitor to city parks and gardens. Anna's hummingbird seems to be in some degree nomadic in its habits, and it probably shifts slightly southward during the colder months, but it performs no true migration, thereby differing from all our other species except that portion or race of Allen's hummingbird resident on the Channel Islands of southern California.

Courtship.—In April, in the blooming orange groves of southern California, at least five of the six species of hummingbirds regularly occurring in that region may sometimes be seen together, in considerable numbers and feverish activity. No small part of that activity consists in the practicing of highly specialized forms of courtship flight. While the males of all California hummingbirds can easily be recognized when clearly seen, identification is more difficult when the bird persists in manifesting itself as a vague streak rather than a definite object. Under these circumstances a knowledge of the specific distinctions in "nuptial flight," and particularly of the peculiar and entirely characteristic utterances accompanying such flight, is often of great assistance in determining species.

The most elaborate of these nuptial flights is that of Anna's hummingbird, in which the bird mounts upward until almost lost to sight, then shoots vertically downward at tremendous speed, finally altering his course to describe an arc of a vertical circle, which carries him as closely as possible past the object of his attention as she sits quietly in some bush or tree. At the lowest point of the circuit he gives utterance to a loud, explosive chirp, which so nearly resembles the "bark" of a California ground squirrel (*Citellus beecheyi*) that one who is familiar with that sound may easily be deceived. From this point he continues along the arc until he arrives at a point directly above his mate, where he hovers for a few seconds with body horizontal and bill directed downward, rendering his squeaky "song." Then, without change of attitude, he begins to rise rapidly and vertically, repeating the entire maneuver until he tires or the other bird departs, with himself in hot pursuit.

Presumably this practice originated strictly as a courtship display, but it now has a much broader application, frequently being directed at other species or at birds of wholly different kinds. Young males begin performing the flight as early as September of their first year, and it is continued through at least the greater part of the year. Anna's hummingbird is not addicted to the shuttling flight so much used by those species in which the wings of the males are modified in such a way as to produce a metallic rattling sound. The actual mating, which is not often witnessed, has been described by Leroy W. Arnold (1930) : "When first observed, the birds were playfully chasing each other about and suddenly swooped down to within about eighteen inches of the ground where the leading bird, which proved to be the female, stopped and faced about. The male approached and the mating was consummated in the air, the birds breast to breast and with the male somewhat under the female. The male then settled down to the ground for a few moments, fanning out his tail and pointing his beak upward, while the female flew to a nearby perch. After a short rest, the male rose and flew after the female who returned to her former position and mating again took place as before."

Nesting.—With reference to the nesting habits of hummingbirds, few distinctions can be drawn between the various species even under quite different ecological conditions, except in the matters of season, locale, type of site, and nest materials. The nesting of Rieffer's hummingbird (*Amazilia tzacatl tzacatl*) in Central America has been carefully observed by Alexander F. Skutch (1931), and the agreement in procedure between this species of the humid Tropics and those of the semiarid Temperate Zone is most striking. The principal specific variations in this connection among North American hummingbirds concern the selection of materials for the nest, but there is also considerable individual latitude that tends to bridge the gaps.

Although Anna's hummingbird is generally distributed west of the Sierra Nevada and the Colorado Desert, it is rather definitely classified as a breeder in the Upper Sonoran Zone and is less partial to arid localities than is Costa's hummingbird. The nesting season begins before the arrival of any of the migrants, sets of eggs having been found by various persons as early as December. The nesting probably continues normally through late winter and spring and sporadically throughout summer, with some evidence of its extending even into the fall. With the breeding season so greatly prolonged, it is of course difficult to determine exactly how many broods are raised each year, but it may be inferred that two is the usual number, as in the cases of the black-chinned and Allen's hummingbirds. During one season throughout which I was able to follow the activities of one pair separately, by the aid of artificial feeding, the movements of the female indicated—though the nest was not found—that the first incubation period began late in January, the second just two months later. Incidentally, it is hard to explain satisfactorily why these species, which quite certainly raise two broods yearly, do not gain in numbers relatively to the Costa's, rufous, and calliope hummingbirds, which usually do not remain on their breeding grounds long enough to permit more than one.

Nests of Anna's hummingbirds have been described or photographed on almost every kind of site to which it would be possible to attach the structure, except on the ground or any extensive horizontal surface. It is usually, without doubt, birds of this species that now and then achieve newspaper publicity by nesting in some unexpected spot in the business district of Los Angeles. The distance from the ground at which the nests are placed is also extremely variable. Of 52 nests found by W. Lee Chambers (1903) between January 1 and February 18, 1903, the heights ranged from 17 inches to 30 feet. James B. Dixon, of Escondido, Calif., writes (MS.) concerning nests and their sites: "The female seems to select the nesting site and so far as I have ever observed did all of the nest building. The nest location may be in a wide variety of locations, as I have seen nests in the following locations: On insulated electric-light wires under the crossarm of a service pole 30 feet from the ground; on a climbing vine on a granite cliff face within a few feet of an occupied nest of the golden eagle; in citrus trees, both oranges and lemons; in brush far removed from any wooded areas; and in dense oak groves in narrow wooded canyons. The last-mentioned place is by far the most favored as to nest location and I should say was typical of this area. The nests are large and well made and are usually devoid of camouflage when first built but are decorated with lichens during the incubation period and by the time the young are hatched are very beautiful structures and in my estimation are the most beautiful of all the hummingbird nests. The nests are made of plant down put together with cobwebs and are often lined with fine bird feathers and plant down. Often eggs are laid in the nest when it is a mere platform and the remaining part of the nest is built up around the eggs and the finishing touches of lichens and plant seed put on last.

Two eggs are usually laid, although I have seen nests with one and three eggs, which I feel sure were sets. The female is usually very tame after brooding a short time and is very curious if disturbed and will fly right into your face to look you over and try to scare you away from the nest. I have never seen the male bird feed the young or help build the nests. Anna's hummingbird does not colonize like some of the others and seems to prefer an area to itself."

W. Leon Dawson (1923) states that "nests of the Anna Hummer vary in construction perhaps more widely than those of any other local species. Some are massive and as heavily adorned with lichens as those of the eastern Ruby-throat." According to all available data, however, they can probably be regarded as essentially similar to those of Costa's hummingbird except for their slightly larger size; fibers and stemmy materials usually being used in the walls, and ornamentation on the exterior, while feathers are frequent in the lining. An interesting account of the nesting activities has been given by A. W. Anthony (1897):

Sometime about April 1, an Anna's Hummingbird began her nest in a cypress in front of my residence in San Diego. I could not be sure as to the exact date of beginning, but on the 6th, when I first noticed the bird at work, there was nothing but a little platform the size of a silver twenty-five cent piece, fastened to the upper side of a twig which nearly overhung the front walk, and was but just high enough to escape being struck by anyone passing below.

From an upper window I could look down upon the growth of the downy cup, and watch the diminutive builder from a distance of but a few feet, as she brought almost imperceptible quantities of cotton and tucked them into the sides and rim of the prospective nest. In working the material into the structure she always used her body as a form around which to build, tucking the cottony substance into the side and pushing it with her breast, frequently turning about to see if it were the right size all around.

On April 12, when the nest was apparently but half finished, and little better than a platform with a raised rim, I was surprised to see an egg, which the mother carefully guarded as she buzzed about, still bringing nesting material.

The following morning the second egg was added, and on one or two occasions the male made his appearance, and tried, seemingly, to coax the female to leave the nest, even making several attempts to push her from the eggs when other means failed. He soon became discouraged, however, and departed for parts unknown, leaving his demure little spouse to care for the eggs and complete the half finished nest.

For several days incubation progressed just about two minutes at a time. The Hummer, after arriving with material and building it into the slowly rising rim, would incubate for two minutes, seldom more than a few seconds more or less, before leaving for another consignment.

Her periods of absence were of almost exactly the same duration. It was not until incubation was more than half complete that the nest was finally finished, but unadorned by the usual bits of lichen. These were added from day to day until May 1, when the first egg hatched, either eighteen or nineteen days after incubation began. Owing to the unsettled actions of the bird on the 12th and 13th of April I could not satisfy myself as to when incubation really began.

The second egg never hatched, and after the nest was abandoned the broken shell was found buried in the bottom of the nest.

Eggs.—[AUTHOR'S NOTE: The usual two eggs of Anna's hummingbird are indistinguishable from the eggs of other hummingbirds of similar size. The measurements of 50 eggs average 13.31 by 8.65 millimeters; the eggs showing the four extremes measure 14.3 by 9.0, 12.7 by 9.4, and 11.3 by 7.7 millimeters.]

Young.—It will be noted from Mr. Anthony's account that the incubation period is considerably longer than that of most common passerine birds, despite the smaller size of the eggs. This is confirmed in the following description by J. H. Bowles (1910) of the nesting of an Anna's hummingbird at Santa Barbara:

The first egg was laid January 3, but during the following night a heavy frost left ice more than a quarter of an inch in thickness on the puddles. * * * I think the icy weather must have been too severe for the first egg, for, whatever the cause, only one egg hatched. This took place on January 22, showing the period of incubation to be just seventeen days. It may be interesting to note here that I have found thirteen days to be the period of incubation for eggs of the Black-chinned Hummer (*Archilochus alexandri*). This great difference I think may be attributed in part to the consistency of the albumen, which in eggs of *C. anna* is thick and almost gummy, while in *A. alexandri* it is thin as in eggs of other small birds.

In spite of the very cold, rainy weather my young hummer grew very rapidly; but it was not until he was thirteen days old that his eyes opened. * * * On February 13, when he was just three weeks old, the young bird left the nest.

I believe, however, that the difference in incubating time between Anna's hummingbird and other species cannot be so great as assumed by Mr. Bowles, as I have found the period for both black-chinned and Costa's to be about 16 days, while, on the other hand, Donald R. Dickey (1915) gives an even shorter time for Anna's hummingbird, as observed in the Ojai Valley of Ventura County:

Finally, on the fourteenth day of incubation—a long period for so small a bird—the young hatched into black, grubby caterpillars, with smoky fuzz in two lines down the back, and squat, yellowish mouths that gave no hint of the future awl-like bills. Now the mother's care was redoubled, and on the fifth day their eyes opened. Two days later respectable pin feathers transformed them from loathsome black worms into tiny porcupines.

Now we saw more and more often the grewsome-seeming spectacle of their feeding. The female's foraged burden of small insect life, culled from the flowers' corollas, and doubtless nectar-sweetened, is transferred to the young by regurgitation, and to avoid waste the mother's needle bill is driven to its hilt down the hungry youngster's throat. It suggests, as someone has said, a "major surgical operation," but the young so obviously enjoy and thrive upon it that we outsiders slowly lost our fear for them. At last the feathers broke their sheaths and the wee mites took on the semblance of real hummers. And then one night the worst happened—a prowling cat found the nest and exacted nature's price of death!

The disagreement in the figures of Bowles and Dickey as to the age at which the eyes are opened is probably due to the fact that the eyes are habitually kept closed for a good while after they are capable of being opened. Despite the great number of nests described or recorded, there seem to be few published figures on the length of time the young Anna's hummingbird remains in the nest. The single occupant of the nest watched by Mr. Anthony left after 18 days, undoubtedly a shorter than average time, since the period of three weeks recorded by Mr. Bowles corresponds very closely with my determinations for Costa's and the black-chinned, which range from 20 to 23 days for each species. This period in the case of the hummingbirds is more uniform than it is with most species of passerine birds and averages at least 50 percent longer.

Plumages.—The molting of the body plumage, as indicated by a slightly unkempt appearance, seems to take place in July and August. The luminous feathers of the crown and gorget are not replaced at that time, however, but begin to be shed in October, the ruff being completely lost and the throat and head becoming decidedly ragged, the former showing streaks of gray. The entire process to the completion of the new gorget requires perhaps a month. During this time the remainder of the plumage shows no sign of molting. The practice of the "nuptial flight," in so far as I have observed, seems to be discontinued during this period.

The outline of the gorget becomes visible on the throat of the young male soon after it has left the nest. The area gradually becomes sooty black, with glints of red, and slowly grows redder, the throat feathers lengthening into a ruff. Even in fall, however, when this first gorget is apparently complete, it still is lacking something in brilliancy and form; but it is almost immediately shed, to be replaced by the full perfection of the adult.

In the male Anna's and Costa's hummingbirds, alone among the species occurring in the United States, the crown is like the throat in color, but the two differ from each other not only in the color of the gorget but in its shape. As viewed from the front, that of Anna's is deeper and its lower border forms nearly a straight line, while the lower outline of the Costa's gorget is decidedly concave and its ruff is narrower and more prolonged. In both, the area of the crown is separated from that of the throat by a light streak running backward and downward from the eye, but in the Anna's only a very narrow gray line divides the luminous area behind the eye from that of the crown.

Among hummingbirds, and especially in the present species, individual variations seem more pronounced than among most birds. The color of the back ranges from slightly bluish metallic green to decidedly bronzy green in different individuals; the rose-red of the crown and gorget changes to purple as a secondary color in some instances, while in others gold and greenish lights are frequently seen. Ridgway (1892) refers to this as "perhaps the most beautiful of North American Humming Birds" and quotes Gould's Monograph of the Trochilidae as follows:

When studying the diversified forms and coloring of the Trochilidae, I have frequently been struck with the fact that those districts or countries having a metalliferous character are tenanted by species of Humming Birds which are more than ordinarily brilliant and glittering. This is especially the case with the species inhabiting Mexico and California: in illustration of this assertion, I may cite the three California species, *Selasphorus rufus*, *Calypte costae*, and the present bird, *C. annae*, all of which are unequaled for the rich metallic brilliancy of certain parts of their plumage, by any other members of the family. The two latter, *C. costae* and *C. annae*, have not only the throat, but the entire head as glitteringly resplendent as if they had been dipped in molten metal.

Food.—The food of the hummingbird is divided quite definitely into two classes: Carbohydrates, consisting of the nectar of flowers and more rarely of fruit juices and the sap of trees; and proteins, as furnished by the minute insects and spiders obtained either in conjunction with the other food or as the product of separate hunting activities. In late afternoon or on a cloudy day a hummingbird may frequently be seen perched upon some exposed twig or wire, from which it sallies forth at intervals to engage in strange aerial evolutions that might well mystify a stranger, since the flying insects it pursues are too small to be discerned at any distance. A specific instance of this sort is thus described by Frank F. Gander (1927): "On the morning of Thanksgiving Day, November 25, 1926, in Balboa Park, San Diego, California, I watched three male Anna Hummingbirds (*Calypte anna*) catching insects on the wing. A rain the night before had cleared the air and I could easily see the sun glistening on the gossamer wings of a host of tiny midges flying all about me in the air. The male hummers would hang on rapidly vibrating wings for a second and then dart suddenly a short distance and one of the glistening insects would disappear. This was repeated time and time again, and the birds seldom missed; on the rare occasions when they did miss they relentlessly pursued their chosen prey until it was captured."

Many observers have mentioned the hummingbirds' habit of searching the trunks and branches of trees for animal food and of extracting from spiders' webs small entangled insects or even the proprietors themselves. In their account of Anna's hummingbird in the Yosemite Valley, Grinnell and Storer (1924) have described some of its lesser-known feeding habits:

During November and December of 1914 we saw individuals almost daily at El Portal. At this time of the year there were no flowers of any sort to be found in the vicinity, but the Anna Hummingbirds seemed to find enough good forage on the foliage of the golden oaks, about which they were seen almost exclusively. The minute insects which live on the leaves of the golden oak probably afforded sufficient forage of one sort, but the hummingbirds had another source of food supply.

It was noted that one or more Anna Hummingbirds were to be found regularly about a certain golden oak, but the reason for their attraction to this particular tree was not discerned for several days. Then, on December 11, one of these birds was seen hovering before, and drinking from, some punctures made by a Red-breasted Sapsucker in the bark of the oak tree. The hummer visited puncture after puncture just as it would the individual blossoms in a spike of flowers, and evidently partook of both the sap and the smaller of the insects which had been attracted by the sap.

It is rather contrary to the traditional conception of hummingbirds that they should deliberately frequent the higher altitudes devoid of flowers, but there are undoubtedly times, following especially severe frosts, when members of this species in many parts of California must be compelled to obtain their living in other than the usual way. Mr. Dawson (1923) also mentions the use of sap: "Anna's Hummer is fond of the sap of our common willows (*Salix laevigata* and *S. lasiolepis*). It will also follow the Red-breasted Sapsucker (*Sphyrapicus ruber*) into the orchards and glean eagerly from its deserted borings. A catalogue of Anna's favorite flowers would be nearly equivalent to a botany of southern California. But if one had to choose *the* favorite it would probably be *Ribes speciosum*, our handsome red flowering gooseberry, for it is upon the abundance of this flower that Anna relies for her early nesting."

Naturalists in the eastern and northern parts of the country have found that hummingbirds are more attracted to red flowers than to those of any other color. The early-flowering gooseberry above mentioned and the paintbrush growing along a creek, which M. P. Skinner, in his notes, tells of seeing an Anna's hummingbird visit to the exclusion of other flowers, are both red; but in all these cases the flowers are probably seen against a green background, and since red is the complementary color of green, the greater visibility of that color may be more of a factor than any preference which the birds might feel. At any rate, there seems to be no such favoritism in the more arid parts of the Southwest, where the backgrounds are often grayish or tawny. Bits of red and blue cloth seemed to attract equal attention, though green was ignored.

Like most young animals, immature hummingbirds are filled with curiosity and are quick to investigate any brightly colored object; a bunch of carrots will attract them as readily as a flower. Through this process of trial they presently learn to discriminate among the flowers and often to choose those of inconspicuous appearance over the more brilliant kinds. As experience thus supplants curiosity, they cease to show much interest in unfamiliar brightly colored objects, unless it may be in times of food shortage, or when invading new territory where exploration must be carried on to locate its floral resources. Among familiar surroundings, memory for location undoubtedly guides the hummingbird to a large degree in its feeding.

As a general rule, hummingbirds prefer flowers of tubular form and are comparatively indifferent to composites and double flowers, such as roses. Within certain limits, size seems to be of little moment. One of the most valuable plants to Anna's hummingbird, especially, is a naturalized introduction from South America, the tree tobacco (*Nicotiana glauca*). This tall, sparse-foliaged, drought-resistant shrub bears a profusion of narrowly tubular blossoms practically throughout the year. Somewhat sensitive to cold, it is found only in the warmer parts of California. As an example of the hummingbirds' frequent disregard of bright coloring, they will probe the greenish-yellow newly opened flowers of this plant in preference to the purer yellow mature blossoms, which evidently contain less nectar. The greatest concentration of hummingbirds is seen about the tall, treelike flower stalks that culminate the life cycle of the common "century plant" (*Agave americana*), abundantly grown in California. The numerous greenish-yellow blossoms are dull-colored, but evidently they offer a rich store of nectar. Various species of eucalyptus, some of which bloom in winter, also attract large numbers of hummingbirds. The State of California must now be capable of supporting a much larger population of these birds than would have been possible under primitive conditions.

At times when their natural food is scarce, hummingbirds will gladly avail themselves of offerings of saturated sugar solution, which seems to be preferred to commercial honey. When flowers are plentiful and hummingbirds not too numerous they pay less attention to the artificial food than do the orioles and house finches, which are equally fond of sweets and not so well fitted to extract them from the flowers. It is during the latter half of the year that the hummingbirds will make most frequent use of sugar syrup in order to compensate for the comparative scarcity of flowers, though when the habit is once formed it may be continued even through spring. Visits are made at intervals during the day, perhaps only half-hourly when the temperature is high, but with increasing frequency toward evening, the height of this activity occurring between sunset and ten minutes after, when feeding ceases for the day. The use of clear glass vials affords an opportunity to observe the hummingbird's manner of drinking. When the liquid is out of reach of the bill, it is lapped up by rapid movements of the tongue, which can be extended an additional distance equal to the length of the bill. Should the vessel be filled nearly to the top, the syrup is either sipped with the end of the bill submerged or lapped with the tip of the bill held just at the surface and the tongue protruded only slightly. An Anna's hummingbird ordinarily consumes about two teaspoonfuls of saturated solution daily, only a few drops being taken at a time.

Various means may be used for the artificial feeding of the hummingbirds, ranging from small vials tied to the branches of trees to large and elaborate self-feeding devices, with provisions for discouraging the visits of ants, bees, and larger birds. Syrup in ordinary small brown bottles is often discovered by the birds without any kind of lure, but in more complex arrangements it is usually necessary to first guide them by inserting a flower in the opening. A change in the design of the container will cause much confusion and uncertainty for a time. Of other liquids than sugar solution, maple syrup and strained honey are acceptable, though the latter sometimes seemed to cause inconvenience because of its viscosity. Milk was not taken, and preserved fruit juices, though heavy with sugar, were apparently not palatable.

Naturally the proportion of liquid food in the ordinary diet of the hummingbird cannot be determined by an examination of stomachs, but Junius Henderson (1927) lists the identified contents of a large number of stomachs, as reported by Beal and McAtee in Farmers' Bulletin 506 (1912), as follows: Anna hummingbird (*Calypte anna*), 111 stomachs—vegetable matter, only a trace of fruit pulp; Diptera (gnats and small flies, largely neutral), 45.23 percent; Hymenoptera, mostly useful, 35.03 percent; Hemiptera, 17.30 percent; spiders, 2 percent.

F. C. Clark (1902) found that one stomach examined contained 32 treehoppers, 1 spider, 1 fly, and other insect remains. Fruit juices doubtless form only an inconsiderable part of the hummingbird's diet, but occasionally in fall an Anna's hummingbird may be seen sipping the juice of a persimmon that has been pecked by other birds and has softened on the tree, or the juice of a partially eaten tuna or pricklypear (*Opuntia*).

That the females in the nesting season require some additional mineral constituents in their diet was made clear to me upon seeing a female Anna's hummingbird upon several occasions visit a spot where particles of mortar were scattered. Hovering close to the ground, she appeared to be picking up the small grains and at other times would repeatedly plunge her bill into the loose sandy soil near by. Mr. Arnold (1930) tells of seeing Anna's hummingbirds alight on patches of ground where sand and plaster were strewn and seem to be picking up something, which he did not identify.

The changing seasons of the flowers have made expedient for the hummingbirds a somewhat nomadic existence, aside from true migrations. Perhaps this instinct for change has become so strong in the nonmigratory Anna's hummingbirds that they are unable to remain in one locality permanently. The sugar syrup containers maintained for their use have been visited by a constantly changing succession of individuals, some remaining only a few days, a few for a period of months, but all have eventually felt some urge more potent than the desire for a sure and easy living.

Behavior.—The flight of the hummingbird resembles that of no other bird, but rather that of certain insects, such as dragonflies or hawk moths, though stronger and swifter. Some of the earlier ornithologists expressed doubt of any bird's ability actually to fly backward, suggesting that the hummingbird's withdrawal from the depths of a tubular flower was accomplished by a forward flirt of the tail. A little careful observation would soon remove any skepticism as to its ability to easily fly backward, sidewise or in any other direction. While the tail is rhythmically vibrated forward and backward as the bird probes the flowers, it can be seen that its movements are not at all related to the backward flight, and that it is, in fact, seldom widely opened.

A hummingbird's wings are in almost uninterrupted motion while it is in the air; occasionally it will glide for an instant while in rapid flight. The amplitude of the wing beat is variable, but it often describes an arc of nearly 180° when the bird poises in the air. Sometimes the wings seem not to rise above the level of the back, but when the bird hovers over a cluster of upturned blossoms they may travel through the upper portion only of the complete arc. The confidence and sureness with which a hummingbird threads its way through a maze of twigs without injury while apparently devoting all its attention to the flowers cause one to admire, but its instant coordination of perception and movement can perhaps best be appreciated by noting the ease and certainty with which it thrusts its bill into a small tubular flower blown by a gusty wind.

That the flight of the hummingbird is by no means effortless, however, may be realized on a hot day, when one of them, returning to its shaded perch after an extended sortie, will sit for a minute or two with wide-open bill, panting with a violence that shakes its entire body. Though an immense amount of unnecessary flying is done, apparently in sport, the obtaining of food is evidently listed under the heading of work, and a hummingbird will seldom overlook an opportunity to perch, even to the extent of hanging almost upside down while reaching into a flower. The only sound produced by the normal flight of either sex of Anna's hummingbird is a low hum, which rises in volume and pitch when the speed is accelerated and has a slight suggestion of the rustling of silk. In wet weather, however, one may often hear from a flying hummingbird a sort of clapping noise of short duration, as if it were striking its wings together to rid them of moisture.

The sense of hearing, like that of sight, is keen, and a slight crunching of fallen leaves will evoke an attitude of alert apprehension, just as it does in many other wild creatures. The reaction to a sharp noise, though, is likely to be merely a nervous start, instead of the immediate flight, which is precipitated by any abrupt visible movement. This latter response is so invariable that it may well be regarded as a reflex rather than a volitional action. There seems to be no convincing evidence that the sense of smell plays any part in the discovery of food. A perfumed green-wrapped vial of sugar syrup attracted no attention, though a nearby unperfumed red-wrapped vial was quickly investigated. Some of the most heavily scented flowers, such as the jasmine and the large white blossom of the cactus *Trichocereus spachianus*, are comparatively neglected. Sense of location is very well developed, and when a bottle of syrup that has been regularly visited by a hummingbird is moved with its support to a different part of the grounds, the bird upon returning will hover in the exact spot from which the bottle was removed, often making several trips before finally becoming convinced.

Most writers have credited hummingbirds with extreme quarrelsomeness among themselves and a tyrannical disposition toward other birds. Careful observation has convinced me that their pugnacity has been greatly exaggerated, especially with reference to birds of other kinds. I believe that a hummingbird pursues other birds for exactly the same reason that a small dog will run after any passing vehicle, but immediately lose interest in it when it stops. Even the smallest passerine birds show no fear of the hummingbirds, nor are they molested if they fail to enter into the spirit of the game. Furthermore, I have often seen Anna's hummingbirds forced away from their sugar syrup by house finches or Audubon's warblers without the slightest show of resentment. Of course, a hummingbird that has preempted a certain territory resents any trespassing by other hummingbirds, who usually seem to recognize his rights and seldom dispute them; it is when an interloper resists eviction that the most earnest hostilities occur. Among the migrants in spring and among the immature birds late in summer, however, the constant chases and skirmishes appear to be carried on in a spirit of sport much more than of spite.

Probably because of their constant association among the flowers, hummingbirds show little fear of bees. I have sometimes seen an Anna's hummingbird, in order to reach a supply of sugar syrup, thrust its bill through a struggling mass of the insects. In contrast to this, a few small ants walking around the mouth of the bottle will often keep the bird away entirely. Whether this fear is an instinct founded on the occasional destruction of nestlings by ants is, of course, merely a matter of conjecture. Although the hummingbirds ordinarily treat the bees with indifference, I have watched one attack bees flying around an agave stalk, darting at one after another with open bill as if trying to bite them.

When a male hummingbird preempts a certain territory, he chooses one or more elevated exposed perches from which he can survey his domain and quickly detect trespassers. Sometimes he will use the same perch almost constantly through a whole season, seeking a more sheltered place only in very hot or windy weather; other individuals will alternate between two or more favorite perches, or select new ones at intervals without apparent reason. Acknowledging no family responsibilities, the males spend a large proportion of their daylight hours on these perches; but even the females who are caring for the young unaided seem to have an abundance of leisure in which to rest, preen their plumage, and engage in skirmishes.

Hummingbirds are fond of bathing, especially during the cooler part of the year. Often they seem afraid to enter water of any appreciable depth, but they enjoy bathing in a thin film of water flowing over a flat rock. Most of their bathing is done on dew-covered foliage in the early morning and, when available, in the fine spray of a lawn sprinkler. They revel in misty or drizzly rain and are particularly active under such conditions. Carroll Dewilton Scott, of Pacific Beach, Calif., writes (MS.) : "Anna's hummingbirds have a strong attraction for moving water. They will hover over irrigation ditches, evidently fascinated by the running water. I have never seen one drink anywhere or take a bath in still water. But the spray of a hose or a fountain is irresistible for a shower bath, even in January. Whenever I spray the garden a hummer is sure to appear." Unusual actions of a bathing hummingbird are described by F. N. Bassett (1924):

On August 17, 1924, while watering my lawn in Alameda, California, I placed the sprinkler in position and had just turned on the water when an adult male Anna Hummingbird (*Calypte anna*) flew into and poised in the dense spray. After glancing about for a moment he gradually assumed a vertical position and spreading his tail, then slowly settled to the ground, meanwhile drawing the tail back until it nearly reached the horizontal plane, when he actually "sat" on the grass, the body erect and the tail spread out fanwise behind him. The wings continued to vibrate while in this position, but the strokes were much less frequent than when flying, being just sufficient to maintain a vertical balance. In a few seconds he began increasing the wing strokes and slowly ascended about a foot above the ground where he poised a moment and then repeated the entire performance several times, after which he flew to a wire overhead.

Sun-bathing is less frequent and appears to be an individual rather than a general custom. Shortly after noon on a hot July day I saw an immature male Anna's hummingbird alight on a bare patch of ground and, heading directly away from the sun, stretch out flat on the soil with wings fully extended and the feathers of the back erected. Again, about two months later, at about the same time of day, the identical action was repeated on the lawn by the same individual. In both instances he remained on the ground less than a minute.

As to the intelligence of hummingbirds, I find no evidence to support W. H. Hudson's contention that they resemble insects more than birds in their mental processes. Their tameness cannot reasonably be attributed to mere stupidity, but rather to justified confidence in their own agility and swiftness, and perhaps also in human good will, since their power of discrimination is shown by their noticeable wariness toward cats. In their disposition and temperament hummingbirds are hardly comparable to any other birds but remind one most strongly of chipmunks.

Voice.—Of the seven species of hummingbirds found in the State of California, Anna's is the only one that may be said to possess a song. The "song" can hardly be called melodious, being a thin, squeaky warble suggestive of filing a saw. Nevertheless, it is delivered with fervor and remarkable persistence, with little regard for season. This song, which in addition to its use in courtship seems to serve the purpose of a general greeting or challenge, or sometimes merely a form of self-amusement, is peculiar to the males, who begin practicing it almost before their gorgets have started to develop. During the rendition, which often lasts for a rather long time, the bird leans forward on his perch, extends his neck, and holds his bill tightly closed, as far as can be detected at a distance of several feet. The clear, high-pitched, 2- or 3-syllabled whistling call of the male Costa's hummingbird, though less persistently used, appears to be entirely analogous to the Anna's song.

The ordinary notes common to both sexes are similar to those of other species. They consist of the feeding note, a mechanical "tick" or a more liquid chirp uttered at measured intervals as the bird goes from flower to flower; a similar note repeated more rapidly and animatedly while perching and often accompanied by a wagging of the head from side to side, expressing excitement or warning to trespassers; and the shrill twittering, which indicates a chase or skirmish. The begging call of the newly fledged young is much like that of other young birds.

Field marks.—Anna's hummingbird is the largest species found within its ordinary range, but there is integradation in measurements with all but the calliope hummingbird, whose small size is usually sufficient to distinguish it from Anna's at any time. Both sexes of Anna's can be separated from the rufous, Allen's, and broad-tailed hummingbirds by the entire absence of rufous or brownish coloring in the plumage. The male differs from the black-chinned and Costa's in the color of its throat and crown and in the fact that the gorget is bordered below by gray instead of white. The adult female usually has a central patch or scattered spots of luminous red on the throat; otherwise it can generally be distinguished from Costa's by its larger size and darker underparts, and from the black-chinned by its stouter form. In size and general appearance, including the color of the throat, Anna's is probably most like the broad-tailed, but the normal ranges of the two species are entirely separate.

Enemies.—The hummingbird is one of the most notable exceptions to the rule that smaller animals must be more prolific than larger ones in order to compensate for an inherently higher mortality rate. Nevertheless, the eggs and young of hummingbirds seem to be subject to more than ordinary vicissitudes. The small size and fragility of the nest, together with its usually exposed situation, make it liable to destruction by storms or accidents, while the long period between the laying of the eggs and the fledging of the young increases the possibility of loss. The eggs are said to be often taken by the California jay (*Aphelocoma californica*), and quite possibly they may be eaten by the banded racer (*Bascanion laterale*) and the alligator lizard (*Gerrhonotus scincicauda*), as these reptiles are frequently seen climbing through the foliage of shrubs and trees. In some cases, also, one of the eggs will fail to hatch, even though not disturbed. In their earlier stages, the young are probably threatened by the same enemies previously mentioned, while the spotted skunk (*Spilogale phenax*) is always a definite peril if the nest is within its reach. Another source of danger to the young birds is mentioned by Mr. Anthony (1923):

The ornithologist visiting San Diego is usually impressed with the surprising scarcity of nesting birds in Balboa Park, though the surroundings seem to be ideal. It was not until I had been at the San Diego Museum of Natural History a year, that the possible explanation was presented. A swarm of bees that had been installed as an exhibit in the museum was destroyed in a few days by an insignificant ant. This ant, I was told, had in all probability reached our shores with some of the trees or shrubs brought in from South America. It was known as the Argentine Ant. * * *

If bees were killed by ants, why not young birds? Several nests of the Anna Hummingbird (*Calypte anna*) were located and kept under observation and in every case the young were killed and eaten within two or three days of the time they hatched.

Dependence upon one parent alone would also theoretically increase the chances of failure. All in all, it would seem that the number of young fledged could not represent a very large proportion of the eggs laid. Once the young bird is able to fly, however, the situation is wholly changed, and the fledgling may look forward to the expectancy of a long life. If this were not true, the members of this family could not have maintained their present abundance with their small annual increase. The adult hummingbird seems to have no enemies of importance; certainly no predatory bird could capture it except by accident. On rare occasions a cat will catch one, in all probability an immature individual that has not yet learned caution, as seems to be generally the case among other birds. There are a few accounts of disaster through the agency of an unintentional enemy, such as the following from the manuscript notes of Carroll Dewilton Scott: "On one occasion I rescued a female Anna from impending death. A giant black spider had hung an enormous orb web among pendant eucalyptus limbs about 8 feet from the ground. One spring morning after a foggy night I noticed a female Anna fluttering on the edge of the web. The spider was nowhere to be seen and had not herself entangled the bird who had been snared, possibly, while gathering webs for binding her nest. But she was hopelessly caught by both wings in the tough, elastic, wet, sticky strands of the spider. After I pulled the webs from her wings she flew to an adjoining tree and sat quite still for several minutes."

That these incidents happen so seldom is a tribute to the hummingbird's alertness and quick perception, since the opportunities for such mishaps are very numerous, and the webs of these large orb-weaving spiders have been proved capable of holding considerably larger birds. Mr. Scott also mentions finding a dead Anna's hummingbird at the base of a window, presumably killed by striking the glass. Eric C. Kinsey states, however, that hummingbirds kept in glass-sided cages soon become accustomed to the glass and do not injure themselves by flying against it.

Of Anna's hummingbird, specifically, it would appear that the most destructive enemy is the exceptional period of cold weather that comes once in a cycle of years and, with native plants and animals alike, may overcome the powers of resistance built up to withstand ordinary winters. In this connection Mr. Dawson (1923) says:

Hummingbirds, one sees, even though they be so frail, possess an amazing vitality or recuperative power. But it is not too rare an experience to find one stranded, or numbed with the cold; and, to cite the extreme instance, the big freeze of January 2nd, 1913, undoubtedly cut down the resident hummer population of southern California (all Annas) one-half. It is quite worth while upon finding such a waif to try various methods of first-aid. The first expedient is, of course, heat—that of the closed hand may suffice. Or, it may be that the little engine only lacks "gas". Sweetened water, of a pretty strong solution, offered in a pipette, or medicine dropper (pressed upon attention, or flooding the bill until the tongue gets the flavor), will sometimes resuscitate a fallen hummer like a magic potion.

Nevertheless, the hardiness of Anna's hummingbird is greater than might be expected of so small a bird, belonging to a family predominantly tropical. In January 1937, during the most prolonged period of freezing weather in the history of southern California, when the temperature repeatedly fell to 24° F. at my home in the San Gabriel Valley, when ice remained on pools and birdbaths throughout the days and the sky was dark with soot from orchard heaters, half a dozen or more hummingbirds buzzed and twittered about a tall blooming eucalyptus tree and seemed not in the least distressed.

DISTRIBUTION

Range.—Chiefly California and Baja California; east casually in winter to Arizona and the mainland of Mexico; apparently not regularly migratory.

The breeding range extends **north** to northern California (Yreka and Mount Shasta. **East** in this State to Mount Shasta, Pyramid Peak, Big Creek, and the San Bernardino Mountains; and Baja California (San Pedro Martir Mountains). **South** to northern Baja California (San Pedro Martir Mountains, San Quintin, and San Telmo). The western boundary of the breeding range extends north from this point along the coast of Baja California and California to Red Bluff and Yreka.

During the winter season there is only a slight withdrawal from the northern parts of the summer range, as the species has been recorded at this time north in California to Ferndale and Red Bluff. The most southerly record at this season is Cerros Island, Baja California, about 200 miles south of known breeding areas. During the winter the species also is sometimes common in the southern part of Arizona (Roosevelt Lake and probably Salt River Reservation).

Casual records.—This species has been reported from the following other localities in Arizona: Camp Grant (September), Santa Catalina Mountains (October), and the Huachuca Mountains (October). A specimen was taken on February 21, 1934, at Punta Penascosa, Sonora.

Egg dates.—California: 86 records, December 21 to August 17; 43 records, February 22 to May 18, indicating the height of the season.

SELASPHORUS PLATYCERCUS PLATYCERCUS (Swainson)

BROAD-TAILED HUMMINGBIRD

PLATES 63, 64

HABITS

The broad-tailed hummingbird is *the* hummingbird of the Rocky Mountain region, ranging from southern Idaho, Montana, and Wyoming to the Valley of Mexico, and it is essentially a mountain bird.

It has been recorded from extreme eastern California, Inyo Mountains, and eastward as far as western Nebraska and western Texas.
M. P. Skinner says, in his notes from Yellowstone National Park:
"I have seen this little bird at all altitudes from the lowest up to
8,000 feet above sea level. I have seen it in the open, in lodge-pole
pine forest, and in alder thickets." Mr. Ridgway (1892) says: "In
the Rocky Mountain district proper, as in Colorado, for example, it
breeds at an elevation of from 4,000 to 11,000 feet, and I found it
having about the same vertical range in the East Humboldt Mountains." Dr. Jean M. Linsdale (1938) found that "the broad-tailed
hummingbird made up almost the entire hummingbird population
of the Toyabe Mountains," in Nevada, where "observations indicated
that the normal habitat for this species is close to mountain streams."
We found it in the Huachuca Mountains, Ariz., mainly along the
swift mountain streams, at altitudes of from about 5,000 to 7,000 feet.
Mr. Swarth (1904) says: "It is possible that this species remains in
the Huachucas through the winter as I saw a male bird near the
base of the mountains on February 28, 1903; and though not at all
common, I saw and heard them a number of times through the month
of March. It was the middle of April before they began to appear
in any numbers, and from then on they became more and more
abundant. At this time they were seen at a low altitude and along
the canyons; but after the summer rains began and the grass and
flowers sprung up, I found them mostly in the highest parts of the
range. * * * They breed in the highest parts of the mountains,
often in the pines and at a considerable distance from the ground."

Dr. Mearns (1890) writes: "This beautiful hummingbird is an
inhabitant of the highest land of Arizona, being rarely encountered
until one is well within the spruce belt, when it suddenly becomes
extremely plentiful. About springs and willow-edged water-courses
swarms of these gay birds congregate. * * * It ranges to the
very summit of San Francisco Mountain, being abundant in the highest timber." And Mrs. Bailey (1928) says:

The Broad-tailed Hummingbird, with the deep rose gorget and green crown,
is one of the most abundant birds of the New Mexico mountain region. Its
characteristic machine-like clicking, suggestive of the buzz of the cicada, made,
Mr. Henshaw explains, by the "attenuation of the outer primaries," was heard
by us at all levels from the foot of the Sangre de Cristo Mountains at 7,400
feet up to 12,700 feet at the highest terrace on the side of Wheeler Peak where
there was water; for during the season it follows the successively blooming
flowers up the mountain sides. * * *

The Broad-tails are seen not only in the uninhabited mountains but occasionally in towns. On the campus of the Santa Fe Indian School Mr. Jensen
found two pairs nesting in 1921 and 1922; and in front of a hotel in Rincon in
1920 Mr. Ligon saw one playing in the spray of a lawn sprinkler.

Major Bendire (1895) writes: "On the first arrival of this species in the spring it is comparatively common in the lower foothills and valleys, and unquestionably breeds here. By the time the young are large enough to leave the nest the majority of the flowers have ceased blooming, and as the country begins to dry up more and more these Hummingbirds retire to higher altitudes in the mountain parks, where everything is now as green and bright looking as it was in the lower valleys two or three months earlier. Here they raise their second broods under nearly similar conditions as the first; the former are by this time well able to take care of themselves and can be seen frolicking about everywhere."

Courtship.—Dr. Linsdale (1938) watched two hummers of this species on June 5, 1932, "that were definitely distinguished as a male and female which were going through mating antics. At first both were in flight together. Then the male flew up into the air about 30 feet and made a U-shaped dive. Next, both birds flew up in the air for about 90 feet, one lower than the other by 4 or 5 feet, and they came down at the same time. One flew off to the side but returned immediately. Both flew up and repeated the dive. Then the male hovered for half a minute, over birches and cottonwoods along the stream, until the female disappeared. No noise was made by the male bird while hovering."

Alexander F. Skutch sends me the following note on the courtship of the Guatemalan race of this species: "It was during the brightest, warmest hours of the day that I saw the broad-tailed hummingbirds rising and falling above the brushy growth on the sunny mountain-side where the salvias bloomed. One morning I watched a female as she perched within 2 feet of the ground in a little thicket where there was an abundance of flowers. Presently a male of her kind appeared; and she rose a few inches into the air and hovered with her bill pointed toward him, while he poised motionless on beating wings in front of and a little above her, displaying his brilliant red gorget before her eyes. Then of a sudden he rose almost vertically 30 or 40 feet into the air, whence he dropped straight downward and shot through the edge of the thicket directly in front of the female, who meanwhile had resumed her perch. Once past her, he inclined his course slightly upward and darted away over the mountainside."

Nesting.—Major Bendire (1895) makes the following general statement about the nests of the broad-tailed hummingbird:

Nests from different localities vary considerably in make-up as well as in size. Nests saddled on good-sized limbs, like those found in the mountains of Colorado, are occasionally almost as large again as others placed on small twigs. One now before me, from the Ralph collection, taken by Mr. William G. Smith, at Pinewood, Colorado, on June 23, 1892, measures 2 inches in outer diameter by 1⅜ inches in depth, while one taken by Mr. Ridgway, in Parley's Park, Utah, on July 23, 1869, measures only 1⅝ by 1 inch outside measurement. The difference in size of the inner cups of these two nests is even more noticeable, the former measuring 1 inch by three-fourths of an inch, the latter three-fourths by one-half of an inch. While the walls of both of these nests are mainly composed of willow or cottonwood down, their outer covering is entirely dissimilar. The outside of the larger one is profusely covered with small bits of lichens, like the nest of the Ruby-throat; the smaller one is decorated with shreds of bark, fine leaves, and dry plant fibers, resembling more the nests of Costa's Hummingbird in this respect. * * * The inner lining appears to be composed entirely of willow or cottonwood down, and none of the specimens before me contain even a single feather. The outer covering or thatching is firmly secured to the walls of the nest with spider webs or silk from cocoons. The majority of the nests of the Broad-tailed Hummingbird are placed on low, horizontal branches of willows, alders, cottonwoods, etc., at no great heights from the ground, or overhanging small mountain streams, while others are saddled on boughs or limbs of pine, fir, spruce, or aspens, from 4 to 15 feet from the ground, rarely higher. Occasionally a nest may be placed on a curled-up piece of bark or on a splinter of a broken limb.

Robert B. Rockwell tells me that "the broad-tailed hummingbird seems to be the only really common species about Colorado Springs. I have seen it as late as September 18, 1911. In 1923 one built a nest on a small branch of an elm tree overhanging a porch outside of our dining room. The nest was about 7 feet above the porch." He tells in his notes of another nest in a yellow pine tree, 8 feet above ground, and of another that was saddled on a dead limb of a small cottonwood, about 5 feet from the ground. He says (1908), in his paper on the birds of Mesa County, Colo., that it "frequents the timber along the streams from 6000 feet up and raises two broods in a season and possibly three. I found them breeding abundantly on Buzzard Creek at about 8000 and found nests containing fresh eggs, freshly hatched young and fledglings just ready to leave the nest on the same day and within a radius of half a mile. * * * One nest found was built on a root protruding from a bank directly over and within 2 feet of the swift running water of Buzzard Creek." Aiken and Warren (1914) say that "one confiding bird built its nest on the electric light fixture directly before the front door of a house, on a porch where people were continually going and coming, and raised two young."

R. C. Tate (1926) says that Oklahoma nests that he has examined were made of "rock-moss, lint from cottonwoods and willows, fine willows, fine shreds of thin inner bark from cottonwoods, and fine rootlets of blue-stem and gama grass."

Frank C. Willard's notes contain the records of six nests in the mountains of southern Arizona, at altitudes ranging from 4,900 to 6,000 feet. One nest was 8 feet up in a scrub oak, three were in sycamores 3 to 20 feet above ground, and two were in pines 20 and 30 feet from the ground.

The six nests of the broad-tailed hummingbird in the Thayer collection in Cambridge show about the same range of variation in size, shape, and make-up as those described by Bendire above. One nest, however, is decidedly smaller, measuring only 1¼ inches in diameter and 1 inch in height externally; the walls are very thin and the cup is very shallow; it is made of the usual materials, mixed with the winged seeds of milkweed or thistle. Another nest is worthy of mention, as illustrating camouflage to match its surroundings; it was built on a sycamore branch, composed of sycamore or willow cotton, and was decorated on the outside, almost completely covered, with pale gray and buff lichens, producing a soft, buffy effect to harmonize with the branch that held it.

Eggs.—The broad-tailed hummingbird lays almost invariably two eggs; I have no record of more or fewer. These are like those of other hummingbirds, pure white, without gloss, and about elliptical-oval in shape. The measurements of 62 eggs average 13 by 8.8 millimeters; the eggs showing the four extremes measure **14.5** by 9.9, 13.8 by **10.0, 11.9** by 8.4, and 12.2 by **7.9** millimeters.

Young.—The period of incubation is probably about 14 days, as with other related species. Incubation is performed wholly by the female, and she takes full care of the young; she is a brave and devoted mother. The young are fed at first on regurgitated, semi-digested food, but as they grow older they are given an increasing amount of minute insects; they are fed at more or less irregular intervals. Dr. Linsdale (1938) says of a nest that he watched: "At 10 o'clock I saw the female go to the nest and feed 5 times, the last for only a short period, and then brood. The first thrust was deep down the gullet of the young, and then the bill was withdrawn gradually. At 10:12 the female was off the nest. At 10:19 it returned and fed 4 times and brooded. Each feeding required between 5 and 10 seconds. It was not more than a minute from the time of arrival to time of settling on the nest. The bird faced at least 3 directions while brooding but always stood on the north rim to feed. When it left at 10:27, there were clouds and a cold wind. At 10:31 it returned directly to the nest and began to brood."

Plumages.—I have no data on the development of the juvenal plumage in the nestling broad-tailed hummingbird, but it probably does not differ materially from that of the rufous hummingbird, described under that species.

Ridgway (1911) describes the young male, in juvenal plumage, as "similar to the adult female but feathers of upper parts (especially rump and upper tail-coverts) indistinctly margined terminally with pale brownish buff or cinnamon, and lateral rectrices with much less of cinnamomeous on basal portion." The young female, he says, is "similar to the young male but rectrices as in adult female."

Young males begin to acquire some red in the throat before the end of July and assume the fully adult plumage late in the following winter, or early in the spring, at the complete annual molt.

Food.—Mrs. Bailey (1928) gives, as the food of the broad-tailed hummingbird in New Mexico, "insects found in flowers, as pentstemon, larkspur, agave, gilia, gooseberry, and on willow catkins." Elsewhere (1904), she says that "the throat of one shot was full of honey and long-tailed, wasp-like insects." Bendire (1895) mentions the flowers of *Scrophularia* and *Ocotilla* as favorite feeding places. Mr. Rockwell says in his notes: "August 3, 1902, at some willows on a ranch near Crested Butte, I saw four hummingbirds. They seemed to be interested with something in the willows, and I found many perforations in the bark made by sapsuckers; many ants and other insects were about these perforations; whether it was the sap or the insects that attracted the birds I could not tell."

Dr. Linsdale (1938) writes: "On June 18, 1930, at 7,000 feet on Kingston Creek, a female broad-tailed hummingbird was watched which apparently was feeding upon flying insects caught in the air. It was in a small clearing near the creek. After a poise the bird would dart 3 feet after an insect, then poise and go after another. This was repeated half a dozen times, the bird being about 10 feet above the ground."

Apparently this, like other hummingbirds, lives to a large extent on small spiders and minute insects of the orders Diptera, Hymenoptera, Hemiptera, Coleoptera, etc., which it finds in the flowers; nectar, honey, or sap may not be what at first attracted the birds, but they have proved to be very acceptable foods, just as the eastern rubythroat has learned to feed freely from glass containers filled with syrup. Sugar is a very nourishing and strengthening food.

Behavior.—Robert Ridgway (1877) writes thus attractively of the behavior of the broad-tailed hummingbird:

The flight of this Humming-bird is unusually rapid, and that of the male is accompanied by a curious screeching buzz, while it is followed through an undulating course. Long before the author of this curious sound was detected its source was a mystery to us. This shrill screeching note is heard only when the bird is passing rapidly through the air, for when hovering among the flowers its flight is accompanied by only the usual muffled hum common to all the species of the family. During the nesting-season the male is of an exceedingly quarrelsome disposition, and intrepid, probably beyond any other bird, the Flycatchers not excepted. All birds that approach the vicinity of his nest, whether they be his own species or of the size of hawks, are immediately assaulted with great force and pertinacity by this seemingly insignificant little creature, the vigor of whose attacks, accompanied as they are by the shrill piercing noise we have mentioned, invariably puts to flight any bird assaulted. We have thus seen the Western Kingbird (*Tyrannus verticalis*), the Black-headed Grosbeak (*Hedymeles melanocephalus*), and the Sharp-shinned Hawk (*Nisus fuscus*) beat a hasty retreat before the persevering assaults of this Humming-bird. When thus teasing an intruder the little champion ascends almost perpendicularly to a considerable height, and then descends with the quickness of a flash at the object he would annoy, which is probably more frightened by the accompanying noise than by the mere attack itself. As we chanced, while hunting on the mountains, to pass through the haunts of this Hummer, it frequently happened that one of the little creatures, prompted apparently by curiosity, would approach close to us and remain poised in one spot, its wings vibrating so rapidly as to appear as a mere haze around the body; now and then it would shift from one side to another, its little black eyes sparkling as it eyed us intently. So close would it finally approach that to strike it with a hat or a stick seemed to be quite an easy matter, but upon the slightest motion on our part the little thing would vanish so quickly that its direction could scarcely be traced.

Mr. Swarth (1904) testifies on the swiftness of the flight of this bird, as follows: "The shrill buzz of its wings, that is of the male bird, is frequently heard; and time and again as the sound approached, passed, and died away in the distance, I watched, but in vain, to catch sight of the author of it. Several times I have seen one leave its perch on a twig and dart off in pursuit of another of the same species, and even then was unable to follow him with my eye; and though presently the sound of wings announced his return, I was seldom able to see the bird before he dropped onto his perch. * * * The flight of the female is not accompanied by the buzzing noise made by the male bird, and from their habits they are more inconspicuous and less frequently seen than their mates."

Curiosity is shown in various ways, beside the case cited above. Mr. Rockwell tells, in his notes, of one that flew against the window of a laboratory where he was sitting; another "hovered before a mirror that was hanging to a tent pole outside" of his camp, but "it made no attempt to fight its image"; again it, or another, alighted "on a guy rope, then hovered before the tent, and finally flew over to the car, and in front of every window, apparently attracted by its image." Dr. Mearns (1890) writes: "Its boldness is without parallel; it knows no fear. A member of our party on San Francisco Mountain wore a scarlet cap, but he found these audacious birds so troublesome from their constant attacks upon it that he was glad to pocket it in order to be rid of the irate little furies."

All hummingbirds are fond of bathing, and this species is no exception. On May 15, 1922, while climbing to the summit in the Huachuca Mountains, and following the course of a little mountain stream that flowed swiftly over its stony bed, we stopped to watch a pair of broad-tailed hummingbirds that were bathing in the brook. They chose a spot where the water barely covered a flat stone, settled down in the shallow water, which barely covered their little bodies, and fluttered their wings as they faced upstream; after a few seconds in the cold water, they flew off to a nearby branch to shake themselves and preen their plumage. Dr. Merriam (1890) says that, on San Francisco Mountain—

They wake up very early in the morning and go to water at daylight no matter how cold the weather is. During the month of August, and particularly the first half of the month, when the mornings were often quite frosty, hundreds of them came to the spring to drink and bathe at break of day. They were like a swarm of bees, buzzing about one's head and darting to and fro in every direction. The air was full of them. They would drop down to the water, dip their feet and bellies, and rise and shoot away as if propelled by an unseen power. They would often dart at the face of an intruder as if bent on piercing the eye with their needle-like bill, and then poise for a moment almost within reach before turning, when they were again lost in the busy throng.

Voice.—The loud, screeching sound, referred to by several observers, is probably mechanical, made by the rushing of the air through the flight feathers. Mrs. Bailey (1928) says that "besides their squeaky little song they gave some small staccato notes." And Robert S. Woods (1927b) says: "A rather faint, muffled staccato note is uttered twice in quick succession at the lowest point of its vertically diving nuptial flight."

Field marks.—The broad-tailed hummingbird suggests the ruby-throated in general appearance, but the rufous edgings in the tail will mark the former, and the ranges of the two hardly come together. Mr. Woods (1927b) writes:

The appearance of the Broad-tailed Hummingbird is not especially distinctive in any way. The color of the gorget, aside from its somewhat inferior brilliancy, is very similar to that of Anna's Hummingbird, though showing at some angles a more purplish cast. A convenient recognition mark of the male is the rufous edging of certain of the tail feathers, in conjunction with the solid green color of the back and upper tail-coverts. It may be safely said that the Broad-tailed Hummingbird is much more readily identified by ear than by eye. The loud metallic noise produced by the flight of the male is an agreeable, almost musical sound, clearer in tone than that made by the Rufous, Allen's or Black-chinned Hummingbirds, while the notes of the female seem more liquid than those of other species.

The rose-pink gorget and the green crown distinguish the broad-tailed from the males of other western hummers. But the females are not so easily recognized; the female broadtail has less rufous in the tail than the rufous or calliope, only the three outer tail feathers being basally rufous; the calliope is considerably smaller; the female broadtail may be distinguished from the female black-chinned by the presence of some rufous in the flanks of the former.

Fall.—Mr. Henshaw (1886) found the broad-tailed hummingbirds "extremely numerous" late in summer in the mountains of New Mexico. He says:

Young birds were noticed August 1, and by the 10th they became common. By August 1 the males of this species began to get less numerous, and by the 10th there were none; in fact, I saw very few after that date. * * *

In this locality at least there is an evident reason for this. Just about this date the *Scrophularia*, which is the favorite food plant of the Hummers, begins to lose its blossoms, and in a comparatively short time the flowers give place to the seed pods. Though there are other flowers which are resorted to by the Hummers, particularly several species of *Pentstemon*, they by no means afford the luxurious living the former plant does. It seems evident therefore, that the moment its progeny is on the wing, and its home ties severed, warned of the approach of fall alike by the frosty nights and the decreasing supply of food, off go the males to their inviting winter haunts, to be followed not long after by the females and young. The latter—probably because they have less strength—linger last, and may be seen even after every adult bird has departed.

DISTRIBUTION

Range.—Western United States and Central America.

Breeding range.—The breeding range of the broad-tailed hummingbird extends **north** to central Nevada (White Mountains, Toquima Mountains, Monitor Mountains, and the Snake Mountains); northern Utah (Brighton, Salt Lake City, and Parleys Park); and northern Wyoming (Yellowstone National Park and Midwest). **East** to eastern Wyoming (Midwest, Douglas, Wheatland, and Laramie); eastern Colorado (Greeley, Denver, Colorado Springs, and Beulah); New Mexico (Culebra Mountains, Pecos, and the Sacramento Mountains); and southwestern Texas (Chisos Mountains). **South** to southwestern Texas (Chisos Mountains); northeastern Sonora (Oposura); southern Arizona (Huachuca Mountains and Santa Rita Mountains); southern Nevada (Charleston Mountains); and east-central California (Inyo Mountains). **West** to eastern California (Inyo Mountains and Cottonwood Creek); and western Nevada (Davis Creek, Chiatovich Creek, and White Mountains). It has been stated that this species breeds south to the "Valley of Mexico," but the evidence is unconvincing, particularly in view of the absence of breeding data through the mountainous regions of northern Mexico. A closely related subspecies is found in the highlands of Guatemala.

Winter range.—During the winter season the broad-tailed hummingbirds appear to be concentrated in west-central Mexico, as in the States of Zacatecas (Bolanos), Jalisco (Volcano de Colima), Mexico (Eslava), and Guerrero (Taxco).

Spring migration.—Early dates of spring arrival are: Arizona—Tucson, March 25; Tombstone, April 1. New Mexico—Apache, April 9; Chloride, April 13. Colorado—Beulah, April 23; Durango, April 26; Boulder, May 4. Wyoming—Laramie, May 20. Utah—Salt Lake City, May 3.

Fall migration.—Late dates of fall departure as: Wyoming—Fort Sanders, September 3; Laramie, September 16. Colorado—Durango,

September 12; Colorado Springs, September 21.   New Mexico—
Apache, October 5.

Casual records.—A specimen was collected at Mount Vernon, Oreg.,
on June 30, 1915, and another was seen at Enterprise on July 27,
1921; one was taken at Big Butte, Idaho, on July 19, 1890, and one
was seen at Spencer on July 9, 1916; in Montana one was obtained at
Chico in 1902, while two have been taken in Glacier National Park,
one on May 23 and the other on June 17, 1895; a pair were reported
as seen daily between August 18 and 22, 1906, at Glen, Nebr., and one
was collected at Kearney on July 22, 1914.

Egg dates.—Arizona: 20 records, May 8 to July 30; 10 records,
June 11 to July 16, indicating the height of the season.

Colorado: 18 records, May 22 to July 17; 9 records, June 13 to 26.
Utah: 10 records, June 6 to July 23.

SELASPHORUS RUFUS (Gmelin)

RUFOUS HUMMINGBIRD

PLATES 65–67

HABITS

Although I have always considered Costa's hummingbird to be the
most beautiful of our North American hummingbirds, on account of
the charming colors reflected in its crown and gorget, it must yield
the palm for brilliancy to the rufous hummingbird and its near
relative, Allen's.   The brilliant scarlet of the rufous hummer's gorget,
which often glows like burnished gold, puts it in the front rank
as a gleaming gem, a feathered ball of fire.   It is not only fiery
in appearance, but it has a fiery temper and makes things lively for
any rivals near its feeding stations or its nest.

It ranges farther north than any of our other hummingbirds,
breeding from about latitude 61° N. in Alaska and southern Yukon
southward to Oregon and southwestern Montana.   It is exceedingly abundant from the Rocky Mountains westward on its migrations to and from its winter home in southern Mexico.   And it
may yet be found breeding at high elevations in some of the mountain ranges south of its present known breeding range.   Henshaw
(1886) was perhaps mistaken in assuming that this hummer was
breeding in the region of the upper Pecos River in New Mexico,
though he states that it was abundant at altitudes of from 8,000 to
9,000 feet "during the entire summer"; but he found only one nest,
"and this after it was deserted."   Mrs. Bailey (1928) says: "There
seems to be no known instance of the Rufous Hummingbird nesting
in Arizona, Colorado, or New Mexico, though the species has been
included in the breeding lists of these States for the last thirty

years." Mr. Ridgway (1911) includes these States, as well as some mountains in California, in the breeding range. The fact that early migrants appear in these regions in July may have led to the assumption that the species was breeding in the vicinity, but no occupied nest seems to have been reported.

Spring.—The rufous hummingbird apparently makes its northward migration in spring mainly to the westward of the Rocky Mountains; according to Mrs. Bailey (1928) "it is unknown in spring in both New Mexico and Colorado"; and Mr. Swarth (1904) did not see it in the Huachuca Mountains at any time in the spring and considers it of comparatively rare occurrence in Arizona at this season. In southern California, and probably throughout the State, it is a very common spring migrant, especially through the valleys and foothills of the Pacific slope. Referring to Los Angeles County, Robert S. Woods (1927b) says that, after the arrival of Anna's hummingbird, "the Rufous Hummingbird is the next of the migrants to appear, usually arriving early in March and leaving late in April. During part of this time it is the commonest species. My earliest record for the Rufous is February 17 (1926) and the latest for the spring migration May 1 (1924)."

Leslie L. Haskin writes to me from Oregon: "In the Willamette Valley the rufous hummingbird is the first of the family to arrive. It appears normally about the first of March, although an occasional earlier individual may often be seen. The males precede the females by a considerable time. My observation is that, while the males are very abundant throughout March, few females will be seen before the last week of that month. The main body of the rufous hummingbird migration arrives just as the crimson-flowered currant (*Ribes sanguineum*) is bursting into bloom, and of the flowers of this shrub the hummingbirds are especially fond. At that time every bush is alive with the darting hummers, and it is one of the most brilliant bird and flower spectacles of the West. The glittering, coppery sheen of the birds and the crimson flowers, borne in profuse drooping panicles, make a brilliant combination."

Courtship.—A very good account of this bird's courtship is given by G. D. Sprot (1927) as follows:

In the displays I have witnessed, which have been many, a careful survey of the ground beneath the performer invariably revealed the female sitting motionless on some twig of the low-growing underbrush, and as the aerial acrobat reached the limit of his upward flight she was seen to turn her head slightly and glance admiringly aloft. The male ascended usually with his back towards his mate, then turning, faced her, and with gorget fully expanded descended swiftly until within an inch or two of her, when spreading both wings and tail he checked himself and soared aloft again to repeat the performance, or else settled on some near-by bush. As he so checked his flight the whining note was produced, undoubtedly by the rush of air through the outspread feathers.

On two occasions, in May, 1925, and May, 1926, I witnessed in connection with the above performance what I believe to be the actual mating of the birds. After one or two towering flights by the male, the female rose from her perch and the male immediately closed with her. Then over a distance of some ten or twelve feet, and horizontally, they swung together backwards and forwards through the air, just as one often sees insects so doing. The regular swinging hum of the wings is hard to describe but is just what one might expect. So fast is this swinging flight, and so close was I, not over four or five feet away in one instance, that I was totally unable to see the birds except as a blurred streak of color. As the flight ceased I saw them separate, and in one instance the female was seen to fall to the ground, but later to regain her perch, while the male continued his towering flights.

Mr. Haskin says in his notes: "Besides the diving act it has another modified performance. In this act the male 'teeters' in the air above the female who is hidden in the grass below. It is like the dive, but the arc is much shorter and flatter—a shallow curve of only 6 or 8 inches. The male in this stunt shoots forward with the tail spread and much elevated, followed by a quick backward dart, tail lowered, and twittering and buzzing to his utmost. This is repeated again and again."

Nesting.—A. Dawes DuBois has sent me some very elaborate notes on the nesting habits and home life of the rufous hummingbird in the vicinity of Belton, Mont., subsequently published by him (1938). The nest that he studied "was five feet from the ground, in a small balsam fir, among the branches of a close-standing birch. It was situated at the bottom of the slope of a foothill. The foothills were wooded chiefly with larch, spruce, hemlock, fir and cedar, and on this particular slope was a growth of birch. It was constructed of soft, cottony, plant materials felted together and thickly covered exteriorly with lichens held in place by cob-webs." He gives the dimensions of the nest as diameter at the rim 1 inch, diameter at the bulge 1⅞, inside depth ⅞, and outside depth 1¼ inches.

D. E. Brown has sent me the following notes: "The rufous hummingbird returns to western Washington by the middle of March and commences nest building a month later. They colonize to a certain extent in favorable localities, and I have seen as many as 10 nests in a small patch of gorse. The nest is near the ground as a rule, but sometimes it is placed higher up in either conifers or deciduous trees. The drooping branches of conifers are favorite sites, the nest often being placed on the lowest branch; and a branch that has a sharp downward bend is so well liked that the bird often returns to the same place the next year, and even the third year. A nest built on such a branch is fastened to it from the bottom to the very top, which is built out to level things up. The next year's nest is placed on the old one but securely tied to the stem, and the third nest is built the same way. Double nests are not at all uncommon, and I have seen three where the third nest had been added."

J. H. Bowles (Dawson and Bowles, 1909) writes:

There is scarcely a conceivable situation, except directly on the ground, that these birds will not select for a nesting site. Such odd places have been chosen as a knot in a large rope that hung from the rafters of woodshed; and again, amongst the wires of an electric light globe that was suspended in the front porch of a city residence. It may be found fifty feet up in some huge fir in the depths of the forest, or on the stem of some blackberry bush growing in a city lot.

Very often they form colonies during the nesting season, as many as twenty nests being built in a small area. Some large fir grove is generally chosen for the colony, but a most interesting one was located on a tiny island in Puget Sound. This island has had most of its large timber cut away, and is heavily overgrown with huckleberry, blackberry, and small alders. In the center is the colony, the nests placed only a few yards apart on any vine or bush that will serve the purpose. Huckleberry bushes seem the favorites, but many nests are built in the alders and on the blackberry vines.

A. W. Anthony wrote to Major Bendire (1895): "I found the Rufous Hummingbird very abundant at Beaverton, Oregon. Here they nested in oaks, blackberry vines, and on dry roots projecting from upturned trees. One nest hung from the end of a tall fern, while others, drooping over it from above, hid the beautiful structure from all but accidental discovery. Their favorite sites, however, seemed to be the long, trailing vines overhanging embankments and upturned trees. A number were found in railroad cuts; frequently several nests were situated within a few feet of each other, a slight preference being shown for embankments having a southern exposure."

What few nests of the rufous hummingbird I have seen are rather large, well made, and handsome structures; the body of the nest, including the lining, is made up mainly of pale buff cottony substances, apparently from willow blossoms; but this is mixed with and profusely covered externally with bright-green moss, so that the nest appears to be made largely of this moss; it is often more or less decorated on the outside with leaf or bud scales, shreds of inner bark, lichens, and various other plant fibres, all of which are securely bound on with spider web, making a firm compact structure. Bendire (1895) says that "an average nest measures 1½ inches in outer diameter by 1¼ inches in depth; the inner cup is about seven-eighths of an inch in width by one-half inch deep." One that I measured was 1¾ inches in outside diameter. The favorite nesting trees seem to be firs, spruces, and other conifers, but nests have also been found in willows, cypresses, ashes, apple trees, various oaks, and probably other trees, as well as numerous bushes, such as wild currant, salmonberry, hazel, etc. The nests are usually artfully decorated to match their surroundings. Dawson and Bowles (1909) say that "the nesting season is greatly protracted, for fresh eggs may be found from April till July. This makes it seem probable that each pair raises at least two broods during the spring and summer."

Eggs.—Two eggs almost invariably make up the full set for the rufous hummer, but Major Bendire (1895) records a set of three, taken by Clyde L. Kellar, of Salem, Oreg. D. E. Brown tells me that often there is only one, and he has "seen one nest that contained four, evidently contributed by two females." The eggs are like other hummingbirds' eggs, dead pure white and varying from oval to elliptical-oval in shape. The measurements of 53 eggs average 13.1 by 8.8 millimeters; the eggs showing the four extremes measure **14.0** by 8.7, 13.1 by **10.0, 11.4** by 8.9, and 13.0 by **7.7** millimeters.

Young.—The period of incubation is said to be 12 days (Burns, 1921), but probably it is nearer 13 or 14 days, as with some other hummingbirds. This duty and the care of the young are performed entirely by the female; the male seldom, if ever, comes near the nest after the eggs are laid. William L. Finley (1905) writes:

As soon as the cottony cup was finished and the mother had cradled her twin white eggs, the father disappeared. He merely dropped out of existence, as Bradford Torrey says, leaving a widow with twins on her hands. This generally seems to be the case, for at the different nests where I have watched, I never but once saw a male hummer near the nest after the young were hatched. I was lying in the shade of the bushes a few feet from the nest one afternoon. For two whole days, I had been watching and photographing and no other hummer had been near. Suddenly a male darted up the canyon and lit on a dead twig opposite the nest. He hadn't settled before the mother hurtled at him. I jumped up to watch. They shot up and down the hillside like winged bullets, through trees and over stumps, the mother, with tail spread and all the while squeaking like mad. It looked like the chase of two meteors, that were likely to disappear in a shower of sparks, had they struck anything. If it was the father, he didn't get a squint at the bantlings. If it was a bachelor a-wooing, he got a hot reception.

On the other hand, Alfred M. Bailey (1927) saw, in southeastern Alaska, an adult male incubating on a set of eggs nearly ready to hatch, of which he says: "I was walking along the base of a precipitous cliff when I noticed the handsome little male hovering over my head, about twenty feet up, and was then surprised to see him climb into a nest, in the terminal branches of a drooping spruce. When incubating, the little male squatted far down in the nest, with tail and beak pointed almost vertically, and he proved so tame that I believe I could have touched him."

The following statements are based on, and the quotations are taken from, some elaborate notes sent to me by A. Dawes DuBois, who made an intensive study of a nest of the rufous hummingbird near Belton, Mont. In order to be able to study the parent and the single young bird at close range, he concealed himself in a "balsam cloak," which was "prepared by sewing balsam boughs all over the outside of an old brown bathrobe. An old felt hat was covered with boughs, which hung down all around to hide the observer's head and face while permitting observation through the interstices of the foliage." Under this disguise, he could stand, motionless as a tree, with his eyes within 10 or 12 inches of the nest and slightly above it.

Before the eggs hatched the female incubated almost constantly with absences of only a few minutes; one day, while the sun was shining on the nest most of the time, she was gone for more than an hour; during two hours of watching, on the day before the one egg hatched, the bird left the nest five times, for intervals varying from 5 to 19 minutes. One of the two eggs did not hatch, and, as the bird did not remove the remnants, Mr. DuBois did so.

After the one young bird hatched the female brooded it with frequent intervals of absence, much like those taken during incubation, up to the time that it was seven days old; from that time on, she "was absent much of the time during the mornings. In the afternoons she had to shelter the nestling from the sun."

When the nestling was two days old, it was fed only three times between 8:45 a. m. and 6 p. m., but the observer was absent from 12 m. to 1:33 p. m. and from 3:30 to 3:45 p. m. "When four days old, the average of seven known intervals was about 44 minutes. When six days old, the average of 11 known intervals was 32 minutes. The frequency of feeding increased in the latter portion of the day."

The number of regurgitations for each feeding varied from two to five; the total time occupied for five pumpings and subsequent examination and tidying of the nest was somewhat less than one minute. On July 20, when the nestling was two days old, "at 10:30, there was no pushing up and down; the parent seemed to pump the fluid by the slightest visible motion of her own throat. At 5:35 the same day she poked rather vigorously while regurgitating, and two days later, the poking was extremely vigorous. As observed on the 24th, the young bird's head moved up and down with the mother's bill. During one of the feedings, as I stood close to the nest with my head covered, I could see the liquid welling up in the young bird's mouth. At the age of 5½ days, the young one responded very vigorously and took the whole length of the parent's bill into his throat.

"The alvine discharges of the young hummingbird were forcibly ejected in a manner to render nest cleaning unnecessary. Very close observation from the balsam cloak, on July 22, indicated that the parent did not take excrement from the young or nest; nor did the young emit excrement after being fed. On the 23d, while the parent was absent, I observed the method employed by the nestling, then five days old. Following a slight shaking of the nest, it struggled to reach the top of the high nest wall. The great depth of the nest made this very difficult, but the young bird accomplished it, standing literally on its head, braced against the wall of the nest. The discharge was projected to a distance of several inches beyond the nest."

Mr. DuBois could not mention in his notes the length of time that his young bird remained in the nest, as it died prematurely, but Gladys Hammersley (1928) observed that the altricial period is about 20 days; she writes:

As the young hummers grew bigger they gradually tramped the nest out of shape, so that when they flew away on June 23rd it was no longer a dainty little cup, but an almost shapeless platform in comparison. There were no flying lessons; the little hummers buzzed fearlessly out into the world as though they had been accustomed to flying every day of their lives. They were not so expert with their feet, however, making several ineffectual attempts before securing a safe landing. I never found any young return to the nest having once left it, but they will return regularly to a chosen perch day after day, even when disturbed several times during the day, generally returning to precisely the same spot on the same twig each time.

Plumages.—Mr. DuBois says that the young rufous hummingbird, when first hatched, is about as large as a honey bee, nearly black and quite naked, except for two slight tracts of grayish natal down extending longitudinally along the back. It is blind at first, but when six days old a slit begins to show in the membrane covering the eye, and by the twelfth day the eyes are well opened. The natal down grows longer day by day, and pinfeathers begin to show on the sixth and seventh days. From that time on the juvenal plumage continues to grow.

When fully fledged in fresh juvenal plumage the young male is similar to the adult female, the back largely green, but the upper tail coverts are "cinnamon-rufous" with terminal spots of metallic bronze-green; the throat is dull white, spotted with dark bronzy; the chest is dull white, and the sides and flanks are heavily washed with "cinnamon-rufous." Usually in August, but sometimes as early as the middle of July, some metallic red feathers begin to appear in the throat, increasing more or less during fall and winter; but I have seen one young male, taken as late as March 17, that still shows no red in the throat, though the back and rump are practically all rufous. The juvenal tail, with terminal white spots on the three outer rectrices somewhat smaller than those of the female, is worn all through fall and winter, until the complete annual molt, late in winter and early in spring, produces the adult plumage; I have seen one young male, taken on April 15, that was just completing this molt. Young females are like young males but have more green on the back. Adults apparently molt at the same time as young birds, late in winter and early in spring.

Food.—The rufous hummingbird finds its nectar and probably its insect food in a great variety of flowers and in the blossoms of trees and shrubs, showing a decided preference for red flowers. Mr. Haskin, writing from Oregon, tells me that "early in spring the crimson-flowered currant is their favorite flower, next to that they resort in great numbers to another red flower, the columbine. Of white flowers, their favorite is the blossom of the madrona tree (*Arbutus menziesii*), whose flowers are perfect honey pots. A tree of the madrona in full bloom attracts them literally by the hundreds." Frank L. Farley writes to me that in Alberta in July and August "its favorite flower appears to be the bright-colored nasturtium."

M. P. Skinner says, in his notes from California, that it feeds on red columbine and "paint brush." Of its insect hunting, he says: "Another individual alighted on some willow twigs beside a river and watched for the insects that flew by at frequent intervals. Twice it rose 5 or 6 feet for one and then dropped back to its perch. Twice it caught an insect 40 feet above its perch, showing what keen eyes it had. Then it made a dizzying swift dart down among the willows. After that this bird came back at intervals all through the morning to do the same kind of insect hunting over the willows and over the river waters."

Mrs. Bailey (1902) writes:

On the birds' breeding ground the flowers they feed on, as far as I have observed, are mainly red, as the hummer's coloration might suggest. On San Francisco Mountain, Arizona, they were especially fond of the scarlet pentstemons. On Mount Shasta they fed from the painted-cups, tiger lilies, and columbines. Any spot of red would attract them as it does other hummers, and they investigated it fearlessly even when it adorned the person of a collector.

One of the birds actually crossed a wide meadow of green brakes straight to a single columbine standing most inconspicuously near the woods. But the painted-cups were their especial delight on Shasta, and a meadow full of the flowers was fairly alive with them.

William H. Kobbé (1900) says that, in Washington, about Cape Disappointment, "they are particularly abundant about the flowering salmon-berry bushes and also the thimble-berry, but they seemed to be fonder of the honeysuckle blossoms than of either of the others." Dr. A. M. Woodbury (1938) saw a rufous hummingbird feeding at the working of a red-naped sapsucker on some willows; they were apparently eating the sap that exuded, but may have been obtaining some of the insects that were attracted to the workings.

Harry S. Swarth (1922) relates the following story: "For a hummingbird to appear as a menace to a farm crop was a new rôle for a member of that family, but we heard of one such complaint of damage done. Mr. W. E. Parrott, of Sergief Island, had a large strawberry patch, the fruit of which he marketed in the nearby town of Wrangell. Time and again, so he told us, he had seen a hummingbird dash at one of the bright red berries, apparently under the impression that it was a flower, and the bird's bill would be thrust through the fruit, which, of course, was ruined. He had found a number of berries pierced in this way, and was puzzled to account for the damage until he saw a hummingbird in the act."

Mr. DuBois says, in his notes, that the bird he was watching paid no attention to a red-clover blossom that he dipped in diluted honey and hung on a branch near the nest. He saw one "feeding in a novel manner over the small garden in the clearing. The bird was about 30 feet in the air, now poised on vibrating wings, now darting here and there like a dragonfly, apparently catching small insects on the wing. One day (July 22) I saw her drinking at the spring. She hovered above the pool, as she would above a flower, dipping her bill into the water several times. On the 27th, I again saw her getting water at the spring, but in a different manner. She stood, for a second or two at a time, in the film of water that flowed over a board, and dipped her bill into it several times."

Behavior.—All observers seem to agree that jealous courage and pugnacity are among the chief attributes of the rufous hummingbird; it seems to be the dominant species in the vicinity of its nest and about its feeding places, driving away, not only other hummingbirds, but other species of larger birds and animals; it seems to love to fight and often appears to provoke a quarrel unnecessarily. Mr. DuBois has sent me the following note: "Once during the afternoon of July 17, while the hummingbird was incubating, an olive-backed thrush inadvertently came too close to the nest. The little bird darted after him so suddenly and violently that she made him squawk as he hurried away. Another intruder was a chipmunk. He was searching for huckleberries—running on the ground and climbing in the small bushes—and at length his occupation brought him almost beneath the hummer's nest. She darted after him; and the sudden onslaught evidently filled him with terror. He beat a hasty retreat, squealing lustily as he ran. It is not surprising that the sudden movements of the hummingbird and the ominous sound of her wings, at close quarters, are terrorizing to any trespasser. On another occasion she chased a good sized bird away from the neighborhood."

Mrs. Wheelock (1904) saw a male rufous hummer attack and drive away a Brewer's blackbird that had chanced to alight in the bush containing the hummer's nest. "This blackbird was nesting in a hollow post which stood in four feet of water fifty feet from the bush. His usual course in leaving his nest was over the hummer's bush, and the male seldom failed to dart out at him from his watch tower near by."

Mr. Kobbé (1900) writes:

The pugnacity of these birds is the most prominent characteristic of the species and when they are not fighting among themselves they make war upon other birds. The males are nearly always the participants and seem to take great delight in fighting each other with their utmost strength. It is a very common sight to see a male Hummer perched upon a telegraph wire or exposed twig watching for others of his own sex with which to do battle. Although they sometimes fall over and over toward the ground like two huge bees, they seldom disable one another, since their bills are very weak. The greatest efforts on the part of one of the Hummers only succeed in pulling out a few feathers of his adversary, who is finally driven away in a rather bedraggled condition. * * * On several occasions I have seen male Hummers fight and drive off Swallows from the vicinity of their nest, particularly when it contained eggs. During the nesting season the males frequently, but not always, sit near the tree in which their home is placed and attempt to drive all birds from the vicinity of the nest. They pay great attention to their duty and seldom fail to dart after other Hummers, even if they are simply passing the tree in which the nest is placed. I have good reasons to believe that they do this more from a love of fighting than from parental instinct or devotion, since the male birds rarely appear upon the scene when their nest is being taken.

Henshaw (1886) writes of behavior on their feeding grounds in New Mexico:

Males and females all flock to the common feeding ground, and as the Hummers, especially of the Rufous-backed species, are pugnacious and hot tempered in the extreme, the field becomes a constant battle-ground whereon favorite flowers and favorite perching grounds are contested for with all the ardor that attaches to more important conquests. The fiery red throat of the Rufous-backed Hummer is an index of its impetuous, aggressive disposition, and when brought into conflict with the other species it invariably asserts its supremacy and drives its rival in utter rout from the fields. Nor do the males of this species confine their warfare to their own sex. Gallantry has no place apparently in their breasts, and when conquest has put them in possession of a perch near a clump of flowers they wage war on all comers, females as well as males. * * *

When the attack is urged against the males of the Broad-tailed species the contest is less fierce, the latter species usually abandoning the ground in hot haste. The latter result always follows the assault of a male upon the females who, if less valiant in battle, are scarcely less backward when it comes to the assertion of their rights against intruders of their own sex. The rivalry the females display is not less marked if the battles it prompts are less fierce than when the males are engaged; occasionally the females will fight with all the ardor displayed by the males.

The elaborate notes that Mr. DuBois has sent me on his intensive study of the home life of this species well illustrate its tameness, its devotion to its young, and its lack of fear after it had learned to trust him. He was able to approach cautiously, without any concealment, to within about 18 inches of the nest and to take numerous photographs at short range, without causing the bird much concern. On the second day the camera was placed on the tripod close to the nest; she examined it thoroughly several times and from all sides but did not seem much afraid of it; and on the following day she sat with her tail toward the instrument, thus showing her indifference to it. For a close study of the care of the young, he disguised himself as a balsam tree, being well covered with balsam boughs and twigs; the bird paid almost no attention to him with this disguise, and he was able to watch proceedings for long periods with his face within about a foot of the nest. At first she was suspicious and would not go to the nest but buzzed all around him, chirping and examining his make-up very minutely, and when she came within an inch or two of his ear, he found the boom of her wings a formidable sound; she repeated this examination twice more before she settled on the nest for any length of time.

It is a well-known fact that hummingbirds are attracted to investigate any red object that might suggest a flower. Dr. Grinnell (1909) records that, on Admiralty Island, Alaska, a brilliant male rufous hummer "buzzed about some bright red tomato cans that had been thrown out. Stephens records that at the same place, May 2, a male came around camp investigating everything that was red, such as a red-bordered towel, the red places on the end of a fruit box, an empty salmon can, and particularly a red bandana handkerchief hanging on a bush; this the bird went to three times."

Voice.—During the courtship performance a twittering note is heard from the male, as well as a whining sound, which is probably caused by the rush of air through the wings. Ralph C. Tate (1928) heard "a peculiar sound, somewhere between a buzz and a grunt," from a male that was feeding at the flowers of a trumpetvine on his porch. Dr. Wetmore (1921) says that "in flying their wings made a subdued humming and the birds called *chewp chewp* in a low tone."

G. Hammersley (1928) writes from Crofton, British Columbia:

When the fruit trees came into blossom, Mr. Hummer was in the orchard every day. One does not have to see him in order to know that he is there, as he has his own peculiar song or "drumming." It is uttered as he swoops past one or shoots swiftly overhead and might be written *ch-ch-ch chut-churrr* or *tut-ut-ut-ut-turrre.* Immediately after making this sound he darts straight upwards until reaching the desired height when he comes to a sudden and complete full stop, remaining stationary in the air like a glittering ruby set in the blue sky. Whilst in this position he will repeat the ordinary call note of *tchik* which is common to both the sexes, then dropping suddenly he flies back to his "watch-tower". I think that the drumming sound is probably produced by the tail feathers. The male hummer has the monopoly of another and quite different sound also. This sound is produced continually as long as the bird is on the wing, and only varies by increasing in volume each time the bird moves from its position in the air. The sound is difficult to describe, but might be likened to tiny beads vibrating regularly in a thin metal box. Although, as far as my own observations go, the male rufous never flies without making this vibrating sound, the female never at any time produces it.

Mr. DuBois says in his notes: "Usually the mother bird was silent; but when the nestling was two days old I once heard the mother chirping for a moment, from among the branches of a fallen tree, before she came to settle in the nest." When agitated she chirped while on the nest.

Field marks.—The male rufous hummingbird can be easily recognized by the large amount of rufous on the upper parts, including the posterior portion of the crown, the back, and most of the tail; the brilliant metallic scarlet gorget is very conspicuous and shines like burnished gold in some lights; the chest is white, but otherwise the underparts are pale rufous. The only species that closely resembles it is Allen's hummingbird, which has a green back.

The female can hardly be distinguished in the field from the female of Allen's, as both have much light rufous on the underparts, and their tails are largely rufous basally, the three outer rectrices being broadly tipped with white. A close inspection of the tails will show slight differences between the two species. The outer tail feathers of the rufous are broader at the black space, about 0.15, as against about 0.10 of an inch in Allen's. Ridgway (1911) says that in the rufous "middle pair of rectrices metallic bronze-green (usually more dusky terminally), both webs broadly edged basally with cinnamon-rufous (sometimes with whole basal half or more of this color) ; next pair with more than basal half cinnamon-rufous, then metallic bronze-green, the terminal portion purplish black." And, of Allen's, he says: "Middle pair of rectrices with basal half (laterally, at least) cinnamon-rufous, the terminal half (more or less) metallic bronze-green; next pair similar, but terminal portion (extensively) black, the tip of inner web sometimes with a small spot of white."

Enemies.—Mr. Sprot (1927) tells of a male rufous hummer that tried its towering flight once too often, "when he staged a drop on a Black Pigeon Hawk, and got caught." Probably other hawks, and perhaps owls, have taken their toll. Mr. Skinner says in his notes: "One was seen resting on a willow twig in the sun until an irascible Audubon's warbler made a dive at it and drove it away, but in a moment the hummer was back again. After its return, it seemed very nervous, as if the rowdy Audubon had ruffled its feelings. Another one was chased away by a lutescent warbler."

Mr. DuBois (1938) saw a large black and yellow fly attack the young hummer that he was watching and slightly wound it; it might have killed it, if he had not driven it away. The mother of this young bird disappeared mysteriously, and he suspected a weasel might have been the cause.

Fall.—The fall migration from its breeding grounds in Alaska starts early, and sometimes these hummers wander out over the ocean. S. F. Rathbun tells me that on July 20, 1914, while he was crossing the Gulf of Alaska and was just within sight of land, off Nespina Glacier, a male rufous hummingbird came aboard and alighted on one of the stays of the ship's stack. It showed no alarm, and after about 15 minutes it flew off toward the land.

After the breeding season the summer wanderings of this hummingbird extend well up into the mountains, even in Washington. On Mount Rainier, on August 6, Taylor and Shaw (1927) saw individuals flying over the glaciers at 6,000 and at 9,000 feet altitude. "We were now hung, as it were, between earth and heaven, 2,500 feet above timber line. The water supply froze shortly after 5 o'clock p. m., and the midsummer breeze was cold and cheerless. What was our surprise to find the hummers still with us. One whizzed past us as we were making camp, and two more were observed the following morning."

On the southward migration through the Rocky Mountain region, the rufous hummingbird is sometimes very abundant at high altitudes, wherever it can find flowers in bloom; it has been seen as high as 12,600 feet on Truchas Peak in the Upper Pecos region, N. Mex., according to Mrs. Bailey (1904). Henshaw (1886), writing of this same region, says:

The number of representatives of this and the preceding species that make their summer homes in these mountains is simply beyond calculation. No one whose experience is limited to the Eastern United States can form any adequate idea of their abundance. They occur from an altitude of about 7,500 feet far up on the mountain sides, as high up, in fact, as suitable flowers afford them the means of subsistence. They are most numerous at an altitude of from 8,000 to 9,000 feet. During the entire summer they frequent almost exclusively a species of *Scrophularia* which grows in clumps in the sunnier spots in the valleys. From early dawn till dusk the Hummingbirds throng around these plants intent in surfeiting themselves on honey and the minute insects that the honey attracts. The scene presented in one of these flowering areas is a most attractive one. * * *

Some idea of the number of Hummingbirds in this locality—and in this respect this whole mountain area is alike—may be gained from the statement that in a single clump of the *Scrophularia* I have counted eighteen Hummers, all within reach of an ordinary fishing rod. There was scarcely a moment in the day when upwards of fifty could not be counted within an area of a few yards in any of the patches of this common plant.

Mr. Swarth (1904) says of its appearance in the Huachuca Mountains, Arizona: "I have not seen this species at any time in the spring, but about the middle of July they begin to make their appearance; and throughout the month of August I found them very abundant, but frequenting the highest parts of the mountains, principally; more being seen between 8000 and 9000 feet than elsewhere.

"The flowering mescal stalks are a great attraction to them, and they seem to frequent them in preference to anything else. I have seen as many as twenty Rufous Hummingbirds around a single stalk, mostly immature birds, but with a fair sprinkling of adult males. No adult females were taken at any time."

Grinnell and Storer (1924) say of the migration in the Yosemite region, in California:

Most of the northbound movement probably takes place at low altitudes and in any event occurs too early in the spring to be observed by most visitors in the Yosemite section. But the migration initiated in late June or early July continues until the middle of September, and especially at the higher altitudes is much in evidence. * * *

The first representatives of the species to be seen in the southbound migration are males. Thus the bird seen near Yosemite Point on July 1 was a fully adult male, as it showed an all-rufous back. But later in the same month the females and their young began to pass through. Of the birds seen in Lyell Cañon on July 23 at least one was a female (immature). The southbound migration was evidently in full swing by that date as no less than 5 separate individuals were seen during two or three hours spent on the meadows and adjacent slopes.

A visit to Parsons Peak on September 6, 1915, showed that the migration was still in progress, and further, that the Rufous Hummingbirds were evidently using the crest of the Sierra Nevada as a fly-way. During the short time spent at the top of the peak, 12,120 feet, two of these dimunutive travelers were seen flying southward, laboring against the strong southerly breeze; both took advantage of the same gap in the rocks to gain a slight respite from the buffeting of the wind. Other observers have told us of similar incidents noted by them while visiting peaks elsewhere along the backbone of the Sierra Nevada.

Mr. Woods (1927) says of Los Angeles County lowlands: "The adult male is only an occasional visitant on the southward migration in late summer, though the females, or more probably immature birds of both sexes, are seen more frequently." The inference from all the foregoing observations is that the northward migration in spring is mainly through the lower levels and chiefly to the westward of the main mountain chains and that the southward migration in fall follows mainly the crests of the Rocky Mountains and the Sierra Nevada.

DISTRIBUTION

Range.—Western North America.

Breeding range.—The breeding range of the rufous hummingbird extends **north** to southeastern Alaska (Montague Island, probably Cordova, and Carcross). **East** to eastern Alaska (Carcross); British

Columbia (Telegraph Creek and Fort St. James); southwestern Alberta (Banff); and western Montana (Belton, Anaconda, and Red Lodge). **South** to southern Montana (Red Lodge); southern Idaho (Blue Lake); and east-central California (Silver Creek). **West** to California (Silver Creek and Mount Shasta); Oregon (Newport and Netarts); Washington (Gig Harbor, Lake Crescent, and Tatoosh Island); western British Columbia (Courtenay and Graham Island); and southeastern Alaska (Ketchikan, Sitka, Point Couverden, and Montague Island).

Winter range.—During the winter months this species is more or less concentrated in the Mexican States of Zacatecas (La Parada), Jalisco (Volcano de Colima), Mexico (Tlalpam), and Michoacan (Lake Patzcuaro).

Spring migration.—Early dates of spring arrival are: California—Haywards, February 11; Berkeley, February 12. Oregon—Newport, March 4; Corvallis, March 11. Washington—Tacoma, February 26; Ilwaco, March 9; North Yakima, March 12. British Columbia—Massett, April 2; Chilliwack, April 11. Idaho—Rathdrum, May 5. Montana—Missoula, April 30. Alaska—Ketchikan, April 10; Juneau, April 18.

Fall migration.—Late dates of fall departure are: Alaska—Craig, September 9; St. Lazaria Island, September 30. British Columbia—Arrow Lakes, September 22; Courtnay, October 4. Washington—Seattle, September 26; Clallam Bay, October 7. Oregon—Newport, October 18; Coos Bay, October 28. Montana—Fortine, September 13; Belton, September 14.

Casual records.—The rufous hummingbird has been detected outside its normal range on several occasions, some cases being notable records. It was reported as observed at Camrose, Alberta, on August 24, 1930, and there are at least two and probably three specimen records for the vicinity of Eastend, Saskatchewan, the dates being August 11, 1939, August 18, 1932, and July 31, 1933. The species was reported from Kenton, Okla., under date of August 10, 1927, and a specimen was collected at Brownsville, Tex., on January 19, 1892. One was found dead at Pensacola, Fla., on November 29, 1934, two others being seen in the same area until December 13, while it was again recorded from this point on December 8, 12, 14, and 17, 1935. A specimen was taken in Charleston, S. C., on December 18, 1909.

Egg dates.—British Columbia: 7 records, May 6 to July 6.

Oregon: 11 records, April 27 to June 29.

Washington: 12 records, April 22 to June 7; 6 records, May 3 to 30, indicating the height of the season.

SELASPHORUS ALLENI Henshaw

ALLEN'S HUMMINGBIRD

PLATES 68, 69

HABITS

This is another very brilliant hummingbird, which is closely related to the rufous hummingbird, and much like it in appearance and behavior. It seems to be confined, in the breeding season at least, to the coastal district of California, from Humboldt County to Ventura County and the Santa Barbara Islands. It may possibly be found breeding in Oregon, and there are two authentic records of its occurrence in Washington. There was formerly a specimen in the United States National Museum, which has since been destroyed, that was collected at Fort Steilacoom, on April 26, 1856, and was identified by both Henshaw and Ridgway. S. F. Rathbun collected an adult male near Seattle on May 27, 1894, which is apparently the only Washington specimen in existence; he tells me that this specimen is now in the State Museum, at the University of Washington, in Seattle. Dr. Tracy I. Storer (1921) has made a careful study of all other records north of California and reports that no others are authentic.

Courtship.—Robert S. Woods (1927b) says on this subject: "Allen's Hummingbird flies rather slowly back and forth along a path such as would be described by a giant pendulum, with a sort of lateral writhing movement of the body and extended tail and a vibratory metallic noise, but without vocal sound. Again it will poise itself close in front of another bird and rapidly shuttle to and fro sidewise through a space of perhaps a foot or two."

Frank N. Bassett (1921) gives a somewhat different and more elaborate account of it, as follows:

On the afternoon of April 16, 1920, I was walking through the hills back of the Claremont Club golf links when I was brought to a halt by a rather prolonged buzzing sound, very penetrating and metallic in quality, somewhat similar to the sound produced by drawing a fine-grained file over the edge of a piece of sheet steel with a sudden jerk. Looking in the direction of the sound I saw poised in the air about twenty feet from the ground, a male Allen Hummingbird (*Selasphorus alleni*), uttering his commonly heard mouse-like squeaks. Then followed the performance of the nuptial flight, similar to that of the Anna Hummingbird, though the path described in the air was somewhat different. He "rocked" back and forth over the female, which was perched on a twig of a low poison oak (*Rhus diversiloba*), describing a semi-circle about twenty-five feet in diameter. There was a pause at each end of the arc, and before the pause he spread his tail and shook his whole body so violently that I wondered how his feathers remained fast. During this time he continued uttering the characteristic squeaks. After several of these semi-circles were described he began his climb to a height of about seventy-five feet; and then came the "high dive." He swooped down with the speed of a comet, and on passing over the female gave the low-pitched but resonant buzzing sound which had first attracted my attention; then he curved upward and came to a pause about twenty-five feet in the air, where I had first seen him. The sound emitted on passing over the female was of a second or more in duration, and differed greatly from the instantaneous, metallic *clink* of the Anna Hummingbird.

Nesting.—Charles A. Allen, of Nicasio, Calif., who discovered this species, and for whom it was named, wrote to Major Bendire (1895) as follows:

Allen's Hummingbird arrives in the vicinity of Nicasio, California, about the middle of February, and commences to nest soon after arrival. The earliest date on which I found one was February 27, 1879; this was then about half finished, when a heavy storm set in which lasted about five days, and I did not visit the locality again until March 8, when the nest was completed and contained two fresh eggs. I have taken their nests as late as July 3, and am well convinced that two broods are raised in a season, at least by all of the earlier breeding birds. They select all sorts of situations and various kinds of trees and bushes to nest in. I have found their nests as low as 10 inches and again as high as 90 feet from the ground.

All the nests and eggs of this species [continues Bendire] in the United States National Museum were taken by Mr. Allen near Nicasio, California; one of these, now before me, is attached to the side of a small oak limb which turns abruptly at an angle of about 45° directly over the cup of the nest, protecting it above; another is likewise attached to the side of a small pendant oak twig, its base being supported by a bunch of moss. Some are securely saddled on small twigs of raspberry bushes, and several of these are usually incorporated in the walls of the nest. Occasionally they nest in hedges, on weed stalks, or on bushes overhanging water.

The nests are well and compactly built, the inside being lined with vegetable down, while the outer walls are composed of green tree mosses, and a few bits of lichens, securely fastened in place with a spider web. Nests built on trees seem to be generally somewhat larger than those found in bushes. The average measurements of one of the former is 1½ inches outer diameter and the same in depth; the inner cup is seven-eighths of an inch in width by three-fourths of an inch in depth. On the whole they resemble the nests of Anna's Hummingbird more than those of the Rufous, and appear to me to be better and more neatly built than either.

James B. Dixon has sent me the following note: "The only place where I have contacted this hummingbird in the breeding season was in San Luis Obispo County, in the dense willow montes where they were nesting in large numbers and were as common as the black-chinned hummingbirds are farther south. Here the nests were often found within 50 feet of each other. As with all the other hummingbirds, there seemed to be a wide variation in the breeding season, as nests with young half grown would be found close to nests with fresh eggs. The nests are larger and better built than those of most other hummingbirds. They have a habit of saddling the nests on a small limb growing away from the butt or main stem of a willow sapling, in much the same manner as the wood pewee; I have never found the other hummingbirds doing this. Nests are made of dried weed stems, weed seed, and plant down, bound together with cobwebs, and decorated outwardly with lichens; they do more toward decorating the outside with lichens as incubation advances."

Dr. Harold C. Bryant (1925) gives an interesting account of the colonial nesting habits of this species:

Heretofore I had believed along with others * * * that the favorite nesting place of the Allen Hummingbird (*Selasphorus alleni*) is the tangle of berry vines along a stream. But a recent experience in Golden Gate Park, San Francisco, has led me to alter my view. * * *

On April 19, a trip through a growth of cypress and Monterey pines netted eleven hummingbirds' nests, all, with the possible exception of one, being those of the Allen Hummingbird. Three of the nests found were in pine trees; all the rest of them were in Monterey cypress. The lowest one was about 5½ feet above the ground, the highest 15 feet. Measurement of the inside diameter of two nests showed them to be 1¼ to 1½ inches. Most of the nests contained eggs, but in one instance young birds ready to fly were found. In fact, one of the young birds launched out of the nest and had to be replaced. At least two nests were incomplete. One of these a week later was found to contain eggs.

In most instances the incubating female, frightened from the nest, helped in determining the location. On one area of less than an acre in extent, an unsystematic search disclosed five nests. In one instance nests were hardly 15 feet apart. Another casual search on April 26 disclosed three more nests on this same limited area, and undoubtedly several more nests could have been found had each tree been searched systematically. * * *

When we stop to think that the Rufous Hummingbird, a close relative, breeds commonly in coniferous forests of northwestern North America, it does not seem unreasonable that the Allen should chose a similar habitat in the humid coast belt of California. And evidently it was choice in this instance, for extensive tangles of berry vines near water were close at hand but were not chosen for nesting places.

Grinnell and Linsdale (1936) report two nests found in the Point Lobos Reserve, Monterey County, Calif.; one "found on April 18, was four and one-half feet up on a twig one-eighth inch in diameter, at the lower, outer end of a limb of live oak. * * * Another nest, found on May 18, was at least seventy feet above the ground on a small stub beneath a slender limb of pine in the woods."

Ernest D. Clabaugh (1936) tells of an Allen's hummingbird that built its nest on an ivy vine hanging down about 6 inches from the ceiling of a covered entrance to his house; one young was successfully raised and left the nest on May 11; "the old nest was removed, and on June 4, another nest was built in the same spot." Joseph Mailliard (1913) records three nests built "inside of buildings more or less in use"; two of these were under the rafters of a wagon shed, one on a hanging pulley, and the other on the loop of a rope sling; the third was in a carriage house, on an iron hook that was used in cleaning harnesses, and about 5 feet from the ground; broods were raised in the first two, but the third was abandoned.

W. L. Dawson (1923) writes: "As for the Allen Hummer the blackberry tangles are her home, and all such other situations as assure a measure of protection from above. Thus, drooping vines falling over boulders offer ideal sites; for *alleni* is also fond of a swing. The most remarkable nest of our experience, a *five-story* one, was saddled upon the hook of a broken root, which was, in turn, caught upon a sprangle of roots above, unearthed by the under-cutting of the stream. This root could be lifted clear and replaced without injury; and its mistress added, in one season, stories No. 4 and No. 5, to our knowledge."

Two of the four nests of Allen's hummingbird in the Thayer collection in Cambridge are large handsome nests, suggesting the best types of nests of the rufous hummingbird. One of these was 8 feet from the ground and 20 feet out from the trunk on a branch of a spruce; it is composed of fine green moss, decorated with flakes of pale-gray lichens, bound on with spider web, and lined with willow cotton; it measures approximately 2 inches wide and 1 inch high externally; the inner cup is about 1 inch in diameter by five-eighths of an inch deep. The other large nest was built on a branch of a young live oak between upright twigs; it measures about 2 inches in diameter and 1½ inches in height externally; it appears to be made almost entirely, including all the rim, of the pale buff cottony down from willow blossoms; only the lower and external part of the nest is composed of green mosses and various brown fibers; it is a very pretty nest. The smallest nest in the lot was 2 feet from the ground in a shallow bend of a horizontal branch of a sagebrush; it measures 1¾ by 1¼ inches in external diameter, and is only three-quarters of an inch high, the inner cavity being very shallow; this is a very drab-looking nest, with no green moss in its composition; it is made of various gray and brown fibers and similar material, with very little cotton and a few small feathers in the lining; apparently it matched its surroundings in the gray sage.

Since the above was written Ernest I. Dyer (1939) has published a detailed account of the nesting of Allen's hummingbird, to which the reader is referred.

Eggs.—Allen's hummingbird lays almost invariably two eggs; I have no record of more or fewer. They are like other hummers' eggs, varying in shape from oval to elliptical-oval, and are pure white without gloss. The measurements of 55 eggs average 12.7 by 8.6 millimeters; the eggs showing the four extremes measure **14.0** by 8.9, 13.8 by **10.0**, and **11.7** by **7.6** millimeters.

Young.—The incubation period of this hummingbird is said to be 14 or 15 days, as is the case with several other hummingbirds. The female doubtless does all the incubating and assumes full care of the young. After describing so fully the home life of the preceding species, to which the present species is so closely related, it hardly seems necessary to enlarge here on the activities of the mother at the nest or on the development of the young. The rufous hummingbird and Allen's are much alike in appearance and behavior; their nesting habits are similar; and probably, although I have no notes on the subject, the care and development of the young follow along the same lines.

Since the above was written, Robert T. Orr (1939) has published a very full account of the incubation behavior and the care and development of the young, to which the reader is referred.

Plumages.—So far as I can learn from the literature and from the examination of specimens, the development of the juvenal plumage of Allen's hummingbird and its subsequent molts and plumages are the same as in the rufous hummingbird. The two species are almost exactly alike, except for the specific differences explained under the field marks of the two, the very narrow lateral rectrices and the greater amount of green in Allen's being the principal differences. Young male Allen's hummers begin to show red in the throat early in July. I have seen a young male, taken on June 1, that was molting into the adult plumage, some red coming in on the throat, and some of the outer rectrices still white-tipped, as in the juvenal tail, probably a belated molt.

Food.—I cannot find much in print about the food of Allen's hummingbird, which probably does not differ materially from that of other California hummers. Whatever brightly colored flowers happen to be in bloom are resorted to for honey and minute insects and spiders. That they are of service to the plants in cross fertilization is evident from the amount of pollen so often seen on their heads. The tree tobacco is popular with this hummingbird, as are the blossoms of *Ceanothus*, madroña, and the flowering stalks of the century plant; the scarlet sage, brightly colored mints, and various other flowers are attractive. Dr. Grinnell (1905b) says that, on Mount Pinos, in July, "masses of monkeyflowers (*Mimulus langsdorfi* and *cardinalis*), columbines (*Aquilegia* sp.?), and other plants (*Stachys albens, Castilleia grinnelli*, etc.) began to burst into bloom during the first week in July about the wet places in the cañon bottoms. And these flower masses were the scenes of many noisy revels among the Allen Hummers, sometimes as many as five of the birds taking part in what looked like a free-for-all fight."

Mr. Woods (1927) says that, on Santa Catalina Island, "towards evening, like other species, they make short sallies in Flycatcher fashion after passing insects too minute to be discerned by the human eye."

Behavior.—Henshaw (1877), with his original description of Allen's hummingbird, makes the following comparison of this species with the rufous hummingbird:

I am in possession of but few notes bearing upon the habits of this Hummer. Mr. Allen remarks incidentally in a letter that the Green-backs are much the livelier and more active of the two, keeping constantly in the open, and always perching upon the most prominent dead twigs they can find. Their extreme shyness, as contrasted with the unsuspicious nature of the Rufous-backed, is quite remarkable. They seem to possess a larger share than usual of the courage and pugnacity which is so constantly displayed in birds of this family. Not only do they always come off the victors when chance encounters take place between them and the Rufous-backs, but Mr. Allen has seen a pair attack and put to rout a Red-tailed Hawk; while, as he remarks, "Sparrow-Hawks have no chance at all with them." He has often seen the little fellows in hot chase after these latter birds, and their only care seemed to be to get out of the way as soon as possible of foes so determined.

Each male seems to claim a particular range, which he occupies for feeding and breeding purposes, and every other bird seen by him encroaching on his preserve is at once so determinedly set upon and harassed that he is only too glad to beat a hasty retreat. During their quarrels these birds keep up an incessant, sharp chirping, and a harsh, rasping buzzing with their wings, which sounds very different from the low, soft humming they make with these while feeding. Every action and motion at such times indicates that they are as mad as can be; the poor Anna Hummers have to get out of their way pretty quickly at any time, but especially when they encroach on their breeding grounds. The males very often have quarrels among themselves, and are then very noisy, while the females are more orderly and quiet; but even they have occasional little misunderstandings with each other, especially when a pair meet while feeding on the same bush; one generally vacates the premises very quickly, and as soon as she does all becomes quiet again.

Field marks.—The male Allen's hummingbird looks very much like the male rufous, but can be distinguished from it by the large amount of green in the back. Both sexes can be distinguished from other California hummingbirds, except migrating rufous, by the large amount of rufous in the plumage, especially in the tail. The female Allen's is practically indistinguishable, in the field, from the female rufous hummingbird; only a close comparison of the tails will distinguish the two species. The difference in the color patterns of the tails of the two females is described, as quoted from Ridgway (1911), under the field marks of the rufous hummingbird; but the difference seems to be very slight. The best distinguishing character, which might under favorable circumstances be seen in the field, is the width of the two outer tail feathers, as illustrated in Henshaw's cut (1877); in *S. rufus* the four lateral rectrices are "successively graduated in size, the outer the smallest"; and they are of normal hummingbird width; whereas in *S. alleni* the two outer feathers are "very narrow, linear, the outer nearly acicular," a well-marked difference.

Range.—Coastal regions of California and northwestern Mexico; casual in Washington, Oregon, and Arizona.

Breeding range.—Allen's hummingbird is found during the nesting season only in the narrow coastal district that extends nearly the full length of California from San Clemente and Santa Catalina Islands northward to San Francisco, Berkeley, and Eureka. Four specimens taken on July 10, 1905, in the San Pedro Martir Mountains, Baja California, may possibly indicate a more southern limit of the breeding range.

Winter range.—In winter the species is found **north** to southern California (Santa Cruz Island) ; and **south** to central Baja California (San Quintin and Santo Domingo). It also has been detected at Santa Barbara, Chihuahua, in the latter part of September.

Spring migration.—Early dates of spring arrival in California are: Berkeley, February 13; Haywards, February 16; Escondido, February 22.

Fall migration.—The species appears to retire from the northern parts of its range during August and September, late dates being: Palo Alto, August 24: Berkeley, September 29; Presidio of San Francisco, September 30.

Casual records.—Two specimens were collected at the mouth of the Pistol River, Curry County, Oreg., on June 23, 1929; and one was taken at Seattle, Wash., on May 27, 1894. In Arizona there are several records as follows: One was secured in the Santa Catalina Mountains, July 23, 1884; specimens were taken near Bisbee during August and September 1892 (?) ; and in the Huachuca Mountains in July 1896, in July 1902, and on July 10 and August 1, 1929.

Egg dates.—California: 100 records, February 2 to June 28; 50 records, March 21 to May 22, indicating the height of the season.

ATTHIS HELOISA HELOISA (De Lattre and Lesson)

HELOISE'S HUMMINGBIRD

HABITS

On July 2, 1896, two female hummingbirds were taken in Ramsay Canyon, in the Huachuca Mountains, Ariz., by H. G. Rising. These two specimens were sent to Mr. Ridgway, who described and named them (1898) as a new species, Morcom's hummingbird (*Atthis morcomi*), in honor of G. Frean Morcom. In his description he states that "the adult male of this species is unfortunately unknown. The adult female differs from that of *A. heloisa* in being pure bronze-green above instead of almost coppery bronze inclining to greenish only on upper tail-coverts and middle tail-feathers; in having the cinnamon-rufous on basal portion of the tail far more extensive, there being more on the middle rectrices in *A. heloisa*, while on the others it occupies very much less than the basal half, and is entirely hidden by the coverts; the sides and flanks are less deeply, and apparently less extensively, cinnamon-rufous, and the under tail-coverts are white or but very faintly buffy, instead of being deep cinnamon-buff."

In his "Birds of North and Middle America" (1911), Ridgway treats Morcom's hummingbird as a subspecies of *Atthis heloisa*, under the name *Atthis heloisa morcomi*, which he characterizes as "similar to *A. h. heloisa*, but smaller (except bill); adult female paler below, with bronzy spots on chin and throat much smaller, sides less extensively cinnamon-rufous, and under tail-coverts pure white."

According to our 1931 Check-list, *morcomi* is not accorded even subspecific rank and is regarded as identical with *A. h. heloisa*, to which race our Arizona specimens are now understood to belong. This is the race that is found in central and southern Mexico, from the States of Tamaulipas, Guanajuato, and San Luís Potosí to Guerrero and Tepic.

Nothing seems to be known about the habits of this subspecies and, so far as I know, the nest of the *species* has never been found. But Alexander F. Skutch has sent me the following notes on a closely related form, Elliot's hummingbird (*Atthis heloisa ellioti*), the Guatemalan race.

"Like so many of the Central American hummingbirds, the male Elliot's hummingbirds gather in definite assemblies to sing. Although I have found them in western Guatemala from 6,000 to 11,000 feet above sea level, they appear to be nowhere common. Yet where one finds a male singing persistently, day after day, from the same perch, there will generally be one or more others within hearing. About the middle of October 1933, I found an assembly of four males on a steep, bushy slope at an altitude of about 9,000 feet. Each bird had chosen as his singing perch the bare, exposed twig of a bush or the low branch of a tree. Their headquarters were separated from each other by 25 or 30 yards. They were stretched out in a line; and the birds in the middle could each hear two of their neighbors, but those in the end positions could hear only the one nearest to them—unless their ears were sharper than mine, which is certainly not improbable. These hummingbirds did not perch so close together by chance, for I found none other of the kind within a mile of this assembly.

"The assembly was established in a spot not far from the highway that crossed the mountain; and whenever I passed that way I would pause to listen, enchanted, to a song that amazed me, coming from so small a bird. The voice, although weak, was not squeaky. In its intensity, its variety of phrasing, and its rising and falling cadences the song reminded me not a little of the higher notes of a small finch and often suggested the impassioned conclusion of the lay of the little black-and-white Morellet's seedeater (*Sporophila morelletii*) of the lowlands. The hummingbird frequently sang without a pause for thirty or forty seconds. Were his song only a little more forceful, without any change of tune or phrasing, Elliot's hummingbird would be famous as a musician.

"As he poured forth his sweet, impassioned little lay, the hummingbird spread the stiff feathers of his gorget, which then appeared to form a scaly shield covering the throat, and turned his head from side to side. The feathers at the sides of the shield, longer than the rest, formed sharp points at the lower corners. When the bird faced directly toward me, the gorget reflected an intense magenta light; but as the head slowly turned away the color was gradually extinguished, and the shield, seen from the side, appeared velvety black. At certain angles, it sent a metallic-green reflection to my eye. At times the little singer vibrated his wings in his ecstasy, and either floated slowly to another perch or suspended himself in mid-air on invisible pinions, all without interrupting his song. At times he made a long, looping flight, returning again to the perch from which he started, and continued his singing during the entire journey."

Robert T. Moore found four species of hummingbirds feeding on the flowering tree in southeastern Sinaloa, referred to in his notes on the white eared hummingbird. Among them was another race of this species, Margaret's hummingbird (*Atthis heloisa margarethae*), of which he says in his notes:

"Much the smallest of the four and one of the tiniest members of the family, this near relative of the so-called Morcom's hummingbird of Arizona flew into the tree at rare intervals. If the broad-tailed and Calliope hummers, of which there were always five or six, were feeding from the tree, *Atthis* would be permitted to probe the least attractive blooms. She experienced little difficulty in finding a few of the forty thousand flowerets, which had not already been deprived of their sweets. But when a single male white-ear blustered in among the busy gleaners, he would invariably launch an assault on the rare gem of the mountain and drive it away to the thicker growth of pines. For the time *Atthis* had to be content with a more frugal repast on the scarce blooms of *labiatae*, which starred the pine-needle floor of the forest with spikes of maroon-colored flowers. Margaret's hummingbird probably feeds from several kinds of flowers, but we actually observed it doing so from only three. In addition to the two mentioned, it sometimes prospected the exquisite tawny flowers of the huge Opuntias near our camp site, but the bird seemed to prefer those of the purple-bracted shrub, referred to above.

"No larger than a huge orange-marked bee, which was intoxicated by the same flowers, *Atthis heloisa margarethae* was not much larger than its name on this sheet. Slower in its movements than the other four hummingbirds, the revolution of its wings created only an infinitesimal murmur. As compared with the energetic nervous course of the white-ear, that of *Atthis* is slow and unwavering. It resembles more closely that of the calliope than either of the other two hummers. It is not nearly so swift as that of the broadtail.

"In northwestern Mexico Margaret's hummingbird seems to be confined to the Transition Zone, not descending very far below its lower margin, as all of our specimens have come from 5,700 feet to 7,500 feet. Occasionally occurring elsewhere at lower levels, a female was taken by Chester Lamb near the city of Tepic, Nayarit, at an altitude of 3,000 feet.

"I have no doubt that Margaret's hummingbird breeds in the lower margin of the Transition Zone in Sinaloa, but we have never found the nest."

DISTRIBUTION

Range.—Central Mexico south to Honduras; accidental in south-ern Arizona; not generally migratory.

The range of this species extends **north** to San Luis Potosi (Al-varez); and central Veracruz (Jalapa). **East** to Veracruz (Jalapa and Cordoba); and Honduras (San Juancito). **South** to Honduras (San Jauncito); Guatemala (Fuego Volcano and Atitlan); and Guerrero (Omilteme). **West** to Guerrero (Omilteme), Mexico (Santa Lucia); and southwestern San Luis Potosi (Alvarez).

Casual records.—The only records for the United States are for two specimens collected in Ramsay Canyon, in the Huachuca Moun-tains, Ariz., on July 2, 1896.

STELLULA CALLIOPE (Gould)

CALLIOPE HUMMINGBIRD

PLATE 70

HABITS

This tiny mite is the smallest member of the group containing the smallest North American birds. Grinnell and Storer (1924) state that "its average weight is only about 3 grams (one-tenth of an ounce) which is about half that of an Anna Hummingbird, or of a kinglet or bush-tit." The length of the male is about 2¾ inches and that of the female is less than 3 inches. But it is a hardy little midget and a long-distance traveler, migrating from northern British Columbia to Mexico City; it spends its summers in the Canadian zones at high altitudes in the mountains and at lower levels farther north.

Its generic name was well chosen, *Stellula*, little star, for the long, narrow, metallic purple feathers rise and spread, under excitement, above the snow-white background of the gorget, like a scintillating star. The choice of the specific name, *calliope*, was not so fortunate; Calliope was the muse of eloquence, and this is a very silent bird.

At least throughout the southern portion of its breeding range, and to some extent farther north, the calliope hummingbird is essentially a mountain species, though it breeds in the lower valleys and near sea level in some of the more northern portions of its range. Dawson (1923) says that in California—

it is essentially a mountain-loving species, and is, so far as we have been able to prove, the only breeding Hummer of the higher Sierran slopes. There is a 3000 foot record, by Stephens, of a nest in the San Bernardinos; but 4000 is the usual minimum, and 8000 a better average. In the Canadian zone, therefore, the bird knows no restrictions, save that it does not favor the densely timbered sections. In the Sierras it nests nearly up to timber line, 10,000 to 11,500 feet, and follows the advancing season to the limit of flowers. * * * A bit of heather on a northern peak, where we camped at an elevation of 8,000 feet, yielded thirty-two species of plants in conspicuous bloom within a stone's throw of the breakfast table.

Elsewhere (Dawson and Bowles, 1909) he says: "We have found it commonly in the northern and eastern portions of Washington at much lower altitudes, and have taken its nest in the Burning Gorge of the Columbia at an altitude of only six hundred feet."

James B. Dixon writes to me: "In the San Bernardino country it was a rare breeder at elevations from 6,000 to 8,500 feet above sea level, and there it nested along the stream beds where water ran all summer. In the Mono Basin they were found along running streams, generally in the aspen thickets, but sometimes out in the open forests high on the mountain sides and some distance from running water; they were much more common, however, in the aspen groves."

Ralph Hoffmann (1927) writes: "The flowering shrubs and vines about dwellings attract nearly all the different hummingbirds of the coast. One species, however, still keeps to the natural gardens on mountain slopes, where Indian paint-brush, mountain heather and columbine splotch the springy slopes with red, or wild currant forms extensive thickets. Here the little Calliope Hummer, the smallest and most delicately adorned of them all, flashes the lavender streaks on its gorget as it chases off some rival or pursues a female."

J. A. Munro (1919) says that in the Okanagan Valley, British Columbia, "a birch and maple draw is the favorite home of *Stellula calliope*, and one can often see six or eight, buzzing around a birch tree, which a Red-naped Sapsucker has girdled." Winton Weydemeyer (1927), writing of its haunts in northwestern Montana, where it is a common breeder, says:

In Lincoln County the Calliope Hummingbird (*Stellula calliope*) nests along streams throughout most of the Canadian zone and downward into the upper borders of the Transition zone. During the nesting season and late summer it also frequents open mountains, ranging into the Hudsonian zone, and during May and August is commonly seen in the breeding areas of lower Transition zone species. Tree associations evidently have greater influence on its range than does elevation. In the eastern part of the country I have found the species to be common during the nesting season at 7,000 feet, although I have never chanced actually to see a nest above 4,800 feet. In the Kootenai Valley, near Libby, I have found it nesting abundantly at an elevation of less than 2,100 feet, and I have no doubt that it breeds below 1,900 feet a few miles distant, in the lower end of the valley, the only place in Montana where so low an elevation occurs.

Courtship.—The courtship performances of the hummingbirds all follow the same general pattern, with only slight variations, and this species is no exception to the rule. Grinnell, Dixon, and Linsdale (1930) describe it very well as follows:

An exhibition of courting flight that seemed fairly typical for this species was observed on May 16, 1924. A female was down in a blossoming currant (*Ribes cereum*) bush. A male started towering from her vicinity, slowly at first and with an audible buzz, then faster until he reached a height of fully twenty-two meters. Then he shot down in a broadly U-shaped course, passing the bush closely (barely missing it) and ascended to an equal height on the opposite tip of the "U." At the moment of passing the bush, within which the female was perched, he gave out a droll, flatted sound *bzt*—short, not loud, like a bee held down. After making three complete sky-dives, the male, on coming down the last time, perched six meters away at the tip of a stem of budding service-berry bush. The female began at once to feed at the currant flowers within the abundantly white-flowering bush.

The following variation in the antics was observed by L. E. Wyman (1920):

On one occasion an angry buzzing, almost terrifying in volume, resolved itself into a pair of these birds holding to each other's beaks and revolving like a horizontal pinwheel, *less than four feet from my eyes*. Around they went, a half-dozen times, then parted, the female perching and preening on a twig of the oak-scrub just beyond arm's reach, with the male two feet farther away and giving vent at three-second intervals to an explosive metallic *tzing*. This was, of course, made with the wings, but the bird was sufficiently screened so that I could not see it clearly.

On another occasion a female sat preening on a horizontal dead weed, when a male shot up the hill-side close to the ground, passed the female, mounted about twenty-five feet and darted down again in a long, narrow, vertical ellipse that flattened where it touched the hill-side. As he passed the female she fluttered and swung head downward on her perch. The male alighted above her, with vibrating wings, and coition took place in this position.

Nesting.—Major Bendire (1895) gives an interesting account of the nesting of the   calliope hummingbird near Fort Klamath, Oreg., where he said that this species outnumbered the common rufous hummingbird about three to one. His first nest was found by the actions of the bird; he writes:

> I had taken quite a long walk along the banks of Fort Creek on June 10, and, the day being a hot one, sat down with my back resting against the trunk of a bushy black pine whose lower limbs had been killed by fire; while resting thus one of these Hummers buzzed repeatedly about my head for a few seconds at a time, and then rose perpendicularly in the air, only to repeat the performance again. I had no idea then that this species nested in pines, but in order to give me an opportunity to watch its performance better I moved out from under the tree, and a few minutes later saw the bird settle on what I at first supposed to be an old clump of pine cones. On looking closer, however, I noticed its nest, which was ingeniously saddled on two small cones, and its outward appearance resembled a cone very closely. * * * Knowing now where to look for them, I had no further difficulty in finding their nests, and all of those observed by me were built in exactly similar situations. * * * They were usually placed on or against a dry cone on small dead limbs of *Pinus contorta*, from 8 to 15 feet from the ground, and on account of the brittle nature of these limbs they were rather hard to secure. The nests, while outwardly not as handsome as those of the majority of our Hummers, are nevertheless marvels of ingenuity, all those I have seen mimicking a small dead pine cone so perfectly as to almost defy detection unless one sees the bird fly on or off the nest. The majority found were saddled on one or two such cones, or on a small limb and resting against the sides of a cone. The outer walls are composed of bits of bark and small shreds of cone, and the inner cup is softly lined with willow down. An average nest measures about 1¼ inches in outer diameter by the same in depth; the inner cup being three-quarters of an inch in width by one-half inch in depth. The nests were generally so placed that the contents were protected by larger limbs or green boughs above.

He says of another nest: "This is composed interiorly of fine moss and willow down, and the outer walls are decorated with tiny shreds of bark, fine flakes of wood, and flakes of whitewash, fastened securely with cobwebs; it was placed on a knot in a rope hanging from the roof of a woodshed and within 5 feet of an occupied dwelling house. The materials out of which the nest is composed closely assimilate the rope and knot on which it is placed."

It seems to be the prevailing custom of this hummingbird to build its nest on a small branch or twig directly under a larger branch, or under a canopy of foliage, which serves to protect or conceal the nest from overhead; many observers have noticed this, and numerous photographs illustrate this type of location. This hummer has also developed to a high degree its skill in so placing its nest and so artfully camouflaging it that it fades into the picture as a natural part of its environment. James B. Dixon says in his notes that in the shaded portions of the aspen groves there are numerous dead, black or gray mistletoe knots, about the size of hummingbirds' nests, and the birds seem to realize the value of the protection thus offered; most of the nests that he found there were built either upon one of these knots or in such a position that the nest would look exactly like one of them; and he had difficulty in recognizing a nest until he could see a bird alight upon it.

Nine nests that Dr. Joseph Grinnell (1908) recorded in the San Bernardino Mountains of southern California "varied in height above the ground from twenty-two inches (measured) to seventy feet (estimated); I should judge the average height to have been about thirty-five feet, as the majority were above that height. The nests were all in cañons, though none were directly over or very near the water, as with some other species of hummingbirds. One was located in an alder, two in silver firs, and six in yellow and Jeffrey pines."

The first nest mentioned above, as 22 inches above the ground, is in the Thayer collection in Cambridge; it was near the end of a drooping bough of a young silver fir growing on a canyon side and only 15 inches from the face of a huge overhanging boulder; its general appearance is dark gray, being made of various gray and brown fibers, bark scales, and bits of inner bark; the bottom of the cavity only is lined with grayish-white down; it measures 1½ by 1¾ inches in outside diameter and 1⅛ inches by seven-eighths of an inch in inner diameter; it is only seven-eighths of an inch high outside and five-eighths of an inch deep inside.

Mr. Weydemeyer (1927) says of its nesting habits in northwestern Montana:

The nest of this Hummingbird is placed in a coniferous tree. Within this limit, the choice of an individual tree appears to depend more upon the location than upon the species. In the higher elevations of Lincoln County, nests are placed in alpine firs. Along the streams of the Transition zone, the trees most commonly used are the Engelmann spruce, western hemlock, and arborvitae. I have found one nest in a Douglas fir, but have seen none in pines. Near Libby I have observed nests in three species of trees within a few yards of each other along a stream. Evidently, to suit the requirements of the birds, the tree must be a conifer standing on the bank of a creek, or beside a road or other opening in the forest, with one of its lowermost branches swinging free from all other foliage and commanding a clear view in practically all directions.

The word "lowermost" is used with a purpose. All the nests of this species that I have seen have been placed on the lowermost living branch on its side of the tree. This habit determines the height of the nest above the ground or water. In the region considered here the distance generally ranges from four to ten feet. * * *

But little variation occurs in the general types of materials used in constructing the nests. In comparative bulk the average nest is composed approximately as follows: plant down, 60 per cent; tree lichens, 20 per cent;

ground and rock mosses, 10 per cent; tree mosses, 5 per cent; spider webs and fibers of insect cocoons, 1 per cent; miscellaneous material, 4 per cent.

The "shell" of the nest is formed principally of ground and rock mosses mixed with more or less plant down, strongly bound together with cocoon fibers, especially at the rim. Many species of moss are utilized, but generally only one kind is used in an individual nest. In many cases black fibrous tree moss also is used. This part of the nest contains the "miscellaneous material." In the fourteen nests examined this included conifer needles, grass, aspen bark, rotted wood, feathers (from the birds themselves), small leaves, and pieces of spider and insect skeletons (Diptera, Coleoptera, and Hymenoptera).

The exterior of this framework is thickly covered with gray or greenish lichens of the kind occurring on the tree in which the nest is placed. The pieces are bound to the moss by shreds of insect webs and cocoons, or by fibrous tree moss. The main body of the nest, within the sustaining framework, is composed of a thick, soft layer of various kinds of plant down, firmly compacted to form the interior cup. This down retains its shape without being bound with any other material.

Second year additions to a nest are composed mainly of down. Often the only added material is a thick layer of down in the bottom of the cup, and a thinner one on its sides. This method of addition decreases the depth of the cup about a quarter of an inch. In other cases, the rim of the nest is heightened also. If this is done, a new layer of lichen is added to the outside of the nest, making it impossible to determine, from the appearance of the exterior, how many years the nest has been used.

The foregoing paragraph indicates the methods employed by hummingbirds in repairing, or adding to, a last year's nest, a common practice among some species. But often, with this and other species, an entirely new nest is attached to or built upon the remains of a last year's nest; in this case the old nest can be easily recognized by its faded appearance. A series of two, three, or even four such nests, perhaps built during successive seasons, may occasionally be seen. Ridgway (1892, pl. 1) shows a cut of a 4-story nest of a calliope hummingbird.

Eggs.—The calliope hummingbird lays the usual set of two eggs. These are like other hummingbirds' eggs, pure white, without gloss, and varying in shape from oval to elliptical-oval. The measurements of 45 eggs average 12.1 by 8.3 millimeters; the eggs showing the four extremes measure 13.0 by 9.6 and 10.7 by 7.4 millimeters.

Plumages.—No information seems to be available about the development of the juvenal plumage, or about the early nest life of the young calliope hummingbird. In the full juvenal plumage, just after leaving the nest, the young male is practically indistinguishable from the adult female, as it still has the throat more or less streaked or spotted with bronzy brownish or dusky and with no sign of any purple in the gorget; I have seen birds in this plumage up to the first of July; some, but not all, young males have rather more rufous in the tail than the adult female has. Specimens taken in August begin to show more or fewer metallic-purple feathers in the gorget; slight advance toward maturity seems to continue during fall and winter, until the prenuptial molt, late in winter or early in spring, produces the fully adult plumage. The young female is like the adult female, but the upper parts are more bronzy and the feathers are indistinctly margined with dull brownish.

Food.—The calliope, like other hummingbirds, feeds on nectar from flowers and on the minute insects and small spiders that frequent the flowers. The sweet nectar in the flowers undoubtedly attracted the insects, but whether it was the nectar or the insects that first attracted the hummingbird is an open question; the insects may have been the original objects of their search, and the nectar developed a taste for sweets. Any brightly colored flowers are likely to attract these birds, but they seem to show a preference for red flowers, such as the scarlet paintbrush and the red columbine. The yellow flowers of *Mimulus implexus* also furnish a food supply for them. And Grinnell, Dixon, and Linsdale (1930) write: "In early May in the vicinity of Mineral this species appeared to have just one plant, a species of lousewort (*Pedicularis semibarbata*), which it frequented. The flowers grew on long spikes from leaf rosettes under snow-brush. The hummers had to fly down among close-set twiggage of the bushes to get at these flowers. Often they alighted almost on the ground to get at the horizontal tubes. By May 28 they were very active in a tract of blossoming manzanita at 6000 feet, even among snow banks. A female was seen at a snow-plant (*Sarcodes*) where these plants were first coming up, on June 26, beneath red firs."

The calliope hummingbird also hawks for insects on the wing, much after the manner of flycatchers; probably any small insect that becomes available is acceptable, but small species of Diptera, Hymenoptera, or Coleoptera seem to be most often taken. Milton P. Skinner tells me that he has seen one perched on a willow, turning its head and upper body from side to side with an almost clocklike motion, while watching for insects. Others have noticed its sallies into the air for passing insects, which its keen eyes have detected.

Behavior—Several observers have written of the territorial relations of this hummingbird and of its aggressiveness in defending its nesting territory and its foraging range. Grinnell, Dixon, and Linsdale (1930) write:

On a six-acre plot of ground where the activities of individual birds were observed closely through several nesting seasons four separate males kept distinct "stands" each for itself. As nearly as could be determined all the females that were seen on this plot were visitors whose nests were off in a belt of lodgepole pines on Battle Creek Meadows. Females came onto the plot to forage about flowers (*Castilleia*) that were plentiful there, and were then shown attention by the males.

The stand of one male was on a telephone wire directly above quantities of flowers to which a female frequently came. Another male divided his time among the growing tips of three closely adjacent young yellow pines slightly overtopping a sea of snow-brush. Another perched chiefly on one of the highest twigs of a service-berry thicket in an opening among firs. One male was established on the tallest, scrub black oak tip, driving away from the vicinity any approaching forager.

Grinnell and Storer (1924) write:

The males of all our hummingbirds are accustomed to harass birds many times their own size. A Calliope at Mono Meadow was seen to put a Wright Flycatcher to rout, the latter seeking seclusion in a ceanothus thicket. In Yosemite Valley another was seen driving at a Western Robin that was on the ground. The hummer would mount as much as 30 feet into the air and then dash down at the robin. Even Red-tailed Hawks are sometimes "attacked" by these pugnacious midgets. * * *
Like other hummingbirds the Calliope is often attracted by red objects. Whether this is a voluntary action based on esthetic appeal, or a reflex based on food-getting instinct, is problematic. At Chinquapin, on June 14, a female of this species darted into the front of our open tent and poised with seeming interest before a red-labeled baking powder can on the table. Then the bird went out into the sunshine, but it returned again twice before finally going away. Two of our three August records of this species were of individuals which were attracted in the same manner, the object being a red handkerchief in one case, and a sweater of the same color in the other.

Apparently the calliope is not always so aggressive or so pugnacious as are some other hummingbirds, for Henshaw (1886) says that it is "much less obtrusive, and in the contests of its larger neighbors it takes no part. When assailed, as it promptly is by the other kinds, it at once darts away to another spot where it can feed without molestation. It appears to be timid in every way, so much so that it is not an easy bird to collect."

Mr. Wyman (1920) says: "Ordinarily the Black-chins, of which a few haunted the same locality, would drive the Calliopes unmercifully. Once, however, a male Calliope shot close beside me up the hillside, just grazing the grass-tips, driving at a Black-chin that was quietly feeding. Within two feet of the latter he mounted vertically about thirty feet, then dropped like a plummet on the feeding bird, and both flashed down the hill-side with Calliope doing the chasing."

Aretas A. Saunders (1915) observed a bird of this species that "was very belligerent in protecting her home from all birds and other animals that approached too closely. A pine squirrel had ventured into the tree and the mother hummer chased it away immediately, following it a long way through the trees and darting at it first from one side and then from the other. The nest contained half-grown young when first found."

Field marks.—The small size of the calliope hummingbird will help to distinguish it from others, when the opportunity for comparison is favorable. The male is, of course, easy to recognize by the long, spreading, metallic-purple feathers against the snow-white background of its gorget. Aside from its small size, the female can be distinguished from the three species with which it is most likely to be associated by the amount of rufous in the tail; in the female calliope all but the central pair of rectrices have some rufous at the base; in the rufous female all the rectrices are more or less basally rufous; in the female broad-tailed only the three outer feathers are so marked; and in the female black-chinned there is no rufous in the tail.

Fall.—The males start on the southward migration rather early in the summer, or at least desert the females and move away from the breeding grounds. The females and young follow later. In the Yosemite region Grinnell and Storer (1924) saw no males after the end of June. Henshaw (1886), referring to New Mexico, says: "An utterly unaccountable fact noticed in connection with this species was the apparent rarity of females. Up to August 10 I had seen perhaps half a dozen, though constantly on the watch for them, while I had certainly seen not less than ten times that number of males. Subsequently to that date I saw a few more, but nothing like the number of males. By September the young were numerous in certain localities, notably in a large sunflower patch."

Of the migration in the Huachuca Mountains, Arizona, Harry S. Swarth (1904) writes: "After the summer rains the mountains present an exceedingly inviting appearance, particularly so in the higher parts, along the ridges and on various pine covered 'flats,' where, with the green grass, a multitude of brilliantly colored wild flowers springs up, often waist high, and in many places in solid banks of bright colors. In such places, in the late summer of 1902, I found the Calliope Hummingbird quite abundant, feeding close to the ground, and when alighting usually choosing a low bush. * * * The first one was shot August 14, and from then up to the time we left the mountains, September 5, they remained abundant in certain localities; none being seen below 9000 feet."

DISTRIBUTION

Range.—Western North America and Mexico.

Breeding range.—The breeding range of the calliope hummingbird extents **north** to southern British Columbia (150-mile House, Okanagan Landing, and Deer Park); and southwestern Alberta (Banff). **East** to southwestern Alberta (Banff); Montana (Fortine, Polson, rarely Sheep Creek, and Red Lodge) ; northwestern Wyoming (Yellowstone National Park) ; Utah (Escalante Mountains) ; and northern Baja California (Vallecitos). **South** to northern Baja California (Vallecitos) ; and southern California (Grant Creek, Mount Waterman and Mount Pinos). **West** to western California (Mount Pinos, Glenbrook, Battle Creek, and Steward Springs) ; Oregon (Gold Hill, Fort Klamath, and Weston) ; Washington (Yakima, Bumping Lake, and Lake Chelan) ; and British Columbia (probably Chilliwack and 150-mile House).

Winter range.—During the winter season the species appears to be concentrated in the southern Mexican States of Michoacan (Lake Patzcuaro) ; Mexico (Ajusco) ; and Guerrero (Taxco and Amula).

Spring migration.—Early dates of spring arrival are: California—Yosemite Valley, March 2; Azusa, March 6; Whittier, March 20; Grass Valley, April 23. Oregon—Weston, May 3; Anthony, May 6; Fort Klamath, May 16. Washington—Grays Harbor, April 22; Tacoma, May 10; Pullman, May 12. British Columbia—Okanagan Landing, April 25; Burrard Inlet, May 7. Arizona—Superstition Mountain, March 22; Santa Catalina Mountains, April 14. Idaho—Coeur d'Alene, May 20. Montana—Missoula, May 9; Fortine, May 11; Bozeman, May 25.

Fall migration.—Late dates of fall departure are: Montana—Corvallis, September 7; Fortine, September 14. Idaho—Priest River, August 24. New Mexico—Albuquerque, September 16. Arizona—Fort Verde, August 27; Apache, August 28; San Bernardino Ranch, September 11. British Columbia—Okanagan Landing, August 25. Washington—Ahtanum, August 12; Mount Adams, August 14. Nevada—East Humboldt Mountains, September 7. California—Yosemite Valley, September 4; Santa Barbara, September 11; San Bernardino Mountains, September 16.

Casual records.—A specimen was taken at El Paso, Tex., in 1851. Colorado has several records, as follows: One was collected at Breckenridge on June 30, 1882; one was found dead in Cheyenne Canyon, near Colorado Springs, on July 25, 1897; specimens also were reported from this general vicinity on July 18, 1915, and in August 1915; while several were seen on August 27, 1904, at Antonito. One was found dead near Shaunavon, Saskatchewan, on August 22, 1935. The species has been reported as occasional at Wrangell, Alaska, but the evidence is not considered satisfactory.

Egg dates.—California: 46 records, May 27 to July 30; 23 records, June 10 to 28, indicating the height of the season.

Utah: 7 records, July 3 to 23.

CALOTHORAX LUCIFER (Swainson)

LUCIFER HUMMINGBIRD

HABITS

This brilliant little hummer, with its deeply forked gorget of a vivid violet-purple, changing to reddish purple or blue in different lights, is only rarely found across our southwestern border in Arizona and western Texas. Its main range is on the tablelands of Mexico as far south as the City of Mexico, Puebla, and Chiapas. It was first added to our fauna by Henry W. Henshaw (1875), who took a female near Camp Bowie, Ariz., on August 8, 1874, and doubtfully recorded it as *Doricha enicura;* it was later determined to be a lucifer hummingbird. Some years later, in 1901, it was taken in the Chisos Mountains in western Texas by a Biological Survey party. It is apparently fairly common in these mountains, for Mrs. Bailey (1902) says that Mr. Bailey found it "with several other species common in June about the big agaves, which were then in full flower." Still later, Van Tyne and Sutton (1937) report the capture of two specimens in this region but say that the nest has not yet been found there. The lucifer hummingbird may be commoner along our southwestern border than is generally known, for it somewhat resembles Costa's hummingbird in size and color and might easily be overlooked.

Nesting.—Comparatively few nests of the lucifer hummingbird have been found. Wm. Bullock (1825), in his "Six Months in Mexico," gives us the first account of it: "They breed in Mexico in June and July; and the nest is a beautiful specimen of the architectural talen of these birds: it is neatly constructed with cotton, or the down of thistles, to which is fastened on the outside, by some glutinous substance, a white flat lichen resembling ours."

W. W. Brown collected four nests of this species in Tamaulipas, Mexico, between June 15 and July 4, 1924. Three of these are now in the Thayer collection in Cambridge, and one is in the Doe collection in Gainesville, Fla. All the nests were built in shrubs and only a few feet above ground; one was recorded as 4 and one 6 feet up. The nests were made of soft vegetable fibers and down, mixed with the scales of buds, blossoms or seeds, and bits of lichen, all completely covered and held in place with cobwebs or very fine fibers.

Eggs.—The lucifer hummingbird lays the usual hummingbird set of two eggs, which are indistinguishable from the eggs of other hummingbirds of similar size. The measurements of 6 eggs average 12.7 by 9.7 millimeters; the eggs showing the four extremes measure **13.8** by 10.0, 12.4 by **10.1**, and **12.0** by **9.2** millimeters.

Plumages.—Not much seems to be known about the immature plumages of this species, but the sexes are apparently alike in juvenal plumages and resemble the adult female, though a little grayer on the under parts. One young male, collected September 15, has one violet-purple feather on its throat, indicating an approach to the adult plumage during the fall and winter. I have seen adults of both sexes molting from September to December, during which time the complete annual molt probably occurs.

Food.—We have no definite data on the food of this species, which probably does not differ materially from that of other humming-birds. It is said to be devoted to the flower clusters of the tall, flowering agave, where it finds a bountiful supply of nectar, as well as numerous small insects and spiders.

Mr. Bullock (1825) gives the following interesting account of its spider hunting:

The house I resided in at Xalapa for several weeks was only one story high, enclosing, like most of the Spanish houses, a small garden in the centre, the roof projecting six or seven feet from the walls, covering a walk all round, and leaving a small space only between the tiles, and the trees which grew in the centre. From the edges of these tiles to the branches of the trees in the garden, the spiders had spread their innumerable webs so closely and compactly that they resembled a net. I have frequently watched with much amusement the cautious peregrination of the humming bird, who, advancing beneath the web, entered the various labyrinths and cells in search of entangled flies, but as the larger spiders did not tamely surrender their booty, the invader was often compelled to retreat; being within a few feet, I could observe all their evolutions with great precision. The active little bird generally passed once or twice round the court, as if to reconnoitre his ground, and commenced his attack by going carefully under the nets of the wily insect, and seizing by surprise the smallest entangled flies, or those that were most feeble. In ascending the angular traps of the spider great care and skill was required; sometimes he had scarcely room for his little wings to perform their office, and the least deviation would have entangled him in the complex machinery of the web, and involved him in ruin. It was only the works of the smaller spider that he durst attack, as the larger sort rose to the defence of their citadels, when the besieger would shoot off like a sunbeam, and could only be traced by the luminous glow of his refulgent colors. The bird generally spent about ten minutes in this predatory excursion, and then alighted on a branch of the Avocata to rest and refresh himself, placing his crimson star-like breast to the sun, which then presented all the glowing fire of the ruby and surpassing in lustre the diadem of monarchs.

Behavior.—The same observer writes:

When attending their young, they attack any bird indiscriminately that approaches the nest. Their motions, when under the influence of anger or fear, are very violent, and their flight rapid as an arrow; the eye cannot follow them, but the shrill, piercing shriek which they utter on the wing may be heard when the bird is invisible. They attack the eyes of the larger birds, and their sharp, needle-like bill is a truly formidable weapon in this kind of warfare. Nothing can exceed their fierceness when one of their own species invades their territory during the breeding season. Under the influence of jealousy they become perfect furies; their throats swell, their crests, tails, and wings expand; they fight in the air (uttering a shrill noise) till one falls exhausted to the ground. I witnessed a combat of this kind near Otumba, during a heavy fall of rain, every separate drop of which I supposed sufficient to have beaten the puny warriors to the earth.

Field marks.—The lucifer hummingbird might be mistaken, by the casual observer, for Costa's hummingbird, as the two are somewhat alike in size and in the shape and color of the gorget, but there are decided differences in shape and color pattern. In Costa's the entire top of the head is of the same brilliant violet-purple as the gorget, whereas in the lucifer hummer only the throat gorget, with its elongated lateral extension is of this brilliant color. Furthermore, the male lucifer has a deeply forked tail, with very narrow lateral feathers. The female lucifer has a rounded, or double rounded, tail and buffy under parts. But the best field mark for both sexes is the long, decidedly decurved bill; no other North American hummingbird has such a curved bill.

DISTRIBUTION

Range.—Southern Mexico; accidental in Arizona and Texas.

The normal range of the lucifer hummingbird is from Jalisco (Bolanos) south to Guerrero (Taxco and Chilpancingo) and east to Puebla (Chalchicomula).

Casual records.—A specimen was collected in the Chisos Mountains, Texas, on June 7, 1901; and an adult female was taken at Fort Bowie, Ariz., on August 8, 1874.

Egg dates.—Mexico: 6 records, June 15 to July 4.

AMAZILIA TZACATL TZACATL (de la Llave)

RIEFFER'S HUMMINGBIRD

PLATES 71, 72

HABITS

CONTRIBUTED BY ALEXANDER FRANK SKUTCH

This glittering green hummingbird, with a bright chestnut tail, abundant and familiar over a wide range in the warmer portions of both Americas, is merely a wandering straggler within the territory of the United States, where it has been recorded only twice, both times in the neighborhood of Brownsville, Tex., just north of the Mexican border. Its breeding range extends from the Mexican State of Tamaulipas to eastern Ecuador. In the Central American portion of this range it is, from Panama to Guatemala, the member of the family most numerous in the cultivated areas of the humid Caribbean lowlands. Thus Charles W. Richmond (quoted by Bendire, 1895) wrote that it "is extremely abundant in the lowlands of eastern Nicaragua. It outnumbers in individuals all the other (five) species of Hummingbirds found in the same region. On the Escondido River this species is confined to the banana plantations and the shrubbery around the houses, where it finds an abundance of food and good nesting sites. It is the plantation Hummer, only two other species occasionally wandering into the plantations from the forest, which is the home of the other species." Similarly George K. Cherrie (1892) affirms that in Costa Rica it is "the most abundant species about San José, and indeed the most abundant species found on either coast." This is certainly true, in my own experience, of the Caribbean coastlands of Costa Rica; but on the Pacific side of the country Rieffer's hummingbird is abundant only in the more humid regions from the Gulf of Nicoya southward. About the shores of the Gulf it mingles with the related cinnamomeous hummingbird (*Amazilia cinnamomea*), and along the Pacific side of Central America to the northward, where the dry season is long and severe, it is entirely replaced by the latter species, which here is almost as familiar and abundant on the plantations, in the flower gardens, and in the light, open woodlands as its green-breasted relative on the opposite coast.

A bird of the clearings, Rieffer's hummingbird is found in the forest only in the more open glades and seldom far from its edge. While most abundant in the lowlands, it extends upward into the highlands to an altitude (in Costa Rica) of about 5,000 feet and (on the authority of Mr. Cherrie) is found occasionally as high as 6,000 feet.

Courtship.—No hummingbirds, so far as we know, actually associate in pairs; and the male never joins a female in the duties of a nest. The purpose of the male's courtship, then, is to effect temporary union with the female, resulting in the fecundation of the eggs, not to attach unto himself a mate. Two strikingly different modes of courtship are found in this great family, and may be characterized as "dynamic" and "static." In the former, well exemplified by the broad-tailed hummingbird (*Selasphorus platycercus*), the male gives a thrilling aerial display, which centers around the female, rising high into the air and swooping down in front of her as she perches, swinging back and forth in a great, open **U**, the arms of which may be 50 or 60 feet high. In the "static" courtship the male establishes his headquarters in one particular spot, where he is to be found day after day during the breeding season. Usually he has a favorite perch, where he rests to deliver untiringly the calls, frequently weak and unmelodious, which draw the females' attention to himself. Among many species, the males group themselves into assemblies made up of two to many individuals, but frequently they are found "singing" alone. This "static" form of courtship is far more prevalent among the Central American hummingbirds than the set aerial display. So far as we know, the same species does not practice both types of courtship.

The courtship of Rieffer's hummingbird is neither persistent nor likely to draw the bird-watcher's attention. In a number of years past, in districts where the species is abundant, I have not once witnessed an aerial display of definite form comparable to that of the broad-tailed hummingbird. So far as it has any particular mode of courtship, this appears to be of the "static" type; but even in the less arduous occupation of sitting and calling, Rieffer's hummingbird is far less assiduous than many others of the Central American species. The scanty information I have on this subject is summarized in an entry made in my notebook on October 17, 1936, while I lived at Rivas de El General, in southwestern Costa Rica:

"These mornings, when I stand in the old cornfield at dawn to watch the golden-naped woodpeckers arise, I hear the quaint little songs of the Rieffer's hummingbirds. This morning I distinctly heard three of them, apparently situated at different points along the edge of the forest, at the head of the clearing. The one I watched was perching on a twig in the top of a fallen tree, 6 feet above ground, just outside the edge of the forest. The 'song' is quite distinct from that of any other hummingbird that I know, and easy to recognize once it has been heard; but as usual with hummingbirds' songs, I find it difficult to paraphrase in human words, or to describe it in such a fashion as to give anyone who has not heard it a notion of its quaint pleasantness. *Tse-we ts' we* is as near as I can come to it in alphabetical notation; but I am not well satisfied with what I have written. Sometimes the phrase is repeated several times continuously; sometimes the bird sings *Tse-we ts' we tse-we*. These hummingbirds sing most actively in the dawn, and less and less as the day grows older.

"I first heard Rieffer's hummingbirds singing here last December, when I watched a bird that perched very near the position of the one I watched this morning. Probably he was the same individual. During the greater part of the dry season I failed to notice the odd little song; but now it has been a month or so since it was resumed. The males seem to have a singing assembly here at the edge of the forest, where they are to be found every morning; but they perform less constantly than many other kinds of hummingbirds."

Nesting.—In the Caribbean lowlands of Central America Rieffer's hummingbird has been found nesting at all seasons, and there are records of nests, from one part or the other of this region, for each of the 12 months. In the Province of Bocas del Toro in western Panama the majority of the nests were discovered during the drier weather from January until May. Although in the lowlands the nesting period, for the species as a whole, is unusually long, even for tropical birds, and is peculiar in including both the dry and rainy seasons, we do not know how many broods each female may raise in a year, or what period the breeding activities of a single individual may cover.

At Rivas, on the Pacific slope of southern Costa Rica, the hummingbirds of several species, including Rieffer's, behave in their choice of a breeding season essentially as the members of the family that dwell in the higher mountains, although here the altitude is only 3,000 feet and the avifauna in general is that of the humid lowlands, with a slight admixture of species representative of the subtropical zone. In this region there is, in most years, a pronounced dry season of four months, from December to March, inclusive, while the remaining eight months are very wet. The great majority of birds of all kinds breed between the vernal equinox and the June solstice; but there is a scattering of nests of birds belonging to the most diverse families at all periods of the year. The hummingbirds, however, breed chiefly during October, November, December, and January, the very months when nests belonging to birds of other families are fewest.

During a residence of a year and a half at Rivas, I recorded six nests of Rieffer's hummingbirds during November, December, and January but not a single one during the other nine months, when nests were just as assiduously sought by myself and the boys I had reporting them to me. Flowers, although many are to be found throughout the year, reach their maximum profusion in the clearings during December and January, and their minimum abundance at the end of the dry season in March.

The highest point at which I have seen a nest of Rieffer's hummingbird is the Hacienda Las Cóncavas, near Cartago, Costa Rica, where, at an altitude of 4,500 feet, I found a nest with two well-feathered nestlings on November 3, 1935. The bird was nesting in the wettest and least agreeable season of the year, at a time when scarcely any of the Central American birds of other families breed at so high an elevation.

The nests of *Amazilia* are placed in trees or bushes in the clearings where the birds reside, without any distinct preference for any particular type. Frequently a thorny lime or orange tree is chosen, or a bougainvillea vine; but as often a thornless kind is selected for the nesting site. Sometimes even a low herbaceous plant is favored. I have found their elevation to vary from 2 to 20 feet from the ground. The open cup is constructed in a variety of situations but almost invariably on some slender support. If some variety of citrus tree has been chosen, it may rest in the angle between an upright branch and one of its large thorns attached to both by cobwebs; or in another kind of plant it may be placed in the axil of a slender leaf stalk or in the angle between a thin horizontal branch and a vertical stem. Sometimes a leaf alone suffices for its foundation. One of the most attractively situated I ever found was attached near the drooping tip of a large frond of the thorny pejibaye palm (*Guilielma utilis*); another was fastened to the palmately compound leaf of the Brazilian rubber tree; a third straddled the slender rhachis of the pinnately compound leaf of an akee (*Blighia sapida*), supported on each side by the opposite leaflets. At times the bird selects a very inadequate foundation. I once found a nest attached to a frail and decaying twig, which in its descent from somewhere higher in the tree had caught on a horizontal branch and hung loosely beneath it, draped about with the fronds of a slender, creeping species of polypody fern, which covered the bough and dropped in festoons below it. The one requirement of a nesting site is a horizontal support sufficiently slender to be grasped by the bird's feet—for from such a perch the building operations are always begun—close to some vertical or oblique support to which the side of the nest may be anchored. Frequently the nest is situated above or close beside a path along which people are constantly passing.

The nest is an open cup, formed exteriorly of weathered strips of grass, leaves, bits of weed, fibers, and the like, and abundantly lined with soft, felted plant down, the whole bound together by cobwebs liberally supplied. The outer surface is tastefully decorated with gray lichens and green mosses, which sometimes are allowed to hang in long, waving festoons beneath it. Rarely, as in the nest I found on Barro Colorado Island, this ornamentation is very sparingly applied, so that the prevailing color of the exterior is grayish or tawny, from the fibers and down employed in its construction. Sometimes an otherwise beautiful nest is marred by a long piece of withered grass leaf, used in building the foundation, and carelessly allowed to hang beneath it. The dimensions of a typical nest are: External diameter 1¾ inches, height 1¼ inches; internal diameter 1¼ inches, depth ⅞ inch.

The moss- and lichen-covered nests blend so well with the green foliage among which they are usually placed that it would be extremely difficult to find them, especially when the white eggs are hidden by the emerald bird, if the female sat more closely. The locations of several nests, which otherwise I should probably never have found, were betrayed by the birds' darting off as I passed within a few yards of them. The instinct that leads the birds to build a nest to blend so well with its setting lacks fulfillment in a corresponding instinct to utilize this advantage by remaining motionless. Perhaps at the approach of really formidable enemies other than man the female does remain motionless on her nest; but when most small creatures, lizards or birds even many times her size, venture too near, she merely darts at them and usually puts them promptly to flight. Individual birds, however, differ greatly in the closeness with which they cover their eggs and young. One female, the closest sitter of all I found, whose nest was built in a young lime tree in a nursery where men were frequently at work, would allow me to approach within arm's length before deserting, to return within a few minutes and settle down on her eggs directly before me if I waited quietly at this distance.

I could scarcely have desired a nest located more conveniently for study than the first of this species I ever found. I was at the time engaged chiefly in work with the microscope in a little frame building that served as office and laboratory at the now abandoned experiment station of the United Fruit Co. beside the great Changüinola Lagoon, 20 miles from Almirante, Panama. On the afternoon of December 19, I raised my head from my work and noticed a hummingbird, of a kind still unknown to me, perched on the petiole of a ramie plant (*Boehmeria nivea*) just outside the window, scarcely 3 yards from where I sat and separated from me only by a screen. An oddness in her manner of perching attracted my attention, and, looking more intently, I perceived something light colored almost hidden beneath her. When she flew off, I went out to examine her perch and found there a little tuft of plant down, fastened in the angle between the hairy petiole and the stem with cobweb, a piece of white thread, and several hairs from cattle, which grazed all about the small enclosure. During the succeeding days, as I sat at my work table poring over bits of banana tissue, *Amazilia* labored steadily at her growing nest. The rite of adding a new bit of material followed an invariable routine. Returning with a tuft of down in her slender bill, she would alight softly on the incipient nest, push in the stuff where it was needed, and then proceed with the shaping of the structure. She bent down her head and, moving around and around, with her long bill shaped the substance to the contour of her body. As she pressed the yielding down more closely to her breast, she erected the bronze-green feathers of her crown, and her folded wings vibrated as if she thrilled in anticipation of the completed nest and the nestlings it was intended to cradle. Then she sat facing in a set direction; and from the way her body bounced up and down I concluded she must be kneading the material together with her toes, although, as they were hidden beneath her, I was unable to see them in action. Sometimes she would dart away and then, as if the kneading and shaping had not been done to her satisfaction, return with empty bill to continue the moulding operations. So, as the nest grew, it became just large enough to fit snugly about the central portion of her body, leaving neck and head and rump and tail protruding beyond its rim.

Hummingbirds of this species do not seem to have any prescribed order for the addition of the various elements of which the nest is composed. This particular bird began with a wad of down, then bound around it strips of fibrous vegetable material, such as grass blades softened by partial decay, and fastened them there with cobweb. Others begin with strips of grass and banana-leaf epidermis, adding the down later when they can get it. It seems to be merely a matter of convenience or luck in finding the proper materials. I once found a nest built entirely of fine grass and pieces of weeds but so devoid of lining that the eggs touched the branch on which it rested. This was doubtless because down for the lining was not available; and under favorable conditions the downy lining is added simultaneously with the fibrous materials, which impart rigidity to the structure. Although the lichens and mosses appear to be merely an ornament of the nest, and do not constitute an essential part of the structure, they are often added before the foundation portions of the walls are completed.

Because of torrential rains that interrupted her work, this hummingbird required 12 days for the completion of her nest; but others, building during more favorable weather, may finish their task in a week.

The attachment of Rieffer's hummingbird to a nest site once chosen is very strong. Soon after the eggs had hatched in the nest whose construction has been described, the nestlings were attacked and killed by ants. The deserted nest was then used as a quarry by another hummingbird, who removed most of the down to her own new structure on the opposite side of the building. Six weeks after the destruction of the nestlings, all that remained of their nest was its basal portion, a shallow cup of grass and fibers with hardly any lining, darkened and discolored by the elements. The original builder now reclaimed it, added fresh bits of grass to the walls, increasing their height, and attached new lichens to the exterior. With the nest in this condition, she laid her two eggs upon the hard, impacted bottom; but afterward, in the intervals of incubation, she continued to build up and line the old structure, until at length it was as comfortable, and appeared as solid, as when new. In Guatemala I once found a nest containing eggs, built upon an older nest of the same kind that had turned sideways.

Eggs.—As with the great majority of hummingbirds, Rieffer's lays two eggs. The interval between the laying of the first and second is two days (about 48 hours). The eggs are pure white and oblong or oblong-ovate, often with little difference between the two ends. The measurements of six eggs removed temporarily from their nests in Honduras average 14 by 8.7 millimeters; the eggs showing the four extremes measure 14.2 by 8.6, 14 by 9.1, and 13.5 by 8.6 millimeters.

Young.—As she builds, so the female hummingbird incubates quite alone; and no male of her kind takes an interest in her labors. During her recesses she continues to seek fresh downy material and cobweb to add to her nest, even when it is already well padded. The period of incubation is normally 16 days. I have never enjoyed a better opportunity to watch the care and development of the young than was offered by the nest in the ramie plant, just outside the window before my work table in Panama.

The newly emerged nestlings were like ugly grubs, blind, black-skinned, and naked except for two lines of short, tawny down extending the length of the back, one on each side of the middle line. The slender bill of the adult was represented by a mere bump, hardly longer than that of a newly hatched pauraque (*Nyctidromus albicollis*). At intervals one of the graceless creatures reared up spasmodically, opening wide its yellow-lined mouth in a voiceless call for nourishment, to sink again exhausted, with drooping head, into the nest. The mother's time for the first week was divided between brooding and feeding her offspring, which she did in the customary manner of the family, by regurgitation. Sitting upright on the rim of the nest, she thrust the rapierlike bill into the nearest gaping mouth, pushing it down until it seemed that it must pierce the en trails of the nestling. Then with a convulsive jerking of the body she regurgitated a portion of the contents of her crop into that of her infant. Both nestlings were as a rule fed at each return to the nest, and often each was given food twice, alternately. When the nestlings are older, sometimes each is fed four times at a single visit of their mother. After feeding, she usually returned to brooding, repeatedly thrusting out her long, white tongue as she sat on the nest. Although during the day she flew off, twittering her complaint, at my too near approach, at night she would permit me to advance and touch her on the nest, in the beam of a flashlight.

With these constant ministrations the youngsters grew amazingly, and at the age of six days, when the beady black eyes first began to peep out of the still-naked head, and the bill had lengthened considerably, they quite filled the bottom of their downy cup. The next

day the eyes were fully open, and the tawny tips of the feathers began
to protrude from their sheaths. But at this stage the nest was invaded by fire ants, and my observations temporarily interrupted.
Six weeks later the mother returned, repaired the old nest, laid two
more eggs, and hatched from them two nestlings, which lived to
take wing. They passed through a most eventful infancy, attended
by many mishaps and tribulations. First the renovated nest became
loose on the supporting stem; and I was obliged to fasten it up with
pins to save the occupants from spilling out. The leaves that had
originally shaded it died and fell away with age, exposing the still
unfeathered nestlings to the full glare of the afternoon sun. They sat
with necks stretched upward, mouths widely gaping, and glassy,
staring eyes. Once I saw the mother perch on the rim of the nest
with wings partly spread, attempting to shield them from the sun's
rays; but her position was not well chosen and her shadow fell to one
side of them, and they continued to pant. Later she covered them
on the nest; but one nestling, pushing its head out between her wing
and body, continued to gasp. Fearing they might succumb, I attempted to arrange a sunshade; but I had not yet learned the toughness of young hummingbirds.

Their vitality was amazing. Exposure to the sun, a 4-foot fall
when the old nest finally broke to pieces, and repeated handling by
fingers many times larger than themselves had not killed them. Now
a still more severe ordeal awaited them—24 hours of rain with hardly
a let-up, and some beating tropical downpours in the interval. The
mother had definitely ceased to cover them, and the scant foliage of
the ramie, which remained above the nest I had improvised for
them, afforded slight protection. After a night of this severe pun-
ishment, I watched them through much of the dreary day. When the
heavy downpours came, and the big drops beat ceaselessly upon them,
the 2-week-old birds sat in the improvised nest with eyes closed and
bills pointing straight to heaven, shaking their heads from side to
side when struck by a particularly large drop. Their budding plumage gave little comfort; and the cool rain soaked them to the skin.
Amazilia attended them faithfully the whole day. At intervals between the heavy showers she came, her black bill dusted with the
white pollen of the banana flowers in which she had been probing,
perched on the rim of the paper cup, and fed her wet offspring.
Often one or the other or sometimes both of the nestlings refused
to accept nourishment, when she gently touched its bill once or
twice with hers as if to coax it to take food; but often it was too
wet and miserable to be tempted. At each visit she ran over the
plumage of the nestlings, or a part of the nest, with her tongue, an
act I never witnessed in dry weather; and from the way her throat

worked, I concluded she was sucking up some of the excess water. And with these unfailing maternal ministrations, the unfledged birds pulled through the ordeal. Then I began to understand something of the secret of the wide distribution and great abundance of the species. Their nesting habits appear very imperfect, for the nest seems to sacrifice utility to beauty, and in a region where a large proportion of the birds build some sort of covered nest to protect its occupants from burning sun and beating rain, theirs is open to the sky, and moreover is too small to accommodate the two nestlings until they are ready to leave it. Their success as a species resides rather in the inherent toughness of fiber of the nestlings, coupled with the indefatigable attentions of the devoted mother.

Before leaving the nest, the fledglings acquired the plumage of the adults, although the colors were not so bright, and tufts of brown down still adhere to the tips of the green feathers, giving them a rather rough appearance. Two days before their departure from the nest, when I attempted to touch them they would ruffle up their feathers and attack a finger with their bills, which were still considerably shorter than the adult's. The first bird flew off as I was examining the nest, at an age of 21 days. The folded wings spread and began to whir, in a moment it rose into the air, and, uttering a low twitter as it went, flew away until it was lost from sight among the bananas. The maiden flight showed power and control. The second bird left two days later, aged 22 days. The mother continued to feed them by regurgitation for a number of days after their departure; but I am unable to state just how long.

The nestling period of these birds was perhaps a few days longer than normal because of the untoward circumstances attending it. In the case of another nest I watched in Panama, the nestlings took flight at the ages of 19 and 20 days, respectively. From a nest near Tela, Honduras, the nestlings departed at ages of 18 to 19 days, respectively, while from a second nest both departed at the age of 19 days.

Rieffer's hummingbird sits lightly on her nest, and a greater portion of her body protudes above it than is the case with most other birds. This is the outcome of the closeness with which she molds it to the central portion of her body and then often continues to add down to the interior after the eggs have been laid, further decreasing the size of the cavity. The nestling, at the time of its departure, is almost as large as the adult, and naturally the two are very much crowded in the small nest. Before they depart the wall is always more or less flared outward by the pressure of their bodies, while one or the other is forced to an uncomfortable position on the rim. Especially when the nest is softened by water during rainy periods, it is sometimes literally burst asunder by the pressure of the growing bodies it contains. In one case that came under my observation the nest split down the side, then turned almost inside out and dropped its two helpless occupants on the ground. I found them next morning, after a showery night, in the grass beneath the ruined structure, among wandering fire ants, which probably would eventually have devoured them had I not replaced them on the remains of their nest, where they sat a week more before they were able to fly away.

Plumages.—Dr. Frank M. Chapman (1925) states that "there is but little variation with sex, age, or season in this species. The male usually has the throat more solid green and the abdomen darker than the female, from which young males are not distinguishable."

Behavior.—About the habitations of men, where these hummingbirds seem most at home, they spend their time probing for insects or nectar in the great red blossoms of *Hibiscus sinensis*, which is everywhere a favorite shrub for hedges, dooryards, and the town plaza, or else in the blue trumpets of the *Thunbergia*, which scrambles over fences and up the sides of houses; or they hover before the coral vine, the blue flowers of *Clitoria*, or the blossoms of some fruit tree. At other times they enter the banana groves and poise beside the long, pendent inflorescences, where they probe the white blossoms clustered beneath their heavy red bracts, swarming with the little, black, stingless bees, which gather their pollen and rich nectar. Early in the morning one may see them bathing on the dewy surface of the broad banana leaves, over which they glide with vibrant wings, gathering up the heavy dew drops in their plumage. They are no more sociable than other kinds of hummingbirds and dart fiercely at another of the same or a different species if he ventures too near; but the bird attacked almost invariably retreats at the first dashing onslaught, closely followed by the pursuer; and I have never witnessed two birds engage in an encounter face to face, or one inflict injury on another.

A surprising aspect of the behavior of the Rieffer's hummingbirds, as I watched them near Almirante, Panama, during the early part of 1929, was the frequency with which they pilfered material from one another's nests. About our house at the research station larceny of this kind was shockingly prevalent; and I believe that about half of the failures to rear a brood that came to my attention were to be attributed to this unsocial practice. The condition was probably local and possibly even seasonal; I have never noticed it elsewhere; but then never elsewhere have I seen so great a concentration of hummingbirds' nests. It was induced to a large extent, I think, by the inadequate supply of down for lining the nests, added to the close proximity in which they were placed, sometimes 100 feet or less from each other, which made robbery easier than a long expedition afield to gather soft materials. To this may be added the hummingbird's passion for bringing more down to a nest in which incubation is already in progress and which is already quite adequately lined. The presence of eggs did not render a nest sacred to other hummingbirds, which sometimes continued to tear away material until they fell to the ground.

One unfortunate Rieffer's hummingbird, which tried to establish a nest in a cashew tree growing in a corner of our yard, was so impeded in her efforts to build by the thievery of her neighbors that at the end of a month of fairly continuous effort she had nothing to show for her labor. With the usual attachment of her kind to one particular location, she tried to build only in the cashew tree and an avocado tree standing close beside it. A removal to a more distant site might have brought her better fortune. In these two trees she made at least 12 fresh beginnings of her nest, each of which was in a short time more or less completely obliterated. The behavior of this bird is recorded in detail in my article in The Auk (Skutch, 1931); and to this the reader must be referred.

DISTRIBUTION

Range.—Eastern Mexico, Central America, and northwestern South America; casual in southern Texas; nonmigratory.

Rieffer's hummingbird ranges **north** to northern Veracruz (Tampico); and British Honduras (Orange Walk and Corosal). **East** to British Honduras (Corosal and Belize); Honduras (Tela and La Ceiba); Nicaragua (Matagalpa, La Libertad, and Bluefields); Panama (Gatun and Barro Colorado Island); western Venezuela (Chama); central Colombia (Puerto Berrio, Bogota, and Fusugasugo); and western Ecuador (Perucho, Babohoyo, and Chimbo). **South** to Ecuador (Chimbo); Costa Rica (Boruca, Puntarenas, and Barranca); and southwestern Guatemala (Santa Lucia). **West** to Guatemala (Santa Lucia); western Tabasco (Teapa); eastern Oaxaca (Choapan, Playa Vincente, and Tuxtepec); and Veracruz (Orizaba, Cordoba, and Tampico).

The birds found in Ecuador have been described as a geographic race or subspecies.

The claim of this species to a place in the list of birds of the United States rests upon two specimens captured at Fort Brown, Tex., in June and July 1876.

Egg dates.—Central America, Caribbean lowlands from Panama to Guatemala: 24 records, January to December, covering every month.

Costa Rica, Pacific slope, 3,000 feet: 6 records, November 7 to January 9. Caribbean slope, 4,500 feet: 1 record (nestlings), November 3.

AMAZILIA YUCATANENSIS CHALCONOTA Oberholser

BUFF-BELLIED HUMMINGBIRD

HABITS

This is another Mexican species that extends its range northward into the valley of the lower Rio Grande in Texas. It is the northern form of a species inhabiting eastern Mexico and Yucatan, from the Rio Grande to extreme southeastern Mexico, which has been divided into three subspecies. This race is described by Ridgway (1911) as "similar to *A. y. cerviniventris*, but under parts of body much paler (light cinnamon buff to pale pinkish buff) and green of upper parts averaging more bronzy."

The buff-bellied hummingbird was added to our fauna by Dr. James C. Merrill (1878), who took the first specimen within our borders on the military reservation of Fort Brown, Tex., on August 17, 1876. He found it to be an "abundant summer visitor" and says that "it seems perfectly at home among the dense, tangled thickets, darting rapidly among the bushes and creeping vines, and is with difficulty obtained. A rather noisy bird, its shrill cries usually first attract one's attention to its presence."

While George F. Simmons and I were collecting with R. D. Camp, near Brownsville, Tex., in 1923, Captain Camp told us that this hummingbird had become very rare in that vicinity, but we saw two or three in the tangled thickets along a resaca near town; they tried unsuccessfully to shoot one, but I could plainly see the long, rufous tail and the buff underparts, which served to identify the species. As many nests have been taken in Cameron County, Tex., this hummingbird is probably still rather common in the open woodlands and chaparral thickets in that vicinity, coming out occasionally into the open gardens and about the plantations, though much of its original habitat has been destroyed to make room for citrus orchards and vegetable farms.

Nesting.—The first nest found within the United States is thus described by Dr. Merrill (1878): "A Hummer's nest, undoubtedly made by this species, was found in September, 1877, within the fort. It was placed on the fork of a dead, drooping twig of a small tree on the edge of a path through a thicket; it was about seven feet from the ground, and contained the shrivelled body of a young bird. The nest is made of the downy blossoms of the tree on which it is placed, bound on the outside with cobwebs, and rather sparingly covered with lichens."

Major Bendire (1895) writes:

I have eight of these nests before me, all taken in Cameron County, Texas, which are readily distinguishable from those of other species breeding in the United States whose nests are known. They are composed of shreds of vegetable fiber, thistle down, and an occasional specimen is lined with a vegetable substance resembling brown cattle hair; but the majority are lined with thistle down. The outside is covered with bits of dry flower blossoms, shreds of bark, and small pieces of light-colored lichens, securely fastened in place by spider webs. The nests are neatly built, and are usually saddled on a small, drooping limb, or placed on a fork of a horizontal twig, at distances of from 3 to 8 feet from the ground. Small trees or bushes of the Anachuita (*Cordia boissieri*) ebony and hackberry seem to furnish their favorite nesting sites, though occasionally a nest is found in a willow. An average-sized nest measures 1⅜ inches in outer diameter by 1¼ inches in height; the inner cup is seven-eighths of an inch in width by five-eights of an inch in depth. Open woods and the edges of chaparral thickets near roads or paths seem to be preferred for purposes of nidification. Probably two broods are raised in a season. The earliest nesting record I have is April 23; the latest June 16.

There are three nests of the buff-bellied hummingbird in the Thayer collection in Cambridge, one collected in Tamaulipas, Mexico, and two in Cameron County, Tex. The latter two compare very well with the nests described above, in location, in size, and in materials used in construction. But the Tamaulipas nest, collected on April 15, 1908, is quite different; it is a very tall structure, apparently a series of three nests built upon the top of one another, perhaps the work of three seasons or the home of three broods; it measures 2½ inches in overall height and 1½ inches in external diameter; the inner cavity is 1 inch in diameter and is hollowed to the depth of 1 inch, this hollow being nearly twice as deep as in the other nests. The nest is made of thistledown, some with the seeds attached, and other woolly substances, reinforced with very fine twigs, weed stems, small dry leaves, strips of inner bark and lichens, all bound together with spider webs; and it is lined with pale buff down.

Eggs.—So far as I know, the buff-bellied hummingbird always lays two eggs. These are oval or elliptical-oval and pure white. The measurements of 50 eggs average 13.24 by 8.65 millimeters; the eggs showing the four extremes measure **15.3** by 8.9, 14.0 by **9.4**, and **11.8** by **7.7** millimeters.

Plumages.—The sexes are alike in all plumages, and young birds are much like their parents, although the green of the throat is more mixed with grayish buff.

DISTRIBUTION

Range.—Coastal regions of southern Texas and eastern Mexico.

The buff-bellied hummingbird breeds **north** to the lower Rio Grande Valley in Texas (Brownsville). From this point the range extends southward through eastern Tamaulipas (Matamoros and Altamira); eastern San Luis Potosi (Valles); Veracruz (Tampico, Cordoba, and Tlacotalapan); Yucatan (Merida); Quintana Roo (Palmul and Acomal); to Chiapas (Ocozucuantla).

The race of this species that is found in Texas and northeastern Mexico is known as *Amazilia y. chalconota*. Other races occur in southern Mexico and in Yucatan.

While apparently not regularly migratory, nevertheless it appears that those birds breeding in the Rio Grande Valley leave in October for winter quarters in southern Tamaulipas and Veracruz, returning in April.

Egg dates.—Texas: 30 records, March 24 to July 16; 15 records, May 9 to June 9, indicating the height of the season.

AMAZILIA SALVINI (Brewster)

SALVIN'S HUMMINGBIRD

HABITS

This seems to be a doubtful species, and evidently is only a hybrid. Only two specimens are known. The type, an adult male, was taken at Nacosari, Sonora, Mexico, by John C. Cahoon, on March 31, 1887, for William Brewster (1893); this specimen is now in the collection of the Museum of Comparative Zoology at Cambridge. The other specimen, now in the collection of Dr. Louis B. Bishop (1906), was taken for him by H. W. Marsden at Parmerlee, Cochise County. Ariz., on July 4, 1905; this is a young female.

The best authorities seem to agree that *salvini* is a hybrid between one of the races of *Amazilia violiceps* and one of the races of *Cynanthus latirostris*, but which race of each is involved seems open to discussion. Ludlow Griscom (1934) writes:

A careful study of the color and structural characters of the type convinces me that *Cyanomyia salvini* Brewster is a hybrid between *Amazilia violiceps conjuncta* and *Cynanthus latirostris* Swainson. These closely related genera differ in (1) *Amazilia* has the frontal feathering extending forward to and partially concealing the nasal operculum; (2) the tail is slightly forked in *Cynanthus*, truncate in the section of *Amazilia* with which we are here concerned. In these respects *salvini* is an *Amazilia* as to the frontal feathering, but the tail is slightly forked as in *Cynanthus*. In size *salvini* resembles the *Cynanthus*, a considerably smaller bird than *A. violiceps*. The color characters combine the two supposed parents perfectly. The glittering violet crown plaque of *violiceps* combined with the plain green of *Cynanthus* produces a glittering bluish green plaque. The green upper back fading to dusky green is a perfect combination of the dusky versus dark green upperparts of the supposed parents. The tail is dark green instead of steel blue versus dull dusky bronzy green, and the feathers have the gray tips of *Cynanthus*. The underparts are white medially as in the *Amazilia*, but the sides of the neck and chest are glittering bluish green, passing to green on the sides and flanks, just as in *Cynanthus*.

The nest of the hybrid form has, apparently, never been found, but Robert T. Moore has sent me the following note on a nest of *Amazilia violiceps ellioti*, which very likely is one of the parent forms:

"This was found by Chester Lamb on a 'thorny bush overhanging a creek' in a wooded arroyo at Copalito, northeastern Sinaloa, July 29, 1936. The *situ* was the crotch of a dead twig 3 feet up from the ground at the extremity of a branch of the bush. The bulk of the nest is composed of the whitish cotton from the pod of the palo-blanco tree. The body of the structure is completely and tightly bound together on the entire external portion with very fine webbing, which may have been obtained from a spiderweb but looks surprisingly like the fine threads of the cotton itself. If so, they have been very carefully pulled out and each one worked separately into the nest. Three small dead twigs are attached to the external part, but the chief decoration is a very beautiful 'pale glaucous-green' lichen. I have not seen this particular lichen used elsewhere, and I am sure it is not the oak lichen, commonly used by the white-eared hummingbird. The interior of the nest has no lining other than the cotton itself, but there are four lichens well inside of the margin of the nest. The characteristic feature of the structure, which differentiates it from the nest of most other species I have seen in northwestern Mexico, is the use of the fine tendrils of cotton or cobwebs to swathe the external part of it."

HYLOCHARIS XANTUSI (Lawrence)

XANTUS'S HUMMINGBIRD

HABITS

The type specimen of this hummingbird, a female now in the United States National Museum, was taken in 1859 near Cape San Lucas, Baja California, by John Xantus and was named in his honor. Its center of abundance is in the vicinity of the Cape, but it ranges northward to about the twenty-ninth parallel of latitude, where it becomes rare.

William Brewster (1902) says:

This Hummingbird is peculiar to Lower California, but it is not strictly confined to the Cape Region, for Mr. Frazar found it common at a point about one hundred and fifty miles north of La Paz among the mountains opposite Carmen Island in latitude 26°, and Mr. Bryant has traced its extension still farther northward to about latitude 29°. It seems to be most abundant, however, in the mountains south of La Paz, especially on the Sierra de la Laguna, where it ranges from the highest elevations down to the lower limits of the oaks among the foothills. It also occurs—at least sparingly and locally at certain seasons—in the low arid country near the coast, for Mr. Frazar took a male at La Paz on February 11, and saw upward of a dozen at San José del Cabo in September. At the latter place, Mr. Belding found it "common in orchards" about the last of April, 1882. Among the mountains it shows a marked preference for cañons, especially such as have pools or small streams of water. Mr. Belding says that "in winter" it is "found only in mountain cañons," but Mr. Frazar's experience was exactly the reverse of this, for during his winter visit to the Sierra de la Laguna (November 27–December 2), the "whole top of the cold, sleety mountain was alive with Xantus's Hummers, which seemed to be attracted there by an abundant shrub covered with *dry* yellow blossoms, whereas in May and June they were confined quite closely to the cañons." The truth of the matter probably is that their movements, like those of most other members of this family, are dependent largely on the presence or absence, at any given locality or season, of the flowers on which they feed.

Chester C. Lamb (1925) evidently agrees with Mr. Brewster as to the center of abundance of this hummingbird, which he says is "in Laguna Valley, in the heart of the Sierra de la Laguna, situated south of La Paz." He continues:

These mountains are difficult of access, and it takes two days on mule back, over tortuous trails, to reach Laguna Valley, a small, uninhabited valley at an elevation of about 5500 feet. The Xantus Hummingbirds radiate out from this valley in all directions, and are very common in all the mountain canyons, right down to the open deserts. One may get into some of the favorable hummingbird localities of California and believe he has seen a great concourse of hummingbirds, but half an hour's walk across Laguna Valley and around the lower rim will astound one at the numbers seen. One day I endeavored in the course of a short morning's walk to count the number of Xantus Hummingbirds, but, going up to two hundred before the first hour, I gave up the actual count and started to estimate. One cannot see this large number of hummingbirds at any hour of the day, however. The very early morning hours are when they appear in the greatest abundance. At this time they come out of the oak and pine forests around the rim of the valley and seek a place to bathe, and also to feed and play around a red flowering shrub that grows along the stream on the floor of the valley.

Nesting.—Mr. Lamb (1925) was at "Comondu from March 30 to April 11, 1924, and during that interval twelve nests were discovered." He says:

At this altitude, 800 feet, the birds must start nesting early in February, as all but three nests contained large young or eggs about to hatch. I would not be surprised if they raised two broods annually at Comondu, though I did not stay long enough to prove the fact or to learn the period of incubation.

In their courting, the male Xantus Hummingbird does not fly up in the air and make the parabolic dive that the Costa Hummingbird does, but there is considerable chasing by individuals of one another around through the trees. The nesting birds of Comondu, where there are no oaks, have an entirely different style of nest building from those of the oak regions of the Sierra de la Laguna. The Comondu birds are not particular as to what kind of a tree they select in which to build their nests. The nests are usually placed low above the ground, and they are always very close to running water. * * *

At Comondu I noted two exceptions to the usual method of suspending nests to twigs. In one case a nest was found saddled to the dry spike of a date palm tree, and another was saddled on a dead limb of a fig tree. Other trees in which nests were found at Comondu were avocado, olive, lemon, orange, water willow and cottonwood. * * *

In the Sierra de la Laguna (Laguna Valley), nests are always in live oak trees, not necessarily near water. I made diligent searches in the pines and white oak trees, which, especially the latter, are much more abundant than the live oaks, but discovered no nests. Nearly all the nests found were hung at the ends of small twigs, from four to six feet from the ground, in very small live oaks. Two exceptions were nests found twelve feet up in large oaks. * * *

The nesting material of the Comondu birds and the Laguna birds was about the same, the nests being composed of fine plant down, dried flower heads, plant fibers and small feathers, all bound together with spider webbing. A nest from Comondu is covered on the outside with strips of bark of the water willow. Without exception all the nests of the Sierra birds are beautifully decorated with lichens from the oaks. The Comondu birds do not decorate their nests with lichens, these not being available, but sometimes they do attempt a little decoration with bits of bark or leaves.

The nesting dates of the Laguna birds are also different from those at Comondu. We arrived in the Sierra de la Laguna on June 16 and remained until July 7, and in that time no nests were found, though I am not sure that the birds were not nesting. August 3 I re-visited the mountains and remained in Laguna Valley and vicinity until September 3, and in this month discovered twenty-five nests. On September 1 I found a nest just ready for eggs. Of those found, the greater number contained young or heavily incubated eggs, so it might be said that the nesting season in Laguna Valley started about the middle of July and continued to the middle of September.

Mr. Brewster (1902) gives the following detailed description of a nest, found by Mr. Frazar:

A nest found at San José del Rancho, on July 28, was placed at the extremity of a slender, drooping oak twig, about eight feet above the ground. One side is built against and around the main stem (here only .12 inches in diameter), and the bottom rests securely on a terminal fork, from the ends of which hang a number of dry, bleached oak leaves, apparently of the previous year's growth. The chief, if not only, material composing the walls of this nest consists of small, woolly leaves of a pale sage-green color, intermixed with reddish-brown, catkin-shaped objects, which appear to be made up of numerous minute seed vessels attached in double, triple, or quadruple rows or clusters to stems an inch or more in length. The entire outer surface of the nest is wrapped with a net-work of spider-web silk so fine as to be well-nigh invisible but sufficiently strong and taughtly drawn to give the walls a firm, smooth outline. The interior is not lined save at the bottom, which is furnished with a soft bed of whitish down, evidently that of some bird. This nest measures externally 1.60 inches in diameter by 1.65 in depth; internally, .73 inches in diameter by .50 in depth.

Eggs.—The two eggs laid by Xantus's hummingbird are practically indistinguishable from those of other hummingbirds of similar size. They are pure dull white and vary in shape from oval to elliptical-oval. The measurements of 26 eggs average 12.3 by 8.4 millimeters; the eggs showing the four extremes measure **13.5 by 9.9, 11.4 by 7.8, 1.9 by 7.5** millimeters.

Plumages.—I have no information on the early plumages of the nestling, but in the juvenal plumage, which is probably fully acquired before the young bird leaves the nest, the sexes are apparently alike and closely resemble the adult female. The adult female is like the adult male, but she has no black on the head, no green on the throat, and the postocular stripe is buffy instead of white. Mr. Ridgway (1911) says that the young male has the "throat spotted with metallic emerald green or yellowish green." And the young female, he says, is "similar to the young male but without green on the throat."

Mr. Brewster (1902), who had a large series of these birds, taken every month in the year except October and January, makes the following general remarks on the seasonal variations in plumages:

The summer and autumn birds are by far the brightest colored, having the green of the back quite pure; the black of the forehead, sides of head and chin, deep velvety often glossed with violet or blue; the metallic green of the throat, clear and brilliant; the cinnamon rufous of the under parts, rich and pure. The spring birds (March, April, and May) are uniformly much duller and paler, the green of the back being much tinged with ashy or rusty, and the black of the head with brown, while the green of the throat is muddy in tone and but slightly iridescent.

One bird (No. 17,031, Triunfo, April 11, 1887) has the black of the head confined to the auriculars, and the green of the throat to a few central spots, the rest of the under parts being dull cinnamon rufous, and the entire upper parts dull green with most of the feathers tipped with rusty cinnamon.

This specimen is evidently a young male that is beginning to assume the adult plumage at its annual complete molt. Judged from what is available in the literature and what can be learned from the study of specimens, it seems that the young of both sexes are, at first, like the adult female with no green on the throat; and that the young male soon begins to acquire some metallic green feathers on the throat, but does not assume the fully adult plumage until the next spring; I have seen young males acquiring the green throat in April and in July, and in full molt in July. I have seen adults molting in July.

Food.—Not much is definitely known about the food of Xantus's hummingbird, which probably does not differ essentially from that of other hummingbirds, with due allowance for the species of insects and feeding plants to be found in its habitat. Dr. Frederic A. Lucas (1893) lists: "*Cecidomyia, Phora,* three specimens of *Solenopsis geminatus,* elytra of beetle, *Psyllus,* parts of spiders."

Behavior.—Mr. Lamb (1925) has this to say about the habits of this hummer:

At one place the hummingbirds' bath was discovered, where a trickle of water flowed over a flat rock a short distance and then dropped in a tiny waterfall. At one time I counted nine birds at once taking a bath. They would sit in the water and give themselves a thorough shower with their wings; then, to finish off, they would fly against the falls, breast first, and then they would back up to the falling water. Besides the birds busily bathing, there were as many more sitting around on the bushes, drying themselves.

Towards dark, in the winter time, the adult males have a habit of perching on some dead twig, and there, remaining motionless for a considerable period, give themselves up to song, uttering at regular short intervals their quite pleasing little tune. During the heavy tropical rains of that region the hummingbirds would disappear, but the minute the rain ceased they would be out again. These birds love the pines and live oaks of the high mountain regions, and are to be seen at all hours of the day hunting around those trees for the minute insects that constitute their food.

They seem to be of gentle disposition, though they do not permit the too close proximity of another species while feeding or at their nests. They are tame, but not so much so that the brooding female will ever allow a person to touch her. At most any time, a little squeak will bring one or two birds buzzing around one's head. When I had my work table out under the oaks the hummingbirds seemed much interested in my work, buzzing around the table and inspecting my instrument box. I had a fluff of cotton hanging nearby, which they soon learned made excellent nest building material.

Enemies.—Mr. Lamb (1925) says that ravens are very common in the Cape region of Baja California and are very destructive; one was caught in the very act of destroying a hummingbird's nest that he had just examined.

Field marks.—The only hummingbird with which Xantus's is likely to be confused is the white-eared, as both have the white postocular stripe; but, fortunately, their ranges do not overlap. The adult male *xantusi* is easily recognized by its blue-black face, white postocular stripe, bright metallic-green throat, cinnamon-rufous under parts, largely chestnut tail, and reddish bill. The female is similar but with no black on the head, no green on the throat, and has a black bill and a buffy postocular stripe. The young are similar to the adult female, though the young male may have the throat flecked with green.

DISTRIBUTION

Range.—The southern half of the peninsula of Baja California; nonmigratory. This species is normally found from about the central part of this Mexico State (Purissima) south to the cape district (San Jose del Cabo). A specimen was collected at Todos Santos Island off the northern part of the west coast on November 14, 1923. There are no records for the United States.

Egg dates.—Lower California (lowlands) : 12 records, April 5 to May 17.

Lower California (mountains) : 14 records, July 19 to August 5.

Mr. Lamb (1925) says that at Comodu they must start nesting in February and that in the Laguna Valley they probably nest from July 15 to September 15.

HYLOCHARIS LEUCOTIS LEUCOTIS (Vieillot)

WHITE-EARED HUMMINGBIRD

PLATE 73

HABITS

CONTRIBUTED BY ALEXANDER F. SKUTCH

The white-eared hummingbird is a common and widespread species of northern Central America and Mexico, occurring in the United States only in southern Arizona, where it was first discovered in the Chiricahua Mountains by Dr. A. K. Fisher (1894). Near the southern extremity of its range, in Guatemala, it is a bird of the highlands found chiefly at elevations between 4,000 and 9,000 feet, although in favorable localities it may extend upward to 11,000 feet above sea level. Here its favorite haunts are the more open woods of oak, pine, and alder and the clearings and bushy mountainsides where there is a profusion of flowering shrubs. Over much of the Guatemalan highlands, at the altitudes it prefers, it is one of the most abundant and familiar hummingbirds of the cultivated areas and the flower gardens, but it is rarely seen in the darker and more humid forests and almost never in the heavy cypress forests of the mountaintops. In the southern part of its range it is resident at all seasons, or at most performs short altitudinal migrations occasioned by the local abundance of flowers. But in Arizona, according to Oberholser (1925), the species is migratory, arriving probably in April and remaining until August or possibly September, although definite dates of arrival and departure are lacking. It is said to winter as far north as the Valley of Mexico and the State of Colima.

In El Salvador and Nicaragua the species is represented by the race *pygmaea*, which in the former country, according to Dickey and van Rossem (1938), ranges between 3,500 and 8,000 feet above sea level, dwelling in the undergrowth of the oak forests and in various sorts of scrubby growth.

Courtship.—In the highlands of western Guatemala, the rainy season normally extends from the middle of May to the middle of October. In November and December, the first months of clear, sunny weather, there is a greater profusion of bright, conspicuous blossoms than at any other period of the year. Hummingbirds of all kinds nest during this flowery season, despite frequent cold, biting winds, and the frosts that from November to the end of March form almost nightly on open fields above 7,500 feet. By the end of January blossoms have become far fewer as a result of continued dryness and frosts increasingly severe, and the nesting season of the hummingbirds is drawing to a close. During the period between the vernal equinox and the June solstice, when the vast majority of birds of all kinds raise their young, nests of the hummingbirds are unknown at higher elevations. During the season when the hummingbirds breed, the only other bird whose nests I have found, at altitudes in excess of 7,000 feet, is *Diglossa baritula*, an aberrant honeycreeper, which, like them, sucks the nectar of flowers.

Just as many of the plants that blossom during the dry season anticipate the return of bright weather and open their earliest flowers during the gloomy days of the later part of the rainy season, so the male white-eared hummingbirds prepare for their courtship well in advance of the cessation of the rains. By the end of August 1933, some of the male white-ears, on the mountains above Tecpán in west-central Guatemala, had chosen the positions they would occupy during the following months, and from time to time sounded in a tentative fashion the clear little notes that advertise their presence to the females. As September advanced with increasing mist and rain they lapsed into silence, but with the advent of October they became vocal again, and some tinkled from the same bushes where I had first heard them a month earlier.

As I roamed the bushy mountainsides and the open oak woods, it soon became clear to me that the male white-ears were not distributed uniformly or at random over the territory suitable to them but had congregated into definite groups which I came to call "singing assemblies." The largest of these assemblies that I discovered was made up of seven birds, whose perches were in the pine and oak trees surrounding an irregular open pasture. This group was very much spread out, with the two most distant individuals about 600 feet apart and out of hearing of each other (unless the hummingbirds' ears are sharper than my own); but each member of the assembly could certainly hear the calls of two or more of his neighbors. Another assembly consisted of five birds, scattered among tall raijón bushes that had taken possession of an abandoned pasture, the birds so spaced that each was about 90 to 100 feet from his neighbors. Other assemblies contained three or only two white-ears. Sometimes the birds perched as close as 60 feet from each other. Between these groups of hummingbirds were considerable stretches of similar terrain where one listened in vain for their reiterated notes.

Scattered here and there, however, were lone males, which remained aloof from the assemblies. One of these made his headquarters in a raijón bush beside the road, and here I frequently met him, perched on a dead twig and tinkling persistently. Another, with a weak, plaintive little voice, called from a low perch on a bush in an overgrown pasture, beyond hearing of all others of his kind.

The male white-ears sometimes chose low perches in the midst of a thicket, only 2 or 3 feet above ground, sometimes high, exposed ones, such as the dead twig of a pine tree 40 feet in the air. One bird, which engaged much of my attention, regularly alternated between a perch less than a yard from the ground in a thicket of raijón bushes, and an exposed dead twig in the top of an alder tree growing beside the thicket, fully a dozen times as high. Sometimes a strong wind caused a white-ear whose favorite perch was lofty and exposed to descend to some lower, more protected position close at hand. Whatever the nature of the station he had chosen, the bird was to be found there day after day, week after week, throughout the months of October, November, and December. When I departed the region at the end of the year, a number still sounded their little calls from the very spots where I first encountered them early in September.

Perhaps the most typical note of the male white-eared hummingbird in the singing assembly is a low, clear *tink tink tink*, sounding like the chiming of a small, sweet-toned silver bell. At least this is the note that I first discovered, and the one that I like best to remember. Some individuals toll their little bells very rapidly, others more slowly and deliberately. But as I began to know more and more white-ears, scattered over miles of mountainside, I came to realize that there was a surprising degree of variation in their voices. Many individuals persistently sounded notes so different from the usual clear tinkle that I did not recognize them as the utterances of white-ears until I had laboriously stalked the birds and actually watched them as they called. These notes were dull and flat, with no trace of the clear timbre characteristic of the majority of the species, or else high and squeaky, or low and melancholy. One that I frequently visited uttered rapidly and monotonously a single clicking note, a kind of harsh metallic buzzing almost painful to hear.

These individual differences in voice were surprising enough in themselves, but even more remarkable was the fact that the same type of voice was likely to be common to all the members of a singing assembly. If one bird of a group uttered a clear, silvery tinkle, his neighbors would be found to sing in the same strain; if I happened to be attracted to an assembly by a chirping note, I usually found that this note was common to all the members of the group. There were, of course, exceptions to this rule, but these were not sufficiently numerous to make me doubt its validity. But what is the explanation of this phenomenon? Not impossibly it was the result of imitation, and all the members of an assembly merely copied the vocal peculiarities of one bird that happened to be the first to begin to sing, or in some manner dominated his neighbors by his personality. But I suspect that the real cause was deeper. The individual variations in voice were so great that they seemed to me to result from variations in the structure of the vocal organs. I never heard the white-ear that produced the metallic rattle utter the clear, silvery tinkle, or *vice versa*. More than this, I find it difficult to believe that the same individual was physically capable of producing sounds so distinct. It is not impossible, although the point would be difficult of actual proof, that these peculiarities of voice are inherited, and that the males of the same assembly are somehow related by ties of blood.

Whether a clear dawn revealed the pastures white with frost, or day broke sadly over a world drenched in gray, wind-blown cloud mist, dreary and penetratingly chill, the white-eared hummingbirds always began to sing in the dim light of early dawn. Once the season of song was at its height, neither wind nor rain or cold, driving cloud mist could utterly quench the spirits or extinguish the voices of these tiny hummers. They sang most vigorously early in the morning, and less and less as the day advanced. In the afternoon their song was rather inconstant, for they were far less persevering in their vocal exercises than the violet-ears (*Colibri thalassinus*), one of which made almost as much volume of sound as a whole assembly of white-ears, and continued his chant far more constantly through the day. As he sang the male white-ear tilted upward his coral-red, black-tipped bill and turned his head restlessly from side to side. Sometimes he would interrupt his tinkling to utter a rapid twittering, which ran off into a very low buzz of a most peculiar tone. Perhaps this twittering and buzzing represented his true song, but it was far less melodious than the tinkling of those individuals with the clearest voices and would not bear comparison with the inspired little song of Elliot's hummingbird (*Atthis heloisa*). At intervals he vibrated his wings in the midst of his tinkling, or paused and slowly stretched them. Finally, becoming hungry, he flew off to suck nectar from the flowers, the nearest of which were often at a considerable distance from the singing-perch.

The territorial rights of each white-ear were respected by the others, and as a rule each sounded his little tinkle without much interference from his neighbors. But occasionally one invaded the domain of another, and a vigorous but inconsequential pursuit resulted. Sometimes one settled down close to the perch of a second, and the two sang face to face or side by side for a few moments, until one dashed at the other and both winged rapidly out of sight. Or else the two rose, spiring about each other, high into the air, only to separate without having come to grips or inflicted injury on each other. Then, the momentary flareup over, each would return peaceably to his own post and continue his tireless calling.

The purpose of so much vocal activity on the part of the males is without much doubt to attract the opposite sex. Their season of song coincides roughly with the nesting period of the females. Yet, in spite of many hours of watching, I was not able to determine the behavior of the males when a female approached or to witness actual pairing. The white-ears are so small and withal so shy that they are difficult to keep in sight; on the wing their movements are so swift that it is impossible to distinguish male from female, or even to follow them long with the eye. I saw three or four of these hummingbirds flying together, pursuing and pursued, so frequently that I suspect that they do not honor the rights of their neighbors when a female approaches, as manakins, which form similar assemblies for courtship, almost invariably do.

In January, when the blossoms become less abundant with increasing drought, the white-ears disperse and cease to call. During most of the year they are silent; and one is not likely to notice them unless he watches before a stand of flowers, which they visit for the purpose of sipping the nectar.

Nesting.—In the middle of October 1933, six or seven weeks after the males had selected their posts and begun to sing in a tentative fashion, I found a female just beginning her nest. Later I found a dozen more, which, together with four I had discovered in November 1930, brought the total up to 17; but some were never completed, all were well removed from the singing assemblies of the males, some far away, others just sufficiently distant to be out of hearing of the nearest male—that is, of course, too far away for *me* to hear his voice. With a single exception, all these nests were placed among the slender twigs of the raijón (*Baccharis vaccinioides*), a composite shrub common everywhere on the mountains, at heights varying from 5 to 20 feet above ground. The one nest not in a raijón bush had been built in the crotch of an ascending branch of a bushy *Eupatorium*. The nests were situated in bushy clearings or light, open woodland.

The female white-ear built her nest alone, without the assistance or even the encouragement of one of the males that sang so tirelessly beyond sight and hearing. The raijón bush she chose as its site was never far distant from the oak trees upon which she depended for the downy materials she needed. The leaves of several species, belonging to both the white and black oak groups, are covered on the lower surface with a dense, woolly cloak composed of rather short, crinkled, tawny hairs. This hairy covering is firmly attached to the epidermis and difficult to remove, except in places where a leaf-mining larva has devoured the underlying tissues. By seeking out the spots where the larva has separated the epidermis from the body of the leaf, the hummingbirds materially diminish the labor of gathering the down. But an even greater proportion of the material used in the nests is derived from the woolly insect galls growing on the oak leaves. The color of these galls varies from rusty brown or reddish brown to light buff. Although the dark-colored galls on the upper sides of the leaves are more abundant, the hummingbirds prefer the pale ones, which are found only on the lower sides of the foliage, and neglect, or use very sparingly, those with brownish hairs.

Thus insects, either indirectly, by laying the eggs that stimulate the leaves to produce hairy galls, or directly, by freeing the normal woolly covering from the body of the leaf and making it easy to remove, supply the white-eared hummingbird with practically all the downy stuff for her nest. Spiders, in spinning their webs, furnish her the material necessary to bind the down together and to attach the nest to the supporting twigs. Green mosses and grayish lichens are attached to the exterior for decoration. Some nests are very well covered with these plants, which give the prevailing color to the exterior, while others are so sparingly decorated that much of the down shows through. In form, the nest is roughly a hollow sphere with the upper quarter cut away. The outside diameter of the open cup varies from 1¾ to 2 inches; the height from 1¼ to 2¾ inches. The interior of the cozy little nest is very nearly as broad as deep and measures about an inch in both diameter and depth. The rim is quite noticeably incurved, and this helps to hold the eggs inside when fierce November winds whip the slender branches of the raijón bushes and threaten to roll them out.

Robert T. Moore contributes the following notes on nests of the white-eared hummingbird, found by Chester C. Lamb and himself in Chihuahua and Sinaloa, Mexico: "In his journal Mr. Lamb states that the Laguna Juanota nest was found 'in a small oak, 6 inches in diameter and 25 feet tall, growing in a grove of the same on the north hillside of a rocky butte at the lake.' It was saddled on a twig among the leafy extremities of a branch 2 feet from the trunk. The nest is composed almost entirely of a buff-colored plant down, the only exceptions consisting of one small oak twig woven loosely to the bottom of the nest and greenish gray lichens ornamenting the exterior portion. Measuring 1 by 1⅛ inches on the inside, it has no other lining except the plant down. The outside measurements are 1⅞ by 1½ inches."

He tells of a second nest, twice as large as the above, which resembles it closely, "except that two oak catkins have been woven into the sides and the lichen decorations are more complete."

Then, of a third nest, he says: "Its total bulk is nearly five times that of the first nest and four times that of the second, and yet the internal dimensions are actually less than either, namely 1 by $\frac{11}{16}$ inch. The internal depth, however, is almost twice as great as that of nest No. 1. The external measurements are length 3⅛, width 2¼, and depth 2⅛ inches. Furthermore, the structure of the external part of the nest is almost totally different, being completely swathed with a fine green moss, and having pine needles, dried twigs, and four or five small leaves, as well as a few lichens, woven into the external construction. There is no evidence whatever that this is a double nest.

"It is quite probable that the environment of the nest site had a great deal to do with the type of construction. This moss-covered abode was placed on a small shrub, growing out of rocks 4 feet up from the base of a cliff in a very dark and deep arroyo. In such a place much moss is available, whereas lichens are difficult to find. Three nest sites so dissimilar could hardly have been chosen as these three structures—an oak tree on the very highest point of a wind-blown mountain range, a cliff jutting out on the shore of a wind-protected small lake, and the bottom of a deeply shaded gorge. Dissimilarity of nesting period is also indicated—March, May, and August."

Eggs.—The number of eggs laid by the white-eared hummingbird appears invariably to be two. They are pure white and narrowly oblong. The measurements of six eggs, removed temporarily from their nests in the highlands of Guatemala, average 12.5 by 8.0 millimeters. The eggs showing the four extremes measure **12.7** by 7.9, 12.3 by **8.3**, and **11.9** by **7.9** millimeters.

Young.—Incubation is carried on by the female alone, without ever so much as a visit from one of the males, which continue to sing as if oblivious of all the cares and labor of the other sex. Both of the female white-ears I watched sat deeply in their nests. When perfectly at rest, the eyes were only a trifle above the rim, the sides were entirely protected, the back was invisible to a person slightly below the level of the nest, while the tail and the tips of the longest wing plumes projected beyond the rim at the rear. They were far better protected than the Rieffer's hummingbirds of the warm lowlands, for the nests of these are comparatively broad and shallow, and much of the body of the sitting bird remains on the outside.

The white-eared hummingbirds' mode of entering and leaving their nests demonstrated clearly their lightness and skill upon the wing. Upon returning to their eggs after a recess, heavier birds alight upon the rim of the nest, or even upon a branch at a little distance, and walk or hop into the cup. The white-ears never alighted on the rim but invariably flew directly into the nest and, as they settled neatly over the eggs, folded their wings about them and were at once at rest. Most birds of other families, when they wish to leave the nest, step on the rim before taking flight, but the hummingbirds showed their mastery of the air by making their departure in a more direct manner. Still sitting on the eggs, they spread and vibrated their wings and rose directly into the air, with as little apparent effort as if they were lighter than the atmosphere, and ascended because their hidden moorings had been severed. Frequently they flew upward and backward until they had cleared the nest, then quickly reversed and darted forward and away. When they wished to turn their eggs, they flew backward from the bowl onto the rim, alighted on that portion that had been beneath the tail as they sat, bent down the bill into the cup, and in an instant flew away. Of course, I could not see the eggs or what was done to them, for the nests were above the level of my eyes as I watched; but this is the only significance I can find in the oft-repeated act; and moreover, if the hummingbirds did not turn their eggs on these occasions, they never turned them at all. They never rose up while incubating to adjust their eggs beneath them, as other birds do, doubtless because the length of the bill, coupled with the narrowness of the bowl, would have made this an awkward and difficult performance.

During the morning hours the white-ears devoted much time to seeking down and cobweb and bringing these materials to the nest. The down was deposited inside the cup, the cobweb wiped from the bill to the outer surface; and in addition an occasional lichen was attached there. Since the nests had been completed before the eggs were laid, these additions to its bulk appeared to be made from force of habit rather than from necessity; and it was interesting to find that the new materials were brought chiefly at the time of day when the birds had built most actively. The daily application of fresh cobweb was useful in that it served to prevent the binding of the nest, and its attachment to the supporting twigs, losing their strength with age. During the hours when the gathering of material claimed their attention, the birds spent very brief periods on the eggs, often only a minute and sometimes less; but in the afternoon, when they brought nothing back with them on returning from their recesses, they sometimes sat continuously for 20 or 30 minutes, rarely slightly longer. During the course of an entire day the average period of incubation of one white-ear was 9.7 minutes; her average recess was five minutes. Her separate sessions on the eggs during the forenoon ranged from less than 1 minute to 15 minutes, with an average of 7.4 minutes; her recesses varied from 1 to 10 minutes, with an average of 3.7 minutes. During the afternoon, when she sat more constantly, her sessions varied from 7 to 24 minutes, with an average of 15 minutes, and her recesses were of 2 to 17 minutes' duration. From her first departure in the morning until her final return in the evening, she devoted 7 hours 47 minutes to warming her eggs, while 3 hours 59 minutes were spent away from the nest.

When at length they are hatched, the new-born hummingbirds appear more like black grubs than the nestlings of a feathered creature. Their eyes are completely hidden by the tightly closed lids; the bill is represented by a mere bump; and the line of sparse brown fuzz along the center of the back does little to cover their bareness. They seem very small and very naked to survive the cold blustery days that during November and December are frequent on the higher mountains where they are raised. During the nights they are well protected from exposure, for their downy nests are thick-walled and warm, and their mother fits into the space above them as snugly as a cork in the mouth of a bottle, maintaining the vital spark within her children by means of her own marvelous capacity for heat production. It is during the day that the endurance of the nestlings is put to the most severe test, because they must be left uncovered at intervals while the mother forages for food. If ever nestlings seem to need the ministrations of a father, to help feed them and to warm them while the mother takes her recesses and seeks her food, it is these little hummingbirds; yet no male ever appears to aid in their care, for this is not the custom among hummingbirds. On cruel days when a wind that is half a gale drives the chilling cloud mist through the treetops and whips the limber branches that support the nests, one marvels that such minute creatures, smaller even than a honey bee, can maintain the temperature of their bodies above the death point, even during the few minutes for which they are left exposed while the mother forages. Sometimes, indeed, a tiny hummer only a few days old is found dead in its nest, apparently having succumbed to the inclement weather, in spite of the devoted attention of the mother.

Before the nestlings are large and strong enough to raise up and eject their droppings beyond the rim of the nest, these are removed from the interior by the mother, who, standing on the rim, grasps the particles between the tips of her mandibles and throws them out by sideways jerks of her heard, or else swallows them, and by this means keeps the nest decently clean. When they are slightly older, the young hummers barely manage to deposit their excrement on the rim, and then the parent, less careful than most passerine birds in the sanitation of her nest, no longer takes the trouble to remove it. Finally, with increasing size and strength, the nestlings are able to eject their droppings beyond the rim of the nest and no longer soil it.

When the young hummingbirds are seven or eight days old their pinfeathers begin to sprout. At the age of nine or ten days the eyelids begin to part, and the brown tips of the feathers to peep from the ends of their sheaths. Four days later the green portions of the contour feathers become visible; but still the black skin of the little birds is not entirely covered. They are 16 days old before the wing plumes begin to push from the ends of their sheaths, and 18 days of age before the rectrices escape their horny covering. The nestlings are brooded nightly by their mother until 17 or 18 days old, when they are well clothed with feathers. If frightened, they may fly from the nest at the age of 23 days, but if unmolested they do not depart until their twenty-sixth day. At the time of their departure they fly with strength and ease and never again return to the shelter of the nest. The fledgling white-ears closely resemble their mothers, except that the white postocular line is slightly tinged with buff. It is perhaps significant that these hummingbirds raised during cool and frosty weather in the highlands remain in the nest several days longer than the Rieffer's hummingbirds of the warm lowlands, which quit the nest at the age of 18 to 23 days.

The white-eared hummingbirds may raise two broods in a season. One female, which succeeded in raising a single nestling in her first nest, built a second structure, 40 feet from the first, during the week after her fledgling took wing. She had a busy week, for she satisfied the hunger of the young hummingbird in the intervals of working on the new nest. As a result of her divided attention, the second nest was far less perfect than the first. It was shallower, thinner walled, and carelessly finished; in fact, it seemed scarcely completed when the first egg was laid in it, ten days after the fledgling departed his cradle.

From my tent I watched this hummingbird as she incubated her second set of eggs. Her fledgling, a young male, was now 40 days old and had been out of the nest just two weeks. In size he was scarcely to be distinguished from his mother. His bill seemed slightly shorter, and his back was not such a bright green, because many of the feathers still bore the downy-brown tips which characterize the nestling plumage. He flew very well, and spent much time sucking nectar from the red blossoms of the salvias, which I could watch through the right window of the tent. When not occupied with visiting the flowers, he rested among the low branches of a little bushy thicket about 30 feet from his mother's second nest. Here she came to feed him during her absences from the eggs, in spite of the fact that he could now forage very well for himself. Once, indeed, he visited the flowers while his mother gathered food for him, then came to supplement his meal by what she had to offer. Perching beside him upon a low twig, she delivered the food, as always, by regurgitation, which she began with very violent convulsive movements of the body. He was a well-behaved youngster and never came to pester his mother with demands for food while she warmed her eggs, but always waited patiently for her to come to him. As he waited in his little thicket, he called slowly *tink tink tink*, an utterance that somewhat resembled the calls of the adult males on their singing perches, but was much fainter and weaker.

While she incubated her first set of eggs, the mother found much time for bringing additional cobweb and down to the nest, which was so well finished that it did not appear to require further attention. The hastily built second nest was in far greater need of additional material; but now the hummingbird was too busy with other things to give time to this and brought nothing to the nest during the morning which I passed with her. She was now more attentive to her duties and incubated more steadily; she came to and left the nest only eight times in four hours, as compared with 23 times during the same period of a morning while she incubated her first set of eggs. Even during a seven minutes' recess from the nest, she found time to satisfy her own hunger and to gather food for her fledgling.

It seems to be the unhappy fate of hummingbirds that their nests come to disaster even more frequently than those of other kinds of birds, and the white-ears are no exception to this rule. The nine completed nests I found in Guatemala in 1933 contained two eggs each, making a total of 18. Three of these nests were destroyed in some unknown manner while they still contained eggs, and one was deserted. Only nine eggs hatched. Of the nine nestlings, one succumbed to the cold, two were probably taken by the Indians, and three met unknown ends. Only three lived to leave the nest.

Plumages.—Dr. Frank M. Chapman (1925) writes: "Young females have the crown and upper parts more rusty than the adult, the under-parts buffy white, the sides rusty rather than green. Young males resemble the adult female, but usually have a few metallic blue feathers on the throat or forehead."

Dickey and van Rossem (1938) write of the closely allied race *pygmaea* in El Salvador, where apparently the species breeds in November and December, just as in the neighboring Republic of Guatemala: "A young male taken February 21 has nearly completed the postjuvenal body molt, and the iridescent blue and green feathers are rapidly filling in the chin and throat."

Food.—Like other hummingbirds, the white-ears subsist largely upon the nectar of flowers, which they supplement by minute spiders plucked from their webs and small volitant insects deftly snatched from the air. They seem to have no particular preferences as to the source of their nectar but visit indifferently a great variety of blossoms. At the beginning of their nesting season in the Guatemalan highlands, a bur-marigold (*Bidens refracta*), common in the open oak woods, is one of their principal food plants. With great patience the hummingbird poises on vibrant wings before a yellow flowerhead and rapidly moves its bill from floret to floret, an instant in each, and usually probes many in each head, before flying on to the next. Each tiny floret yields at best a minute quantity of nectar, but there are so many in a flowerhead that in aggregate they must supply a considerable amount. Later in the season, various species of *Salvia*, in particular the red *Salvia cinnabarina*, yield an abundance of nectar, which is secreted as a single large drop at the base of the corolla tube, and so is far more conveniently sipped than the sweet secretions of the bur-marigold heads, divided among a multitude of separate florets. Though usually the white-ear reaches the nectar through the throat of the corolla, once I watched an eccentric individual puncture the side of the tube of the lovely blue flowers of *Salvia cacalioefolia*, easily pushing his sharp bill through the delicate tissue of the corolla.

Behavior.—In April 1938, in southeastern Sinaloa, Mr. Moore observed four species of hummingbirds "feeding from the flowers of one large shrub at an altitude of about 6,000 feet. Approaching the proportions of a tree, this remarkable shrub, 20 feet in height and of the same width, was completely covered with globelike clusters of grayish-lavender blooms. At no time from sunrise to sunset were there less than four hummingbirds in this tree. Often there were as many as 20 of four different species, white-eared, broad-tailed, calliope, and Margaret's hummingbirds. The white-ears, like irascible knights of the air, were always ready to thrust lance at an assumed affront. It made no difference whether it was the tiny Margaret's or the larger broad-tailed, some white-ear would dive viciously at any intruder that dared to approach too close. The broad-tailed hummingbird, heavier and more powerful, would dart into the tree with direct flight and pompous hum, but his assurance would be quickly dispelled. A male white-ear would immediately launch an assault and drive the larger bird up the mountainside in ignominious retreat.

"The same dominance was exhibited on several afternoons in May 1937, when I visited the mammoth paintbrush beds on the slopes of Mount Mohinora at the 10,000-foot level. Here the white-ears outnumbered all the broad-billed, blue-throated, and Rivoli's together. In one of these astounding fields of color, perhaps 100 yards long and 100 feet wide, a dozen white-ears were feeding at one time. If one of the other larger species dived into the flower masses, even if at a point far removed from the nearest white-ear, one of the latter would immediately whirl to the attack and drive the Rivoli's and blue-throated hummingbirds, twice their size, into headlong flight.

During the drowsy hours of midday the white-ears would cease feeding and rest quietly at various points among the oak trees, generally choosing some spot in the shade. Should a blue-throated or Rivoli's choose this propitious moment to glide quietly into the flowerbeds, the nearest white-ear would come to life and volplane down in a surprise attack. Not once out of many hundred times did I observe any of these three other species attempt to resist. It might seek some other point in the large mass of flowers, but the white-ear invariably pursued until the other bird had left the food area.

"The wing action of the white-eared hummingbird I compared with that of the calliope and the other species at Rancho Batel in 1936. Its wings beat more slowly, so that when poising in front of a flower they are not an indistinguishable blur, as in the case of the calliope, but there is a slightly visible wing stroke. Possibly because of this slower wing stroke, as well as the heavier, longer body, the rear end of the bird gradully drops as it continues to poise in front of the flower. If it feeds continuously from one cluster of small blooms, a curious rhythmic, but irregular motion of the tail up and down is created. At first the tail is horizontal and in the same plane with the body. When the tail begins to drop, the bird, in order to compensate for the increasing lack of balance, forcibly lifts it into the air. Timing these vertical beats, I found they averaged three to the second. At first I thought this downward and alternate upward sweep of the tail was for the purpose of moving the bird from one flower to another, but this was not the case. I never observed the calliope or Margaret's hummingbird doing this."

He says that, in spite of its pugnacious behavior, the white-eared hummingbird is the shiest of the four species mentioned above; and refers to its voice as "exceedingly high-pitched and sharply staccato."

DISTRIBUTION

Range.—Central America; casual in southeastern Arizona; not regularly migratory.

The range of the white-eared hummingbird extends **north** to central Sonora (Oposura); northern Chihuahua (Carmen); and northern Tamaulipas (Bravo). **East** to Tamaulipas (Bravo and Golindo); Veracruz (Jalapa and Orizaba); Honduras (San Juancito); and Nicaragua (Jinotego). **South** to Nicaragua (Jinotego and Matagalpa); Oaxaca (Totontepec and Villa Alta); and Guerrero (Amula and Chilpancingo). **West** to Guerrero (Chilpancingo and Taxco); State of Mexico (Coatepec and Jalapa); Durango (Durango); western Chihuahua (Jesus Maria and Pinos Altos); and Sonora (Oposura).

This range is occupied chiefly by the typical race, *H. l. leucotis*, but according to some systematists those in the north (which include the individuals noted casually in Arizona) are a distinct race to which the name *H. l. borealis* has been given. The birds found in Nicaragua also have been recognized as a distinct subspecies.

Casual records.—The species has been recorded a number of times from southeastern Arizona as follows: The first United States specimen was collected on June 9, 1894, at Fly Park, in the Chiricahua Mountains; one was taken in the Santa Rita Mountains on June 24, 1903; in 1915 a specimen was taken in the Santa Catalina Mountains; during the period from June 10 to December 31, 1919, 12 specimens were obtained in the Huachuca Mountains; and on August 11, 1933, an adult male was captured in Miller Canyon, of the Huachucas.

Egg dates.—Chihuahua and Sinaloa: March 26, May 23 and August 12 (Moore).

Guatemala: Sierra de Tecpán, Department of Chimaltenango, west-central Guatemala, 8,000–9,000 feet: 12 records, November and December. In 1933, nest building began about the middle of October. The earliest date of laying for which there is a record (computed from date of hatching) is about October 23; the latest, December 22 (Skutch).

CYNANTHUS LATIROSTRIS Swainson

BROAD-BILLED HUMMINGBIRD

HABITS

Robert T. Moore has kindly lent me a portion of his unpublished manuscript on the life habits of the birds of Sinaloa, and, with his permission, I am quoting from it most of what follows in the account of this species. As to the subspecific status of our form of the broadbilled hummingbird, he writes: "The comparison of our large series of 31 males and 24 females from northwestern Mexico, with 9 males and 3 females in the Moore collection, as well as others, from east-central Mexico, has convinced me that the northwestern birds, originally given the name of *magica* by Mulsant and Verreaux, should be differentiated on the basis of darker-green posterior underparts, whiter under tail coverts, and definitely smaller size. The Arizona form resembles this northwestern Mexican bird, rather than the eastern."

As to his personal experience with it in the field, he says: "My first acquaintance with the broad-billed hummingbird was made at the base of the great Butte, at Peña Blanca Spring, southern Arizona. A large group of ocotillos fringed the eastern ledges below the cliff, their red pennants providing an irresistible attraction. The birds did not seem to be interested in any other flowers. My real knowledge of the habits of this hummingbird has been acquired in the States of Sonora, Sinaloa, and Chihuahua, of northwestern Mexico.

"Our four nests have been found at altitudes from 45 feet at Culiacan, Sinaloa, to 1,450 feet at Guirocoba, Sonora. Specimens have been collected at the highest elevations—Palo Verdes Mines, 4,900 feet; on the Urique River, Chihuahua, taken by myself, 5,000 feet; and even on Mount Mohinora at nearly 10,000 feet—but no nests have been secured at these altitudes. Although I observed both sexes repeatedly during May on Mohinora, feeding within a few feet of me among the flowers in extraordinary mammoth beds of paintbrush, they showed no indications of breeding."

Courtship.—Mrs. Bailey (1928) refers to this briefly, as follows: "The courtship 'pendulum swing back and forth in front of a female,' when given by the Broad-bill, Mr. Willard says is 'higher pitched than that of any of the other small hummers,' having 'the *zing* of a rifle bullet' (MS.). It is of peculiar interest to hear from Mr. O. W. Howard that while in Arizona he saw several of the male Broad-bills in the vicinity of their completed nests."

Nesting.—Mr. Moore's (MS.) remarks on nesting follow: "The finding of my first nest at the Guirocoba Ranch, Sonora, was a welcome goad to a brain completely fagged by the terrific heat. The tropical sun was desiccating a tiny arroyo with relentless power. A female propelled its tiny atom of a body straight to a nest on the branch of a small tree, overhanging the bank of the arroyo and not 5 feet from the ground. It was an unusual demonstration of courage and confidence in human beings, for the nest on May 2, 1934, contained no eggs, being only half finished. I have known many ruby-throated hummingbirds to desert an unfinished home, if one climbed the nest tree, and never in my experience with some dozen of them has a single male or female protected an eggless nest, as this tiny parent did repeatedly during the next few days.

"When it came to the more arduous operation of nest building, involving the carrying of material and weaving instead of resting, she preferred the cooler hours of the day from 3:30 until dark, and did a prodigious amount of work. A red letter day of accomplishment was May 2. At 5:30 p. m. the nest had attained one half its final height, but at 9 o'clock the next morning the complete altitude of the walls had been erected. As the nest, now before me, is approximately 1 inch high on the outside, the above statement means that the bird built half an inch of wall material during the late afternoon and early morning hours. In addition, she added the lining and attached a considerable number of white cobweb strands, completely swathing the bottom of the nest with them and supporting and connecting its outer rim to the leaves and tiny branchlets in the vicinity. However, free access to the nest was not obstructed.

"The most interesting nest-building technique was displayed a number of times when I was within a few feet of the nest. The bird molded the bottom of it with quivering, caressing motions of the body. Often in the process the wings revolved at almost full velocity, certainly until they were blurred to sight, and yet the body of the bird appeared to be sitting in the nest throughout the action. I saw it performed a number of times; sometimes it gave the impression of a swaying motion, from one side to the other, without the body leaving the nest, or the wings ceasing to revolve. When the wings did not revolve, the bill moved rapidly along the outside of the abode, tucking in protruding ends of grasses.

"The bulk of the nest is composed of exceedingly fine material, mostly tiny shreds of buff-colored or brownish bark, grasses, and bits of dried leaves. The only larger pieces are three strips of bark placed upright, parallel with the tiny twig on which the nest is placed. I imagine these came from the sabino, a cypress that grows to a great height along a small stream not far away. Part of the inside of the nest is lined with a white material, probably some kind of minute plant down, but possibly cotton of fine texture. All these materials could be obtained from the fields nearby, which are cultivated by the Indians of the Guirocoba Plantation.

"Three other nests were secured by our expedition in Sinaloa, two of them in March at Culiacan and one on January 16, 1936, at San Lorenzo, Sinaloa. Examination of the sex organs of our numerous specimens proves that the birds are apt to breed at any time from January to August.

"As these last three nests contain two eggs each, it can be presumed that they are finished creations, although some hummingbirds attach ornamental bits of lichen to the exterior, even during the period of incubation. Not the slightest indication of this appears in any of these four nests. The January nest was taken at San Lorenzo by Chester C. Lamb, which differs somewhat from the other three. Like the March 1 nest, it was attached to the stalk of a vine. Placed 4 feet up in an espino tree, the body of the nest is composed almost entirely of cotton, but lined with a glossy-white plant down. The base is supported by a dried pod of the vine itself. On the outside are attached pieces of dried leaves and, according to Mr. Lamb, some 'short fibers of the palo-blanco pods.' The entire exterior is bound together with spiderwebs. The March 1 and March 7 nests from Culiacan display a lining of white plant down, covered on the periphery with bits of bark and leaves, but the bodies of the nests seem to be made of grasses and exceedingly fine, threadlike stalks of dried plants. The March 1 nest was placed in a 'dry bush, covered with dry vines' and the March 7 in an espino tree.

"In spite of these minor differences, these abodes are so similar that I think I could recognize them at random among a large number of other hummingbird nests. They all have some grass stalks in the body, are lined with white plant down, are all adorned with bits of leaves and bark on the outside, and not one of them has a single lichen on any part of the nest. In addition, they are all very small, with an inside diameter of only about three-quarters of an inch, and all were placed within 5 feet of the ground. They differ markedly from our nests of other hummingbirds of Sinaloa, such as the white-ear, azurecrown, and the violaceous, all these having lichen adornments. The eggs are white, two in number, and at least in the case of the San Lorenzo nest, were laid two days apart."

Roy W. Quillin (1935) records the finding of a nest of the broad-billed hummingbird in Texas, the only nest so far reported for that State:

"A nest of this species containing two eggs was found on May 17, 1934, at Talley's (Johnson's) Ranch, on the Rio Grande, southwest of Mariscal Mountain, Brewster County, Texas. The nest was on the very bank of the Rio Grande, on a drooping twig in a triple fork of a small willow tree some ten or twelve feet above the ground on a steep bank of the river and almost overhung the water. The nest was composed almost entirely of the down of the willows ornamented on the outside with yellow blooms and tiny mesquite leaves and bound with spider or insect webs. The materials of the nest lashed it firmly to the twigs on which it rested in an upright fork."

My acquaintance with the broad-billed hummingbird was a brief one in Sabino Canyon, at the southern end of the Santa Catalina Mountains, Ariz. In the rough, rocky bed of the stream flowing through this rugged canyon, Frank Willard and I made a long and laborious search for the nests of this hummingbird. It has been found nesting here in a species of shrub that grows profusely along the rough banks of the stream and among the rocks in its bed. Two or three of the birds dashed by us at different times, in such rapid flight that it seemed as if a whistling bullet had whizzed past us; but we did not succeed in finding a nest; it was in April, and we were perhaps too early. Mr. Willard had previously found a nest here, 5 feet up in a small willow over the water; he told me that O. W. Howard had also found it nesting here. There is a nest from this locality in the P. B. Philipp collection, taken by H. H. Kimball on April 20, 1923, that was placed "in a hackberry bush growing against a small sycamore at the edge of a creek, 4 feet from the water."

There are three nests in the Thayer collection, taken by W. W. Brown, Jr., near Opodepe, Sonora, Mexico, on May 3, 10, and 13, 1905; one of these was in an apricot tree and the other two in mesquites; the construction of these nests compares very closely with the excellent description given above by Mr. Moore.

Eggs.—Two eggs seem to be the usual, if not the invariable, rule with the broad-billed hummingbird. These are pure white, without gloss, and otherwise indistinguishable from the eggs of other hummingbirds of similar size. The measurements of 27 eggs average 12.6 by 8.5 millimeters; the eggs showing the four extremes measure 13.5 by 9.7, 13.4 by 9.8, and 11.5 by 7.5 millimeters.

Plumages.—Mr. Moore says (MS.) : "The Moore collection contains no young, actually taken from a nest, but a young male, obviously not long out of the nest, was secured at the Guirocoba Ranch in extreme southeastern Sonora on March 26, 1931. The bill is only half the length of the adult, the tail the same, and the wings two-thirds, the postnatal molt being about four-fifths complete on wings, tail, entire upper parts, under tail coverts, and portions of the neck. Possessing very loose margins, the remiges are recurved. Two nearly parallel feather tracts on the throat are sharply defined, because the new feathers are still in their sheaths, and areas on throat and breast are bare.

"As to coloration, it is significant that the tail plainly shows the male characteristics, being almost identically like the fully adult male tail in miniature, revealing no white tips to the lateral rectrices as in the female and having the median pair blue, tipped with gray, instead of entirely bronzy green. The longest upper tail coverts show full development and might easily be mistaken for the median pair of rectrices. Therefore, it is clear that the sexes can be differentiated in this species, even in the juvenal plumage, when a few weeks old. Cinnamon-buff covers a large part of crown and occiput and reveals much wider margins on the back than in the May, June, and September worn juvenal plumage. The lesser and middle wing coverts show irridescent green, instead of bronzy.

"On the under tail coverts, although the plumage is looser than in the first winter plumage, the general appearance is immaculate white, as in practically all adult *magicus*, contrasting them sharply with *Cynanthus latirostris*. So many spots on the underparts are not feathered that, except for the under tail coverts, they are blotched with black and light buff.

"The most interesting peculiarity consists in a prominent white postocular streak. This is represented by a narrow streak, half the length, in the adult female and juvenile male of first winter plumage, which is reduced to dot or is obsolete in the adult male. This streak consists of nonpennaceous feathers, very loose in texture, as in the juvenile male, and contracts with the typical feathers of the adult female.

"Five representatives of juvenile males in their first winter plumage form part of the Moore collection. They resemble the female coloration, except that the feathers of the upper parts are margined with buffy, much more narrowly than in the juvenal plumage, and the rectrices are exactly like the adult males. A female, from Los Leones, Sinaloa, March 22, 1934, which has acquired the complete juvenal plumage, has feathers of upper parts margined just as broadly with cinnamon-buff, as the young male in partial juvenal plumage, but differs in having a fully developed tail, just like the adult females. Consequently, the differences of the sexes can be determined in every plumage."

Young males begin to acquire some of the bluish-green feathers in the throat patch early in their first year but, apparently, do not acquire the full bluish-green gorget and the metallic bronze-green of the breast and sides until the first annual molt the next summer, when old and young become indistinguishable.

Food.—The broad-billed hummingbird evidently lives on similar food to that of other members of the family, the nectar of flowers and the minute insects that the flowers attract. Mr. Moore (MS.) mentions the red flowers of the ocotillo as attracting it and seeing it feeding in the beds of the paint brush, but probably any brightly colored blossoms would serve equally well as feeding places. He says: "A small shrub, the 'tavachin,' flaunts an extraordinary flower, resembling the royal poinciana, and fairly startles one with its scarlet glory. Belonging to the genus *Caesalpinia* or *Poinciana*, it provides the favorite rendezvous for *Cynanthus*, as well as many species of butterflies. The tiny homesteader made many excursions to obtain food from this plant, whose vivid red and yellow flowers flamed in the sunlit spaces across the sandy arroyo. She apportioned part of her time to the yellow flowers of a huge opuntia, which hung out perilously over her side of the arroyo. During the hottest period of the day she drowsed on a branch of the nesting tree, within 10 feet of the nest, not usually making food rounds until 3:30 in the afternoon. Between each round she would spend several minutes resting in the nest tree. At the beginning of each circuit I timed the average of inception, which was approximately 15 minutes, and each time she visited apparently every flower over again. A few less conspicuous blooms were also probed."

Cottam and Knappen (1939) examined four stomachs collected in Arizona, which "show that the bird feeds primarily on small insects and spiders." In their summary they mention fragments of plant lice, leafhoppers, jumping plant lice, miscellaneous bugs, root gnats, flower flies, miscellaneous flies including dance flies, ants, parasitic wasps, miscellaneous Hymenoptera, some undertermined insects, spiders, daddy-longlegs, and pollen grains.

Behavior.—Referring to the behavior of the female in the defense of her eggless nest, an unusual occurrence among hummingbirds, Mr. Moore (MS.) writes: "It is true that her little majesty was never real rude about it, for when I set up my camera without camouflage this bit of animated lightning betrayed no resentment, flew straight to the nest, twirled about on it two or three times, and showed no irritation because of the huge eye of the graflex. Curiously enough, the only time she really attacked was when I photographed her with moving picture camera 20 yards from the nest, as she fed from the scarlet flowers of the 'tavachin.' A formal visit to her home seemed perfectly proper, but an intrusion at the dinner hour was the epitome of rudeness. Even then the attack was only half-hearted, and chronic good nature took possession immediately, as she whirled from one brilliant flower to another.

"A male broadbill was observed feeding from the 'tavachin' and, although he several times flew within 10 feet of the nest tree, he never landed on it, nor did the female appear to object to his feeding 20 feet away across the sandy wash. The broadbill is a common bird of the region and the male bird might not have been the 'mate'. Although the males of United States hummingbirds do not make a practice of assisting about the nest, southern species often do. In Ecuador I have observed the male as well as the female violet-ear take turns incubating the same nest. Both individuals were collected to prove this habit.

"Such evidences of anger as the female exhibited were directed not so much at me as at the large blue swallowtail that insisted on appropriating the sweets from her flower garden. Several times she, as well as the male, chased it away, but they did not attempt to pursue the smaller butterflies. The flight of this bird from flower to flower is so characteristic that it can be recognized at some distance. Instead of darting straight to its object, as many hummingbirds do, *Cynanthus* progresses with a somewhat jerky, irregular flight. At least its short flight has an exceedingly nervous kind of movement, the tail bobbing up and down, lacking the precision of the Rivoli's undeviating course."

Dr. Alexander Wetmore (1932) says: "The broad-bill seems quieter and less active than some of the species that have been described, and frequently, after aggressive flight in pursuit of some intruder, I have seen the two combatants perch four or five inches from one another for a few seconds, while with raised wings they gave a low, chattering call." He also refers to the ordinary flight as "accompanied by a subdued humming sound." The sound produced by this bird in flight, as I have heard it, is more like the shriek of a passing bullet, far from subdued.

Field marks.—The most conspicuous and diagnostic field mark of the broad-billed hummingbird is the broad, purplish-red or carmine bill; the bill of the adult male is wholly red, except for the dusky tip; that of the young male and the female is basally red. The color pattern of the adult male is distinctive, green upper parts and breast, bluish-green throat, white posterior under parts, and glossy blue-black tail. The female, adult or young, has a grayish breast and some green in the tail. The young male has a tail like his father, and the young female one like her mother.

DISTRIBUTION

Range.—Southern Arizona, south to central Mexico.

Breeding range.—The broad-billed hummingbird breeds **north** to southeastern Arizona (Santa Catalina Mountains and Sabino Canyon); probably rarely southwestern New Mexico (Cloverdale Range); and central Nuevo Leon (Monterey). **East** to western Nuevo Leon (Monterey); and the State of Mexico (Chimalcoyoc). **South** to the State of Mexico (Chimalcoyoc); Jalisco (Lake Chapala); and southern Sinaloa (Escuinapa). **West** to Sinaloa (Escuinapa); Sonora (Tesia, San Javier, Moctezuma, and Saric); and southeastern Arizona (Santa Rita Mountains, probably Fresnal Canyon, and Santa Catalina Mountains).

Winter range.—The species appears to be resident throughout the Mexican portion of the range, although at this season it has been recorded south to Taxco, State of Guerrero. It withdraws entirely from the United States but winters north to central Sonora (Guaymas and Oposura).

Migration.—Little information is available concerning the short migratory flights that are made but early dates of arrival in Arizona are: Rillito Creek, near Tucson, March 13, and Santa Catalina Mountains, April 5. It leaves this region during the last of August and early part of September.

Egg dates.—Mexico: 16 records, January 16 to May 21; 8 records, March 25 to May 11, indicating the height of the season.

Arizona: 5 records, April 14 to July 15.

LITERATURE CITED

ABBOTT, CLINTON GILBERT.
    1914. City nighthawks. Bird-Lore, vol. 16, pp. 10–13.
AIKEN, CHARLES EDWARD HOWARD, and WARREN, EDWARD ROYAL.
    1914. The birds of El Paso County, Colorado. II. Colorado Coll. Publ.,
        sci. ser., vol. 12, pp. 497–603.
ALDRICH, ELMER C.
    1935. Nesting of the dusky poor-will. Condor, vol. 37, pp. 49–55.
ALLARD, HARRY ARDELL.
    1934. Speed of the ruby-throated hummingbird's flight. Auk, vol. 51, p. 84.
ALLEN, ARTHUR AUGUSTUS.
    1930. Rubythroat. Bird-Lore, vol. 32, pp. 223–231.
    1933. The nighthawk's story. Bird-Lore, vol. 35, pp. 171–179.
ALLEN, CHARLES ANDREW.
    1880. Habits of Vaux's swift. Bull. Nuttall Orn. Club, vol. 5, pp. 55–56.
ALLEN, JOEL ASAPH.
    1871. On the mammals and winter birds of east Florida, with an examina-
        tion of certain assumed specific characters in birds, and a sketch
        of the bird-faunae of eastern North America. Bull. Mus. Comp.
        Zool., vol. 2, pp. 161–426.
ALLEN, MARY PIERSON.
    1908. Hummingbird eccentricities. Bird-Lore, vol. 10, pp. 198–200.
ALLEN, W. E.
    1932. Note on food of California roadrunner (Geococcyx californianus).
        Bird-Lore, vol. 34, pp. 264–265.
AMERICAN ORNITHOLOGISTS' UNION.
    1910. Check-list of North American birds. Ed. 3.
    1931. Check-list of North American birds. Ed. 4.
ANTHONY, ALFRED WEBSTER.
    1892. Birds of southwestern New Mexico. Auk, vol. 9, pp. 357–369.
    1896. The roadrunner as a rat-killer. Auk, vol. 13, pp. 257–258.
    1897. Habits of Anna's hummingbird. Nidologist, vol. 4, pp. 31–33.
    1923. Ants destructive to bird life. Condor, vol. 25, pp. 132–133.
"ARKANSAS HOOSIER."
    1890. The Caprimulgidae in Arkansas. Oologist, vol. 7, pp. 155–156.
ARNOLD, LEROY W.
    1930. Observations upon hummingbirds. Condor, vol. 32, pp. 302–303.
ATTWATER, HENRY PHILEMON.
    1892. List of birds observed in the vicinity of San Antonio, Bexar County,
        Texas. Auk, vol. 9, pp. 229–238.
AUDUBON, JOHN JAMES.
    1840. The birds of America, vol. 1.
    1842. The birds of America, vol. 4.

BAILEY, ALFRED MARSHALL.
   1927. Notes on the birds of southeastern Alaska. Auk, vol. 44, pp. 351–367.
BAILEY, FLORENCE AUGUSTA MERRIAM.
   1896. Notes on some of the birds of southern California. Auk, vol. 13, pp. 115–124.
   1902. Handbook of birds of the Western United States.
   1904. Additional notes on the birds of the Upper Pecos. Auk, vol. 21, pp. 349–363.
   1907. White-throated swifts at Capistrano. Condor, vol. 9, pp. 169–172.
   1922. Koo. Bird-Lore, vol. 24, pp. 260–265.
   1923. Birds recorded from the Santa Rita Mountains in southern Arizona. Pacific Coast Avifauna, No. 15.
   1928. Birds of New Mexico.
BAILEY, GUY ANDREW.
   1905. The chimney swift. Bird-Lore, vol. 7, pp. 130–132.
BAILEY, HAROLD HARRIS.
   1907. Mortality among kingfishers. Auk, vol. 24, p. 439.
   1913. The birds of Virginia.
BAILEY, HARRY BALCH.
   1883. Memoranda of a collection of eggs from Georgia. Bull. Nuttall Orn. Club, vol. 8, pp. 37–43.
BAILEY, WILLIAM LLOYD.
   1900. The kingfishers' home life. Bird-Lore, vol. 2, pp. 76–80.
BAIRD, SPENCER FULLERTON.
   1858. Reports of explorations and surveys to ascertain the most practicable and economical route for a railroad from the Mississippi River to the Pacific Ocean, part 2. Birds. Vol. 9.
BANCROFT, GRIFFING.
   1930. The breeding birds of central Lower California. Condor, vol. 32, pp. 20–49.
BANGS, OUTRAM.
   1913. An unnamed race of the Carolina paroquet. Proc. New England Zool. Club, vol. 4, pp. 93–94.
BANGS, OUTRAM, and PENARD, THOMAS EDWARD.
   1921. Notes on some American birds, chiefly neotropical. Bull. Mus. Comp. Zool., vol. 64, pp. 365–397.
BANGS, OUTRAM, and PETERS, JAMES LEE.
   1928. Birds collected by Dr. Joseph F. Rock in western Kansu and eastern Tibet. Bull. Mus. Comp. Zool., vol. 68, pp. 313–381.
BARBOUR, THOMAS.
   1923. The birds of Cuba.
BARROWS, WALTER BRADFORD.
   1912. Michigan bird life.
BARTRAM, BENJAMIN SMITH.
   1799. Fragments of the natural history of Pennsylvania.
BASSETT, FRANK NEWTON.
   1921. The nuptial flight of the Allen hummingbird. Condor, vol. 23, p. 37.
   1924. The Anna hummingbird takes a shower bath. Condor, vol. 26, p. 227.
BATCHELDER, CHARLES FOSTER.
   1882. Notes on the summer birds of the upper St. John. Bull. Nuttall Orn. Club, vol. 7, pp. 147–152.
BAYNES, ERNEST HAROLD.
   1915. Wild bird guests.

BEAL, FOSTER ELLENBOROUGH LASCELLES.

1897. Some common birds in their relation to agriculture. U. S. Dept. Agr. Farmers' Bull. 54.

1915. Some common birds useful to the farmer. U. S. Dept. Agr. Farmers' Bull. 630.

BEAL, FOSTER ELLENBOROUGH LASCELLES, and McATEE, WALDO LEE.

1912. Food of some well-known birds of forest, farm, and garden. U. S. Dept. Agr. Farmers' Bull. 506.

BEAL, FOSTER ELLENBOROUGH LASCELLES ; McATEE, WALDO LEE ; and KALMBACH, EDWIN RICHARD.

1916. Common birds of Southeastern United States in relation to agriculture. U. S. Dept. Agr. Farmers' Bull. 755.

BEAL, MARY.

1933. The black-chinned hummingbird. Bird-Lore, vol. 35, pp. 96–97.

BECK, ROLLO HOWARD.

1897. Watching a poor-will. Nidologist, vol. 4, p. 105.

BEEBE, CHARLES WILLIAM.

1905. Two bird-lovers in Mexico.

BELDING, LYMAN.

1883. Catalogue of a collection of birds made near the southern extremity of the peninsula of Lower California. Proc. U. S. Nat. Mus., vol. 5, pp. 532–550.

BENDIRE, CHARLES EMIL.

1895. Life histories of North American birds. U. S. Nat. Mus. Spec. Bull. 3.

BERGTOLD, WILLIAM HARRY.

1906. Concerning the thick-billed parrot. Auk. vol. 23, pp. 425–428.

BEYER, GEORGE EUGENE ; ALLISON, ANDREW ; and KOPMAN, HENRY HAZLITT.

1908. List of the birds of Louisiana, pt. 5. Auk, vol. 25, pp. 439–448.

BISHOP, LOUIS BENNETT.

1896. Description of a new horned lark and a new song sparrow, with remarks on Sennett's nighthawk. Auk, vol. 13, pp. 129–135.

1906. *Uranomitra salvini* in Arizona. Auk, vol. 23, pp. 337–338.

BLAKISTON, THOMAS WRIGHT, and PRYER, HENRY JAMES STOVIN.

1878. A catalogue of the birds of Japan. Ibis, 1878, pp. 209–250.

BOLLES, FRANK.

1894. From Blomidon to Smoky.

1912. Notes on whip-poor-wills and owls. Auk, vol. 29, pp. 150–159.

BOWLES, JOHN HOOPER.

1895. Further notes on Antrostomus vociferous whip-poor-will. The Museum, vol. 1, pp. 152–153.

1910. The Anna hummingbird. Condor, vol. 12, pp. 125–127.

1921. Nesting habits of nighthawks at Tacoma, Wash. Auk, vol. 38, pp. 203–217.

BRADBURY, WILLIAM CHASE.

1918. Notes on the nesting habits of the white-throated swift in Colorado. Condor, vol. 20, pp. 103–110.

BRALLIAR, FLOYD.

1922. Knowing birds through stories.

BREWER, THOMAS MAYO.

1874. A history of North American birds. Land birds. By Baird, Brewer, and Ridgway. Vol. 2.

BREWSTER, WILLIAM.

1879. On the habits and nesting of certain birds in Texas. Bull. Nuttall Orn. Club, vol. 4, pp. 75–80.

1881. Notes on some birds from Arizona and New Mexico, with a description of a supposed new whip-poor-will. Bull. Nuttall Orn. Club, vol. 6, pp. 65–73.

1882. On a collection of birds lately made by Mr. F. Stephens in Arizona. Bull. Nuttall Orn. Club, vol. 7, pp. 193–212.

1889. Nesting habits of the parrakeet (*Conurus carolinensis*). Auk, vol. 6, pp. 336–337.

1890. Food of young hummingbirds. Auk, vol. 7, pp. 206–207.

1893. Description of a new hummingbird from northern Mexico. Auk, vol. 10, pp. 214–215.

1895. The land-birds and game-birds of New England, by H. D. Minot. Ed. 2.

1902. Birds of the Cape region of Lower California. Bull. Mus. Comp. Zool., vol. 41, pp. 1–241.

1906. The birds of the Cambridge region of Massachusetts.

1937a. The birds of the Lake Umbagog region of Maine, part 3.

1937b. Concord River.

BRYANT, HAROLD CHILD.

1916. Habits and food of the roadrunner in California. Univ. California Publ. Zool., vol. 17, pp. 21–58.

1925. Nesting of the Allen hummingbird in Golden Gate Park. Condor, vol. 27, pp. 98–100.

BULLOCK, WILLIAM.

1825. Six months residence and travels in Mexico . . ., ed. 2. Vol. 2.

BURMEISTER, HERMAN.

1856. Thiere Brasiliens. Vol. 1.

BURNS, FRANKLIN LORENZO.

1915. Comparative periods of deposition and incubation of some North American birds. Wilson Bull., vol. 27, pp. 275–286.

1921. Comparative periods of nestling life of some North American Nidicolae. Wilson Bull., vol. 33, pp. 4–15.

BURROUGHS, JULIAN.

1922. A chimney swift invasion. Bird-Lore, vol. 24, pp. 210–211.

BUTLER, AMOS WILLIAM.

1892. Notes on the range and habits of the Carolina parrakeet. Auk, vol. 9, pp. 49–56.

1898. The birds of Indiana.

CAMERON, EWEN SOMERLED.

1907. The birds of Custer and Dawson Counties, Montana. Auk, vol. 24, pp. 289–406.

CAMPBELL, ARCHIBALD JAMES.

1901. Nests and eggs of Australian birds.

CAMPBELL, E. K. and D.

1926. Roosting swifts. Bird-Lore, vol. 28, pp. 395–396.

CANFIELD, JOSEPH BUCKINGHAM.

1902. A note on the night hawk. Amer. Orn., vol. 2, p. 217.

CAREY, HENRY REGINALD.

1909. Remarks on the habits of the kingfisher on the New Hampshire seacoast. Bird-Lore, vol. 11, pp. 161–164.

CARPENTER, FREDERIC HOWARD.
1886. Some ornithological explorations in the Dead River region of Maine. Ornithologist and Oologist, vol. 11, pp. 161–163.
CARTER, THOMAS DONALD.
1924. Nesting of chimney swifts. Bird-Lore, vol. 26, p. 330.
CASSIN, JOHN.
1862. Illustrations of the birds of California, Texas, Oregon, British and Russian America.
CHAMBERS, WILLIE LEE.
1901. Curious nest of Anna's hummingbird. Condor, vol. 3, p. 105.
1903. Early nesting of *Calypte anna* in the vicinity of Santa Monica, California. Condor, vol. 5, p. 133.
CHANCE, EDGAR.
1922. The cuckoo's secret.
CHANEY, RALPH WORKS.
1910. Summer and fall birds of the Hamlin Lake region, Mason County, Mich. Auk, vol. 27, pp. 271–279.
CHAPMAN, FRANK MICHLER.
1888. A list of birds observed at Gainesville, Florida. Auk, vol. 5, pp. 267–277.
1890. Notes on the Carolina paroquet (*Conurus carolinensis*) in Florida. Abstr. Proc. Linn. Soc. New York, year ending March 7, 1890, pp. 4–6.
1896. Notes on birds observed in Yucatan. Bull. Amer. Mus. Nat. Hist., vol. 8, pp. 271–290.
1912. Handbook of birds of eastern North America.
1915. The Carolina paroquet in Florida. Bird-Lore, vol. 17, p. 453.
1925. Notes on the plumages of North American birds. Bird-Lore, vol. 27, pp. 104, 327.
1931. The winter range of the chimney swift (*Chaetura pelagica*). Auk, vol. 48, pp. 119–121.
CHENEY, SIMEON PEASE.
1891. Some bird songs. Auk, vol. 8, pp. 32–37.
CHERRIE, GEORGE KRUCK.
1892. A preliminary list of the birds of San José, Costa Rica. Auk, vol. 9, pp. 322–329.
1896. An apparently new *Chordeiles* from Costa Rica. Auk, vol. 13, pp. 135–136.
CHILDS, JOHN LEWIS.
1905. Eggs of the Carolina paroquet. Warbler, vol. 1, pp. 97–98.
1906a. Nest and eggs of the blue-throated hummingbird. Warbler, vol. 2, p. 65.
1906b. Eggs of the Carolina paroquet. Warbler, vol. 2, p. 65.
CHRISTY, BAYARD HENDERSON.
1932. A hummingbird nest. Condor, vol. 34, pp. 241–242.
CLABAUGH, ERNEST DWIGHT.
1936. Nesting of the Allen hummingbird. Condor, vol. 38, pp. 176–177.
CLARK, FRANK CUTHBERT.
1902. Food of Anna hummingbird. Condor, vol. 5, p. 18.
CLARK, JOSIAH HUNTOON.
1900. Notes on the nesting of the blue-throated hummingbird. Auk, vol. 17, p. 294.

CLAY, MARCIA B.
  1929. The yellow-billed cuckoo. Bird-Lore, vol. 31, pp. 189–190.
COALE, HENRY KELSO.
  1920. Curious habits of the whip-poor-will. Auk, vol. 37, pp. 293–294.
COCHRANE, HENRY LANE.
  1914. A note on the breeding of the white-rumped swift (*Micropus pacificus*). Ibis, 1914, pp. 586–588.
COOKE, WELLS WOODBRIDGE.
  1884. Bird nomenclature of the Chippewa Indians. Auk, vol. 1, pp. 242–250.
CORDIER, ALBERT HAWES.
  1923. Birds, their photographs and home life.
COTTAM, CLARENCE.
  1932. Nocturnal habits of the chimney swift. Auk, vol. 49, pp. 479–481.
COTTAM, CLARENCE, and KNAPPEN, PHOEBE.
  1939. Food of some uncommon North American birds. Auk, vol. 56, pp. 138–169.
COUES, ELLIOTT.
  1874. Birds of the Northwest.
  1878. Habits of the kingfisher (*Ceryle alcyon*). Bull. Nuttall Orn. Club, vol. 3, p. 92.
  1888. New forms of North American *Chordiles*. Auk, vol. 5, p. 37.
  1897. How the chimney swift secures twigs for its nest. Auk, vol. 14, pp. 217–218.
  1900. The "churca" (*Geococcyx californianus*). Auk, vol. 17, p. 66.
  1903. Key to North American birds.
COUPER, WILLIAM.
  1876. Naturalist for April. Forest and Stream, vol. 6, p. 132.
DANFORTH, RALPH EMERSON.
  1921. An unusual accident. Bird-lore, vol. 23, p. 246.
DANIEL, JOHN WARWICK, Jr.
  1902. Summer birds of the Great Dismal Swamp. Auk, vol. 19, pp. 15–18.
DAVIS, WILLIAM B.
  1937. A Vaux swift and its young. Condor, vol. 39, vol. 222–223.
DAVISON, JOHN LESTER.
  1887. Birds laying their eggs in the nest of other birds. Auk, vol. 4, pp. 263–264.
DAWSON, WILLIAM LEON.
  1903. The birds of Ohio.
  1923. The birds of California. Vol. 2.
DAWSON, WILLIAM LEON, and BOWLES, JOHN HOOPER.
  1909. The birds of Washington. Vol. 1.
DAY, MARY F.
  1899. Home-life in a chimney. Bird-Lore, vol. 1, pp. 78–81.
DEKAY, JAMES ELLSWORTH.
  1844. Zoology of New York, or the New-York fauna, part 2. Birds.
DE LAUBENFELS, MAX WALKER.
  1925. Unusual notes of Texas nighthawk. Condor, vol. 27, p. 210.
DICKEY, DONALD RYDER.
  1915. The hummers in a foothill valley. Country Life in America, vol. 28, No. 2, pp. 35–39.
  1928. A new poor-will from the Colorado River Valley. Condor, vol. 30, pp. 152–153.

DICKEY, DONALD RYDER, and VAN ROSSEM, ADRIAAN JOSEPH.
  1938. The birds of El Salvador. Field Mus. Nat. Hist. Publ., zool. ser.,
    vol. 23.
"DIDYMUS" [=HEADE, MARTIN JOHNSON].
  1891. Florida hummingbirds. Forest and Stream, vol. 36, p. 455.
DIXON, JAMES BENJAMIN.
  1912. The Costa hummingbird. Condor, vol. 14, pp. 75–77.
DIXON, JOSEPH SCATTERGOOD.
  1935. Nesting of the black swift in Sequoia National Park. Condor, vol.
    37, pp. 265–267.
DREW, FRANK MAYO.
  1882. Notes on the plumage of *Nephoecetes niger borealis*. Bull. Nuttall
    Orn. Club, vol. 7, pp. 182–183.
DRURY, CHARLES.
  1887. Migration of night hawks. Journ. Cincinnati Soc. Nat. Hist., vol.
    10, pp. 148–149.
DuBOIS, ALEXANDER DAWES.
  1911. A note on the nesting of the whip-poor-will. Auk, vol. 28, pp. 469–
    471.
  1938. Observations at a rufous hummingbird's nest. Auk, vol. 55, pp. 629–
    641.
DUTCHER, WILLIAM.
  1902. Results of special protection to gulls and terns obtained through the
    Thayer fund. Auk, vol. 19, pp. 34–64.
DYER, ERNEST I.
  1939. More observations on the nesting of the Allen hummingbird. Con-
    dor, vol. 41, pp. 62–67.
EATON, ELON HOWARD.
  1914. Birds of New York.
EATON, WARREN FRANCIS.
  1936. Former occurrence of Carolina paroquet in New Jersey. Auk, vol.
    53, p. 82.
EIFRIG, CHARLES WILLIAM GUSTAVE.
  1919. Notes on birds of the Chicago area and its immediate vicinity. Auk,
    vol. 36, pp. 513–524
ELZEY, M. G.
  1876. Game bag and gun. Forest and Stream, vol. 6, p. 122.
EVERETT, CONSTANCE and E. A.
  1927. The fun of banding chimney swifts. Wilson Bull., vol. 39, pp. 111–
    112.
EVERMANN, BARTON WARREN.
  1889. Birds of Carroll County, Indiana. Auk, vol. 6, pp. 22–30.
FINLEY, WILLIAM LOVELL.
  1905. Hummingbird studies. Condor, vol. 7, pp. 59–62.
FINLEY, WILLIAM LOVELL and IRENE.
  1915. With the Arizona road-runners. Bird-Lore, vol. 17, pp. 159–165.
  1924. Changing habits of Vaux swift and western martin. Condor, vol. 26,
    pp. 6–9.
FISHER, ALBERT KENRICK.
  1894. The capture of *Basilinna leucotis* in southern Arizona. Auk, vol. 11,
    pp. 325–326.
FISHER, WALTER KENRICK.
  1904. Road-runners eat young mockingbirds. Condor, vol. 6, p. 80.

FLOYD, CHARLES BENTON.
    1937. Ruby-throated hummingbirds (*Archilochus colubris*) in cold weather. Bird-Banding, vol. 8, p. 79.
FORBUSH, EDWARD HOWE.
    1907. Useful birds and their protection.
    1927. Birds of Massachusetts and other New England States. Vol. 2.
FOREMAN, GRANT.
    1924. Cuckoos and jays. Bird-Lore, vol. 26, p. 182.
FOWLER, FREDERICK HALL.
    1903. Stray notes from southern Arizona. Condor, vol. 5, pp. 68–71, 106–107.
FRIEDMANN, HERBERT, and RILEY, JOSEPH HARVEY.
    1931. The genus *Cuculus* in North America. Auk, vol. 48, p. 269.
GANDER, FRANK FORREST.
    1927. The fly-catching habits of the Anna hummingbird. Condor, vol 29, p. 171.
GENTRY, THOMAS GEORGE.
    1877. Life-histories of the birds of eastern Pennsylvania. Vol. 1.
GILMAN, MARSHALL FRENCH.
    1915. A forty acre bird census at Sacaton, Arizona. Condor, vol. 17, pp. 86–90.
GOFF, MILTON.
    1932. Roof drama. Bird-Lore, vol. 34, p. 202.
GOSS, NATHANIEL STICKNEY.
    1891. History of the birds of Kansas.
GOSSE, PHILIP HENRY.
    1847. The birds of Jamaica.
GRINNELL, JOSEPH.
    1898. Birds of the Pacific slope of Los Angeles County. Pasadena Acad. Sci. Publ. 11.
    1905a. The Pacific nighthawk. Condor, vol. 7, p. 170.
    1905b. Summer birds of Mount Pinos, California. Auk, vol. 22, pp. 378–391.
    1908. The biota of the San Bernardino Mountains. Univ. California Publ. Zool., vol. 5, pp. 1–170.
    1909. Birds and mammals of the 1907 Alexander expedition to southeastern Alaska. Univ. California Publ. Zool., vol. 5, pp. 171–264.
    1910. Birds of the 1908 Alexander Alaska expedition, with a note on the avifaunal relationships of the Prince William Sound district. Univ. California Publ. Zool., vol. 5, pp. 361–428.
    1914. An account of the mammals and birds of the lower Colorado Valley, with especial reference to the distributional problems presented. Univ. California Publ. Zool., vol. 12, pp. 51–294.
    1928. Notes on the systematics of west American birds, II. Condor, vol. 30, pp. 153–156.
GRINNELL, JOSEPH; DIXON, JOSEPH; and LINSDALE, JEAN MYRON.
    1930. Vertebrate natural history of a section of northern California through the Lassen Peak region. Univ. California Publ. Zool., vol. 35, pp. 1–594.
GRINNELL, JOSEPH, and LINSDALE, JEAN MYRON.
    1936. Vertebrate animals of Point Lobos Reserve, 1934–35.
GRINNELL, JOSEPH, and STORER, TRACY IRWIN.
    1924. Animal life in the Yosemite.
GRISCOM, LUDLOW.
    1934. The ornithology of Guerrero, Mexico. Bull. Mus. Comp. Zool., vol. 75, pp. 367–422.

HAMMERSLEY, GLADYS.
1928. Observations on the rufous hummingbird (*Sclasphorus rufus*), 1927. Can. Field-Nat., vol. 42, pp. 149–150.
HANNA, WILSON CREAL.
1909. The white-throated swifts on Slover Mountain. Condor, vol. 11, pp. 77–81.
1917. Further notes on the white-throated swifts of Slover Mountain. Condor, vol. 19, pp. 3–8.
1937. California cuckoo in the San Bernardino Valley, California. Condor, vol. 39, pp. 57–59.
HARRIS, HARRY.
1919. Birds of the Kansas City region. Trans. Acad. Sci. St. Louis, vol. 23, pp. 213–371.
HARTERT, ERNST.
1912. Die Vögel der paläarktischen Fauna. Vol. 2.
HARTERT, ERNST, and HALL, ROBERT.
1904. On the birds collected by Mr. Robert Hall, of Melbourne, on the banks of the Lena River between Gigalowa and its mouth. Ibis, 1904, pp. 415–446.
HARTMAN, FRANK ALEXANDER.
1914. The cause of the peculiar sound made by nighthawks when volplaning. Science, new ser., vol. 39, pp. 326–327.
HASBROUCK, EDWIN MARBLE.
1891. The Carolina paroquet (*Conurus carolinensis*). Auk, vol. 8, pp. 369–379.
HENDERSON, JUNIUS.
1927. The practical value of birds.
HENSHAW, HENRY WETHERBEE.
1875. Report upon the ornithological collections made in portions of Nevada, Utah, California, Colorado, New Mexico, and Arizona, during the years 1871, 1872, 1873, and 1874. Wheeler's Rept. Expl. Surv. West 100th Merid., vol. 5, pp. 131–507.
1877. Description of a new species of humming-bird from California. Bull. Nuttall Orn. Club, vol. 2, pp. 53–58.
1886. List of birds observed in summer and fall on the upper Pecos River, New Mexico. Auk, vol. 3, pp. 73–80.
HERRICK, FRANCIS HOBART.
1901. The home life of wild birds.
1935. Wild birds at home.
HERSEY, FRANK SEYMOUR.
1923. Observations on the habits of the whip-poor-will (*Antrostomus v. vociferus*). Auk, vol. 40, pp. 534–536.
HESS, ISAAC ELNORE.
1910. One hundred breeding birds of an Illinois ten-mile radius. Auk, vol. 27, pp. 19–32.
HINE, JANE L.
1894. Observations on the ruby-throated hummingbird. Auk, vol. 11, pp. 253–254.
HOFFMANN, RALPH.
1927. Birds of the Pacific States.
HOLLISTER, NED.
1908. Birds of the region about Needles, California. Auk, vol. 25, pp. 455–462.

HOPKINS, H. C.
  1892. Oyster vs. kingfisher. Ornithologist and Oologist, vol. 17, p. 109.
HOWELL, ALFRED BRAZIER.
  1916. Some results of a winter's observations in Arizona. Condor, vol. 18,
      pp. 209–214.
  1927. Poor-wills attracted by arc light. Condor, vol. 29, p. 76.
HOWELL, ARTHUR HOLMES.
  1932. Florida bird life.
HOWES, PAUL GRISWOLD.
  1908. Notes on the black-billed cuckoo. Oologist, vol. 25, pp. 171–172.
HOXIE, WALTER [JOHN].
  1887. The capacity of eggs. Ornithologist and Oologist, vol. 12, p. 207.
HUEY, LAURENCE MARKHAM.
  1924. Nuptial flight of the black-chinned hummingbird. Condor, vol. 26,
      p. 229.
HUNT, RICHARD [MONTAGUE].
  1920. How fast can a roadrunner run? Condor, vol. 22, pp. 186–187.
HYDE, ARTHUR SIDNEY.
  1924. Chimney swift nesting in a cistern. Auk, vol. 41, pp. 157–158.
INGERSOLL, ERNEST.
  1920. The wit of the wild.
INGRAM, COLLINGWOOD.
  1908. Ornithological notes from Japan. Ibis, 1908, pp. 129–169.
JASPER, THEODORE.
  1878. The birds of North America.
JENCKS, FRED TINGLEY.
  1881. Kingbird and kingfisher. Ornithologist and Oologist, vol. 6, p. 64.
JENSEN, JENS KNUDSON.
  1923. Notes on the nesting birds of northern Santa Fe County, New Mexico.
      Auk, vol. 40, pp. 452–569.
JEWELL, H. W.
  1908. Nighthawks rear young in robin's nest. Journ. Maine Orn. Soc., vol.
      10, p. 25.
JOHNSON, CHARLES EUGENE.
  1920. Summer bird records from Lake County, Minnesota. Auk, vol. 37, pp.
      541–551.
JONES, A. E.
  1937. A cuckoo (*C. canorus* Linn.) incident. Journ. Bombay Nat. Hist.
      Soc., vol. 39, pp. 175–177.
JONES, LYNDS.
  1909. The birds of Cedar Point and vicinity. Wilson Bull., vol. 21, pp.
      187–204.
JUDD, SYLVESTER DWIGHT.
  1902. Birds of a Maryland farm. Biol. Surv. Bull. 17.
KEMERY, V. MAX.
  1925. A nighthawk's unusual home ties. Bird-Lore, vol. 27, pp. 251–252.
KENNARD, FREDERIC HEDGE.
  1895. Two unique nesting-sites in and about camp buildings in Hamilton
      County, New York. Auk, vol. 12, p. 314.
KENNERLY, CALEB BURWELL ROWAN.
  1857. Description of a new species of *Cypselus* [*C. borealis*], collected on the
      North Western Boundary Survey, Archibald Campbell, Esq., Com-
      missioner. Proc. Acad. Nat. Sci. Philadelphia, vol. 9, pp. 202–203.

KERSHAW, J. G.
1904. List of the birds of the Quangtung coast, China. Ibis, 1904, pp. 235–248.
KING, FRANKLIN HIRAM.
1883. Economic relations of Wisconsin birds. Geology of Wisconsin, vol. 1, pp. 441–610.
KNAPPEN, PHOEBE.
1934. Plecoptera as a bird food. Auk, vol. 51, pp. 103–104.
KNIGHT, ORA WILLIS.
1908. The birds of Maine.
KNOWLTON, FRANK HALL.
1896. Nighthawk catching insects by electric light. Osprey, vol. 1, p. 53.
KOBBÉ, WILLIAM HOFFMAN.
1900. The rufous hummingbirds of Cape Disappointment. Auk, vol. 17, pp. 8–15.
KOPMAN, HENRY HAZLITT.
1915. List of the birds of Louisiana, pt. 6. Auk, vol. 32, pp. 15–29.
KOZLOVA, E. V.
1932. The birds of south-west Transkaikalia, northern Mongolia, and central Gobi. Ibis, 1932, pp. 567–596.
LACEY, HOWARD [GEORGE].
1911. The birds of Kerrville, Texas, and vicinity. Auk, vol. 28, pp. 200–219.
LAMB, CHESTER CONVERSE.
1912. Birds of a Mohave Desert oasis. Condor, vol. 14, pp. 32–40.
1925. Observations on the Xantus hummingbird. Condor, vol. 27, pp. 89–92.
LATHAM, ROY.
1920. Unusual habits of chimney swift. Auk, vol. 37, pp. 132–133.
LA TOUCHE, JOHN DAVID DIQUES.
1914. The spring migration at Chiawangtao in north-east Chihli. Ibis, 1914, pp. 560–586.
1931. A handbook of the birds of eastern China. Vol. 2, pt. 1.
LAW, JOHN EUGENE.
1923. A guilty road-runner: Circumstantial evidence. Condor, vol. 25, pp. 133–134.
LAWRENCE, GEORGE NEWBOLD.
1874. Birds of western and northwestern Mexico, based upon collections made by Col. A. J. Grayson, Capt. J. Xantus and Ferd. Bischoff, now in the museum of the Smithsonian Institution, at Washington, D. C. Mem. Boston Soc. Nat. Hist., vol. 2, pp. 265–319.
LEMMON, ISABELLA McC.
1901. Two young hummingbirds. Bird-Lore, vol. 3, p. 108.
LEOPOLD, ALDO.
1922. Road-runner caught in the act. Condor, vol. 24, p. 183.
LEWIS, JOHN BARZILLAI.
1927. Chimney swifts nesting in a well. Bird-Lore, vol. 29, p. 265.
1929. Feeding habits of chimney swifts. Auk, vol. 46, pp. 546–547.
LINCOLN, FREDERICK CHARLES.
1917. Some notes on the birds of Rock Canyon, Arizona. Wilson Bull., vol. 29, pp. 65–73.
1924. A "territory" note on the belted kingfisher. Wilson Bull., vol. 36, pp. 113–115.

LINSDALE, JEAN MYRON.
    1938. Environmental responses of vertebrates in the Great Basin. Amer.
        Midl. Nat., vol. 19, pp. 1–206.
LINTON, EDWIN.
    1924. Chimney swifts at bedtime. Bird-Lore, vol. 26, pp. 252–253.
LIVESEY, T. R.
    1936. Cuckoo problems. Journ. Bombay Nat. Hist. Soc., vol. 38, pp. 735–758.
LOCKWOOD, MARY E.
    1922. Hummingbird and bass. Bird-Lore, vol. 24, p. 94.
LONG, WILBUR S.
    1935. Spring notes from Lawrence, Kansas. Auk, vol. 52, pp. 466–467.
LONGSTREET, RUBERT JAMES.
    1930. Bird study in Florida.
LORD, JOHN KEAST.
    1866. The naturalist in Vancouver Island and British Columbia. Vol. 2.
LOWERY, GEORGE HINES, JR.
    1938. Hummingbird in a pigeon hawk's stomach. Auk, vol. 55, p. 280.
LUCAS, FREDERIC AUGUSTUS.
    1893. The food of hummingbirds. Auk, vol. 10, pp. 311–315.
LUSK, RICHARD DeWITT.
    1900. Parrots in the United States. Condor, vol. 2, p. 129.
MACFARLANE, RODERICK ROSS.
    1891. Notes on and list of birds and eggs collected in Arctic America,
        1861–1866. Proc. U. S. Nat. Mus., vol. 14, pp. 413–446.
MAILLIARD, JOSEPH.
    1913. Some curious nesting places of the Allen hummingbird on the Rancho
        San Geronimo. Condor, vol. 15, pp. 205–207.
MAILLIARD, JOSEPH, and HANNA, G. DALLAS.
    1921. New bird records for North America with notes on the Pribilof
        Island list. Condor, vol. 23, pp. 93–95.
MAYFIELD, GEORGE RADFORD.
    1921. Roof-nesting nighthawks. Wilson Bull., vol. 33, pp. 147–148.
MAYNARD, CHARLES JOHNSON.
    1896. The birds of eastern North America.
McATEE, WALDO LEE.
    1908. The value of the nighthawk. Bird-Lore, vol. 10, pp. 150–151.
    1916. Common birds of Southeastern United States in relation to agricul-
        ture. U. S. Dept. Agr. Farmers' Bull. 755.
    1926. The relation of birds to woodlots in New York State. Roosevelt Wild
        Life Bull., vol. 4, pp. 1–152.
    1931. A little essay on vermin. Bird-Lore, vol. 33, pp. 381–384.
McBRIDE, JOHN M.
    1933. Unusual roosting of the chuck-will's-widow. Auk, vol. 50, p. 107.
McILWRAITH, THOMAS.
    1894. The birds of Ontario.
MEARNS, EDGAR ALEXANDER.
    1890. Observations on the avifauna of portions of Arizona. Auk, vol. 7,
        pp. 251–264.
MERRIAM, CLINTON HART.
    1890. Results of a biological survey of the San Francisco Mountain region
        and desert of the Little Colorado in Arizona. North Amer. Fauna,
        No. 3.

MERRILL, JAMES CUSHING.
1878. Notes on the ornithology of southern Texas, being a list of birds observed in the vicinity of Fort Brown, Texas, from February, 1876, to June, 1878. Proc. U. S. Nat. Mus., vol. 1, pp. 118–173.
MICHAEL, CHARLES WILSON.
1927. Black swifts nesting in Yosemite National Park. Condor, vol. 29, pp. 89–97.
MICHAEL, ENID.
1926. The habits of swifts in Yosemite Valley. Condor, vol. 28, pp. 109–114.
1933. A young black swift. Condor, vol. 35, p. 30.
MILLER, ALDEN HOLMES.
1925. The boom-flight of the Pacific nighthawk. Condor, vol. 27, pp. 141–143.
1932. Observations on some breeding birds of El Salvador, Central America. Condor, vol. 34, pp. 8–17.
1937. The nuptial flight of the Texas nighthawk. Condor, vol. 39, pp. 42–43.
MILLER, OLIVE THORNE.
1892. Little brothers of the air.
MINOT, HENRY DAVIS.
1877. The land-birds and game-birds of New England.
MOORE, WILLIAM HENRY.
1902a. Notes on some Canadian birds. Ottawa Nat., vol. 16, pp. 130–134.
1902b. Nesting habits of the chimney swift. Bird-Lore, vol. 4, p. 102.
MOUSLEY, WILLIAM HENRY.
1938. A study of the home life of the eastern belted kingfisher. Wilson Bull., vol. 50, pp. 3–12.
MUNRO, JAMES ALEXANDER.
1918. Notes on some British Columbia birds. Auk, vol. 35, pp. 234–235.
1919. Notes on some birds of the Okanagan Valley, British Columbia. Auk, vol. 36, pp. 64–74.
MUNSTERHJELM, L.
1922. Meddelanden f. Goteborgs Musei. Zoolog. Avdelning, 13.
MUSSELMAN, THOMAS EDGAR.
1926. Chimney swift banding. Wilson Bull., vol. 38, pp. 120–121.
1931. Disasters to swifts. Bird-Lore, vol. 33, p. 397.
NOWOTNY, Dr.
1898. The breeding of the Carolina paroquet in captivity. Auk, vol. 15, pp. 28–32.
OBERHOLSER, HARRY CHURCH.
1896. A preliminary list of the birds of Wayne County, Ohio. Bull. Ohio Agr. Exper. Sta., techn. ser., vol. 1, pp. 243–354.
1914. A monograph of the genus *Chordeiles* Swainson, type of a new family of goatsuckers. U. S. Nat. Mus. Bull. 86.
1918. Description of a new subspecies of *Cyanolaemus clemenciae*. Condor, vol. 20, pp. 181–182.
1925. The migration of North American birds. Bird-Lore, vol. 27, pp. 103–104, 326.
1926. The migration of North American birds. Bird-Lore, vol. 28, pp. 255–261.
ORR, ROBERT THOMAS.
1939. Observations on the nesting of the Allen hummingbird. Condor, vol. 41, pp. 17–24.

PALMER, THEODORE SHERMAN.
1918. Costa's hummingbird—its type locality, early history and name. Condor, vol. 20, pp. 114–116.
PALMER, WILLIAM.
1894. An Asiatic cuckoo on the Pribylof Islands, Alaska. Auk, vol. 11, p. 325.
PATTON, F. A.
1924. Birds of the foot hills. Nesting of the Sennett's night hawk. Oologist, vol. 41, p. 111.
PEARSON, THOMAS GILBERT.
1911. The chimney swift. Bird-Lore, vol. 13, pp. 115–118.
PEMBERTON, JOHN ROY.
1916. Variation of the broken-wing stunt by a roadrunner. Condor, vol. 18. p. 203.
PICKENS, ANDREW LEE.
1927. Unique method of pollination by the ruby-throat. Auk, vol. 44, pp. 24–27.
1930. Favorite colors of hummingbirds. Auk, vol. 47, pp. 346–352.
PICKWELL, GAYLE BENJAMIN.
1937. Winter habits of the white-throated swift. Condor, vol. 39, pp. 187–188.
PICKWELL, GAYLE BENJAMIN, and SMITH, EMILY.
1938. The Texas nighthawk in its summer home. Condor, vol. 40, pp. 193–215.
POLING, OTHO CURTIS.
1890. Notes on *Eugenes fulgens*. Auk, vol. 7, pp. 402–403.
QUILLIN, ROY WILLIAM.
1935. New bird records from Texas. Auk, vol. 52, pp. 324–325.
RATHBUN, SAMUEL FREDERICK.
1925. The black swift and its habits. Auk, vol. 42, pp. 497–516.
RAY, ROSE CAROLYN.
1925. Discovery of a nest and eggs of the blue-throated hummingbird. Condor, vol. 27, pp. 49–51.
RESSEL, CYRUS B.
1889. Birds of Chester County, Penn. Ornithologist and Oologist, vol. 14, pp. 97–101.
RICHMOND, CHARLES WALLACE.
1893. Notes on a collection of birds from eastern Nicaragua and the Rio Frio, Costa Rica, with a description of a supposed new trogon. Proc. U. S. Nat. Mus., vol. 16, pp. 479–532.
RIDGWAY, ROBERT.
1877. United States geological exploration of the fortieth parallel. Part 3: Ornithology.
1892. The humming birds. Rep. U. S. Nat. Mus. for 1890, pp. 253–383.
1898. Description of a new species of hummingbird from Arizona. Auk, vol. 15, pp. 325–326.
1911. The birds of North and Middle America, U. S. Nat. Mus. Bull. 50, pt. 5.
1912. Color standards and color nomenclature.
1914. The birds of North and Middle America. U. S. Nat. Mus. Bull. 50, pt. 6.
1916. The birds of North and Middle America. U. S. Nat. Mus. Bull. 50, pt. 7.
ROBERTS, THOMAS SADLER.
1932. The birds of Minnesota. Vol. 1.

ROBERTSON, JOHN McBRAIR.
   1933. An unusual nesting of the black-chinned hummingbird. Condor, vol. 35, pp. 241–242.
ROCKWELL, ROBERT BLANCHARD.
   1908. An annotated list of the birds of Mesa County, Colorado. Condor, vol. 10, pp. 152–180.
RUST, HENRY JUDSON.
   1911. Western nighthawks. Oologist, vol. 28, pp. 186–190.
SAMUELS, EDWARD AUGUSTUS.
   1872. Birds of New England and adjacent States.
   1883. Our northern and eastern birds.
SAUNDERS, ARETAS ANDREWS.
   1915. A summer at Flathead Lake, Montana. Condor, vol. 17, pp. 109–115.
   1929. The summer birds of the northern Adirondack Mountains. Roosevelt Wild Life Bull., vol. 5, pp. 327–499.
   1936. Ecology of the birds of Quaker Run Valley, Allegany State Park, New York. New York State Mus. Handbook, 16.
SAUNDERS, WILLIAM EDWIN.
   1917. City nesting of nighthawks. Wilson Bull., vol. 29, p. 105.
SCHLAG, CARL W.
   1930. Hummingbirds and their nests. Cardinal, vol. 2, pp. 195–200.
SCOTT, WILLIAM EARL DODGE.
   1886. On the avifauna of Pinal County, with remarks on some birds of Pima and Gila Counties, Arizona. Auk, vol. 3, pp. 431–432.
   1889. A summary of observations on the birds of the gulf coast of Florida. Auk, vol. 6, pp. 245–252.
   1890. On the birds observed at the Dry Tortugas, Florida, during parts of March and April, 1890. Auk, vol. 7, pp. 301–314.
   1892. Observations on the birds of Jamaica, West Indies. Auk, vol. 9, pp. 369–375.
SELLECK, G. H.
   1916. A nighthawk family. Guide to Nature, vol. 9, pp. 4–6.
SENNETT, GEORGE BURRITT.
   1878. Notes on the ornithology of the lower Rio Grande of Texas. Bull. U. S. Geol. and Geogr. Surv., vol. 4, pp. 1–00.
   1879. Further notes on the ornithology of the lower Rio Grande of Texas. Bull. U. S. Geol. and Geogr. Surv., vol. 5, pp. 371–440.
   1888. Descriptions of a new species and two new subspecies of birds from Texas. Auk, vol. 5, pp. 43–46.
SETON, ERNEST THOMPSON.
   1890. The birds of Manitoba. Proc. U. S. Nat. Mus., vol. 13, pp. 457–643.
SHARP, CLARENCE SAUGER.
   1907. The breeding birds of Escondido. Condor, vol. 9, pp. 84–91.
SHAW, TSEN-HWANG.
   1936. The birds of Hopei Province.
SHELDON, HARRY HARGRAVE.
   1922a. Top speed of the road-runner. Condor, vol. 24, p. 180.
   1922b. Vaux swift in migration. Condor, vol. 24, pp. 184–185.
SHELLEY, LEWIS ORMAN.
   1929. Twig gathering of the chimney swift. Auk, vol. 46, p. 116.
SHELTON, ALFRED COOPER.
   1911. Nesting of the California cuckoo. Condor, vol. 13, pp. 19–22.

SHERMAN, ALTHEA ROSINA.
   1913. Experimenting in feeding hummingbirds during seven summers. Wilson Bull., vol. 25, pp. 153–166.
SHUFELDT, ROBERT WILSON.
   1885. On the feeding habits of *Phalaenoptilus nuttalli*. Auk, vol. 2, pp. 382–383.
SIMMONS, GEORGE FINLAY.
   1915. On the nesting of certain birds in Texas. Auk, vol. 32, pp. 317–331.
   1925. Birds of the Austin region.
SIMPSON, CHARLES TORREY.
   1920. In lower Florida wilds.
SKINNER, MILTON PHILO.
   1928. Kingfisher and sharp-shinned hawk. Auk, vol. 45, pp. 100–101.
SKUTCH, ALEXANDER FRANK.
   1931. The life history of Rieffer's hummingbird (*Amazilia tzacatl tzacatl*) in Panama and Honduras. Auk, vol. 48, pp. 481–500.
SLOANAKER, JOSEPH L.
   1913. Bird notes from the South-west. Wilson Bull., vol. 25, pp. 187–199.
SMITH, AUSTIN PAUL.
   1907. The thick-billed parrot in Arizona. Condor, vol. 9, p. 104.
   1915. Birds of the Boston Mountains, Arkansas. Condor, vol. 17, pp. 41–57.
SMITH, EMILY.
   1928. Black swifts nesting behind a waterfall. Condor, vol. 30, pp. 136–138.
SMITH, EVERETT.
   1883. The birds of Maine. Forest and Stream, vol. 19, pp. 504–505.
SMITH, HUGH McCORMICK, and PALMER, WILLIAM.
   1888. Additions to the avifauna of Washington and vicinity. Auk, vol. 5, pp. 147–148.
SMITH, PHILO W.
   1900. Nesting of Stephens's whippoorwill. Osprey, vol. 4, p. 89.
SMITH, WILBUR F.
   1920. A hummingbird story. Bird-Lore, vol. 22, pp. 274–275.
SNYDER, LESTER LYNNE, and LOGIER, E. B. S.
   1931. A faunal investigation of Long Point, and vicinity, Norfolk County, Ontario. Contr. Roy. Ontario Mus. Zool., vol. 18, pp. 117–236.
SOULE, CAROLINE GRAY.
   1900. A hummingbird experiment. Bird-Lore, vol. 2, p. 158.
SPIKER, CHARLES JOLLEY.
   1935. A popular account of the bird life of the Finger Lakes section of New York, with main reference to the summer season. Roosevelt Wild Life Bull., vol. 6, No. 3.
SPROT, GEORGE DOVETON.
   1927. Notes on the courtship of the rufous hummingbird. Condor, vol. 29, pp. 71–72.
SPRUNT, ALEXANDER, Jr., and CHAMBERLAIN, EDWARD BURNHAM.
   1931. Second supplement to Arthur T. Wayne's birds of South Carolina. Charleston Mus. Contr. No. 6.
STEARNS, WINFRID ALDEN.
   1883. New England bird life, pt. 2. Edited by Elliott Coues.
STEPHENS, FRANK.
   1913. Nighthawk drinking. Condor, vol. 15, p. 184.

STERLING, E.
  1885. Night hawks nesting. Forest and Stream, vol. 25, p. 4.
STEVENS, HERBERT.
  1925. Notes on the birds of the Sikkim Himalayas. Journ. Bombay Nat. Hist. Soc., vol. 30, pp. 664–685.
STOCKARD, CHARLES RUPERT.
  1905. Nesting habits of birds in Mississippi. Auk, vol. 22, pp. 146–158.
STONE, WITMER.
  1894. Capture of *Ceryle torquata* (Linn.) at Laredo, Texas. A species new to the United States. Auk, vol. 11, p. 177.
STORER, TRACY IRWIN.
  1921. The northward range of the Allen hummingbird. Condor, vol. 23, pp. 160–162.
STROTHER, W. A.
  1886. An albino nighthawk. American Field, vol. 26, p. 415.
SUTTON, GEORGE MIKSCH.
  1922. Notes on the road-runner at Fort Worth, Texas. Wilson Bull., vol. 34, pp. 3–20.
  1928. Notes on the flight of the chimney swift. Cardinal, vol. 2, pp. 85–92.
  1935. An expedition to the Big Bend country. Cardinal, vol. 4, pp. 1–7.
  1936. Birds in the wilderness.
SWARTH, HARRY SCHELWALD.
  1904. Birds of the Huachuca Mountains, Arizona. Pacific Coast Avifauna, No. 4.
  1912. Differences due to sex in the black swift. Auk, vol. 29, pp. 241–242.
  1920. Birds of the Papago Saguaro National Monument and the neighboring region, Arizona.
  1922. Birds and mammals of the Stikine River region of northern British Columbia and southeastern Alaska. Univ. California Publ. Zool., vol. 24, pp. 125–314.
  1929. The faunal areas of southern Arizona: A study in animal distribution. Proc. California Acad. Sci., vol. 18, pp. 267–383.
SWENK, MYRON HARMON.
  1934. The interior paroquet as a Nebraska bird. Nebraska Bird Rev., vol. 2, pp. 55–59.
SWINHOE, ROBERT.
  1860. Letter on birds of Lam-yit. Ibis, 1860, pp. 428–429.
  1870. On the ornithology of Hainan. Ibis, 1870, pp. 77–97.
  1874. Ornithological notes made at Chefoo. Ibis, 1874, p. 435.
TATE, RALPH C.
  1926. Some materials used in nest construction by certain birds of the Oklahoma Panhandle. Univ. Oklahoma Bull., vol. 5, pp. 103–104.
  1928. Rufous hummingbird in the Oklahoma Panhandle. Condor, vol. 30, pp. 252–253.
TAVERNER, PERCY ALGERNON, and SWALES, BRADSHAW HALL.
  1907. The birds of Point Pelee. Wilson Bull., vol. 19, pp. 133–153.
TAYLOR, WALTER PENN, and SHAW, WILLIAM THOMAS.
  1927. Mammals and birds of Mount Rainier National Park.
THAYER, GERALD HENDERSON.
  1899. The chuck-will's-widow on shipboard. Auk, vol. 16, pp. 273–276.
  1903. The mystery of the black-billed cuckoo. Bird-Lore, vol. 5, pp. 143–145.

THAYER, JOHN ELIOT.
    1906. Eggs and nests of the thick-billed parrot (*Rhyncopsitta pachyrhyncha*).
        Auk, vol. 23, pp. 223–224.
THOMAS, EDWARD S.
    1932. Chuck-will's-widow, a new bird for Ohio. Auk, vol. 49, p. 479.
THOMPSON, ALBERT ERVIN.
    1937. A swift in a granite wall. Nature Mag., vol. 30, p. 141.
TODD, WALTER EDMOND CLYDE.
    1916. The birds of the Isle of Pines. Ann. Carnegie Mus., vol. 10, pp.
        146–296.
TORREY, BRADFORD.
    1892. The foot-path way.
    1903. The clerk of the woods.
TOWNSEND, CHARLES WENDELL.
    1906. Notes on the birds of Cape Breton Island. Auk, vol. 23, pp. 172–179.
    1912. Notes on the summer birds of the St. John valley, New Brunswick.
        Auk, vol. 29, pp. 16–23.
    1918. Ipswich bird notes. Auk, vol. 35, pp. 182–185.
    1920a. Supplement to the birds of Essex County, Massachusetts. Mem.
        Nuttall Orn. Club, No. 5.
    1920b. Courtship in birds. Auk, vol. 37, pp. 380–393.
TULLSEN, H.
    1911. My avian visitors: Notes from South Dakota. Condor, vol. 13, pp.
        89–104.
TURNBULL, WILLIAM PATTERSON.
    1869. The birds of eastern Pennsylvania and New Jersey.
TUTTLE, HENRY EMERSON.
    1911. The nesting of the whip-poor-will. Bird-Lore, vol. 13, pp. 235–238.
TYLER, JOHN GRIPPER.
    1913. Some birds of the Fresno district, California. Pacific Coast Avifauna,
        No. 9.
VAN ROSSEM, ADRIAAN JOSEPH.
    1927. Eye shine in birds, with notes on the feeding habits of some goat-
        suckers. Condor, vol. 29, pp. 25–28.
    1936. Notes on birds in relation to the faunal areas of south-central Arizona.
        Trans. San Diego Soc. Nat. Hist., vol. 8, pp. 121–148.
    1938. See Dickey and van Rossem, 1938.
VAN ROSSEM, ADRIAAN JOSEPH, and BOWLES, JOHN HOOPER.
    1920. Nesting of the dusky poor-will near Saugus, Los Angeles County,
        California. Condor, vol, 22, pp. 61–62.
VAN TYNE, JOSSELYN, and SUTTON, GEORGE MIKSCH.
    1937. The birds of Brewster County, Texas. Univ. Michigan Mus. Zool.,
        Misc. Publ. No. 37.
VAUGHAN, ROBERT E., and JONES, KENNETH HURLSTONE.
    1913. The birds of Hong Kong, Macao, and the West River or Si Kiang in
        south-eastern China, with special reference to their nidification
        and seasonal movements. Ibis, 1913, pp. 163–201.
VISHER, STEPHEN SARGENT.
    1910. Notes on the birds of Pima County, Arizona. Auk, vol 27, pp. 279–
        288.
VORHIES, CHARLES TAYLOR.
    1934. Arizona records of the thick-billed parrot. Condor, vol. 36, pp. 180–181.

VROOMAN, ALBERT GEORGE.
  1901. Discovery of the egg of the black swift (*Cypseloides niger borealis*).
    Auk, vol. 18, pp. 394–395.
WARREN, BENJAMIN HARRY.
  1890. Report on the birds of Pennsylvania. Ed. 2.
WARREN, EDWARD ROYAL.
  1916. Notes on the birds of the Elk Mountain region, Gunnison County,
    Colorado. Auk, vol. 33, pp. 292–317.
WATSON, SHEPPARD ARTHUR.
  1933. The Vaux swift at Whittier, California. Condor, vol. 35, pp. 203–204.
WAYNE, ARTHUR TREZEVANT.
  1910. Birds of South Carolina.
WELLS, JOHN GRANT.
  1902. Birds of the island of Carriacou. Auk, vol. 19, pp. 343–349.
WELTER, WILFRED AUGUST.
  1935. Nesting habits of ruby-throated hummingbird. Auk, vol. 52, pp.
    88–89.
WESTOVER, MYRON F.
  1932. The flight of swifts. Bird-Lore, vol. 34, pp. 253–254.
WETMORE, ALEXANDER.
  1916. Birds of Porto Rico. U. S. Dept. Agr. Bull. 326.
  1920. Observations on the habits of birds at Lake Burford, New Mexico.
    Auk, vol. 37, pp. 393–412.
  1921. Further notes on birds observed near Williams, Arizona. Condor,
    vol. 23, pp. 60–64.
  1927. The birds of Porto Rico and the Virgin Islands. New York Acad. Sci.,
    vol. 9, pt. 4, pp. 409–571.
  1932. Seeking the smallest feathered creatures. Nat. Geogr. Mag., vol.
    62, pp. 65–89.
  1935. The thick-billed parrot in southern Arizona. Condor, vol. 37, pp.
    18–21.
WEYDEMEYER, WINTON.
  1927. Notes on the location and construction of the nest of the calliope
    hummingbird. Condor, vol. 29, pp. 19–24.
WHEELER, HARRY EDGAR.
  1922. Random notes from Arkansas. Wilson Bull., vol. 34, pp. 221–224.
WHEELOCK, IRENE GROSVENOR.
  1904. Birds of California.
  1905. Regurgitative feeding of nestlings. Auk, vol. 22, pp. 54–70.
WHITTLE, CHARLES LIVY.
  1937. A study of hummingbird behavior during a nesting season. Bird-
    Banding, vol. 8, pp. 170–173.
WIDMANN, OTTO.
  1907. A preliminary catalog of the birds of Missouri.
WILLARD, FRANCIS COTTLE.
  1899. Notes on *Eugenes fulgens*. Osprey, vol. 3, pp. 65–66.
  1911. The blue-throated hummingbird. Condor, vol. 13, pp. 46–49.
WILSON, ALEXANDER.
  1828–1832. American ornithology. Vols. 1, 2.
WOODBURY, ANGUS M.
  1938. Red-naped sapsucker and rufous hummingbird. Condor, vol. 40,
    p. 125.

WOODS, ROBERT S.

1922. The development of young Costa hummingbirds. Condor, vol. 24, pp. 189–193.

1924a. Some birds of the San Gabriel wash. Bird-Lore, vol. 26, pp. 1–9.

1924b. Notes on the life history of the Texas nighthawk. Condor, vol. 26, pp. 3–6.

1927a. Road-runner versus mockingbird. Condor, vol. 29, p. 273.

1927b. The hummingbirds of California. Auk, vol. 44, pp. 297–318.

1934. A hummingbird entangled in a spider's web. Condor, vol. 36, p. 242.

WRIGHT, ALBERT HAZEN, and HARPER, FRANCIS.

1913. A biological reconnaissance of Okefinokee Swamp: The birds. Auk, vol. 30, pp. 477–505.

WYMAN, LUTHER EVERET.

1920. Notes on the calliope hummingbird. Condor, vol. 22, pp. 206–207.

ZAREGA, LOUIS AUGUSTUS DI.

1882. The nighthawk in cities. Forest and Stream, vol. 18, p. 467.

INDEX

This index covers both Parts of this work. Part I contains pages 1 to 244 and Part II contains pages 244 through 506.

493

...

Plates

PLATE 37

W. M. Pierce.

NESTING OF TEXAS NIGHTHAWK.

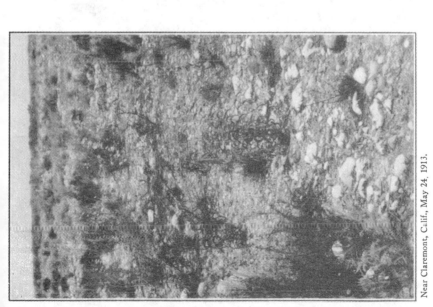

Near Claremont, Calif., May 24, 1913.

PLATE 38

May 16, 1923.

Downy young 2 or 3 days old.

Azusa, Calif., May 24, 1923.   R. S. Woods.

Young 10 days old.

TEXAS NIGHTHAWKS.

PLATE 39

May 30, 1923.

Young 16 or 17 days old.

Azusa, Calif., May 19, 1923.

R. S. Woods.

Female brooding young.

TEXAS NIGHTHAWKS

PLATE 40

HISTORIC NESTING SITE OF NORTHERN BLACK SWIFT (A. G. VROOMAN AT NEST).

Santa Cruz, Calif., June 22, 1914.

PLATE 41

California State Redwood Park, 1926.   Emily Smith; F. R. Fulmer.

NESTING SITE OF NORTHERN BLACK SWIFT UNDER BERRY CREEK FALLS.

PLATE 42

Nesting site under shadow of a rock beside a cascade.

Fresno County, Calif.   A. E. Thompson.

Adult on nest.

NESTING OF NORTHERN BLACK SWIFT.

PLATE 43

Sequoia National Park, Calif., August 7, 1933.

J. S. Dixon.
Courtesy of National Park Service.

Yosemite, Calif., August 22, 1926.

C. W. Michael.

Five weeks old.

YOUNG NORTHERN BLACK SWIFTS.

PLATE 44

Branchport, N. Y., June 17, 1900.　　　　　　　　　　　　C. F .Stone.

Quincy, Ill.　　　　　　　　　　　　　　　　　　T. E. Musselman.

NESTS OF CHIMNEY SWIFTS.

PLATE 45

Adult on nest in a silo.

Ithaca, N. Y.

Young.

A. A. Allen.

CHIMNEY SWIFTS.

PLATE 46

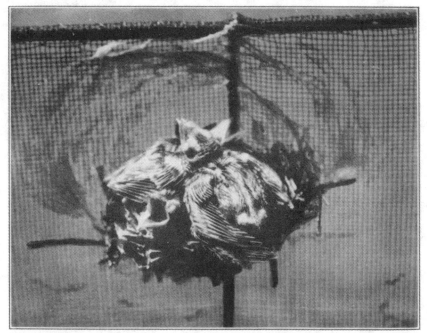

Arnprior, Ontario.   C. Macnamara.

NESTING OF CHIMNEY SWIFTS ON A FIREGUARD ON A HEARTH.
(Note the circle of glue.)

PLATE 47

Colton, Calif., May 1916.

W. C. Hanna.

NESTS OF WHITE-THROATED SWIFTS.

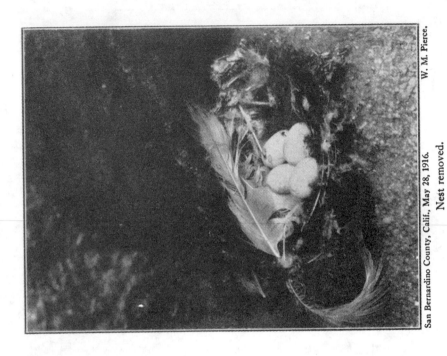

San Bernardino County, Calif., May 28, 1916.

W. M. Pierce.

Nest removed.

Colton, Calif.

W. C. Hanna.

Collector at nest site.

WHITE-THROATED SWIFT

PLATE 48

PLATE 49

F. C. Willard.

Huachuca Mountains, Ariz.

NESTING SITES OF RIVOLI'S HUMMINGBIRD.

PLATE 50

Huachuca Mountains, Ariz.   F. C. Willard.

NESTS OF RIVOLI'S HUMMINGBIRD.

PLATE 51

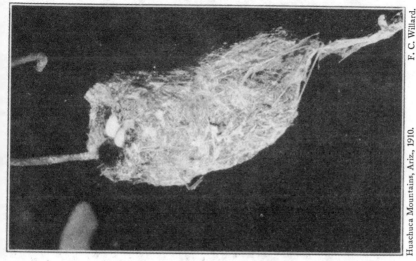

Huachuca Mountains, Ariz., 1910.   F. C. Willard.
Nest on a bucket bail in a greenhouse.

ARIZONA BLUE-THROATED HUMMINGBIRD.

Huachuca Mountains, Ariz., May 10, 1922.   A. C. Bent.
Nesting site in a clump of *Mimulus cardinalis* (lower right).

PLATE 52

Two young nearly grown.

Huachuca Mountains, Ariz.

F. C. Willard.

Nest under roof of a pavilion.

ARIZONA BLUE-THROATED HUMMINGBIRD

PLATE 53

Plymouth, Mass., June 8, 1902.   A. C. Bent.

Nest in a pitch pine.

Sangamon County, Ill., June 3, 1908.   A. D. DuBois.

Nest in an oak.

RUBY-THROATED HUMMINGBIRD.

PLATE 54

Oakland County, Mich., June 19, 1921.   W. E. Hastings.

Adult female.

Ithaca, N. Y.   A. A. Allen.

Female feeding full-grown young.

RUBY-THROATED HUMMINGBIRDS.

PLATE 55

Holderness, N. H.   H. F. Edgerton.

Mrs. Laurence J. Webster and her pets.

RUBY-THROATED HUMMINGBIRDS.

PLATE 56

C. F. Stone.

Branchport, N. Y., August 27. 1900.

RUBY-THROATED HUMMINGBIRDS.

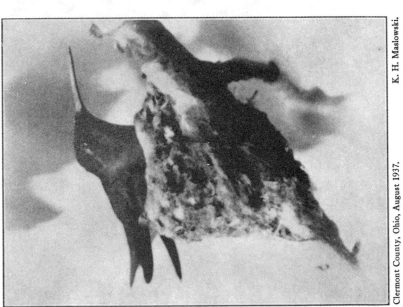

K. H. Maslowski.

Clermont County, Ohio, August 1937.

PLATE 57

Holderness, N. H.   H. E. Edgerton.

RUBY-THROATED HUMMINGBIRDS AT MRS. WEBSTER'S FEEDING STATION.

PLATE 58

Azusa, Calif., July 17, 1923.   R. S. Woods.

Adult male.

Azusa, Calif., June 13, 1938.   R. S. Woods.

A durable used nest.

BLACK-CHINNED HUMMINGBIRD.

PLATE 59

Azusa, Calif., April 19, 1923.   R. S. Woods.

Nest in a feijoa bush.

May 15, 1913.   W. M. Pierce.

Nest in a white-sage bush.

COSTA'S HUMMINGBIRD.

PLATE 60

Azusa, Calif., May 22, 1925. R. S. Woods.

Young about 11 days old.

Azusa, Calif., June 2, 1933. R. S. Woods.

COSTA'S HUMMINGBIRDS.

PLATE 61

Azusa, Calif., June 8, 1923.   R. S. Woods.

Adult male.

COSTA'S HUMMINGBIRD.

Mojave Desert, Calif., May 7, 1916.   W. M. Pierce.

Nest in *Opuntia ramosissima.*

PLATE 62

Azusa, Calif., February 22, 1931.   R. S. Woods.

Adult male feeding.

Claremont, Calif.   W. M. Pierce.

Nest in a lemon tree.

ANNA'S HUMMINGBIRD.

PLATE 63

Arizona.   F. C. Willard.

NEST OF BROAD-TAILED HUMMINGBIRD

PLATE 64

Colorado Springs, Colo., July 16, 1906.   E. R. Warren.

BROAD-TAILED HUMMINGBIRD.

PLATE 65

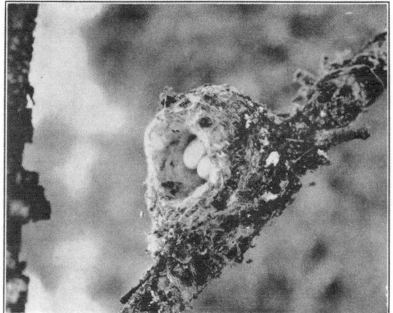

J. E. Patterson.

Bear Creek, Oreg., May 29, 1925.

NEST OF RUFOUS HUMMINGBIRD IN AN OAK TREE.

PLATE 66

July 17, 1914.

Female shading eggs.

Flathead County, Mont., July 20, 1914.

A. D. DuBois.

Young 2 days old.

RUFOUS HUMMINGBIRDS.

PLATE 67

W. L. Finley and H. T. Bohlman.

Portland, Oreg.

NEST OF RUFOUS HUMMINGBIRD IN A VIRGINIA CREEPER.

PLATE 68

Ynes Mexía.

Nest in a eucalyptus.

ALLEN'S HUMMINGBIRD.

Berkeley, Calif.

Nest in a Monterey pine.

PLATE 69

Nest and small young in a Monterey cypress.

Berkeley, Calif.   Ynes Mexía.

Nest and two large young in a Monterey cypress.

ALLEN'S HUMMINGBIRD.

PLATE 70

Jackson County, Oreg., June 8, 1925.   J. E. Patterson.

Blue Mountains, Wash.   S. H. Lyman.

NESTS OF CALLIOPE HUMMINGBIRD.

PLATE 71

Almirante, Panama, March 6, 1929.   A. F. Skutch.

Nest in a bougainvillea bush.

Tela, Honduras, September 7, 1930.   A. F. Skutch.

Nest in a lime tree.

RIEFFER'S HUMMINGBIRD.

PLATE 72

A. F. Skutch.

Tela, Honduras, September 8, 1930.

Young 16 days old.

RIEFFER'S HUMMINGBIRDS.

A. F. Skutch.

Almirante, Panama, March 25, 1929.

Young 13 days old.

PLATE 73

Near Tecpan, Guatemala, December 11, 1933.   A. F. Skutch.

NEST OF WHITE-EARED HUMMINGBIRD.

A CATALOG OF SELECTED DOVER
BOOKS IN ALL FIELDS OF INTEREST

DRAWINGS OF REMBRANDT, edited by Seymour Slive. Updated Lippmann, Hofstede de Groot edition, with definitive scholarly apparatus. All portraits, biblical sketches, landscapes, nudes. Oriental figures, classical studies, together with selection of work by followers. 550 illustrations. Total of 630pp. 9⅛ × 12¼.
21485-0, 21486-9 Pa., Two-vol. set $25.00

GHOST AND HORROR STORIES OF AMBROSE BIERCE, Ambrose Bierce. 24 tales vividly imagined, strangely prophetic, and decades ahead of their time in technical skill: "The Damned Thing," "An Inhabitant of Carcosa," "The Eyes of the Panther," "Moxon's Master," and 20 more. 199pp. 5⅜ × 8½. 20767-6 Pa. $3.95

ETHICAL WRITINGS OF MAIMONIDES, Maimonides. Most significant ethical works of great medieval sage, newly translated for utmost precision, readability. Laws Concerning Character Traits, Eight Chapters, more. 192pp. 5⅜ × 8½.
24522-5 Pa. $4.50

THE EXPLORATION OF THE COLORADO RIVER AND ITS CANYONS, J. W. Powell. Full text of Powell's 1,000-mile expedition down the fabled Colorado in 1869. Superb account of terrain, geology, vegetation, Indians, famine, mutiny, treacherous rapids, mighty canyons, during exploration of last unknown part of continental U.S. 400pp. 5⅜ × 8½. 20094-9 Pa. $6.95

HISTORY OF PHILOSOPHY, Julián Marías. Clearest one-volume history on the market. Every major philosopher and dozens of others, to Existentialism and later. 505pp. 5⅜ × 8½. 21739-6 Pa. $8.50

ALL ABOUT LIGHTNING, Martin A. Uman. Highly readable non-technical survey of nature and causes of lightning, thunderstorms, ball lightning, St. Elmo's Fire, much more. Illustrated. 192pp. 5⅜ × 8½. 25237-X Pa. $5.95

SAILING ALONE AROUND THE WORLD, Captain Joshua Slocum. First man to sail around the world, alone, in small boat. One of great feats of seamanship told in delightful manner. 67 illustrations. 294pp. 5⅜ × 8½. 20326-3 Pa. $4.95

LETTERS AND NOTES ON THE MANNERS, CUSTOMS AND CONDITIONS OF THE NORTH AMERICAN INDIANS, George Catlin. Classic account of life among Plains Indians: ceremonies, hunt, warfare, etc. 312 plates. 572pp. of text. 6⅛ × 9¼. 22118-0, 22119-9 Pa. Two-vol. set $15.90

ALASKA: The Harriman Expedition, 1899, John Burroughs, John Muir, et al. Informative, engrossing accounts of two-month, 9,000-mile expedition. Native peoples, wildlife, forests, geography, salmon industry, glaciers, more. Profusely illustrated. 240 black-and-white line drawings. 124 black-and-white photographs. 3 maps. Index. 576pp. 5⅜ × 8½. 25109-8 Pa. $11.95

THE BOOK OF BEASTS: Being a Translation from a Latin Bestiary of the Twelfth Century, T. H. White. Wonderful catalog real and fanciful beasts: manticore, griffin, phoenix, amphivius, jaculus, many more. White's witty erudite commentary on scientific, historical aspects. Fascinating glimpse of medieval mind. Illustrated. 296pp. 5⅝ × 8¼. (Available in U.S. only) 24609-4 Pa. $5.95

FRANK LLOYD WRIGHT: ARCHITECTURE AND NATURE With 160 Illustrations, Donald Hoffmann. Profusely illustrated study of influence of nature—especially prairie—on Wright's designs for Fallingwater, Robie House, Guggenheim Museum, other masterpieces. 96pp. 9¼ × 10¾. 25098-9 Pa. $7.95

FRANK LLOYD WRIGHT'S FALLINGWATER, Donald Hoffmann. Wright's famous waterfall house: planning and construction of organic idea. History of site, owners, Wright's personal involvement. Photographs of various stages of building. Preface by Edgar Kaufmann, Jr. 100 illustrations. 112pp. 9¼ × 10.
23671-4 Pa. $7.95

YEARS WITH FRANK LLOYD WRIGHT: Apprentice to Genius, Edgar Tafel. Insightful memoir by a former apprentice presents a revealing portrait of Wright the man, the inspired teacher, the greatest American architect. 372 black-and-white illustrations. Preface. Index. vi + 228pp. 8¼ × 11. 24801-1 Pa. $9.95

THE STORY OF KING ARTHUR AND HIS KNIGHTS, Howard Pyle. Enchanting version of King Arthur fable has delighted generations with imaginative narratives of exciting adventures and unforgettable illustrations by the author. 41 illustrations. xviii + 313pp. 6⅛ × 9¼. 21445-1 Pa. $6.50

THE GODS OF THE EGYPTIANS, E. A. Wallis Budge. Thorough coverage of numerous gods of ancient Egypt by foremost Egyptologist. Information on evolution of cults, rites and gods; the cult of Osiris; the Book of the Dead and its rites; the sacred animals and birds; Heaven and Hell; and more. 956pp. 6⅛ × 9¼.
22055-9, 22056-7 Pa., Two-vol. set $20.00

A THEOLOGICO-POLITICAL TREATISE, Benedict Spinoza. Also contains unfinished *Political Treatise*. Great classic on religious liberty, theory of government on common consent. R. Elwes translation. Total of 421pp. 5⅜ × 8½.
20249-6 Pa. $6.95

INCIDENTS OF TRAVEL IN CENTRAL AMERICA, CHIAPAS, AND YUCATAN, John L. Stephens. Almost single-handed discovery of Maya culture; exploration of ruined cities, monuments, temples; customs of Indians. 115 drawings. 892pp. 5⅜ × 8½. 22404-X, 22405-8 Pa., Two-vol. set $15.90

LOS CAPRICHOS, Francisco Goya. 80 plates of wild, grotesque monsters and caricatures. Prado manuscript included. 183pp. 6⅝ × 9⅝. 22384-1 Pa. $4.95

AUTOBIOGRAPHY: The Story of My Experiments with Truth, Mohandas K. Gandhi. Not hagiography, but Gandhi in his own words. Boyhood, legal studies, purification, the growth of the Satyagraha (nonviolent protest) movement. Critical, inspiring work of the man who freed India. 480pp. 5⅜ × 8½. (Available in U.S. only)
24593-4 Pa. $6.95

ILLUSTRATED DICTIONARY OF HISTORIC ARCHITECTURE, edited by Cyril M. Harris. Extraordinary compendium of clear, concise definitions for over 5,000 important architectural terms complemented by over 2,000 line drawings. Covers full spectrum of architecture from ancient ruins to 20th-century Modernism. Preface. 592pp. 7½ × 9⅜.   24444-X Pa. $14.95

THE NIGHT BEFORE CHRISTMAS, Clement Moore. Full text, and woodcuts from original 1848 book. Also critical, historical material. 19 illustrations. 40pp. 4⅝ × 6.   22797-9 Pa. $2.25

THE LESSON OF JAPANESE ARCHITECTURE: 165 Photographs, Jiro Harada. Memorable gallery of 165 photographs taken in the 1930's of exquisite Japanese homes of the well-to-do and historic buildings. 13 line diagrams. 192pp. 8⅜ × 11¼.   24778-3 Pa. $8.95

THE AUTOBIOGRAPHY OF CHARLES DARWIN AND SELECTED LETTERS, edited by Francis Darwin. The fascinating life of eccentric genius composed of an intimate memoir by Darwin (intended for his children); commentary by his son, Francis; hundreds of fragments from notebooks, journals, papers; and letters to and from Lyell, Hooker, Huxley, Wallace and Henslow. xi + 365pp. 5⅜ × 8.
                                                              20479-0 Pa. $6.95

WONDERS OF THE SKY: Observing Rainbows, Comets, Eclipses, the Stars and Other Phenomena, Fred Schaaf. Charming, easy-to-read poetic guide to all manner of celestial events visible to the naked eye. Mock suns, glories, Belt of Venus, more. Illustrated. 299pp. 5¼ × 8¼.   24402-4 Pa. $7.95

BURNHAM'S CELESTIAL HANDBOOK, Robert Burnham, Jr. Thorough guide to the stars beyond our solar system. Exhaustive treatment. Alphabetical by constellation: Andromeda to Cetus in Vol. 1; Chamaeleon to Orion in Vol. 2; and Pavo to Vulpecula in Vol. 3. Hundreds of illustrations. Index in Vol. 3. 2,000pp. 6⅛ × 9¼.   23567-X, 23568-8, 23673-0 Pa., Three-vol. set $38.85

STAR NAMES: Their Lore and Meaning, Richard Hinckley Allen. Fascinating history of names various cultures have given to constellations and literary and folkloristic uses that have been made of stars. Indexes to subjects. Arabic and Greek names. Biblical references. Bibliography. 563pp. 5⅜ × 8½.   21079-0 Pa. $7.95

THIRTY YEARS THAT SHOOK PHYSICS: The Story of Quantum Theory, George Gamow. Lucid, accessible introduction to influential theory of energy and matter. Careful explanations of Dirac's anti-particles, Bohr's model of the atom, much more. 12 plates. Numerous drawings. 240pp. 5⅜ × 8½.   24895-X Pa. $4.95

CHINESE DOMESTIC FURNITURE IN PHOTOGRAPHS AND MEASURED DRAWINGS, Gustav Ecke. A rare volume, now affordably priced for antique collectors, furniture buffs and art historians. Detailed review of styles ranging from early Shang to late Ming. Unabridged republication. 161 black-and-white drawings, photos. Total of 224pp. 8⅜ × 11¼. (Available in U.S. only) 25171-3 Pa. $12.95

VINCENT VAN GOGH: A Biography, Julius Meier-Graefe. Dynamic, penetrating study of artist's life, relationship with brother, Theo, painting techniques, travels, more. Readable, engrossing. 160pp. 5⅜ × 8½. (Available in U.S. only)
                                                              25253-1 Pa. $3.95

HOW TO WRITE, Gertrude Stein. Gertrude Stein claimed anyone could understand her unconventional writing—here are clues to help. Fascinating improvisations, language experiments, explanations illuminate Stein's craft and the art of writing. Total of 414pp. 4⅝ × 6⅜. 23144-5 Pa. $5.95

ADVENTURES AT SEA IN THE GREAT AGE OF SAIL: Five Firsthand Narratives, edited by Elliot Snow. Rare true accounts of exploration, whaling, shipwreck, fierce natives, trade, shipboard life, more. 33 illustrations. Introduction. 353pp. 5⅜ × 8½. 25177-2 Pa. $7.95

THE HERBAL OR GENERAL HISTORY OF PLANTS, John Gerard. Classic descriptions of about 2,850 plants—with over 2,700 illustrations—includes Latin and English names, physical descriptions, varieties, time and place of growth, more. 2,706 illustrations. xlv + 1,678pp. 8½ × 12¼. 23147-X Cloth. $75.00

DOROTHY AND THE WIZARD IN OZ, L. Frank Baum. Dorothy and the Wizard visit the center of the Earth, where people are vegetables, glass houses grow and Oz characters reappear. Classic sequel to *Wizard of Oz*. 256pp. 5⅜ × 8. 24714-7 Pa. $4.95

SONGS OF EXPERIENCE: Facsimile Reproduction with 26 Plates in Full Color, William Blake. This facsimile of Blake's original "Illuminated Book" reproduces 26 full-color plates from a rare 1826 edition. Includes "The Tyger," "London," "Holy Thursday," and other immortal poems. 26 color plates. Printed text of poems. 48pp. 5¼ × 7. 24636-1 Pa. $3.50

SONGS OF INNOCENCE, William Blake. The first and most popular of Blake's famous "Illuminated Books," in a facsimile edition reproducing all 31 brightly colored plates. Additional printed text of each poem. 64pp. 5¼ × 7. 22764-2 Pa. $3.50

PRECIOUS STONES, Max Bauer. Classic, thorough study of diamonds, rubies, emeralds, garnets, etc.: physical character, occurrence, properties, use, similar topics. 20 plates, 8 in color. 94 figures. 659pp. 6⅛ × 9¼. 21910-0, 21911-9 Pa., Two-vol. set $15.90

ENCYCLOPEDIA OF VICTORIAN NEEDLEWORK, S. F. A. Caulfeild and Blanche Saward. Full, precise descriptions of stitches, techniques for dozens of needlecrafts—most exhaustive reference of its kind. Over 800 figures. Total of 679pp. 8⅛ × 11. Two volumes. Vol. 1 22800-2 Pa. $11.95
Vol. 2 22801-0 Pa. $11.95

THE MARVELOUS LAND OF OZ, L. Frank Baum. Second Oz book, the Scarecrow and Tin Woodman are back with hero named Tip, Oz magic. 136 illustrations. 287pp. 5⅜ × 8½. 20692-0 Pa. $5.95

WILD FOWL DECOYS, Joel Barber. Basic book on the subject, by foremost authority and collector. Reveals history of decoy making and rigging, place in American culture, different kinds of decoys, how to make them, and how to use them. 140 plates. 156pp. 7⅞ × 10¾. 20011-6 Pa. $8.95

HISTORY OF LACE, Mrs. Bury Palliser. Definitive, profusely illustrated chronicle of lace from earliest times to late 19th century. Laces of Italy, Greece, England, France, Belgium, etc. Landmark of needlework scholarship. 266 illustrations. 672pp. 6⅛ × 9¼. 24742-2 Pa. $14.95

ILLUSTRATED GUIDE TO SHAKER FURNITURE, Robert Meader. All furniture and appurtenances, with much on unknown local styles. 235 photos. 146pp. 9 × 12. 22819-3 Pa. $7.95

WHALE SHIPS AND WHALING: A Pictorial Survey, George Francis Dow. Over 200 vintage engravings, drawings, photographs of barks, brigs, cutters, other vessels. Also harpoons, lances, whaling guns, many other artifacts. Comprehensive text by foremost authority. 207 black-and-white illustrations. 288pp. 6 × 9. 24808-9 Pa. $8.95

THE BERTRAMS, Anthony Trollope. Powerful portrayal of blind self-will and thwarted ambition includes one of Trollope's most heartrending love stories. 497pp. 5⅜ × 8½. 25119-5 Pa. $8.95

ADVENTURES WITH A HAND LENS, Richard Headstrom. Clearly written guide to observing and studying flowers and grasses, fish scales, moth and insect wings, egg cases, buds, feathers, seeds, leaf scars, moss, molds, ferns, common crystals, etc.—all with an ordinary, inexpensive magnifying glass. 209 exact line drawings aid in your discoveries. 220pp. 5⅜ × 8½. 23330-8 Pa. $3.95

RODIN ON ART AND ARTISTS, Auguste Rodin. Great sculptor's candid, wide-ranging comments on meaning of art; great artists; relation of sculpture to poetry, painting, music; philosophy of life, more. 76 superb black-and-white illustrations of Rodin's sculpture, drawings and prints. 119pp. 8⅜ × 11¼. 24487-3 Pa. $6.95

FIFTY CLASSIC FRENCH FILMS, 1912–1982: A Pictorial Record, Anthony Slide. Memorable stills from Grand Illusion, Beauty and the Beast, Hiroshima, Mon Amour, many more. Credits, plot synopses, reviews, etc. 160pp. 8¼ × 11. 25256-6 Pa. $11.95

THE PRINCIPLES OF PSYCHOLOGY, William James. Famous long course complete, unabridged. Stream of thought, time perception, memory, experimental methods; great work decades ahead of its time. 94 figures. 1,391pp. 5⅜ × 8½. 20381-6, 20382-4 Pa., Two-vol. set $19.90

BODIES IN A BOOKSHOP, R. T. Campbell. Challenging mystery of blackmail and murder with ingenious plot and superbly drawn characters. In the best tradition of British suspense fiction. 192pp. 5⅜ × 8½. 24720-1 Pa. $3.95

CALLAS: PORTRAIT OF A PRIMA DONNA, George Jellinek. Renowned commentator on the musical scene chronicles incredible career and life of the most controversial, fascinating, influential operatic personality of our time. 64 black-and-white photographs. 416pp. 5⅜ × 8¼. 25047-4 Pa. $7.95

GEOMETRY, RELATIVITY AND THE FOURTH DIMENSION, Rudolph Rucker. Exposition of fourth dimension, concepts of relativity as Flatland characters continue adventures. Popular, easily followed yet accurate, profound. 141 illustrations. 133pp. 5⅜ × 8½. 23400-2 Pa. $3.95

HOUSEHOLD STORIES BY THE BROTHERS GRIMM, with pictures by Walter Crane. 53 classic stories—Rumpelstiltskin, Rapunzel, Hansel and Gretel, the Fisherman and his Wife, Snow White, Tom Thumb, Sleeping Beauty, Cinderella, and so much more—lavishly illustrated with original 19th century drawings. 114 illustrations. x + 269pp. 5⅜ × 8½. 21080-4 Pa. $4.50

SUNDIALS, Albert Waugh. Far and away the best, most thorough coverage of ideas, mathematics concerned, types, construction, adjusting anywhere. Over 100 illustrations. 230pp. 5⅜ × 8½. 22947-5 Pa. $4.50

PICTURE HISTORY OF THE NORMANDIE: With 190 Illustrations, Frank O. Braynard. Full story of legendary French ocean liner: Art Deco interiors, design innovations, furnishings, celebrities, maiden voyage, tragic fire, much more. Extensive text. 144pp. 8⅜ × 11¾. 25257-4 Pa. $9.95

THE FIRST AMERICAN COOKBOOK: A Facsimile of "American Cookery," 1796, Amelia Simmons. Facsimile of the first American-written cookbook published in the United States contains authentic recipes for colonial favorites—pumpkin pudding, winter squash pudding, spruce beer, Indian slapjacks, and more. Introductory Essay and Glossary of colonial cooking terms. 80pp. 5⅜ × 8½. 24710-4 Pa. $3.50

101 PUZZLES IN THOUGHT AND LOGIC, C. R. Wylie, Jr. Solve murders and robberies, find out which fishermen are liars, how a blind man could possibly identify a color—purely by your own reasoning! 107pp. 5⅜ × 8½. 20367-0 Pa. $2.50

THE BOOK OF WORLD-FAMOUS MUSIC—CLASSICAL, POPULAR AND FOLK, James J. Fuld. Revised and enlarged republication of landmark work in musico-bibliography. Full information about nearly 1,000 songs and compositions including first lines of music and lyrics. New supplement. Index. 800pp. 5⅜ × 8¼. 24857-7 Pa. $14.95

ANTHROPOLOGY AND MODERN LIFE, Franz Boas. Great anthropologist's classic treatise on race and culture. Introduction by Ruth Bunzel. Only inexpensive paperback edition. 255pp. 5⅜ × 8½. 25245-0 Pa. $5.95

THE TALE OF PETER RABBIT, Beatrix Potter. The inimitable Peter's terrifying adventure in Mr. McGregor's garden, with all 27 wonderful, full-color Potter illustrations. 55pp. 4¼ × 5½. (Available in U.S. only) 22827-4 Pa. $1.75

THREE PROPHETIC SCIENCE FICTION NOVELS, H. G. Wells. *When the Sleeper Wakes, A Story of the Days to Come* and *The Time Machine* (full version). 335pp. 5⅜ × 8½. (Available in U.S. only) 20605-X Pa. $5.95

APICIUS COOKERY AND DINING IN IMPERIAL ROME, edited and translated by Joseph Dommers Vehling. Oldest known cookbook in existence offers readers a clear picture of what foods Romans ate, how they prepared them, etc. 49 illustrations. 301pp. 6⅛ × 9¼. 23563-7 Pa. $6.50

SHAKESPEARE LEXICON AND QUOTATION DICTIONARY, Alexander Schmidt. Full definitions, locations, shades of meaning of every word in plays and poems. More than 50,000 exact quotations. 1,485pp. 6½ × 9¼. 22726-X, 22727-8 Pa., Two-vol. set $27.90

THE WORLD'S GREAT SPEECHES, edited by Lewis Copeland and Lawrence W. Lamm. Vast collection of 278 speeches from Greeks to 1970. Powerful and effective models; unique look at history. 842pp. 5⅜ × 8½. 20468-5 Pa. $11.95

THE BLUE FAIRY BOOK, Andrew Lang. The first, most famous collection, with many familiar tales: Little Red Riding Hood, Aladdin and the Wonderful Lamp, Puss in Boots, Sleeping Beauty, Hansel and Gretel, Rumpelstiltskin; 37 in all. 138 illustrations. 390pp. 5⅜ × 8½.   21437-0 Pa. $5.95

THE STORY OF THE CHAMPIONS OF THE ROUND TABLE, Howard Pyle. Sir Launcelot, Sir Tristram and Sir Percival in spirited adventures of love and triumph retold in Pyle's inimitable style. 50 drawings, 31 full-page. xviii + 329pp. 6½ × 9¼.   21883-X Pa. $6.95

AUDUBON AND HIS JOURNALS, Maria Audubon. Unmatched two-volume portrait of the great artist, naturalist and author contains his journals, an excellent biography by his granddaughter, expert annotations by the noted ornithologist, Dr. Elliott Coues, and 37 superb illustrations. Total of 1,200pp. 5⅜ × 8.
Vol. I 25143-8 Pa. $8.95
Vol. II 25144-6 Pa. $8.95

GREAT DINOSAUR HUNTERS AND THEIR DISCOVERIES, Edwin H. Colbert. Fascinating, lavishly illustrated chronicle of dinosaur research, 1820's to 1960. Achievements of Cope, Marsh, Brown, Buckland, Mantell, Huxley, many others. 384pp. 5¼ × 8¼.   24701-5 Pa. $6.95

THE TASTEMAKERS, Russell Lynes. Informal, illustrated social history of American taste 1850's–1950's. First popularized categories Highbrow, Lowbrow, Middlebrow. 129 illustrations. New (1979) afterword. 384pp. 6 × 9.
23993-4 Pa. $6.95

DOUBLE CROSS PURPOSES, Ronald A. Knox. A treasure hunt in the Scottish Highlands, an old map, unidentified corpse, surprise discoveries keep reader guessing in this cleverly intricate tale of financial skullduggery. 2 black-and-white maps. 320pp. 5⅜ × 8½. (Available in U.S. only)   25032-6 Pa. $5.95

AUTHENTIC VICTORIAN DECORATION AND ORNAMENTATION IN FULL COLOR: 46 Plates from "Studies in Design," Christopher Dresser. Superb full-color lithographs reproduced from rare original portfolio of a major Victorian designer. 48pp. 9¼ × 12¼.   25083-0 Pa. $7.95

PRIMITIVE ART, Franz Boas. Remains the best text ever prepared on subject, thoroughly discussing Indian, African, Asian, Australian, and, especially, Northern American primitive art. Over 950 illustrations show ceramics, masks, totem poles, weapons, textiles, paintings, much more. 376pp. 5⅜ × 8. 20025-6 Pa. $6.95

SIDELIGHTS ON RELATIVITY, Albert Einstein. Unabridged republication of two lectures delivered by the great physicist in 1920–21. *Ether and Relativity* and *Geometry and Experience*. Elegant ideas in non-mathematical form, accessible to intelligent layman. vi + 56pp. 5⅜ × 8½.   24511-X Pa. $2.95

THE WIT AND HUMOR OF OSCAR WILDE, edited by Alvin Redman. More than 1,000 ripostes, paradoxes, wisecracks: Work is the curse of the drinking classes, I can resist everything except temptation, etc. 258pp. 5⅜ × 8½.   20602-5 Pa. $4.50

ADVENTURES WITH A MICROSCOPE, Richard Headstrom. 59 adventures with clothing fibers, protozoa, ferns and lichens, roots and leaves, much more. 142 illustrations. 232pp. 5⅜ × 8½.   23471-1 Pa. $3.95

PLANTS OF THE BIBLE, Harold N. Moldenke and Alma L. Moldenke. Standard reference to all 230 plants mentioned in Scriptures. Latin name, biblical reference, uses, modern identity, much more. Unsurpassed encyclopedic resource for scholars, botanists, nature lovers, students of Bible. Bibliography. Indexes. 123 black-and-white illustrations. 384pp. 6 × 9. 25069-5 Pa. $8.95

FAMOUS AMERICAN WOMEN: A Biographical Dictionary from Colonial Times to the Present, Robert McHenry, ed. From Pocahontas to Rosa Parks, 1,035 distinguished American women documented in separate biographical entries. Accurate, up-to-date data, numerous categories, spans 400 years. Indices. 493pp. 6½ × 9¼. 24523-3 Pa. $9.95

THE FABULOUS INTERIORS OF THE GREAT OCEAN LINERS IN HISTORIC PHOTOGRAPHS, William H. Miller, Jr. Some 200 superb photographs capture exquisite interiors of world's great "floating palaces"—1890's to 1980's: *Titanic, Ile de France, Queen Elizabeth, United States, Europa,* more. Approx. 200 black-and-white photographs. Captions. Text. Introduction. 160pp. 8⅞ × 11¾. 24756-2 Pa. $9.95

THE GREAT LUXURY LINERS, 1927–1954: A Photographic Record, William H. Miller, Jr. Nostalgic tribute to heyday of ocean liners. 186 photos of Ile de France, Normandie, Leviathan, Queen Elizabeth, United States, many others. Interior and exterior views. Introduction. Captions. 160pp. 9 × 12. 24056-8 Pa. $9.95

A NATURAL HISTORY OF THE DUCKS, John Charles Phillips. Great landmark of ornithology offers complete detailed coverage of nearly 200 species and subspecies of ducks: gadwall, sheldrake, merganser, pintail, many more. 74 full-color plates, 102 black-and-white. Bibliography. Total of 1,920pp. 8⅝ × 11¼. 25141-1, 25142-X Cloth. Two-vol. set $100.00

THE SEAWEED HANDBOOK: An Illustrated Guide to Seaweeds from North Carolina to Canada, Thomas F. Lee. Concise reference covers 78 species. Scientific and common names, habitat, distribution, more. Finding keys for easy identification. 224pp. 5⅜ × 8½. 25215-9 Pa. $5.95

THE TEN BOOKS OF ARCHITECTURE: The 1755 Leoni Edition, Leon Battista Alberti. Rare classic helped introduce the glories of ancient architecture to the Renaissance. 68 black-and-white plates. 336pp. 8⅜ × 11¼. 25239-6 Pa. $14.95

MISS MACKENZIE, Anthony Trollope. Minor masterpieces by Victorian master unmasks many truths about life in 19th-century England. First inexpensive edition in years. 392pp. 5⅜ × 8½. 25201-9 Pa. $7.95

THE RIME OF THE ANCIENT MARINER, Gustave Doré, Samuel Taylor Coleridge. Dramatic engravings considered by many to be his greatest work. The terrifying space of the open sea, the storms and whirlpools of an unknown ocean, the ice of Antarctica, more—all rendered in a powerful, chilling manner. Full text. 38 plates. 77pp. 9¼ × 12. 22305-1 Pa. $4.95

THE EXPEDITIONS OF ZEBULON MONTGOMERY PIKE, Zebulon Montgomery Pike. Fascinating first-hand accounts (1805-6) of exploration of Mississippi River, Indian wars, capture by Spanish dragoons, much more. 1,088pp. 5⅜ × 8½. 25254-X, 25255-8 Pa. Two-vol. set $23.90

A CONCISE HISTORY OF PHOTOGRAPHY: Third Revised Edition, Helmut Gernsheim. Best one-volume history—camera obscura, photochemistry, daguerreotypes, evolution of cameras, film, more. Also artistic aspects—landscape, portraits, fine art, etc. 281 black-and-white photographs. 26 in color. 176pp. 8⅜ × 11¼. 25128-4 Pa. $12.95

THE DORÉ BIBLE ILLUSTRATIONS, Gustave Doré. 241 detailed plates from the Bible: the Creation scenes, Adam and Eve, Flood, Babylon, battle sequences, life of Jesus, etc. Each plate is accompanied by the verses from the King James version of the Bible. 241pp. 9 × 12. 23004-X Pa. $8.95

HUGGER-MUGGER IN THE LOUVRE, Elliot Paul. Second Homer Evans mystery-comedy. Theft at the Louvre involves sleuth in hilarious, madcap caper. "A knockout."—Books. 336pp. 5⅜ × 8½. 25185-3 Pa. $5.95

FLATLAND, E. A. Abbott. Intriguing and enormously popular science-fiction classic explores the complexities of trying to survive as a two-dimensional being in a three-dimensional world. Amusingly illustrated by the author. 16 illustrations. 103pp. 5⅜ × 8½. 20001-9 Pa. $2.25

THE HISTORY OF THE LEWIS AND CLARK EXPEDITION, Meriwether Lewis and William Clark, edited by Elliott Coues. Classic edition of Lewis and Clark's day-by-day journals that later became the basis for U.S. claims to Oregon and the West. Accurate and invaluable geographical, botanical, biological, meteorological and anthropological material. Total of 1,508pp. 5⅜ × 8½.
21268-8, 21269-6, 21270-X Pa. Three-vol. set $25.50

LANGUAGE, TRUTH AND LOGIC, Alfred J. Ayer. Famous, clear introduction to Vienna, Cambridge schools of Logical Positivism. Role of philosophy, elimination of metaphysics, nature of analysis, etc. 160pp. 5⅜ × 8½. (Available in U.S. and Canada only) 20010-8 Pa. $2.95

MATHEMATICS FOR THE NONMATHEMATICIAN, Morris Kline. Detailed, college-level treatment of mathematics in cultural and historical context, with numerous exercises. For liberal arts students. Preface. Recommended Reading Lists. Tables. Index. Numerous black-and-white figures. xvi + 641pp. 5⅜ × 8½.
24823-2 Pa. $11.95

28 SCIENCE FICTION STORIES, H. G. Wells. Novels, *Star Begotten* and *Men Like Gods,* plus 26 short stories: "Empire of the Ants," "A Story of the Stone Age," "The Stolen Bacillus," "In the Abyss," etc. 915pp. 5⅜ × 8½. (Available in U.S. only)
20265-8 Cloth. $10.95

HANDBOOK OF PICTORIAL SYMBOLS, Rudolph Modley. 3,250 signs and symbols, many systems in full; official or heavy commercial use. Arranged by subject. Most in Pictorial Archive series. 143pp. 8⅛ × 11. 23357-X Pa. $5.95

INCIDENTS OF TRAVEL IN YUCATAN, John L. Stephens. Classic (1843) exploration of jungles of Yucatan, looking for evidences of Maya civilization. Travel adventures, Mexican and Indian culture, etc. Total of 669pp. 5⅜ × 8½.
20926-1, 20927-X Pa., Two-vol. set $9.90

DEGAS: An Intimate Portrait, Ambroise Vollard. Charming, anecdotal memoir by famous art dealer of one of the greatest 19th-century French painters. 14 black-and-white illustrations. Introduction by Harold L. Van Doren. 96pp. 5¾ × 8½.
25131-4 Pa. $3.95

PERSONAL NARRATIVE OF A PILGRIMAGE TO ALMANDINAH AND MECCAH, Richard Burton. Great travel classic by remarkably colorful personality. Burton, disguised as a Moroccan, visited sacred shrines of Islam, narrowly escaping death. 47 illustrations. 959pp. 5¾ × 8½. 21217-3, 21218-1 Pa., Two-vol. set $19.90

PHRASE AND WORD ORIGINS, A. H. Holt. Entertaining, reliable, modern study of more than 1,200 colorful words, phrases, origins and histories. Much unexpected information. 254pp. 5¾ × 8½. 20758-7 Pa. $4.95

THE RED THUMB MARK, R. Austin Freeman. In this first Dr. Thorndyke case, the great scientific detective draws fascinating conclusions from the nature of a single fingerprint. Exciting story, authentic science. 320pp. 5¾ × 8½. (Available in U.S. only) 25210-8 Pa. $5.95

AN EGYPTIAN HIEROGLYPHIC DICTIONARY, E. A. Wallis Budge. Monumental work containing about 25,000 words or terms that occur in texts ranging from 3000 B.C. to 600 A.D. Each entry consists of a transliteration of the word, the word in hieroglyphs, and the meaning in English. 1,314pp. 6⅜ × 10.
23615-3, 23616-1 Pa., Two-vol. set $27.90

THE COMPLEAT STRATEGYST: Being a Primer on the Theory of Games of Strategy, J. D. Williams. Highly entertaining classic describes, with many illustrated examples, how to select best strategies in conflict situations. Prefaces. Appendices. xvi + 268pp. 5¾ × 8½. 25101-2 Pa. $5.95

THE ROAD TO OZ, L. Frank Baum. Dorothy meets the Shaggy Man, little Button-Bright and the Rainbow's beautiful daughter in this delightful trip to the magical Land of Oz. 272pp. 5¾ × 8. 25208-6 Pa. $4.95

POINT AND LINE TO PLANE, Wassily Kandinsky. Seminal exposition of role of point, line, other elements in non-objective painting. Essential to understanding 20th-century art. 127 illustrations. 192pp. 6½ × 9¼. 23808-3 Pa. $4.50

LADY ANNA, Anthony Trollope. Moving chronicle of Countess Lovel's bitter struggle to win for herself and daughter Anna their rightful rank and fortune—perhaps at cost of sanity itself. 384pp. 5¾ × 8½. 24669-8 Pa. $6.95

EGYPTIAN MAGIC, E. A. Wallis Budge. Sums up all that is known about magic in Ancient Egypt: the role of magic in controlling the gods, powerful amulets that warded off evil spirits, scarabs of immortality, use of wax images, formulas and spells, the secret name, much more. 253pp. 5¾ × 8½. 22681-6 Pa. $4.00

THE DANCE OF SIVA, Ananda Coomaraswamy. Preeminent authority unfolds the vast metaphysic of India: the revelation of her art, conception of the universe, social organization, etc. 27 reproductions of art masterpieces. 192pp. 5¾ × 8½.
24817-8 Pa. $5.95

CHRISTMAS CUSTOMS AND TRADITIONS, Clement A. Miles. Origin, evolution, significance of religious, secular practices. Caroling, gifts, yule logs, much more. Full, scholarly yet fascinating; non-sectarian. 400pp. 5⅜ × 8½.
23354-5 Pa. $6.50

THE HUMAN FIGURE IN MOTION, Eadweard Muybridge. More than 4,500 stopped-action photos, in action series, showing undraped men, women, children jumping, lying down, throwing, sitting, wrestling, carrying, etc. 390pp. 7⅞ × 10⅝.
20204-6 Cloth. $21.95

THE MAN WHO WAS THURSDAY, Gilbert Keith Chesterton. Witty, fast-paced novel about a club of anarchists in turn-of-the-century London. Brilliant social, religious, philosophical speculations. 128pp. 5⅜ × 8½.   25121-7 Pa. $3.95

A CEZANNE SKETCHBOOK: Figures, Portraits, Landscapes and Still Lifes, Paul Cezanne. Great artist experiments with tonal effects, light, mass, other qualities in over 100 drawings. A revealing view of developing master painter, precursor of Cubism. 102 black-and-white illustrations. 144pp. 8¾ × 6⅜.   24790-2 Pa. $5.95

AN ENCYCLOPEDIA OF BATTLES: Accounts of Over 1,560 Battles from 1479 B.C. to the Present, David Eggenberger. Presents essential details of every major battle in recorded history, from the first battle of Megiddo in 1479 B.C. to Grenada in 1984. List of Battle Maps. New Appendix covering the years 1967–1984. Index. 99 illustrations. 544pp. 6½ × 9¼.   24913-1 Pa. $14.95

AN ETYMOLOGICAL DICTIONARY OF MODERN ENGLISH, Ernest Weekley. Richest, fullest work, by foremost British lexicographer. Detailed word histories. Inexhaustible. Total of 856pp. 6½ × 9¼.
21873-2, 21874-0 Pa., Two-vol. set $17.00

WEBSTER'S AMERICAN MILITARY BIOGRAPHIES, edited by Robert McHenry. Over 1,000 figures who shaped 3 centuries of American military history. Detailed biographies of Nathan Hale, Douglas MacArthur, Mary Hallaren, others. Chronologies of engagements, more. Introduction. Addenda. 1,033 entries in alphabetical order. xi + 548pp. 6½ × 9¼. (Available in U.S. only)
24758-9 Pa. $11.95

LIFE IN ANCIENT EGYPT, Adolf Erman. Detailed older account, with much not in more recent books: domestic life, religion, magic, medicine, commerce, and whatever else needed for complete picture. Many illustrations. 597pp. 5⅜ × 8½.
22632-8 Pa. $8.50

HISTORIC COSTUME IN PICTURES, Braun & Schneider. Over 1,450 costumed figures shown, covering a wide variety of peoples: kings, emperors, nobles, priests, servants, soldiers, scholars, townsfolk, peasants, merchants, courtiers, cavaliers, and more. 256pp. 8⅜ × 11¼.   23150-X Pa. $7.95

THE NOTEBOOKS OF LEONARDO DA VINCI, edited by J. P. Richter. Extracts from manuscripts reveal great genius; on painting, sculpture, anatomy, sciences, geography, etc. Both Italian and English. 186 ms. pages reproduced, plus 500 additional drawings, including studies for *Last Supper*, *Sforza* monument, etc. 860pp. 7⅞ × 10¾. (Available in U.S. only) 22572-0, 22573-9 Pa., Two-vol. set $25.90

THE ART NOUVEAU STYLE BOOK OF ALPHONSE MUCHA: All 72 Plates from "Documents Decoratifs" in Original Color, Alphonse Mucha. Rare copyright-free design portfolio by high priest of Art Nouveau. Jewelry, wallpaper, stained glass, furniture, figure studies, plant and animal motifs, etc. Only complete one-volume edition. 80pp. 9⅜ × 12¼. 24044-4 Pa. $8.95

ANIMALS: 1,419 COPYRIGHT-FREE ILLUSTRATIONS OF MAMMALS, BIRDS, FISH, INSECTS, ETC., edited by Jim Harter. Clear wood engravings present, in extremely lifelike poses, over 1,000 species of animals. One of the most extensive pictorial sourcebooks of its kind. Captions. Index. 284pp. 9 × 12.
23766-4 Pa. $9.95

OBELISTS FLY HIGH, C. Daly King. Masterpiece of American detective fiction, long out of print, involves murder on a 1935 transcontinental flight—"a very thrilling story"—NY Times. Unabridged and unaltered republication of the edition published by William Collins Sons & Co. Ltd., London, 1935. 288pp. 5⅜ × 8½. (Available in U.S. only) 25036-9 Pa. $4.95

VICTORIAN AND EDWARDIAN FASHION: A Photographic Survey, Alison Gernsheim. First fashion history completely illustrated by contemporary photographs. Full text plus 235 photos, 1840–1914, in which many celebrities appear. 240pp. 6½ × 9¼. 24205-6 Pa. $6.00

THE ART OF THE FRENCH ILLUSTRATED BOOK, 1700–1914, Gordon N. Ray. Over 630 superb book illustrations by Fragonard, Delacroix, Daumier, Doré, Grandville, Manet, Mucha, Steinlen, Toulouse-Lautrec and many others. Preface. Introduction. 633 halftones. Indices of artists, authors & titles, binders and provenances. Appendices. Bibliography. 608pp. 8⅜ × 11¼. 25086-5 Pa. $24.95

THE WONDERFUL WIZARD OF OZ, L. Frank Baum. Facsimile in full color of America's finest children's classic. 143 illustrations by W. W. Denslow. 267pp. 5⅜ × 8½. 20691-2 Pa. $5.95

FRONTIERS OF MODERN PHYSICS: New Perspectives on Cosmology, Relativity, Black Holes and Extraterrestrial Intelligence, Tony Rothman, et al. For the intelligent layman. Subjects include: cosmological models of the universe; black holes; the neutrino; the search for extraterrestrial intelligence. Introduction. 46 black-and-white illustrations. 192pp. 5⅜ × 8½. 24587-X Pa. $6.95

THE FRIENDLY STARS, Martha Evans Martin & Donald Howard Menzel. Classic text marshalls the stars together in an engaging, non-technical survey, presenting them as sources of beauty in night sky. 23 illustrations. Foreword. 2 star charts. Index. 147pp. 5⅜ × 8½. 21099-5 Pa. $3.50

FADS AND FALLACIES IN THE NAME OF SCIENCE, Martin Gardner. Fair, witty appraisal of cranks, quacks, and quackeries of science and pseudoscience: hollow earth, Velikovsky, orgone energy, Dianetics, flying saucers, Bridey Murphy, food and medical fads, etc. Revised, expanded In the Name of Science. "A very able and even-tempered presentation."—The New Yorker. 363pp. 5⅜ × 8.
20394-8 Pa. $6.50

ANCIENT EGYPT: ITS CULTURE AND HISTORY, J. E Manchip White. From pre-dynastics through Ptolemies: society, history, political structure, religion, daily life, literature, cultural heritage. 48 plates. 217pp. 5⅜ × 8½. 22548-8 Pa. $4.95

SIR HARRY HOTSPUR OF HUMBLETHWAITE, Anthony Trollope. Incisive, unconventional psychological study of a conflict between a wealthy baronet, his idealistic daughter, and their scapegrace cousin. The 1870 novel in its first inexpensive edition in years. 250pp. 5⅜ × 8½. 24953-0 Pa. $5.95

LASERS AND HOLOGRAPHY, Winston E. Kock. Sound introduction to burgeoning field, expanded (1981) for second edition. Wave patterns, coherence, lasers, diffraction, zone plates, properties of holograms, recent advances. 84 illustrations. 160pp. 5⅜ × 8¼. (Except in United Kingdom) 24041-X Pa. $3.50

INTRODUCTION TO ARTIFICIAL INTELLIGENCE: SECOND, ENLARGED EDITION, Philip C. Jackson, Jr. Comprehensive survey of artificial intelligence—the study of how machines (computers) can be made to act intelligently. Includes introductory and advanced material. Extensive notes updating the main text. 132 black-and-white illustrations. 512pp. 5⅜ × 8½. 24864-X Pa. $8.95

HISTORY OF INDIAN AND INDONESIAN ART, Ananda K. Coomaraswamy. Over 400 illustrations illuminate classic study of Indian art from earliest Harappa finds to early 20th century. Provides philosophical, religious and social insights. 304pp. 6⅝ × 9⅝. 25005-9 Pa. $8.95

THE GOLEM, Gustav Meyrink. Most famous supernatural novel in modern European literature, set in Ghetto of Old Prague around 1890. Compelling story of mystical experiences, strange transformations, profound terror. 13 black-and-white illustrations. 224pp. 5⅜ × 8½. (Available in U.S. only) 25025-3 Pa. $5.95

ARMADALE, Wilkie Collins. Third great mystery novel by the author of *The Woman in White* and *The Moonstone*. Original magazine version with 40 illustrations. 597pp. 5⅜ × 8½. 23429-0 Pa. $9.95

PICTORIAL ENCYCLOPEDIA OF HISTORIC ARCHITECTURAL PLANS, DETAILS AND ELEMENTS: With 1,880 Line Drawings of Arches, Domes, Doorways, Facades, Gables, Windows, etc., John Theodore Haneman. Sourcebook of inspiration for architects, designers, others. Bibliography. Captions. 141pp. 9 × 12. 24605-1 Pa. $6.95

BENCHLEY LOST AND FOUND, Robert Benchley. Finest humor from early 30's, about pet peeves, child psychologists, post office and others. Mostly unavailable elsewhere. 73 illustrations by Peter Arno and others. 183pp. 5⅜ × 8½. 22410-4 Pa. $3.95

ERTÉ GRAPHICS, Erté. Collection of striking color graphics: *Seasons, Alphabet, Numerals, Aces* and *Precious Stones*. 50 plates, including 4 on covers. 48pp. 9⅜ × 12¼. 23580-7 Pa. $6.95

THE JOURNAL OF HENRY D. THOREAU, edited by Bradford Torrey, F. H. Allen. Complete reprinting of 14 volumes, 1837–61, over two million words; the sourcebooks for *Walden*, etc. Definitive. All original sketches, plus 75 photographs. 1,804pp. 8½ × 12¼. 20312-3, 20313-1 Cloth., Two-vol. set $80.00

CASTLES: THEIR CONSTRUCTION AND HISTORY, Sidney Toy. Traces castle development from ancient roots. Nearly 200 photographs and drawings illustrate moats, keeps, baileys, many other features. Caernarvon, Dover Castles, Hadrian's Wall, Tower of London, dozens more. 256pp. 5⅜ × 8¼. 24898-4 Pa. $5.95

AMERICAN CLIPPER SHIPS: 1833–1858, Octavius T. Howe & Frederick C. Matthews. Fully-illustrated, encyclopedic review of 352 clipper ships from the period of America's greatest maritime supremacy. Introduction. 109 halftones. 5 black-and-white line illustrations. Index. Total of 928pp. 5⅜ × 8½.
25115-2, 25116-0 Pa., Two-vol. set $17.90

TOWARDS A NEW ARCHITECTURE, Le Corbusier. Pioneering manifesto by great architect, near legendary founder of "International School." Technical and aesthetic theories, views on industry, economics, relation of form to function, "mass-production spirit," much more. Profusely illustrated. Unabridged translation of 13th French edition. Introduction by Frederick Etchells. 320pp. 6⅛ × 9¼. (Available in U.S. only)
25023-7 Pa. $8.95

THE BOOK OF KELLS, edited by Blanche Cirker. Inexpensive collection of 32 full-color, full-page plates from the greatest illuminated manuscript of the Middle Ages, painstakingly reproduced from rare facsimile edition. Publisher's Note. Captions. 32pp. 9⅜ × 12¼.
24345-1 Pa. $4.95

BEST SCIENCE FICTION STORIES OF H. G. WELLS, H. G. Wells. Full novel *The Invisible Man*, plus 17 short stories: "The Crystal Egg," "Aepyornis Island," "The Strange Orchid," etc. 303pp. 5⅜ × 8½. (Available in U.S. only)
21531-8 Pa. $4.95

AMERICAN SAILING SHIPS: Their Plans and History, Charles G. Davis. Photos, construction details of schooners, frigates, clippers, other sailcraft of 18th to early 20th centuries—plus entertaining discourse on design, rigging, nautical lore, much more. 137 black-and-white illustrations. 240pp. 6⅛ × 9¼.
24658-2 Pa. $5.95

ENTERTAINING MATHEMATICAL PUZZLES, Martin Gardner. Selection of author's favorite conundrums involving arithmetic, money, speed, etc., with lively commentary. Complete solutions. 112pp. 5⅜ × 8½.
25211-6 Pa. $2.95

THE WILL TO BELIEVE, HUMAN IMMORTALITY, William James. Two books bound together. Effect of irrational on logical, and arguments for human immortality. 402pp. 5⅜ × 8½.
20291-7 Pa. $7.50

THE HAUNTED MONASTERY and THE CHINESE MAZE MURDERS, Robert Van Gulik. 2 full novels by Van Gulik continue adventures of Judge Dee and his companions. An evil Taoist monastery, seemingly supernatural events; overgrown topiary maze that hides strange crimes. Set in 7th-century China. 27 illustrations. 328pp. 5⅜ × 8½.
23502-5 Pa. $5.95

CELEBRATED CASES OF JUDGE DEE (DEE GOONG AN), translated by Robert Van Gulik. Authentic 18th-century Chinese detective novel; Dee and associates solve three interlocked cases. Led to Van Gulik's own stories with same characters. Extensive introduction. 9 illustrations. 237pp. 5⅜ × 8½.
23337-5 Pa. $4.95

Prices subject to change without notice.

Available at your book dealer or write for free catalog to Dept. GI, Dover Publications, Inc., 31 East 2nd St., Mineola, N.Y. 11501. Dover publishes more than 175 books each year on science, elementary and advanced mathematics, biology, music, art, literary history, social sciences and other areas.